MOLECULAR BIOLOGY
OF THE GENE

RNA polymera
on promotor?

DNA

See the polymerases?

mRNA degradation?

J. D. WATSON
Harvard University and
Cold Spring Harbor Laboratory

MOLECULAR
BIOLOGY
OF THE GENE

SECOND EDITION

With illustrations by Keith Roberts

W. A. BENJAMIN, INC.   New York   1970

MOLECULAR BIOLOGY OF THE GENE, *Second Edition*

Standard Book Number 8053-9020-0 (Clothbound Edition)
8053-9603-9 (Paperback Edition)

Library of Congress Catalog Card Number 72-134173

Manufactured in the United States of America
12345K43210

W. A. BENJAMIN, INC.
New York, New York 10016

*Frontispiece: Electron micrograph of polyribosomes attached to a section of
the E. coli genome. (Kindly supplied by O. L. Miller, Jr., Biology Division,
Oak Ridge National Laboratory, Barbara A. Hamkalo, and C. A. Thomas, Jr.,
Department of Biological Chemistry, Harvard Medical School.)*

to S. E. LURIA

PREFACE

THE ORIGINAL VERSION OF THIS TEXT MIGHT NEVER HAVE BEEN
written if I had known how much of my time it would eventually consume. The same is true of this revision. What started
out as a summer's part-time task has lasted exactly a year, almost
as long as writing the original text. In part this interval reflects
the enormous changes which have occurred in molecular biology
in just five years. I also mistakenly thought I could produce the
new version by merely inserting new sentences, not by the
more serious task of starting anew. But later on, I faced up to
the fact that turgidity in style must not be given the permanence
of type. Also, I saw the need to include new facts or delete passages that I found no longer to be true. So as each month passed
this revision grew longer and longer. Even so, many changes had
to be made at the last minute.

Through all of this effort, I have hoped that this version, like
the original, would be useful to a wide audience ranging from
college freshmen to practicing biologists who want a concise
reference source for the new facts of molecular biology. At many
points in the text I was tempted to leave out a given item, knowing that most introductory students would not need it. On the
other hand, I suspect that many such students will have first
learned about the double helix and ribosomes in primary school

and if they are to read about them once again, they should have the opportunity to learn where such topics now stand. So, more apparent "details" are included than some readers will like. Naturally they interest me or I would not have lengthened this book so perilously close to being too long.

As in the first edition, I have taken chances, presenting some new facts as perhaps more solid than they now are. Hopefully most of my hunches will prove to be solid and teachers who use this book as a text will not have to correct many misinterpretations. In some places I know I have oversimplified, but to have given all the facts would have made this book unsuitable for a general biological audience, most of whom do not want to be subjected to unending complexities.

Many of my friends have looked at one or more chapters, given me much advice, and kept me from making a variety of loose oversimplifications, if not bad mistakes. Most useful comments were made by Ann Burgess, John Cairns, Lionel Crawford, David Dressler, Bernard Hirt, Raymond Kaempfer, Jeffrey Miller, Carel Mulder, Keith Roberts, Bob Schlief, Andrew Travers, Rudolf Werner and John Wolfson. In particular, I wish to thank Nancy Hopkins for her very careful reading of the entire manuscript, which cut out innumerable outrages against the English language, as well as many scientifically sloppy passages. In some instances, however, I have not agreed with a given comment and I am clearly responsible for all the errors which remain.

In the actual preparation of the text, the Radcliffe students Lili Gottfried and Helen Trilling have immeasurably lessened my load, as has the continued good nature and competence of my secretary, DeeDee Skiff. Again I was very lucky in obtaining the artistic services of Keith Roberts of St. John's College, Cambridge, England. Without his unparalled ability to clearly illustrate molecular biology, my text would have grown even longer.

J. D. WATSON

Cold Spring Harbor, New York
July, 1970

CONTENTS

1

THE
MENDELIAN
VIEW OF
THE WORLD

IT IS EASY TO CONSIDER MAN UNIQUE among living organisms. He alone has developed complicated languages that allow meaningful and complex interplay of ideas and emotions. Great civilizations have developed and changed our world's environment in ways inconceivable for any other form of life. Thus there has always been a tendency to think that something special differentiates man from everything else. This belief has found expression in man's religions, by which he tries to find an origin for his existence and, in so doing, to provide workable rules for conducting his life. It seemed natural to think that, just as every human life begins and ends at a fixed time, man had not always existed but was created at a fixed moment, perhaps the same moment for man and for all other forms of life.

This belief was first seriously questioned just over 100 years ago when Darwin and Wallace proposed their theories of evolution, based upon selection of the most fit. They stated that the various forms of life are not constant, but are continually giving rise to slightly different animals and plants, some of which are adapted to survive and to multiply more effectively. At the time of this theory, they did not know the origin of this continuous variation, but they did correctly realize that these new characteristics must persist in the progeny if such variations were to form the basis of evolution.

1

At first, there was a great deal of furor against Darwin, most of it coming from people who did not like to believe that man and the rather obscene-looking apes could have a common ancestor, even if this ancestor had occurred some 50 to 100 million years in the past. There was also initial opposition from many biologists, who failed to find Darwin's evidence convincing. Among these was the famous Swiss-born naturalist Agassiz, then at Harvard, who spent many years writing against Darwin and Darwin's champion, T. H. Huxley, the most successful of the popularizers of evolution. But by the end of the nineteenth century, the scientific argument was almost complete; both the current geographic distribution of plants and animals and their selective occurrence in the fossil records of the geologic past were explicable only by postulating that continuously evolving groups of organisms had descended from a common ancestor. Today, the theory of evolution is an accepted fact for everyone but a fundamentalist minority, whose objections are based not on reasoning but on doctrinaire adherence to religious principles.

An immediate consequence of the acceptance of Darwinian theory is the realization that life first existed on our Earth some 1 to 2 billion years ago in a simple form, possibly resembling the bacteria—the simplest variety of life now existing. Of course, the very existence of such small bacteria tells us that the essence of the living state is found in very small organisms. Nonetheless, evolutionary theory further affects our thinking by suggesting that the same basic principles of life exist in all living forms.

THE CELL THEORY

The same conclusion was independently reached by the second great principle of nineteenth century biology, the *cell theory*. This theory, first put forward convincingly in 1839 by the German microscopists Schleiden and Schwann, proposes that all the plants and animals are constructed from small fundamental units called cells. All cells are surrounded by a membrane, and usually contain an inner body, the nucleus, which is

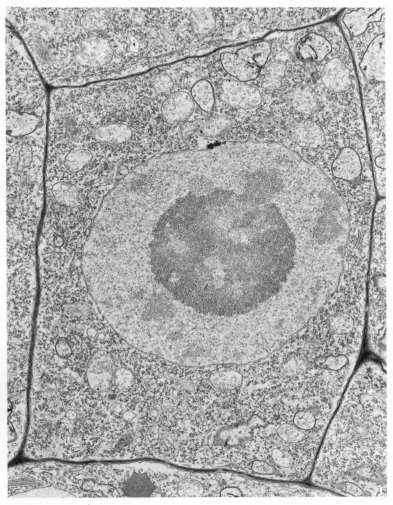

FIGURE 1–1   *Electron micrograph of a thin section from a cell of the African violet. The thin primary cellulose cell wall and the nucleus, containing a prominent nucleolus, are clearly visible. The cytoplasmic ground substance is heavily laden with spherical particles, the ribosomes, visible as small black dots. The profiles of a network of hollow membranes, the endoplasmic reticulum, can be seen scattered throughout the cell (courtesy of Drs. K. R. Porter and M. C. Ledbetter, Biological Laboratories, Harvard University).*

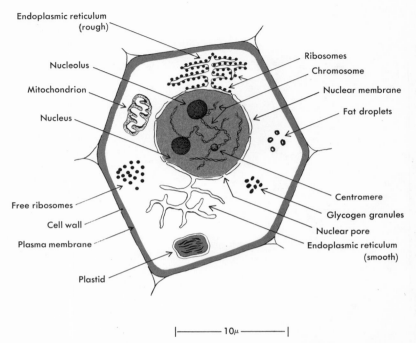

Endoplasmic reticulum (rough)

Nucleolus

Mitochondrion

Nucleus

Free ribosomes

Cell wall

Plasma membrane

Plastid

Ribosomes

Chromosome

Nuclear membrane

Fat droplets

Centromere

Glycogen granules

Nuclear pore

Endoplasmic reticulum (smooth)

|——— 10μ ———|

FIGURE 1–2   *A schematic view of the plant cell shown in Figure 1–1. The various components are not always drawn to scale.*

also surrounded by a membrane, called the nuclear membrane (Figures 1–1 and 1–2). Most important, cells arise only from other cells by the process of cell division. Most cells are capable of growing and of splitting roughly equally to give two daughter cells. At the same time, the nucleus divides so that each daughter cell can receive a nucleus.

MITOSIS MAINTAINS THE PARENTAL CHROMOSOME NUMBER

Each nucleus encloses a fixed number of linear bodies, called chromosomes (Figure 1–3). Before cell division, each chromosome divides to form two chromosomes identical to the parental body. This process, first accurately observed by Flemming in

1879, doubles the number of nuclear chromosomes. During nuclear division, one of each pair of daughter chromosomes moves into each daughter nucleus (Figure 1–4). As a result of these events (now collectively termed *mitosis*), the chromosomal complement of daughter cells is usually identical to that of the parental cells.

During most of a cell's life, its chromosomes exist in a highly extended linear form. Prior to cell division, however, they condense into much more compact bodies. The duplication of chromosomes occurs chiefly when they are in the extended state characteristic of interphase (the various stages of cell division are defined in Figure 1–4). One part of the chromosome, however, always duplicates during the contracted metaphase state; this is the *centromere*, a body that controls the movement of the chromosome during cell divisions. The centromere always has

F I G U R E 1–3 *The haploid complement of chromosomes from the leopard frog (Rana pipens), magnified 2125 times. This photograph was taken with a light microscope by T. E. Powell, of the Biological Laboratories, Harvard University. It shows the chromosomes when they have duplicated to form two chromatids held together by a single centromere.*

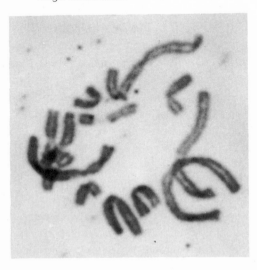

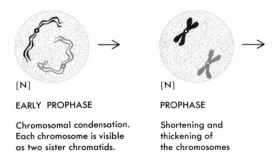

[N]   [N]

EARLY PROPHASE   PROPHASE

Chromosomal condensation.   Shortening and
Each chromosome is visible   thickening of
as two sister chromatids.   the chromosomes

FIGURE 1-4   *Diagram of mitosis in the nucleus of a haploid cell containing two nonhomologous chromosomes.*

a fixed location specific to a given chromosome; in some it is near one end, and in others it occupies an intermediate region.

When a chromosome is completely duplicated except for the centromere, it is said to consist of two *chromatids*. A chromatid is transformed into a chromosome as soon as its centromere has divided and is no longer shared with another chromatid. As soon as one centromere becomes two, the two daughter chromosomes begin to move away from each other.

The regular lining up of chromosomes during the metaphase stage is accompanied by the appearance of the *spindle*. This is a cellular region, shaped like a spindle, through which the chromosomes of higher organisms move apart during the anaphase stage. Much of the spindle region is filled with long, thin fibers, which some people think are similar to the contractile proteins of muscles. If this resemblance is genuine, then perhaps the same mechanism that underlies the contraction of muscles also underlies the movement of chromosomes through the spindle.

Objects called the *nucleoli* are also present in the nucleus of practically every plant and animal cell. There is often one nucleolus per haploid set of chromosomes, and in some cells the nucleolus is connected to a specific chromosome. Until recently, the functional role of the nucleolus was completely obscure, though some biologists originally thought that it might be related to the formation of the spindle. Now, however,

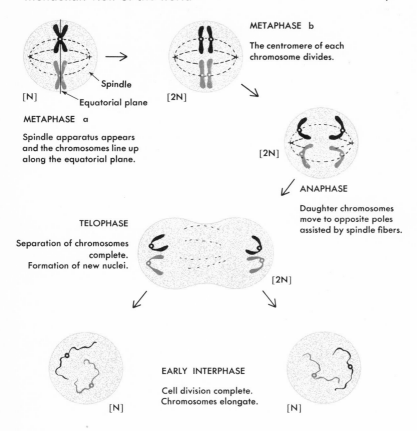

METAPHASE a

[N]

Spindle

Equatorial plane

Spindle apparatus appears and the chromosomes line up along the equatorial plane.

METAPHASE b

The centromere of each chromosome divides.

[2N]

[2N]

ANAPHASE

Daughter chromosomes move to opposite poles assisted by spindle fibers.

[2N]

TELOPHASE

Separation of chromosomes complete. Formation of new nuclei.

[N]

EARLY INTERPHASE

Cell division complete. Chromosomes elongate.

[N]

there are some strong hints that the nucleolus is involved in the synthesis of ribosomes, small particles within the cell upon which all proteins are synthesized.

MEIOSIS REDUCES THE PARENTAL CHROMOSOME NUMBER

One important exception was found to the mitotic process. After the conclusion of the two cell divisions that form the sex cells, the sperm, and the egg (*meiosis*), the number of chromosomes is reduced to one-half of its previous number (Figure 1–5). In higher plants and animals each specific type of chromosome is normally present in two copies: the homologous chromo-

PROPHASE I

Two pairs of homologous chromosomes
are shown in this imaginary diploid cell.
Chromosomes become visible as single
strands.

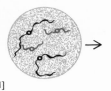

[2N]

FIGURE 1-5   *Schematic diagram of meiosis in the cell of an organism containing two pairs of homologous chromosomes.*

somes (the *diploid* state). In sex-cell formation the resulting
sperm and egg each usually encloses only one of each type (the
haploid state). Union of sperm and egg during fertilization
results in a fertilized egg (*zygote*) containing one homologous
chromosome from the male parent and another from the
female parent. Thus the normal diploid chromosome constitution is restored.

Although most cells are diploid in higher plants and animals,
the haploid state is the most frequent condition in lower plants
and bacteria, the diploid number existing only briefly following
sex-cell fusion. Usually meiosis occurs almost immediately
after fertilization to produce haploid cells (Figure 1-6).

The cell theory thus tells us that all cells come from preexisting cells. All the cells in adult plants and animals are
derived from the division and growth of a fertilized egg, itself
formed by the union of two other cells, the sperm and the egg.
All growing cells contain chromosomes, usually two of each
type, and here again, new chromosomes always arise through
division of previously existing bodies.

THE CELL THEORY IS UNIVERSALLY APPLICABLE

Although the cell theory developed from observations about
higher organisms, it holds with equal force for the more simple
forms of life, such as protozoa and bacteria. Each bacterium or
protozoan is a single cell, whose division ordinarily produces a
new cell identical to its parent, from which it soon separates.
In the higher organisms, on the other hand, the daughter cells

PROPHASE Ia

Homologous chromosomes undergo pairing. Later, each chromosome becomes visible as two chromatids (crossing over occurs at this point).

[2N]

METAPHASE I

Orientation of paired chromosomes in the equatorial plane. Formation of spindle apparatus.

[4N]

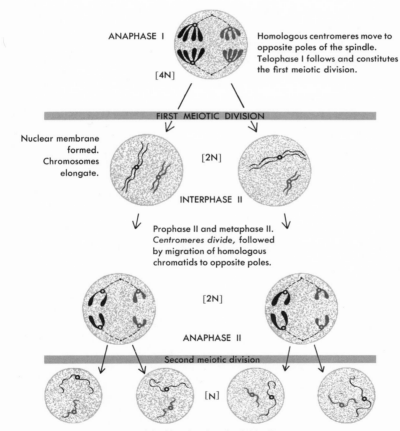

ANAPHASE I

[4N]

Homologous centromeres move to opposite poles of the spindle. Telophase I follows and constitutes the first meiotic division.

FIRST MEIOTIC DIVISION

Nuclear membrane formed. Chromosomes elongate.

[2N]

INTERPHASE II

Prophase II and metaphase II. *Centromeres divide,* followed by migration of homologous chromatids to opposite poles.

[2N]

ANAPHASE II

Second meiotic division

[N]

Final result is four haploid cells.

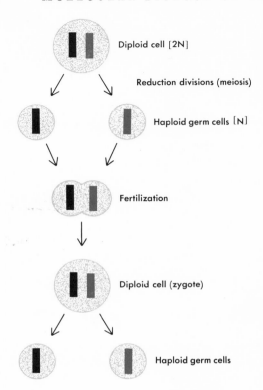

FIGURE 1–6   *Diagram of the alternation of haploid and diploid states, which comprise the sexual cycle. The chromosome set derived from one parent is shown in black, that from the other parent in color.*

not only often remain together, but also frequently differentiate into radically different cell types (such as nerve or muscle cells), while maintaining the chromosome complement of the zygote. Here, new organisms arise from the highly differentiated sperm and egg, whose union initiates a new cycle of division and differentiation.

Thus, although a complicated organism like man contains a large number of cells (up to 5×10^{12}), all these cells arise initially from a single cell. The fertilized egg contains all the information necessary for the growth and development of an adult

plant or animal. Again the living state per se does not demand
the complicated interactions that occur in complex organisms;
its essential properties can be found in single growing cells.

MENDELIAN LAWS

The most striking attribute of a living cell is its ability to trans-
mit hereditary properties from one cell generation to another.
The existence of heredity must have been noticed by early man
as he witnessed the passing of characteristics, like eye or hair
color, from parents to their offspring. Its physical basis,
however, was not understood until the first years of the
twentieth century, when, during a remarkable period of cre-
ative activity, the chromosomal theory of heredity was established.

Hereditary transmission through the sperm and egg became
known by 1860, and in 1868 Haeckel, noting that sperm
consisted largely of nuclear material, postulated that the
nucleus was responsible for heredity. Almost 20 years passed
before the chromosomes were singled out as the active factors,
because the details of mitosis, meiosis, and fertilization had to
be worked out first.

When this was accomplished, it could be seen that, unlike
other cell constituents, the chromosomes were equally divided
between daughter cells. Moreover, the complicated chromosomal changes which reduce the sperm and egg chromosome
number to the haploid number during meiosis became under-
standable as necessary for keeping the chromosome number
constant. These facts, however, merely suggested that chromosomes carry heredity.

Proof came at the turn of the century with the discovery of
the basic rules of heredity. These rules, named after their
original discoverer, Mendel, had in fact been first proposed in
1865, but the climate of scientific opinion had not been ripe
for their acceptance. They were completely ignored until 1900,
despite some early efforts on Mendel's part to interest the
prominent biologists of his time. Then de Vries, Correns, and
Tschermak, all working independently, realized the great im-

portance of Mendel's forgotten work. All three were plant breeders, doing experiments related to Mendel's, and each reached similar conclusions before they knew of Mendel's work.

PRINCIPLE OF INDEPENDENT SEGREGATION

Mendel's experiments traced the results of breeding experiments (genetic crosses) between strains of peas differing in well-defined characteristics, like seed shape (round or wrinkled), seed color (yellow or green), pod shape (inflated or wrinkled), and stem length (long or short). His concentration on well-defined differences was of great importance; many breeders had previously tried to follow the inheritance of more gross qualities, like body weight, and were unable to discover any simple rules about their transmission from parents to offspring. After ascertaining that each type of parental strain bred true (that is, produced progeny with particular qualities identical to those of the parents), Mendel made a number of crosses between parents (P) differing in single characteristics (such as seed shape *or* seed color). All the progeny (F_1 = first filial generation) had the appearance of *one* parent. For example, in a cross between peas having yellow seeds and peas having green seeds, all the progeny had yellow seeds. The trait that appears in the progeny is called *dominant*, whereas that not appearing in F_1 is called *recessive*.

The meaning of these results became clear when Mendel made genetic crosses between F_1 offspring. These crosses gave the most important result that the recessive trait reappeared in approximately 25 per cent of the progeny, whereas the dominant trait appeared in 75 per cent of them. For each of the seven traits he followed, the ratio in F_2 of dominant to recessive traits was always approximately 3:1. When these experiments were carried to a third (F_3) progeny generation, all the F_2 peas with recessive traits bred true (produced progeny with the recessive traits). Those with dominant traits fell into two groups: one-third bred true (produced only progeny with the dominant trait); the remaining two-thirds again produced mixed progeny in a 3:1 ratio of dominant to recessive.

Mendel correctly interpreted his results as follows (Figure 1–7): The various traits are controlled by pairs of factors (which we now call *genes*), one factor derived from the male parent, the other from the female. For example, pure-breeding strains of round peas contain two genes for roundness (RR), whereas pure-breeding wrinkled strains have two genes for wrinkledness (rr). The round-strain gametes each have one gene for roundness; the wrinkled-strain gametes each have one gene for wrinkledness (r). In a cross between RR and rr, fertilization produces an F_1 plant with both genes (Rr). The

FIGURE 1–7 *Representation of how Mendel's first law (independent segregation) explains the 3:1 ratio of dominant to recessive phenotypes among the F_2 progeny. (A) represent the dominant gene and (a) the recessive gene. The shaded circles represent dominance, the gray circles the recessive phenotype.*

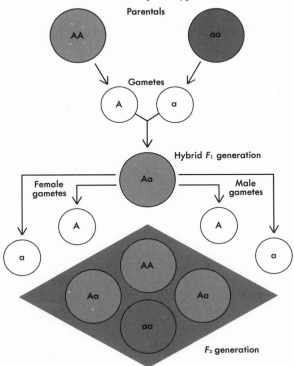

seed looks round because R is dominant over r. We refer to the appearance (physical structure) of an individual as its *phenotype*, and to its genetic composition as its *genotype*. Individuals with identical phenotypes may possess different genotypes; thus, to determine the genotype of an organism, it is frequently necessary to perform genetic crosses for several generations. The term *homozygous* refers to a gene pair in which both the maternal and paternal genes are identical (e.g., RR or rr). In contrast, those gene pairs in which paternal and maternal genes are different (e.g., Rr) are called *heterozygous*.

It is important to notice that a given gamete contains only one of the two genes present in the organism it comes from (for example, either the R or the r, but never both) and that the two types of gamete are produced in equal numbers. Thus there is a 50:50 chance that a given gamete from an F_1 pea will contain a particular gene (R or r). This choice is purely random. We do not expect to find *exact* 3:1 ratios when we examine a limited number of F_2 progeny. The ratio will sometimes be slightly higher and other times slightly lower. But as we look at increasingly larger samples, we expect that the ratio of peas with the dominant trait to peas with the recessive trait will approximate the 3:1 ratio more and more closely.

The reappearance of the recessive character in the F_2 generation indicates that recessive genes are neither modified nor lost in the *hybrid* (Rr) generation, but that the dominant and recessive genes are independently transmitted, and so are able to segregate independently during the formation of sex cells. *This principle of independent segregation is frequently referred to as Mendel's first law.*

SOME GENES ARE NEITHER DOMINANT NOR RECESSIVE

In the crosses reported by Mendel, one of each gene pair was clearly dominant, and the other recessive. Such behavior, however, is not universal. Sometimes the heterozygous phenotype is intermediate between the two homozygous phenotypes.

For example, the cross between a pure-breeding red snapdragon (*Antirrhinum*) and a pure-breeding white variety gives
F_1 progeny of the intermediate pink color. If these F_1 progeny
are crossed among themselves, the resulting F_2 progeny contain
red, pink, and white flowers in the proportion of 1:2:1 (Figure
1–8). Thus it is possible here to distinguish heterozygotes
from homozygotes by their phenotype. We also see that
Mendel's laws do not depend for their applicability on
whether one *gene* of a gene pair is dominant over the other.

FIGURE 1–8   *The inheritance of flower color in the snapdragon.
One parent is homozygous for red flowers (AA) and
the other homozygous for white flowers (aa).   No
dominance is present, and the heterozygous flowers
are pink.   The 1:2:1 ratio of red:pink:white flowers
is shown by appropriate coloring.*

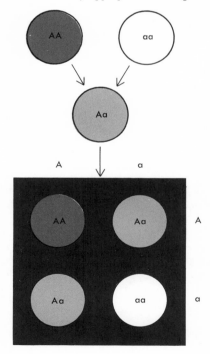

PRINCIPLE OF INDEPENDENT ASSORTMENT

Mendel extended his breeding experiments to peas differing by more than one character. As before, he started with two strains of peas, each of which bred pure when mated with itself. One of the strains had round yellow seeds, the other, wrinkled green seeds. Since round and yellow are dominant over wrinkled and green, the entire F_1 generation produced round, yellow seeds. The F_1 generation was then crossed within itself to produce a number of F_2 progeny, which were examined for seed appearance (phenotype). In addition to the two original phenotypes (round yellow; wrinkled green), two new types (*recombinants*) emerged: wrinkled yellow and round green.

Again Mendel found he could interpret the results by the postulate of genes, if he assumed that, during sex-cell formation, each gene pair was independently transmitted to the sex cell (gamete). This interpretation is shown in Figure 1–9. Any one gamete contains only one type of inherited factor from each gene pair. Thus the gametes produced by an F_1 (RrYy) will have the composition RY, Ry, rY, or ry, but never Rr, Yy, YY, or RR. Furthermore, in this example, all four possible gametes are produced with equal frequency. There is no tendency of the genes arising from one parent to stay together. As a result, the F_2 progeny phenotypes appear in the ratio: 9 round yellow, 3 round green, 3 wrinkled yellow, and 1 wrinkled green. *This phenomenon of independent assortment is frequently called Mendel's second law.*

CHROMOSOMAL THEORY OF HEREDITY

A principal reason for the original failure to appreciate Mendel's discovery was the absence of firm facts about the behavior of chromosomes during meiosis and mitosis. This knowledge was available, however, when Mendel's laws were reannounced in 1900, and was seized upon in 1903 by the American Sutton. In his classic paper, *The Chromosomes in Heredity*, he emphasized the importance of the fact that the diploid chromosome group consists of two morphologically

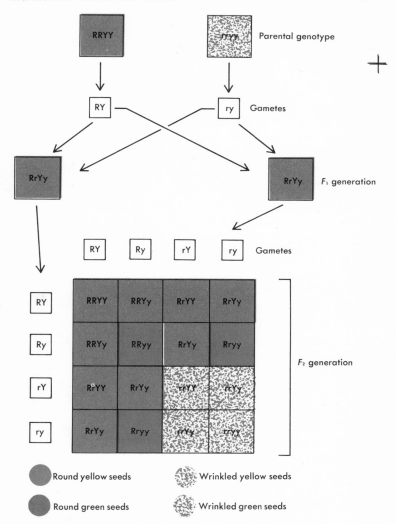

Round yellow seeds   Wrinkled yellow seeds

Round green seeds   Wrinkled green seeds

FIGURE 1-9   Schematic drawing of how Mendel's second law (independent assortment) operates. In this example, the inheritance of yellow (Y) and green (y) seed color is followed together with the inheritance of round (R) and wrinkled (r) seed shapes. The (R) and (Y) alleles are dominant over (r) and (y). The genotypes of the various parents and progeny are indicated by letter combinations, and four different phenotypes distinguished by appropriate shading.

similar sets and that, during meiosis, every gamete receives only one chromosome of each homologous pair. He then used this fact to explain Mendel's results by the assumption that genes are parts of the chromosome. He postulated that the yellow-and-green-seed genes are carried on a certain pair of chromosomes, and that the round- and wrinkled-seed genes are carried on a different pair. This hypothesis immediately explains the experimentally observed 9:3:3:1 segregation ratios. Though Sutton's paper did not prove the chromosomal theory of heredity, it was immensely important; it brought together for the first time the independent disciplines of genetics (the study of breeding experiments) and cytology (the study of cell structure).

CHROMOSOMAL DETERMINATION OF SEX

There exists one important exception to the rule that all chromosomes of diploid organisms are present in two copies. It was observed as early as 1890 that one chromosome (then called an accessory chromosome and now the x chromosome) does not always possess a morphologically identical mate. The biological significance of this observation was clarified by the American cytologist Wilson and his student Stevens, in 1905. They showed that, although the female contains a pair of x chromosomes, the male contains only one. In addition, in some species (including man), the male cells contain a unique chromosome, not found in females, called the y chromosome. They pointed out how this situation provides a simple method of sex determination; whereas every egg will contain one x chromosome, only half the sperms will carry one. Fertilization of an ovum by an x-bearing sperm leads to an xx zygote, which becomes a female; fertilization by a sperm cell lacking an x chromosome gives rise to male offspring (Figure 1–10). These observations provided the first clear linking of a definite chromosome to a hereditary property. In addition they elegantly explained how male and female zygotes are created in equal numbers.

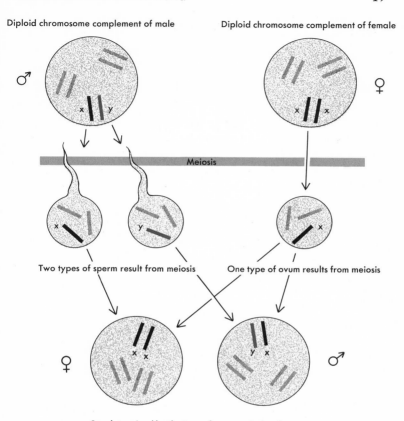

Diploid chromosome complement of male

Diploid chromosome complement of female

Meiosis

Two types of sperm result from meiosis

One type of ovum results from meiosis

Sex determined by the type of sperm entering the ovum

FIGURE 1–10   *Schematic representation of how sex chromosomes operate. Here is shown a case in which males contain one x and one y chromosome, and females, two x chromosomes. This is the situation in both humans and Drosophila. In some other species there is no y chromosome, so that diploid male cells contain one less chromosome than diploid female cells.*

THE IMPORTANCE OF DROSOPHILA

Initially, all breeding experiments used genetic differences already existing in nature. For example, Mendel used seeds obtained from seed dealers who must have obtained them from farmers. The existence of alternative forms of the same gene (alleles) raises the question of how they arose. One obvious hypothesis states that genes can change (mutate) to give rise to new genes (mutant genes). This hypothesis was first seriously tested, beginning in 1908, by the great American biologist Morgan and his young collaborators, the geneticists Bridges, Muller, and Sturtevant. They worked with the tiny fly *Drosophila*. This fly, which normally lives on fruit, was found to be easily maintained under laboratory conditions, where a new generation can be produced every 14 days. Thus by using *Drosophila* instead of more slowly multiplying organisms like peas, it was possible to work at least 25 times faster, and also much more economically. The first mutant found was a male with white eyes instead of the normal red eyes. It spontaneously appeared in a culture bottle of red-eyed flies. Because essentially all *Drosophila* found in nature have red eyes, the gene leading to red eyes was referred to as the *wild-type* gene; the gene leading to white eyes was called a *mutant gene* (allele).

The white-eye mutant gene was immediately used in breeding experiments (Figure 1–11*a* and *b*), with the striking result that the behavior of the allele completely paralleled the distribution of an *x* chromosome (i.e., was sex linked). This immediately suggested that this gene might be located on the *x* chromosome, together with those genes controlling sex. This hypothesis was quickly confirmed by additional genetic crosses using newly isolated mutant genes. Many of these additional mutant genes also were sex linked.

GENE LINKAGE AND CROSSING OVER

Mendel's principle of independent assortment is based on the fact that genes located on different chromosomes behave independently during meiosis. Often, however, two genes do not assort independently, because they are located on the same chromosome (*linked genes*). Numerous examples of non-random assortment were found as soon as a large number of mutant genes became available for breeding analysis. In every well-studied case, the number of linked groups was identical with the haploid chromosome number. For example, there are four groups of linked genes in *Drosophila* and four morphologically distinct chromosomes in a haploid cell.

Linkage, however, is in effect never complete. The probability that two genes on the same chromosome will remain together during meiosis ranges from just less than 100% to about 50%.

This means that a mechanism must exist for exchanging genes on homologous chromosomes. This mechanism is called *crossing over*. Its cytological basis was first described by the Belgian cytologist Janssens. At the start of meiosis, the homologous chromosomes form pairs (*synapse*) with their long axes parallel. At this stage, each chromosome has duplicated to form two chromatids. Thus synapsis brings together four chromatids (a tetrad), which coil about each other. Janssens postulated that, possibly because of tension resulting from this coiling, two of the chromatids might sometimes break at a corresponding place on each. This could create four broken ends, which might rejoin crossways, so that a section of each of the two chromatids would be joined to a section of the other (Figure 1–12). Thus recombinant chromatids might be produced that contain a segment derived from each of the original homologous chromosomes.

Morgan and his students were quick to exploit the implication of Janssens' still unproved theory: that genes located close to each other on a chromosome would assort with each other much more regularly (close linkage) than genes located far apart on a chromosome. This immediately suggested a way to locate (map) the relative positions of genes on the various chromosomes (see Chapter 7 for details). By 1915, more than 85 mutant genes in *Drosophila* had been assigned locations, each a distinct spot on one of the four linkage groups or chromosomes (Table 1–1). The definitive volume which Morgan then published, *The Mechanism of Mendelian Heredity*, showed the general validity of the chromosomal basis of heredity, a concept ranking with the theories of evolution and the cell as one of the main achievements of the biologist's attempt to understand the nature of the living world.

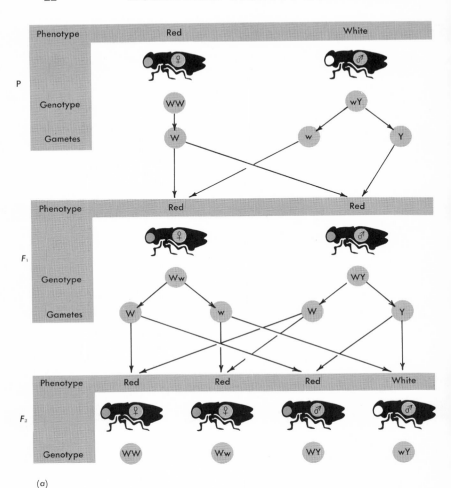

(a)

FIGURE 1–11   *The inheritance of a sex-linked gene in Drosophila. Genes located on sex chromosomes can express themselves differentially in male and female progeny because, if there is only one x chromosome present, recessive genes present on this chromosome are always expressed. Here are shown two crosses, both involving a recessive gene (w, for white eye) located on the x chromosome. In (a) the male parent is a white-eyed*

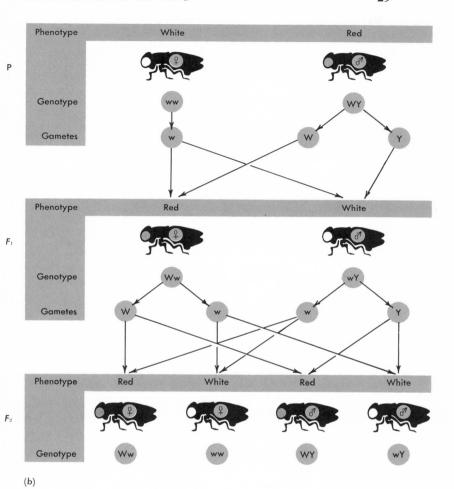

(b)

(wY) fly, and the female, homozygous for red eye
(WW). In (b) the male has red eyes (WY) and
the female, white eyes (ww). The letter (Y) stands,
here, not for an allele, but for the y chromosome,
present in male *Drosophila* in place of a homologous
x chromosome. There is no gene on the y chromosome corresponding to the (w) or (W) gene on the
x chromosome.

MANY GENES CONTROL THE RED EYE

Mere inspection of the list of mutant genes in Table 1–1 reveals an important fact; many different genes act to influence a single character. For example, 13 of the genes discovered by

TABLE 1–1   *The eighty-five mutant genes reported in Drosophila melanogaster in 1915[a]*

Group I

Name	Region affected	Name	Region affected
Abnormal	Abdomen	Lethal, 13	Body, death
Bar	Eye	Minature	Wing
Bifid	Venation	Notch	Venation
Bow	Wing	Reduplicated	Eye color
Cherry	Eye color	Ruby	Leg
Chrome	Body color	Rudimentary	Wing
Cleft	Venation	Sable	Body color
Club	Wing	Shifted	Venation
Depressed	Wing	Short	Wing
Dotted	Thorax	Skee	Wing
Eosin	Eye color	Spoon	Wing
Facet	Ommatidia	Spot	Body color
Forked	Spine	Tan	Antenna
Furrowed	Eye	Truncate	Wing
Fused	Venation	Vermilion	Eye color
Green	Body color	White	Eye color
Jaunty	Wing	Yellow	Body color
Lemon	Body color		

Group II

Name	Region affected	Name	Region affected
Antlered	Wing	Jaunty	Wing
Apterous	Wing	Limited	Abdominal band
Arc	Wing	Little crossover	II chromosome
Balloon	Venation	Morula	Ommatidia
Black	Body color	Olive	Body color
Blistered	Wing	Plexus	Venation
Comma	Thorax mark	Purple	Eye color
Confluent	Venation	Speck	Thorax mark
Cream II	Eye color	Strap	Wing
Curved	Wing	Streak	Pattern
Dachs	Leg	Trefoil	Pattern
Extra vein	Venation	Truncate	Wing
Fringed	Wing	Vestigial	Wing

T A B L E 1–1   (*continued*)

Group III

Name	Region affected	Name	Region affected
Band	Pattern	Pink	Eye color
Beaded	Wing	Rough	Eye
Cream III	Eye color	Safranin	Eye color
Deformed	Eye	Sepia	Eye color
Dwarf	Size of body	Sooty	Body color
Ebony	Body color	Spineless	Spine
Giant	Size of body	Spread	Wing
Kidney	Eye	Trident	Pattern
Low crossing over	III chromosome	Truncate intensf.	Wing
Maroon	Eye color	Whitehead	Pattern
Peach	Eye color	While ocelli	Simple eye

Group IV

Name	Region affected	Name	Region affected
Bent	Wing	Eyeless	Eye

ᵃ The mutations fall into four linkage groups. Since four chromosomes were cytologically observed, this indicated that the genes are
situated on the chromosomes. Notice that mutations in various
genes can act to alter a single character, such as body color, in different ways.

1915 affect eye color. When a fly is homozygous for a mutant
form of any of these genes, the eye color is not red, but a
different color, distinct for the mutant gene (e.g., carnation,
vermillion). Thus there is no one-to-one correspondence between genes and complex characters like eye color or wing
shape. Instead, the development of each character is controlled by a series of events, each of which is controlled by a
gene. We might make a useful analogy with the functioning
of a complex machine like the automobile: There are clearly a
number of separate parts, like the motor, the brakes, the radi-
ator, and the fuel tank, all of which are essential for its proper
operation. Although a fault in any one part may cause the car
to stop functioning properly, there is no reason to believe that
the presence of that component alone is sufficient for proper
functioning.

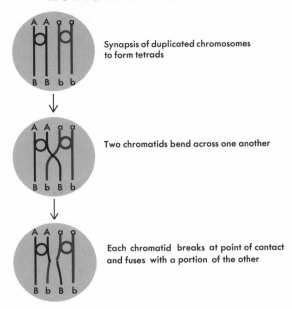

Synapsis of duplicated chromosomes
to form tetrads

Two chromatids bend across one another

Each chromatid breaks at point of contact
and fuses with a portion of the other

FIGURE 1–12   *Janssens' theory of crossing over.*

ORIGIN OF GENETIC VARIABILITY
THROUGH MUTATIONS

It now became possible to understand the hereditary variation
that is found throughout the biological world and that forms
the basis of the theory of evolution.   Genes are normally
copied exactly during chromosome duplication.   Rarely, however, changes (*mutations*) occur in genes to give rise to altered
forms most, *but not all*, of which function less well than the
wild-type alleles.   This process is necessarily rare; otherwise
many genes would be changed during every cell cycle, and
offspring would not ordinarily resemble their parents.   There
is instead a strong advantage in there being a small but finite
mutation rate; it provides a constant source of new variability,
necessary to allow plants and animals to adapt to a constantly
changing physical and biological environment.

Surprisingly, however, the results of the Mendelian geneticists were not avidly seized upon by the classical biologists,
then the authorities on the evolutionary relations between the
various forms of life. Doubts were raised about whether genetic changes of the type studied by Morgen and his students
were sufficient to permit the evolution of radically new structures, like wings or eyes. Instead, they believed that there
must also exist more powerful "macromutations," and that it
was these which allowed great evolutionary advances.

Gradually, however, doubts vanished, largely as a result of the
efforts of the mathematical geneticists Wright, Fisher, and
Haldane. Considering the great age of the earth, they showed
that the relatively low mutation rates found for *Drosophila*
genes, together with only mild selective advantages, would be
sufficient to allow the gradual accumulation of new favorable
attributes. By the 1930s, biologists themselves began to re-
evaluate their knowledge on the origin of species, and to understand the work of the mathematical geneticists. Among these
new Darwinians were the biologist Julian Huxley (a grandson
of Darwin's original publicist T. H. Huxley), the geneticist
Dobzhansky, the paleontologist Simpson, and the ornithologist
Mayr. In the 1940s, all four wrote major works, each showing
from his special viewpoint how Mendelianism and Darwinism
were indeed compatible.

EARLY SPECULATIONS ABOUT WHAT GENES ARE AND HOW THEY ACT

Almost immediately after the rediscovery of Mendel's laws,
geneticists began to speculate about both the chemical structure
of the gene and how it acts. No real progress could be made,
however, since the chemical identity of the genetic material
remained unknown. Even the realization that both nucleic
acids and proteins are present in chromosomes did not really
help, since the structure of neither was at all understood. The
most fruitful speculations focused attention on the fact that
genes must be, in some sense, self-duplicating: Their structure

must be exactly copied every time one chromosome becomes two. This fact immediately raised the profound chemical question of how a complicated molecule could be precisely copied to yield exact replicas.

Some physicists also became intrigued with the gene, and when quantum mechanics burst on the world in the late 1920's the possibility arose that, to understand the gene, it would be necessary to master the subtleties of the most advanced theoretical physics. Such thoughts, however, never really took root, since it was obvious that even the best physicists or theoretical chemists could not worry about a substance whose structure still awaited elucidation. There was only one fact which they might ponder: Muller's 1927 discovery that x rays induce mutation. Since there is a greater probability that an x ray will hit a larger gene than a smaller one, the frequency of mutations induced in a given gene by a given x-ray dose yields an estimate of the size of this gene. But even here so many special assumptions had to be made that virtually no one, not even the estimators themselves, took the estimates very seriously.

PRELIMINARY ATTEMPTS TO FIND A GENE–PROTEIN RELATIONSHIP

The most fruitful endeavors to find a relationship between genes and proteins examined the ways in which gene changes affect what proteins are present in the cell. At first this study was difficult, since no one really knew anything about the proteins that were present in structures such as the eye or the wing. It soon became obvious that genes with simple metabolic functions would be easier to study than genes affecting gross structures. One of the first useful examples came from a study of an hereditary disease affecting amino acid metabolism. Spontaneous mutations occur in humans, affecting the ability to metabolize the amino acid phenylalanine. When individuals homozygous for the mutant trait eat food containing phenylalanine, their inability to convert it to tyrosine causes a toxic level of phenylpyruvic acid to build up in the blood stream.

The existence of such diseases, an example of the so-called "inborn errors of metabolism," suggested as early as 1909 to the physician Garrod that the wild-type gene is responsible for the presence of a particular enzyme and that, in a homozygous mutant, the enzyme is congenitally absent.

Garrod's general hypothesis of a gene-enzyme relationship was extended in the 1930s by work on flower pigments and the pigments of insect eyes. In both cases evidence was obtained that a particular gene affected a particular step in the formation of the pigment. However, the absence of fundamental knowledge about the structures of the relevant proteins ruled out deeper examination of the gene-protein relationship, and no assurance could be given either that most genes control the synthesis of proteins (by then it was suspected that all enzymes were proteins), or that all proteins are under gene control.

As early as 1935, it became obvious to the Mendelian geneticists that future experiments of the sort successful in elucidating the basic features of Mendelian genetics were unlikely to yield productive evidence about how genes act. Instead it would be necessary to find biological objects more suitable for chemical analysis. They were aware, however, that the contemporary state of nucleic acid and protein chemistry was completely inadequate for a fundamental chemical attack on even the most suitable biological systems. Fortunately, however, the limitations in chemistry did not deter them from learning how to do genetic experiments with chemically simple molds, bacteria, and viruses. As we shall see, the necessary chemical facts became available almost as soon as the geneticists were ready to use them.

SUMMARY

The study of living organisms at the biological level has led to three great generalizations: (1) Darwin's and Wallace's theory of evolution by natural selection, which tells us that today's complex plants and animals are derived by a continuous evo-

lutionary progression from the first primitive organisms; (2) the cell theory, the realization that all organisms are built up of cells; (3) the chromosomal theory of heredity, the understanding that the function of chromosomes is the control of heredity.

All cells contain chromosomes, normally duplicated prior to a cell-division process (mitosis) which produces two daughter cells, each with a chromosomal complement identical to that of the parental cell. In haploid cells there is just one copy of each type of chromosome; in diploid cells there are usually two copies (pairs of homologous chromosomes). A diploid cell arises by fusion of a male and a female haploid cell (fertilization), whereas haploid cells are formed from a diploid cell by a distinctive form of cell division (meiosis), which reduces the chromosome number to one-half of its previous number.

Chromosomes control heredity because they are the cellular locations of genes. Genes were first discovered by Mendel in 1865, but their importance was not realized until the start of the twentieth century. Each gene can exist in a variety of different forms called alleles. Mendel proposed that a gene for each hereditary trait is given by each parent to each of its offspring. The physical basis for this behavior is in the distribution of homologous chromosomes during meiosis: One (randomly chosen) of each pair of homologous chromosomes is distributed to each haploid cell. When two genes are on the same chromosome, they tend to be inherited together (linked genes). Genes affecting different characters are sometimes inherited independently of each other: this is because they are located on different chromosomes. In any case, linkage is seldom complete, because homologous chromosomes attach to each other during meiosis and often break at identical spots and rejoin crossways (crossing over). This attaches genes initially found on a paternally derived chromosome to gene groups originating from the maternal parent.

Different alleles of the same gene arise by inheritable changes (mutations) in the gene itself. Normally genes are extremely stable and are exactly copied during chromosome duplication; mutation normally occurs only rarely and usually has harmful consequences. It does, however, play a positive role, since the accumulation of the rare favorable mutations provides the basis for the genetic variability that the theory of evolution presupposes.

For many years the structure of the genes and the chemical way in which they control cellular characteristics were a mystery. As soon as large numbers of spontaneous mutations had been described, it became obvious that a one genome character relationship does not exist, but that all complex characters are under the control of many genes. The most sensible idea, postulated clearly by Garrod as early as 1909, was that genes affect the synthesis of enzymes. However, in general, the tools of the Mendelian geneticists, organisms such as the corn plant, the mouse, and even the fruit fly, Drosophila, were not suitable for chemical investigations of gene-protein relations. For this type of analysis, work with much simpler microorganisms became indispensable.

REFERENCES

Swanson, D. P., *The Cell*, 2nd ed., Prentice-Hall, Englewood Cliffs, N.J., 1964. An introductory survey of the cell theory.

Moore, J. A., *Heredity and Development*, Oxford, New York, 1963. An elegant introduction to genetics and embryology, with emphasis on the historical approach.

Sturtevant, A. H., and G. W. Beadle, *An Introduction to Genetics*, Dover, New York, 1962. Now available in paperback form, this book, originally published in 1939, remains a classic statement of the results of *Drosophila* genetics.

Levine, R. P., *Genetics*, 2nd ed., Holt, New York, 1968. A rapid survey of genetics, with emphasis on the use of microorganisms in establishing a chemical basis of genetics.

Srb, A., R. Owen, and R. Edgar, *General Genetics*, 2nd ed., Freeman, San Francisco, 1965. Excellent introduction to genetics.

Peters, J. A., *Classic Papers in Genetics*, Prentice-Hall, Englewood Cliffs, N.J., 1959. A collection of reprints of many of the most significant papers in the history of genetics, up to Benzer's fine-structure analysis of the gene.

Carlson, E. J., *The Gene Theory: A Critical History*, W. B. Saunders, Philadelphia, 1966. Surveys the development of genetical ideas from Mendel to the present.

Mayr, E., *Animal Species and Evolution*, Harvard University Press, Cambridge, 1963. The most complete statement of the facts supporting the theory of evolution.

2

CELLS OBEY
THE LAWS OF
CHEMISTRY

IN DARWIN'S TIME CHEMISTS WERE AL-
ready asking whether living cells
worked by the same chemical rules as
nonliving systems. By then, cells had
been found to contain no atoms peculiar to living material. Also recognized early was the predominant role
of carbon, a major constituent of almost all types of biological molecules.
A reflection of the initial tendency to
distinguish between carbon compounds like those in living matter and
all other molecules is retained in the
division of modern chemistry into organic chemistry (the study of most
compounds containing carbon atoms)
and inorganic chemistry. Now we
know that this distinction is artificial
and has no biological basis. There is
no purely chemical way to decide
whether a compound has been synthesized in a cell or in a chemist's
laboratory.

Nonetheless, through the first quar-
ter of this century, a strong feeling
existed in many biological and chemical laboratories that some vital force
outside the laws of chemistry differentiated between the animate and the
inanimate. Part of the reason for the
persistence of this "vitalism" was that
the success of the biologically oriented
chemists (now usually called biochemists) was limited. Although the
techniques of the organic chemists were
sufficient to work out the structures of
relatively small molecules like glucose
(Table 2–1), there was increasing

awareness that many of the most important molecules in the cell were very large—the so-called macromolecules—too large to be pursued by even the best of organic chemists.

The most important group of macromolecules was for many years believed to be the proteins, because of the growing evidence that all enzymes are proteins. Initially, there was controversy as to whether enzymes were small molecules or macromolecules. It was not until 1926 that the enzymatic nature of a crystalline protein was demonstrated by the American biochemist Sumner; the controversy was then practically settled. But even this important discovery did not dispel the general aura of mystery about proteins. Then, the complex structures of proteins were undecipherable by available chemical tools, so it was still possible, as late as 1940, for some scientists to believe that these molecules would eventually be shown to have features unique to living systems.

The general belief also existed that the genes, like the enzymes, might be proteins. There was no direct evidence, but the high degree of specificity of genes suggested to most people who speculated on their nature that they could only be proteins, by then known to occur in the chromosomes. Another class of molecules, the nucleic acids, were also found to be a common chromosomal component, but these were thought to be relatively small and incapable of carrying sufficient genetic information.

Besides general ignorance of the structures of the large molecules, the feeling was often expressed that something unique about the three-dimensional organization of the cell gave it its living feature. This argument was sometimes phrased in terms of the impossibility of ever understanding all the exact chemical interactions of the cell. More frequently, however, it took the form of the prediction that some new natural laws, as important as the cell theory or the theory of evolution, would have to be discovered before the essence of life could be understood. But these almost mystical ideas never led to meaningful experiments and, in their vague form, could never be tested. Progress was made instead only by biologically oriented chemists and physicists patiently at-

T A B L E 2-1 *Some important classes of small biological molecules*

Class	Characteristics	Example
Aliphatic hydrocarbon	Linear or branched molecules containing only carbon and hydrogen	Ethane
Aromatic hydrocarbon	Ring-shaped hydrocarbons containing alternating single and double bonds	Benzene
Pyrimidine	An aromatic compound of the formula $C_4H_4N_2$ (or a derivative thereof)	Uracil

Purine

Guanine

An aromatic compound of the formula $C_5H_4N_4$ (or a derivative)

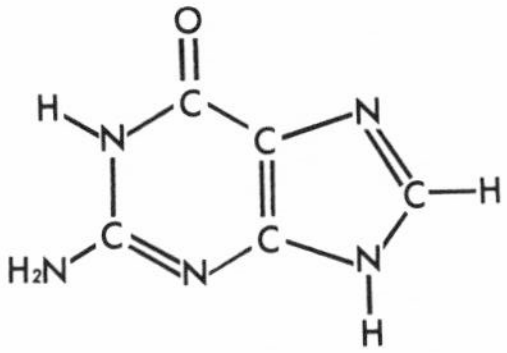

Alcohol

Ethanol

A hydrocarbon skeleton substituted with one to several OH groups

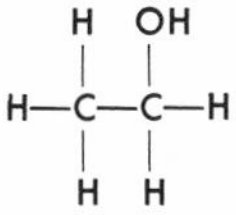

Phosphate ester

Glucose-1-℗

Molecule formed from alcohols and phosphoric acids with the elimination of H_2O.

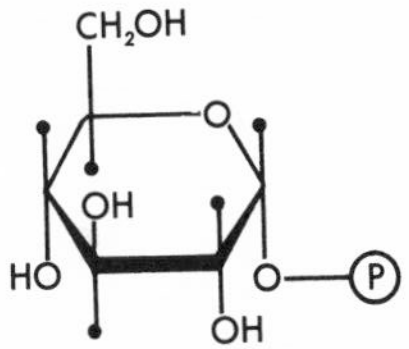

(continued)

TABLE 2-1 (continued)

Class	Characteristics	Example
Nucleoside	Contains a pentose sugar linked to either a purine or pyrimidine base, through a C–N bond	Adenosine
Nucleotide	Phosphate ester of a nucleoside	Adenosine-5-℗ or Adenylic acid

Carboxylic acid	Hydrocarbon skeleton containing one to several COO^- groups	Acetate
Hydroxy acid	Substituted hydrocarbon containing both an OH and a COO^- group	Lactate
Keto acid	Substituted hydrocarbon containing both a keto group and a COO^- group	Pyruvate
Amino acid	Contains both NH_2 and COOH groups; both groups are usually charged. The general formula is [structure] where (R) represents a group that varies from amino acid to amino acid. There are 20 amino acids, each with a distinctive R group.	Glycine
Sugar (monosaccharide)	Polyhydroxyl molecule containing a $C=O$ group (either an aldehyde or a ketone). The most common sugars have 3 (triose), 4 (tetrose), 5 (pentose), or 6 (hexose) carbon atoms.	Ribose

tempting to devise new ways of solving more and more complex biological structures. But for many years, there were no triumphs to shout. The chemists and biologists usually moved in different and sometimes hostile worlds, the biologist often denying that the chemist would ever provide the real answers to the important riddles of biology. Always not too far back in some biologists' minds was the feeling, if not the hope, that something more basic than mere complexity and size separated biology from the bleak, inanimate world of a chemical laboratory.

THE CONCEPT OF INTERMEDIARY METABOLISM

As soon as the organic chemists began to identify some of the various cellular molecules, it became clear that food molecules are extensively transformed after they enter an organism. In no case does a food source contain all the different molecules present in a cell. On the contrary, in some cases practically all the organic molecules within an organism are synthesized inside it. This point is easily seen by observing cellular growth on well-defined food sources: for example, the growth of yeast cells using the simple sugar glucose as the sole source of carbon. Here, soon after its cellular entry, glucose is chemically transformed into a large variety of molecules necessary for the building of new structural components. Usually these chemical transformations do not occur in one step; instead intermediate compounds are produced. These intermediate compounds often have no cellular function besides forming part of a pathway leading to the synthesis of a necessary structural component like an amino acid.

The sum total of all the various chemical reactions occurring in a cell is frequently referred to as the *metabolism* of the cell. Correspondingly, the various molecules involved in these transformations are often called *metabolites*. *Intermediary metabolism* is the term used to describe the various chemical reactions involved in the transformation of food molecules into essential cellular building blocks.

ENERGY GENERATION BY OXIDATION–
REDUCTION REACTIONS

By the middle of the nineteenth century, it was known that the food (initially of plant origin) eaten by animals and bacteria is only in part transformed into new cellular building blocks, some of it being burned by combustion with oxygen to yield CO_2 and H_2O and energy. At the same time it was becoming clear that the reverse process also operates in green plants.

Respiration:

$C_6H_{12}O_6$ (glucose) $+ 6O_2 \rightarrow 6CO_2 + 6H_2O +$ energy (in form of heat)

(occurs both in plants and animals)   (2–1)

Photosynthesis:

$6CO_2 + 6H_2O +$ energy (from the sun) $\rightarrow C_6H_{12}O_6$ (glucose) $+ 6O_2$

(occurs only in plants)   (2–2)

Both these equations can be thought of as the sum total of a lengthy series of oxidation-reduction reactions.

In respiration, organic molecules such as glucose are oxidized by molecular oxygen to form $C{=}O$ bonds (Table 2–2), which contain *less* usable energy (energy which can do work) than the starting C—H, C—OH, and C—C bonds. Energy is given off in respiration, just as it is when glucose burns at high temperatures outside the cell to produce CO_2, H_2O, and energy in the form of heat. In contrast, during photosynthesis, the energy from the light quanta of the sun is used to reduce CO_2 to molecules which contain *more* usable energy.

When these relationships were first worked out, no one knew how the energy obtained during respiration was put to advantage. It was clear that somehow a useful form of energy had to be available to enable living organisms to carry out a variety of forms of work, such as muscular contraction and selective transport of molecules across cell membranes. Even then it seemed unlikely that the energy obtained from food was first released as heat, since, at the temperature at which life exists, heat energy cannot be effectively used to synthesize new

TABLE 2-2 *Important functional groups in biological molecules*

Group	Molecular Example	Biological Significance
Methyl	Methyl group of alanine	Highly insoluble in water; does not form hydrogen bonds
—OH Hydroxyl	Ethanol (ethyl alcohol)	Water soluble; forms hydrogen bonds
Carboxyl	Acetic acid	Usually charged: $\rightleftharpoons$ + H$^+$ good acceptor of hydrogen bonds
Amino	Glycine	Often charged: $-NH_2 + H^+ \rightleftharpoons -NH_3^+$ forms hydrogen bonds
Carbonyl C=O	Acetaldehyde	Forms hydrogen bonds; usually exists in keto form: R—C—CH$_3$

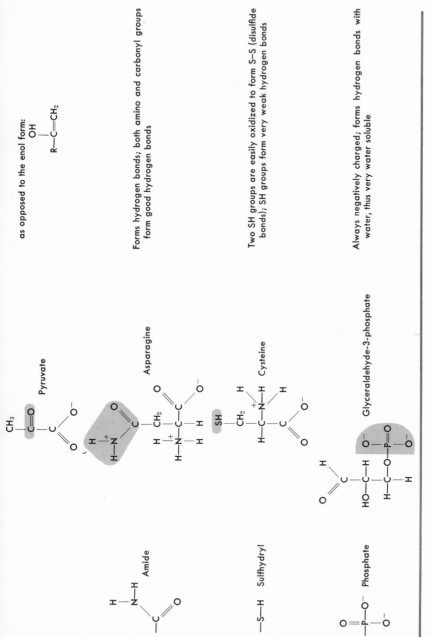

as opposed to the enol form:

Pyruvate

Amide

Forms hydrogen bonds; both amino and carbonyl groups form good hydrogen bonds

Asparagine

Sulfhydryl

Two SH groups are easily oxidized to form S—S (disulfide bonds); SH groups form very weak hydrogen bonds

Cysteine

Phosphate

Always negatively charged; forms hydrogen bonds with water, thus very water soluble

Glyceraldehyde-3-phosphate

41

chemical bonds. Thus since the awakening of an interest in the chemistry of life, a prime challenge has been to understand the generation of energy in a useful form.

MOST BIOLOGICAL OXIDATIONS OCCUR WITHOUT DIRECT PARTICIPATION OF OXYGEN

Because oxygen is so completely necessary for the functioning of animals, it was natural to guess that oxygen would participate directly in all oxidations of carbon compounds. Actually, most biological oxidations occur in the absence of oxygen. This is possible because, as first proposed around 1912 by the German biochemist Wieland, most biological oxidations are actually dehydrogenations. A compound is oxidized when we remove a pair of hydrogen atoms from it (Figure 2–1). It is not possible, however, merely to remove the hydrogen atoms. They must be transferred to another molecule, which is then said to be reduced (Figure 2–2). In these reactions, as in all other oxidation-reduction reactions, every time one molecule is oxidized, another must be reduced. There are several different molecules whose role is to receive hydrogen atoms. All are medium-sized (MW $\sim$ 500) organic molecules that associate with specific proteins to form active enzymes. The protein components alone have no enzymatic activity. Only when the small partner is present will activity be present. Hence these small molecules are named *coenzymes* (we should note that not all coenzymes participate in oxidation-reduction reactions; some coenzymes function in other types of metabolic reactions).

FIGURE 2–1   *Oxidation of an organic molecule by removal of a pair of hydrogen atoms. This figure shows the oxidation of lactate to pyruvate.*

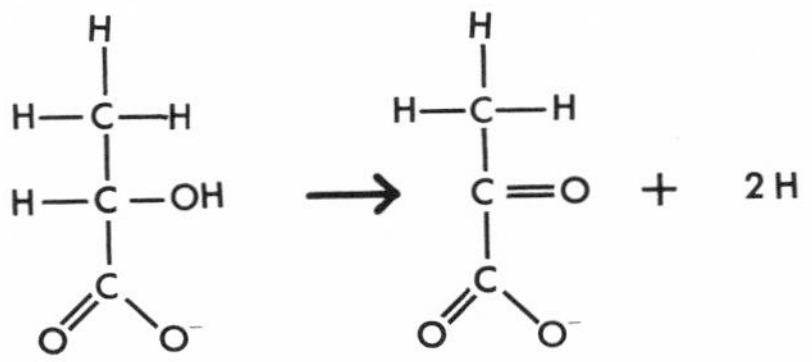

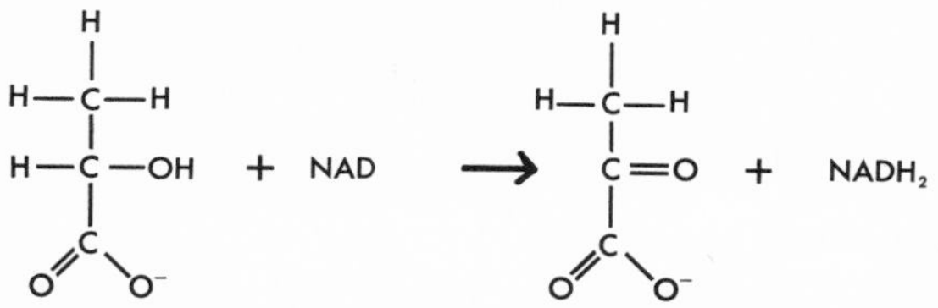

FIGURE 2-2 *The participation of NAD in the oxidation of lactate to pyruvate. The oxidizing agent here is NAD, and the hydrogen donor is lactate.*

Although the involvement of coenzymes in oxidative reactions was hinted at by 1910, it was not until the early 1930s that their cardinal significance was appreciated. Then the work of the great German biochemist, Otto Warburg, and the Swedish chemists, von Euler and Theorell, established the structure and action of several of the most important coenzymes: nicotinamide adenine dinucleotide (NAD, earlier called diphosphopyridine nucleotide or DPN, Figure 2-3), flavin mononucleotide (FMN), and flavin adenine dinucleotide (FAD).

Coenzymes, like enzymes, function many different times and are not used up in the course of functioning. This is because the hydrogen atoms transferred to them do not remain permanently attached, but are transferred by a second oxidation-reduction reaction, usually to another coenzyme, or to oxygen itself (Figure 2-4). Coenzymes are thus being continually oxidized and reduced. Furthermore, we see that, although oxygen is not directly necessary for a given reaction, it is often necessary indirectly, since it must be available to oxidize the coenzyme molecules to make them available for accepting additional pairs of hydrogen atoms (or electrons).

THE BREAKDOWN OF GLUCOSE

Much of the early work in intermediary metabolism dealt with the transformation of glucose into other molecules. Glucose was emphasized, not only because it played a central role in the economy of cells, but also for a practical reason: The alcohol (ethanol) produced when wine is made from grapes is derived from the breakdown of glucose. As early as 1810, the chemist Gay-Lussac demonstrated the production of ethyl alcohol by this process, and by 1837 the essential role of yeast was established. The production of the alcohol in wine is not a spontaneous process but normally requires the presence of living yeast cells.

Also important in the initial work with glucose was the French microbiologist Pasteur, who discovered that the process does not require air; to distinguish it from reactions requiring oxygen, he used the term *fermentation*. He also showed that

FIGURE 2–3   *The oxidation and reduction of a coenzyme. Shown here are both the oxidized and reduced forms of the very important coenzyme nicotinamide adenine dinucleotide, NAD (the oxidized form), an acceptor of hydrogen atoms, and NADH$_2$ (the reduced form), a donor of hydrogen atoms. The release of hydrogen atoms decreases the free energy of a molecule; the acceptance of them increases its free energy.*

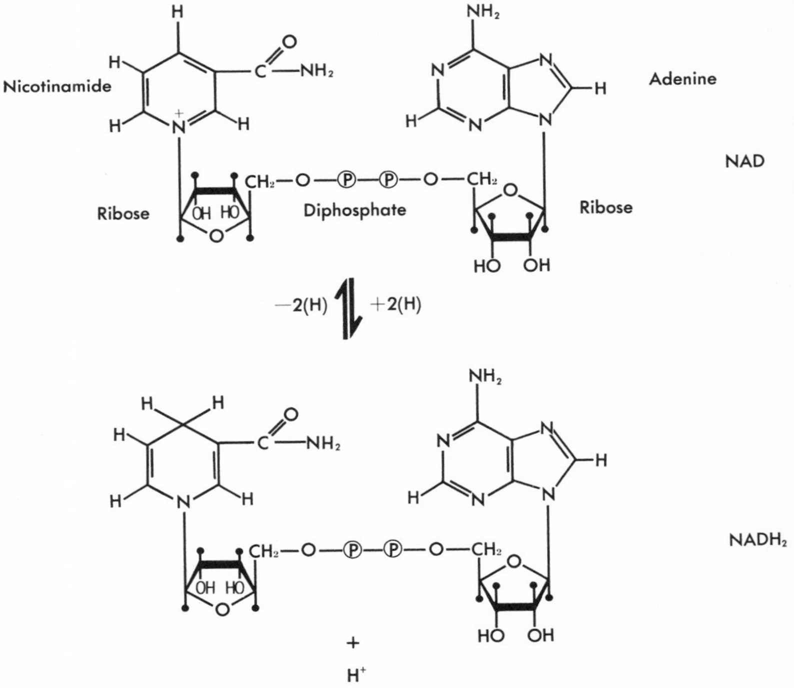

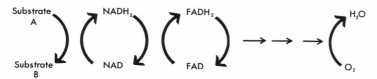

FIGURE 2–4 *The transfer of a pair of hydrogen atoms from one coenzyme to another. In this series of reactions, the final hydrogen acceptor is oxygen* (O_2). *FAD is flavin adenine dinucleotide, which exists not free, but usually in combination with a specific protein, to form a flavoprotein.*

ethanol is not the only product of glucose fermentation, but that there are other products, such as lactic acid and glycerol.

The next great advance came with Buchner's discovery in 1897 that the living cell per se is not necessary for fermentation, but that a cell-free extract from yeast can, by itself, transform glucose into ethanol. This step was not only conceptually important, but also provided a much more practical system for studying the chemical steps of fermentation. When working with cell-free systems, it is relatively easy to add or subtract components thought to be involved in the reaction; when living cells are being used, it is often very difficult, and sometimes impossible, to transfer specific compounds in an unmodified form across the cell membrane.

Over the next 40 years, cell-free extracts were used by a large number of distinguished biochemists, including the Englishmen Harden and Young, and the Germans Embden and Meyerhof, to work out the exact chemical pathways of glucose degradation (Figure 2–5). During this period, the important generalization emerged that the reactions involved (collectively called the Embden-Meyerhof pathway) were not peculiar to alcoholic fermentation in yeast, but occurred in many other cases of glucose utilization as well. Perhaps the most significant discovery was made by Meyerhof. He showed that, when muscles contract in the absence of oxygen, the carbohydrate food reserve of glycogen is broken down, via glucose, to lactic acid (anaerobic *glycolysis*). Thus it became clear that, not only can microorganisms obtain their energy and carbon

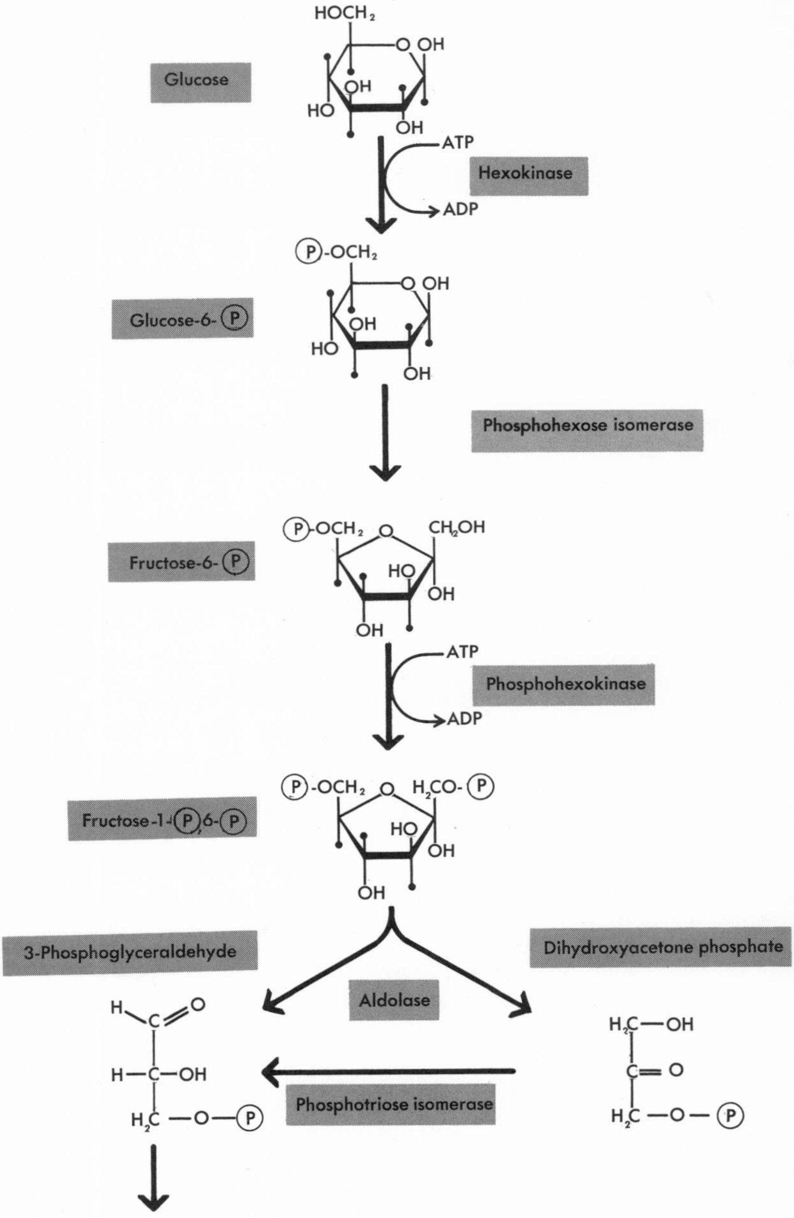
Glucose
HOCH₂
ATP
Hexokinase
ADP
Glucose-6-(P)
(P)-OCH₂
Phosphohexose isomerase
Fructose-6-(P)
ATP
Phosphohexokinase
ADP
Fructose-1-(P),6-(P)
3-Phosphoglyceraldehyde
Aldolase
Dihydroxyacetone phosphate
Phosphotriose isomerase

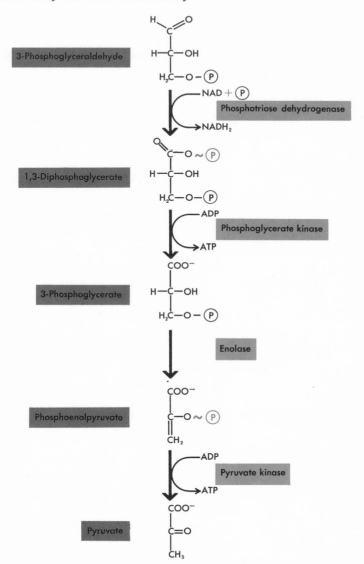

FIGURE 2–5   *The stepwise degradation of glucose to pyruvic acid. This collection of consecutive reactions is often called the Embden-Meyerhof pathway.*

via the Embden-Meyerhof pathway, but energy involved in the contraction of muscles is also generated by the same pathway.

A feeling often expressed as "the unity of biochemistry" began to develop. By this we mean the realization that the basic biochemical reactions upon which cell growth and division depend are the same, or very similar, in all cells, those of microorganisms as well as of higher plants and animals. This unity was not surprising to the more astute biologists, many of whom were largely preoccupied with the consequences of evolutionary theory: Given that a man and a fish are descended from a common ancestor, it should not be surprising that many of their cell constituents are similar.

INVOLVEMENT OF PHOSPHORUS AND THE GENERATION OF ATP

As early as 1905 the phosphorus atom was implicated in a vital role in metabolism. Then Harden and Young found that alcoholic fermentation occurs only when inorganic phosphate (PO_4^{3-}) is present. This discovery was followed by the eventual isolation of a large number of intermediary metabolites containing PO_4^{3-} (Ⓟ) groups attached to carbon atoms by phosphate ester linkages $\left(-\overset{|}{\underset{|}{C}}-O-Ⓟ \right)$.

The significance of phosphorylated intermediates was unclear for 25 years. Then, about 1930, Meyerhof and Lipmann realized the crucial fact that it is by means of the phosphate esters that cells are able to trap some of the energy of the chemical bonds present in their food molecules. During fermentation several intermediates (Figure 2–6) are created (e.g., D-1,3-diphosphoglyceric acid), which contain what are popularly known as high-energy phosphate bonds (see Chapter 5 for more details). These high-energy phosphate groups are usually transferred to acceptor molecules, where they can serve as sources of chemical energy for vital cellular processes, such as motion, generation of light, and (as we shall see in Chapters 5 and 6) the efficient biosynthesis of necessary cellular molecules. The most important of the acceptor molecules is adenosine diphosphate (ADP, Figure 2–7). Addition of a high-energy ℗ group to ADP forms *adenosine triphosphate (ATP)*.

ADP + ℗ ⇌ ATP

The discovery of the role of ADP as an acceptor molecule and that of ATP as a donor of high-energy phosphate groups was one of the most important discoveries of modern biology. Until the roles of these molecules were known, there was complete mystery about how cells obtained energy. There was constant speculation about how cellular existence was compatible with the second law of thermodynamics [in a closed system the amount of disorder (entropy) invariably increases]. What was conceivably a paradox ceased to exist as soon as it was seen how animal cells could trap and utilize the energy in food molecules. At that time the mechanism by which the sun's energy was trapped in photosynthesis was not known. Here again, the primary action of the sun's energy is now known to be the generation of ATP.

FIGURE 2–6 *The formation of an energy-rich phosphate ester bond, coupled with the oxidation of 3-phosphoglyceraldehyde by NAD.*

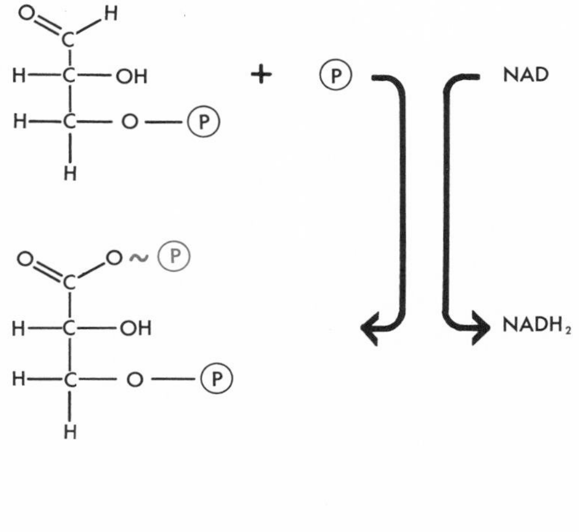

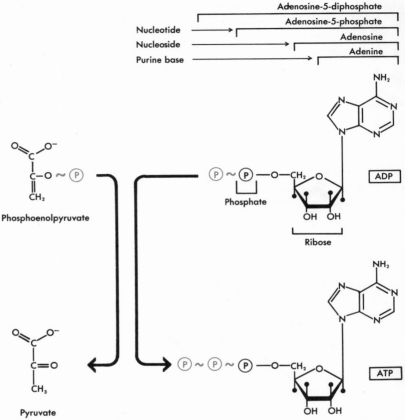

FIGURE 2–7   *The formation of ATP (adenosine-5′-triphosphate) from ADP and an energy-rich phosphate bond. Here the donor of the high-energy bond is phosphoenolpyruvate. The symbol ~ signifies that the bond is of the high-energy variety.*

MOST SPECIFIC CELLULAR REACTIONS REQUIRE A SPECIFIC ENZYME

The idea that most specific metabolic steps require a specific enzyme was realized only when a number of specific reactions were unraveled. As the Embden-Meyerhof pathway was being worked out, it became clear that each step required a separate enzyme (see Figure 2–5). Each of the enzymes acts by combining with the molecules involved in the particular reaction (the substrates of the enzymes). For example, glucose and ATP are substrates for the enzyme hexokinase. When these molecules interact on the surface of hexokinase, the terminal P of ATP is transferred to a glucose molecule to form glucose-6-Ⓟ.

The essence of an enzyme is its ability to speed up (catalyze) a reaction involving the making or breaking of a specific covalent bond (a bond in which atoms are held together by the sharing of electrons). In the absence of enzymes, most of the covalent bonds of biological molecules are very stable, and decompose only under high nonphysiological temperatures; only at several hundred degrees centigrade is glucose, for example, appreciably oxidized by O_2 in the absence of enzymes. Enzymes must therefore act by somehow lowering the temperature at which a given bond is unstable. A physical chemist would say that an enzyme lowers the "activation energy." How this is done is just being understood at the molecular level. The 3-D structure of several enzymes is now known, and plausible chemical theories about how they work exist. Thus, there is no reason to suspect that still undiscovered laws of chemistry underlie enzyme action. Numerous examples already exist where well-defined molecules speed up reactions between other molecules.

A very important characteristic of enzymes is that they are never consumed in the course of reaction; once a reaction is complete, they are free to adsorb new molecules and function again (Figure 2–8). On a biological time scale (seconds to years), enzymes can work very fast, some being able to catalyze as many as 10^6 reactions per minute; often no successful collision of substrates will occur in this time interval when enzymes are absent.

Not all enzymatic reactions, however, are specific. There exist, for example, various enzymes which break down a variety of different proteins to their component amino acids. They are specific only in the sense that they catalyze the breakdown of a specific type of covalent bond, the peptide bond, and will not, for example, degrade the phosphodiester linkages of the nucleic acids.

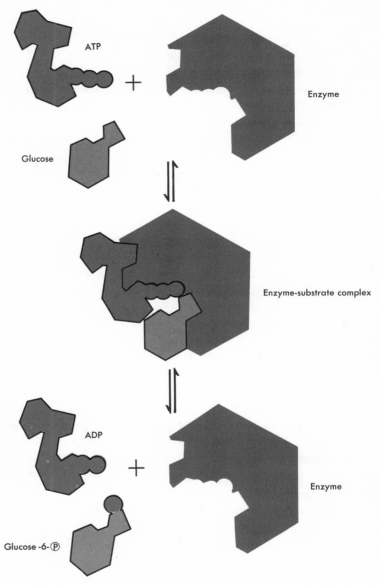

FIGURE 2–8 *The formation of an enzyme-substrate complex, followed by catalysis.*

THE KEY ROLE OF PYRUVATE: * ITS
UTILIZATION VIA THE KREBS CYCLE

Attempts to understand the generation of ATP in the presence of oxygen occurred parallel with the study of fermentation and glycolysis. It was immediately obvious from consideration of the amounts of ATP generated by fermentation and glycolysis that these processes could account for only a small fraction of total ATP production in the presence of oxygen. This means that ATP production in the presence of oxygen does not cease once glucose has been degraded as far as pyruvic acid (pyruvate), but that pyruvic acid itself must be further transformed, via energy-yielding reactions requiring the presence of oxygen.

The first real breakthrough in understanding how this happens came with the discoveries made by the biochemists Szent-Györgyi, Martius, and Krebs. Their work revealed the existence of a cyclic series of reactions (now usually called the *Krebs cycle*) by which pyruvate is oxidatively broken down to yield carbon dioxide (CO_2) and a series of pairs of hydrogen atoms that attach to oxidized coenzyme molecules. Before pyruvate enters the Krebs cycle, it is transformed into a key molecule called acetyl-CoA (Figure 2–9), known before its chemical identification as "active acetate." This important intermediate, discovered in 1949 by Lipmann, working in Boston, then combines with oxaloacetate to yield citrate. A series of at least nine additional steps (see Figure 2–10) then occur to yield four pairs of H atoms and two molecules of CO_2. The pairs of hydrogen atoms never exist free, but are transferred to specific coenzyme molecules.

The Krebs cycle should be viewed as a mechanism for breaking down acetyl-CoA to two types of products: the completely oxidized CO_2 molecules, which cannot be used as energy sources, and the reduced coenzymes, whose further oxidation yields most of the energy used by organisms growing in the presence of oxygen.

---

* The terms pyruvic acid and pyruvate are used interchangeably. Technically, pyruvate refers to the negatively charged ion. Likewise, lactic acid is often called lactate, glutamic acid–glutamate, citric acid–citrate, etc.

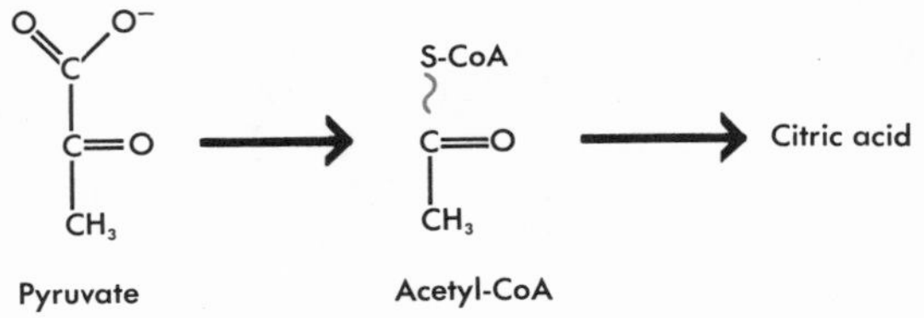

Pyruvate   Acetyl-CoA

FIGURE 2–9   *The transformation of pyruvate to acetyl-CoA. CoA refers to coenzyme A. The transformation, as written, is greatly simplified. Several steps are required in which the coenzymes thiamine pyrophosphate and lipoic acid are both involved. Acetyl-CoA is an extremely important intermediate, for it is formed not only from glucose via pyruvate, but also by the degradation of fatty acids.*

OXIDATION OF REDUCED COENZYMES BY RESPIRATORY ENZYMES

During the functioning of the Krebs cycle there is no direct involvement of molecular oxygen. Oxygen is involved only after the hydrogen atoms (or electrons) have been transferred through an additional series of oxidation-reduction reactions that involve a series of closely linked enzymes, all of which contain iron atoms. These enzymes are often collectively called the respiratory enzymes.

Their existence was hinted at late in the nineteenth century, but it was not until the period of 1925 to 1940 that their significance was appreciated, largely as a result of the work of Warburg and the Polish-born David Keilin, who spent most of his scientific life in England. Even today there remains uncertainty about the exact number of enzymes involved. Nevertheless, the correctness of the general picture is not disputed. Figure 2–11 shows the general features of the respiratory chain.

The chain operates by a series of coupled oxidation-reduction reactions, during each of which energy is released. Thus the energy present in the reduced coenzymes is released not all at once but in a series of small packets. If $NADH_2$ were instead directly oxidized by molecular oxygen, a great amount of energy would be released, which it would be impossible to couple efficiently with the formation of the high-energy bonds of ATP.

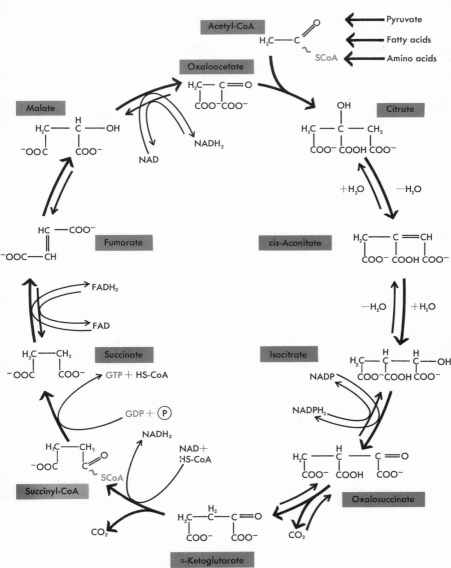

FIGURE 2-10 *The citric acid cycle (often called the Krebs cycle).*

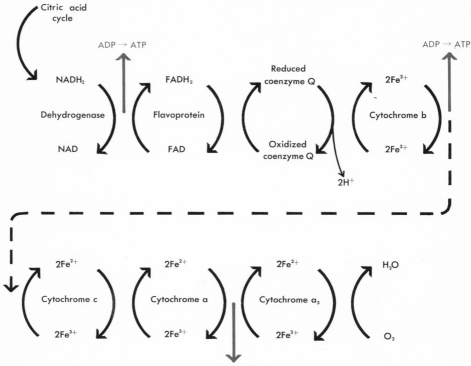

FIGURE 2–11   *The respiratory chain. Here are shown schematically the successive oxidation-reduction reactions which release, in small packets, the energy present in NADH$_2$ molecules. Whether all the cytochromes operate in a single cycle is not known. The exact sites of ATP formation have not been unambiguously determined.*

SYNTHESIS OF ATP IN THE PRESENCE OF OXYGEN (OXIDATIVE PHOSPHORYLATION)

During the period 1925 to 1940, most biochemists concentrated on following the path of hydrogen atoms (or electrons) through the linked, energy-yielding oxidation-reduction reactions. Until the end of this period, only slight attention was given to how the energy was released in a useful form. Then the Dane, Kalckar, and the Russian, Belitzer, observed ATP formation coupled with oxidation-reduction reactions in cell-free systems (1938–1940).

Further understanding did not come quickly, since most of the enzymes involved could not be obtained in pure soluble form. These troubles were not resolved until it was realized that the normal sites of *oxidative phosphorylation* in plant and animal cells are large, highly organized subcellular particles, the *mitochondria*. Using intact mitochondria, it is easy to observe the oxidative generation of ATP; this was first demonstrated in 1947 by the Americans Lehninger and Kennedy. Now there is evidence for the generation of three ATP molecules for each passage of a pair of hydrogens through the respiratory chain. There are believed to exist, however, at least six separate oxidation-reduction steps in the chain. Future work may reveal that one ATP molecule is generated during each distinct oxidation-reduction step.

Roughly 20 times more energy is released by the respiratory chain than by the initial breakdown of glucose to pyruvate. This explains why growth of cells under aerobic conditions is

FIGURE 2–12   The fermentation of glucose to yield lactate. Here the NADH₂ produced during pyruvate formation is oxidized to reduce pyruvate to lactate. When oxygen is present, the NADH₂ is oxidized through the respiratory chain, and no lactate is produced.

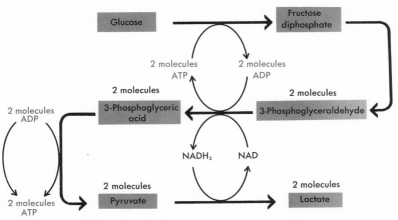

so much more efficient than growth without air: If oxygen is not present, pyruvate cannot accumulate, since its formation (see Figure 2–5) demands a supply of unreduced NAD. The amount of NAD within cells, like that of other coenzymes, is, however, very small. In the absence of oxygen, it is rapidly converted to $NADH_2$ as glucose is oxidized by the Embden-Meyerhof pathway. Thus for the continued generation of ATP without oxygen (fermentation), a device must be used to oxidize the reduced $NADH_2$. This is often achieved by reducing pyruvate itself, using $NADH_2$ as the hydrogen donor. This explains the appearance of lactic acid both during the anaerobic contraction of muscles and during the anaerobic growth of many bacteria (Figure 2–12).

GENERATION OF ATP DURING PHOTOSYNTHESIS

Today the ultimate source of the various food molecules used by microorganisms and animals is the photosynthetic plants. Thus the energy of the sun's light quanta must somehow be converted into the energy present in covalent bonds. How this happens chemically did not become clear until the basic energy relations within animals and bacteria were understood. Largely as a result of the work of the American biochemist Arnon, it was discovered in 1959 that the primary action of the sun's light quanta is to phosphorylate ADP to ATP.

This phosphorylation takes place in the chloroplasts, which are complicated, chlorophyll-containing cellular particles found in most cells capable of usefully trapping the energy of the sun. Thus we realize that the controlled release of energy in plants depends upon the same energy carrier important in bacterial and animal cells, ATP. The details of the process remain unclear. An initial step must be the capture of the light quantum by the green pigment molecule chlorophyll, to excite one of its electrons to a high-energy state. Much of what happens between this initial energy adsorption and the phosphorylation of ATP remains to be elucidated.

It is most important to realize the uniqueness of photosynthesis. It is the only significant cellular event that utilizes any

energy source other than the covalent bond. All other important cellular reactions are accompanied by a decrease in the
energy included in covalent bonds. Superficially, we might thus
guess that the ability to photosynthesize must have been a primary feature of the first forms of life. It is, however, difficult
to imagine that very early forms possessed the complicated
chloroplast structures necessary for photosynthesis. Instead
there is good reason to believe that, early in the history of the
earth, a unique chemical environment allowed the creation of
a large number of carbon-containing compounds using the
energy of light quanta originating from the sun. These spontaneously formed organic molecules then served as the energy
(food) supply for the first forms of life. As these original organic molecules were depleted and living matter increased, a
strong selective advantage developed for those cells which
evolved a photosynthetic structure to provide a means of increasing the amount of organic molecules. Today essentially all
glucose molecules are formed using chemical energy originating
in photosynthesis.

VITAMINS AND GROWTH FACTORS

Although some microorganisms, such as the bacteria *Escherichia coli*, can use glucose as their sole carbon and energy source,
not all bacteria and none of the higher animals can use glucose
to synthesize all the necessary metabolites. For example, rats
are unable to synthesize 11 of the 20 amino acids present in
their proteins; thus their food supply must contain substantial
amounts of these molecules.

In addition to dietary requirements (necessary growth factors) for compounds with important structural roles, requirements often exist for very small amounts of certain specific
organic molecules. These molecules, needed in just trace
amounts, are called vitamins (vital molecules). For many years
they seemed quite mysterious. Now we realize that the vitamins
are closely related to the coenzymes. Some are precursors of
coenzymes and some are coenzymes themselves. For example,
the vitamin niacin is used in the synthesis of NAD. The fact

that coenzymes, like enzymes, are able to function over and over explains why they are needed only in trace amounts.

Thus there is nothing unusual about the fact that a molecule is sometimes required as a growth factor or a vitamin; such requirements are fully explicable in chemical terms. It seems most likely that the genes necessary for the synthesis of certain molecules were lost during evolution, bringing specific growth-factor requirements into existence. There would be no selective advantage to an organism's retaining a specific gene if the corresponding metabolite were always available in its food supply.

THE LABILITY OF LARGE MOLECULES

In striking contrast with the splendid success of biochemists in understanding the behavior of small molecules like the amino acids and nucleotides, scientists interested in the large molecules had arrived at only partial answers before 1950. Their only real success involved a number of polysaccharide molecules (e.g., glycogen). They were relatively easy to understand, because they are built up by the regular polymerization of a smaller subunit (e.g., glucose). Their understanding, however, had no real biological impact because molecules like glycogen are, in most respects, structurally uninteresting. Their sole purpose is to serve as a reserve form of energy-yielding glucose residues. The molecules that people most wanted to unravel were the proteins, because many of them are enzymes, and the nucleic acids, because they were thought to be involved in the hereditary mechanism. Both these classes of molecules were, however, initially refractory to investigation.

One major reason why they were difficult to study was that they appeared to be much less stable (more labile) than most small molecules. Extremes of temperature and pH (acidity or alkalinity) cause them to lose their natural shapes (denaturation) and sometimes to precipitate irreversibly out of solution in an inactive form. Thus great care had to be taken in their isolation; sometimes it was necessary to perform the entire isolation process at temperatures near 0°C. At first it was thought that only proteins were subject to denaturation, but now it is clear that nucleic acid molecules also denature during isolation if proper precautions are not taken.

Until 1945 (after the Second World War), the commonly used techniques of organic chemistry were the main tools for studying most of the small molecules. Thus the success of a biochemist working on intermediary metabolism often depended on his ability as an organic chemist. In work with proteins and nucleic acids, however, most of the initial stages of research did not rely on the analytical techniques of the organic chemist. Instead the protein chemist, before he could even start worrying about the detailed structure of a protein, needed to work very hard to be sure his protein was both chemically pure and biologically active. He had to devise gentle techniques for isolation, which avoided the usual strong acids and alkalies of organic analysis. Then he needed techniques to reveal whether his product was homogeneous, and hopefully, also to provide data on molecular size. For this sort of answer, the help of physical chemists was indispensable, and there developed a well-recognized new line of research investigating the physical-chemical properties of macromolecules in solution. It concerned itself with topics like the osmotic properties of macromolecular solutions and the movement of macromolecules under electrical and centrifugal forces.

Perhaps the most striking contribution of physical chemistry to the study of biological macromolecules was the development, in the 1920s, of centrifuges that rotated at high speed (ultracentrifuges) and that could cause the rapid sedimentation of proteins and nucleic acids. The development of the ultracentrifuge was the work of the Swede Svedberg, after whom the unit of sedimentation (S = Svedberg) was named. Ultracentrifuges equipped with optical devices to observe exactly how fast the molecules sedimented were extremely valuable in obtaining data on the molecular weight of proteins and establishing the concept that proteins, like smaller biological molecules, are of discrete molecular weights and shapes. This work revealed that the sizes of proteins vary greatly, with a continuous range in weights between the extremes of approximately 10,000 and 1,000,000.

IMPLICATIONS OF CHROMATOGRAPHY

Early in the twentieth century, the work of the great German chemist Emil Fischer had established that protein molecules are largely composed of amino acids linked together by peptide bonds. The determination of the exact way in which the amino acids are linked together to form proteins remained, however, a great puzzle until 1951. This was partly because there are 20 different amino acids and their proportions vary from one type of protein to another. Until about 1942, the methodological problems involved in amino acid separation and identification were formidable, and most organic chemists chose to work with simpler molecules.

This state of affairs changed completely in 1942, when the Englishmen Martin and Synge developed separation methods that depended on the relative solubilities of the several amino acids in two different solvents (partition chromatography). Particularly useful were separation methods by which the amino acids were separated on strips of paper. With these new tricks, it became a routine matter to separate quantitatively the 20 amino acids found in proteins. These methods were quickly seized upon by the English biochemist Sanger, who used them to establish all the covalent linkages in the protein hormone insulin (see Chapter 6 for details of the insulin structure). Sanger's work was a milestone in the study of proteins, for it demonstrated that each type of protein contains a specific arrangement of amino acids.

THE 25–YEAR LONELINESS OF THE PROTEIN CRYSTALLOGRAPHERS

An equally significant step in understanding macromolecules was the effective extension of x-ray crystallographic techniques to their study. This approach utilizes the diffraction of x rays by crystals to give precise data about the three-dimensional arrangement of the atoms in molecules. The first successful use of x-ray diffraction was in 1912, when the Englishman Bragg solved the NaCl structure. This success immediately initiated research on the structures of molecules of increasing complexity.

The technique used in the initial x-ray diffraction studies of small molecules consisted of guessing the structure, calculating the theoretical diffraction pattern predicted by this structure, and comparing the calculated with the observed pattern. This method was practical for studying relatively simple structures, but was not usually useful in the study of larger structures. It took much insight on the part of Bragg and the great American chemist Pauling, in the 1920s, to solve the structures of some complicated inorganic silicate molecules. Clearly, however, proteins were too complicated for even the best chemist to guess their 3-D structures. Thus the early protein crystallographers knew that, until new methods for structural determination were found, they would have no results to present to the impatient biochemists, who were increasingly anxious to know what proteins actually looked like.

The first serious x-ray diffraction studies on proteins began in the mid-1930s in Bernal's laboratory in Cambridge, England. Here it was found that although dry protein crystals gave very poor x-ray patterns, wet crystals often gave beautiful pictures. Unfortunately, however, there was no logical method available for their interpretation. Nonetheless, Bernal's student Perutz, an Austrian then in England, slowly increased the pace of his work (begun in 1937) with the oxygen-carrying blood protein, hemoglobin. He had chosen hemoglobin for several reasons: Not only is it one of the most important of all animal proteins, but it is also easy to obtain, and forms crystals that lend themselves well to crystallographic analysis. For many years, however, no very significant results emerged either from Perutz's work on hemoglobin structure or from that begun in 1947 by Kendrew, on the structure of the muscle protein myoglobin. This protein, which, like hemoglobin, combines with oxygen, had the added advantage of being four times smaller ($MW = 17,000$) than hemoglobin.

During the lonely period of no real results there was only one triumph. Pauling correctly guessed from stereochemical considerations that amino acids linked together by peptide bonds would sometimes tend to assume helical configurations, and proposed in 1951 that a helical configuration, which he called the alpha helix (see Chapter 4 for details), would be an important element in protein structure. Support for Pauling's α-helix theory came soon after its announcement, when Perutz demonstrated that several synthetic polypeptide chains containing only one type of amino acid exist as α-helices.

It was not until 1959 that Perutz and Kendrew got their answers. An essential breakthrough, which occurred in 1953, showed how the attachment of heavy atoms to protein molecules could logically lead from the diffraction data to the correct structures. For the next several years, these heavy-atom methods were exploited at a pace undreamed of 20 years before, largely thanks to the availability of high-speed electronic computers. Then, to everyone's delight, the x-ray diffraction measurements could at last be translated into the arrangement of atoms in myoglobin and (in somewhat less detail) in hemoglobin. Both molecules were found to be enormously complicated, with their amino acid chains folded as α-helices in some regions, and very irregularly in others. Furthermore, their molecular configurations were found to obey in every respect the chemical laws that govern the shape of smaller molecules. Absolutely no new laws of nature are involved in the construction of proteins; this was no surprise to the biochemists.

AVERY'S BOMBSHELL: NUCLEIC ACIDS CAN CARRY GENETIC SPECIFICITY

Until 1944, the number of chemists working on the nucleic acids was but a tiny fraction of the number attempting to understand proteins. Two nucleic acids, DNA (*deoxyribonucleic acid*) and RNA (*ribonucleic acid*), were known to exist, but the general features of their chemical structures had not been elucidated. Although DNA was found only in nuclei (hence the name nucleic acids), there was general agreement that it probably was not a genetic substance, since chemists thought that its four types of nucleotide (see Chapter 3 for details of their structures) were present in equal amounts, giving DNA a repetitive structure like that of glycogen (the tetranucleotide hypothesis).

In the middle 1930s, the Swedish chemists Hammarsten and Caspersson found by physical-chemical techniques that DNA molecules, prepared by gentle procedures, have molecular weights even larger (>500,000) than most proteins. At the same time, chemical analysis of purified plant viruses by the American Stanley and the Englishmen Bawden and Pirie suggested the generalization that all viruses contain nucleic acid, hinting that nucleic acids might have a genetic role.

The first real proof, however, of the genetic role for nucleic acids came from the work of the noted American microbiologist Avery and his colleagues MacLeod and McCarty at the Rockefeller Institute in New York. They made the momentous discovery in 1944 that the hereditary properties of pneumonia bacteria can be specifically altered by the addition of carefully prepared DNA of high molecular weight.

Even though there was momentary hesitation in accepting its implications, their discovery provided great stimulation for a detailed chemical investigation of nucleic acids. Here also paper chromatography became immensely useful, and quickly allowed the biochemist Chargaff, then working in New York, to analyze the nucleotide composition of DNA molecules from a number of different organisms. In 1947, his experiments showed not only that the four nucleotides are not present in equal amounts, but also that exact ratios of the four nucleotides varied from one species to another. This finding meant that much more variation was possible among DNA molecules than the tetranucleotide hypothesis had allowed, and immediately opened up the possibility that the precise arrangement of nucleotides within a molecule is related to its genetic specificity.

It also became obvious from Chargaff's work in the next several years that the relative ratios of the four bases were not random. The amount of adenine in a DNA sample was always found to be equal to the amount of thymine, and the amount of guanine equal to the amount of cytosine. The fundamental significance of these relationships did not become clear, however, until serious attention was given to the 3-D structure of DNA.

THE DOUBLE HELIX

Parallel with work on the x-ray analysis of protein structure, a still smaller number of scientists concentrated on trying to solve the x-ray diffraction pattern of DNA. The first diffraction patterns were taken in 1938 by the Englishman Astbury and used DNA supplied by Hammarsten and Caspersson. It was not until after the war (1950–1952), however, that high quality photographs were taken, by Wilkins and Franklin, working in London at King's College. Even then, however, the chemical bonds linking the various nucleotides were not unambiguously established. This was accomplished in 1952 by a group of organic chemists working in the Cambridge, England, laboratory of Alexander Todd.

Because of interest in Pauling's α-helix, in 1951 an elegant theory of the diffraction of helical molecules was developed. The existence of this theory made it easy to test possible DNA structures on a trial and error basis. The correct solution, a complementary double helix (see Chapter 9 for details), was found in 1953 by Crick and Watson, then working in England in the laboratory of Perutz and Kendrew. Their arrival at the correct answer was in large part dependent on finding the stereochemically most favorable configuration compatible with the x-ray diffraction data of the King's College group.

The establishment of the double helix immediately initiated a profound revolution in the way in which many geneticists analyzed their data. The gene was no longer a mysterious entity whose behavior could be investigated only by breeding experiments. Instead it quickly became a real molecular object about which chemists could think objectively in the same manner as smaller molecules, such as pyruvate or NAD. Most of the excitement, however, came not merely from the fact that the structure was solved, but also from the nature of the structure. Before the answer was known, there had always been the mild fear that it would turn out to be dull, and reveal nothing about how genes replicate and function. Fortunately, however, the answer was immensely exciting. The structure appeared to be two intertwined strands of complementary structures, suggesting that one strand serves as the specific surface (*template*) upon which the other strand is made. If this hypothesis were true (which it is now known to be!), then the fundamental problem of gene replication, about which the geneticists had puzzled for so many years, was, in fact, solved.

There were thus initiated over the past 12 years a variety of experiments designed to study, at a molecular level, how DNA molecules control what a cell is like. These studies have brought many discoveries, unforeseen in 1953, about how the genetic material functions. Because these answers are, for the first time, consistently at the molecular level, it is convenient to refer to the subject matter at this level as molecular genetics.

THE GOAL OF MOLECULAR BIOLOGY

Until recently, heredity has always seemed the most mysterious of life's characteristics. The current realization that the structure of DNA already allows us to understand practically all its fundamental features at the molecular level is thus most significant. We see not only that the laws of chemistry are sufficient for understanding protein structure, but also that they are consistent with all known hereditary phenomena. Complete certainty now exists among essentially all biochemists that the other characteristics of living organisms (for example, selective permeability across cell membranes, muscle contraction, nerve conduction, and the hearing and memory processes) will all be completely understood in terms of the coordinative interactions of small and large molecules. Much is already known about the less complex features, enough to give us confidence that further research of the intensity recently given to genetics will eventually provide man with the ability to describe with completeness the essential features that constitute life.

SUMMARY

The growth and division of cells are based upon the same laws of chemistry that control the behavior of molecules outside of cells. Cells contain no atoms unique to the living state; they can synthesize no molecules which the chemist, with inspired, hard work, cannot some day make. Thus there is no special chemistry of living cells. A biochemist is not someone who studies unique types of chemical laws, but a chemist interested in learning about the behavior of molecules found within cells (biological molecules).

The growth and division of cells depend upon the availability of a usable form of chemical energy. This energy now initially comes from the energy of the sun's light quanta, which is converted by photosynthetic plants into cellular molecules, some of which are then used as food sources by various microorganisms and animals. The most striking initial triumphs of the biochemists told us how food molecules are transformed into other cellular molecules and into useful forms of chemical energy. The energy within food molecules largely resides in the covalent bonds of reduced carbon compounds; it is released when these molecules are transformed by oxidation-reduction reactions to carbon compounds of a higher degree of oxidation. For most forms of life, the ultimate oxidizing agent is molecular O_2. The products of the complete oxidation of organic molecules like glucose are CO_2 and H_2O.

Most organic molecules, however, are not oxidized directly by oxygen. They are oxidized instead by diverse organic molecules, often coenzymes, such as the coenzyme NAD. The reduced coenzyme (for example, $NADH_2$) is itself oxidized by another molecule (such as FAD) to yield a new reduced coenzyme ($FADH_2$) and the original coenzyme, in the oxidized form (NAD). After several such cycles, molecular oxygen directly participates, to end the oxidation-reduction chain, giving off water (H_2O).

The energy released during the oxidation-reduction cycles is not released entirely as heat. Instead, more than half the energy is converted into new chemical bonds. Phosphorus atoms play a key role in this transformation. Phosphate esters are formed that have a higher usable energy content than most covalent bonds. These phosphate groups are transferred in a high-energy form to acceptor molecules. The most important acceptor of such groups is ADP; a phosphate group is added to ADP to yield ATP. Very recently, experiments revealed that the phosphorylation of ADP to ATP is a primary step in photosynthesis, where it is called photophosphorylation. The ADP $\rightarrow$ ATP transformation is at the heart of energy relations in all cells.

Until a few years ago, the chemists' understanding of the cell's very large molecules, the proteins and nucleic acids, was much less firm than it is now. Most of these molecules are in a size range several orders of magnitude larger than the largest "small molecules" studied by organic chemistry (molecules of protein and nucleic acid run from MW 10^4 to 10^9). Both proteins and nucleic acids are complex, and only recently have physical and chemical techniques been developed to allow a concerted attack on their structure. Among the most important techniques have been partition chromatography, analytical ultracentrifugation, and x-ray crystallography as extended to the study of large molecules. Now practically all the important features of the protein myoglobin and the primary genetic material DNA are known. In both cases the chemical laws applicable to small molecules also apply. So far the greatest impact on biological thought has come from the realization that DNA has a complementary double-helical structure. This structure immediately suggested a mechanism for the replication of the gene, and initiated a revolution in the way biologists think of heredity. These successes have created a firm belief that the current extension of our understanding of biological phenomena to the molecular level (molecular biology) will soon enable us to understand all the basic features of the living state.

REFERENCES

McElroy, W. D., *Cell Physiology and Biochemistry*, 2nd ed., Prentice-Hall, Englewood Cliffs, N.J., 1964. A concise introductory statement of many of the important principles of biochemistry.

Lehninger, A. L., *Bioenergetics*, Benjamin, New York, 1965. An introduction to the chemical reactions by which cells trap, store, and utilize chemical energy. Emphasis is placed on generation of ATP in mitochondria and chloroplasts.

Bennett, T. P., and E. Frieden, *Modern Topics in Biochemistry*, Macmillan, New York, 1966. A good beginner's introduction to biochemistry.

Baldwin, E., *Dynamic Aspects of Biochemistry*, 3rd ed., Cambridge, New York, 1959. This is one of the few texts in biochemistry deserving to be called a classic. Now it is best read for the way in which coenzymes participate in hydrogen transfers.

Conn, E. E., and P. K. Stumpf, *Outlines of Biochemistry*, Wiley, New York, 1963. An introductory text that emphasizes metabolic pathways.

Kamen, M. D., *Primary Processes in Photosynthesis*, Academic, New York, 1963. A concise statement, available in paperback form, about what we do and do not understand about photosynthesis.

Kaleker, H. M., *Biological Phosphorylations*, Prentice-Hall, Englewood Cliffs, N.J., 1969. Contains a collection of many of the classic papers which lead to the understanding of the manyfold importance of high-energy phosphate bonds.

3

A CHEMIST'S LOOK AT THE BACTERIAL CELL

THE MOST IMPORTANT ASPECT OF LIVING cells is their tendency to grow and divide. In this process, food molecules are absorbed from the external environment and transformed into cellular constituents. The rates of cell growth vary tremendously, but in general the smallest cells grow the fastest. Under optimal conditions some bacteria double their number every 20 minutes, whereas most larger mammalian cells can divide only once about every 24 hours. But, independent of the length of the time interval, growth and division necessarily demand that the number of cellular molecules double with each cell generation. One way, therefore, of asking the question, "What is life?" is to ask how a cell doubles its molecular content, that is, how biological molecules are replicated as a cell grows.

BACTERIA GROW UNDER SIMPLE, WELL–DEFINED CONDITIONS

Today most serious questions about cell growth and division are studied by using microorganisms, especially the bacteria. The tendency to concentrate on microorganisms does not arise from a belief that bacteria are fundamentally more important than higher organisms. The converse is obviously true to human beings, naturally curious to know about themselves and anxious to use information about their own

71

chemical makeup to combat the various diseases threatening their existence. Nonetheless, upon even a superficial examination, the difficulties of thoroughly mastering the chemical events in a higher organism are staggering. There are about 5×10^{12} cells in a human being, each of whose existence is intimately related to the behavior of many other cells. It is therefore difficult to study the growth of a single cell within a multicellular organism without taking into consideration the influence of its surrounding cells.

Much effort has been devoted to learning how to grow the cells of multicellular organisms in an isolated system. In this work (often called *tissue culture*) small groups of cells, or sometimes single cells, are removed from a plant or animal and placed under controlled laboratory conditions in a solution containing a variety of food molecules. In the first experiments, the isolated cells almost invariably died, but now, partly because of a better understanding of the nutritional requirements of cells, they often grow and divide to form large numbers of new cells. Such freely growing plant and animal cells have been of much value in showing how cells aggregate to form organized groups of similar cells (tissues), and even more striking, how tissues unite in the test tube to form bodies morphologically identical to small regions of organs, such as the liver or the kidney. On the other hand, tissue culture cells are not ideal objects for studying cell growth and division. Even though many cells of higher organisms will grow in isolation, it must be remembered that this is not their normal way of existence, and, unless precautions are taken, they tend to aggregate quickly into multicellular groups. Thus even today the isolated growth of cells from higher organisms can be difficult and time consuming.

In contrast, the cells of many microorganisms normally grow free, as single cells, separating from each other as soon as cell division occurs. It is thus fairly easy to grow such single-celled organisms under well-defined laboratory conditions, since the conditions of growth in the scientist's test tube are not radically different from the conditions under which they normally grow outside the laboratory. In contrast to mammalian cells, which require a large variety of growth supplements, many bacteria will grow on a simple, well-defined diet or medium. For ex-

T A B L E 3–1 *A simple synthetic growth medium for E. coli*[a]

NH$_4$Cl	1.0 g
MgSO$_4$	0.13 g
KH$_2$PO$_4$	3.0 g
Na$_2$HPO$_4$	6.0 g
Glucose	4.0 g
Water	1000 ml

[a] Traces of other ions (e.g., Fe^{2+}) are also required for growth. Usually these are not added separately, since they are normally present as contaminants in either the added inorganic salts or the water itself.

ample, the bacteria *Escherichia coli* will grow on an aqueous solution containing just glucose and several inorganic ions (Table 3–1).

The growth of a specific bacterium is usually not dependent on the availability of a specific carbon source. Most bacteria are highly adaptable as to which organic molecules they can use as their carbon and energy sources. Glucose can be replaced by a variety of other organic molecules, and the greater the variety of food molecules supplied, the faster a cell generally grows. For example, if *E. coli* grows upon only glucose, about 60 minutes are required at 37°C to double the cell mass. But if glucose is supplemented by the various amino acids and purine and pyrimidine bases (the precursors of nucleic acids), then only 20 minutes are necessary for the doubling of cell mass. This effect is due to the direct incorporation of these components into proteins and nucleic acids, sparing the cell the task of carrying out the synthesis of the building blocks. There is a lower limit, however, to the time necessary to double the cell mass (often called the *generation time*): No matter how favorable the growth conditions, bacteria are unable to divide more than once every 20 minutes.

E. COLI IS THE BEST UNDERSTOOD ORGANISM AT THE MOLECULAR LEVEL!

Over the past 20 years there has been an increasing concentration of effort toward work with the bacterium *E. coli* and evolutionarily related organisms. Because of its small size, normal lack of pathogenicity to any common organism, and ease of growth under laboratory conditions, E. coli is now the most intensively studied organism except for man. Many other bacteria besides E. coli possess the same favorable attributes, and the original reasons for choosing E. coli are essentially accidental. Once serious work had started on E. coli, however, it obviously made no sense to switch to another organism if E. coli could be used. Even now the tendency to concentrate on E. coli is increasing, because parallel with the chemical studies, extensive successful genetic analysis has also been carried out. Our knowledge of the genetics of E. coli is thus much more complete than our knowledge of that of any other bacterium or lower plant. As we shall see, the combined methods of genetics and biochemistry are so powerful that it is often just not sensible to use in biochemical studies an organism with which genetic analysis is not possible.

The average E. coli cell (Figure 3–1) is rod-shaped and about 2μ in length and 1μ in diameter. It grows by increasing in length, followed by a fission process that generates two cells of equal length. Growth occurs best at temperatures about 37°C, perhaps to suit it for existence in the intestines of higher mammals, where it is frequently found as a harmless parasite. It will, however, regularly grow and divide at temperatures as low as 20°. Cell growth proceeds much more slowly at these low temperatures; the generation time under otherwise optimal conditions is about 120 minutes at 20°C.

Cell number and size are often measured by observation under the light microscope (and occasionally the electron microscope). Such observation, however, cannot reveal whether a visible cell is alive or dead. This can be determined only by seeing whether a given cell forms daughter cells. This determination is usually made by spreading a small number of cells on top of a solid agar surface (Figure 3–2), which has been supplemented with the nutrients necessary for cell growth. If a cell is alive, it will grow to form two daughter cells which in turn give rise to subsequent generations of daughter cells. The net result after 12 to 24 hours of incubation at 37°C is discrete masses (*colonies*) of bacterial cells. Provided that the colonies do not overlap, each must have arisen from the initial presence of a single bacterial cell.

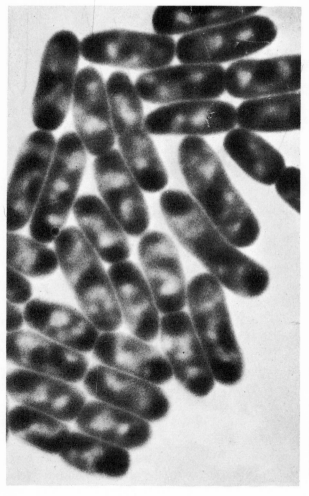

FIGURE 3–1 Electron micrograph of a group of intact E.coli cells. The light regions inside the bacteria represent areas where DNA is concentrated. Magnification is 12,000. This photograph was taken in the laboratory of E. Kellenberger, University of Geneva (reproduced with permission).

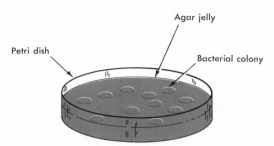

FIGURE 3–2   *The multiplication of single bacterial cells to form colonies.   E. coli cells are usually not motile.   Thus when a cell has divided on a solid surface, the two daughter cells and all their descendants will tend to remain next to each other.   After 24 hours at 37°C, each initial living cell has given rise to a solid mass of cells.*

   The growth of bacteria may also be followed in liquid nutrient solutions. If a nutrient medium is inoculated with a small number of rapidly dividing bacteria from a similar medium, the bacteria will continue dividing with a constant division time, doubling the number of bacteria each generation time. Thus the number of bacteria increases in an exponential (logarithmic) fashion (Figure 3–3). *Exponential growth* continues until the number of cells reaches such a high level that the initial optimal nutritional conditions no longer exist. One of the first factors that usually limits growth is the supply of oxygen. When the number of cells is low, the oxygen available by diffusion from the liquid interface is sufficient, but as the number of cells rises additional oxygen is needed. It is often supplied either by bubbling oxygen through the solution or by shaking the solution rapidly. Even with violent aeration, the growth rates begin to slow down after the cell density reaches about 10^9 cells per milliliter, and a tendency develops for the cells being produced to be shorter. Finally, at cell densities of about 5×10^9 cells per milliliter, cell growth is discontinued, for still unclear nutritional reasons. The term *growth curve* is frequently used to describe the increase of cell numbers as a function of time.

In most growing bacterial cultures, the exact division time of the cells varies, so that even if a culture has started from a single cell, after a few generations, cells can be found at various stages of the division cycle at any given moment. Such growth is frequently called *unsynchronized growth*. Over the past 10 years, tricks have been developed to isolate bacterial cells at the same stage of the cell cycle. These can be used to obtain several generations of *synchronized cell growth* (Figure 3–4). Then, because of slightly unequal divisions, the resulting growth curve again acquires an unsynchronized appearance.

During exponential growth each cell contains between two and four chromosomes. All these chromosomes have identical genetic compositions since they are all descendants of the same parental chromosome. Why each healthy cell contains several

FIGURE 3–3 Growth curve of E. coli cells at 37°C. The gray line shows the increase in cell number following the inoculation of a sterile, nutrient-rich solution (glucose, salts, amino acids, purines, pyrimidines) with 10^5 cells from an E. coli culture in an exponential phase of growth. If this growth curve had been started, instead, from cells in a slow-multiplying, nearly saturated culture, the growth would not have begun immediately, but rather (colored curve) a lag period of approximately 1 hour would have preceded exponential growth.

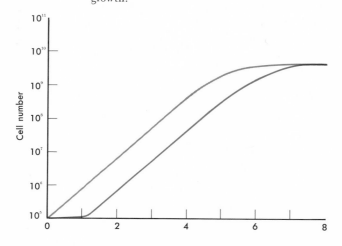

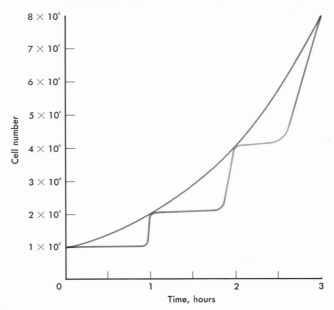

FIGURE 3–4   *The growth curve (colored line) of a synchronized E. coli culture growing upon glucose as the sole carbon source. The gray line shows the increase in cell number of an unsynchronized culture. Here we show an example in which the degree of synchronization noticeably lessens in the second and third cycles of growth.*

identical chromosomes is not known. It is not an intrinsic feature of the *E. coli* life cycle, since when the nutritional conditions are poor, chromosome duplication sometimes lags behind cell division (Figure 3–5), resulting in viable cells with just one chromosome apiece.

In *E. coli*, as in most if not all bacteria, the chromosome is not enclosed within a nuclear membrane. There is no structural distinction between the nucleus and the cytoplasm. Nonetheless, bacterial cytologists often refer to the region occupied by the chromosomes as the *nuclear region*. This term, however, is a misnomer. It is still very unclear what separates the chromosomes during cell division. There is no evidence of a spindle-like region even under the electron microscope, which hints that the spindle is a specialized structure developed at the point in evolution when the nuclear and cytoplasmic regions were differentiated. Thus the only essential parallel between mitotic divisions in higher organisms and in the bacteria is that in both the accurate duplication and partition of the chromosomes is essential.

For many years it was believed that bacteria, including *E. coli*, had no sexual process involving cell fusion. Since 1947, however, it has been known that male and female cells do exist, and that there is a very rare cell-fusion process which produces diploid cells (see Chapter 7 for details). These diploid cells usually do not exist for long intervals, segregating out haploid cells within one or two cell division cycles. Here, as in the case of bacterial mitosis, no evidence is available about the me-

FIGURE 3–5   *The life cycle of* E. coli *cells. Under optimal growth conditions the average cell contains from two to four chromosomes, depending upon its exact stage in the division cycle. All these chromosomes are descended from the same parental chromosome, and so are genetically identical.*

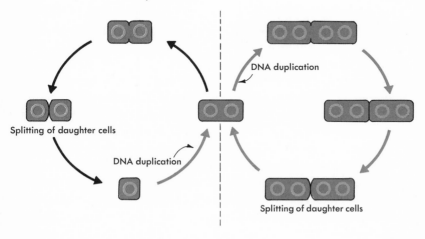

DNA duplication

Splitting of daughter cells

DNA duplication

Splitting of daughter cells

▬ Optimal growth conditions
▬ Poor growth conditions

Under optimal nutritional conditions at 37°C, the cell cycle takes about 20 min.

chanics of chromosome separation, which must underlie the reduction of chromosome number back to the haploid condition.

EVEN SMALL CELLS ARE COMPLEX

Even cells as small as those of *E. coli* present great difficulties when we study them at the molecular level. At first sight, the problem of soon, if ever, understanding the essential features of *E. coli* should seem insuperable to an honest chemist. He realizes immediately that, on a chemical scale, even the smallest cells are fantastically large. Although an *E. coli* cell is about 500 times smaller than an average cell in a higher plant or animal (which has a diameter of approximately 10μ), it nonetheless weighs approximately 2×10^{-12} gram (MW $\sim 10^{12}$ daltons; a dalton has a MW $= 1$). This number, which initially may seem very small, is immense on the chemist's scale, since it is 6×10^{10} times greater than the weight of a water molecule (MW $= 18$). Furthermore, this mass reflects the highly complex arrangement of a large number of different carbon-containing molecules.

There is also seemingly infinite variety in the chemical nature of these molecules. But fortunately, it is possible to distribute most molecules in terms of mass into several well-defined classes possessing common arrangements of some atoms. These classes are the carbohydrates, lipids, proteins, and nucleic acids (Table 3–2). Many molecules possess chemical groups common to several of these categories, so that the classification of such molecules is necessarily arbitrary. Also in the cell are many smaller molecules, such as amino acids, purine and pyrimidine nucleotides, various coenzymes, very small molecules (e.g., O_2 and CO_2), and numerous electrically charged inorganic ions, (e.g., Na^+, K^+ and PO_4^{3-}). Finally, there is H_2O, the most common molecule in all cells, and a solvent for most biological molecules, through which diffusion from one cellular location to another can occur quickly.

A glimpse into the cellular organization of *E. coli* is shown in an electron micrograph of a very thin section cut from a rapidly growing cell (Figure 3–6). On the outside is the rigid cell wall,

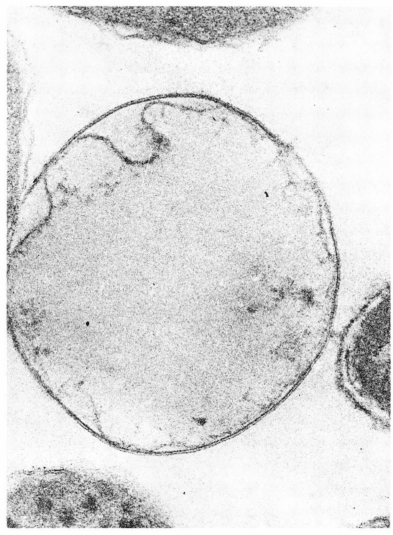

FIGURE 3-6 *Electron micrograph of a very thin cross section of an E. coli cell. The magnification is ×105,000. The outer membrane is the protective cell wall; inside this is the cell membrane, which controls permeability. Normally the cell membrane lies tightly next to the cell wall; here, for illustrative purposes, we show an accidental situation in which the membrane has in a few places separated from the cell wall. (Supplied by E. Kellenberger; reproduced with permission.)*

TABLE 3-2   *The main classes of biological molecules*

	General description	Functions
Proteins	Molecules containing C, H, O, N, and sometimes S, which are built up from amino acids.	Most proteins are enzymes—some, usually present in very large numbers per cell, are used to build up essential structures, such as the cell wall, the cell membrane, the ribosomes, muscle fiber, nerves, etc.
Lipids	Molecules insoluble in water, that are sometimes built up by the combination of glycerol and three long-chain fatty acids (triglycerid). Sometimes one fatty acid is replaced by choline (lecithins). Sometimes glycerol is replaced by sphingosine. Phosphorus is present in a large number of the lipids (phospholipids).	Triglycerids are a main storehouse of energy-rich food. They degrade to give acetyl-CoA. Phospholipids are an essential component of all membranes. Their insolubility in water is related to their control of permeability.
Carbohydrates	Molecules containing C, H, and O, usually in ratios near 1:2:1; polysaccharides are built up from simple sugars (monosaccharides) such as glucose and galactose. In some cases the sugars contain amino groups (e.g., glucosamine).	Some, such as cellulose and pectin, are used to construct strong, protective cell walls; others, such as glycogen, provide a form of storing glucose.
Nucleic acids	Long, linear molecules containing P, as well as C, H, O, and N, which are built up from pentose (5-carbon) nucleotides.	There are two main classes of nucleic acids in cells: DNA is the primary genetic component of all cells; RNA usually functions in the synthesis of proteins. In some viruses, RNA is the genetic material.

a 100-A thick mosaic structure built up of protein, polysaccharide, and lipid molecules. Just inside the cell wall is a flexible, 100-A thick cell membrane, largely composed of protein and lipid. This membrane is semipermeable and controls which molecules enter and leave the cell. Of vital importance is its ability to maintain a concentration gradient, since most molecules, both small and large, are present at much higher levels

T A B L E 3–2 (*continued*)

Building blocks

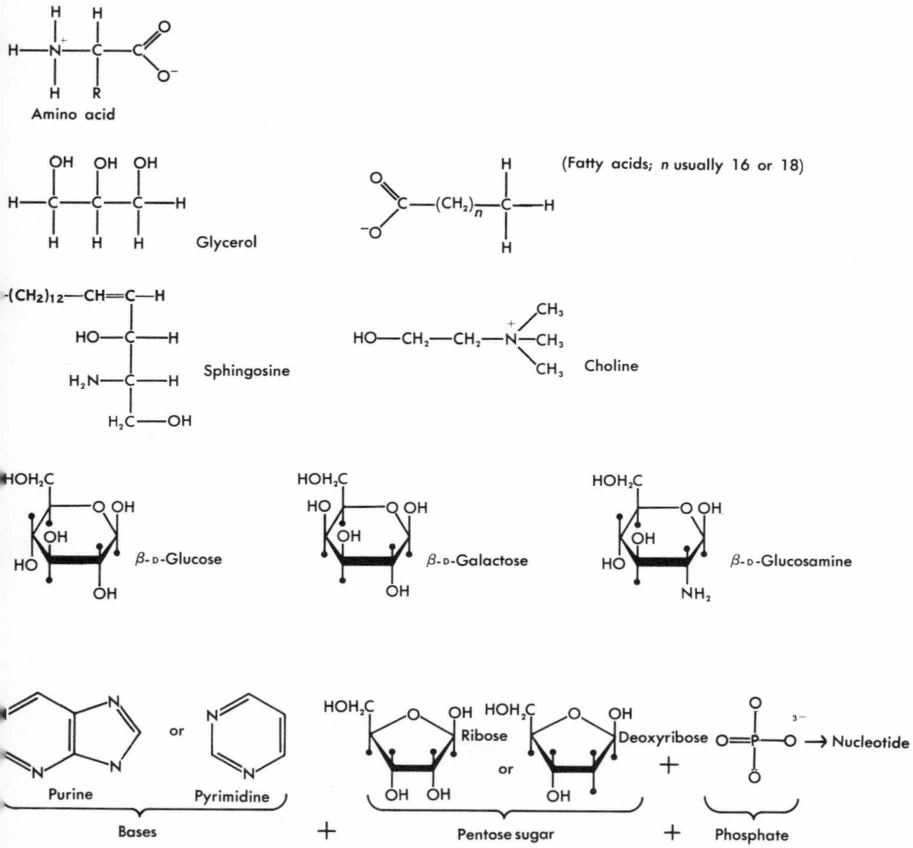

Amino acid

Glycerol

(Fatty acids; *n* usually 16 or 18)

Sphingosine

Choline

β-D-Glucose

β-D-Galactose

β-D-Glucosamine

Purine   or   Pyrimidine

Bases   +   Ribose   Deoxyribose   or   Pentose sugar   +   Phosphate → Nucleotide

---

inside than outside the cell membrane. This is true for both inorganic ions (e.g., K^+ and Mg^{2+}) and most important organic molecules. The membrane must actively prevent molecules from diffusing into the outside area of very much lower concentrations.

A schematic view of a typical *E. coli* cell is shown in Figure 3–7. About one-fifth of the interior of the cell is occupied by deoxyribonucleic acid (DNA), the compound responsible for the transmission of genetic material from one cell to another. Immediately surrounding the DNA occur 20,000 to 30,000 spherical particles, 200 A thick. These are the ribosomes, usually present in aggregates called polyribosomes. The cellular sites of protein synthesis, they contain approximately 40 per cent protein and 60 per cent ribonucleic acid (RNA). The remainder of the cell's interior is filled with water, water-soluble enzymes, and a large number of various small molecules.

At present we can make only an approximate guess of the number of chemically different molecules within a single *E. coli* cell. Each year many new molecules are discovered. The best guess is that between 3000 and 6000 different types of molecules are present (Table 3–3). Some of these, such as H_2O and CO_2, are chemically simple. Others, such as the common sugar glucose or the nitrogen-containing purine adenine, are more complex but nonetheless rather easily studied by current chemical

FIGURE 3–7 *Schematic view of an E. coli cell containing two identical chromosomes.*

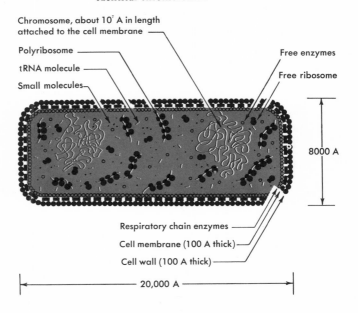

techniques. Still other cellular molecules, in particular the proteins and nucleic acids, are very large, and even today their chemical structures are immensely difficult to unravel. Most of these macromolecules are not being actively studied, since their overwhelming complexity has forced chemists to concentrate on relatively few of them. Thus we must immediately admit that the structure of a cell will never be understood in the same way as that of water or glucose molecules. Not only will the exact structures of most macromolecules remain unsolved, but their relative locations within cells can be only vaguely known.

It is thus not surprising that many chemists, after brief periods

T A B L E 3–3 *Approximate chemical composition of a rapidly dividing Escherichia coli cell*[a]

Component	Per cent of total cell weight	Average MW	Approximate number per cell	Number of different kinds
H_2O	70	18	4×10^{10}	1
Inorganic ions (Na+, K+, Mg^{2+}, Ca^{2+}, Fe^{2+}, Cl−, PO$_4^{4-}$, SO$_4^{2-}$, etc.)	1	40	2.5×10^8	20
Carbohydrates and precursors	3	150	2×10^8	200
Amino acids and precursors	0.4	120	3×10^7	100
Nucleotides and precursors	0.4	300	1.2×10^7	200
Lipids and precursors	2	750	2.5×10^7	50
Other small molecules (heme, quinones, breakdown products of food molecules, etc.)	0.2	150	1.5×10^7	200
Proteins	15	40,000	10^6	2000 to 3000
Nucleic acids				
DNA	1	2.5×10^9	4	1
RNA	6			
16s rRNA		500,000	3×10^4	1
23s rRNA		1,000,000	3×10^4	1
tRNA		25,000	4×10^5	40
mRNA		1,000,000	10^3	1000

[a] Weight 10^{12} daltons.

TABLE 3-4 Structural organization of several important biological macromolecules

Macromolecule	Monomeric units	Number of different monomers	General monomer formula	Fixed or irregular chain length	Linkage between monomers
Glycogen (a polysaccharide)	Glucose	One		Indefinite—may be > 1000	1–4-Glycosidic linkage
DNA (deoxyribonucleic acid)	Deoxynucleotides	Four: deoxyadenylate deoxyguanylate deoxythymidylate deoxycytidylate	Purine-deoxyribose-P (or pyrimidine-deoxyribose-P)	Genetically fixed—may be $> 10^7$	3′–5′-Phosphodiester linkage
RNA (ribonucleic acid)	Ribonucleotides	Four: adenylate guanylate uridylate cytidylate	Purine-ribose-P (or pyrimidine-ribose-P)	Genetically fixed, often > 3000	3′–5′-Phosphodiester linkage
Protein	L-Amino acids	Twenty: glycine, alanine, serine, etc.		Genetically fixed, usually varies between 100 and 1000	Peptide linkage

of enthusiasm for studying "life," silently return to the world of pure chemistry. Others, however, become more optimistic when they understand (1) that all macromolecules are polymeric molecules built up from smaller monomers, (2) that there exist well-defined chains of successive chemical reactions in cells (metabolic pathways), and (3) that a limit is placed on the number of enzymes (and hence small molecules) that can exist in a cell by the fact that each contains a finite amount of DNA.

MACROMOLECULES CONSTRUCTED
BY LINEAR LINKING OF SMALL MOLECULES

Most of the mass of E. coli (excluding water), like that of all other cells, is composed of macromolecules. Most of these large molecules are proteins, about half of which function as enzymes. The remainder of the proteins are used to help construct the ribosomes, the cell wall, etc. Table 3–3 shows that the number of atoms in a macromolecule is 25 to 50 times the number in a small molecule. Thus one might initially guess that most biochemists concerned with synthesis would be directly concerned with the frightfully complicated task of understanding the atom by atom growth of big molecules. Furthermore, one might also guess that their relatively immense size would lead to a very slow pace of research. Fortunately, however, the existence of three simplifying structural generalizations reduces the problem to a difficult, but not impossible, task.

First, all macromolecules are polymeric molecules formed by the condensation of small molecules. Macromolecule biosynthesis thus occurs in two stages: (1) the formation of the smaller subunits, and (2) the systematic linking together of these subunits. An analogy can be made to the building of a house from preconstructed bricks.

Second, the building blocks for a given macromolecule have common chemical groupings as illustrated in Table 3–4, which describes the main structural features of several important macromolecules. For example, proteins form by the condensation of nitrogen-containing organic molecules called amino

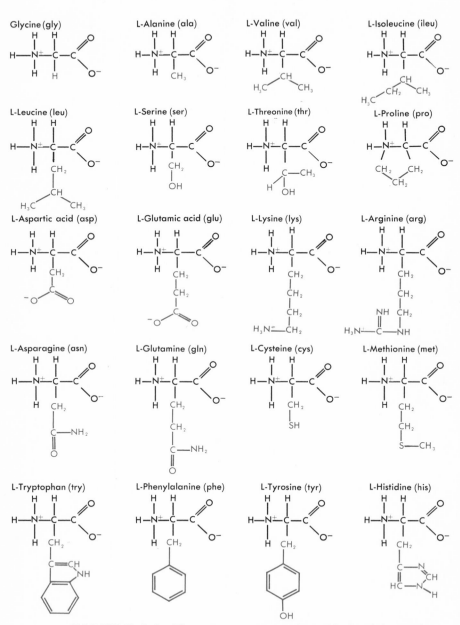

FIGURE 3–8 *The twenty common amino acids found in proteins.*

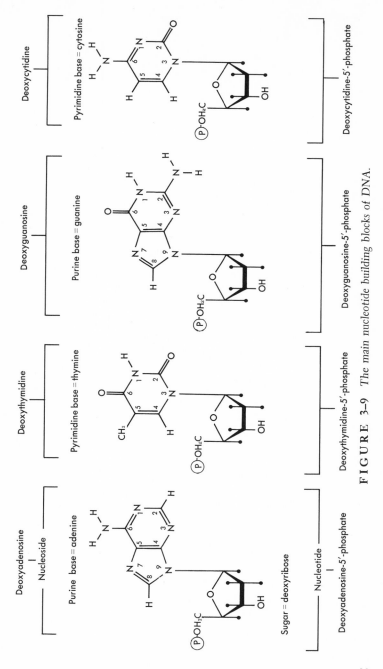

FIGURE 3-9 *The main nucleotide building blocks of DNA.*

89

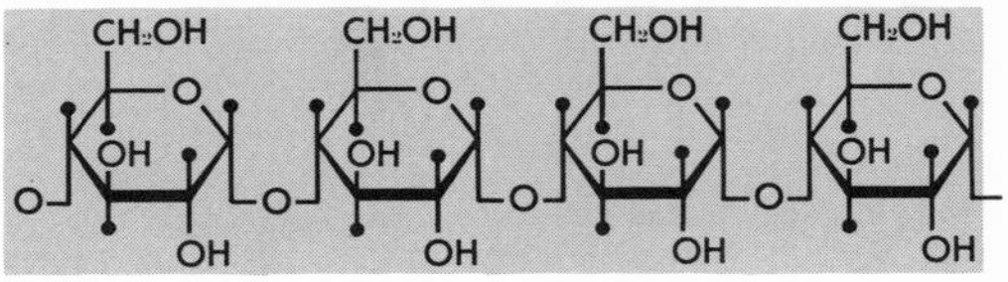

(a)

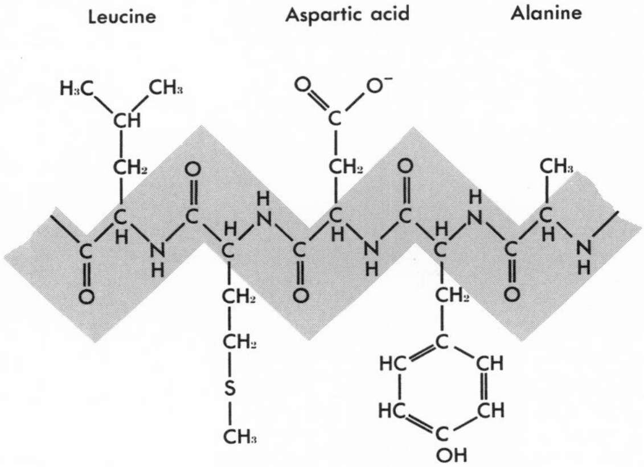

(b)

FIGURE 3–10   *The structure of some biological macromolecules. The backbones are shown in color.* (a) *The structure of a portion of a glycogen chain composed of glucose subunits.* (b) *A portion of a polypeptide chain of a protein.   The amino acid subunits are, from left to right: leucine, methionine, aspartic acid, tyrosine, and alanine.* (c) *A portion of the polynucleotide chain of a deoxyribonucleic acid.*

acids.   The chemical bond that links two amino acids together is the peptide bond.   There are 20 important amino acids, each of which has part of its structure identical to that of comparable regions in the other amino acids.   Attached to the regular region is a "side group," specific for each amino acid (Figure 3–8). Each amino acid thus has a *specific* region (the side group) and a *nonspecific* region.   The nucleic acids, DNA and RNA, are also formed by the union of smaller molecules called nucleotides.   The nucleotides of RNA, since they contain the sugar

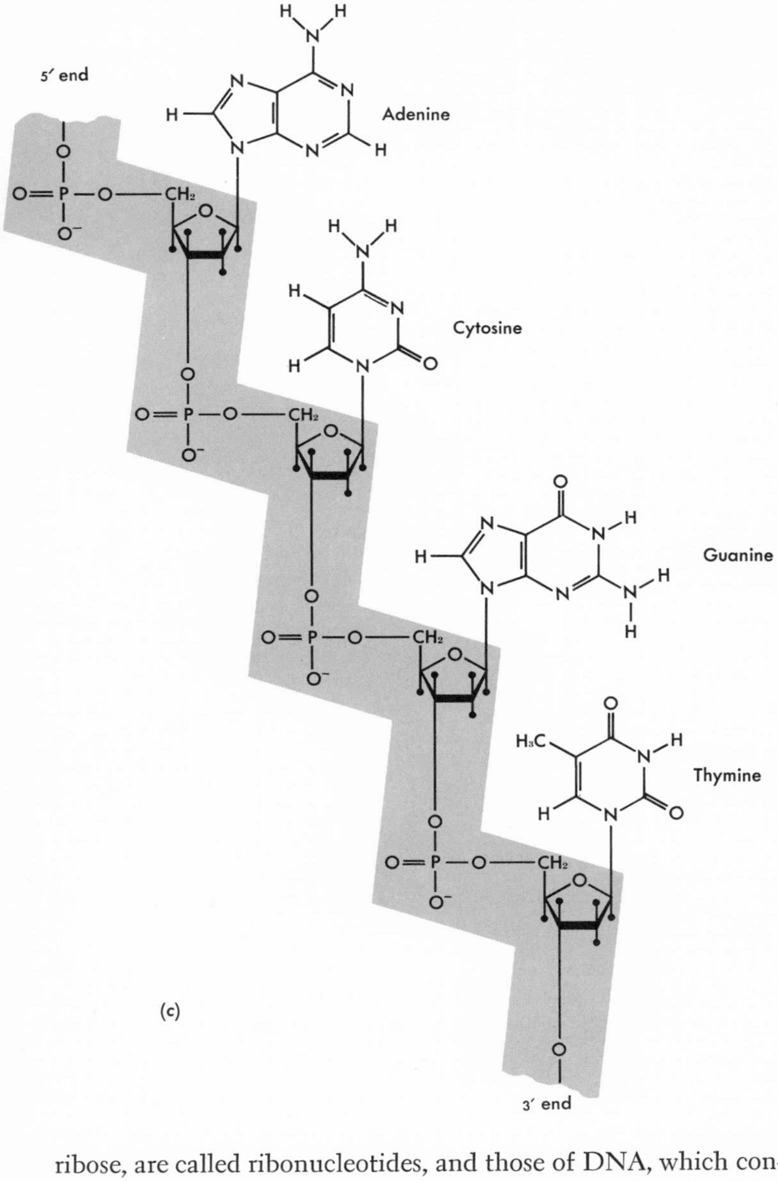

5′ end

Adenine

Cytosine

Guanine

Thymine

(c)

3′ end

ribose, are called ribonucleotides, and those of DNA, which contain deoxyribose instead, are called deoxyribonucleotides (Figure 3–9; see Chapter 9 for details). The nucleotides are always linked together through a phosphate group and a hydroxyl group on the sugar component (Table 3–4). Hence these linkages are called phosphodiester bonds. Each nucleotide, like each amino acid, contains both a specific and a nonspecific region. The phosphate and sugar groups comprise the nonspecific portion of a nucleotide, while the purine and pyrimidine bases make up the specific portion. DNA and RNA each contain four main bases: two purines and two pyrimidines.

Third, most macromolecules (nucleic acids, proteins, and

FIGURE 3–11   *Hydrolysis of a polypeptide to form amino acids. Here we show a very simple polypeptide containing only three amino acids.*

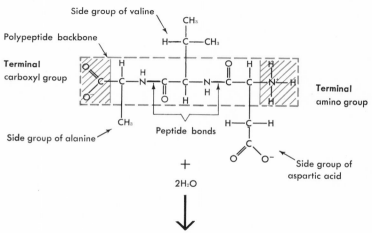

some polysaccharides) are *linear* aggregates in which the subunits are linked together by a chemical bond between atoms in the nonspecific regions. Their linear configuration follows from the fact that most subunits possess only two atoms that form bonds with other subunits. Thus a large fraction of most macromolecules consists of a repeating series of identical chemical groups (the *backbone*, Figure 3–10).

A feature common to all these biological polymers is that the individual subunits in the polymer chain contain two hydrogen atoms and one oxygen atom less than the simple monomers from which they are synthesized. Synthesis thus involves the release of water. When the polymers are degraded to yield smaller molecules, one H_2O molecule is incorporated by each peptide bond broken (Figure 3–11).

Degradative reactions in which H_2O uptake is required are known as hydrolytic reactions. There are many types of hydrolytic reactions, since numerous small molecules can be broken down to still smaller products by the addition of water. Under normal cell conditions, hydrolysis of any of the important polymers or small molecules is very rare. Hydrolysis is, however, speeded up by the presence of specific enzymes. For example, the enzymes pepsin and trypsin specifically catalyze the hydrolytic breakdown of proteins.

DISTINCTION BETWEEN REGULAR AND IRREGULAR POLYMERS

Table 3–4 also reveals an important difference between the polysaccharides, like glycogen, and the proteins and nucleic acids. Polysaccharides are usually constructed by *regular* (or semiregular) aggregation of one or two different kinds of monosaccharide building blocks. In contrast, proteins contain 20 different amino acids, and nucleic acids contain 4 different nucleotides. Moreover, in the nucleic acids and proteins, the order of subunits is highly *irregular* and varies greatly from one specific molecule to another. Polysaccharide synthesis from monosaccharides generally involves only the making of the same backbone bond; the synthesis of nucleic acids and proteins demands in addition a highly efficient mechanism for choosing and ordering the correct subunits.

METABOLIC PATHWAYS

We can see directly that all the molecules in a cell arise from cellular transformation of food molecules if we allow the bacterium *E. coli* to grow in a simple, well-defined medium containing the sugar glucose (Table 3–1). Under these conditions glucose is the only organic source of carbon. In effect, all the carbon atoms of the *E. coli* molecules (a few are derived from CO_2) must result from chemical transformations by which glucose molecules are either broken down to smaller fragments or added to each other to form large molecules like the nucleotides or glycogen. The exact way in which all these transformations (collectively known as intermediary metabolism) occur is enormously complex, and most biochemists concern themselves with studying (or even knowing about!) only a small fraction of the total interactions.

Fortunately, some basic simplicity to the general pattern of metabolism is now beginning to emerge. Figure 3–12 shows some of the more important types of chemical events that occur after glucose is taken into an *E. coli* cell. Much of this information comes from experiments in which *E. coli* is fed molecules specifically labeled with radioactive isotopes. For example, if we expose *E. coli* for several seconds (a pulse) to C^{14}-labeled glucose, the radioactive atoms can be detected almost immediately in molecules chemically similar to glucose, such as glucose-6-phosphate. Only later do the labeled atoms find their way into the various amino acids and nucleotides. The amount of time before radioactivity appears in the various compounds corresponds roughly to the number of biochemical reactions separating glucose from the various metabolites.

Figure 3–12 shows that various key intermediates in glucose degradation often have several possible fates. They may be completely degraded via the Embden-Meyerhof pathway, the Krebs cycle, and the respiratory chain, to yield CO_2 and H_2O.

During this process, ADP is converted to ATP. Alternatively, various intermediates may be used to initiate a series of successive chemical reactions that end with the synthesis of vital molecules, such as the amino acids or the nucleotides. For example, dihydroxyacetone-(P) is used as a precursor for the lipid constituent glycerol, whereas 3-phosphoglyceric acid is the beginning metabolite in a series of reactions that leads to the amino acids serine, glycine, and cysteine.

Connected groups of biosynthetic (degradative) reactions are referred to as *metabolic pathways*. Once a molecule has started on a pathway it often has no choice but to undergo a series of successive transformations. All pathways, however, are not necessarily linear. Some may be branched. Intermediates at branch points are transformed into one of two or more possible compounds. Those intermediates that are subject to several alternative fates are very important in cellular metabolism. Prominent among them are glucose-6-(P), pyruvate, α-ketoglutarate, and oxaloacetate; each serves as a starting point for several important pathways. Perhaps the most important such compound is acetyl-CoA, which is not only the main precursor of lipids, but also contains the acetate residue consumed by the citric acid cycle.

The metabolic fates of the majority of molecules are, however, much more limited. An average molecule can be either broken down to compound x or used as an intermediate in the biosynthesis of compound y; correspondingly, each such metabolite is able to combine specifically with only two different enzymes.

DEGRADATION PATHWAYS DISTINCT FROM BIOSYNTHETIC PATHWAYS

When *E. coli* is growing upon glucose as its sole carbon source, all its amino acids must be synthesized from metabolites derived from glucose. Thus there exists a distinct biosynthetic pathway for each of the 20 amino acids (Figure 3–12). *E. coli* can also grow, however, in the absence of a sugar, using any of the 20 amino acids as a *sole* carbon source. This means that there

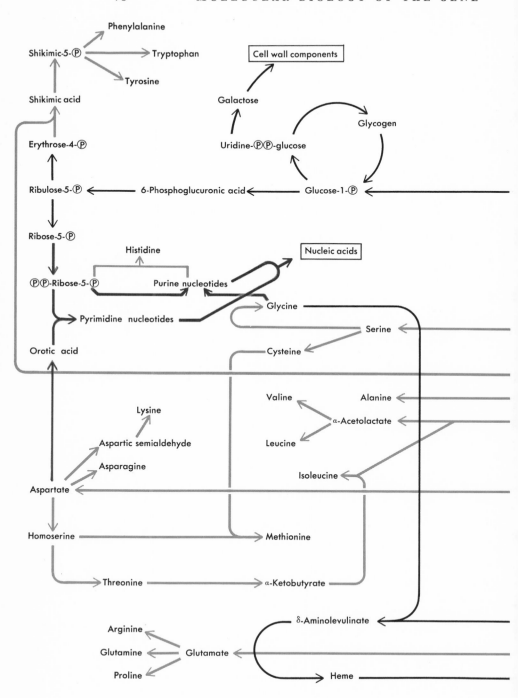

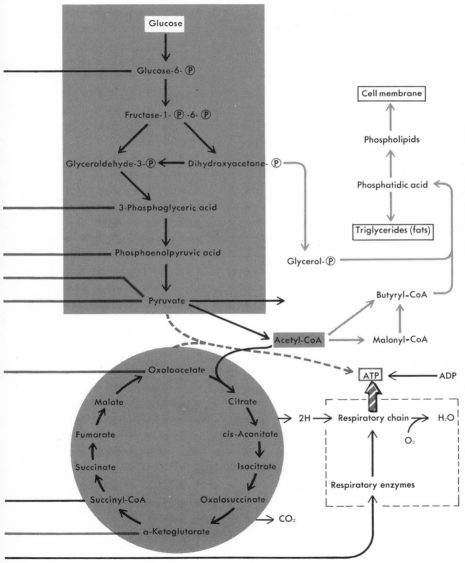

FIGURE 3–12 *Schematic view of some of the main metabolic pathways in E. coli.*

must also exist 20 pathways of amino acid degradation, by which the carbon and nitrogen atoms of the amino acids are usefully freed to form key metabolite compounds such as α-ketoglutarate and acetyl-CoA. These compounds can then be used in the synthesis of other amino acids. Degradative pathways also exist for various lipids, the purine and pyrimidine nucleotides, many pentose and hexose sugars, etc. Most of the degradative pathways are quite specific, and thus a very large number (perhaps 200 to 300) of different degradative intermediates may be found in E. coli. The number must be even larger in many other bacteria, particularly the Pseudomonads, since they degrade a larger, more varied collection of organic molecules than E. coli.

The generalization is beginning to emerge that degradative pathways are usually quite different from pathways of biosynthesis. This observation is not surprising. As we shall see in Chapter 5, most biosynthetic reactions require energy, and often involve the breakdown of ATP, whereas degradative reactions, by their very function, must eventually generate ATP, in addition to supplying carbon and nitrogen skeletons.

THE SIGNIFICANCE OF A FINITE AMOUNT OF DNA

It is easy for the sophisticated pure chemist to look at Figure 3–12 with initial skepticism. Its neatness and clarity cannot obscure the fact that seemingly each week a new enzyme with its corresponding newly discovered metabolic reaction is reported. The question arises whether Figure 3–12, by its simplification, completely misses the point of metabolism in E. coli. This would certainly be the case if there were not just one or two ways of degrading glucose, but 50 to 100 ways, and likewise if there were 20 different pathways leading to the biosynthesis of each of the nucleotides, amino acids, etc.

However, there exists a simple way to refute the "heretical thought" that only an insignificant fraction of the metabolic reactions that occur in E. coli have to date been described. The argument is based on the fact, which we shall prove in later chapters, that the sequence of nucleotides in DNA carries the genetic information that orders (codes) the sequence of amino acids in proteins. It is now clear that successive groups of three nucleotide pairs code for each amino acid. Thus the average-size protein, containing about 300 amino acids, requires a code of 900 nucleotide pairs. Since each nucleotide pair has a $MW = 660$, DNA units of $MW = (660)(900) \cong 6 \times 10^5$ are needed for each protein. Thus the number of different proteins within a cell can be no greater than the amount of haploid $DNA/6 \times 10^5$.

This figure can be used further to estimate the number of different types of small molecules a cell can possess. The majority of kinds of proteins in a cell are enzymes, each of which catalyzes a specific metabolic reaction. The approximate number of types of small molecules can be estimated if we know, on the average, how many specific enzymes are needed for the metabolism of the average small molecule. At present it seems a good guess that the number lies between one and two.

ONE—FIFTH TO ONE—THIRD OF THE CHEMICAL REACTIONS IN E. COLI ARE KNOWN

Our best estimate for the haploid MW of DNA in *E. coli* is $2.5 \times 10^9 \pm 0.5 \times 10^9$. This figure corresponds to 2000 to 3000 average size protein molecules, and suggests that the number of different small molecules will be somewhat under 2000. Most pleasingly we find by looking at Table 3–3 that our best guess of the number of different small metabolites involved in already known metabolic pathways is between 600 and 800. This means that we already know at least 1/5, and maybe more than 1/3 of all the metabolic reactions that will ever be described in *E. coli*. The conclusion is most satisfying, for it strongly suggests that within the next 10 to 20 years we shall approach a state in which it will be possible to describe essentially all the metabolic reactions involved in the life of an *E. coli* cell.

Therefore even a cautious chemist, when properly informed, need not look at a bacterial cell as a hopelessly complex object. Instead he might easily adopt an almost joyous enthusiasm, for it is clear that he, unlike his nineteenth-century equivalent, at last possesses the tools to describe completely the essential features of life.

SUMMARY

At the chemical level even the smallest cells are fantastically complicated. Most scientists interested in the essential chemical features of cell growth and division now concentrate on bacteria, since bacterial cells are about 500 times smaller than the average cell of a higher plant or animal. The most commonly employed bacterium, Escherichia coli, weighs about 2×10^{-12} gram (10^{12} daltons), of which about 70 per cent is water. The number of different types of molecules within an E. coli cell probably lies between 3000 and 6000. Approximately half are "small" molecules and the remainder, macromolecules. The large number of different macromolecules means that we shall not know in the near (or conceivably, even in the distant) future the exact 3-D structures of all the molecules in even the smallest cell.

We do, however, know some rules about cell chemistry that make it possible to understand the growth of a cell without knowing the exact molecular structure of all its constituents. We know, for example, that all cellular macromolecules are polymeric molecules built up from much smaller monomers. Proteins are polymers containing amino acids as their monomers; the polymeric nucleic acids are built by the linking of nucleotides. Further simplicity comes from the fact that most polymers, including all the proteins and nucleic acids, are essentially linear molecules.

Another simplifying rule concerns the complexity of intermediary metabolism. Generally compounds cannot be directly transformed into a large number of other compounds. Instead each compound comprises a step in a series of reactions (pathway) leading either to the degradation of a food molecule or to the biosynthesis of a necessary cellular molecule such as amino acid or a fatty acid. Cellular metabolism is the sum total of a large number of such pathways (on metabolic maps) connected in such a way that products of degradative pathways can be used to initiate specific biosynthetic pathways.

The complexity of the metabolic map of an organism is related to the amount of genetic information (DNA) in the organism. The amount of DNA in a cell places an upper limit on the number of different enzymes the cell can produce. E. coli possess sufficient DNA to code for the amino acid sequence in at most 2000 to 3000 different proteins. Some 600 different small molecules have now been detected in E. coli. This indicates that those metabolic reactions which we know of in E. coli account for one-fifth to one-third of its total metabolism.

REFERENCES

Sistrom, W., *Microbial Life*, 2nd ed., Holt, New York, 1969. A brief paperback introduction to the biology and chemistry of microbes.

Stanier, R. Y., M. Doudoroff, and E. A. Adelberg, *The Microbial World*, 3rd ed; Prentice-Hall, Englewood Cliffs, N.J., 1970. A superb treatment of microbiology that can be read by any beginning college student.

Loewy, A., and P. Siekevitz, *Cell Structure and Function*, 2nd ed., Holt, New York, 1969. Essentials of the physiology of the cell, often with emphasis on the problems of multicellular organization.

Gunsalus, I. C., and R. Y. Stanier, *The Bacteria: A Treatise on Structure and Function* (5 vols.), Academic, New York, 1960–1964. A series of reviews and articles on essentially everything interesting about bacteria.

4

THE

IMPORTANCE

OF WEAK

CHEMICAL

INTERACTIONS

UNTIL NOW WE HAVE FOCUSED OUR attention on the existence of discrete organic molecules and, following classical organic chemistry, have emphasized the covalent bonds which hold them together. It takes little insight, however, to realize that this type of analysis is inadequate for describing a cell, and that we must also concern ourselves with the exact shape of molecules and with the several factors which bind them together in an organized fashion. The distribution of molecules in cells is not random, and we must ask ourselves what chemical laws determine this distribution. Clearly, covalent bonding cannot be involved; by definition, atoms united by covalent bonds belong to the same molecule.

The arrangement of distinct molecules in cells is controlled instead by chemical bonds much weaker than covalent bonds. Atoms united by covalent bonds are capable of weak interactions with nearby atoms. These interactions, sometimes called "secondary bonds," occur not only between atoms in different molecules, but also between atoms in the same molecule. Weak bonds are important not just in deciding which molecules lie next to each other, but also in giving shape to flexible molecules such as the polypeptides and polynucleotides. It is, therefore, useful to have a feeling for the nature of weak chemical interactions and to understand how their "weak" character makes them indispensable to cellular existence. The most important include van der Waals bonds, hydrogen bonds, and ionic bonds.

DEFINITION AND SOME CHARACTERISTICS OF CHEMICAL BONDS

A chemical bond is an attractive force that holds atoms together. Aggregates of finite size are called molecules. Originally, it was thought that only covalent bonds hold atoms together in molecules, but now, as we shall show later in this chapter, weaker attractive forces are known to be important in holding together many macromolecules. For example, the four polypeptide chains of hemoglobin are held together by the combined action of several weak bonds. It is thus now customary also to call weak positive interactions chemical bonds, even though they are not strong enough, when present singly, to effectively bind two atoms together.

Chemical bonds are characterized in several ways. A most obvious characteristic of a bond is its strength. Strong bonds almost never fall apart at physiological temperatures. This is why atoms united by covalent bonds always belong to the same molecule. Weak bonds are easily broken, and when they exist singly, they exist fleetingly. Only when present in ordered groups do weak bonds exist for a long time. The strength of a bond is correlated with its length, so that two atoms connected by a strong bond are always closer together than the same two atoms held together by a weak bond. For example, two hydrogen atoms bound covalently to form a hydrogen molecule (H:H) are 0.74 A apart, whereas the same two atoms, when held together by the van der Waals forces instead, are held 1.2 A apart.

Another important bond characteristic is the maximum number of bonds that a given atom can make. The number of covalent bonds an atom forms is called its valence. Oxygen, for example, has a valence of two: It can never form more than two covalent bonds. There is more variability in the case of van der Waals bonds, where the limiting factor is purely steric: The

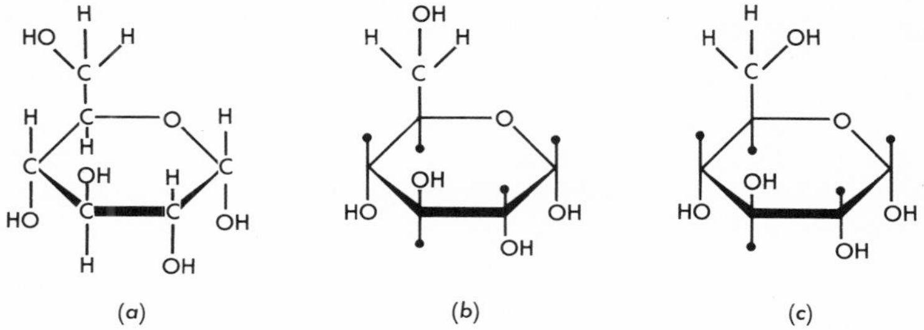

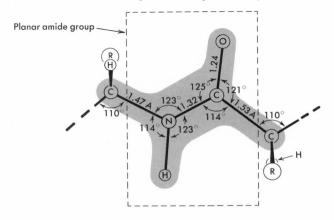

(a)   (b)   (c)

FIGURE 4-1   Rotation about the C_5–C_6 bond in glucose. This carbon-carbon bond is a single bond, and so any of the three configurations (a), (b), (c) may occur.

FIGURE 4-2   The planar shape of the peptide bond. Shown is a portion of an extended polypeptide chain. Almost no rotation is possible about the peptide bond because of its partial double-bond character:

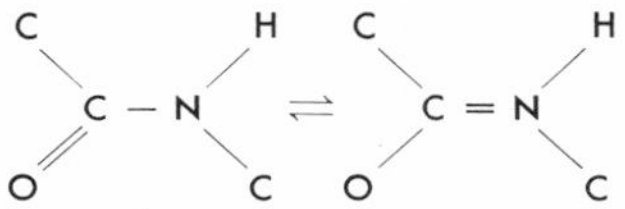

All the atoms in the grey must lie in the same plane. Rotation is possible, however, around the remaining two bonds, which make up the polypeptide configurations. (Redrawn from L. Pauling, *The Nature of the Chemical Bond*, 3rd ed., Cornell Univ. Press, Ithaca, N.Y., 1960, p. 498, with permission.)

number of possible bonds is limited only by the number of atoms that can simultaneously touch each other. The formation of hydrogen bonds is subject to more restrictions. A covalently bonded hydrogen atom usually participates in only one hydrogen bond, whereas an oxygen atom seldom participates in more than two hydrogen bonds.

The angle between two bonds originating from a single atom is called the bond angle. The angle between two specific covalent bonds is always approximately the same. For example, when a carbon atom has four single bonds, they are directed tetrahedrally (bond angle $= 109°$). In contrast, the angles between weak bonds are much more variable.

Bonds differ also in the freedom of rotation they allow. Single covalent bonds permit free rotation of bound atoms (Figure 4-1), whereas double and triple bonds are quite rigid. For example, the carbonyl ($C{=}O$) and imino (N—H) groups bound together by the rigid peptide bond must lie in the same plane (Figure 4-2), because of the partial double-bond character of the peptide bond. Much weaker, ionic bonds show completely opposite behavior; they impose no restrictions on the relative orientations of bonded atoms.

CHEMICAL BONDS ARE EXPLAINABLE IN QUANTUM–MECHANICAL TERMS

The nature of the forces, strong as well as weak, that give rise to chemical bonds remained a mystery to chemists until the quantum theory of the atom (quantum mechanics) was developed in the 1920s. Then, for the first time, the various empirical laws about how chemical bonds are formed were put on a firm theoretical basis. It was realized that all chemical bonds, weak as well as strong, were based on electrostatic forces. Quantum-mechanical explanations were provided not only for covalent bonding by the sharing of electrons, but also for the formation of weaker bonds.

CHEMICAL–BOND FORMATION INVOLVES A CHANGE IN THE FORM OF ENERGY

The spontaneous formation of a bond between two atoms always involves the release of some of the internal energy of the unbonded atoms and its conversion to another energy form. The stronger the bond, the greater the amount of energy which is released upon its formation. The bonding reaction between two atoms A and B is thus described by

$$A + B \rightarrow AB + \text{energy} \tag{4-1}$$

where AB represents the bonded aggregate. The rate of the reaction is proportional to the frequency of collision between A and B. The unit most commonly used to measure energy is the calorie, the amount of energy required to raise the temperature of 1 gram of water from 14.5°C to 15.5°C. Since thousands of calories are usually involved in the breaking of a mole of chemical bonds, most chemical-energy changes in chemical reactions are expressed in kilocalories per mole.

Atoms joined by chemical bonds, however, do not forever remain together. There also exist forces which break chemical bonds. By far the most important of these forces arises from heat energy. Collisions with fast-moving molecules or atoms can break chemical bonds. During a collision, some of the kinetic energy of a moving molecule is given up as it pushes apart two bonded atoms. The faster a molecule is moving (the higher the temperature), the greater the probability that, upon collision, it will break a bond. Hence, as the temperature of a collection of molecules is increased, the stability of their bonds decreases. The breaking of a bond is thus always indicated by the formula

$$AB + \text{energy} \rightarrow A + B \tag{4-2}$$

The amount of energy that must be added to break a bond is exactly equal to the amount which was released upon its formation. This equivalence follows from the first law of thermodynamics, which states that energy (except as it is interconvertible with mass) can be neither made nor destroyed.

EQUILIBRIUM BETWEEN BOND MAKING
AND BREAKING

Every bond is thus a result of the combined actions of bond-making (arising from electrostatic interactions) and bond-breaking forces. When an equilibrium is reached in a closed system, the number of bonds forming per unit time will equal the number breaking. Then the proportion of bonded atoms is described by the following mass action formula:

$$K_{eq} = \frac{conc^{AB}}{conc^{A} \times conc^{B}}$$

(4–3)

where K_{eq} is the equilibrium constant, and $conc^{A}$, $conc^{B}$, and $conc^{AB}$ are the concentrations of A, B, and AB in moles per liter, respectively. Whether we start with only free A and B, with only the molecule AB, or with a combination of AB and free A and B, at equilibrium the proportions of A, B, and AB will reach the concentration given by K_{eq}.

THE CONCEPT OF FREE ENERGY

There is always a change in the form of energy as the proportion of bonded atoms moves toward the equilibrium concentration. Biologically, the most useful way to express this energy change is through the physical chemists' concept of *free energy, G*.* Here we shall not give a rigorous description of free energy nor show how it differs from the other forms of energy. For this, the reader must refer to a chemistry text which discusses the second law of thermodynamics. We must suffice by saying that *free energy is energy that has the ability to do work.*

The second law of thermodynamics tells us that a decrease of free energy (ΔG is negative) always occurs in spontaneous reactions. When equilibrium is reached, there is no further change in the amount of free energy ($\Delta G = 0$). The equilib-

* It was the custom in the United States until recently to refer to free energy by the symbol F. Now, however, most new texts have adopted the international symbol G, which honors the great nineteenth-century physicist Gibbs.

rium state for a closed collection of atoms is thus that state that contains the least amount of free energy.

The free energy lost as equilibrium is approached is either transformed into heat or used to increase the amount of entropy. Here, we shall not attempt to define entropy (again this task must be left to a chemistry text), except to say that the amount of entropy is a measure of the amount of disorder. The greater the disorder, the greater the amount of entropy. The existence of entropy means that many spontaneous chemical reactions do not proceed with an evolution of heat. For example, in the dissolving of NaCl in water, heat is absorbed. There is, nonetheless, a net decrease in free energy because of the increase of disorder of the Na^+ and Cl^- ions as they move from a solid to a liquid phase.

K_{eq} IS EXPONENTIALLY RELATED TO ΔG

It is obvious that the stronger the bond, and hence the greater the change in free energy (ΔG) which accompanies its formation, the greater the proportion of atoms that must exist in the bonded form. This common-sense idea is quantitatively expressed by the physical-chemical formula

$$\Delta G = -RT \ln K_{eq} \quad \text{or} \quad K_{eq} = e^{-\Delta G/RT} \tag{4-4}$$

where R is the universal gas constant, T the absolute temperature, $e = 2.718$, ln the logarithm of K to the base e, and K_{eq} the equilibrium constant.

TABLE 4-1 *The numerical relationship between the equilibrium constant and ΔG at $25°C$*

K_{eq}	ΔG, kcal/mole
0.001	4.089
0.01	2.726
0.1	1.363
1.0	0
10.0	−1.363
100.0	−2.726
1000.0	−4.089

Insertion of the appropriate values of R ($= 1.987$ cal/deg/mole) and T ($= 298$ at 25°C) tells us (Table 4–1) that ΔG values as low as 2 kcal/mole can drive a bond-forming reaction to virtual completion if all reactants are present at molar concentrations.

COVALENT BONDS ARE VERY STRONG

The ΔG values accompanying the formation of covalent bonds from free atoms such as hydrogen or oxygen are very large and negative in sign, usually -50 to -110 kcal/mole. Application of Eq. (4–4) tells us that K_{eq} of the bonding reaction will be correspondingly large, and so the concentration of hydrogen or oxygen atoms existing unbound will be very small. For example, a ΔG value of -100 kcal/mole tells us that, if we start with 1 mole/liter of the reacting atoms, only one in 10^{40} atoms will remain unbound when equilibrium is reached.

WEAK BONDS HAVE ENERGIES BETWEEN 1 AND 7 KCAL/MOLE

The main types of weak bonds important in biological systems are the van der Waals bonds, hydrogen bonds, and ionic bonds. Sometimes, as we shall soon point out, the distinction between a hydrogen bond and an ionic bond is arbitrary. The weakest bonds are the van der Waals bonds. These have energies (1 to 2 kcal/mole) that are only slightly greater than the kinetic energy of heat motion. The energies of hydrogen and ionic bonds range between 3 and 7 kcal/mole.

In liquid solutions, almost all molecules are forming a number of weak bonds to nearby atoms. All molecules are able to form van der Waals bonds; hydrogen and ionic bonds can also form between molecules (ions) which have a net charge or in which the charge is unequally distributed. Some molecules thus have the capacity to form several types of weak bonds. Energetic considerations, however, tell us that molecules always have a greater tendency to form the stronger bond.

WEAK BONDS CONSTANTLY MADE AND BROKEN AT PHYSIOLOGICAL TEMPERATURES

The energy of the strongest weak bond is only about ten times larger than the average energy of kinetic motion (heat) at 25°C (0.6 kcal/mole). Since there is a significant spread in the energies of kinetic motion, many molecules with sufficient kinetic energy to break the strongest weak bond always exist at physiological temperatures.

ENZYMES NOT INVOLVED IN MAKING (BREAKING) OF WEAK BONDS

The average lifetime of a single weak bond is only a fraction of a second. Cells thus do not need a special mechanism to speed up the rate at which weak bonds are made and broken. Correspondingly, enzymes never participate in reactions of weak bonds.

DISTINCTION BETWEEN POLAR AND NONPOLAR MOLECULES

All forms of weak interactions are based upon attractions between electric charges. The separation of electric charges can be permanent or temporary, depending upon the atoms involved. For example, the oxygen molecule (O:O) has a symmetric distribution of electrons between its two oxygen atoms, and so each of its two atoms is uncharged. In contrast, there is a nonuniform distribution of charge in water (H:O:H), where the bond electrons are unevenly shared (Figure 4–3). They are held more strongly by the oxygen atom, which thus carries a considerable negative charge, whereas the two hydrogen atoms together have an equal amount of positive charge. The center of the positive charge is on one side of the center of the negative charge. A combination of separated positive and negative charges is called an electric dipole moment. Unequal electron sharing reflects dissimilar affinities of the bonding atoms for electrons. Atoms which have a tendency to gain electrons are called electronegative atoms. Electropositive atoms have a tendency to give up electrons.

Molecules such as H_2O, which have a dipole moment, are called *polar molecules*. *Nonpolar molecules* are those with no effective dipole moments. In CH_4 (methane), for example, the carbon and hydrogen atoms have similar affinities for their shared electron pairs, and so neither the carbon nor the hydrogen atom is noticeably charged.

The distribution of charge in a molecule can also be affected by the presence of nearby molecules, particularly if the affected molecule is polar. This effect may cause a nonpolar molecule to acquire a slight polar character. If the second molecule is not polar, its presence will still alter the nonpolar molecule, establishing a fluctuating charge distribution. Such induced effects, however, give rise to a much smaller separation of charge than is found in polar molecules, thus resulting in smaller interaction energies and, correspondingly, weaker chemical bonds.

FIGURE 4–3   *The structure of a water molecule.*

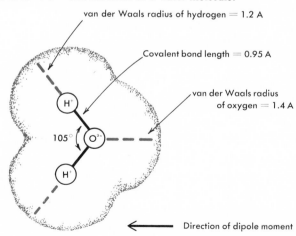

van der Waals radius of hydrogen = 1.2 A

Covalent bond length = 0.95 A

van der Waals radius
of oxygen = 1.4 A

H^+

105° O^{2-}

H^+

⟵————   Direction of dipole moment

VAN DER WAALS FORCES

Van der Waals bonding arises from a nonspecific attractive force originating when two atoms come close to each other. It is based not upon the existence of permanent charge separations, but rather upon the induced fluctuating charges caused by the nearness of molecules. It therefore operates between all types of molecules, polar as well as nonpolar. It depends heavily upon the distance between the interacting groups, since the bond energy is inversely proportional to the sixth power of distance (Figure 4–4).

There also exists a more powerful van der Waals repulsive force, which comes into play at even shorter distances. This repulsion is caused by the overlapping of the outer electron shells of the atoms involved. The van der Waals attractive and repulsive forces balance at a certain distance specific for each type of atom. This distance is the so-called van der Waals radius (Table 4–2 and Figure 4–5). The van der Waals bonding energy between two atoms separated by the sum of their van der Waals radii increases with the size of the respective atoms. For two average atoms it is only about 1 kcal/mole, which is just slightly more than the average thermal energy of molecules at room temperature (0.6 kcal/mole).

This means that van der Waals forces are an effective binding force at physiological temperatures only when several atoms in a given molecule are bound to several atoms in another molecule. Then the energy of interaction is much greater than the

T A B L E 4–2   *van der Waals radii of the atoms in biological molecules*

Atom	van der Waals radius, Å
H	1.2
N	1.5
O	1.4
P	1.9
S	1.85
CH₃ group	2.0
Half thickness of aromatic molecule	1.7

dissociating tendency resulting from random thermal movements. In order for several atoms to interact effectively, the
molecular fit must be precise, since the distance separating
any two interacting atoms must not be much greater than the

FIGURE 4-4 *Diagram illustrating van der Waals attraction and repulsion forces in relation to electron distribution of
monoatomic molecules on the inert rare gas argon.
(Redrawn from L. Pauling, General Chemistry, 2nd
ed., Freeman, San Francisco, 1958, p. 322, with permission.)*

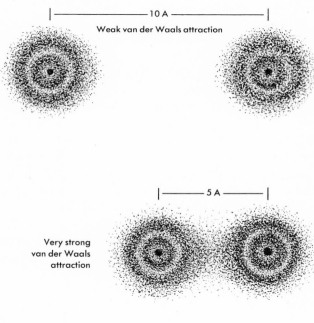

|———————— 10 A ————————|

Weak van der Waals attraction

|——— 5 A ———|

Very strong
van der Waals
attraction

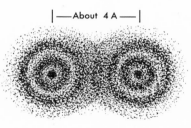

|—About 4 A —|

van der Waals attraction just balanced
by repulsive forces, owing to inter-
penetration of outer electron shells

sum of their van der Waals radii (Figure 4–6). The strength of interaction rapidly approaches zero when this distance is only slightly exceeded. Thus, the strongest type of van der Waals contact arises when a molecule contains a cavity exactly complementary in shape to a protruding group of another molecule (Figure 4–7). This is the type of situation thought to exist between an antigen and its specific antibody (see Chapter 15). In this instance, the binding energies sometimes can be as large as 10 kcal/mole, so that antigen-antibody complexes seldom fall apart. Many polar molecules are only seldom af-

FIGURE 4–5   *Drawings of several molecules with the van der Waals radii of the atoms outlined.*

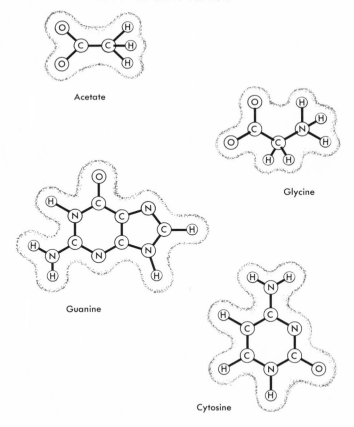

Acetate

Glycine

Guanine

Cytosine

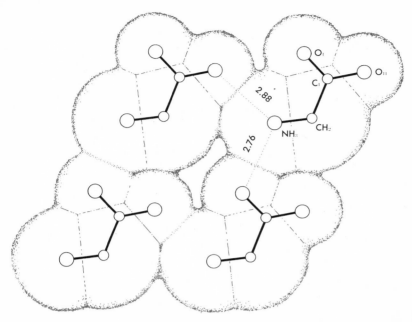

FIGURE 4–6 *The arrangement of molecules in a layer of a crystal formed by the amino acid glycine. The packing of the molecules is determined by the van der Waals radii of the groups, except for the N–H····O contacts, which are shortened by the formation of hydrogen bonds. (Redrawn from L. Pauling, The Nature of the Chemical Bond, 3rd ed., Cornell Univ. Press, Ithaca, N.Y., 1960, p. 262, with permission.)*

fected by van der Waals interactions, since such molecules can acquire a lower energy state (lose more free energy) by forming other types of bonds.

HYDROGEN BONDS

A hydrogen bond arises between a covalently bound hydrogen atom with some positive charge and a negatively charged, covalently bound acceptor atom (Figure 4–8). For example, the hydrogen atoms of the imino group (N—H) are attracted by the negatively charged keto oxygen atoms (C=O). Some-

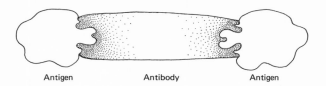

Antigen   Antibody   Antigen

FIGURE 4–7   *Schematic drawing showing the complementary relation
between the surface configurations of an antigen and
an antibody, allowing the formation of secondary
bonds between them.*

times the hydrogen-bonded atoms belong to groups with a unit
of charge (e.g., NH_3^+ or COO^-).   In other cases, both the
donor hydrogen atoms and the negative acceptor atoms have less
than a unit of charge.

The biologically most important hydrogen bonds involve
hydrogen atoms covalently bound to oxygen (O—H) or nitrogen atoms (N—H).   Likewise, the negative acceptor atoms are
usually nitrogen or oxygen. Table 4–3 lists some of the most
important hydrogen bonds.   Bond energies range between 3 and
7 kcal/mole, the stronger bonds involving the greater charge
differences between donor and acceptor atoms.   Hydrogen
bonds are thus weaker than covalent bonds, yet considerably

TABLE 4–3   *Approximate bond lengths of biologically important hydrogen bonds*

Bond	Approximate bond length, A
O–H — — — O	2.70 ± .10
O–H — — — O⁻	2.63 ± .10
O–H — — — N	2.88 ± .13
N–H — — — O	3.04 ± .13
N⁺H — — — O	2.93 ± .10
N–H — — — N	3.10 ± .13

stronger than van der Waals bonds. A hydrogen bond, therefore, will hold two atoms closer together than the sum of their
van der Waals radii, but not so close together as a covalent bond
would hold them.

Hydrogen bonds, unlike van der Waals bonds, are highly

FIGURE 4-8 *Examples of hydrogen bonds in biological molecules.*

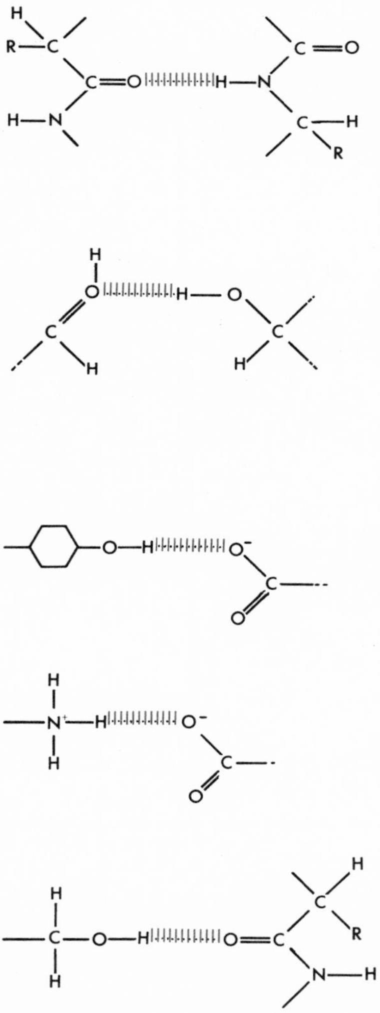

Hydrogen bond between peptide groups

Hydrogen bond between two hydroxyl groups

Hydrogen bond between a charged carboxyl group and the hydroxyl group of tyrosine

Hydrogen bond between a charged amino group and a charged carboxyl group

Hydrogen bond between a hydroxyl group of serine and a peptide group

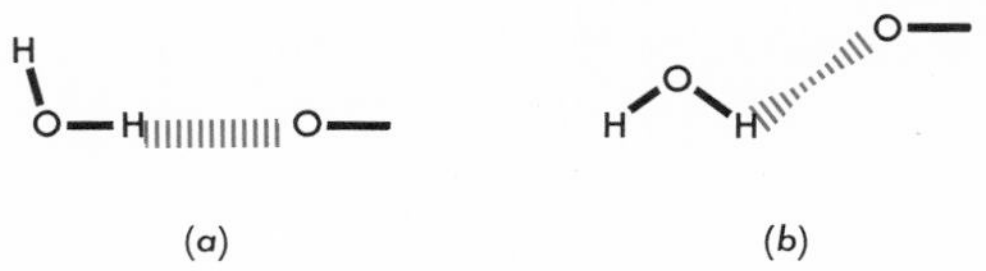

(a)   (b)

FIGURE 4-9   *Directional properties of hydrogen bonds. In (a) the vector along the covalent O—H bond points directly at the acceptor oxygen, thereby forming a strong bond. In (b) the vector points away from the oxygen atom, resulting in a much weaker bond.*

directional. In optimally strong hydrogen bonds, the hydrogen atom points directly at the acceptor atom (Figure 4-9). If it points indirectly, the bond energy is much less. Hydrogen bonds are also much more specific than van der Waals bonds, since they demand the existence of molecules with complementary donor hydrogen and acceptor groups.

SOME IONIC BONDS ARE, IN EFFECT, HYDROGEN BONDS

Many organic molecules possess ionic groups that contain one or more units of net positive or negative charge. The negatively charged mononucleotides, for example, contain phosphate groups (PO_3^{3-}) with three units of negative charge, whereas each amino acid (except proline) has a negative carboxyl group (COO^-) and a positive amino group (NH_3^+), both of which carry a unit of charge. These charged groups are usually neutralized by nearby, oppositely charged, groups. The electrostatic forces acting between the oppositely charged groups are called ionic bonds. Their average bond energy in an aqueous solution is about 5 kcal/mole.

In many cases, either an inorganic cation like Na^+, K^+, or Mg^{2+}, or an inorganic anion like Cl^- or SO_4^{2-}, neutralizes the charge of the ionized organic molecules. When this happens in aqueous solution, the neutralizing cations and anions do not occupy fixed positions, because inorganic ions are usually surrounded by shells of water molecules and so do not directly bind to oppositely charged groups. Thus it is now believed that, in water solutions, electrostatic bonds to surrounding inorganic cations or anions are not of primary importance in determining the molecular shapes of organic molecules.

On the other hand, highly directional bonds result if the oppositely charged groups can form hydrogen bonds to each other. For example, both the COO^- and NH_3^+ groups are often held together by strong hydrogen bonds. Since these hydrogen bonds are stronger than those that involve groups with less than a unit of charge, they are correspondingly shorter. A strong hydrogen bond can also form between a group with a unit charge and a group having less than a unit charge. For example, a hydrogen atom belonging to an amino group ($-NH_2$) bonds strongly to an oxygen atom of a carboxyl group (COO^-).

WEAK INTERACTIONS DEMAND COMPLEMENTARY MOLECULAR SURFACES

Weak binding forces are effective only when the interacting surfaces are close. This proximity is possible only when the molecular surfaces have *complementary structures*, so that a protruding group (or positive charge) on one surface is matched by a cavity (or negative charge) on another; i.e., the interacting molecules must have a lock-and-key relationship. In cells this requirement often means that some molecules hardly ever bond to other molecules of the same kind, because such molecules do not have the properties of symmetry necessary for self-interaction. For example, some (polar) molecules contain donor hydrogen atoms and no suitable acceptor atoms, whereas others can accept hydrogen bonds but have no hydrogen atoms to donate. On the other hand, many molecules do exist with the symmetry to permit strong self-interaction in cells, water being the most important example.

H_2O MOLECULES FORM HYDROGEN BONDS

Under physiological conditions, water molecules rarely ionize to form H^+ and OH^- ions. Instead, they exist as polar $H-O-H$ molecules. Both the hydrogen and oxygen atoms form strong hydrogen bonds. In each H_2O molecule, the oxygen atom can bind to two external hydrogen atoms, whereas each hydrogen atom can bind to one adjacent oxygen atom. These bonds are directed tetrahedrally (Figure 4–10), so that, in its solid and liquid forms, each water molecule tends to have four nearest neighbors, one in each of the four directions of a tetrahedron. In ice the bonds to these neighbors are very rigid and the arrangement

FIGURE 4–10   *Schematic diagram of a lattice formed by H_2O molecules. The energy gained by forming specific hydrogen bonds (||||||) between H_2O molecules favors the arrangement of the molecules in adjacent tetrahedrons. Oxygen atoms are indicated by large circles, and hydrogen atoms by small circles. Although the rigidity of the arrangement depends upon the temperature of the molecules, the pictured structure is, nevertheless, predominant in water as well as in ice. (Redrawn from L. Pauling, The Nature of the Chemical Bond, 3rd ed., Cornell Univ. Press, Ithaca, N.Y., 1960, p. 465, with permission.)*

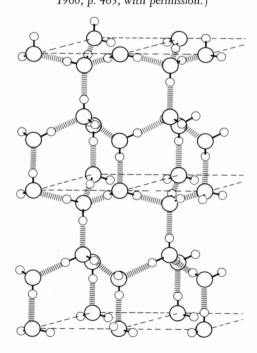

of molecules fixed. Above the melting temperature (0°C) the energy of thermal motion is sufficient to break the hydrogen bonds and to allow the water molecules to change their nearest neighbors continually. Even in the liquid form, however, at a given instant most water molecules are bound by four strong hydrogen bonds.

WEAK BONDS BETWEEN MOLECULES IN AQUEOUS SOLUTIONS

The average energy of a secondary bond, though small compared to that of a covalent bond, is nonetheless strong enough compared to heat energy to ensure that most molecules in aqueous solution will form secondary bonds to other molecules. The proportion of bonded to nonbonded arrangements is given by Eq. (4–4), corrected to take into account the high concentration of molecules in a liquid. It tells us that interaction energies as low as 2 to 3 kcal/mole are sufficient at physiological temperatures to force most molecules to form the maximum number of good secondary bonds.

The specific structure of a solution at a given instant is markedly influenced by which solute molecules are present, not only because molecules have specific shapes, but also because molecules differ in which types of secondary bonds they can form. These differences mean that a molecule will tend to move until it is next to a molecule with which it can form the strongest possible secondary bond.

Solutions of course are not static. Because of the disruptive influence of heat, the specific configuration of a solution is constantly changing from one arrangement to another of approximately the same energy content. Equally important in biological systems is the fact that metabolism is continually transforming one molecule into another and so automatically changing the nature of the secondary bonds that can be formed. The solution structure of cells is thus constantly disrupted not only by heat motion, but also by the metabolic transformations of the cell's solute molecules.

ORGANIC MOLECULES THAT TEND TO FORM HYDROGEN BONDS ARE WATER SOLUBLE

The energy of hydrogen bonds per atomic group is much greater than that of van der Waals contacts. Thus those molecules that can form hydrogen bonds will form them in preference to van der Waals contacts. For example, if we try to mix water with a compound which cannot form hydrogen bonds, such as benzene, the water and benzene molecules rapidly separate from each other, the water molecules forming hydrogen bonds among themselves, while the benzene molecules attach to each other by van der Waals bonds. Thus it is effectively impossible to insert a non-hydrogen-bonding organic molecule into water.

On the other hand, polar molecules such as glucose and pyruvate, which contain a large number of groups that form excellent hydrogen bonds (e.g., $=O$ or $—OH$), are somewhat soluble in water (hydrophilic as opposed to hydrophobic). This effect occurs because, while the insertion of such groups into a water lattice breaks water-water hydrogen bonds, it results simultaneously in hydrogen bonds between glucose and water. These alternative arrangements, however, are not usually as energetically satisfactory as the water-water arrangements, so that even the most polar molecules ordinarily have only limited solubility.

Thus almost all the molecules which cells are constantly acquiring, either through food intake or biosynthesis, are somewhat insoluble in water. These molecules, by their thermal movements, randomly collide with other molecules until they find complementary molecular surfaces on which to attach and thereby release water molecules for water-water interactions.

THE UNIQUENESS OF MOLECULAR SHAPES; THE CONCEPT OF SELECTIVE STICKINESS

Even though most cellular molecules are built up from only a small number of groups, such as OH, NH_2, and CH_3, great specificity exists as to which molecules tend to lie next to each other. This is because each molecule has unique bonding properties. One very clear demonstration comes from the specificity of stereoisomers. For example, proteins are always constructed from L-amino acids, never from their mirror images, the D-amino acids (Figure 4–11). Though the D- and L-amino acids have identical covalent bonds, their binding properties to asymmetric molecules are often very different. Thus most enzymes are specific for L-amino acids. If an L-amino acid is able to attach to a specific enzyme, the D-amino acid is unable to bind.

The general rule exists that most molecules in cells can make good "weak" bonds with only a small number of other molecules. This is partly because all molecules in biological systems exist in an aqueous environment. The formation of a bond in a cell depends not only upon whether two molecules bind well to each other, but also upon whether the bond will permit their water solvent to form the maximum number of good hydrogen bonds.

FIGURE 4–11   *The two stereoisomers of the amino acid alanine. (Redrawn from L. Pauling, General Chemistry, 2nd ed., Freeman, San Francisco, 1958, p. 598, with permission.)*

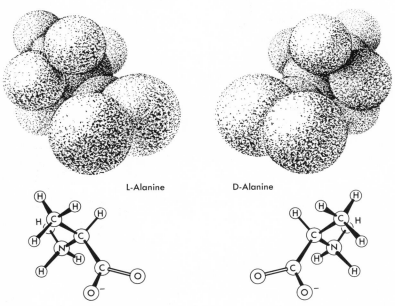

L-Alanine   D-Alanine

The strong tendency of water to exclude nonpolar groups is frequently referred to as *hydrophobic bonding*. Some chemists like to call all the bonds between nonpolar groups *in a water solution* hydrophobic bonds (Figure 4–12). In a sense this term is a confusing misnomer, for the phenomenon that it seeks to emphasize is the absence, not the presence, of bonds. (The bonds that tend to form between the nonpolar groups are due to van der Waals attractive forces.) On the other hand, the term

FIGURE 4–12   *Illustrative examples of van der Waals (hydrophobic) bonds between the nonpolar side groups of amino acids. The hydrogens are not indicated individually. For the sake of clarity, the van der Waals radii are reduced by 20 per cent. The structural formulas adjacent to each space-filling drawing indicate the arrangement of the atoms; (a) phenylalanine-leucine bond; (b) phenylalanine-phenylalanine bond. (Redrawn from H. A. Scheraga, in The Proteins, H. Neurath (ed.), 2nd ed., Vol. I, Academic Press, New York, 1963, p. 527, with permission.)*

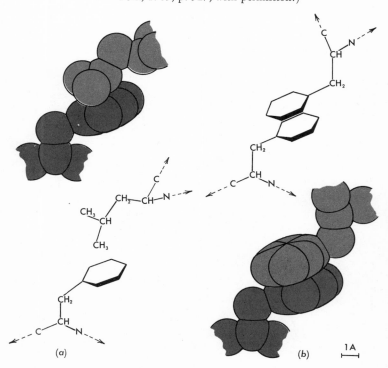

(a)   (b)   1A

hydrophobic bond is often useful, since it emphasizes the fact that nonpolar groups will try to arrange themselves so that they are not in contact with water molecules.

Consider, for example, the energy difference between the binding in water of the amino acids alanine and glycine to a third molecule which has a surface complementary to alanine. Alanine differs from glycine by the presence of one methyl group in the former. When alanine is bound to the third molecule, the van der Waals contacts around the methyl group yield 1 kcal/mole of energy, which is not released when glycine is bound instead. This small energy difference alone would give [using Eq. (4–4)] only a factor of 6 between the binding of alanine and glycine. This calculation does not take into consideration, however, the fact that water is trying to exclude alanine much more than glycine. The presence of alanine's CH_3 group upsets the water lattice much more seriously than does the hydrogen atom side group of glycine. At present it is still difficult to predict how large a correction factor must be introduced for this disruption of the water lattice by the hydrophobic side groups. A current guess is that the water tends to exclude alanine, thrusting it toward a third molecule with a hydrophobic force 2 to 3 kcal/mole larger than the force excluding glycine.

We thus arrive at the important conclusion that the energetic difference between the binding of even the most similar molecules to a third molecule (when the difference involves a nonpolar group) is at least 2 to 3 kcal/mole greater in the aqueous interior of cells than under nonaqueous conditions. Frequently, the energetic difference is 3 to 4 kcal/mole, since the molecules involved often contain polar groups which can form hydrogen bonds.

THE ADVANTAGE OF ΔG'S BETWEEN 2 AND 5 KCAL/MOLE

We have seen that the energy of just one secondary bond (2 to 5 kcal/mole) is often sufficient to ensure that a molecule preferentially binds to a selected group of molecules. Equally important, these energy differences are not so large that rigid lattice arrangements develop within a cell—the interior of a cell never crystallizes as it would if the energy of secondary bonds were several times greater. Larger energy differences would mean that the secondary bonds break only seldom, resulting in low diffusion rates incompatible with cellular existence.

WEAK BONDS ATTACH ENZYMES TO SUBSTRATES

Secondary forces are necessarily the basis by which enzymes and their substrates initially combine with each other. Enzymes do not indiscriminantly bind all molecules but, in general, have noticeable affinity only for their own substrates.

Since enzymes catalyze both directions of a chemical reaction, they must have specific affinities for both sets of reacting molecules. In some special cases it is possible to calculate an equilibrium constant for the binding of an enzyme and one of its substrates, which consequently enables us [Eq. (4–4)] to calculate the ΔG upon binding. This calculation in turn hints at which types of bonds may be involved. ΔG values ranging between 5 and 10 kcal/mole suggest that from one to several good secondary bonds are the basis of specific enzyme-substrate interactions. Also worth noting is that the ΔG of binding is never exceptionally high; thus enzyme-substrate complexes can be both made and broken apart rapidly as a result of random thermal movement. This fact explains why enzymes can function so quickly, sometimes as often as 10^6 times per second. If enzymes were bound to their substrates by more powerful bonds, they would act much more slowly.

MOST MOLECULAR SHAPES DETERMINED BY WEAK BONDS

The shapes of numerous molecules are automatically given by the distribution of covalent bonds. This inflexibility occurs when groups are attached by covalent bonds about which free rotation is impossible. Rotation is only possible when atoms are attached by single bonds. (For example, the methyl groups of ethane, H_3C—CH_3, rotate about the carbon-carbon bond.) When more than one electron pair is involved in a bond, rotation does not occur; in fact, the atoms involved must lie in the same plane. Thus the aromatic purine and pyrimidine rings are planar molecules 3.4 A thick. There is no uncertainty about the shape of any aromatic molecules. They are almost always flat, independent of their surrounding environment.

On the contrary, for molecules containing single bonds, the possibility of rotation around the bond suggests that a covalently bonded molecule exists in a large variety of shapes. This theoretical possibility, however, is seldom in fact realized, because the various possible 3-D configurations differ in the number of good weak bonds which can be formed. Generally, there is one configuration that has significantly less free energy than any of the other geometric arrangements.

Two classes of secondary bonds may be important in determining 3-D shapes. One class is internal, forming between atoms connected by a chain of covalent bonds. Internal bonds often cause a linear molecule to bend back upon itself, allowing contacts between atoms separated by a large number of covalent bonds. In such molecules the final shape is usually compact (globular). The other class of bonds is external, forming between atoms not connected by covalent bonds. In cases in which the optimal 3-D configuration is achieved by forming external bonds, molecules most often have extended (fibrous) configurations.

It is no simple matter to guess the correct shape of a large molecule from its covalent-bond structure; although one configuration for a protein or a nucleic acid may be energetically much more suitable than any other, we cannot yet derive it from our knowledge of bond energies. There are two reasons for this difficulty. One is purely logistical. The number of possible configurations of a nucleic acid or even a small protein molecule is immense. Given present techniques for building molecular models, a single person (or even a small group of people) cannot rapidly calculate the sum of the energies of the weak bonds for each possible configuration; years would be required. Future work using electronic computers, however, should simplify some of this task. The second reason for our present inability to derive protein and nucleic acid structures is that our knowledge about the nature of weak bonds is still very incomplete; in many cases, we are not sure about either the exact bond energies or of the possible angles they form to each other.

Today, protein and nucleic acid shapes can be revealed only by x-ray diffraction analysis. Fortunately these experimental structure determinations are beginning to reveal some general rules that tell us which weak chemical interactions are most important in governing the molecular shapes of large molecules. In particular, these rules emphasize the vital importance of interactions of the macromolecules with water, by far the most common molecule in all cells.

POLYMERIC MOLECULES ARE SOMETIMES HELICAL

Earlier we emphasized that polymeric molecules, like proteins and nucleic acids, have regular linear backbones in which specific groups (e.g., —CO—NH—) repeat over and over along the molecule.

Often these regular groups are arranged in helical configurations held together by secondary bonds. The helix is a natural conformation for regular linear polymers, since it places each monomer group in an identical orientation within the molecule (Figure 4–13). Each monomer thereby forms the same group of secondary bonds as every other monomer. On the contrary, when a regular linear polymer has a nonhelical arrangement, different monomers must form different secondary bonds. Clearly, an unstable state occurs if any one set of secondary bonds is much stronger than any of the other arrangements. Thus, helical symmetry does not evolve from the particular shape of the monomer, but is instead the natural consequence of the existence of a unique monomer arrangement which is significantly more stable than all other arrangements.

It is important to remember that most biopolymers are not regular polymers containing identical monomers. Instead they often have irregular side groups attached to a regular backbone. When this happens, as it does in both nucleic acids and proteins, we need not necessarily expect a helical structure: A 3-D arrangement that is energetically very satisfactory for the backbone groups often produces very unsatisfactory bonding of the side groups. The 3-D structure of many irregular polymers is thus a compromise between the tendency of regular backbones

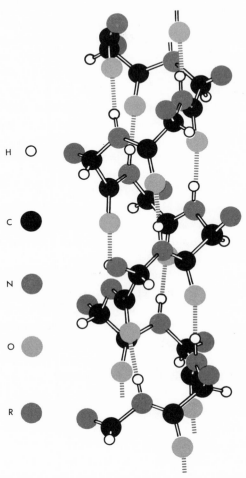

H O

C ●

N ●

O ●

R ●

FIGURE 4–13   *A polypeptide chain folded into a helical configuration called the α-helix. All the backbone atoms have identical orientations within the molecule. It may be looked at as a spiral staircase in which the steps are formed by amino acids. There is an amino acid every 1.5 A along the helical axis. The distance along the axis required for one turn is 5.4 A, giving 3.6 amino acids per turn. The helix is held together by hydrogen bonds between the carbonyl group of one residue and the imino group of the fourth residue down along the chain. (Redrawn from L. Pauling, The Nature of the Chemical Bond, 3rd ed., Cornell Univ. Press, Ithaca, N.Y., 1960, p. 500, with permission.)*

to form a regular helix and the tendency of the side groups to twist the backbone into a configuration that maximizes the strength of the secondary bonds formed by the side groups.

PROTEIN STRUCTURES ARE USUALLY IRREGULAR

In the case of proteins, the compromise between the side groups and the backbone groups is usually decided in favor of the side groups. Thus, as we shall show in much greater detail in Chapter 6, most amino acids in proteins are not part of regular helices. This is because almost one half of the side groups are nonpolar and can be placed in contact with water only by a considerable input of free energy. This conclusion was at first a surprise to many chemists, who were influenced by the fact that backbone groups could form strong internal hydrogen bonds, whereas the nonpolar groups could form only the much weaker van der Waals bonds. Their past reasoning was faulty, however, because it did not consider either the fact that the polar backbone can form almost as strong external hydrogen bonds to water, or the equally important fact that a significant amount of energy is necessary to push nonpolar side groups into a hydrogen-bonded water lattice.

This argument leads to the interesting prediction that in aqueous solutions macromolecules containing a large number of nonpolar side groups will tend to be more stable than molecules containing mostly polar groups. If we disrupt a polar molecule held together by a large number of internal hydrogen bonds, the decrease in free energy is often small, since the polar groups can then hydrogen bond to water. On the contrary, when we disrupt molecules having many nonpolar groups, there is usually a much greater loss in free energy, because the disruption necessarily inserts nonpolar groups into water.

DNA CAN FORM A REGULAR HELIX

At first glance, DNA looks even more unlikely to form a regular helix than does an irregular polypeptide chain. DNA not only has an irregular sequence of side groups, but in addition, all its side groups are hydrophobic. Both the purines (adenine and guanine) and the pyrimidines (thymine and cytosine), even though they contain polar $C=O$ and NH_2 groups, are quite insoluble in water because their flat sides are completely hydrophobic.

Nonetheless, DNA molecules usually have regular helical configurations. This is because most DNA molecules contain two polynucleotide strands that have complementary structures (see Chapter 9 for more details). Both internal and external secondary bonds stabilize the structure. The two strands are held together by hydrogen bonds between pairs of complementary purines and pyrimidines (Figure 4-14). Adenine (amino) is always hydrogen bonded to thymine (keto), whereas guanine (keto) is hydrogen bonded to cytosine (amino). In addition, virtually all the surface atoms in the sugar and phosphate groups form bonds to water molecules.

The purine-pyrimidine base pairs are found in the center of the DNA molecule. This arrangement allows their flat surfaces to stack on top of each other and so limits their contact with water. This stacking arrangement would be much less satisfactory if only one chain were present. A single chain could not have a regular backbone because its pyrimidines are smaller than the purines, and so the angle of helical rotation would have to vary with the sequence of bases. The presence of complementary base pairs in double-helical DNA makes a regular structure possible, since each base pair is of the same size.

DNA MOLECULES ARE STABLE AT PHYSIOLOGICAL TEMPERATURES

The double-helical DNA molecule is very stable at physiological temperatures, for two reasons. First, disruption of the double helix breaks the regular hydrogen bonds and brings the hydrophobic purines and pyrimidines into contact with water. Second, individual DNA molecules have a *very large number of weak bonds,* arranged so that most of them cannot break without the simultaneous breaking of many others. Even though thermal motion is constantly breaking apart the terminal purine-pyrimidine pairs at the ends of each molecule, the two chains do not usually fall apart, because the hydrogen bonds in the

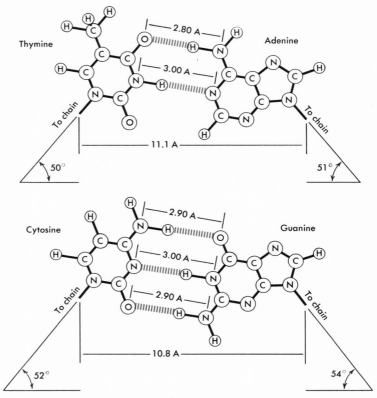

FIGURE 4-14   *The hydrogen-bonded base pairs in DNA. Adenine is always attached to thymine by two hydrogen bonds, whereas guanine always bonds to cytosine by three hydrogen bonds. The obligatory pairing of the smaller pyrimidine with the larger purine allows the two sugar-phosphate backbones to have identical helical configurations. All the hydrogen bonds in both base pairs are strong, since each hydrogen atom points directly at its acceptor atom (nitrogen or oxygen).*

middle are still intact (Figure 4–15). Once a break occurs, the most likely next event is the reforming of the same hydrogen bonds to restore the original molecular configuration. Sometimes, of course, the first breakage is followed by a second one,

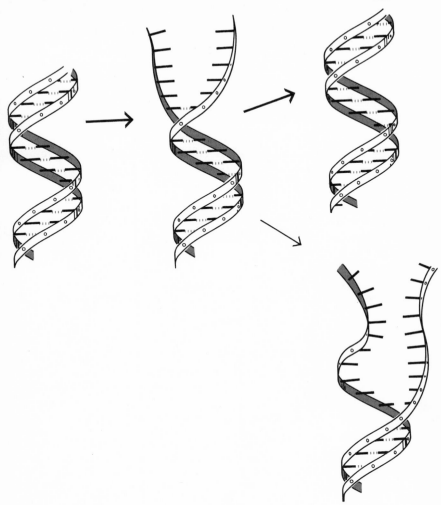

FIGURE 4–15   The breaking of terminal hydrogen bonds in DNA by
random thermal motion.   Because the internal hydrogen bonds continue to hold the two chains together, the immediate reforming of the broken bonds
is highly probable.   Also shown is the very rare alternative: the breaking of further hydrogen bonds, and
the consequent disentangling of the chains.

and so forth. Such multiple breaks, however, are quite rare, so that double helices held together by more than ten nucleotide pairs are very stable at room temperature.

The same principle also governs the stability of most protein molecules. Stable protein shapes are never due to the presence of just one or two weak bonds, but must always represent the cooperative result of a number of weak bonds.

Ordered collections of hydrogen bonds become less and less stable as their temperature is raised above physiological temperatures. At physiologically abnormally high temperatures, the simultaneous breakage of several weak bonds is more frequent. After a significant number have broken, a molecule usually loses its original form (the process of denaturation) and assumes an inactive (denatured) configuration.

MOST MEDIUM SIZE AND ALMOST ALL LARGE PROTEIN MOLECULES ARE AGGREGATES OF SMALLER POLYPEPTIDE CHAINS

Earlier we pointed out how the realization that macromolecules are all polymers constructed from small regular monomers, such as the amino acids, greatly simplified the problem of solving macromolecule structure. It has recently become clear that most of the very large proteins are regular aggregates of much smaller polypeptide chains, containing up to 400 amino acids apiece. For example, the protein ferritin, which functions in mammals to store iron atoms, has a molecular weight of about 480,000. It contains, however, not just one long polypeptide chain of 4000 amino acids, but instead 20 identical smaller polypeptide chains of about 200 amino acids each. Similarly, the protein component of tobacco mosaic virus was originally thought to have the horrendous molecular weight of 36,000,000. Most fortunately, it was subsequently discovered (see Chapter 12) that each TMV protein contains 2150 identical smaller protein molecules, each containing 158 amino acids. Even much smaller protein molecules are frequently constructed from a number of polypeptide chains. Hemoglobin, which has a molecular weight of only 64,500, contains four polypeptide chains, 2 α chains, and 2 β chains, each of which has a molecular weight of about 16,000.

In all three examples, as with most other protein aggregates, the smaller units are held together by secondary bonds. This fact is known because they can be dispersed by the addition of reagents (e.g., urea), which tend to break secondary bonds but not covalent bonds. But weak bonds are not the only force holding macromolecular units together. In some cases, for example, the protein insulin, disulfide bonds (S—S) between cysteine residues are also a binding force.

SUBUNITS ARE ECONOMICAL

Both the construction of polymers from monomers and the use of polymeric molecules themselves as subunits to build still larger molecules reflect a general building principle applicable to all complex structures, nonliving as well as living. This principle states that it is much easier to reduce the impact of construction mistakes if we can discard them before they are incorporated into the final product. For example, let us consider two alternative ways of constructing a molecule with 1,000,000 atoms. In scheme (a) we build the structure atom by atom; in scheme (b) we first build 1000 smaller units, each with 1000 atoms, and subsequently put the subunits together into the 1,000,000-atom product. Now consider that our building process randomly makes mistakes, inserting the wrong atom with a frequency of 10^{-5}. Let us assume that each mistake results in a nonfunctional product.

Under scheme (a), each molecule will contain, on the average, 10 wrong atoms, and so almost no good products will be synthesized. Under scheme (b), however, mistakes will occur in only 1 per cent of the subunits. If there is a device to reject the bad subunits, then good products can be easily made and the cell will hardly be bothered by the presence of the 1 per cent of nonfunctional subunits. This concept is the basis of the assembly line in which complicated industrial products such as radios and automobiles are constructed. At each stage of assembly there are devices to throw away bad subunits. In industrial assembly lines, mistakes were initially removed by human hands; now automation often replaces manual control. In cells, mistakes are sometimes controlled by the specificity of enzymes: if a monomeric subunit is wrongly put together, it usually will not be recognized by the polymer-making specific enzyme, and hence not incorporated into a macromolecule. In other cases, faulty substances are rejected because they are unable spontaneously to become part of stable molecular aggregates.

THE PRINCIPLE OF SELF-ASSEMBLY

ΔG values of 1 to 5 kcal/mole mean not only that single weak bonds will be spontaneously made, but also that structures held together by several weak bonds will be spontaneously formed. For example, an unstable, unfolded polypeptide chain tends to assume a large number of random configurations as a result of thermal movements. Most of these conformations are thermodynamically unstable. Inevitably, however, thermal movements bring together groups that can form good weak bonds. These groups tend to stay together, because more free energy is lost when they form than can be regained by their breakage. Thus, by a random series of movements, the polypeptide chain gradually assumes a configuration in which most of, if not all, the atoms have fixed positions within the molecule.

Aggregation of separate molecules also occurs spontaneously. The protein hemoglobin furnishes a clear example (Figure 4-16). It can be broken apart by the addition of reagents such as urea, which break secondary bonds to yield half molecules of MW = 32,000. If, however, the urea is removed, the half molecules quickly aggregate to form functional hemoglobin molecules. The surface structure of the half molecules is very specific, for they bind only to each other and not with any other cellular molecules.

This same general principle of self-assembly operates to build even larger and more complicated structures, like the cell membrane and the cell wall. Both are mosaic surfaces containing large numbers of various molecules, some large, like proteins, and others much smaller, like lipids. At present, practically nothing is known about the precise arrangement of the molecules in these very large, complicated structures. Nonetheless, there is every reason to believe that the constituent molecules form stable contacts only with other molecules in the cell membrane (or wall). This situation is easy to visualize in the case of lipids, which are extremely insoluble in water because of their long, nonpolar hydrocarbon chains. Newly synthesized lipids have a stronger tendency to attach to other lipids in the cell membrane or cell wall by van der Waals forces than to enter some other more polar area, such as the aqueous (polar) interior of the cell.

FIGURE 4–16   *Formation of an active hemoglobin molecule from two half molecules. Each hemoglobin molecule contains two α and two β chains. When placed in urea (a reagent which destabilizes weak bonds), the native molecule falls apart to two halves, containing one α and one β chain. Upon removal of the urea, the halves reassociate to form the complete molecule.*

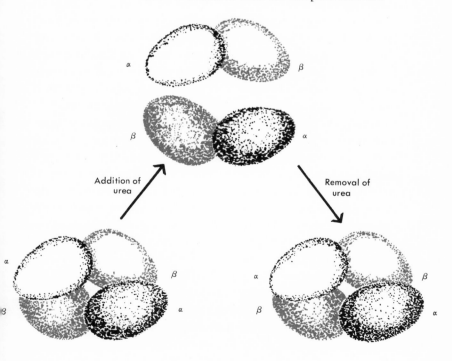

SUMMARY

Many important chemical events in cells do not involve the making or breaking of covalent bonds. The cellular location of most molecules depends on the existence of "weak" (secondary) attractive or repulsive forces. In addition, weak bonds are important in determining the shape of many molecules, especially very large ones. The most important of these "weak" forces are: hydrogen bonding, van der Waals interactions, and ionic bonds. Even though these forces are relatively weak, they are still large enough to ensure that the right molecules (groups) interact with each other. For example, the surface of an enzyme is uniquely shaped to allow specific attraction of its substrates.

The formation of all chemical bonds, weak interactions as well as strong covalent bonds, proceeds according to the laws of thermodynamics. A bond tends to form when the result would be a release of free energy (ΔG negative). In order for the bond to be broken, this same amount of free energy must be supplied. Because the formation of covalent bonds between atoms usually involves a very large negative ΔG, covalently bound atoms almost never separate spontaneously. In contrast, the ΔG values accompanying the formation of weak bonds are only several times larger than the average thermal energy of molecules at physiological temperatures. Single weak bonds are thus frequently being made and broken in living cells.

Molecules having polar (charged) groups interact quite differently from nonpolar molecules (in which the charge is symmetrically distributed). Polar molecules can form good hydrogen bonds, whereas nonpolar molecules can form only van der Waals bonds. The most important polar molecule is water. Each water molecule can form four good hydrogen bonds to other water molecules. Although polar molecules tend to be soluble in water (to various degrees), nonpolar molecules are insoluble, because they cannot form hydrogen bonds with water molecules.

Every distinct molecule has a unique molecular shape that restricts the number of molecules with which it can form good secondary bonds. Strong secondary interactions demand both a complementary (lock-and-key) relationship between the two bonding surfaces, and the involvement of many atoms. Although molecules bound together by only one or two secondary bonds frequently fall apart, a collection of these weak bonds can result in a stable aggregate. The fact that double-helical DNA never falls apart spontaneously demonstrates the extreme stability possible in such an aggregate. The formation of such aggregates can proceed spontaneously, with the correct bonds forming in a step-by-step fashion (the principle of self-assembly).

 The shape of polymeric molecules is determined by secondary bonds. All biological polymers contain single bonds about which free rotation is possible. They do not, however, exist in a variety of shapes as might be expected, because the formation of one of the possible configurations generally involves a maximum decrease in free energy. This energetically preferred configuration thus is formed exclusively. Some polymeric molecules have regular helical backbones held in shape by sets of regular internal secondary bonds between backbone groups. Regular helical structures cannot be formed, however, if they place the specific side groups in positions in which they cannot form favorable weak bonds. This situation occurs in many proteins where an irregular distribution of nonpolar side groups forces the backbone into a highly irregular conformation, permitting the nonpolar groups to form van der Waals bonds with each other. Irregularly distributed side groups do not always lead, however, to nonhelical molecules. In the DNA molecule, for example, the specific pairing of purines with pyrimidines in a double-stranded helix allows the nonpolar aromatic groups to stack on top of each other in the center of the molecule.

REFERENCES

Lehninger, A. L., *Bioenergetics*, Benjamin, New York, 1965. A concise description of the laws of thermodynamics written for the beginning biology student appears in the first several chapters.

Blum, H. F., *Time's Arrow and Evolution*, Princeton University Press, Princeton, N.J., 1951. Chapter 3 provides an exceptionally clear introduction to the thermodynamics applicable to biological systems.

Klotz, I. M., *Some Principles of Energetics in Biochemical Reactions*, Academic, New York, 1957. A somewhat advanced discussion of thermodynamics as it relates to biochemical reactions.

Pauling, L., *The Nature of the Chemical Bond*, 3rd ed., Cornell University Press, Ithaca, N.Y., 1960. One of the great classics of all chemical literature; a treatment of structural chemistry with considerable emphasis on the hydrogen bond.

Haggis, G. H., D. Michie, A. R. Muir, K. B. Roberts, and P. M. B. Walker, *Introduction to Molecular Biology*, Wiley, New York, 1964. A college-level text emphasizing the relation between the structure and function of macromolecules.

5

COUPLED
REACTIONS
AND GROUP
TRANSFERS

IN THE PREVIOUS CHAPTER WE LOOKED at the formation of weak bonds from the thermodynamic viewpoint. Each time a potential weak bond was considered, the question was posed, "Does its formation involve a gain or a loss of free energy?", because only when ΔG is negative does the thermodynamic equilibrium favor a reaction. This same approach holds with equal validity for covalent bonds. The fact that enzymes are usually involved in the making or breaking of a covalent bond does not in any sense alter the requirement of a negative ΔG.

On superficial examination, however, many of the important covalent bonds in cells appear to be formed in violation of the laws of thermodynamics, particularly those bonds joining small molecules together to form large polymeric molecules. The formation of such bonds involves an increase in free energy. Originally this fact suggested to some people that cells had the unique property of working somehow in violation of thermodynamics, and that this property was, in fact, the real "secret of life."

Now, however, it is clear that these biosynthetic processes do not violate thermodynamics but, instead, that they are based upon different reactions from those originally postulated. Nucleic acids, for example, do not form by the condensation of nucleoside phosphates; glycogen is not formed directly from glucose residues; proteins are not

141

formed by the union of amino acids. Instead, the monomeric precursors, using energy present in ATP, are first converted to high-energy "activated" precursors, which then spontaneously (with the help of specific enzymes) unite to form larger molecules. In this chapter we shall illustrate these ideas by concentrating on the thermodynamics of peptide (protein) and phosphodiester (nucleic acid) bonds. First, however, we must briefly look at some general thermodynamic properties of covalent bonds.

FOOD MOLECULES ARE THERMODYNAMICALLY UNSTABLE

There is great variation in the amount of free energy possessed by specific molecules. This is a consequence of the fact that all covalent bonds do not have the same bond energy. As an example, the covalent bond between oxygen and hydrogen is considerably stronger than the bonds between hydrogen and hydrogen or oxygen and oxygen. The formation of an O—H bond at the expense of O—O or H—H will thus release energy. Energetic considerations tell us that a sufficiently concentrated mixture of oxygen and hydrogen will be transformed into water.

A molecule thus possesses a larger amount of free energy if linked together by weak covalent bonds than if it is linked together by strong bonds. This idea seems almost paradoxical at first glance, since it means that the stronger the bond the less energy it can give off. But the notion automatically makes sense when we realize that an atom that has formed a very strong bond has already lost a large amount of free energy in this process. Therefore, the best food molecules (molecules which donate energy) are those molecules that contain weak covalent bonds and are, thereby, thermodynamically unstable.

For example, glucose is an excellent food molecule, since there is a great decrease in free energy when it is oxidized by O_2 to yield CO_2 and H_2O. On the contrary, CO_2 is not a food molecule in animals, since, in the absence of the energy donor ATP, it cannot spontaneously be transformed to more complex organic molecules even with the help of specific enzymes. CO_2

can be used as a primary source of carbon in plants only because the energy supplied by light quanta during photosynthesis results in the formation of ATP.

DISTINCTION BETWEEN DIRECTION AND RATE OF A REACTION

The chemical reactions by which molecules are transformed into other molecules which contain less free energy do not occur at significant rates at physiological temperatures in the absence of a catalyst. This is because even a "weak covalent bond" is, in reality, very strong and is only rarely broken by thermal motion within a cell. In order for a covalent bond to be broken in the absence of a catalyst, energy must be supplied to push apart the bonded atoms. When the atoms are partially apart, they can recombine with new partners to form stronger bonds. In the process of recombination, the energy released is the sum of the free energy supplied to break the old bond plus the difference in free energy between the old and the new bond (Figure 5–1).

The energy that must be supplied to break the old covalent

FIGURE 5–1 *The energy of activation of a chemical reaction* (A–B) + (C–D) → (A–D) + (C–B).

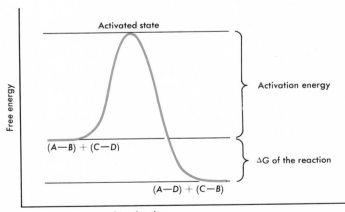

bond in a molecular transformation is called the *activation energy*. The activation energy is usually less than the energy of the original bond because molecular rearrangements generally do not involve the production of completely free atoms. Instead, a collision between the two reacting molecules is required, followed by the temporary formation of a molecular complex (the *activated state*). In the activated state, the close proximity of the two molecules makes each other's bonds more labile, so that less energy is needed to break a bond than when the bond is present in a free molecule.

Most reactions of covalent bonds in cells are, therefore, described by

$$A\text{-}B + C\text{-}D \rightarrow A\text{-}D + C\text{-}B - \Delta G \tag{5-1}$$

The mass action expression for such reaction is

$$K_{eq} = \frac{\text{conc}^{A-D} \times \text{conc}^{C-B}}{\text{conc}^{A-B} \times \text{conc}^{C-D}} \tag{5-2}$$

where conc^{A-B}, conc^{C-D}, etc., are the concentrations of the several reactants in moles per liter. Here also, the value of K_{eq} is related to ΔG by Eq. (4-4).

Since energies of activation are generally between 20 and 30 kcal/mole, activated states practically never occur at physiological temperatures. High activation energies should thus be considered barriers preventing spontaneous rearrangements of cellular covalent bonds.

These barriers are enormously important. Life would be impossible if they did not exist, for all atoms would be in the state of least possible energy. There would be no way to temporarily store energy for future work. On the other hand, life would also be impossible if means were not found to selectively lower the activation energies of certain specific reactions. This also must happen if cell growth is to occur at a rate sufficiently fast so as not to be seriously impeded by random destructive forces, such as ionizing or ultraviolet radiation.

ENZYMES LOWER ACTIVATION ENERGIES

Enzymes are absolutely necessary for life because they lower activation energies. The function of enzymes is to speed up the rate of the chemical reactions requisite to cellular existence by lowering the activation energies of molecular rearrangements to values that can be supplied by the heat of motion. When a specific enzyme is present, there is no longer an effective barrier preventing the rapid formation of the reactants possessing the lowest amounts of free energy. Enzymes never affect the nature of an equilibrium: They merely speed up the rate at which it is reached. Thus, if the thermodynamic equilibrium is unfavorable for the formation of a molecule, the presence of an enzyme can in no way bring about its accumulation.

The need for enzymes to catalyze essentially every cellular molecular rearrangement means that knowledge of the free energy of various molecules cannot by itself tell us whether an energetically feasible rearrangement will, in fact, occur. The rate of the reactions must always be considered. Only if a cell possesses a suitable enzyme will the corresponding reaction be important.

A METABOLIC PATHWAY IS CHARACTERIZED BY A DECREASE IN FREE ENERGY

Thermodynamics tells us that all biochemical pathways must be characterized by a decrease in free energy. This is obviously the case for degradative pathways, in which thermodynamically unstable food molecules are converted to more stable compounds, such as CO_2 and H_2O, with the evolution of heat. All degradative pathways have two primary purposes: (1) to produce the small organic fragments necessary as building blocks for larger organic molecules, and (2) to conserve a significant fraction of the free energy of the original food molecule in a form that can do work, by coupling some of the steps in degradative pathways with the simultaneous formation of molecules that can store free energy (high-energy molecules) like ATP.

Not all the free energy of a food molecule is converted into the free energy of high-energy molecules. If this were the case, a degradative pathway would not be characterized by a decrease in free energy. No driving force would exist to favor the breakdown of food molecules. Instead, we find that all degradative pathways are characterized by a conversion of at least one-half the free energy of the food molecule into heat or entropy. For example, it is now believed that, in cells, approximately 40 per cent of the free energy of glucose is used to make new high-energy compounds, the remainder being dissipated into heat energy and entropy.

HIGH–ENERGY BONDS HYDROLYZE WITH LARGE NEGATIVE ΔG'S

A high-energy molecule contains a bond(s) whose breakdown by water (hydrolysis) is accompanied by a large decrease in free energy (5 kcal/mole or more). The specific bonds whose hydrolysis yields these large negative ΔG's are called *high-energy bonds*. Both these terms are, in a real sense, misleading, since it is not the bond energy but the free energy of hydrolysis that is high. Nonetheless, the term high-energy bond is generally employed, and, for convenience, we shall continue this usage by marking high-energy bonds with the symbol ∼.

The energy of hydrolysis of the average high-energy bond (7 kcal/mole) is very much smaller than the amount of energy that would be released if a glucose molecule were to be completely degraded in one step (688 kcal/mole). A one-step breakdown of glucose would be inefficient in making high-energy bonds. This is undoubtedly the reason why biological glucose degradation requires so many steps. In this way, the amount of energy released per degradative step is of the same order of magnitude as the free energy of hydrolysis of a high-energy bond.

The most important high-energy compound is ATP. It is formed from inorganic phosphate Ⓟ and ADP, using energy obtained either from degradative reactions (some of which are shown in Chapters 2 and 3) or from the sun (photosynthesis). There are, however, many other important high-energy compounds. Some are directly formed during degradative reactions;

others are formed using some of the free energy of ATP. Table 5–1 lists the most important types of high-energy bonds. All involve either phosphate or sulfur atoms. The high-energy pyrophosphate bonds of ATP arise from the union of phosphate

T A B L E 5–1　*Important classes of high-energy bonds*

Class	Molecular example	ΔG of reaction, kcal/mole
Pyrophosphate	(P)~(P)pyrophosphate	(P)~(P) $\rightleftharpoons$ (P)+(P)　$\Delta G = -6$
Nucleoside diphosphates	Adenosine − (P)~(P) (ADP)	ADP $\rightleftharpoons$ AMP +(P) $\Delta G = -6$
Nucleoside triphosphates	Adenosine −(P)~(P)~(P) (ATP)	ATP $\rightleftharpoons$ ADP +(P) $\Delta G = -7$ ATP $\rightleftharpoons$ AMP +(P)~(P) $\Delta G = -8$
Enol phosphates	Phosphoenol pyruvate (PEP)	PEP $\rightleftharpoons$ pyruvate +(P) $\Delta G = -12$
Amino acyl adenylates	Adenosine	AMP ~ AA $\rightleftharpoons$ AMP + AA $\Delta G = -7$
Guanidinium phosphates	Creatine phosphate	Creatine ~ P $\rightleftharpoons$ Creatine + P　$\Delta G = -8$
Thioesters	Acetyl-CoA	Acetyl CoA $\rightleftharpoons$ CoA-SH + acetate　$\Delta G = -8$

groups. The pyrophosphate linkage ($\text{P} \sim \text{P}$) is not, however, the only kind of high-energy phosphate bond: The attachment of a phosphate group to the oxygen atom of a carboxyl group creates a high-energy acyl bond. It is now clear that high-energy bonds involving sulfur atoms play almost as important a role in energy metabolism as those involving phosphorus. The most important molecule containing a high-energy sulfur bond is acetyl-CoA. This bond is the main source of energy for fatty acid biosynthesis.

The wide range of ΔG values of high-energy bonds (Table 5–1) means that calling a bond "high-energy" is sometimes arbitrary. The usual criterion is whether its hydrolysis can be coupled with another reaction to effect an important biosynthesis. For example, the negative ΔG accompanying the hydrolysis of glucose-6-P is 3 to 4 kcal/mole. This ΔG is not sufficient for efficient synthesis of peptide bonds, for example, so this phosphate ester bond is not included among high-energy bonds.

HIGH–ENERGY BONDS NECESSARY FOR BIOSYNTHETIC REACTIONS

Often the construction of a large molecule from smaller building blocks requires the input of free energy. Yet a biosynthetic pathway, like a degradative pathway, would not exist if it were not characterized by a net decrease in free energy. This means that many biosynthetic pathways demand the existence of an external source of free energy. These free-energy sources are the "high-energy compounds." The making of many biosynthetic bonds is coupled with the breakdown of a high-energy bond, so that the net change of free energy is always negative. High-energy bonds in cells, therefore, generally have a very short life. Almost as soon as they are formed during a degradative reaction, they are enzymatically broken down to yield the energy needed to drive another reaction to completion.

Not all the steps in a biosynthetic pathway require the breakdown of a high-energy bond. Often only one or two steps involve such a bond. Sometimes this is because the ΔG, even in the absence of an externally added high-energy bond, favors the biosynthetic direction.   In other cases, ΔG is effectively zero, or in some cases may even be slightly positive.   These small positive ΔG's, however, are not significant so long as they are followed by a reaction characterized by the hydrolysis of a high-energy bond.   Instead, it is the *sum* of all the free-energy changes in a pathway that is significant.   It does not really matter that the K_{eq} of a specific biosynthetic step is slightly (80:20) in favor of degradation, if the K_{eq} of the succeeding step is 100:1 in favor of the forward biosynthetic direction.

Likewise, not all the steps in a degradative pathway generate high-energy bonds.   For example, only two steps in the lengthy glycolytic (Embden-Meyerhof) breakdown of glucose generate ATP.   Moreover, there are many degradative pathways that have one or more steps requiring the breakdown of a high-energy bond.   The glycolytic breakdown of glucose is again an example.   It uses up two molecules of ATP for every four that it generates.   Here, of course, as in every energy-yielding degradative process, more high-energy bonds must be made than consumed.

PEPTIDE BONDS HYDROLYZE SPONTANEOUSLY

The formation of a dipeptide and a water molecule from two amino acids requires a ΔG of 1 to 4 kcal/mole, depending upon which amino acids are being bound.   This ΔG value decreases progressively if amino acids are added to longer polypeptide chains; for an infinitely long chain the ΔG is reduced to ~ 0.5 kcal/mole.   This decrease reflects the fact that the free, charged NH_3^+ and COO^- groups at the chain ends favor the hydrolysis (breakdown accompanied by the uptake of a water molecule) of nearby peptide bonds.

These positive ΔG values by themselves tell us that polypeptide chains cannot form from free amino acids.   In addition, we must take into account the fact that water molecules have a much, much higher concentration (generally > 100) than any other cellular molecules.   All equilibrium reactions in which water participates are thus strongly pushed in the direction that consumes water molecules.   This is easily seen in the definition of equilibrium constants. For example, the reaction forming a dipeptide,

amino acid(a) + amino acid(b) $\rightarrow$ dipeptide(a-b) + H_2O (5–3)

has the following equilibrium constant:

$$K_{eq} = \frac{\text{conc } (a) \times \text{conc } (b)}{\text{conc } (a\text{-}b) \times \text{conc } (H_2O)}$$ (5–4)

where concentrations are given in moles/liter. Thus, for a given K_{eq} value (related to ΔG by the formula $\Delta G = - RT \ln K$) a much greater concentration of H_2O means a correspondingly smaller concentration of the dipeptide. The relative concentrations are, therefore, very important. In fact, a simple calculation shows that hydrolysis may often proceed spontaneously even when the ΔG for the nonhydrolytic reaction is -3 kcal/mole.

Thus, in theory, proteins are unstable and, given sufficient time, will spontaneously degrade to free amino acids. On the other hand, in the absence of specific enzymes, these spontaneous rates are too slow to have a significant effect on cellular metabolism. That is, once a protein is made, it remains stable unless its degradation is catalyzed by a specific enzyme.

COUPLING OF NEGATIVE WITH POSITIVE ΔG

Free energy must be added to amino acids before they can be united to form proteins. How this could happen became clear with the discovery of the fundamental role of ATP as an energy donor. ATP contains three phosphate groups attached to an adenosine molecule (adenosine—O—(P)~(P)~(P)). When one or two of the terminal ~(P) groups are broken off by hydrolysis, there is a significant decrease of free energy.

adenosine — O —(P) ~(P) ~(P) + H_2O $\rightarrow$
(ATP)
            adenosine — O —(P) ~(P) + (P)   ($\Delta G = -7$ kcal/mole)   (5–5)
            (ADP)

adenosine — O — Ⓟ ~ Ⓟ ~ Ⓟ + H_2O →
(ATP)

       adenosine — O — Ⓟ + Ⓟ ~ Ⓟ   ($\Delta G = -8$ kcal/mole)   (5–6)
       (AMP)

adenosine — O — Ⓟ ~ Ⓟ + H_2O →
(ADP)

       adenosine — O — Ⓟ + Ⓟ   ($\Delta G = -6$ kcal/mole)   (5–7)
       (AMP)

All these breakdown reactions have negative ΔG values considerably greater in absolute value (numerical value without regard to sign) than the positive ΔG values accompanying the formation of polymeric molecules from their monomeric building blocks. The essential trick underlying those biosynthetic reactions, which by themselves have a positive ΔG, is that they are coupled with breakdown reactions characterized by negative ΔG of greater absolute value. Thus, during protein synthesis, the formation of each peptide bond ($\Delta G = +0.5$ kcal/mole) is coupled with the breakdown of ATP to AMP and pyrophosphate, which has a ΔG of -8 kcal/mole. This results in a net ΔG of -7.5 kcal/mole, more than sufficient to ensure that the equilibrium favors protein synthesis rather than breakdown.

ACTIVATION THROUGH GROUP TRANSFER

When ATP is hydrolyzed to ADP and Ⓟ, most of the free energy is liberated as heat. Since heat energy cannot be used to make covalent bonds, a coupled reaction cannot be the result of two completely separate reactions, one with a positive, the other with a negative, ΔG. Instead, a coupled reaction is achieved by two or more successive reactions. These are always *group-transfer* reactions: reactions, not involving oxidations or reductions, in which molecules exchange functional groups. The enzymes that catalyze these reactions are called transferases.

A-X + B-Y → A-B + X-Y   (5–8)

In this example, groups X and Y are exchanged with components A and B. Group-transfer reactions are arbitrarily defined to exclude H_2O as a participant. When H_2O is involved,

A-B + H-OH → A-OH + BH   (5–9)

the reaction is called a hydrolysis, and the enzymes involved, hydrolases.

The group-transfer reactions which interest us here are those involving groups attached by high-energy bonds (high-energy groups). When a high-energy group is transferred to an appropriate acceptor molecule, it becomes attached to the acceptor by a high-energy bond. Group transfer thus allows the transfer of high-energy bonds from one molecule to another. For example, Eqs. (5–10) and (5–11) show how energy present in ATP is transferred to form GTP, one of the precursors used in RNA synthesis:

$$\text{adenosine} - \text{\textcircled{P}} \sim \text{\textcircled{P}} \sim \text{\textcircled{P}} + \text{guanosine} - \text{\textcircled{P}} \rightarrow$$
$$\text{(ATP)} \qquad\qquad\qquad\qquad \text{(GMP)}$$

$$\text{adenosine} - \text{\textcircled{P}} \sim \text{\textcircled{P}} + \text{guanosine} - \text{\textcircled{P}} \sim \text{\textcircled{P}} \qquad (5\text{–}10)$$
$$\text{(ADP)} \qquad\qquad\qquad \text{(GDP)}$$

$$\text{adenosine} - \text{\textcircled{P}} \sim \text{\textcircled{P}} \sim \text{\textcircled{P}} + \text{guanosine} - \text{\textcircled{P}} \sim \text{\textcircled{P}} \rightarrow$$
$$\text{(ATP)} \qquad\qquad\qquad\qquad \text{(GDP)}$$

$$\text{adenosine} - \text{\textcircled{P}} \sim \text{\textcircled{P}} + \text{guanosine} - \text{\textcircled{P}} \sim \text{\textcircled{P}} \sim \text{\textcircled{P}} \qquad (5\text{–}11)$$
$$\text{(ADP)} \qquad\qquad\qquad \text{(GTP)}$$

The high-energy $\text{\textcircled{P}} \sim \text{\textcircled{P}}$ group on GTP allows it to unite spontaneously with another molecule. GTP is thus an example of what is called an *activated molecule*; correspondingly, the process of transferring a high-energy group is called *group activation*.

ATP VERSATILITY IN GROUP TRANSFER

In Chapter 2 we emphasized the key role of ATP synthesis in the controlled trapping of the energy of food molecules. In both oxidative and photosynthetic phosphorylations, energy is used to synthesize ATP from ADP and P:

$$\text{adenosine} - \text{\textcircled{P}} \sim \text{\textcircled{P}} + \text{\textcircled{P}} + \text{energy} \rightarrow \text{adenosine} - \text{\textcircled{P}} \sim \text{\textcircled{P}} \sim \text{\textcircled{P}} \qquad (5\text{–}12)$$

Since ATP is, thus, the original biological recipient of high-energy groups, it must be the starting point of a variety of reactions in which high-energy groups are transferred to low-energy molecules to give them the potential to react spontaneously. ATP's central role utilizes the fact that it contains two high-energy bonds whose splitting releases specific groups. This is shown in Figure 5–2, which shows three important groups arising from ATP: (1) ℗~℗, a pyrophosphate group, (2) ~AMP, an adenosyl monophosphate group, and (3) ~℗, a phosphate group. It is important to notice that these high-energy groups retain their high-energy quality only when transferred to an appropriate acceptor molecule. For example, although the transfer of a ~℗ group to a COO⁻ group yields a high-energy COO~℗ acyl-phosphate group, the transfer of the same group to a sugar hydroxyl group (—C—OH), as for example in the formation of glucose-6-℗, gives rise to a low-energy bond (<5 kcal/mole decrease in ΔG upon hydrolysis).

FIGURE 5–2 *Important group transfers involving ATP.*

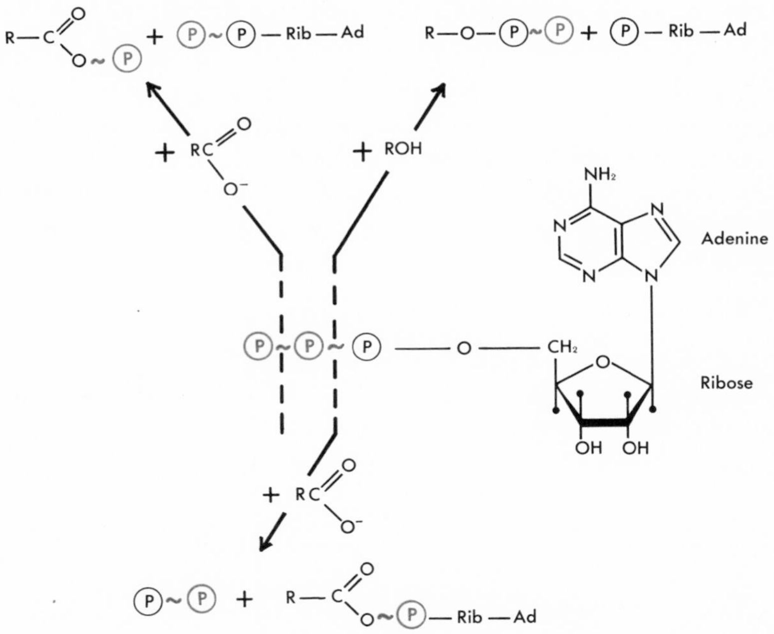

ACTIVATION OF AMINO ACIDS
BY ATTACHMENT OF AMP

The activation of an amino acid is achieved by transfer of an AMP group from ATP to the COO⁻ group of the amino acid:

$$H-\overset{\overset{\displaystyle H}{|}}{\underset{\underset{\displaystyle H}{|}}{N^+}}-\overset{\overset{\displaystyle R}{|}}{\underset{\underset{\displaystyle H}{|}}{C}}-C\overset{\displaystyle O}{\underset{\displaystyle O^-}{\diagdown}} + \text{adenosine}-\text{(P)}\sim\text{(P)}\sim\text{(P)} \rightarrow H-\overset{\overset{\displaystyle H}{|}}{\underset{\underset{\displaystyle H}{|}}{N^+}}-\overset{\overset{\displaystyle R}{|}}{\underset{\underset{\displaystyle H}{|}}{C}}-C\overset{\displaystyle O}{\underset{\displaystyle O\sim\text{(P)}-\text{adenosine}}{\diagdown}} + \text{(P)}\sim\text{(P)}$$

(5–13)

(R represents the specific side group of the amino acid.) The specific enzymes that catalyze this type of reaction are called amino acid-synthetases. Upon activation, an amino acid is thermodynamically capable of being efficiently used for protein synthesis. Nonetheless, the AA~AMP complexes are not the direct precursors of proteins. Instead, for a reason which we shall explain in Chapter 11, a second group transfer must occur to transfer the amino acid, still activated at its carboxyl group, to the end of a tRNA molecule:

$$\text{AA} \sim \text{AMP} + \text{tRNA} \rightarrow \text{AA} \sim \text{tRNA} + \text{AMP} \qquad (5\text{–}14)$$

A peptide bond then forms by the condensation of the AA~ tRNA molecule onto the end of a growing polypeptide chain:

AA ~ tRNA + growing polypeptide chain (of n amino acids) →

tRNA + growing polypeptide chain (of n + 1 amino acids)   (5–15)

Thus the final step of this "coupled reaction," like that of all other coupled reactions, necessarily involves the removal of the activating group and the conversion of a high-energy bond into one with a lower free energy of hydrolysis. This is the source of the negative ΔG which drives the reaction in the direction of protein synthesis.

NUCLEIC ACID PRECURSORS ACTIVATED BY PRESENCE OF (P)~(P)

Both types of nucleic acid, DNA and RNA, are built up of mononucleotide monomers (nucleoside (P)). Mononucleotides, however, are thermodynamically even less likely to combine than amino acids. This is because the phosphodiester bonds which link the former together release considerable free energy upon hydrolysis (-6 kcal/mole). This means that nucleic acids will spontaneously hydrolyze, at a slow rate, to mononucleotides. Thus it is even more important that activated precursors be used in their synthesis than in that of proteins.

Recently it has been found that the immediate precursors for both DNA and RNA are the nucleoside-5'-triphosphates. For DNA these are dATP, dGTP, dCTP, and dTTP (d stands for deoxy); for RNA the precursors are ATP, GTP, CTP, and UTP. ATP thus not only serves as the main source of high-energy groups in group-transfer reactions, but in addition is itself a direct precursor for RNA. The other three RNA precursors all arise by group-transfer reactions like those described in Eqs. (5–10) and (5–11). The deoxytriphosphates are formed in basically the same way: After the deoxymononucleotides have been synthesized, they are transformed to the triphosphate form by group transfer from ATP:

deoxynucleoside — (P)+ ATP → deoxynucleoside — (P)~(P)+ ADP   (5–16)

deoxynucleoside — (P)~(P)+ ATP → deoxynucleoside — (P)~(P)~(P)+ ADP
(5–17)

These triphosphates can then unite to form polynucleotides held together by phosphodiester bonds. In this process (a group-transfer reaction), a pyrophosphate bond is broken and a pyrophosphate group released:

deoxynucleoside — (P)~(P)~(P)+ growing polynucleotide chain (of n nucleotides)

→ (P)~(P)+ growing polynucleotide chain (n +1 nucleotides)   (5–18)

This reaction, unlike that which forms peptide bonds, does not have a negative ΔG. In fact, the ΔG is slightly positive ($\sim$0.5

kcal/mole). This immediately poses the question, since poly-nucleotides obviously form: What is the source of the necessary free energy?

VALUE OF (P)~(P) RELEASE
IN NUCLEIC ACID SYNTHESIS

The needed free energy arises from the splitting of the high-energy pyrophosphate group which is formed simultaneously with the high-energy phosphodiester bond. All cells contain a powerful enzyme, pyrophosphatase, which breaks down pyro-phosphate molecules almost as soon as they are formed:

$$(P)\sim(P) \rightarrow 2\,(P) \quad (\Delta G = -7 \text{ kcal/mole}) \tag{5-19}$$

The large negative ΔG means that the reaction is effectively irreversible: This means that once $(P)\sim(P)$ is broken down it never reforms.

The union of the nucleoside monophosphate group [Eq. (5–16)], coupled with the splitting of the pyrophosphate groups [Eq. (5–19)], has an equilibrium constant determined by the combined ΔG values of the two reactions: (0.5 kcal/mole) + (−7 kcal/mole). The resulting value ($\Delta G = -6.5$ kcal/mole) tells us that nucleic acids almost never break down to reform their nucleoside triphosphate precursors.

Here we see a powerful example of the fact that often it is the free-energy change accompanying a *group of reactions* that determines whether a reaction in the group will take place. Reactions with small, positive ΔG values, which by themselves would never take place, are often part of important metabolic pathways in which they are followed by reactions with large negative ΔG's. At all times we must remember that a single reaction (or even a single pathway) never occurs in isolation, but rather that the nature of the equilibrium is constantly being changed through the addition and through the removal of me-tabolites.

ⓅᐵⓅ SPLITS CHARACTERIZE MOST BIOSYNTHETIC REACTIONS

The synthesis of nucleic acids is not the only reaction where direction is determined by the release and splitting of ⓅᐵⓅ. In fact, the generalization is emerging that essentially all biosynthetic reactions are characterized by one or more steps that release pyrophosphate groups. Consider, for example, the activation of an amino acid by the attachment of AMP. By itself, the transfer of a high-energy bond from ATP to the AAᐵAMP complex has a slightly positive ΔG. Therefore, it is the release and splitting of ATP's terminal pyrophosphate group that provides the negative ΔG that is necessary to drive the reaction.

The great utility of the pyrophosphate split is neatly demonstrated by considering the problems that would arise if a cell attempted to synthesize nucleic acid from nucleoside diphosphates rather than triphosphates. Phosphate, rather than pyrophosphate, would be liberated as the backbone phosphodiester linkages were made. The phosphodiester linkages, however, are not stable in the presence of significant quantities of phosphate, since they are formed without a significant release of free energy. Thus, the biosynthetic reaction would be easily reversible; as soon as phosphate began to accumulate, the reaction would begin to move in the direction of nucleic acid breakdown (mass action law). Moreover, it is not possible for a cell to remove the phosphate groups as soon as they are generated (thus preventing this reverse reaction), since all cells need a significant internal level of phosphate in order to grow. Thus the use of nucleoside triphosphates as precursors of nucleic acids is not a matter of chance.

This same type of argument tells us why ATP, and not ADP, is the key donor of high-energy groups in all cells. At first this preference seemed arbitrary to biochemists. Now, however, we see that many reactions using ADP as an energy donor would occur equally well in both directions.

SUMMARY

The biosynthesis of many molecules appears, at a superficial glance, to violate the thermodynamic law that spontaneous reactions always involve a decrease in free energy (ΔG is negative). For example, the formation of proteins from amino acids has a positive ΔG. This paradox is removed when we realize that the biosynthetic reactions do not proceed as initially postulated. Proteins, for example, are not formed from free amino acids. Instead, the precursors are first enzymatically converted to high-energy activated molecules, which, in the presence of a specific enzyme, spontaneously unite to form the desired biosynthetic product.

Many biosynthetic processes are thus the result of "coupled" reactions, the first of which supplies the energy that allows the spontaneous occurrence of the second reaction. The primary energy source in cells is ATP. It is formed from ADP and inorganic phosphate, either during degradative reactions (e.g., fermentation or respiration) or during photosynthesis. ATP contains several (high-energy) bonds whose hydrolysis has a large negative ΔG. Groups linked by high-energy bonds are called high-energy groups. High-energy groups can be transferred to other molecules by group-transfer reactions, thereby creating new high-energy compounds. These derivative high-energy molecules are then the immediate precursors for many biosynthetic steps.

Amino acids are activated by the addition of an AMP group, originating from ATP, to form an AA $\sim$ AMP molecule. The energy of the high-energy bond in the AA $\sim$ AMP molecule is similar to that of a high-energy bond of ATP. Nonetheless, the group-transfer reaction proceeds to completion because the high-energy $\text{P}\sim\text{P}$ molecule, created when the AA$\sim$AMP molecule is formed, is broken down by the enzyme pyrophosphatase to low-energy groups. Thus, the reverse reaction, $\text{P}\sim\text{P} + \text{AA} \sim \text{AMP} \rightarrow \text{ATP} + \text{AA}$, cannot occur.

The general rule exists that $\text{P}\sim\text{P}$ is released in almost all biosynthetic reactions. Almost as soon as it is made, it is enzymatically broken down to 2P, thereby making impossible a reversal of the biosynthetic reaction. The great utility of the Ⓟ~Ⓟ split provides an explanation for why ATP, not ADP, is the primary energy donor. ADP cannot transfer a high-energy group and, at the same time, produce Ⓟ~Ⓟ groups as a by-product.

REFERENCES

Karlson, P., *Introduction to Modern Biochemistry*, 3rd ed., Academic, New York, 1969. A medium-sized introduction to biochemistry with emphasis on intermediary metabolism.

Mahler, H. R., and E. H. Cordes, *Biological Chemistry*, Harper and Row, New York, 1966. The most complete new text that covers all of biochemistry.

White, A., P. Handler, and E. L. Smith, *Principles of Biochemistry*, 3rd ed., McGraw-Hill, New York, 1964. An admirable survey of cell biochemistry, strongest in its emphasis on intermediary metabolism.

Krebs, H. A., and H. L. Kornberg, "A Survey of the Energy Transformation in Living Material," *Ergeb. Physiol. Biol. Chem. Exptl. Pharmakol.*, **49**, 212 (1957). This comprehensive review is one of the few classics in biochemistry. Though many of its facts have been modified by subsequent research, it can still be used with great profit.

Kornberg, A., "On the Metabolic Significance of Phosphorolytic and Pyrophosphorolytic Reactions," in M. Kasha and B. Pullman (eds.), *Horizons in Biochemistry*, pp. 251–264, Academic, New York, 1962. In this short article are found some detailed arguments about the importance of the release of pyrophosphate.

6

THE CONCEPT
OF TEMPLATE
SURFACES

BY NOW OUR CHEMIST KNOWS THAT there are several "key secrets of life" upon which the ability of a cell to grow and divide depends. First, there must exist a highly organized surface membrane capable of maintaining, through selective permeability, a high concentration of internal molecules. Second, enzymes that catalyze the movement of the atoms from food molecules into new cellular building blocks must exist. Third, useful energy must be derived from food molecules or the sun to ensure that the thermodynamic equilibria favor biosynthetic rather than degradative reactions.

All these properties depend intimately upon the existence of proteins. Only these very large molecules with their 20 different building blocks possess sufficient specificity to build selectively permeable membranes or to catalyze highly specific chemical transformations. We must thus add to the list of key secrets of life the ability to synthesize the physiologically correct amounts of specific proteins. This requirement at first might seem to fall under the more general prerequisite of enzyme-catalyzed biosynthesis. But as we shall soon learn, the synthesis of a protein does not proceed according to rules governing the synthesis of small molecules. This point becomes clear when we look at the way enzymes are used to construct increasingly larger molecules.

160

SYNTHESIS OF SMALL MOLECULES

Let us first look at how the amino acid serine is normally put together in *E. coli* cells growing upon glucose as their sole energy and carbon source. Figure 6–1 illustrates how serine is formed in three steps from 3-phosphoglyceric acid, a key metabolite in the normal degradation of glucose (Figure 2–6). Serine can be further broken down in several more steps (whose exact chemistry has yet to be worked out) to give the simplest amino acid glycine. Each of these steps requires a specific enzyme with a characteristic surface capable of combining only with its correct substrate. Each of the other 18 amino acids is synthesized according to the same principle. In every case, a metabolite derived from glucose serves as the starting point for a series of specific enzymatically mediated reactions leading finally to an amino acid. Likewise, the purine and pyrimidine nucleotides, the building blocks from which the nucleic acids DNA and RNA are constructed, are synthesized by a series of consecutive reactions starting with smaller molecular units whose carbon atoms are derived from glucose molecules.

Some of the reactions leading to the synthesis of the pyrimidine nucleotide, uridine-5'-phosphate, are seen in Figure 6–2. The synthesis of the larger purine nucleotides requires more steps, since more covalent bonds must be built. Again, however, the same basic principles govern: (1) each reaction requires a different specific enzyme and (2) the sum of the reactions results in a release of free energy.

This energy release (usually as heat) means that the thermodynamic equilibrium favors the generation of the biosynthetic reaction products necessary for cell growth. It is often accomplished by having one of the substrates react with the energy-rich molecule ATP to form an activated substrate in which a phosphate ($\sim \circledP$), pyrophosphate ($\sim \circledP \sim \circledP$), or adenylic acid ($\sim$AMP) group is attached to an atom involved in the formation of the desired biosynthetic bond. A typical ATP-driven synthesis is the transformation of ribose-5-$\circledP$ into 5-phosphoribosylamine (PRA) (Figure 6–3). This transformation, one of the initial steps in purine nucleotide formation, occurs in two enzymatic steps. In the first, ribose-5-$\textcircled{P}$ and ATP combine to form ADP and 5-phosphoribosylpyrophosphate (PRPP). The second step involves the reaction of PRPP with glutamine to yield PRA, $\textcircled{P}\sim\textcircled{P}$, and glutamic acid. The equilibrium of the

FIGURE 6–1   *Serine biosynthesis.*

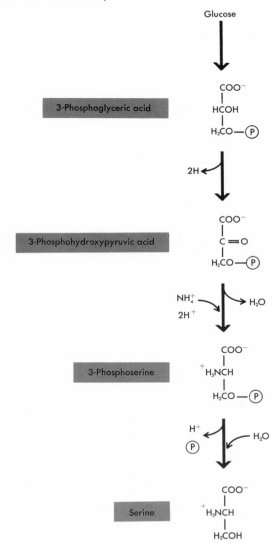

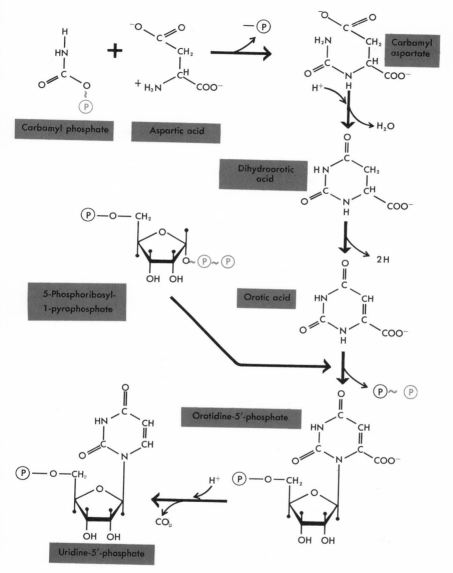

FIGURE 6–2 *The biosynthesis of uridine-5'-phosphate.*

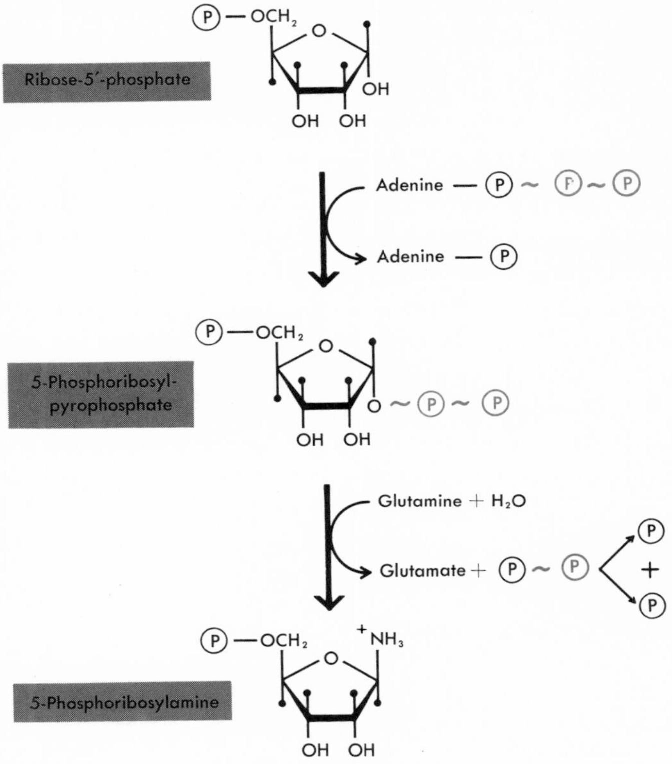

FIGURE 6-3 *Initial steps in purine formation.*

first reaction favors PRPP synthesis because there is more energy in an ATP-pyrophosphate bond than in the phosphate ester
(C—O—Ⓟ) bond attaching Ⓟ~Ⓟ to ribose-5-Ⓟ. Likewise,
the second equilibrium favors PRA formation because the
Ⓟ~Ⓟ product is broken down by pyrophosphatase to 2Ⓟ.

Both biosynthetic steps are thus accompanied by the release
of energy as heat. In contrast there is little energy difference
between the initial C—O bond of ribose-5-Ⓟ and the final
C—N linkage. Hence, activation by an energy donor is a necessary prerequisite for this biosynthetic step. Activation is not,
however, an obligatory feature of all biosyntheses. Sometimes

the relevant covalent bonds in a necessary cell constituent have significantly less free energy than the bonds in the metabolites from which they are derived.

SYNTHESIS OF A LARGE ''SMALL MOLECULE''

The construction of chlorophyll (Figure 6–4) is a good example. Here is a molecule (MW = 892) whose total laboratory synthesis has just recently been achieved, and which still looks very complex even to a first-rate organic chemist. It contains the complicated porphyrin ring, to which is attached a long un-branched alcohol (phytol). As yet, only the broad outlines of its biosynthesis are known. The porphyrin and phytol components are most likely synthesized separately and later joined together. Most of what is now known about its synthesis con-

FIGURE 6–4   *The structure of chlorophyll.*

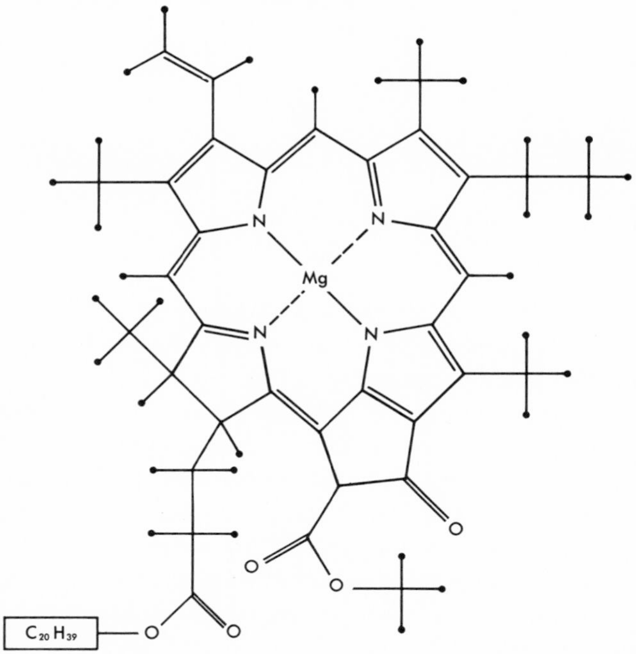

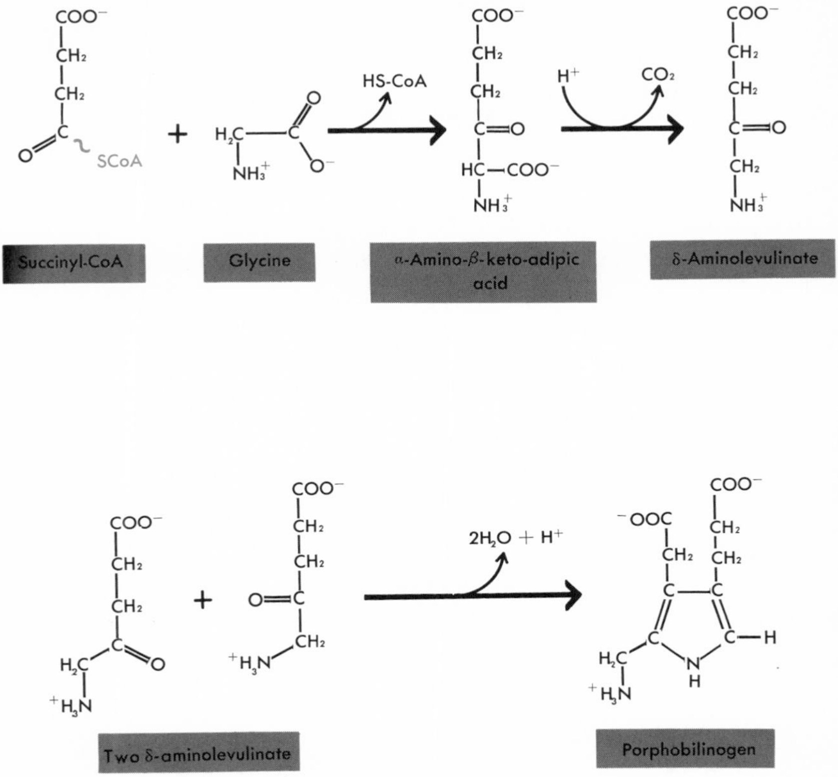

FIGURE 6-5   *The pathway of porphyrin biosynthesis.*

cerns the putting together of the porphyrin ring (Figure 6–5). Here a very large number of different enzymes are used to re-arrange the C, N, O, and H atoms found initially in the much smaller glycine and succinyl~CoA precursors. No new qualita-tive features thus appear to distinguish the synthesis of mole-cules with chlorophyll-like complexity from the construction of small organic molecules. In both cases specific enzymes and favorable thermodynamic equilibria are necessary. There is only the quantitative difference that the biosynthesis of large complex molecules needs more different enzymes and usually more externally added energy.

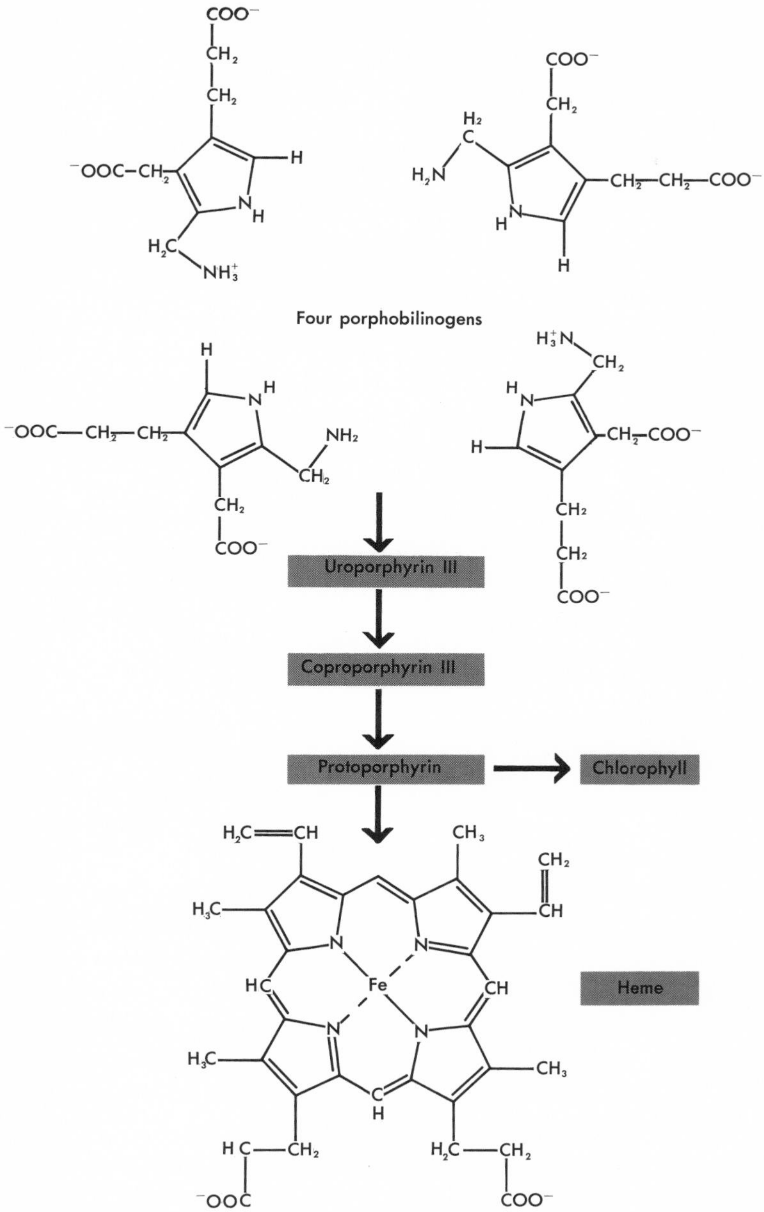

Four porphobilinogens

Uroporphyrin III

Coproporphyrin III

Protoporphyrin → Chlorophyll

Heme

SYNTHESIS OF A REGULAR, VERY LARGE POLYMERIC MOLECULE

Glycogen is a macromolecule whose molecular weight is often above a million. Nonetheless, only four different enzymes are necessary to derive glycogen from glucose, because glycogen is a polymeric molecule built up by the repetitive linking together of glucose units. Figure 6–6 shows the specific chemical steps by which glucose is activated at its number 1 carbon atom and then polymerized. Only one enzyme is required for the final polymerization because each polymerization step makes the same type of chemical bond. Almost all the linkages are glucosidic bonds (C—O—C) between carbon atoms numbers 1 and 4. Much less commonly, another enzyme catalyzes the formation of 1–6 glucosidic bonds. As a result glycogen is often branched.

We thus see that the number of enzymes necessary to synthesize a molecule is related not necessarily to its size, but rather to its chemical complexity. Thus glycogen, which is an easy molecule for the organic chemist to understand, also poses no fundamental problems to the biochemist.

A DEEPER LOOK INTO PROTEIN STRUCTURE

Before we go into the problems involved in protein synthesis, we must first look more closely into protein structure. Proteins are immensely complex macromolecules since they are polymers built up from 20 different building blocks (the amino acids). Thus the organic chemist must determine both how the amino acids are linked together and what their order is within a given linear polypeptide chain. Likewise, the biochemist wishes to know both how the backbone linkages are connected and what trick is used to order the amino acids during synthesis. In both types of work, the questions involving sequence have proved to be the more difficult questions to answer.

It was, in fact, not until 1953 that the first complete amino acid sequence became known. The protein studied was the hormone insulin, a relatively small protein containing 51 amino

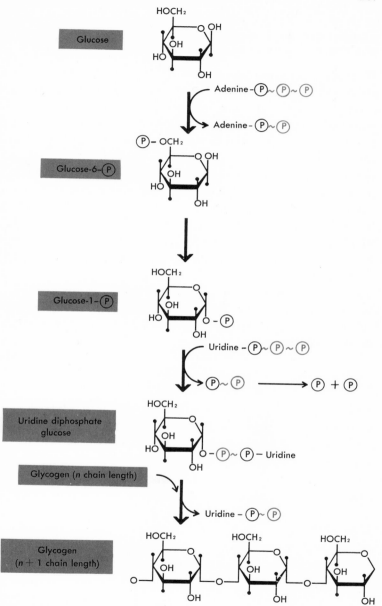

FIGURE 6–6 *The biosynthesis of glycogen from glucose.*

acids (Figure 6–7). More recently, the sequences of a large number of additional proteins have been solved. One of the larger, containing 246 amino acids, is the enzyme chymotrypsinogen, which catalyzes the hydrolysis of peptide bonds. The determination of its sequence (Figure 6–8) required almost 15 man years of work by several talented chemists. Now, new experimental techniques make sequence determinations much easier. Today, with luck, less than a year may be sufficient to solve the structure of a relatively small protein.

Aside from the question of sequence, there is also the problem of how polypeptide chains assume their final 3-D configurations. The correct functioning of almost all proteins depends not only upon possession of the correct amino acid sequence but also upon their exact arrangement in space. As we pointed out in Chapter 4, however, the polypeptide backbone is not completely rigid, for many of its atoms can freely rotate and assume different relative locations. Nonetheless, the tendency to form optimal weak bonds favors a unique conformation for a given protein. Very good indirect evidence indicates that in a given environmental situation all protein molecules with identical sequences have the same "native" 3-D form. Very recently this belief has received direct support from the complete 3-D structural determination of the oxygen-carrying protein myoglobin. In Figure 6–9 is shown its structure as revealed by x-ray diffraction analysis. Though the molecule is immensely complex, detailed inspection shows an important, simplifying structural

FIGURE   6–7   *The amino acid sequence of beef insulin.*

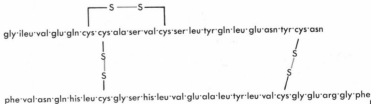

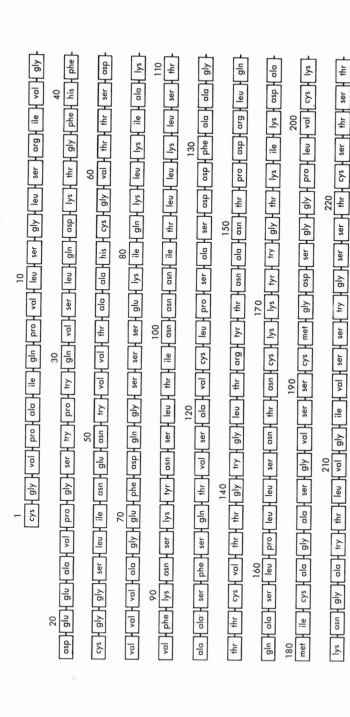

FIGURE 6-8 The amino acid sequence of the protein chymotrypsinogen.

171

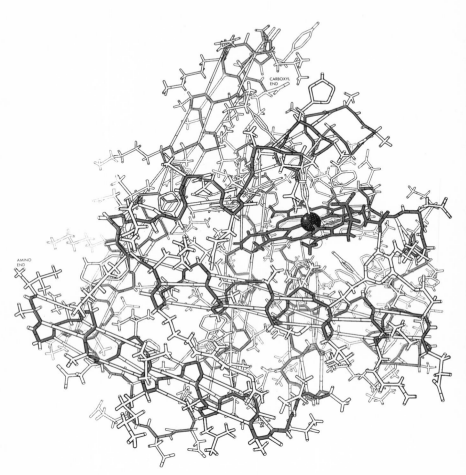

FIGURE 6–9   *The 3-D structure of myoglobin as derived from x-ray diffraction analysis. The polypeptide backbone is shown in color, the heme group in gray. [From J. C. Kendrew, Sci. Am. 205, 100–101 (1961), with permission.]*

characteristic: the chain is folded to bring together atomic groupings that attract each other.

THE PRIMARY STRUCTURES OF PROTEINS

Myoglobin, which has 153 amino acids, is one example of the many proteins that contain only one polypeptide chain.   Many other proteins have two or more chains.   For example, there are four polypeptide chains in the hemoglobin molecule, which has a MW of 64,500.   The number of chains and the sequence of residues within them constitute the *primary*

FIGURE 6–10   *The arrangement of S—S bonds in chymotrypsinogen. Intact chymotrypsinogen molecules are enzymatically inactive. They become active by the enzymatic splitting of the peptide bond between amino acids 15 and 16. The active split product is called chymotrypsin. The 3-D structure of chymotrypsinogen has now been solved through x-ray analysis and its mode of action is partially known. There is evidence that the active center involves the serine residue of position 195 and the histidine residue of position 57. The chain is folded to bring these two amino acids near to each other.*

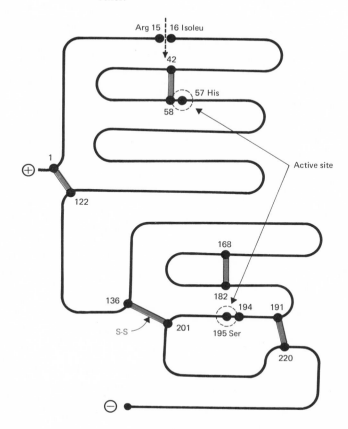

structure of proteins. When several polypeptide chains are present in the same molecule, they are often held together by secondary forces. In other cases, disulfide bonds (S—S) between cysteine side groups keep them together; they are what hold together the two chains of the insulin molecule (Figure 6–7). Disulfide bonds are important also in helping a single chain to maintain a rigid shape. In chymotrypsinogen there are 5 disulfide bridges, each linking specific cysteine residues (Figure 6–10).

In addition, a number of proteins have attached to them nonprotein (prosthetic) groups that play a vital role in their functional activity. They are often metal-organic compounds. Both myoglobin and hemoglobin contain the prosthetic group heme, a metal-organic compound closely related to the porphyrin component of chlorophyll. Heme combines with O_2 and gives to hemoglobin and myoglobin the ability to bind O_2.

A characteristic feature of prosthetic groups is that they possess very little functional activity unless they are attached to a polypeptide partner. Heme by itself, for example, combines with O_2 in an effectively irreversible fashion. Only when heme is attached to either myoglobin or hemoglobin does it possess the quality of reversibly binding oxygen. Then it can release bound oxygen when it is needed under conditions of oxygen scarcity.

SECONDARY STRUCTURES OF PROTEINS MAY BE SHEETS OR HELICES

The term *protein secondary structure* refers to the regular configurations of the polypeptide backbone. One class of these regular arrangements contains hydrogen bonds between groups on different polypeptide chains. These configurations, collectively called β structures, use fully extended polypeptide chains to form sheet-like structures held together by N—H $\cdots$ O=C hydrogen bonds (Figure 6–11). β structures are favored by the presence of large numbers of glycine and alanine residues. In nature they occur chiefly in silk proteins.

The most important regular arrangement of the polypeptide chain, however, is brought about by hydrogen bonding between groups on the same chain. This bonding results in the

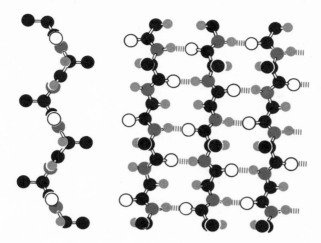

FIGURE 6-11   *An example of extended polypeptide chains held together in sheets by hydrogen bonds (β configuration). (Redrawn from L. Pauling, The Nature of the Chemical Bond, 3rd ed., Cornell Univ. Press, Ithaca, N.Y., p. 501, with permission.)*

twisting of the polypeptide backbone to form a helix. The most important polypeptide helix is the α-helix, which we have shown in Chapter 4 (Figure 4-13) to illustrate helical symmetry. X-ray diffraction analysis tells us that large sections of the polypeptide backbone of myoglobin are folded into α-helices. There is much suggestive evidence for helices in a large variety of proteins.

TERTIARY STRUCTURES OF PROTEINS ARE EXCEEDINGLY IRREGULAR

The *tertiary structure* of a protein is its 3-D form. It is, in many cases, very irregular. Practically no proteins exist in the form of a simple helix: Instead, many proteins contain both helical and nonhelical regions. Some, in fact, seem to have almost no helical regions. There are a number of stereochemical reasons why the α-helix or another regular arrangement is not found more extensively in spite of almost perfectly regular hydrogen bonding in the backbone. One reason is that the amino acid proline does not contain an amino group, and so where it occurs the regular hydrogen bonding must be interrupted. Another reason is the formation of disulfide (S—S) bridges between cysteine residues. When these cysteine residues are on the same polypeptide chain, the helix is necessarily distorted.

Perhaps, however, the most important reason for irregularity in protein structures arises from the diverse chemical nature of the amino acid side groups. Each of these side groups will tend to make the energetically most favorable secondary interactions with other atomic groups. As an example, the free hydroxyl group on tyrosine will tend to assume a position where it can form a hydrogen bond. The considerable energy of the bond would be lost if, for example, it were next to a hydrophobic isoleucine side group.

Furthermore, the side groups of several amino acids, like valine and leucine, are very insoluble in water, whereas others, like those of glutamic acid or lysine, are highly water soluble. It thus makes chemical sense that the water-insoluble side groups are found stacked next to each other in the interior of myoglobin, and the external surface contains groups that mix easily with water. The 3-dimensional configuration represents the energetically most favorable arrangement of the polypeptide chain. Each specific sequence of amino acids takes up the particular "native" arrangement that makes possible a maximum number of favorable atomic contacts between it and its normal environment. This view is strongly supported by very striking experiments in which high temperature or some other unnatural condition breaks down the native 3-D form (denaturation) to give randomly oriented, biologically inactive polypeptide chains. When the denatured chains are carefully returned to their normal environment, some of them can then reassume their native conformation (renaturation) with full biological activity.

S—S BONDS FORM SPONTANEOUSLY
BETWEEN CORRECT PARTNERS

In many cases, renaturation of a disordered protein to an active form involves not only the formation of the thermodynamically favorable weak bonds, but also the making of specific disulfide (S—S) bridges. This was first shown by experiments with the enzyme ribonuclease, a protein constructed from one polypeptide chain of 124 amino acids, cross-linked by four specific S—S bonds. The native, active configuration of the enzyme can be destroyed by reducing the S—S groups to sulfhydryl (SH) groups in the presence of the denaturing agent 8 M urea and the reducing agent mercaptoethanol (Figure 6–12). When the urea is removed, the SH bonds are reoxidized in air to yield S—S bonds identical to

FIGURE 6–12 *Schematic illustration of the fate of S–S bonds during protein denaturation and renaturation. When the denaturing agents are removed, most of the polypeptide chains resume the native configuration with the original S–S bonds. Only a few polypeptide chains fold up in an inactive form characterized by a different set of S–S bonds than those found in the native molecules.*

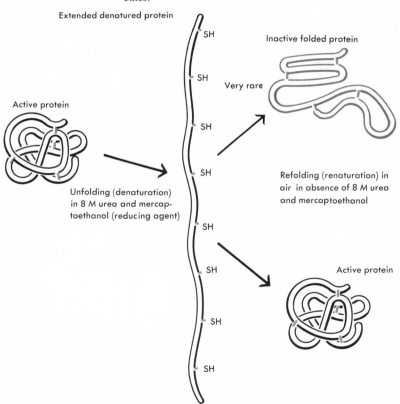

Extended denatured protein

Inactive folded protein

Very rare

Active protein

Unfolding (denaturation) in 8 M urea and mercaptoethanol (reducing agent)

Refolding (renaturation) in air in absence of 8 M urea and mercaptoethanol

Active protein

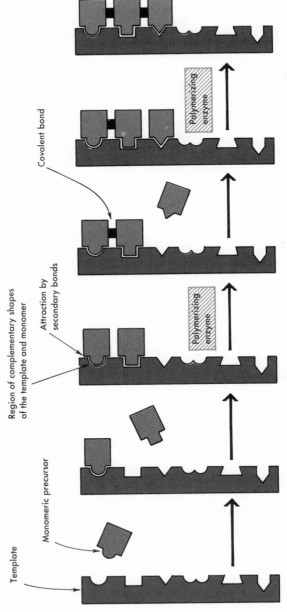

FIGURE 6-13 *Diagrammatic view of the formation of a specific polymeric molecule upon a template surface.*

178

those found in the original molecule. A given SH group re-associates, not randomly with any of the other seven SH groups in the molecule, but rather with a specific SH group brought into close contact with it by the folding of the polypeptide chain. Thus S—S bridges are not a primary reason for the peculiar folding of the chain. They might be better viewed as a device for increasing the stability of an already stable configuration. The presence or absence of S—S bonds does not affect the argument that the final structure of a protein is determined by the amino acid sequence.

ENZYMES CANNOT BE USED TO ORDER AMINO ACIDS IN PROTEINS

We have seen that the sequence of amino acids in the poly-peptide chains largely determines the 3-D structure of a protein. Now we come back to the ordering dilemma with the realization that it is the heart of the matter of protein synthesis. In comparison, the problem of how the connecting links form is minor, for this connective process involves the synthesis of only one type of covalent bond (the peptide bond), a fact that hints a need of only one enzyme or, at most, several enzymes.

On the other hand, the ordering itself cannot be accomplished by recourse to enzymes specific for each amino acid in a protein for the following reason. Such a device would require as many ordering enzymes as there are amino acids in the protein; but since all known enzymes are themselves proteins, still additional ordering enzymes would be necessary to synthesize the enzymes, and so on. This is clearly a paradox, unless we assume a fantastically interrelated series of syntheses in which a given protein can alternatively have many different enzymatic specificities. With such an assumption it might be just possible (and then with great difficulty) to visualize a workable cell. It does not seem likely, however, that most proteins really do have more than one task. All our knowledge, in fact, points toward the opposite general conclusion of one protein, one function.

It is, therefore, necessary to throw out the idea of ordering proteins with enzymes and to predict instead the existence of a specific surface, *the template* (Figure 6–13), that attracts the amino acids (or their activated derivatives) and lines them up in the correct order. Then a specific enzyme common to all protein synthesis could make the peptide bonds. It is, furthermore, necessary to assume that the templates must also have the capacity of serving either directly or indirectly as templates for themselves (self-duplication). That is, in some way their specific surfaces must be exactly copied to give new templates. Again we cannot invoke the help of specific enzymes, for this immediately leads us back to the "enzyme cannot make enzyme" paradox.

TEMPLATE INTERACTIONS ARE BASED ON RELATIVELY WEAK BONDS

The existence of proteins thus simultaneously demands the co-existence of highly specific template molecules. Moreover, the templates themselves must be macromolecules, at least as large as their polypeptide products. This is clear when we examine the rules that govern the selective binding of small molecules to their templates. We first see that the binding is not done by using strong covalent bonds. Instead the attraction is based on relatively weak bonds that can form without enzymes. These are (1) ionic bonds, (2) hydrogen bonds in which an electropositive hydrogen atom is attracted to electronegative atoms, such as oxygen or nitrogen, and (3) van der Waals forces.

Since all these forces operate only over very short distances (< 5 A), templates can order small molecules only when they are in close contact on the atomic level. Thus, it is to be expected that the specific (attracting) regions of the template will be in the same size range as the amino acid side groups in the protein product.

ATTRACTION OF OPPOSITES VERSUS SELF—ATTRACTION

Here we pose the obvious question: Can a polypeptide chain serve as a template for its own synthesis? (If it could, it would make possible a great reduction in the chemical prerequisites for life.) Then the problems of protein synthesis and template replication would be the same, and the additional biochemical complexity required to maintain a special class of template molecules would be unnecessary. This conceptual possibility finds no support, however, from close inspection of the amino acid side groups. There is no chemical reason why, for example, the occurrence of valine on a template should preferentially attract the specific side group of another valine molecule. In fact, none of the amino acid side groups have specific affinities for themselves. Instead it is much easier to imagine molecules with opposite or complementary features attracting each other. Negative charges obviously attract positive groups, and hydrogen atoms can form hydrogen bonds only to electronegative atoms. Similarly, molecules can specifically attract by van der Waals forces only when they possess complementary shapes, to allow a cavity in one molecule to be filled with a protruding group of another molecule.

A formal way remains, however, to save the possibility of protein templates. We might imagine the existence of 20 different specific molecules that we could call connectors. Each would possess two identical surfaces complementary in charge and/or shape to a given amino acid. The intervention of these connector molecules would then make possible the lining up of amino acids in a sequence identical to that of the template polypeptide chain. No evidence exists for such molecules, however. Instead, as we shall shortly show, a specific template class (the nucleic acids) does in fact exist.

A CHEMICAL ARGUMENT AGAINST THE EXISTENCE OF PROTEIN TEMPLATES

The failure of proteins ever to evolve a template role may originate in the composition of the amino acid side groups. The argument can be made that no template whose specificity depends upon the side groups of closely related amino acids, like valine or alanine, could ever be copied with the accuracy demanded for efficient cellular existence. This follows from the fact that some amino acids are chemically similar. For example, valine and isoleucine differ only by the presence of an additional methyl group in isoleucine. Likewise, glycine and alanine also differ by only one methyl group. This close chemical similarity immediately poses the question whether any copying process can be sufficiently accurate to distinguish between such closely related molecules. Our answer depends in part upon what we mean by "sufficiently accurate." A good speculative guess is that each amino acid in an hereditary molecule would have to be copied with an accuracy of not more than one error in 10^8. On the other hand, a semirigorous chemical argument can be made that no chemical reaction could distinguish between molecules differing by only one methyl group with an accuracy of better than one in 10^6. Moreover, when we look at the accuracy of protein synthesis itself, we observe that some amino acids can be inserted into polypeptide chains with no greater than a 99.9 per cent accuracy. Thus proteins do not have the "smell" of an hereditary molecule.

SUMMARY

The frequent occurrence of most chemical reactions within cells depends both on the presence of specific enzymes and on the availability of an external energy supply (the sun or food molecules) to make energy-rich molecules like ATP. There is a different enzyme for almost every specific reaction involved in the synthesis of a small molecule. This rule holds even when the "small molecule" is as large as chlorophyll. The problem arises, however, whether the same general scheme can hold for the biosynthesis of the enzymes themselves. Are a number of specific enzymes used to synthesize each enzyme involved in the metabolism of small molecules? This number would need to be very large, since all enzymes are proteins, themselves very large molecules, constructed by the linear linking together in a definite order of the 20 amino acids. The average protein contains about 300 to 500 amino acids, and so an equivalent number of enzymes would be necessary if enzymes are used to specify amino acid sequences.

This is clearly an unworkable scheme, and the ordering of amino acids in proteins is instead accomplished by template molecules. The templates for protein are also macromolecules. They have surfaces that specifically attract and thereby line up the amino acids in the correct sequence. There is a specific template for each specific protein. No enzymes are involved in the attraction of the amino acid residues to the templates. Attraction is accomplished by weak secondary forces. Specific re-

gions of the template specifically attract one of the 20 different amino acid residues.

When a cell grows and divides, the number of protein template molecules must also double. Templates must in some way also be templates for their own highly exact synthesis. The templates are not protein molecules; there are chemical arguments why proteins should not be highly accurate templates. Instead, all cells contain a special class of molecules specifically devoted to being templates for protein synthesis.

REFERENCES

Kornberg, A. "Pathways of Enzymatic Synthesis of Nucleotides and Polynucleotides," in W. D. McElroy and B. Glass (eds.), *The Chemical Basis of Heredity*, Johns Hopkins, Baltimore, 1957, pp. 579–608. An excellent survey of the biosynthesis of the purine and pyrimidine nucleotides.

Perutz, M. F., "The Hemoglobin Molecule," *Sci. Am.*, November, 1964, pp. 64–76. Relates much of what is currently known about the architecture of the hemoglobin molecule, in the presence or absence of oxygen.

Dickerson, R. E., and I. Geis, *The Structure and Action of Proteins*, Harper and Row, New York, 1969. An extraordinarily well-illustrated introduction to the ways polypeptide chains fold up.

Neurath, H. (ed.), *The Proteins*, 2nd ed., Academic, New York, Vol. 1, 1963, Vol. 2, 1965. A collection of advanced articles about various aspects of protein chemistry.

Muller, H. J., "The Gene," *Proc. Roy. Soc. (London)*, **B134**, 1–37 (1947). A lecture given in 1945 in which a distinguished geneticist traces the history of the gene concept and speculates about how it might function as a template.

Phillips, D., "The Three-Dimensional Structure of an Enzyme Molecule," in R. H. Haynes and P. C. Hanawalt (eds.), *The Molecular Basis of Life*, Freeman, San Francisco, 1968, pp. 52–64. A description of the beautiful work that solved the structure of lysozyme, the first enzyme for which it was possible to correlate structure and function.

Mahler, H. R., and E. H. Cordes, *Biological Chemistry*, Harper and Row, New York, 1966.

Bernhard, S., *Enzymes: Structure and Function*, Benjamin, New York, 1968. A short but excellent introduction to proteins as enzymes.

7

THE ARRANGEMENT OF GENES ON CHROMOSOMES

OUR CHEMICAL INTUITION TELLS US that proteins are unlikely to serve as the templates necessary to order amino acid sequences in proteins. Instead, we must look for a class of molecules capable of both the protein template function and self-replication. Here the direction of our search is completely dictated by the results of modern genetics. This flourishing science has shown in amazing detail how the chromosomes are responsible for the perpetuation of heredity: it is by means of genes, located on the chromosomes, that daughter cells come to resemble parental cells. The major task of the geneticists has been to show how this resemblance occurs.

Parallel to their work in mapping the location of genes, geneticists began to ask the fundamental question of how the genes chemically controlled specific cellular processes. Usually, however, the mutations they studied were not easily analyzed. In the 1920s and the 1930s, as even today, virtually nothing was known of the biochemical basis of development.

Fortunately, however, the mutations affecting color in flowers and eyes were open to a chemical approach. For example, mutations in many genes change the color of the eyes of *Drosophila*. Here biochemical analysis was possible because it was known that eye color is directly related to the presence of definite colored molecules called pigments. It could thus be asked how a gene difference could convert the color of fruit fly eyes from red to white. The obvious and correct answer is that no pigment is found in the eyes of flies thus altered. This in turn hints that an enzyme necessary for its synthesis is absent, a suggestion soon extended to the general hypothesis that genes directly control the synthesis of all proteins, whether or not they are enzymes.

As this way of thinking became generally accepted (about 1946), geneticists began to deal with the deeper problem of how a gene dictates which particular protein is present. Little progress could be made until protein chemists showed unambiguously (in the early 1950s) that proteins were linear collections of the 20 amino acids. It was then a simple matter for the more theoretically inclined geneticists to hypothesize that the chromosomes carry the genetic information that orders amino acid sequences, and to predict that the study of the structure of genes might lead to the elucidation of the molecular basis of the templates that order amino acid sequences. This was, in fact, what did happen. But before we can examine the problem more deeply, some genetic concepts must first be explained.

MUCH REMAINS TO BE LEARNED ABOUT THE MOLECULAR ASPECTS OF CHROMOSOME STRUCTURE

Even today, our knowledge of the molecular structure of chromosomes is very incomplete. This is especially true for the more complex chromosomes of higher plants and animals. In bacteria and viruses there is evidence (which we shall later relate) that the principal chemical component is deoxyribonucleic acid (DNA). The chromosomes of higher organisms, however, also contain a significant fraction (as great as 50 per cent) of protein.

Most of this protein belongs to a class of protein molecules called histones. All histones are basic (have a net positive charge), and it is believed that they neutralize part of the negative charge of the acid DNA molecules. The primary function of histones is still a mystery. Before 1943 many biologists believed that they carried genetic information, but their complete absence in many, if not all, bacteria now argues against the assignment of a fundamental genetic role. Instead there is a growing belief that they have essentially inhibitory functions. When a gene in higher plants and animals is not functioning, it tends to be combined with histones.

Up to now, electron microscopy has provided no useful insight into the structure of chromosomes of higher organisms. This failure is in striking contrast with the success of electron microscopy in examining very thin sections of muscle and nerve fibers. The failure arises from the *irregular* shape not only of the highly extended chromosomes found during interphase, but even of the contracted metaphase chromosomes. At the molecular level the various muscle proteins are nicely lined up in parallel array. In contrast, the path of a chromosome through a cell is excessively irregular: When a thin section is observed, it has so far been impossible even to follow the contour, much less to observe details of molecular structure. Thus, morphological examination by itself has given us no useful information about the chromosomal arrangement of genes; instead genetic crosses are the only way of attacking this problem. Fortunately, as we shall soon see, the powers of resolution of this method are indeed very great.

THE GENETIC CROSS

A variety of devices exist in nature that bring together genetic material from different organisms (the genetic cross) for the purpose of achieving genetic recombination. These devices, collectively known as *sexual processes*, greatly speed up the rate of evolution, since they bring collections of favorable mutations into one cell much faster than successive cycles of favorable mutations could by themselves. Here, however, we are not at all concerned with the evolutionary advantages of the various sexual processes. Our interest in them arises instead from the variety of tools that their existence has provided for finding the location of genes along chromosomes.

The essential trick of locating genes through genetic crosses

involves the determination of whether the genes donated by a
given parent remain together when haploid segregants are
produced. When genes are located on different chromosomes
they will assort randomly, and there will be a 50–50 chance that
they will be found together in a given haploid segregant. When,
on the contrary, they are located on the same chromosome, they
will tend to segregate together, unless they have been separated
by crossing over.

Crossing over occurs at the stage of meiosis where two
homologous chromosomes specifically attract each other to form
pairs. The mechanism of this attraction (*pairing*) remains a
great mystery. It is clearly a very specific process, since it occurs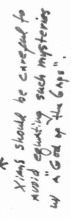
only between chromosomes containing the same genes. Follow-
ing the formation of pairs, both chromosomes occasionally
break at the same point and rejoin crossways. This allows the
formation of recombinant chromosomes containing some genes
derived from the paternal chromosome and some from the
maternal one. Crossing over greatly increases the amount of
genetic recombination and, except in highly specialized cases,
is universally observed. The frequency of crossing over, however,
varies greatly with the particular species involved. On the
average, one to several crossovers occur every time chromosomes pair.

All our early knowledge of gene locations came from the
study of gene segregation after conventional meiotic divisions.
The organisms studied were those in which there is a regular
fusion of the male and the female cells to produce diploid cells
half of whose chromosomes are derived from the male
parent and half from the female. When meiosis occurs, the
diploid chromosome number is regularly reduced to the haploid
number. Crossing over always takes place after each of the
parental chromosomes has split to form two chromatids held
together by a single centromere. Two chromatids are involved
in each crossover event, so that each crossover produces two
recombinant chromatids and leaves the two parental chromosomes intact (Figure 7–1). (This does not mean that half the
chromatids produced during meiosis have the parental genotype. Each chromatid in a pair has an equal chance of crossing

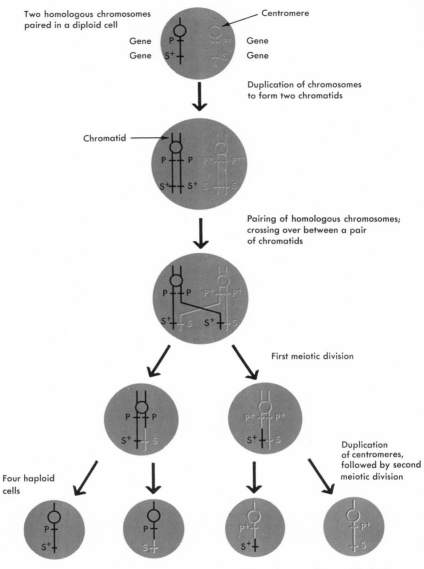

FIGURE 7–1   *Crossing over between homologous chromatids during meiosis.*

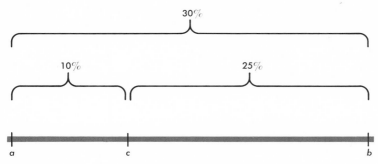

F I G U R E 7–2   *Assignment of the tentative order of three genes on a basis of 3 two-factor crosses (see text for details).*

over, so that, even though a particular chromatid is not involved in a given crossover, it may still participate in another.)

CHROMOSOME MAPPING

The existence of crossing over provides a means of locating genes along chromosomes. Crossing over occurs randomly throughout the length of many chromosomes, so that the farther apart two genes are, the greater the probability that a break will occur between them to cause genetic recombination. The way in which the frequencies of the various recombinant classes are used to locate genes is straightforward. It is especially easy when the progeny are haploid, and the question of dominance versus recessiveness is irrelevant. Consider the segregation pattern of three genes all located on the same chromosome of a haploid organism. The arrangement of the genes can be determined by means of three crosses, in each of which two genes are followed (two-factor crosses). A cross X between a^+b^+ and ab yields four progeny types: the two parental genotypes (a^+b^+ and ab) and two recombinant genotypes (a^+b and ab^+). The cross Y between a^+c^+ and ac similarly gives the two parental combinations as well as the a^+c and ac^+ recombinants, whereas the cross Z between b^+c^+ and bc produces the parental types, and the recombinants b^+c and cb^+. Each cross will produce a specific ratio of parental to recombinant progeny. Consider, for example, the result that cross X gives 30 per cent recombinants, cross Y, 10 per cent, and cross Z, 25 per cent. This hints that genes a and c are closer together than a and b or b and c, and that the genetic distances between a and b and b and c are more similar. The gene arrangement which best fits this data is acb (Figure 7–2).

The correctness of gene orders suggested by crosses of two gene factors can usually be unambiguously confirmed by three-factor crosses. When the three genes used in the above example are followed in the cross a⁺b⁺c⁺ × abc, six recombinant genotypes are found (Figure 7–3). They fall into three groups of reciprocal pairs. The rarest of these groups arises from a double crossover. By looking for the least frequent class, it is often possible instantly to confirm (or deny) a postulated arrangement. The results in Figure 7–3 immediately confirm the order hinted by the two-factor crosses. Only if the order is acb does the fact that the rare recombinants are a⁺cb⁺ and ac⁺b make sense.

FIGURE 7–3   *The use of three-factor crosses to assign gene order. The least frequent pair of reciprocal recombinants must arise from a double crossover. The percentages listed for the various classes are the theoretical values expected for an infinitely large sample. When finite numbers of progeny are recorded, the exact values will be subject to random statistical fluctuations.*

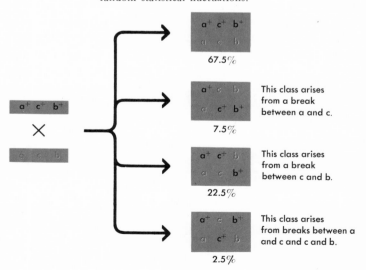

The existence of multiple crossovers means that the amount of recombination (ab) between the outside markers a and b is usually less than the sum of the recombination frequencies (ac and cb) between a and c and c and b. To obtain a more accurate approximation of the distance between the outside markers, we calculate the probability (ac × cb) that, when a crossover occurs between c and b, an ac crossover also occurs, and vice versa (cb × ac). This probability subtracted from the sum of the frequencies expresses more accurately the amount of recombination. This gives the simple formula

$$ab = ac + cb - 2(ac)(cb)$$

It is applicable in all cases where the occurrence of one crossover does not affect the probability of another crossover. Unfortunately, accurate mapping is often disturbed by *interference* phenomena, which can either increase or decrease the probability of correlated crossovers.

The results of a very large number of such crosses have led to an important genetic conclusion: All the genes on a chromosome can be located on a line. The gene arrangement is strictly linear, and never branched. Thus chromosomes are linear, not only in shape, but also in gene arrangement. The arrangement of genes on a particular chromosome is called a *genetic map*, and the locating of genes on a chromosome is often referred to as mapping a gene. Figure 7–4 shows the genetic map of one of the chromosomes of *Drosophila*. Distances between genes on a map are usually measured in map units, which are related to the frequency of recombination between the genes: Thus if the frequency of recombination between two genes is found to be 5 per cent, the genes are said to be separated by five map units. Because of the occurrence of double crossovers, the assignment of map units can be considered accurate only if recombination between closely spaced genes is followed.

Even when two genes are at the far ends of a very long chromosome, they will show not less than 50 per cent linkage (assort together at least 50 per cent of the time), because of multiple crossovers. Genes will be separated if 1,3,5,7 . . .

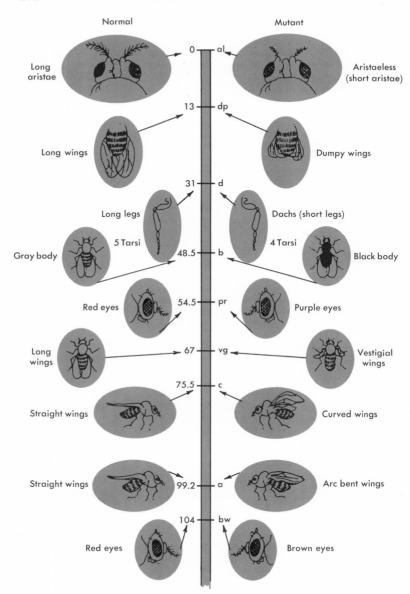

FIGURE 7-4 A portion of the genetic map of Drosophila melanogaster (chromosome 2).

crossovers occur between them; they will end up together if 2,4,6,8 . . . occur between them. Thus in the beginning of the genetic analysis of an organism, it is practically impossible to determine immediately whether two genes are on different chromosomes or are at the opposite ends of one long chromosome. After a large number of genes have been mapped, we often find that two genes thought to be on different chromosomes are, in fact, on the same one. For example, the genes of the phage T4 were thought for many years to lie on three separate chromosomes, until further mapping, using newly discovered genes, revealed that they all lie on a single chromosome.

It is important to remember that a genetic map derived from recombinant frequencies gives only the relative physical distances between mutable sites. It would give the actual physical distances only if the probability of crossing over were the same throughout the length of a chromosome. Thus, just as soon as geneticists made maps, they sought methods that could relate mutational sites to true physical locations. Now a number of tricks, some too complicated to be explained here, tell us that often, *but not always*, genetic maps are a good reflection of the actual chromosome structure. One of these tricks will be described in a subsequent section, in which we discuss the genetic map of *E. coli*.

IMPORTANCE OF WORK WITH MICROORGANISMS

Most of our initial ideas about genes arose from work with large, multicellular plants and animals. Now, however, unless there is an economic or social need for information about a particular species (e.g., the corn plant, man), microorganisms are much more preferable for study. Several important advantages favor work with microorganisms. First, they are usually haploid, so that the ease of genetic analysis does not depend upon whether a mutation is dominant or recessive. Since most mutations are recessive, they cannot be detected when the normal wild-type gene is also present. In work with diploids, several generations of genetic crosses must often be carried out to detect the presence of a particular mutant gene; in a haploid organism the mutant gene can express itself almost immediately. Second, microorganisms multiply very rapidly. There is enormous advantage to working with an organism, such as a bacterium, which has a new cell generation every 20 minutes, rather than with a plant like corn, where at best only two generations per year can be studied, even in tropical environments.

Fifty years ago, *Drosophila*, with its average life cycle of 14 days, looked very attractive. Today it cannot be conveniently used to answer the fundamental questions being asked at the molecular level about what genes are and how they act.

Now the most exciting materials for genetic study are yeasts, molds, bacteria, and viruses, particularly the bacterial viruses, or phages. Genetic work with these effectively began some 25 years ago. Until then their small size was considered an enormous disadvantage. Microorganisms do not have easily recognized morphological features, such as red eyes, and so it was very difficult to know when they contained mutations. Until 1945, it was generally believed that some did not have chromosomes and some biologists even suspected they might not have genes.

THE VALUE OF MUTAGENS

Most mutant genes studied by the early Mendelian geneticists arose spontaneously. Now there is increasing use of mutations specifically induced by external agents, such as ionizing radiation, ultraviolet light, and certain specific chemicals. These agents, collectively called mutagens, greatly increase the rate at which geneticists can isolate mutant genes. For many years the various forms of radiation were the most powerful mutagens known. Now chemical mutagens are more often used, because they produce a much higher fraction of mutated genes. Treatment of bacteria with the highly reactive compound nitrosoguanidine can produce viable mutations in almost 1 per cent of the bacterial genes.

Mutagens act quite indiscriminately. No presently known

mutagen increases the probability of mutating a given gene without also increasing the probability of mutating all other genes. Until recently, the mechanisms of mutagenesis were completely unclear. Now, as we shall point out in Chapter 9, the realization that DNA is the primary genetic material allows the development of precise hypotheses about how several chemical mutagens act.

BACTERIAL MUTATIONS:
THE USE OF GROWTH FACTORS

The essential breakthrough in the use of bacteria as genetic material came in 1944 with the realization that mutations could be obtained affecting the ability of bacteria to synthesize essential metabolites. For example, E. coli ordinarily grows well with only glucose as a carbon source. But as a result of specific mutations, there now exist mutant E. coli strains that will grow only when their normal medium is supplemented with a specific metabolite (*growth factor*). These types of mutation had been described just a few years earlier (1941) in the haploid lower plant Neurospora (a mold). Such mutations are very easy to work with: To test for their presence one need merely grow a suspected mutant both in the presence and in the absence of a metabolite, for example, the amino acid arginine (Figure 7–5). If a mutation inhibiting arginine biosynthesis has occurred, the bacteria will grow only in the presence of arginine. The use of this approach quickly led (with the help of mutagens) to the isolation of a large number of different gene mutations affecting the synthesis of specific molecules.

Another important type of mutation involves the resistance of bacteria to poisonous compounds such as antibiotics. For example, most E. coli cells are rapidly killed by small amounts of streptomycin. Very rarely, however, there occur mutations (Strep^R), which make the cells resistant to certain amounts of the drug. Mutations also can occur to make cells resistant to the growth of viruses. One of the most useful mutations in E. coli strain B confers resistance to the phage T1; these mutant cells are designated B/1. Correspondingly, E. coli strain B

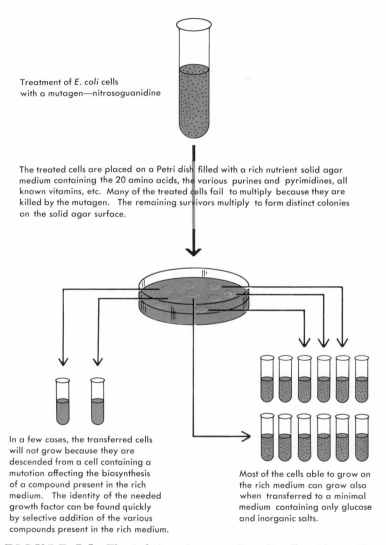

Treatment of E. coli cells with a mutagen—nitrosoguanidine

The treated cells are placed on a Petri dish filled with a rich nutrient solid agar medium containing the 20 amino acids, the various purines and pyrimidines, all known vitamins, etc. Many of the treated cells fail to multiply because they are killed by the mutagen. The remaining survivors multiply to form distinct colonies on the solid agar surface.

In a few cases, the transferred cells will not grow because they are descended from a cell containing a mutation affecting the biosynthesis of a compound present in the rich medium. The identity of the needed growth factor can be found quickly by selective addition of the various compounds present in the rich medium.

Most of the cells able to grow on the rich medium can grow also when transferred to a minimal medium containing only glucose and inorganic salts.

FIGURE 7–5 *The isolation of mutant E. coli cells with specific growth factor requirements.*

cells resistant to phages T2 and T4 are called B/2 and B/4, respectively. Still other mutations affect the ability of E. coli cells to grow upon sugars such as lactose, galactose, or maltose; a specific mutation can cause the loss of the ability of E. coli to use one of these sugars as a sole carbon source.

good exp. evid. for sexuality in E. Coli

The isolation of growth factor, antibiotic resistance, and phage resistance mutations was quickly followed by experiments demonstrating existence of genetic recombination (hence a sexual process) in *E. coli* (Figure 7–6). Twofold use was made of these mutant genes. First, they were used as conventional genetic markers, their segregation patterns revealing the chromosomal arrangement of genes. Second, they provided a method

F I G U R E 7–6 *The use of growth factor requirements to demonstrate sexuality in E. coli.*

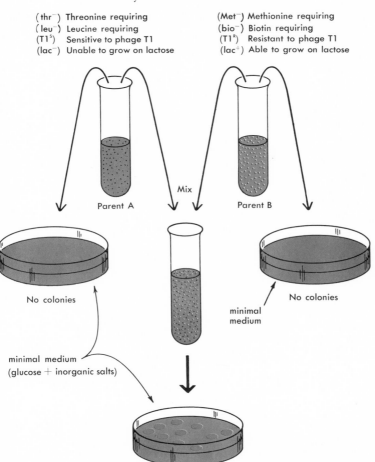

(thr⁻) Threonine requiring
(leu⁻) Leucine requiring
(T1ˢ) Sensitive to phage T1
(lac⁻) Unable to grow on lactose

(Met⁻) Methionine requiring
(bio⁻) Biotin requiring
(T1ᴿ) Resistant to phage T1
(lac⁺) Able to grow on lactose

Parent A   Mix   Parent B

No colonies   No colonies

minimal medium

minimal medium
(glucose + inorganic salts)

A very small fraction of the cells are met⁺, bio⁺, thr⁺, leu⁺. They arise by genetic recombination shown by examination of the lac and T1 markers. In addition to the parental lac⁻T1ˢ and lac⁺T1ᴿ genotypes, there are found lac⁻T1ᴿ and lac⁺T1ˢ cells.

of detecting a genetic recombination process occurring in only a very small fraction of the population at a given time. In *E. coli*, for example, simple morphological examination of bacterial cells gave no clues that cell fusion and genetic recombination existed: To detect recombination it was necessary to devise an experiment in which only the recombinant cells would be able to multiply. This was done by using parental strains with specific growth requirements such that they could not multiply in minimal media.

In these experiments, two strains of bacteria, each possessing specific growth requirements, were mixed together. Neither strain alone was able to grow in the absence of specific metabolites or growth factors (that is, the amino acids threonine and leucine were required by one strain, the vitamin biotin and the amino acid methionine by the other). After the two strains had been mixed together, a small number of cells were able to grow without any growth factors. This meant that they had somehow acquired good copies of each of their mutant genes. This result strongly suggested that *E. coli* has a sexual phase that can bring together the chromosomes of two different cells. Crossing over could then place in one chromosome good copies of all its necessary genes. Further genetic analysis confirmed this hypothesis, and within the past 10 years *E. coli* has become one of the genetically best known of all organisms.

VIRUSES ALSO CONTAIN CHROMOSOMES

Chromosomal control of heredity even extends to viruses. These disease-causing particles, much smaller than bacteria, can enter (infect) cells and multiply to form large numbers of new virus particles. The common cold, influenza, and poliomyelitis are among the many diseases caused by viruses. The relation of viruses to their host cells is very intimate, since they are able to increase in numbers only after they have entered a cell; outside cells they are completely inert. There exist viruses active on most, if not all, plants and animals. Viruses can even multiply in bacteria (bacterial viruses are usually called bacteriophages or phages). The replication of many new virus particles within a single cell usually kills the host cell—hence their disease-causing property.

Our knowledge of the genetics of several bacterial viruses has shown an expansion similar to and simultaneous with the expansion of our knowledge of bacteria. Before 1940, almost no one thought about the genetics of viruses. To most people viruses seemed much too small to be studied unless they caused a disease that we wished to control. They could not be seen in the light microscope, and were generally detected only by their property of killing cells. Several factors changed this outlook. First, it was realized that the bacterial viruses were very easy to experiment with and that the phage-bacterium system was ideally suited to the study of the general problem of how genes multiply and work. Second, it was found that phage mutations were as easy to obtain as mutations in bacteria, if not easier.

Chemically, viruses are extremely heterogeneous both in size and in variety of molecular constituents (Figure 7–7). For many years their biological significance was obscure and the question often asked was, "Are viruses living?" Now we realize that they are small pieces of genetic material, each enclosed within a protective coat, rich in protein, which allows it to be transported from one cell to another. Progeny virus particles resemble their parents because they contain identical chromosomes. We also see that they are no more "alive" than isolated chromosomes; both the chromosomes of cells and those of viruses can duplicate only in the complex environment of a living cell. The study of viruses has been of immense value to the understanding of how cells live: Viruses are almost unique in affording convenient systems for quickly studying the consequences of the sudden introduction of new genetic material into a cell.

VIRUSES DO NOT GROW
BY GRADUAL INCREASE IN SIZE

The life cycle of an average cell involves gradual increase to twice its initial size, followed by a division process (mitosis)

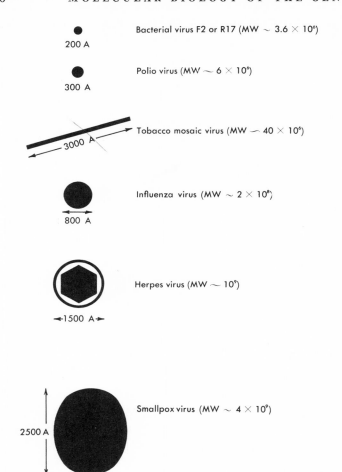

FIGURE 7–7   *Variation in size and shape of a number of viruses.*

producing two identical daughter cells. Viruses, however, do not multiply in this fashion. They are not produced by the fission of a large pre-existing particle—all the virus particles of a given variety have approximately similar (in some cases identical) masses. During viral multiplication there is a temporary disappearance (the eclipse period) of the original parental particle, because the parental particle breaks down upon infection and releases its chromosome from the protective outer shell. Then the free chromosome serves as a template to direct the synthesis of new viral components. This breakdown process is an obligatory feature of viral multiplication, for as long as the chromosome is tightly enclosed within the protein-containing shell, it cannot be a template for the synthesis of either new chromosomes or new shell protein molecules.

VIRUSES ARE PARASITES AT THE GENETIC LEVEL

In most cases, the viral chromosomes (which we shall later show always to be constructed from nucleic acids) and proteins are constructed from the same four main nucleotides and 20 amino acids used in normal cells. All these precursors are usually synthesized by host cell enzymes. Likewise, the energy needed to push the various chemical reactions in the biosynthetic direction usually comes from ATP produced by food molecule degradation controlled by host enzymes.

The parasitism of viruses is thus obligatory. It is impossible to imagine viruses reproducing outside cells, on which they are completely dependent for supply of both the necessary precursors and the ribosomes, the structural machinery for making proteins. The essential aspect of viruses is thus not really their small size, but the fact that they do not possess the capacity to independently construct proteins. Thus for their replication, they must insert their nucleic acid into a functional cell. This fact enables us to distinguish the larger viruses, like smallpox, from very small cellular organisms, like the Rickettsiae. Even though the Rickettsiae are obligatory parasites, they contain both DNA and RNA and grow by increasing in size and splitting into two smaller cells. At no time does their cell membrane break down; moreover, all their protein is synthesized upon their own protein synthesizing machinery.

BACTERIAL VIRUSES (PHAGES)
ARE OFTEN EASY TO STUDY

As mentioned before, the most exciting viruses from the viewpoint of the geneticist are the bacterial viruses (phages). Their discovery in 1914 produced great excitement, for it was hoped that they might afford an effective and simple way to combat bacterial diseases. Phages were unfortunately never medically useful, because their bacterial hosts mutate readily to forms resistant to viral growth. Thus almost everyone lost interest in the phage, and almost no one studied how it multiplied until the late 1930s. Then a small group of biologists and physicists, intrigued by the problem of gene replication, began to investigate the reproduction of several phages which multiplied in *E. coli*. They chose to work with phages

FIGURE 7–8 *Some bacterial viruses that have been important in the study of the chemistry of genetics.*

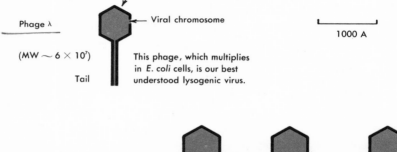

Phage λ

(MW ∼ 6 × 10⁷)

Head — Protective coat

Viral chromosome

Tail

This phage, which multiplies in *E. coli* cells, is our best understood lysogenic virus.

1000 A

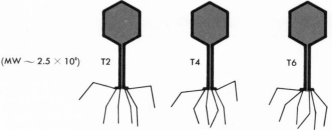

(MW ∼ 2.5 × 10⁸)   T2   T4   T6

These morphologically identical viruses are genetically related. They also multiply in *E. coli* cells and are now the best understood of all genetic objects.

F2   R17   MS2   (MW ∼ 3.6 × 10⁶)

These are the smallest known group of *E. coli* viruses. Even though they have been known only for a few years, they are quickly becoming some of the most intensively studied of all viruses.

rather than with plant or animal viruses because, under laboratory conditions, it is immensely easier to grow bacterial cells than plant or animal cells.

Almost all work with phages has concentrated on several particular phages, arbitrarily given names like T1, T2, P1, F2, or λ (Figure 7–8). Among the best known are the closely related strains T2, T4, T6, and λ. These strains reproduce in essentially the same way. The growth cycle starts when a phage particle collides with a sensitive bacterium and the phage tail specifically attaches to the bacterial wall. An enzyme in the phage tail then breaks down a small portion of the cell wall, creating a small hole through which the viral chromosome enters the cell. The viral chromosome duplicates, and the daughter chromosomes continue to duplicate, to form eventually 100 to 1000 new chromosomes, which become encapsulated with newly synthesized protective coats, to form a large number of new bacteriophage particles. The growth cycle is complete when the bacterial cell wall breaks open (lyses) and releases the progeny particles into the surrounding medium.

PHAGES FORM PLAQUES

The presence of viable phage particles can be quickly demonstrated by adding the virus-containing solution to the surface of a nutrient agar plate, on which bacteria susceptible to this virus are rapidly multiplying. If no virus particles are present, the rapidly dividing bacteria will form a uniform surface layer of bacteria. But if even one virus particle is present, it will attach to a bacterium and multiply to form several hundred new progeny virus particles, which are then suddenly released by dissolution (lysis) of the cell wall, some 15 to 60 minutes after the start of phage infection. Each of these several hundred progeny particles can then attach to a new bacterium and multiply. After several such cycles of attachment, multiplication, and release, all the bacteria in the immediate region of the original virus particle are killed. These regions of killed bacteria appear as circular holes (plaques) in the lawn of healthy bacteria (Figure 7–9).

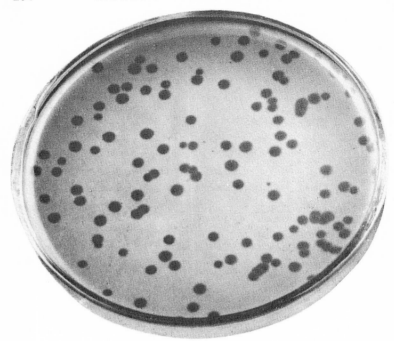

FIGURE 7–9   *Photograph of phage T2 plaques on a lawn of E. coli bacteria growing in a Petri plate. (From G. S. Stent, Molecular Biology of Bacterial Viruses, Freeman, San Francisco, 1963, p. 41, with permission.)*

VIRUS CHROMOSOMES ARE SOMETIMES INSERTED INTO THE CHROMOSOMES OF THEIR HOST CELLS

Some bacterial viruses (e.g., phage λ) do not always multiply upon entering a host cell. Instead their chromosome sometimes becomes inserted into a specific section of a host chromosome. Then the viral chromosome is, for all practical purposes, an integral part of its host chromosome and is duplicated, like the bacterial chromosome, just once every cell generation (Figure 7–10). The virus chromosome when it is integrated into a host chromosome is called the *prophage*; those bacteria containing prophages are called *lysogenic bacteria*; and those types of virus whose chromosomes can become prophages are known as *lysogenic viruses*. In contrast, those viruses (e.g., T2)

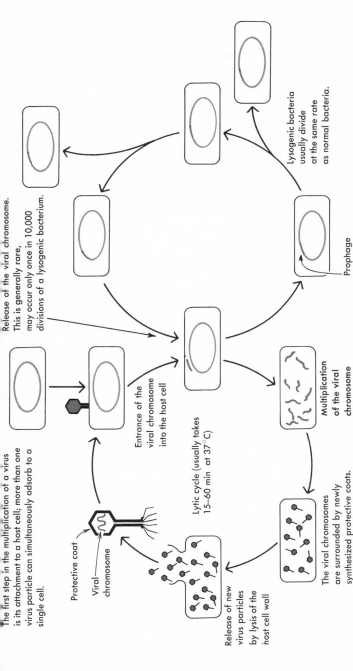

The first step in the multiplication of a virus is its attachment to a host cell; more than one virus particle can simultaneously adsorb to a single cell.

Protective coat

Viral chromosome

Release of new virus particles by lysis of the host cell wall

The viral chromosomes are surrounded by newly synthesized protective coats.

Multiplication of the viral chromosome

Lytic cycle (usually takes 15–60 min at 37°C)

Entrance of the viral chromosome into the host cell

Release of the viral chromosome. This is generally rare, may occur only once in 10,000 divisions of a lysogenic bacterium.

Lysogenic bacteria usually divide at the same rate as normal bacteria.

Prophage

FIGURE 7–10   *The life cycle of a lysogenic bacterial virus. We see that, after its chromosome enters a host cell, it sometimes immediately multiplies like a lytic virus and at other times becomes transformed into prophage. The lytic phase of its life cycle is identical to the complete life cycle of a lytic (nonlysogenic) virus. Lytic bacterial viruses are so called because their multiplication results in the rupture (lysis) of the bacteria.*

205

that always multiply when they enter a host cell are called *lytic viruses*. It is often difficult to know when a bacterium is lysogenic. We can be sure only when the virus chromosome is released from the host chromosome and the multiplication process which forms new progeny particles commences. Why only certain viruses (lysogenic viruses) form lysogenic associations and what advantage they receive from this association is still an open question.

How the viral chromosome is transformed into prophage was until recently very mysterious. Now there is good genetic evidence that the integration of the viral chromosome is achieved by crossing over between the host chromosome and a *circular form* of the viral chromosome. Prior to integration, the viral chromosome forms a circle and attaches to a specific region of the host chromosome. Both the host chromosome and the viral chromosome then break and rejoin in such a way that the broken ends of the viral chromosomes join to the broken ends

FIGURE 7–11   *Insertion of the chromosome of phage λ into the E. coli chromosome by crossing over.*

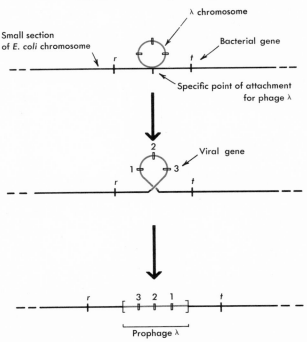

of the bacterial chromosome instead of to each other, thereby inserting the prophage into the host chromosome (Figure 7–11). The prophage detaches from the host chromosome by the reverse process: The two ends of the prophage pair prior to a crossover event which ejects the viral chromosome. The now free viral genome then can begin to multiply as if it were the chromosome of a lytic virus.

BACTERIAL–CHROMOSOME MAPPING BY MATING

Many organisms now of greatest use in revealing what genes are and how they work do not have a conventional meiosis. When sexuality in bacteria was first discovered, it seemed simplest to believe that a conventional cycle of cell fusion followed by meiotic segregation occurred. Now we know, however, that the *E. coli* cycle has distinctive factors complicating conventional genetic analysis. The complications arise from the nature of the mating process. As in higher organisms, there exist male and female cells. The sexual cycle starts when the male and female cells attach to each other by a narrow bridge (Figure 7–12). A male chromosome then begins to move through the bridge to the female cell. Usually the transfer is incomplete, and only part of the male chromosome enters the female cell before the mating cells separate. Thus only rarely are complete diploid cells formed, partially diploid cells usually occurring instead. Crossing over then occurs between the female parent and the male chromosome (or fragment), followed by a segregation process, which yields haploid progeny cells.

The sex difference between the male and female cells is determined by the presence of a specific genetic factor, called the *F(ertility) factor*. When it is present in cells (F^+) the cells are male, and when it is absent (F^-) they are female. The F factor can exist in two alternative states, either as part of the *E. coli* chromosome or as a very small free chromosome that multiplies once per cell division. In the latter case, the F^+ cells are only potentially male, since they cannot transfer their genes to F^- cells; only when the F factor is part of the chromosome can the male cells mate. F^+ cells containing integrated

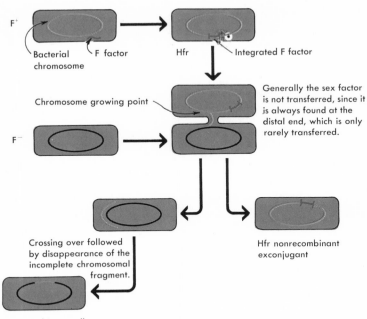

F⁺

Bacterial chromosome   F factor   Hfr   Integrated F factor

Chromosome growing point

F⁻

Generally the sex factor is not transferred, since it is always found at the distal end, which is only rarely transferred.

Crossing over followed by disappearance of the incomplete chromosomal fragment.

Hfr nonrecombinant exconjugant

F⁻ recombinant cell

FIGURE 7–12 Sexuality in E. coli. Chromosomal transfer from male to female cells provides a primitive sexuality in E. coli. When the F agent has become attached to the male chromosome, the male cell, now Hfr, is competent to transfer a chromosome to a female cell. When the Hfr and F⁻ cells join together by a narrow bridge, the Hfr chromosome breaks and begins to duplicate at the site where the F factor has been inserted. A free end of one of the daughter Hfr chromosome segments then begins to move into the F⁻ cell. At 37°C, the transfer of a complete chromosome requires about 90 minutes. Generally, however, only part of the Hfr chromosome moves to the F⁻ cell before the cells separate; crossing over then occurs between the donor genetic material and the F⁻ chromosome. The haploid condition is reestablished by elimination of the supernumerary genes that have not become part of complete chromosomes. The recombinant cells can then be screened for the presence of various Hfr and F⁻ genes, thereby allowing the construction of a genetic map.

sex factors are called *Hfr* (high frequency of recombination).

A variety of different Hfr strains exist, each containing an F factor integrated into a different region of the chromosome. Until recently, there was no good hypothesis about how the F agent becomes part of the host chromosome. Now there are strong hints that the F agent, like the chromosomes of lysogenic phages, has a circular shape and becomes integrated by crossing over.

Both the F factor and the lysogenic phage chromosomes are called *episomes*. An episome is defined as a genetic particle that can exist either free or as a part of a normal cellular chromosome. Now we have good evidence for the existence of episomes only in bacteria; there are hints, however, that they exist in higher plants and animals as well.

At first the fact that only part of the male chromosome enters the female cell made genetic analysis more difficult. Then it was realized that a fixed end of the male chromosome, specific for a given Hfr strain, always enters the female cell first, and that the relative frequency with which male genes are incorporated into the recombinant chromosome is a measure of how close they are to the entering end. Moreover it is possible to break apart the male and female cells artificially by violent agitation (this was first done in a mixing machine called the Waring Blendor); matings can be made and the couples violently agitated at fixed times during the process (the Blendor experiments). If the pairs are disrupted soon after mating, only the genes very close to the forward end will have entered the cell. It is thus possible to obtain the *E. coli* gene positions merely by observing the time intervals at which various male alleles have entered the female cells.

BACTERIAL CHROMOSOMES ARE CIRCULAR

The genetic map obtained through analysis of interrupted matings is the same as that arrived at by analysis of frequencies of various recombinant classes. As in the chromosomal maps of higher organisms, the bacterial genes are arranged on an unbranched line. However, one important distinction exists: The

TABLE 7-1   *Key to the genes of the E. coli chromosome*[a]

Genetic symbols	Mutant character	Enzyme or reaction affected
araD	Cannot use the sugar arabinose as a carbon source	L-Ribulose-5-phosphate-4-epimerase
araA		L-Arabinose isomerase
araB		L-Ribulokinase
araC		
argB	Requires the amino acid arginine for growth	N-Acetylglutamate synthetase
argC		N-Acetyl-γ-glutamokinase
argH		N-Acetylglutamic-γ-semialdehyde dehydrogenase
argG		Acetylornithine-d-transaminase
argA		Acetylornithinase
argD		Ornithine transcarbamylase
argE		Argininosuccinic acid synthetase
argF		Argininosuccinase
aroA, B, C	Requires several aromatic amino acids and vitamins for growth	Shikimic acid to 3-enolpyruvyl-shikimate-5-phosphate
aroD		Biosynthesis of shikimic acid
azi	Resistant to sodium azide	
bio	Requires the vitamin biotin for growth	
cysA	Requires the amino acid cysteine for growth	
cysB		3-Phosphoadenosine-5-phosphosulfate to sulfide
cysC		Sulfate to sulfide; 4 known enzymes
dapA	Requires the cell wall component diaminopimelic acid	Dihydrodipicolinic acid synthetase
dapB		N-Succinyl-diaminopimelic acid deacylase
dap + hom	Requires the amino acid precursor homoserine and the cell-wall component diaminopimelic acid for growth	Aspartic semialdehyde dehydrogenase

T A B L E 7–1 (*continued*)

Genetic symbols	Mutant character	Enzyme or reaction affected
Dsd	Cannot use the amino acid D-serine as a nitrogen source	D-Serine deaminase
fla	Flagella are absent	
galA	Cannot use the sugar galactose as a carbon source	Galactokinase
galB		Galactose-1-phosphate uridyl transferase
galD		Uridine-diphosphogalactose-4-epimerase
gua	Requires the purine guanine for growth	
H	The H antigen is present	
his	Requires the amino acid histidine for growth	10 known enzymes[b]
ile	Requires the amino acid isoleucine for growth	Threonine deaminase
ilvA	Requires the amino acids isoleucine and valine for growth	α-Hydroxy-β-keto acid rectoisomerase
ilvB		α,β-dihydroxyisovaleric dehydrase[b]
ilvC		Transaminase B
ind (indole)	Cannot grow on tryptophan as a carbon source	Tryptophanase
λ	Chromosomal location where prophage λ is normally inserted	
lac Y	Unable to concentrate β-galactosides	Galactoside permease
lac Z	Cannot use the sugar lactose as a carbon source	β-Galactosidase
lac O	Constitutive synthesis of lactose operon proteins (see Chapter 14)	Defective operator
leu	Requires the amino acid leucine for growth	3 known enzymes[b]
lon (long form)	Filament formation and radiation sensitivity are affected	

(continued)

TABLE 7–1 (*continued*)

Genetic symbols	Mutant character	Enzyme or reaction affected
lys	Requires the amino acid lysine for growth	Diaminopimelic acid decarboxylase
lys + met	Requires the amino acids lysine and methionine for growth	
λ rec, malA	Resistant to phage λ and cannot use the sugar maltose	Phage λ receptor, and maltose permease
malB	Cannot use the sugar maltose as a carbon source	Amylomaltase(?)
metA	Requires the amino acid methionine for growth	Synthesis of succinic ester of homoserine
metB	Requires either the amino acid methionine or cobalamine for growth	Succinic ester of homoserine + cysteine to cystathionine
metF		5,10-Methylene tetrahydrofolate reductase
metE		
mtl	Cannot use the sugar mannitol as a carbon source	Mannitol dehydrogenase(?)
muc	Forms mucoid colonies	Regulation of capsular polysaccharide synthesis
O	The O antigen is present	
pan	Requires the vitamin pantothenic acid for growth	
phe A, B	Requires the amino acid phenylalanine for growth	
pho	Cannot use phosphate esters	Alkaline phosphatase
pil	Has filaments (pili) attached to the cell wall	
proA proB proC	Requires the amino acid proline for growth	

T A B L E 7–1 (*continued*)

Genetic symbols	Mutant character	Enzyme or reaction affected
purA		Adenylosuccinate synthetase
purB		Adenylosuccinase
purC, E	Requires certain purines for growth	5-Aminoimidazole ribotide (AIR) to 5-aminoimidazole-4-(N-succino carboximide) ribotide
purD		Biosynthesis of AIR
pyrA	Requires the pyrimidine uracil and the amino acid arginine for growth	Carbamate kinase
pyrB		Aspartate transcarbamylase
pyrC		Dihydroorotase
pyrD	Requires the pyrimidine uracil for growth	Dihydroorotic acid dehydrogenase
pyrE		Orotidylic acid pyrophosphorylase
pyrF		Orotidylic acid decarboxylase
R arg	Constitutive synthesis of arginine (see Chapter 14)	Repressor for enzymes involved in arginine synthesis
R gal	Constitutive production of galactose	Repressor for enzymes involved in galactose production
RI pho, R2 pho	Constitutive synthesis of phosphatase	Alkaline phosphatase repressor
R try	Constitutive synthesis of tryptophan	Repressor for enzymes involved in tryptophan synthesis
RC (RNA control)	Uncontrolled synthesis of RNA	
rha	Cannot use the sugar rhamnose as a carbon source	
serA		3-Phosphoglycerate dehydrogenase
serB	Requires the amino acid serine for growth	Phosphoserine phosphatase

(continued)

TABLE 7–1 (*continued*)

Genetic symbols	Mutant character	Enzyme or reaction affected
str	Resistant to or dependent on streptomycin	
suc	Requires succinic acid	
T1, T5 rec	Resistant to phages T1 and T5 (mutants called B/1,5)	T1, T5 receptor sites absent
T1 rec	Resistant to phage T1 (mutants called B/1)	T1 receptor site absent
T6, colK rec	Resistant to phage T6 and colicine K	T6 and colicine receptor sites absent
T4 rec	Resistant to phage T4 (mutants called B/4)	T4 receptor site absent
thi	Requires the vitamin thiamine for growth	
thr	Requires the amino acid threonine for growth	
thy	Requires the pyrimidine thymine for growth	Thymidylate synthetase
trpA		Tryptophan synthetase, A protein
trpB		Tryptophan synthetase, B protein
trpC	Requires the amino acid tryptophan for growth	Indole-3-glycerolphosphate synthetase
trpD		Phosphoribosyl anthranilate transferase
trpE		Anthranilate synthetase
tyr	Requires the amino acid tyrosine for growth	
uvrA	Resistant to ultraviolet radiation	Ultraviolet-induced lesions in DNA are reactivated
xyl	Cannot use the sugar xylose as a carbon source	

ᵃ Each known gene or gene cluster is listed by its symbol and with the character caused by a mutation in the gene or gene cluster. The enzyme affected or reaction prevented is listed where known.

ᵇ Denotes enzymes controlled by the homologous gene loci of *Salmonella typhimurium.*

genetic map of *E. coli* is a circle (Figure 7–13); the male chromosome must break at a certain point before a free end can move into a female cell. If the point of breakage were not always the same point, we would not observe that in a given bacterial strain some genes tend to be transferred before others. The place where the break occurs, however, is not the same in all strains. This is because the break always occurs at the point where the F factor is integrated. There is one Hfr strain, for example, in which some of the genes connected for the synthesis of threonine and leucine are transferred soon after mating, whereas in another, a gene involved in methionine synthesis is among the first to enter the female cell. The existence of many strains, with various breakage points, has been very important in assigning gene locations. If only one entering point existed, it would be nearly impossible to assign even a rough order to those genes that would always enter last, since they enter the female cell only rarely.

We are still not sure what force drives the male chromosome into the female cell. There are hints that the transfer may be connected to the process of chromosome duplication; that is, the male chromosome does not merely break and one end begin to be transferred. Instead it looks as if the breakage initiates a cycle of chromosome replication, and that as the Hfr chromosome splits to form two chromosomes, one of the progeny chromosomes moves into the female cell. Chromosome transfer may thus accompany the synthesis of a new chromosome or chromosome segment.

The biological significance of circular genetic maps is surrounded with mystery. Circular maps also exist for viral chromosomes, and so the *E. coli* form should not be viewed as a strange exception. We shall return to a discussion of circles when we look at the precise chemistry of the chromosome.

PHAGES OCCASIONALLY CARRY BACTERIAL GENES

Not only can bacterial genes be transferred in mating, but they can also be passively carried from one bacterium to another by phage particles (*transduction*). This happens when a virus particle is formed that accidentally contains a very small

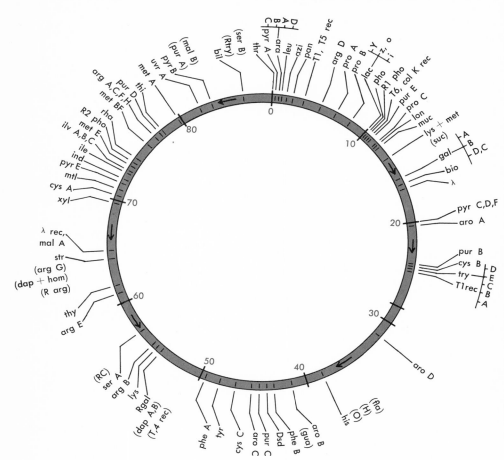

FIGURE 7–13   The genetic map of E. coli. The symbols mark the
locations of genes. A key to the various gene abbre-
viations is found in Table 7–1. Those genes whose
locations are only approximately known are shown in
parentheses. The numbers divide the map into time
intervals corresponding to the time in minutes which
it takes each male chromosomal segment to move into
a female cell. Thus 89 minutes are now thought to
be required for complete transfer. The arrows mark
the points at which various Hfr chromosomes break
prior to transfer into a female cell; the direction of
the arrows indicates transfer direction. [Redrawn
from A. L. Taylor and M. S. Thoman, Genetics, 50,
667 (1964), with permission.]

portion (usually less than 1 to 2 per cent) of its host chromosome (a *transducing phage*). When this virus particle (usually
biologically inactive because its viral chromosome is incomplete
or totally missing) attaches to a host cell, the fragment of
bacterial chromosome is injected into the cell. It then can
engage in crossing over with the host chromosome; if the
transducing phage has been grown on a bacterial strain genetically different from the strain subsequently infected with the
phage, a genetically altered bacterium may be produced
(Figure 7–14). For example, a suspension of phage particles
P1 grown on a strain of *E. coli* that is able to grow on lactose
contains a small number of particles carrying the gene (lac⁺)
involved in lactose metabolism. Addition of these phages to an

FIGURE 7–14   *Passive transfer of genetic material from one bacte-*
rium to another by means of carrier phage particles
(transduction).

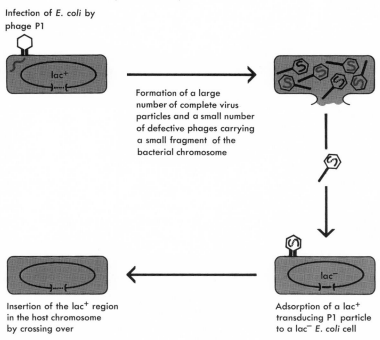

Infection of *E. coli* by
phage P1

Formation of a large
number of complete virus
particles and a small number
of defective phages carrying
a small fragment of the
bacterial chromosome

Insertion of the lac⁺ region
in the host chromosome
by crossing over

Adsorption of a lac⁺
transducing P1 particle
to a lac⁻ *E. coli* cell

E. coli strain unable to use lactose (lac⁻) transforms a small number of the lac⁻ bacteria to the lac⁺ form, by means of genetic recombination.

Because transduction is very rare, it might be guessed that it would not be a useful tool for probing chromosome structure. In fact, it has been most helpful in telling us whether two genes are located close to each other and what their exact order is. This is because the number of bacterial genes carried by a single transducing particle is small so that only genes located very close to each other will be enclosed in the same transducing particle. Thus by determining the frequencies with which groups of genes can be transduced by the same phage particle we can establish very accurately their relative locations.

TRANSFER OF PURIFIED CHROMOSOME FRAGMENTS

Transformation is the name given to genetic recombination brought about by the introduction of purified chromosomes (DNA). It has provided the crucial biological system for the chemical identification of the genetic material (DNA). Transformation was originally discovered in 1928, when the observation was made that the addition of heat-killed cells of a pathogenic strain of *Diplococcus pneumoniae* to a suspension of live, nonpathogenic pneumonia cells caused a small fraction of the live bacteria to become pathogenic. The hereditary nature of this transformation was shown by using descendants of the newly pathogenic strain to transform still other nonpathogenic bacteria. This suggested that when the pathogenic cells are killed by heat, their chromosomes (now known to be DNA) are undamaged, and free chromosomal material, liberated somehow from the heat-killed cells, can pass through the cell wall of the living cells and subsequently undergo genetic recombination with the host chromosome (Figure 7–15).

Subsequent experiments have confirmed the genetic interpretation of the transformation phenomenon. The pathogenic character is caused by a gene S (smooth), which affects the chemistry of the bacterial cell wall and causes the formation of a carbohydrate capsule. When the R (rough) allele of this gene is present instead, no capsule is formed, and the cell is not pathogenic.

Although the first transformation experiments involved only changes in capsule chemistry, it is now clear that all genes can be transformed by means of the addition of extracted chromosomes. Because only small chromosomal fragments are gen-

FIGURE 7–15   *Transformation of the genetic character of a bacterial cell (Diplococcus pneumonia) by addition of heat-killed cells of a genetically different strain. Here we show an R cell receiving a chromosomal fragment containing the S gene. Most R cells, however, receive other chromosome fragments, and so the efficiency of transformation for a given gene is usually less than 1 per cent.*

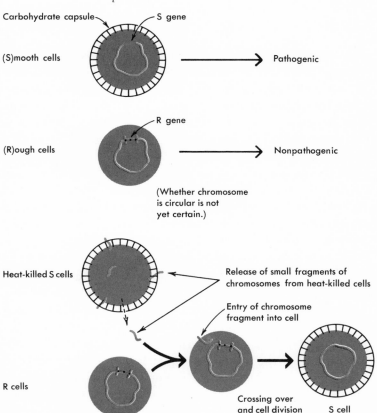

erally transformed in this way, this process can also reveal which genes are located close to each other. The fact that transformation of most types of bacteria is very inefficient has, up to now, severely restricted its general applicability to genetic problems. Thus transduction rather than transformation is our most efficient means of determining the precise order of *E. coli* genes. Transformation has, nevertheless, been very useful in locating the genes of the bacteria *Bacillus subtilis*, for which a useful transducing phage is not yet known.

Ever since transformation was first demonstrated, much speculation has existed whether it is possible in organisms larger than bacteria. Particular attention has been focused on the possibility of transforming mammals, especially man. So far, however, all results have been negative, except for some special cases where viral chromosomes are able to transform normal cells into cancer cells. Here, however, we may be dealing not with the change of an existing gene, but rather with the introduction of entirely new genetic material. In any case, though, too few good experiments have yet been performed to give us a feeling of whether this type of genetic analysis can be extended to higher organisms.

PHAGES ALSO MUTATE

The plaques formed by a given type of phage are quite characteristic and can often be distinguished easily from those of genetically distinct phages. For example, the plaques of phage T2 can easily be separated from those made by phage λ or by phage F2. More significantly, mutations occur that change the morphology of phage plaques. We do not usually know the biochemical basis of these plaque differences, but this does not really matter. The important fact is that these differences are usually reproducible and simple to score. It is easy to look at the morphology of thousands of plaques to see if any differ from the plaques made by the wild-type phage. In this way a large number of different plaque-type mutations were found (Figure 7-16).

Another class of mutations changes the ability of phage to

adsorb to bacteria. For example, wild-type T2 cannot multiply on *E. coli* strain B/2, because the B/2 mutation changes the cell surface, thereby preventing the attachment of T2. Mutant T2 particles can, however, multiply on B/2: They are called T2h, and are able to adsorb because they possess altered tail fibers.

Another very large and important class of mutants exists

FIGURE 7-16 *Photograph of mutant phage plaques. Shown are a mixture of T2r+ (wild-type) plaques and T2r (a rapid lysis mutant) plaques. The mottled plaques arise from the simultaneous growth of both r and r+ phages in the same plaque. (From G. S. Stent, Molecular Biology of Bacterial Viruses, Freeman, San Francisco, 1963, p. 177, with permission.)*

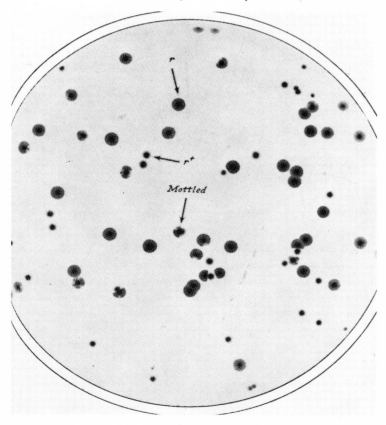

which have the ability to multiply at 25°C, but cannot multiply at 42°C (temperature-sensitive *conditional lethals*). Although we cannot now pinpoint the exact reason why these mutant phages do not multiply at the higher temperature, we suspect that the high temperature destroys the 3–D structure of a protein necessary for their reproduction. This type of mutation has proved useful because a large number of viral genes mutate to a temperature-sensitive form. When we isolate a mutant unable to multiply at the higher temperature, the mutation may be located in a large variety of different genes.

The existence of conditional lethal mutations has allowed phage geneticists to find mutations in essentially all the genes of phages T4 and λ. Despite the fact that genetic recombination between mutant viruses was not discovered until 1945, the phage T4 is now the best and most completely characterized genetic object.

PHAGE CROSSES

More than one phage particle at a time can grow in a single bacterium. If several particles adsorb at once, the chromosomes from all of them enter the cell and duplicate to form large numbers of new copies. So long as the chromosomes exist free (unenclosed by a protective coat) they can cross over with similar chromosomes (Figure 7–17). This is shown by infecting cells with two or more genetically distinct phage particles and finding recombinant genetic types among the progeny particles. For example, it is easy to obtain mutant T4 particles differing from the wild type by two mutations, one in an h gene, which allows them to grow on *E. coli* strain B/4 (a strain resistant to wild-type T4 particles) and the other in an r gene, which causes them to form larger and clearer plaques than wild-type T4 particles. These double mutant phages are designated T4hr, and the wild-type is called T4h⁺r⁺. When an *E. coli* cell is infected simultaneously with a T4h⁺r⁺ and a T4hr phage, four types of progeny particles are found: the parental genotypes h⁺r⁺ and hr, and the recombinant genotypes hr⁺ and h⁺r (Figure 7–18).

The frequency with which recombinants are found depends upon the particular mutants used in the cross. Crosses between some pairs of markers give almost 50 per cent recombinant phage; crosses between others give somewhat lower recombinant values, and sometimes almost no recombinants are found. This immediately suggests that viruses also have unbranched genetic maps, a suggestion now completely confirmed by intense analysis of a large number of independently isolated mutations. At present our best known map is that of phage T4 (Figure

FIGURE 7–17   *Genetic recombination following infection of a bacterium with several genetically distinct phage particles.*

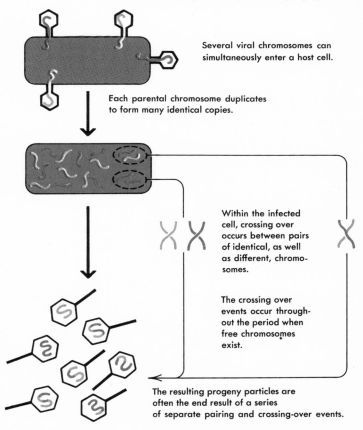

Several viral chromosomes can simultaneously enter a host cell.

Each parental chromosome duplicates to form many identical copies.

Within the infected cell, crossing over occurs between pairs of identical, as well as different, chromosomes.

The crossing over events occur throughout the period when free chromosomes exist.

The resulting progeny particles are often the end result of a series of separate pairing and crossing-over events.

7–19), a circular map, like that of *E. coli*. We do not know whether all viruses will have circular maps; hints now exist that several viruses previously thought to have strictly linear maps will be found to have circular ones.

FIGURE 7–18   *Plaques found after infecting bacteria with T2 hr and T2h⁺r⁺ phages. The technique used to see all four progeny types (hr, h⁺r⁺, h⁺r, hr⁺) is to look for plaques on a mixture of strain B and strain B/2. Only phages possessing the h gene can kill both B and B/2 cells. Phages with the h⁺ gene kill only B cells, and their plaques look turbid because of the presence of live B/2 cells. (From G. S. Stent, Molecular Biology of Bacterial Viruses, Freeman, San Francisco, 1963, p. 185, with permission.)*

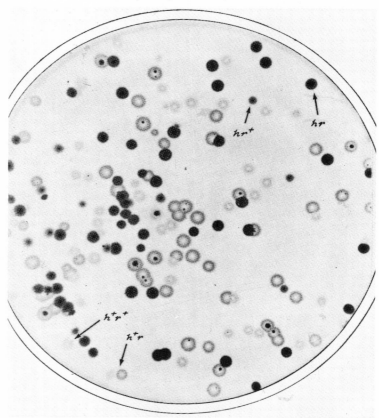

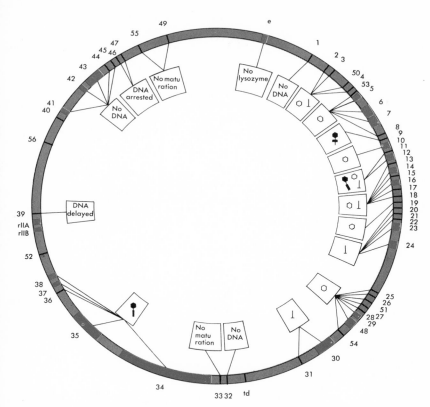

FIGURE 7-19 *The genetic map of T4. The numbers refer to a col-*
lection of 56 genes in which conditional lethal muta-
tions have been located. Their existence as distinct
genes has been shown by complementation studies
(see Chapter 8). The minimal length is shown for
some of the genes (color segments). The length of
other genes (black segments) has not yet been worked
out. The boxes show either deficiencies in synthe-
sis associated with some mutant genes or incomplete
viral components seen by EM investigation of infected
cells. The genes in the upper left of the circle control
functions in the first half of the life cycle. The re-
maining genes function in the last half of the cycle.
Nothing is known about how this differential timing
is accomplished.

VIRAL CROSSES INVOLVE MULTIPLE PAIRINGS

Thus the genetic structure of viral chromosomes appears to be essentially similar to that of cellular chromosomes. Nonetheless, it is worth pointing out a distinct feature of viral crosses. In conventional meiosis each chromosome pairs just once, whereas in a viral cross, pairing and crossing over may occur repeatedly throughout the period when free chromosomes are present. Thus a given chromosome may participate in several pairing and crossing over events. This point is simply demonstrated by infecting a cell with three virus particles, each with a distinct genetic marker, and finding single progeny particles that have derived chromosomal regions from all three particles. The products of a phage cross are essentially, then, the products of a large number of distinct pairings and crossings over. There is great variation among viruses in the amount of crossing over; for example, a chromosome of phage T4 crosses over, on the average, 5 to 10 times, and a phage λ chromosome only 0.5 times, during each growth cycle. The existence of many distinct crossovers does not, however, restrict our ability to map the genetic markers, since the general rule still holds that genes located close together seldom recombine.

Another way in which a viral cross differs from conventional meiosis involving cell fusion is that viruses are not separated into male and female particles. Differentiation into sexes can be considered a device to bring about cell fusion between genetically distinct organisms. Virus particles, however, do not have to fuse, since genetic recombination occurs when two viral chromosomes of different genotypes enter a single host cell. Moreover, in cells infected with several genetically distinct viruses, crossing over can occur between both genetically identical and different chromosomes; thus only a fraction of the crossovers in a cell infected with different viruses result in recombinant chromosomes of a new genotype. Evidence also exists that crossing over occurs after infection with a single virus particle. This phenomenon cannot be revealed by genetic analysis, since all the progeny chromosomes are genetically identical, and so experiments with isotopically labeled virus (see Chapter 9) are necessary for its demonstration.

SUMMARY

Chromosomes control the hereditary properties of all cells and are linear collections of specific genetic factors called genes. Each gene can affect the character of a cell in a highly specific way. This is shown by the striking cellular effects of hereditary changes in gene structures (mutations): Various mutations can alter, for example, the eye color or body size of an organism. Although spontaneous mutations occur only rarely, it is possible to increase mutation rates by applying specific chemicals or radiation (mutagens).

Most of the early work in genetics was with large and complicated diploid plants and animals. Now, however, the most favorable objects for use in studying what a gene is and how it functions are the haploid microorganisms like the bacteria and their viruses, the bacteriophages (phages). They have the advantage of very short life cycles and ease of growth under controllable laboratory conditions.

Bacterial mutations involving growth factors and resistance to specific antibiotics and viruses are particularly useful because of the ease of separating wild-type and mutant particles. The same is true for phage mutations involving host range and temperature requirements.

The location of genes on chromosomes is revealed by a study of the segregation of genes in genetic crosses. Recombination of alleles can be caused by both random assortment of chromosomes and crossing over of homologous chromosomes. We can determine whether given genes are located on different or the same chromosomes by whether they assort randomly, as chromosomes do, or whether they exhibit (more than 50 per cent) linkage. Crossing over of homologous chromosomes provides a basis for determining the relative positions of genes on chromosomes (chromosome mapping). The more frequently crossovers occur between two genes, the farther apart the genes must be. When three genes are considered at once (three-factor cross), the least frequent recombinant type results from a double crossover; the determination of this recombinant type provides a check for the results of several two-factor crosses dealing with the same three factors.

Most genetic crosses designed to reveal what genes are are now performed with bacteria and phages, where typical meiosis does not occur. Bacterial crosses usually involve crossovers between a chromosome fragment and an intact chromosome. Genetic recombination occurs in bacteria as a result of mating between male (Hfr) and female cells (conjugation), attachment of phage particles containing the genes of former bacterial hosts (transduction), and the introduction of foreign chromosomal (DNA) extracts (transformation). Phage crosses take place when a bacterium is infected with two or more genetically distinct phages; they involve many cycles of pairing and crossing over. Despite the difficulties which these phenomena present to the study of phage and bacterial genetics, the chromosomes of the bacterium E. coli and the phage T4 are quickly becoming the best understood of all genetic material.

REFERENCES

Hayes, W., *The Genetics of Bacteria and Their Viruses: Studies in Basic Genetics and Molecular Biology*, 2nd ed., Wiley, New York, 1969. A comprehensive description of the genetic systems of viruses and bacteria showing how they have been used to elucidate many of the fundamental principles of molecular genetics.

Stent, G. S., *Molecular Biology of Bacterial Viruses*, Freeman, San Francisco, 1963. An example of that rare item—a nearly perfect book. Here are lucidly presented both the past and present ideas about bacterial viruses.

Adelberg, E. A. (ed.), *Papers on Bacterial Genetics*, 2nd ed., Little, Brown, Boston, 1966. A collection of significant reprints on the development of bacterial genetics.

Stent, G. S. (ed.), *Papers on Bacterial Viruses*, 2nd ed., Little, Brown, Boston, 1965. A collection of many of the papers that shaped the development of current research with bacterial viruses.

Whitehouse, H. L. K., *Towards an Understanding of the Mechanism of Heredity*, 2nd ed., Edward Arnold, London, 1969. A very good general genetics text with much emphasis on crossing over.

Herskowitz, I. H., *Basic Principles of Molecular Genetics*, Little, Brown, Boston, 1967. A thorough treatment of many aspects of molecular genetics.

8

GENE

STRUCTURE

AND

FUNCTION

FOR MANY YEARS IT WAS GENERALLY thought that crossing over occurred between genes, not within the genes themselves. The chromosome was viewed as a linear collection of genes held together by some nongenetic material, somewhat like a string of pearls. Now, however, we realize that this viewpoint is completely wrong and the exact opposite may be true—all crossing over may occur by breakage and reunion of the genetic molecules themselves. The original impression arose from the fact that crossing over between two regions is much easier to detect if the regions are far apart on a chromosome. If they are very close, recombination is extremely rare and can be detected only by examining a very large number of progeny, too large to make study of intragenic recombination practicable when genetic work was restricted to higher organisms. Even with the intensively studied fruit fly *Drosophila*, it is difficult to look at more than 50,000 progeny from a single cross. Newer techniques, however, permit rapid screening of millions of the progeny from crosses between genetically different molds, yeast, bacteria, or viruses. With these organisms it has been simple to show that crossing over can cause recombination of material within a gene. Each gene contains a number of different sites at which mutations occur and between which crossing over occurs. This result provides a powerful method for investigating topological structures of genes.

RECOMBINATION WITHIN GENES ALLOWS CONSTRUCTION OF A GENE MAP

Up to now, the most striking results on the genetic structure of the gene itself have come from the work with the rIIA and rIIB genes of the bacterial virus T4. These are two adjacent genes which influence the length of the T4 life cycle; mutations in both thereby affect the size of plaques produced in a bacterial layer growing on an agar plate. The presence of either an rIIA or an rIIB mutation can cause a shorter life cycle of T4 phage within an *E. coli* cell. T4-infected cells on an agar plate normally do not break open and release new progeny phage until several hours after they have been infected. Cells infected with rII mutants, however, always break open more rapidly, hence the designation r (II stands for the fact that there do exist other genes which cause rapid cell lysis). Thus rII mutants produce larger plaques than wild-type phage. The rII mutants were chosen to work with because of the possibility of detecting a very small number of wild-type particles among a very large number of mutants. Although the wild-type and the rII mutants grow equally well on *E. coli* strain B, there is another strain, *E. coli* K(λ), on which only the wild-type can multiply. Thus when the progeny of a genetic cross between two different rII mutants are added to K12(λ), only the wild-type recombinants form plaques. Even as few as one wild-type recombinant per 10^6 progeny is easily detected.

Over two thousand independent mutations in the rIIA and rIIB genes have been isolated and used in breeding experiments. In a typical cross, *E. coli* strain B bacteria were infected with two phage particles, each bearing an independently isolated rIIA (or rIIB) mutation. As the virus particles multiplied, genetic recombination occurred. The progeny were then grown on *E. coli* K(λ) to test for the wild type. Normal particles were found in a very large fraction of the crosses, indicating recombination within the gene (Figure 8–1). If recombination occurred only *between* genes it would be impossible to produce wild-type recombinants by crossing two phage particles with mutations in the same gene. A large spectrum of recombination values was found, just as in crosses

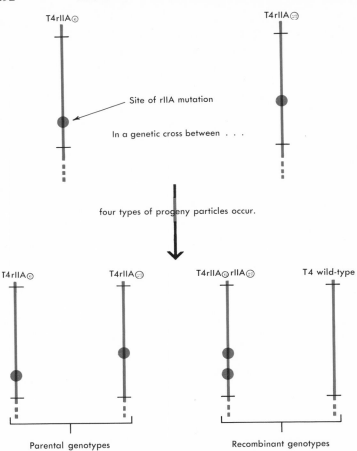

FIGURE 8-1   The use of T4rII mutations in the demonstration of crossing over within the gene. Equal numbers of wild-type and double r recombinants occur. The wild-type recombinants are easily found, because they are the only progeny genotype which will form plaques on $K12(\lambda)$. It is much harder to identify the double $rIIA_6rIIA_{27}$ recombinants, inasmuch as their plaques are indistinguishable from single r plaques. To detect them, it is necessary to isolate a large number of progeny r viruses with the r phenotype and use them for new genetic crosses with both parent r strains. The double r mutants will not produce wild-type recombinants with either of the single r mutants.

between mutants for separate genes. This spread of values indicates that some mutations occur closer together than others, and allows for the construction of genetic maps for the two rII genes. Examination of these genetic maps yields the following striking conclusions:

1. A large number of different sites of mutation (mutable sites) occur within the gene. This number is on the order of 1000 to 1500 altogether for the rIIA and rIIB genes (Figure 8–2).

2. The rIIA and rIIB genetic maps are unambiguously linear, strongly hinting that the gene itself has a linear construction.

3. Most mutations are changes at only one mutable site. Genes containing such mutations are able to be restored to the original wild-type gene structure by the process of undergoing a second (reverse) mutation at the same site as the first mutation.

4. Other mutations cause the deletion of significant fractions of the genetic map. These are the result of a physical deletion of part of the rII gene (Figure 8–3). Mutations deleting more than one mutable site are highly unlikely to mutate back to the original gene form.

The genetic fine structure of a number of other viral and bacterial genes has also been extensively mapped. The lengths of these maps vary from gene to gene, suggesting that some gene products are larger than others. Though no other study has been as extensive as the rII work, each points to the same conclusions—that all genes have a very large number of sites at which mutation can occur, and that these mutable sites are arranged in a strictly linear order. The geneticist's view of a gene is thus: *a discrete chromosomal region which (1) is responsible for a specific cellular product and (2) consists of a linear collection of potentially mutable units (mutable sites), each of which can exist in several alternative forms and between which crossing over can occur.*

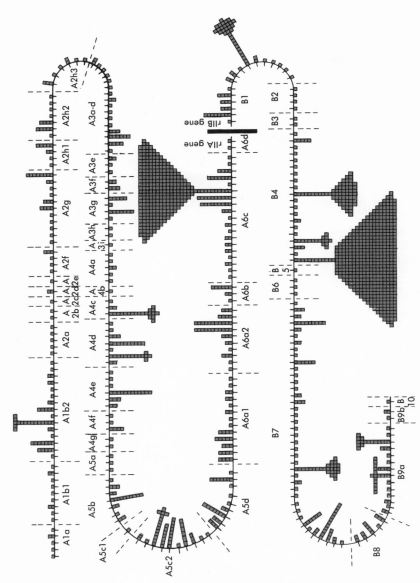

FIGURE 8–2 The genetic map of the rIIA and rIIB genes of phage T4. This map shows the assignment of a large number of different mutations in specific regions (A1a, A1b, etc.) of the gene. In most cases, the order of the mutations within a given region has not yet been determined. Each square corresponds to an independent occurrence of a

234

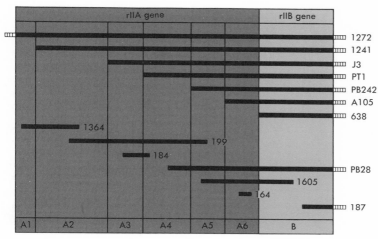

FIGURE 8–3 *Deletion mutations within the rII region of T4. About 10 per cent of the spontaneous rII mutations do not map at a distinct point. They are due to deletions of a large number of adjacent mutable sites. Some deletions, for example 1272, involve both the rIIA and rIIB genes. The small rectangles indicate that the deletion most likely extends into the adjacent gene. The existence of deletion mutations has considerably facilitated genetic mapping. By crossing a newly isolated rII mutant with a number of deletion mutations covering increasingly larger regions, it is quickly possible to assign an approximate map location to the new mutant. In this map the size of the rIIB gene has been arbitrarily reduced.*

THE COMPLEMENTATION TEST DETERMINES IF TWO MUTATIONS ARE IN THE SAME GENE

Since mutations in both the rIIA and rIIB genes result in a larger sized plaque, it is natural to ask why they are considered two genes: Would it not be simpler to consider them parts of the same gene? Our answer is straightforward. If *E. coli* strain K12(λ) is infected simultaneously with a T4rIIA and a T4rIIB mutant, the chromosomes of both viruses multiply, and progeny virus is produced (Figure 8–4). In contrast, simultaneous infection of the K12(λ) with either two different T4rIIA or two different T4rIIB mutants results in no virus multiplication. This demonstrates that rIIA and rIIB genes carry out two different functions, each necessary for multiplication on K12(λ).

In infection with a single T4rIIA mutant, the rIIB gene functions normally, but no active form of the rIIA product is available, so that no viral multiplication is possible. Likewise, in infection with a single rIIB mutant, an active rIIA product results, but only an inactive form of the rIIB product arises. Virus multiplication only occurs when we simultaneously infect a bacterium with an rIIA phage mutant and an rIIB phage mutant because each mutant chromosome is able to produce

FIGURE 8–4   *The demonstration that the rII region consists of two distinct genes which can complement each other during simultaneous infection.*

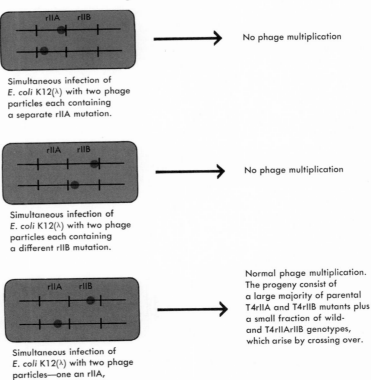

Simultaneous infection of
E. coli K12(λ) with two phage
particles each containing
a separate rIIA mutation.

No phage multiplication

Simultaneous infection of
E. coli K12(λ) with two phage
particles each containing
a different rIIB mutation.

No phage multiplication

Simultaneous infection of
E. coli K12(λ) with two phage
particles—one an rIIA,
the other an rIIB mutation.

Normal phage multiplication.
The progeny consist of
a large majority of parental
T4rIIA and T4rIIB mutants plus
a small fraction of wild-
and T4rIIArIIB genotypes,
which arise by crossing over.

the gene product that its infecting partner is unable to make. Two chromosomes thus can *complement* each other when the mutations are present in distinct genes—*the complementation test.* (This experiment is not affected by the possibility of intragenic crossing over between mutants to produce wild-type phage, because the number of such recombinants is very small; in contrast, complementation between different mutant genes yields a normal number of progeny particles.)

It is easy to perform complementation tests with phage mutants. All that is necessary is to infect a bacterium with two different mutants at once. This automatically creates a cell containing one copy of each mutant chromosome. It is more difficult to carry out complementation tests with normally haploid cells, like *E. coli.* But fortunately, genetic tricks too complicated to be described here enable special strains to be constructed with some chromosome sections present twice (partially diploid strains). These have often been useful in telling us that a chromosomal region thought to contain only one gene actually produces several gene products, and so must contain a corresponding number of genes.

GENETIC CONTROL OF PROTEIN FUNCTION

A direct relationship between genes and enzymes was hypothesized as early as 1909 from a study of the metabolism of phenylalanine in patients suffering from certain hereditary diseases; but it was not until the decade following 1941, when a variety of growth factor mutants became available in *Neurospora* and *E. coli*, that the one gene–one enzyme hypothesis became an established fact. One of the first proofs involved the biosynthesis of the amino acid arginine. Its pathway starts with glutamic acid and proceeds by eight chemical reactions, each catalyzed by a distinct enzyme (Figure 8–5). For each of these eight steps mutant cells have been isolated that fail to carry out that specific enzymatic reaction. This suggests that a separate gene controls the presence of each enzyme, a hypothesis confirmed by the absence of the specific active enzyme in cell extracts prepared from such mutant cells. The biosynthesis of histidine (Figure 8–6) provides another beautiful example of this relationship: There exist specific mutations resulting in the absence of each of the ten enzymes necessary for this biosynthesis.

FIGURE 8–5   *Pathway of arginine biosynthesis in E. coli.*

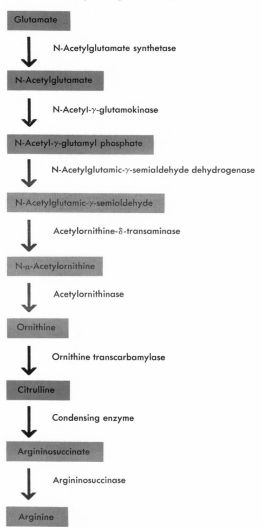

Enzymes are not the only proteins directly controlled by genes. Each specific protein is controlled by a gene unique for that protein. One of the first clean proofs of this idea came from the study of the hemoglobin present in people suffering

FIGURE 8–6 *The pathway for histidine biosynthesis in* Salmonella typhimurium. *This bacterium, which is closely related to* E. coli, *appears to have a chromosome with a similar gene arrangement.*

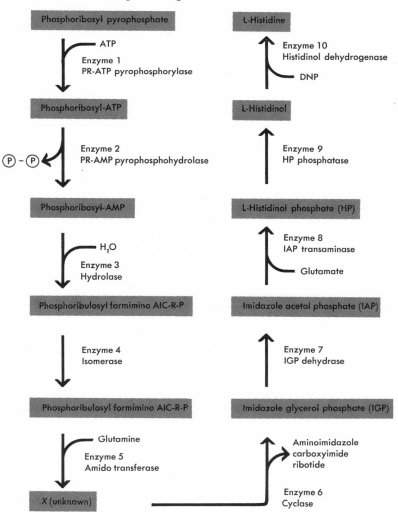

from sickle-cell anemia. This is a disease whose genetic basis is well worked out. If the sickle (*s*) gene is present in both homologous chromosomes, a severe anemia results, characterized by the red blood cells having a sickle shape. If only one *s* gene is present, and the allele in the homologous chromosome is normal (+), the anemia is less severe, and the red blood cells almost normal in shape. The type of hemoglobin in red blood cells is likewise correlated with the genetic pattern. In the *ss* case, all the hemoglobin is of an abnormal type, characterized by a solubility different from that of normal hemoglobin, whereas in the +*s* condition, half the hemoglobin is normal and half sickle.

Even now it is often hard to identify the protein product of a given gene. One of the most annoying cases involves the rII region of T4. We still do not know the biochemical changes that underlie the larger plaques produced by rII mutant phages and, despite much effort, no one has yet found a specific protein absent in *E. coli* cells infected with T4rII mutants and present in cells infected with wild-type phage. Thus there is now a strong tendency to concentrate further genetic analysis on those genes for which we already know how to isolate the corresponding protein.

ONE GENE—ONE POLYPEPTIDE CHAIN

Until recently, the above ideas were stated by the slogan "one gene–one protein (enzyme)." Now we realize that a more correct statement is "one gene–one polypeptide chain." When a protein contains more than one polypeptide chain, each chain is made separately. Only after their synthesis do they aggregate to form the final protein. Generally, the two or more polypeptide chains needed to form a functional protein are controlled by adjacent genes. This is, however, not always the case. The α and β hemoglobin chains are not controlled by linked genes. The complementation test thus tells us not whether two genes control different proteins, but rather, if they control two different polypeptide chains.

RECESSIVE GENES FREQUENTLY DO NOT PRODUCE FUNCTIONAL PRODUCTS

Most mutant genes are recessive with respect to wild-type genes. This fact, puzzling to early geneticists, is now partially understood in terms of the gene-enzyme relation. The recessive phenotype often results from the failure of mutant genes to produce *any* functional protein (enzyme). In heterozygotes, however, there is always present one "good" gene, and correspondingly, a number of good gene products. Because the wild-type gene is present only once in heterozygotes, the possibility exists that there are always fewer good copies of the relevant protein in heterozygotes than in individuals with two wild-type genes. If this were the case, we might guess that the heterozygous phenotype would tend to be intermediate between the two homozygous phenotypes. Usually, however, this does not happen, for one of two reasons. Either there are still enough good enzyme molecules to catalyze the metabolic reaction even though the total number is reduced, or the recessive gene is not noticeable, because control mechanisms cause the wild-type gene in a heterozygote to produce more gene products than does each wild-type gene in a homozygote. In Chapter 14 we shall discuss how the rate at which a gene acts may be controlled.

GENES WITH RELATED FUNCTIONS ARE OFTEN ADJACENT

Until ten years ago, geneticists believed that the chromosomal location of genes was purely random; there seemed to be no tendency for genes with related effects to be located near each other. Now, however, there are strong indications from viral and bacterial genetics that a sizable fraction of genes are situated in groups carrying out related functions. There are two main reasons for this change.

First, many geneticists now study mutations directly affecting the biosynthesis of known cellular molecules. Until the advent of work with microorganisms, most genetic markers involved very complex characters, like eye color or wing shape. The development of wings or eyes is, from a chemical viewpoint, fantastically complicated; clearly there is a large variety of *unrelated chemical reactions* whose absence might lead to a misshapen wing. It is thus not surprising that genes affecting the wings occur in many places on all *Drosophila's* four different chromosomes. In contrast, a mutant character that shows itself as the inability to synthesize a relatively simple molecule like the amino acid serine is most likely due to the absence of one of a much smaller number of *related chemical reactions*. If related genes are, indeed, next to each other on a chromosome, we are more likely to observe this phenomenon when we are studying mutations that we can assign immediately to a particular category of chemical upset.

The second main reason why we now frequently find adjacent genes with related functions is the availability of the complementation test. This often tells us that a chemical phenomenon is more complicated than originally guessed. The splitting of the rII region into the rIIA and rIIB genes is a typical case. Numerous situations now exist where a region previously thought to contain a single gene has been shown by complementation tests to perform a number of different, yet related, tasks. Subsequent biochemical investigations have then revealed that several chemical reactions (enzymes) are involved. One of the most spectacular examples involves the ability of *E. coli* to synthesize histidine. Twenty years ago we would have guessed that a series of mutations blocking histidine synthesis and mapping in the same region all fell in the same gene. Today, however, ten different genes in this region have been identified (Figure 8–7), each concerned with a different enzyme in the biosynthesis of histidine starting from phosphoribosyl pyrophosphate. Likewise, the region concerned with tryptophan biosynthesis contains a cluster of five different genes, each concerned with a distinct step (enzyme) in the biosynthesis of tryptophan.

At first it was thought that the order of genes in the cluster corresponded to the order of their respective enzymes in the biosynthetic pathway. Now, however, there are several known exceptions to the rule. For example, the first two enzymes in histidine biosynthesis are located at opposite ends of the cluster.

Clusters of related genes are not always connected with the biosynthesis of essential metabolites. Degradation of many specific food molecules, such as the sugars galactose and lactose, also involves several consecutive chemical reactions; these also tend to be controlled by adjacent genes. Galactose breakdown requires three specific chemical steps, and lactose utilization at least two, probably three, different genes. Another striking example of adjacent related genes concerns genetic control of various structural proteins found in the protective coat of phage T4: The genes affecting the synthesis of head proteins are in one region, and those affecting the tail fibers in another.

The grouping together of related genes is connected with the fact, which we shall examine in detail in Chapter 14, that all genes do not function at the same time. Mechanisms exist that tell genes whether or not to work. For example, the genes controlling lactose metabolism function only when a cell is growing on lactose; when lactose is absent, there is no need for these genes to work. The switching on and off of the genes is controlled by a specific molecule, the lactose repressor. As we

FIGURE 8–7   *Clustering of the genes involved in the biosynthesis of histidine by the bacterium* Salmonella typhimurium. *The gene order was determined by transduction experiments. Each gene is responsible for the synthesis of one of the 10 enzymes needed to transform phosphoribosyl pyrophosphate into histidine. Here the genes are designated by numbers 1–10. Enzyme 1 is responsible for catalyzing the first reaction in the biosynthesis, enzyme 2 for the second step, etc. The names of these enzymes are given in Figure 8–6.*

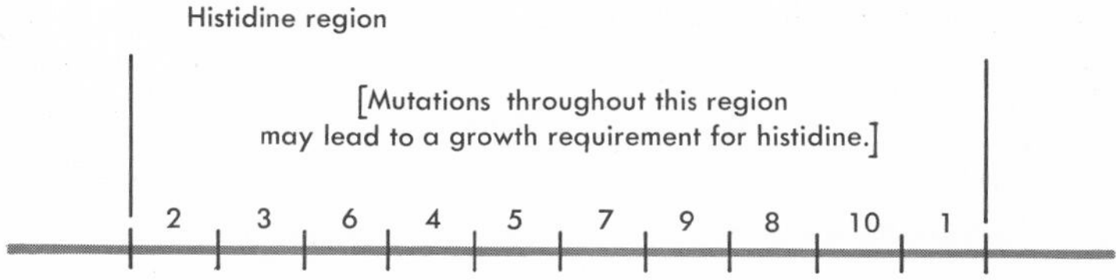

Histidine region

[Mutations throughout this region
may lead to a growth requirement for histidine.]

2   3   6   4   5   7   9   8   10   1

shall see in Chapter 14, the ability of these repressor molecules to simultaneously control the synthesis of several proteins is dependent upon the fact that the corresponding genes are physically adjacent.

PROOF THAT GENES CONTROL
AMINO ACID SEQUENCES IN PROTEINS

The first experimental demonstration that genes control amino acid sequences involved sickle-cell hemoglobin. Wild-type hemoglobin molecules are constructed from two different kinds of polypeptide chains: α chains and β chains. Each chain has a molecular weight of about 16,100. Two α chains and two β chains are present in each molecule, giving hemoglobin a molecular weight of about 64,500. The α and β chains are controlled by two distinct genes, so a single mutation will affect either the α or the β chain but not both. Sickle hemoglobin differs from normal hemoglobin by the change of one amino acid in the β chain: at position 6 (Figure 8–8), the glutamic acid residue found in the wild-type hemoglobin is replaced by valine. Except for this one change the entire amino acid sequence is identical in normal and mutant hemoglobin peptides. This shows that a mutation in a gene results in a specific change in the template for hemoglobin, and strongly hints that all the information required to order hemoglobin amino acid sequences is present in the genes. Strongly supporting this belief are the analyses of amino acid sequences in hemoglobin isolated from persons suffering from other forms of anemia; here sequence analysis shows that each specific anemia is characterized by a single amino acid replacement at a unique site along the polypeptide chain.

The impracticality of large-scale breeding experiments with mammals makes it impossible to correlate the changes in hemoglobin sequences with the location of the various mutations along the genetic map. It is, however, possible to do this form of analysis with altered enzymes found in microorganisms whose genetics are well known.

COLINEARITY OF THE GENE
AND ITS POLYPEPTIDE PRODUCT

The best understood example of the relationship between the order of the mutable sites in a gene and the order of their corresponding amino acid replacements involves the *E. coli* enzyme tryptophan synthetase, one of the several enzymes in-

FIGURE 8–8   *A summary of the established amino acid substitutions in human hemoglobin variants.*

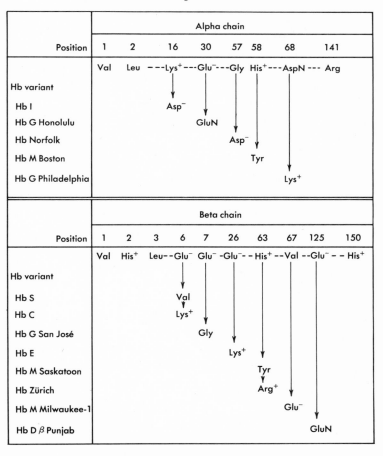

volved in tryptophan synthesis (Figure 8–9). This enzyme consists of two easily separable polypeptide chains, A and B, neither of which is enzymatically active by itself. A large number of mutants unable to synthesize tryptophan have been isolated; they lack a functional A chain and so are enzymatically inactive. When these mutants were genetically analyzed, it was found that changes at a large number of different mutable sites can give rise to inactive A chains. Accurate mapping of these

FIGURE 8–9 *Last steps in the pathway of tryptophan biosynthesis.*

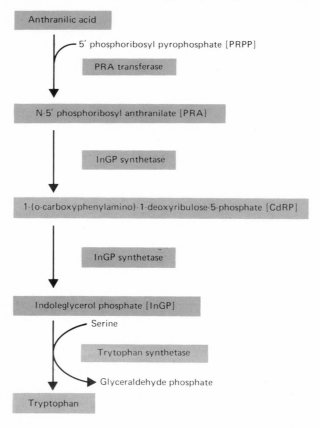

mutants revealed that they all could be unambiguously located on the linear genetic map shown in Figure 8–10. It was possible to isolate the inactive A chains from many of these mutants and to begin to compare their amino acid sequences with the sequence of the wild-type A chain, which contains 267 amino acids. This sequence allows us to see how the location of a mutation within a gene is correlated with the location of amino acid replacements in its polypeptide chain product. Since both genes and polypeptide chains are linear, the simplest hypothesis is that amino acid replacements are in the same relative order as the mutationally altered sites in the corresponding mutant genes. This was most pleasingly demonstrated in 1964. The location of each specific amino acid replacement is exactly correlated (colinearity) with its location along the genetic map (shown in Figure 8–10). Thus each amino acid in a polypeptide chain is controlled (coded) by a specific region of the gene.

A MUTABLE SITE CAN EXIST IN SEVERAL ALTERNATIVE FORMS

Enzymatically inactive tryptophan synthetase molecules resulting from different mutations of the *same* mutable site (as shown by failure to give wild-type recombinants) do not always contain the same amino acid replacement. For example, depending upon the exact mutant strain examined, a change at the same mutable site will result in glycine being replaced by either glutamic acid or valine. This result means that a mutable site can exist in at least three alternative forms. In the next chapter, we shall discuss other evidence which tells us that the mutable sites are the deoxynucleotide building blocks from which the genes (regions of DNA molecules) are constructed. Since only four types of deoxynucleotides exist, this leads us to expect that genetic evidence will never show more than four alternative configurations for a mutable site.

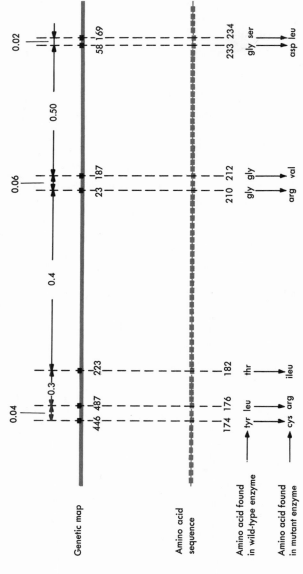

FIGURE 8-10 *Colinearity of the gene and its protein product. Here is illustrated the genetic map for one-fourth of the gene coding for the amino acid sequences in the E. coli protein tryptophan synthetase A. The symbols ←0.04→, etc. refer to map distances (frequencies of recombination) between the various tryptophan synthetase mutations A446, A487, etc. The numbers in the amino acid sequence refer to their position in the 267 residues of the A protein. Following convention, the amino terminal end of the segment is on the left.*

248

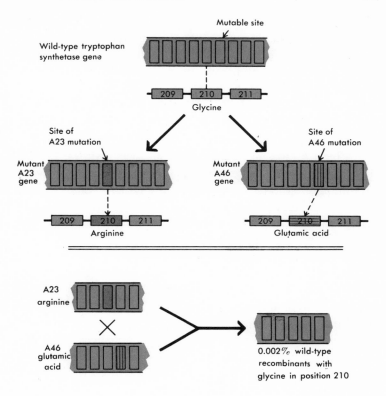

FIGURE 8–11 *Demonstration that a single amino acid is specified by more than one mutable site (see text for details).*

SINGLE AMINO ACIDS ARE SPECIFIED BY SEVERAL ADJACENT MUTABLE SITES

A one-to-one relationship between mutable sites and specific amino acids does not exist. Instead, there is genetic evidence showing that some, if not all, amino acids are jointly specified by several adjacent sites. The relevant evidence comes from the study of residue 47 of the tryptophan synthetase fragment illustrated in Figure 8–10. Treatment with a mutagen of the wild strain has given rise to mutant A23, in which arginine replaces glycine, and the mutant A46, in which glutamic acid replaces glycine. The difference between A23 and A46 does not involve changes to alternative forms of the same mutable site, since a genetic cross between A23 and A46 yields a number of wild-type (glycine in position 210) recombinants (Figure 8–11). If these changes were at the same mutable site, no wild-type recombinants could be produced. The very low frequency of the wild-type recombination suggests that the mutable sites involved may be adjacent to each other.

Another type of evidence suggesting that several mutable sites code for a single amino acid comes from observing how A23 and A46 themselves mutate upon treatment with mutagens. After exposure to a mutagen, both strains can give rise to new strains containing tryptophan synthetase molecules with glycine in position 210. These reverse mutations most likely involve changing the altered mutable sites back to the original wild-type configuration. However, strains also arise in which the amino acid in position 210 is replaced by another amino acid. Most significantly, the type of possible replacement differs for strains A23 and A46. Strain A23, besides back-mutating to glycine, mutates to threonine and serine, whereas A46 mutates to alanine and valine, in addition to glycine. The failure of A23 ever to give rise to alanine or valine, whereas A46 never mutates to threonine or serine, is very difficult to explain if their differences from wild types are based on the possession of alternative configurations of the same mutable site. Instead, if the changes are at two different sites, then a change from arginine to valine might require changes at both sites and so occur at too low a level to be detected under ordinary mutagen treatment.

These experiments by themselves place only the lower limit (two) of the number of mutable sites coding for a single amino acid. Much more extensive results would be necessary before an upper limit could be assigned on the basis of these types of experimentation. In the next chapter we shall talk about other evidence which tells us that three mutable sites (nucleotides) specify a given amino acid.

UNIQUE AMINO ACID SEQUENCES ARE NOT REQUIRED FOR ENZYME ACTIVITY

The ability of a chain to be enzymatically active does not demand a unique amino acid sequence. This is shown by examination of the new mutant strains obtained by treating

strains A23 and A46 with mutagens. The fact that the possession of either glycine or serine in position 210 yields a fully active
enzyme (Figure 8–12), whereas threonine in the same position
yields an enzyme with reduced activity, demonstrates that the
activity of an enzyme does not demand a unique amino acid
sequence. In fact, a variety of evidence now indicates that
amino acid replacements in many parts of a polypeptide chain
can occur without seriously modifying catalytic activity. Most

F I G U R E 8–12   *Evidence that many amino acid replacements do not*
result in loss of enzymatic activity (see text for
details). We have arbitrarily shown the mutations
occurring at the same mutable site.

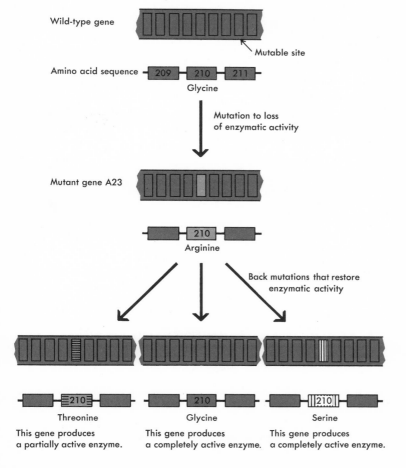

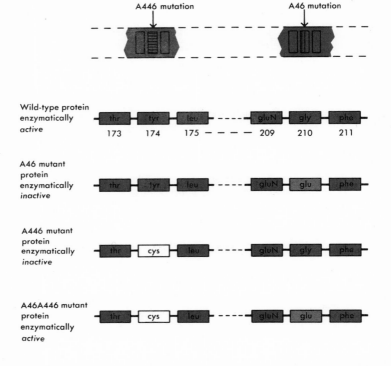

FIGURE 8–13 *Reversal (suppression) of mutant phenotype by a second mutation at a second site in the same gene.*

likely, however, one sequence is best suited to a cell's particular needs, and it is this sequence that is coded for by the wild-type allele. Even though other sequences are almost as good, they will tend to be selected against in evolution unless they are equally functional.

*Why aren't
these equaoluo
& setine
genes in (8-12)?*

"REVERSE" MUTATIONS SOMETIMES CAUSE A SECOND AMINO ACID REPLACEMENT

The conclusion that a unique amino acid sequence is not necessary for enzyme activity is extended by the finding that some mutations, which convert inactive mutant enzyme to an active form, work by causing a second amino acid replacement in the mutant enzyme. If we start with cells of mutant A46, which

produces inactive tryptophan synthetase because of the substitution of arginine for glycine, distant second site mutations
that result in active enzyme occasionally emerge. For example,
the second site mutation A446 is located one-tenth of a gene
length away from the first (Figure 8–13). The double mutant
A46A446 produces active enzyme molecules containing two
amino acid replacements: the original glycine-to-arginine shift,
and a tyrosine-to-cysteine shift located 36 amino acids away.

The second shift can be studied independently of the first
by obtaining recombinant cells with only the A446 mutation.
Most interestingly, the A446 change when present alone also results in an inactive enzyme. We thus see that a combination of
two wrong amino acids can produce an enzyme with an active
3-D configuration. Only sometimes do two wrong amino acids,
however, cancel out each other's faults. For example, double
mutants containing A446 and A23, or A446 and A187, do not
produce active enzyme. It does not now seem wise to speculate
on how the various amino acid residues are folded together in
the 3-D configuration, and why only some combinations are
enzymatically active. This kind of analysis must await the
establishment of the 3-D structure of tryptophan synthetase.

SUMMARY

*Crossing over occurs within the gene, thereby making possible
the mapping of mutations within the gene. Like the order of
genes on a chromosome, the arrangement of mutable sites in a
gene is strictly linear. There appear to be many mutation sites
within an average gene (500 to 1500). Sometimes it is initially
difficult to determine whether a chromosomal region contains
more than one gene; this usually can be resolved by introducing
more than one chromosome (or chromosomal fragment) mutant
for that region into a cell. If two mutants can complement
each other, their mutations must be in different genes (the
complementation test).*

*Genes control a cell's phenotype by determining which pro-
teins the cell can synthesize. Each gene is responsible for the
synthesis of a specific polypeptide. Genes work by controlling
the sequence of amino acids in proteins. This is clearly shown
by the discovery that many mutations cause the production of*

protein molecules that differ from normal protein by a single amino acid replacement. Mutant genes are usually recessive to the wild type because they most often express themselves by the failure to produce a protein product; in such heterozygotes, the wild-type gene dominates by producing enough of its product to bring about the wild-type phenotype.

Good evidence is accumulating that the gene and its polypeptide product are colinear: Mutations that map at an end of a gene affect the amino acid sequence at an end of the polypeptide, and so forth. Genes controlling a series of related biochemical reactions are often adjacent to each other. Various mutants of tryptophan synthetase A demonstrate that a mutable site can exist in at least three alternative states (we shall see in the next chapter that the number is thought to be exactly four). Experiments with these mutants also reveal that each amino acid is under the joint control of more than one (as we shall see, three) mutable site, and that an enzyme does not require a unique amino acid sequence in order to be active.

REFERENCES

Pontecorvo, G., *Trends in Genetic Analysis*, Columbia University Press, New York, 1958. A very readable discussion of the fine-structure analysis of the gene.

Benzer, S., "The Fine Structure of the Gene," *Sci. Am.* January, 1962, pp. 70–84. A lucid presentation of the author's classic investigations of rII gene of phage T4.

Hartman, P. E., and S. R. Suskind, *Gene Action*, 2nd ed., Prentice-Hall, Englewood Cliffs, N.J., 1969. A very clear description of how genes work; introduces many of the experimental details that have led to the general principles.

Wagner, R. P., and H. K. Mitchell, *Genetics and Metabolism*, 2nd ed., Wiley, New York, 1964. A more advanced text illustrating a large number of different gene-enzyme relations.

Ingram, V. M., *The Hemoglobins in Genetics and Evolution*, Columbia University Press, New York, 1963. A description of the variety of ways in which hemoglobin has been used to establish important biological principles. Particularly relevant to this chapter is the discussion of the abnormal hemoglobin molecules.

Yanofsky, C., "Gene Structure and Protein Structure," in R. H. Haynes and P. C. Hanawalt (eds.), *The Molecular Basis of Life*, Freeman, San Francisco, 1968, pp. 224–229. An introductory description of the author's classic work on the tryptophan synthetase system.

9

THE

REPLICATION

OF DNA

GENETICS TELLS US THAT THE INFORMA-
tion that directs amino acid sequences
in proteins is carried by long-chain
polymeric molecules, the deoxyribonucleic acids (DNA).[1] Though DNA
was first recognized in chromosomes
about 70 years ago, it was definitely
identified as having a genetic function
only 20 years ago, and even then many
geneticists thought that some information might also reside in the protein
component of chromosomes. Now,
however, there is no reason to believe
that any genetic information is carried
in other than nucleic acid molecules.

This poses the chemical question of
how the information is transferred at
the molecular level. In addition, we
must ask how the DNA molecules are
exactly copied during chromosome duplication. These questions could not
be immediately attacked in 1943, when
the genetic role of DNA was established. At that time, only fragmentary
information concerning its structure
existed. It was known to be a very
long, large molecule (Figure 9–1), but
the extent of its complexity was unclear. Consequently, there was much
apprehension not only that DNA structure would vary from one gene to another, but that even in the simplest
case, the solution of its structure would

[1] As we shall see in Chapter 15, the chromosomes of some viruses do not contain
DNA but instead are composed of the chemically very similar compound ribonucleic acid
(RNA).

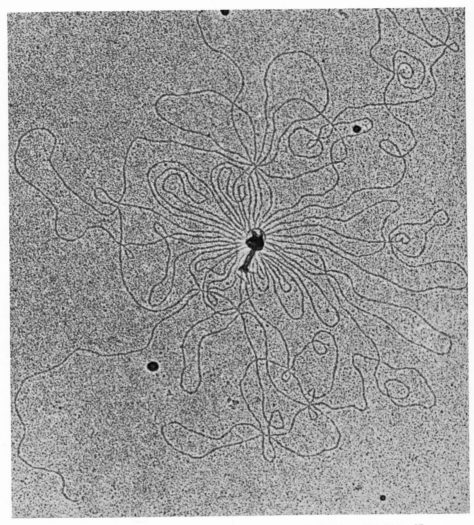

FIGURE 9-1   *Electron micrograph of T2 DNA × 100,000.* [Reproduced from A. K. Kleinschmidt et al., *Biochim. Biophys. Acta,* **61**, *857 (1962), with permission.*]

pose almost insuperable problems. Moreover, there existed an apprehension that, even when the structures of one or more DNA molecules were known, we would not be presented with any obvious clues about how it acted as a template for its self-replication or how it could control the sequence of amino acids in proteins. Fortunately, these fears were unfounded. Only ten years elapsed between the identification of DNA as the transforming substance and the 1953 elucidation of the double-helical structure of most DNA molecules. Moreover, the basic features of the double helix were simple and immediately told how DNA stores genetic information; even more pleasing, they suggested a chemical mechanism for the self-replication of DNA. From this moment on, the way in which geneticists investigated the gene entered a completely new phase. Their hypotheses no longer needed to be based only on genetic crosses. Instead, it made sense always to ask how the structure of DNA affects the interpretation of their genetic crosses. As a consequence, many subjects (e.g., the action of mutagens) previously refractory to a systematic treatment became open to rational analysis.

THE GENE IS (ALMOST ALWAYS) DNA

The first serious assignment of the primary genetic role to DNA arose from experiments (discussed in Chapter 7) involving the genetic transformation of pneumonia bacteria. Soon after the discovery that cell extracts were effective in transformation, careful chemical studies were begun to determine which type of molecule was responsible. Since virtually everybody believed that genes were proteins, there was initially great surprise when Avery and his co-workers reported in 1943 that the active genetic principal was deoxyribonucleic acid (DNA) (Figure 9–2). A major experimental result prompting their conclusion was the observation that the transforming activity of the extract was destroyed by deoxyribonuclease, an enzyme which specifically degrades DNA molecules to their nucleotide building blocks and has no effect on the integrity of protein molecules or ribonucleic acid (RNA). The addition of either the enzyme ribonuclease (which degrades RNA) or various proteolytic (protein-destroying) enzymes had no influence on transforming activity.

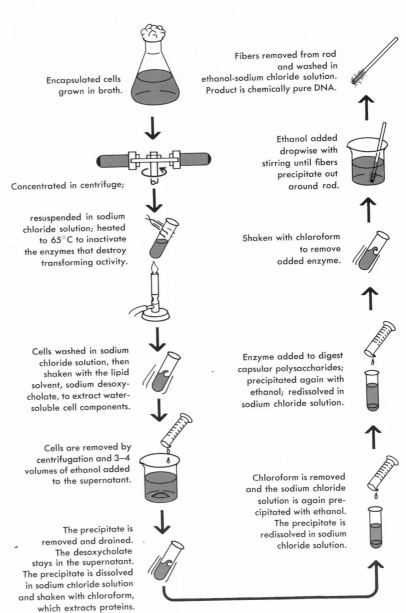

Encapsulated cells grown in broth.

Concentrated in centrifuge; resuspended in sodium chloride solution; heated to 65°C to inactivate the enzymes that destroy transforming activity.

Cells washed in sodium chloride solution, then shaken with the lipid solvent, sodium desoxycholate, to extract water-soluble cell components.

Cells are removed by centrifugation and 3–4 volumes of ethanol added to the supernatant.

The precipitate is removed and drained. The desoxycholate stays in the supernatant. The precipitate is dissolved in sodium chloride solution and shaken with chloroform, which extracts proteins.

Fibers removed from rod and washed in ethanol-sodium chloride solution. Product is chemically pure DNA.

Ethanol added dropwise with stirring until fibers precipitate out around rod.

Shaken with chloroform to remove added enzyme.

Enzyme added to digest capsular polysaccharides; precipitated again with ethanol; redissolved in sodium chloride solution.

Chloroform is removed and the sodium chloride solution is again pre-cipitated with ethanol. The precipitate is redissolved in sodium chloride solution.

FIGURE 9–2 The chemical method used in the original isolation of a chemically pure transforming agent. (Redrawn from F. W. Stahl, The Mechanics of Inheritance, Prentice-Hall, Englewood Cliffs, N.J., 1964, Fig. 2.3, with permission.)

258

THE AMOUNT OF CHROMOSOMAL DNA IS CONSTANT

Even though the transformation results were clear-cut, there was initially great skepticism about their general applicability; people doubted that they would be found relevant to anything but certain strains of bacteria. Thus the momentous nature of Avery's discovery was only gradually appreciated.

One important confirmation came from studies on the chemical nature of chromosomes. DNA was found to be located almost exclusively in the nucleus, and essentially never where detectable chromosomes were absent. Moreover, the amount of DNA per diploid set of chromosomes was constant for a given organism and equal to twice the amount present in the haploid sperm cells. Another type of evidence that favored DNA as the genetic molecule was the observation that it is metabolically stable. It is not rapidly made and broken down like many other cellular molecules: Once atoms are incorporated into DNA they do not leave it as long as healthy cell growth is maintained.

VIRAL GENES ARE ALSO NUCLEIC ACIDS

Even more important confirmatory evidence came from chemical studies with viruses and virus-infected cells. It was possible by 1950 to obtain a number of essentially pure viruses and to determine which types of molecules were present in them. This work led to the very important generalization that all viruses contain nucleic acid. Since there was, at that time, a growing realization that viruses contain genetic material, the question immediately arose of whether the nucleic acid component was the viral chromosome. The first crucial experimental test of the question came from isotopic study of the multiplication of T2, a virus containing a DNA core and a protective shell built up by the aggregation of a number of different protein molecules. In these experiments the protein coat was labeled with a radioactive isotope S^{35}, and the DNA with the radioactive isotope P^{32}. The labeled virus was then used for following the fates of the phage protein and nucleic acid as virus multiplication proceeded, particularly to see which labeled atoms from the parental virus appeared in the progeny phage.

Clear-cut results emerged from these experiments (Figure 9–3): Much of the parental nucleic acid and none of the parental protein was detected in the progeny phage. Moreover, it was possible to show that little of the parental protein ever enters the bacteria—instead it stays attached to the outside of the bacterial cell, performing no function after the DNA component has passed in. This point was neatly shown by violently agitating infected bacteria after the entrance of the DNA: The

FIGURE 9–3 *Demonstration that only the DNA component of T2 carries genetic information and that the protein coat functions as a protective shell which facilitates DNA transfer to new host cells.*

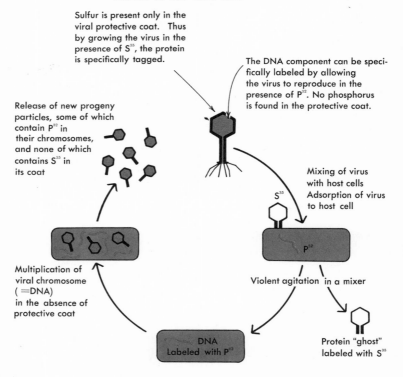

Sulfur is present only in the viral protective coat. Thus by growing the virus in the presence of S^{35}, the protein is specifically tagged.

The DNA component can be specifically labeled by allowing the virus to reproduce in the presence of P^{32}. No phosphorus is found in the protective coat.

Release of new progeny particles, some of which contain P^{32} in their chromosomes, and none of which contains S^{35} in its coat

Multiplication of viral chromosome (=DNA) in the absence of protective coat

Mixing of virus with host cells Adsorption of virus to host cell

S^{35}

P^{32}

Violent agitation in a mixer

DNA Labeled with P^{32}

Protein "ghost" labeled with S^{35}

protein coats were shaken off without affecting the ability of the bacteria to form new virus particles.

With some viruses it is now possible to do an even more convincing experiment. For example, purified DNA from the mouse virus polyoma can enter mouse cells and initiate a cycle of viral multiplication producing many thousands of new polyoma particles. The primary function of viral protein is thus to protect its genetic nucleic acid component in its movement from one cell to another. Thus no reason exists for the assignment of any genetic role to protein molecules.

DNA IS USUALLY A DOUBLE HELIX

The most important feature of DNA is that it usually consists of two very long, thin polymeric chains twisted about each other in the form of a regular double helix (Figures 9–4 and 9–5). The diameter of the helix is about 20 A and each chain makes a complete turn every 34 A. Each chain is a polynucleotide (Figure 3–10), a regular polymeric collection of nucleotides in which the sugar of each nucleotide is linked by a phosphate group to the sugar of the adjacent nucleotide. There are 10 nucleotides on each chain every turn of the helix. The distance per nucleotide base is thus 3.4 A. Four main nucleotides exist, each of them containing a deoxyribose residue, a phosphate group, and a purine or pyrimidine base (Figure 3–9). There are two pyrimidines, thymine (T) and cytosine (C), and two purines, adenine (A) and guanine (G). In the polynucleotide chain the joining together of the sugar and phosphate groups always involves the same chemical groups. Hence, this part of the molecule, called the backbone, is very regular. In contrast, the order of the purine and pyrimidine residues along the chain is highly irregular and varies from one molecule to another. Both the purine and pyrimidine bases are flat, relatively water-insoluble molecules which tend to stack above each other perpendicular to the direction of the helical axis.

The two chains are joined together by hydrogen bonds between pairs of bases. Adenine is always paired with thymine and guanine with cytosine (Figure 4–14). Only these arrangements are possible, for two purines would occupy too much space to allow a regular helix and, correspondingly, two pyrimidines would occupy too little. The strictness of these pairing rules results in a complementary relation between the

FIGURE 9–4   *A space-filling model of double-helical DNA. The size of the circles reflects the van der Waals radii of the different atoms. (Courtesy of M. H. F. Wilkins.)*

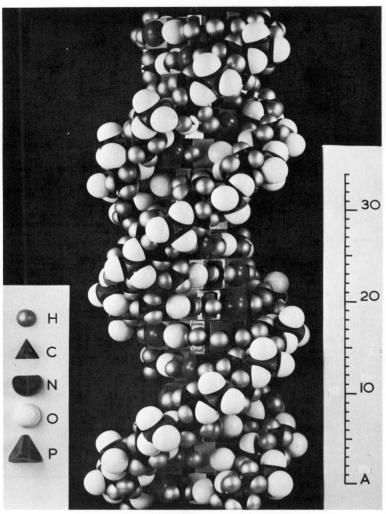

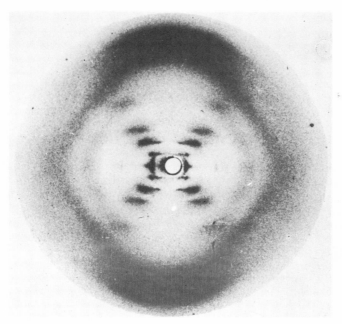

FIGURE 9-5   *The key x-ray photograph involved in the elucidation
of the DNA structure. This photograph, taken at
Kings College, London, in the winter of 1952–1953,
by Rosalind Franklin, experimentally confirmed the
then current guesses that DNA was helical. The helical form is indicated by the crossways pattern of x-ray
reflections (photographically measured by darkening
of the x-ray film) in the center of the photograph.
The very heavy black regions at the top and bottom
tell that the 3.4-A thick purine and pyrimidine bases
are regularly stacked next to each other, perpendicular
to the helical axis. [Reproduced from R. E. Franklin
and R. Gosling, Nature, 171, 740 (1953), with permission.]*

sequences of bases on the two intertwined chains. For example,
if we have a sequence ATGTC on one chain, the opposite chain
must have the sequence TACAG. A stereochemical consequence of the formation of the A · · · · T and G · · · · C base pairs
is that the two polynucleotide chains run in opposite directions.
Thus, if the helix is inverted by 180°, it superficially looks the
same (Figure 9–6).

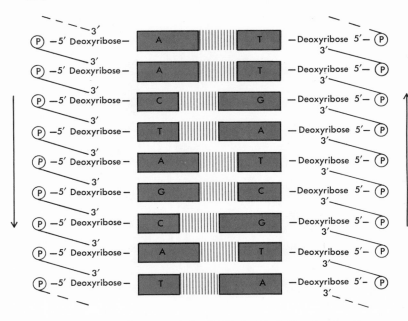

FIGURE 9–6 *Diagram of the DNA double helix, showing the specific pairing of the bases, the unrestricted sequence of bases along any one chain, and the reversed direction of the 3′-5′-phosphodiester linkages of the two chains. The heavy lines indicate the bases, and the interrupted lines the hydrogen bonds between base pairs (A, adenine; G, guanine; T, thymine; C, cytosine). Redrawn from W. Hayes, The Genetics of Bacteria and Their Viruses, Blackwell, Oxford, 1964, p. 229, with permission.)*

An important chemical feature of the structure is the position of the hydrogen atoms in the purine and pyrimidine bases. Before 1953, many people thought that some of the hydrogen atoms were highly mobile, randomly moving from one ring nitrogen or oxygen atom to another, and so could not be assigned a fixed location. Now we realize that, although these movements (called tautomeric shifts) do occur, they are generally quite rare, and most of the time the H atoms are found at precise locations. The N atoms attached to the purine and pyrimidine rings are usually in the *amino* (NH_2) form and only very, very rarely assume the *imino* (NH) configuration. Like-wise, the oxygen atoms attached to the C-6 atoms of guanine and thymine normally have the keto (C=O) form and only rarely take up the enol (COH) configuration.   As we shall see, these relatively stable locations are essential to the bio-logical function of DNA.   For if the H atoms had no fixed locations, adenine could often pair with cytosine, and guanine with thymine.

In contrast to the ratios of A/T and G/C, which must always be 1–1 to satisfy the base-pairing rules, there are wide variations in the $A + T/G + C$ contents of different DNA molecules (Table 9–1).   Higher plants and animals all have an excess of $A + T$ over $G + C$ in their DNA, whereas among the viruses, bacteria, and lower plants, there is much more variation, and both $A + T$-rich and $G + C$-rich species occur.   These varia-tions, however, are not purely random, and the base ratios of taxonomically related organisms are quite similar.   No one yet knows the reason for the wide base-ratio spread.   It may be a consequence of extensive evolution but certainly not a prereq-

T A B L E 9–1   *Examples of the spread of $A + T/G + C$ ratios in the DNA molecules of taxonomically diverse organisms*

Source of DNA	$\dfrac{A+T}{G+C}$	Source of DNA	$\dfrac{A+T}{G+C}$
Pseudomonas aeruginosa (a bacterium)	.51	Paracentrotus lividos (sea urchin)	1.86
Escherichia coli	.97	Locusta migratoria (an insect)	1.41
Bacillus megaterium (a bacterium)	1.66	Trout	1.34
Mycobacterium tuberculosis (a bacterium)	.60	Domestic chicken	1.36
Saccharomyces cerevisiae (a yeast)	1.80	Horse	1.33
Aspergillus niger (a fungus)	1.00	Man	1.40
Scendesmus quadricauda (an alga)	.57	Phage T2	1.84
Rhabdonema adriaticum (an alga = diatom)	1.71	Phage λ	1.06
Wheat	1.22		

uisite. Witness extreme differences between higher plants and animals despite roughly similar percentages of the four main bases. This fact tells us that variation in the sequences of the bases is, by itself, sufficient to produce the gene differences between plants and animals.

DNA molecules with a high G + C content are more resistant to thermal collapse than A + T-rich molecules. When double helical DNA molecules are heated above physiological temperatures (to near 100°C), their hydrogen bonds break and the complementary strands often separate from each other (DNA denaturation). Because the G····C base pair is held together by three hydrogen bonds, higher temperatures are necessary to separate G + C-rich strands than to break apart A + T-rich molecules.

Denaturation is not necessarily an irreversible phenomenon. If a heated DNA solution is slowly cooled, a single strand can often meet its complementary strand and reform a regular double-helical molecule. This ability to renature DNA molecules permits us to show that artificial hybrid DNA molecules can be formed by slowly cooling mixtures of denatured DNA from two different species. For example, hybrid molecules can be formed containing one strand from a man and one from a mouse. Only a fraction (25 per cent) of the DNA strands from a man can form hybrids with mouse DNA. This is, of course, not surprising since it merely means that some genes of a man are very similar to those of a mouse, whereas others have quite different nucleotide sequences. It now appears that this molecular technique may be quite useful in establishing the genetic similarity of the various taxonomic groups.

THE COMPLEMENTARY·SHAPE IMMEDIATELY SUGGESTS SELF-REPLICATION

Earlier, in the discussion of how templates must act, the point was emphasized that, in general, two identical surfaces will not attract each other and that it is instead easier to visualize the attraction of oppositely shaped or charged groups. Thus, without any detailed structural knowledge, we might guess that a molecule as complicated as the gene could not be directly copied. Instead, replication would involve the formation of a molecule complementary in shape, and this in turn would serve as a template to make a replica of the original template. Some geneticists, in the days before detailed knowledge of protein or nucleic acid structure existed, wondered whether DNA might serve as a template for a specific protein that in turn served as a template for a corresponding DNA molecule.

The realization that it is possible to form a DNA molecule in which the specific genetic surfaces (the purine and pyrimidine bases) of the two polynucleotide strands are complementary in shape and charge immediately tells us to reject the possibility, which we already suspected to be chemically tricky if not impossible, of having specific protein formation as the

FIGURE 9–7 *The replication of DNA.*

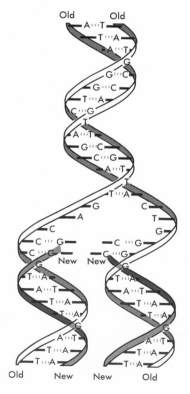

essential aspect of DNA replication. Instead, it is immensely simpler to imagine that DNA replication involves strand separation and formation of complementary molecules on each of the free single strands (Figure 9–7). Under this scheme, each of the two strands of every DNA molecule would serve as the template for the formation of its complement.

No difficulty arises from the need to break the hydrogen bonds joining the base pairs in the parental templates. Though they are highly specific, they are at the same time relatively weak and no enzymes are needed either to make or to break them. Thus they are the ideal means of specifically holding together a template and its complementary replica. Nor does the need to untwist the DNA molecule to separate the two intertwined strands present a real problem. The DNA molecule is very thin (20 A), and rotation about its axis involves almost no energy.

BASE PAIRING SHOULD PERMIT VERY ACCURATE REPLICATION

Earlier we stated that the chemistry of the specific amino acid side groups argued against their employment as accurate templates. Just the opposite, however, is true of the purine and pyrimidine bases, for each of them can form several hydrogen bonds. These bonds are ideal template forces, for they are highly specific, unlike the van der Waals interactions, whose attractive forces are both weaker and virtually independent of specific chemical groupings.

The average energy of a hydrogen bond is about 4 kcal/mole, or eight times the average energy of thermal motion of molecules at room temperature. This value allows us to estimate the ratio of the frequency with which two suitable groups will hydrogen bond to the nonbonding frequency. Under ordinary cellular conditions the ratio of bonding to nonbonding is about 10^4. This means that two molecules held together by several hydrogen bonds are almost never found in the nonbonded form. For example, the frequency with which adenine will attach to cytosine during DNA replication is about 10^{-8} times the frequency of its bonding to thymine ($10^{-4} \times 10^{-4}$ since two hydrogen bonds are involved). Since the G $\cdots$ C pair is held together by three hydrogen bonds, its replication should be even more accurate.

This argument is not affected by the fact that the bases also can form almost equally strong hydrogen bonds with the hydrogen and oxygen atoms of water. It does not matter if, say, the potential thymine site is temporarily filled with several water molecules. They cannot be chemically joined to the growing polynucleotide chain, and they will soon diffuse away and be replaced by the suitable hydrogen-bonding nucleotide.

It is not yet possible to give a similar quantitative argument for why two purines or two pyrimidines never accidentally bond to each other. Though both arrangements seriously distort the sugar-phosphate backbone and clearly are energetically unfavorable, the large number of atoms involved makes the precise calculation of energy differences impossible now. Part of the difficulty arises from the fact that the precise locations of the atoms in DNA are not known at the 0.1 A level. Furthermore, it is unclear what effect this distortion would have on the binding of the enzyme that catalyzes the formation of the internucleotide covalent bonds.

DNA CARRIES ALL THE SPECIFICITY INVOLVED IN ITS SELF-REPLICATION

Proof for this statement came from the 1956 discovery that DNA synthesis could be observed in a cell-free system, prepared from E. coli cells. The enzyme involved, DNA polymerase, was the first to be found involved in the synthesis of polydeoxynucleotides. It links the nucleotide precursors by 3' to 5' phosphodiester bonds (Figure 9–8). Furthermore, it works only in the presence of DNA, which is needed to order the four nucleotides in the polynucleotide product.

The DNA polymerase itself recognizes only the regular sugar-phosphate portion of the nucleotide precursors and so cannot determine sequence specificity. This is neatly demonstrated by allowing the enzyme to work in the presence of DNA molecules

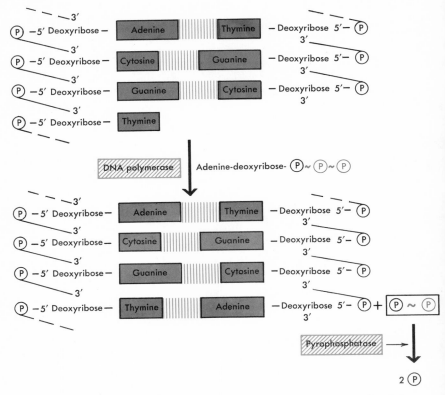

FIGURE 9–8   Enzymatic synthesis of a DNA chain catalyzed by
DNA polymerase.

that contain varying amounts of A····T and G····C base
pairs. In every case, the enzymatically synthesized product has
the base ratios of the primer DNA (Table 9–2). During this
cell-free synthesis, no synthesis of protein or any other molecular class occurs, unambiguously eliminating any non-DNA
componds as intermediate carriers of genetic specificity. There
is thus no doubt that DNA is the direct template for its own
formation. As we might expect, the enzymatic product, like
the primer, has a double-helical structure.

　　Exactly how DNA polymerase works at the molecular level
is not known since little has been determined about its structure. Because it is present in cells in only limited amounts,

T A B L E 9–2   *A comparison of the base composition of enzymatically synthesized DNA and their DNA templates*

Source of DNA template	Base composition of the enzymatic product				$\dfrac{A + T}{G + C}$ in product	$\dfrac{A + T}{G + C}$ in template
	Adenine	Thymine	Guanine	Cytosine		
Micrococcus lysodeiticus (a bacterium)	0.15	0.15	0.35	0.35	0.41	0.39
Aerobacter acrogenes (a bacterium)	0.22	0.22	0.28	0.28	0.80	0.82
Escherichia coli	0.25	0.25	0.25	0.25	1.00	0.97
Calf thymus	0.29	0.28	0.21	0.22	1.32	1.35
Phage T2	0.32	0.32	0.18	0.18	1.78	1.84

purification in large amounts is a horrendous task. It is known, however, to consist of a single polypeptide built from about 1100 amino acids. Eventually, crystallization should be achieved, opening up the prospect of x-ray diffraction studies of its three-dimensional shape.

The ability of DNA polymerase to make complementary copies of DNA chains immediately suggested this must be the major, if not the only, enzyme in *E. coli* involved in linking up nucleotides during DNA replication. But as we shall see later, there are doubts that this is true; the actual replication process seems to be very complicated. Discovery of DNA polymerase, however, was of immense importance in showing that the assembly of complementary nucleotide sequences was amenable to relatively straightforward test-tube analysis.

SOLID EVIDENCE IN FAVOR OF DNA STRAND SEPARATION

To prove this point, methods had to be found for the physical separation of parental and daughter DNA molecules. This was first accomplished through use of heavy isotopes such as N^{15}. Bacteria grown in a medium containing the heavy isotope N^{15} have denser DNA than bacteria grown under normal conditions with N^{14}. Heavy DNA can be separated from light

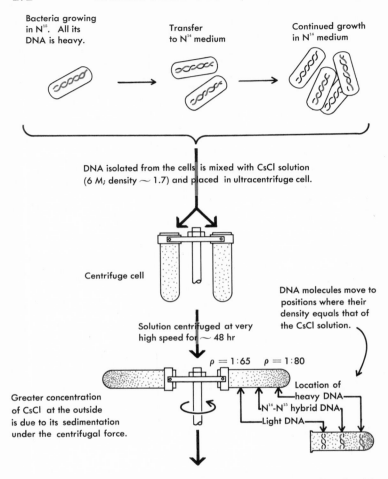

Bacteria growing in N^{15}. All its DNA is heavy.

Transfer to N^{14} medium

Continued growth in N^{14} medium

DNA isolated from the cells is mixed with CsCl solution (6 M; density ~ 1.7) and placed in ultracentrifuge cell.

Centrifuge cell

Solution centrifuged at very high speed for ~ 48 hr

DNA molecules move to positions where their density equals that of the CsCl solution.

$\rho = 1:65$ $\rho = 1:80$

Greater concentration of CsCl at the outside is due to its sedimentation under the centrifugal force.

Location of heavy DNA
N^{14}-N^{15} hybrid DNA
Light DNA

The location of DNA molecules within the centrifuge cell can be determined by ultraviolet optics. DNA solutions absorb strongly at 2600 A.

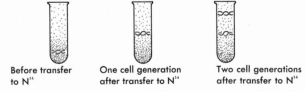

Before transfer to N^{14}

One cell generation after transfer to N^{14}

Two cell generations after transfer to N^{14}

FIGURE 9-9 *Use of a cesium chloride density gradient for the demonstration of the separations of complementary strands during DNA replication.*

DNA by equilibrium centrifugation in concentrated solutions of heavy salts such as cesium chloride. When high centrifugal forces are applied, the solution becomes more dense at the outside of the centrifuge cell. If the correct initial solution density is chosen, the individual DNA molecules will move to the central region of the centrifuge cell where their density equals that of the salt solution. Thus the heavy molecules will band at a higher density than the light molecules. If bacteria containing heavy DNA are transferred to a light medium (containing N^{14}) and allowed to grow, the precursor nucleotides available for use in DNA synthesis will be light; hence, DNA synthesized after transfer will be distinguishable from DNA made before transfer.

If DNA replication involves strand separation, definite predictions can be made about the density of the DNA molecules found after various growth intervals in a light medium. After one generation of growth, all the DNA molecules should contain one heavy and one light strand and thus be of intermediate hybrid density. This result is exactly what is observed. Likewise, after two generations of growth, half the DNA molecules are light and half hybrid (Figure 9–9), just as strand separation predicts.

SINGLE-STRANDED DNA ALSO IS REPLICATED BY BASE PAIRING

At first it was thought that all DNA molecules are double-stranded except during replication, when part is temporarily in a nonhydrogen-bonded, single-stranded form. Many people were surprised, therefore, when conclusive experiments revealed that the DNA of several groups of small bacterial viruses exists normally as circular single-stranded molecules in which $A \neq T$ and $G \neq C$. Among these single-stranded DNA phages are the viruses $\phi \times 174$, s13, and F1.

This discovery of single-stranded DNA immediately posed the question of whether an additional copying mechanism exists in which a single DNA strand serves as a template for an identical copy. This type of replication cannot be accomplished by the formation of a double helix in which identical bases hydrogen bond to each other, because such a structure is stereochemically impossible.   If self-replication were to exist, it would have to use connector molecules of the type discussed when we considered whether a polypeptide chain could be the template for an identical copy.   Four different connectors would have to exist, each having two identical surfaces that could make several hydrogen bonds with a specific base.   The connectors could line up and connect the nucleotides to form a new polynucleotide chain identical to the first.

There is no evidence, however, for the existence of such connectors.   Instead we find that as soon as the single-stranded DNA molecule (which we shall call the "+" strand) enters its

FIGURE 9–10   *The replication of a single-stranded DNA molecule. Each double helix generally serves as the template for the formation of a large number of new "+" strands.*

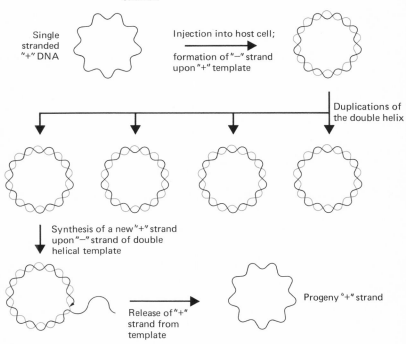

Single stranded "+" DNA

Injection into host cell; formation of "−" strand upon "+" template

Duplications of the double helix

Synthesis of a new "+" strand upon "−" strand of double helical template

Release of "+" strand from template

Progeny "+" strand

host cell, the strand serves as a template for the formation of a complementary "−" strand (Figure 9–10). The resulting double helix in turn serves as a template for the formation of new single "+" strands, which then become incorporated into new virus particles. Thus, the fundamental mechanism for ordering nucleotides during polynucleotide synthesis of single-stranded DNA is basically the same as that used for double-helical DNA. Nucleotide selection always occurs by attraction of the complementary base. The difference is that with the single-stranded viruses, only one (the "−") of two strands in the double helix functions as a template for progeny particle DNA. How this choice is made is not yet known.

Despite the existence of single-stranded DNA in some viruses, most cellular DNA must be double-stranded. This follows from the facts that (1) the two complementary chains do not have identical base sequences and hence (as we shall see later) code for entirely different amino acid arrangements, and (2) in bacteria (and probably in many higher cells) there is usually only one copy of a given gene. Thus, if the single-stranded form were the usual form and the double helix existed only briefly during DNA duplication, then following mitosis the two daughter cells would contain completely different sets of genetic information.

SINGLE DNA MOLECULES ARE THE CHROMOSOMES OF VIRUSES AND E. COLI

Early estimates of the molecular weights of DNA centered at about a million, a size that we shall see is that of the average gene. Therefore, it was natural to equate single DNA molecules with single genes. But these first reports were misleading because of DNA breakage during its isolation and study. Now it is clear that virtually all undegraded DNA molecules contain the information of several genes. Our most convincing molecular weight values come from DNA-containing viruses. For example, the bacterial virus T2 contains one DNA molecule of $MW = 1.3 \times 10^8$ (Figure 9–11), and the bacterial virus λ con-

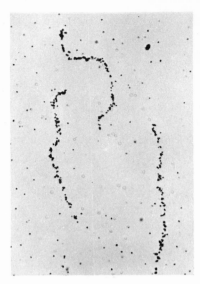

FIGURE 9–11   *Autoradiograph of several T2 chromosomes.   The total length is 52 μ.   (Courtesy of J. Cairns.)*

tains a single molecule of MW = 3.2×10^7 (Figure 9–12). In these cases, we must equate the chromosome, not the gene, with single DNA molecules. This must also be done for the single chromosome of an *E. coli* cell; a single DNA molecule whose molecular weight is about 2×10^9 and whose extended length is almost a millimeter. Exactly how many DNA molecules are contained in the chromosomes of higher plants and animals is not known. Because there are indications that DNA replication occurs simultaneously at many points on a single chromosome, the presence of at least several molecules has been suggested. In any case, some DNA molecules are larger by several powers of 10 than any other biological molecule.

DNA MOLECULES SOMETIMES HAVE A CIRCULAR SHAPE

Initially, our experimental evidence, largely from electron microscopy, suggested that all DNA molecules were linear and had two free ends. As it becomes possible to look more easily

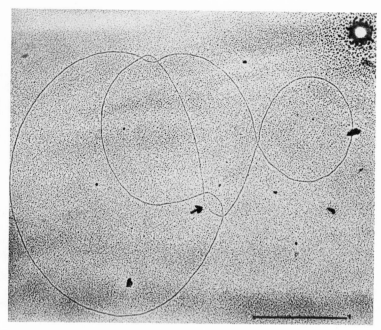

FIGURE 9–12 *Electron micrograph (by B. Chandler, University of Wisconsin) of circular λ DNA molecule. The reference line represents 1 μ. The contour length is 16.3 μ. [Reproduced from H. Ris and B. C. Chandler, Cold Spring Harbor Symp. Quant. Biol., 28, 2 (1963), Fig. 1, with permission.]*

at undegraded DNA molecules, however, the generalization is beginning to emerge that many DNA molecules are normally present in a circular form. For instance, the chromosome of the mouse virus polyoma is isolated from the virus particle as a duplex ring. As already mentioned, the DNA of the virus $\phi \times 174$ is a single-stranded circle; after entrance into the host cell the single-stranded "+" circle is converted to a double-stranded ring by the synthesis of a new "−" strand.

Sometimes a DNA molecule which is linear when isolated from a virus particle (e.g., phage λ) is later found as a circle inside the host cell. This has suggested the important generalization that the linear and circular forms of a DNA molecule

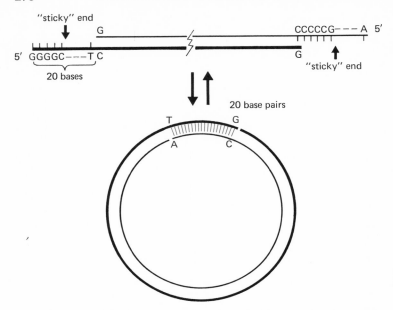

FIGURE 9–13 *Interconversion of the linear and circular forms of λDNA.*

are interconvertible. The basic molecular mechanism which converts a DNA circle to the rod form is shown in Figure 9–13. Starting with a closed circle a specific enzyme(s) introduce(s) two breaks, one in the "+" strand and one in the "−" strand. As these breaks are very close to each other the intervening hydrogen bonds occasionally are broken by thermal agitation and then the circle unfolds. Most importantly, the resulting rod contains single-stranded ends which have complementary nucleotide sequences. Thus at a later time the rod can, by base pairing, resume a circular configuration. If the missing phosphodiester bonds are replaced, then the covalent circle is regenerated.

Solid evidence now exists that λ DNA interconverts between a circular and rod form, using precisely this mechanism. In fact, all DNA rods which have been examined so far, show the ability to form circles under certain conditions. We now think that the relevant form for the duplication process of viral DNA is the circle and that the rod form found in phages is an adaptation for injection of the viral chromosome through the narrow tail.

At first the possibility was considered that circles might represent features peculiar to viruses and their replication. This hypothesis was clearly disproved by the discovery that *E. coli* chromosome (DNA molecule) can also be found as a circle. It is therefore necessary to ask, in general, why DNA molecules should be capable of forming circles. The most appealing hypothesis is that circular DNA is a device for preventing unwanted DNA replication. During cell division each chromosome must replicate once, not twice or more. One conceivable way to achieve this would be to have the DNA molecule in a circular form except for the period in each cell cycle when DNA replication is desired.

TEST TUBE REPLICATION OF A BIOLOGICALLY ACTIVE DNA MOLECULE

Recently, the enzyme DNA polymerase was used in the synthesis of biologically active viral chromosomes. The virus chromosome replicated in these *in vitro* experiments was that of the single-stranded DNA phage $\phi \times 174$. When DNA polymerase and the nucleoside triphosphate precursors were added to circular $\phi \times 174$ DNA molecules, "−" strand synthesis occurred on the "+" parental strands (Figure 9–14). The addition of the DNA-joining enzyme polynucleotide ligase (Figure 9–15) to close the newly synthesized "−" strands resulted in intact circular double helices which had no template activity with DNA polymerase. However, after a nuclease was allowed to nonspecifically nick the circular double helices, it was possible to isolate a number of still intact newly synthesized "−" strands. Use of these intact "−" circles as further templates allowed another round of synthesis, this time of intact "+" strand circles. The progeny "+" circles were shown to be biologically active—capable of initiating virus multiplication. Thus, the copying process accomplished by DNA polymerase

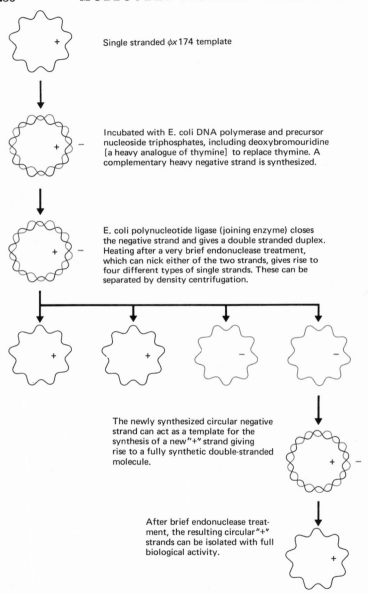

Single stranded φx174 template

Incubated with E. coli DNA polymerase and precursor nucleoside triphosphates, including deoxybromouridine [a heavy analogue of thymine] to replace thymine. A complementary heavy negative strand is synthesized.

E. coli polynucleotide ligase (joining enzyme) closes the negative strand and gives a double stranded duplex. Heating after a very brief endonuclease treatment, which can nick either of the two strands, gives rise to four different types of single strands. These can be separated by density centrifugation.

The newly synthesized circular negative strand can act as a template for the synthesis of a new "+" strand giving rise to a fully synthetic double-stranded molecule.

After brief endonuclease treatment, the resulting circular "+" strands can be isolated with full biological activity.

FIGURE 9–14   *Steps involved in the in vitro synthesis of infectious φ×174 DNA.*

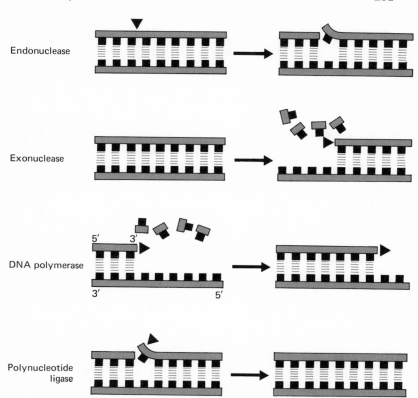

FIGURE 9–15 *Schematic representation of the action of four different enzymes concerned with making and breaking the backbone bonds of DNA.*

is very, very accurate. But this experiment does not answer the question of how double-stranded circular DNA replicates—the template used in these experiments was single-stranded, not the normal double-stranded material.

REPLICATION MUST START WITH AN ENDONUCLEASE CUT

An essential first step in the normal replication of circular duplex DNA must be the enzymatic breaking of at least one of the parental strands. This fact is clearly shown by the inability of covalently closed $\phi \times 174$ double helices to function as templates. Closed circles only become templates after creation of a break which allows the two parental strands to unravel from each other. An early, if not the initial event in replication, thus must be the production by a specific enzyme of one or more specific backbone breaks along the circular chromosome.

Enzymes which break internal phosphodiester bonds are called endonucleases (Figure 9–15). The endonuclease(s) involved in the initiation of DNA replication must begin by recognizing (binding to) a very specific sequence of nucleotides found at the replication origin. Now there is much effort directed toward finding one of the "initiating" nucleases. Though all results so far are negative, a positive result should soon emerge.

EVIDENCE FOR UNIQUE STARTING POINTS

Firm evidence for unique starting points for replication comes from studies of the timing of duplication of specific viral and bacterial genes. With phage λ, DNA replication always initiates upon the parental DNA duplex very near gene O and synthesis proceeds outward from this point (the origin) in both the clockwise and counterclockwise directions. This result was first greeted with much surprise since virtually everyone had assumed that growth would proceed in only one direction. But as we shall show later, growth in both directions does not appear strange when specific molecular models for replication are considered. Studies with E. coli show that DNA replication begins at a fixed point near the arginine H gene (at about 8 o'clock on the genetic map), with some recent experiments suggesting that growth also proceeds in both directions around the circle.

DIRECT VISUALIZATION OF REPLICATING DNA

Now it is easy to isolate DNA in the process of replication and visualize it by autoradiographic techniques and by electron microscopy. Such techniques frequently reveal θ-shaped repli-

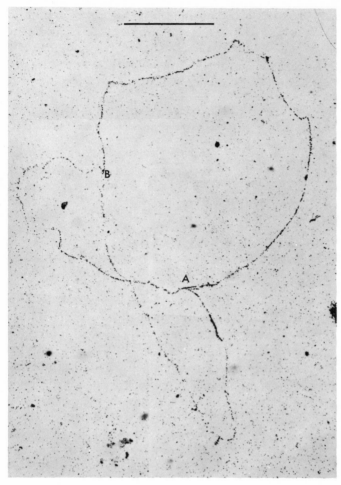

FIGURE 9–16 Autoradiograph showing the Y-shaped growing points
of an E. coli chromosome. The DNA was labeled
with H³-thymidine for two generations of DNA replication. The θ-shaped appearance is the result of
looking at a circular chromosome which has been
two-thirds duplicated. The scale shows 100 μ. [Re-
produced from J. Cairns, Cold Spring Harbor Symp.
Quant. Biol., 28, 44 (1963), with permission.]

cating structures like those shown in Figures 9–16 and 9–17. These structures clearly rule out a two-step replication process in which the parental strands first completely unwind and only later act as templates to form new double helices. In all the replicating structures so far visualized, no evidence can be seen

FIGURE 9–17   *Electron micrographs of three replicating polyoma DNA molecules. (Kindly supplied by Dr. Bernhard Hirt.) Unreplicated circles have a molecular weight of 3×10^6 giving a contour length of 1.5 μ.*

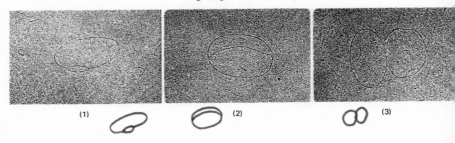

of any extensive regions of single-stranded material. Thus the new polynucleotide strands are synthesized as the parental strands separate.

Other features of these photographs, however, are not so easy to interpret. Particularly puzzling is the absence of free ends and the dilemma it creates about the unraveling of the unreplicated material. Unraveling of such structures demands the presence of a molecular swivel(s) about which the non-replicated material can rotate (Figure 9–18). Unfortunately this idea is very difficult to translate into a precise molecular form. Particularly difficult to comprehend is the process occurring when replication passes over the supposed swivel region. The possibility must also be considered that the θ-shaped structures do not exist within cells but form only during isolation of the replicating material. This point we shall return to later.

CHAIN GROWTH IN BOTH 5′ TO 3′ AND 3′ TO 5′ DIRECTIONS

The existence of double-stranded DNA at the growing points means that both parental strands are serving as templates for the synthesis of new DNA. The elongation of both daughter strands thus occurs virtually simultaneously. This indicates that the overall direction of chain growth must be 5′ to 3′ for one daughter strand and 3′ to 5′ for the other daughter strand. These reversed polarities follow from the opposing chain

FIGURE 9–18   An early model for the replication of a circular DNA molecule. Synthesis always moves in a fixed direction commencing at a specific beginning point. Because the complementary strands are helically twisted about each other, the parent helix must rotate as the strands separate. Under this model some form of molecular swivel exists at the point where replication begins. [Reproduced from J. Cairns, Cold Spring Harbor Symp. Quant. Biol., 28, 43 (1963), with permission.]

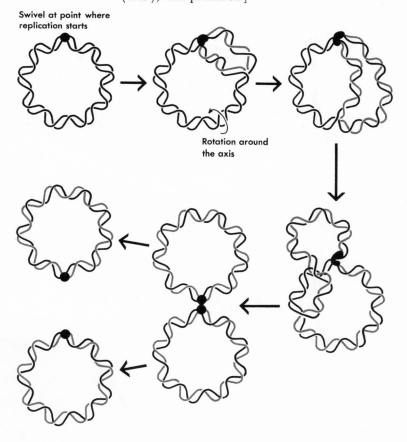

Swivel at point where
replication starts

Rotation around
the axis

directions of the double helix: one runs up $(+)$, the other runs down $(-)$. But the DNA polymerase, the only known enzyme which can add nucleotide precursors to DNA, does so by extending chains only in the 5′ to 3′ direction. The chemical reaction that it catalyzes only allows a nucleoside triphosphate to react with the free 3′ end of a growing polynucleotide strand. The question was thus asked whether another replicating enzyme also exists! Despite extensive searches, however, no

FIGURE 9–19   *Hypothesis that replication of both progeny strands involves joining together of short fragments each synthesized in the 5′-to-3′ direction.*

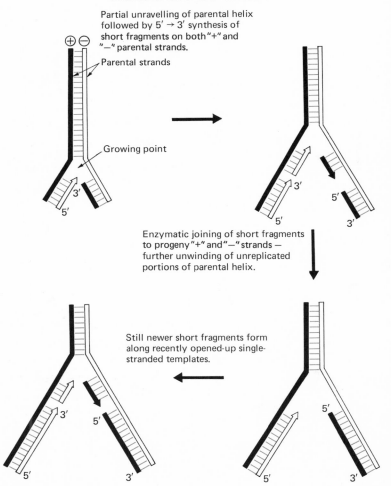

Partial unravelling of parental helix
followed by 5′ → 3′ synthesis of
short fragments on both "+" and
"−" parental strands.

Parental strands

Growing point

Enzymatic joining of short fragments
to progeny "+" and "−" strands —
further unwinding of unreplicated
portions of parental helix.

Still newer short fragments form
along recently opened-up single-
stranded templates.

enzyme with the required 3′ to 5′ specificity has been demonstrated *in vitro*.

MEANING OF THE SMALL FRAGMENTS FOUND NEAR THE GROWING POINTS

Much excitement has been generated by the recent finding that many of the nucleotides incorporated into polynucleotide chains are first observed not in long chains but as part of short polynucleotide fragments. Most importantly, these short fragments have sequences complementary to both "+" and "−" parental strands. These findings open up the possibility that progeny strand replication often involves the stepwise linkup of quite short polynucleotide fragments, each of which grows in the 5′ to 3′ direction (Figure 9–19). In this way, a single enzyme could be responsible for making all progeny chains.

Acceptance of this idea hints that the unraveling of the two parental strands at the replicating fork occurs a short time before the progeny complements are made, thereby creating short stretches of single-stranded parental DNA. This, in turn, leads to the question of whether there is a positive force promoting unraveling. In this connection, the recent discovery (see page 318) of a protein which binds nonspecifically to single-stranded DNA is intriguing. A denaturation protein of this type could facilitate the unwinding of double-stranded DNA at the growing point.

ATTACHMENT OF DAUGHTER POLYNUCLEOTIDE MATERIAL TO PARENTAL STRANDS

For a very long time it seemed simplest to suppose that daughter polynucleotide material would never be covalently attached to parental strands. Attachment obviously should lead to complications in the normal segregation of parental and daughter strands as replication occurs. Thus when the claim first was made that much daughter material was covalently bound to parental material, the sensible course seemed to be to ignore the finding until it could be rechecked. Now, however, there is no doubt that many new strands start growing by adding on to free ends of preexisting strands.   Moreover, subsequent growth of such chains often only goes on until they reach a length two times that of the preexisting strand.

THE ROLLING CIRCLE MODEL

The realization that replication involves extension of preexisting chains inevitably led to the idea of the rolling circle.   This replication scheme starts by a specific cut in one strand of the parental duplex circle, thereby converting this strand to a polynucleotide with two free ends (Figure 9–20).   Each end is chemically different: at one end the nucleotide contains a free 3′OH group on its sugar moiety while at the other end the nucleotide displays a free 5′ phosphate group (see page 91). DNA synthesis begins by the attachment of new nucleotide precursors to the free 3′OH end of the open strand, a chain elongation process which could be catalyzed by DNA polymerase.   Simultaneous with the chain elongation, the other end of the strand (the 5′ end) is rolled out as a free tail of increasing length.   New DNA is laid down on the tails in small fragments, which are eventually pieced together by the DNA-joining enzyme, polynucleotide ligase.

This replicating structure is called a rolling circle since the unraveling of the free single strand is accompanied by rotation of the double helical template about its helical axis.   Such unraveling does not create any topological problems since the circle is held together by only one intact polynucleotide strand which will freely rotate about many of the covalent bonds comprising its backbone.

OPPOSING ROLLING CIRCLE MODELS

The simple rolling circle model by itself, however, does not satisfactorily explain DNA replication.   Firstly, it leads to growth in only one direction, not in both.   Secondly, it provides no explanation for the origin of the θ-shaped replicating intermediates.   Instead it predicts a σ-shaped intermediate in which the free end has no natural reason to bend back onto the circular portion.   Both these objections, however, disappear

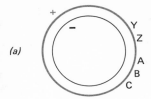

(a)

Replication is initiated upon a closed DNA circle.

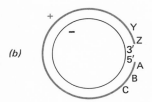

(b)

A sequence-recognizing endonuclease puts a nick into the positive strand.

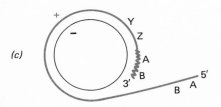

(c)

The DNA polymerase adds nucleotides onto the 3′ end of the open strand, displacing a tail. The correct nucleotides are chosen by hydrogen bonding to the negative strand template. As new nucleotides are chosen, the positive strand becomes longer than unit length.

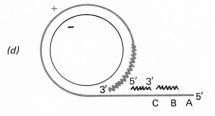

(d)

Complementary fragments begin to be synthesized on the elongating tail thereby converting it to a double-helical form.

FIGURE 9–20 *Creation of a greater-than-unit-length. DNA strand via the Rolling Circle mechanism.*

if we assume that the replicating molecule is the product of two rolling circles moving in opposite directions.

In one model of this type a second nick, near the first nuclease cut, is put into the unnicked strand (Figure 9–21). This allows a second tail to begin to peel back with elongation starting at the newly created 3'OH end. As the tail itself gets longer, complementary fragments are laid down upon it eventually to be joined together by polynucleotide ligase. Most importantly, the ends of the two tails have complementary sequences, which at some later stage can hydrogen bond to each other to form a θ-shaped molecule.

So long as the tails are not hydrogen bonded, there are no unwinding obstacles. But the moment they join, unraveling must stop. Thus the possibility arises that θ structures only form during or after their isolation from the host cell. On the contrary, if θ forms exist in the cell, then replication requires additional nuclease cuts which momentarily permit periods of rapid unwinding. These breaks cannot last very long for they must close up before the replicating forks pass over them—now this seems like a tall order.

The product of this opposing rolling circle model is a double-length DNA circle. This poses the problem of how to cleave the double-size circle into two daughter chromosomes. Conceivably, a sequence-recognizing endonuclease converts such double-size circles into two λ-type DNA rods (Figure 9–21). These could either remain linear, or use their single-stranded complementary ends to circularize. Hints for double-size viral circles already exist in cells, with genetic studies showing that some of these molecules are the product of DNA replication, not of recombination between two unit-size circles.

Despite the pleasing simplicity of this model, however, there is as yet no real reason to believe that all of its features are correct. For example, the second nuclease cut which creates the second rolling circle could be imagined to occur in the same strand broken by the first cut. If so, the resulting products would be two unit-size circles, not a double-size circle. And as we shall mention later, there is considerable doubt about the precise role of DNA polymerase in the replication of most DNA.

SINGLE ROLLING CIRCLES

Some types of DNA replication are best explained on the basis of a replicating intermediate which contains either a clockwise or a counterclockwise tail, but not both. For instance, when

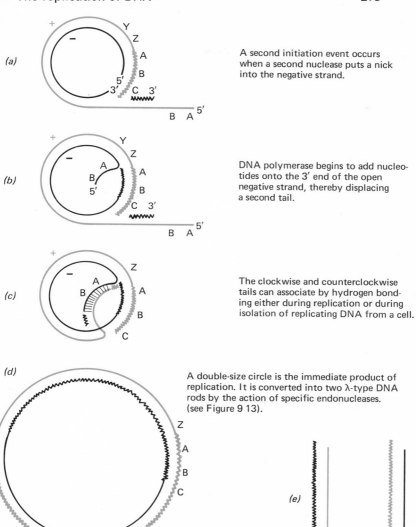

(a) A second initiation event occurs when a second nuclease puts a nick into the negative strand.

(b) DNA polymerase begins to add nucleotides onto the 3′ end of the open negative strand, thereby displacing a second tail.

(c) The clockwise and counterclockwise tails can associate by hydrogen bonding either during replication or during isolation of replicating DNA from a cell.

(d) A double-size circle is the immediate product of replication. It is converted into two λ-type DNA rods by the action of specific endonucleases. (see Figure 9 13).

(e)

FIGURE 9–21   A scheme for DNA replication involving opposing rolling circles.

bacteria mate the DNA that the male transfers into the female is single-stranded, not double-stranded. The mating process starts by the nicking of one strand of the male chromosome. This strand is then elongated at its 3' end, leading to displacement of the 5' end into the female (Figure 9–22). Once the male DNA is inside the recipient, it is converted to normal double-helical DNA. It may then, by genetic recombination, be exchanged for a portion of the original female chromosome. Transfer in this way couples DNA replication and mating in such a way as to never lead to genetically deficient male parents.

REPAIR SYNTHESIS

Until recently, most biochemists believed that their *in vitro* experiments studying incorporation of nucleotide precursors into polynucleotide strands necessarily were related to the normal replication process in cells. Faith in this belief has been seriously shaken by the discovery of several types of repair synthesis. Before, it was thought that a polynucleotide chain must remain intact if it is to be passed on during chromosome replication. Events like x-ray or ultraviolet (uv) irradiation, which broke chains or altered the structure of specific bases,

FIGURE 9–22   *Transfer of single-stranded DNA from a male bacteria into the female via a rolling circle mechanism.*

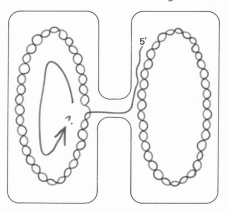

F I G U R E 9–23 *Formation of thymine dimers by uv irradiation.*

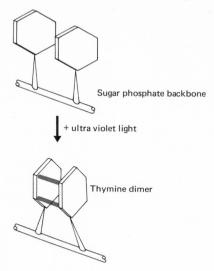

Sugar phosphate backbone

+ ultra violet light

Thymine dimer

were thought to be unconditionally lethal. Now several distinct types of repair processes are known to exist. In large part, they were first revealed by the discovery of mutants with increased sensitivity to radiation damage. Subsequent biochemical work then revealed the lack of a specific repair process in these mutants. Thus, in normal cells, much radiation damage is usually repaired before it has time to express itself.

The best understood case is the creation of thymine-thymine dimers by uv light. When uv light is absorbed by adjacent thymine molecules, they fuse together to form the structure shown in Figure 9–23. If unrepaired, this event is normally lethal; the fused thymine molecules do not act as faithful templates for the production of progeny strains. Normal replication usually takes place only if the dimers are excised. This occurs in several stages, each mediated by a specific enzyme. Conceivably in the first step, a specific endonuclease recognizes the damaged region, cutting the relevant polynucleotide strand on one side of the dimer. In the second step, an exonuclease may digest away nucleotides adjacent to the cut. In the third step, 5′-nucleoside triphosphates bind to the resulting single-stranded region and subsequently become linked by an enzyme, possibly DNA polymerase, to the 3′ end of an adjacent chain fragment. In the last step, the resulting gap is bridged by the joining enzyme polynucleotide ligase (Figure 9–24).

There is evidence for the existence of repair processes in virtually all cells examined, from bacterial to higher plants and animals. This is not surprising, since all cells are constantly subjected to various forms of radiation. During evolution,

FIGURE 9–24 *Some of the enzymatic steps involved in the repair of DNA molecules containing thymine dimers.*

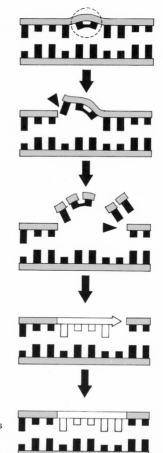

1. A distortion in the DNA molecule caused by a u v light-induced thymine dimer.

2. A specific endonuclease breaks the backbone of one chain near the dimer.

3. The excision of a small region containing the thymine dimer by an exonuclease.

4. 5′–3′ synthesis of new strand. The correct bases are inserted by base pairing with those on the intact strand.

5. Polynucleotide ligase joins up the two ends of the strand and the "repaired" molecule is complete.

those cells possessing better and better enzymatic systems for repairing damaged DNA molecules must have had an enormous selective advantage. In fact, evolution of repair systems might have been a necessary prerequisite for the development of organisms with larger and larger amounts of DNA. For the larger the amount of necessary DNA, the greater the probability that a given dose of radiation would cause a lethal event.

CELLS WITHOUT DNA POLYMERASE

The stepwise addition of nucleotides to growing chains envisioned under rolling circle models requires the functioning of an enzyme with a specificity like that of DNA polymerase. Recently, however, an E. coli mutant was isolated that lacks this enzyme but nonetheless replicates its DNA at the normal rate. Most importantly, this mutant has increased sensitivity to uv and so must lack one of the enzymes involved in repair processes. This is a strong hint that DNA polymerase sometimes plays a repair role. This, however, does not mean that it is not also involved in replication. But for this to be true, we would need to postulate the existence of at least two enzymes with the specificity of DNA polymerase, each of which can do either repair or replication. Under this scheme a cell is viable as long as it possesses at least one of these enzymes. Unfortunately we must again come back to the question of why, despite intensive research, no other enzyme has been found that incorporates nucleotide precursors into polynucleotide strands.

MEMBRANE INVOLVEMENT IN REPLICATION

The answer may be in the need for the simultaneous presence of intact portions of the bacterial membrane. There is excellent cytological evidence for the attachment of bacterial chromosomes to invaginated portions of the cell membrane called mesosomes (Figure 9–25). Moreover, in vivo DNA transformation experiments using fragments of the bacterial chromosome as genetic donors suggest that the DNA section attached

FIGURE 9–25 *Attachment of a Bacillus subtilis chromosome to an invagination (mesosome) of the bacterial membrane. (N) Nuclear chromosomal material; (M) Mesosome. (Photograph kindly supplied by A. Ryter, Institut Pasteur, Paris.)*

to the membrane is close to the region where replication starts. That is, all replication may occur on or near the membrane, with one or more of the replicating enzyme(s) an integral component of the membrane itself. If so, it is not surprising that this (these) enzyme(s) has not yet been discovered. In the preparations of most cell-free systems so far examined, the cell wall and membrane components have been routinely removed. The suspicion that isolation of intact membranes with their attached DNA molecules will be necessary for subsequent progress in understanding how DNA replicates is not completely pleasant. Despite much labor, almost nothing is really known about the structure of any membrane, bacterial or otherwise. Nonetheless, the direction of future progress may finally be clear.

SUMMARY

The primary genetic material is DNA. It usually consists of two polynucleotide chains twisted about each other in a regular helix. Each chain contains a very large number of nucleotides. There are four main nucleotides and their sequence along a given chain is very irregular. The two chains are joined together by hydrogen bonds between pairs of bases. Adenine (purine) is always joined to thymine (pyrimidine) and guanine (purine) is always bonded to cytosine (pyrimidine). The existence of the base pairs means that the sequences of nucleotides along the two chains are not identical but complementary. If the sequence of one chain is known, that of its partner is automatically known.

Cellular duplication of DNA occurs with the two strands separated, allowing the single strands to act as templates for the formation of complementary strands. The strands do not completely separate before the synthesis of the new strands. Instead duplication goes hand in hand with strand separation. The monomeric precursors for DNA synthesis are the deoxynucleoside-triphosphates, which are enzymatically joined together in the presence of DNA template. Selection of the correct nucleotides by hydrogen bonding to the correct template bases is a very accurate process. The average probability of an error in the insertion of a new nucleotide under optimal conditions may be as low as 10^{-8} to 10^{-9}.

Individual DNA molecules may be very large. They either exist as circles or as rods which have the ability to become circles. In fact, the E. coli chromosome appears to be a single circular DNA molecule with a MW of about 2 to 4 $\times 10^9$. It is important for the linear DNA molecules to be able to circularize, since pictures of actively replicating DNA show circular configurations.

Initiation of replication begins at a fixed location on the circular chromosome, with growth of many chains starting by elongation of preexisting strands. Most likely, at least several enzymes (circle opening, elongation, circle closing) are involved in replication. Some of these enzymes probably also function in the repair of damaged DNA molecules. One or more of the enzyme(s) directly connected with the replication process may be associated with portions of the bacterial membrane. Proof of this point, however, may be difficult because of the poverty of knowledge at the molecular level about bacterial membranes.

REFERENCES

Watson, J. D., and F. H. C. Crick, "Genetical Implications of the Structure of Deoxyribonucleic Acid," *Nature*, **177**:964 (1953).

Meselson, M., and F. W. Stahl, "The Replication of DNA in *Escherichia coli*," *Proc. Nat. Acad. Sci.*, **44**:671 (1958). A classic experiment in molecular biology, showing that DNA replication involves the separation of the two complementary polynucleotide chains.

Kornberg, A., "The Synthesis of DNA," *Sci. Am.*, October 1968. A description of the test-tube replication of single-stranded DNA.

Kornberg, A., "Active Center of DNA Polymerase," *Science*, **163**, 1410 (1969). A much more technical description of many of the elegant experiments emanating from the author's Stanford laboratory.

Cairns, J., and C. I. Davern, "Mechanism of DNA Replication in Bacteria," *J. Cell Physiology*, 70: Suppl. I, p. 65 (1967). A short and lucid summary of many of the current dilemmas in the DNA synthesis field.

"Replication of DNA in Microorganisms," *Cold Spring Harbor Symp. Quant. Biol.*, **33** (1968). A very complete summary of all aspects of DNA synthesis may be found in this collection of 89 papers presented during a June 1968 meeting.

Thomas, C. A., Jr., and L. D. MacHattie, "The Anatomy of Viral DNA Molecules," *Ann. Rev. Biochem.*, **36**: Part 2, 485 (1967). An excellent introduction to the ways in which the circular and linear forms of DNA interconvert.

Richardson, C. C. "Enzymes in DNA Metabolism," *Ann. Rev. Biochem.*, **38**, 795 (1969). A most satisfactory survey of the various enzymes now thought to participate in DNA replication and repair.

De Lucia, Paula and J. Cairns, "Isolation of an *E. coli* strain with a mutation affecting DNA polymerase," *Nature*, **224** (1164).

Gross, J. and Marilyn Gross, "Genetic Analysis of an *E. coli* strain with a mutation affecting DNA polymerase," *Nature*, **224** (1166). This and the above paper document the mutant which has lost DNA polymerase activity.

10

THE GENETIC

ORGANIZATION

OF DNA

EVEN BEFORE THE DOUBLE HELIX WAS found, the simplest hypothesis imaginable was that the genetic information of DNA resided in the sequence of its various nucleotides. But until the structure was uncovered, it was possible that knowledge of the nucleotide order was not by itself sufficient. The real key might lie in some weird 3-D form not easily, if at all, deducible from the sequence of bases. Fortunately, the double helix tells us that all nucleotides are geometrically equivalent, unambiguously revealing that the genetic code resides in their linear sequences.

THEORETICALLY, A VERY, VERY LARGE NUMBER OF DIFFERENT SEQUENCES CAN EXIST

Since the sugar-phosphate backbone is the same in all DNA molecules, it necessarily cannot carry any genetic information. The information must instead be carried in the sequence of the four (A, G, C, T) bases. This requirement, however, poses no real restriction on the effective amount of information in DNA. Since each molecule is very long, the number of sequence permutations is 4^n, where n is the number of nucleotides in a given molecule. A virtually infinite number of genetic messages can be coded with the four letters, A, T, C, and G of the nucleic acid alphabet. The possible number of different genes of MW = 10^6 is 4^{1500}, a value very much larger than the number of different genes that have existed in all the chromosomes present since the origin of life.

MUTATIONS ARE CHANGES IN THE SEQUENCE OF BASE PAIRS

The genetic mapping of the T4rIIA gene revealed at least 500 sites at which mutations can occur and between which genetic

FIGURE 10–1   *The relationship of mutations in the rII region of the chromosome of phage T4 to the structure of DNA.*

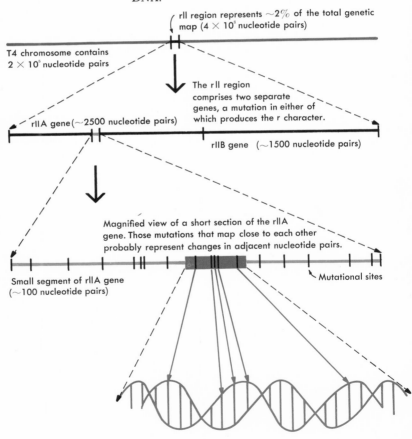

rII region represents ~2% of the total genetic map (4×10^5 nucleotide pairs)

T4 chromosome contains 2×10^5 nucleotide pairs

The rII region comprises two separate genes, a mutation in either of which produces the r character.

rIIA gene (~2500 nucleotide pairs)

rIIB gene (~1500 nucleotide pairs)

Magnified view of a short section of the rIIA gene. Those mutations that map close to each other probably represent changes in adjacent nucleotide pairs.

Small segment of rIIA gene (~100 nucleotide pairs)

Mutational sites

recombination (crossing over) is possible. The magnitude of this number immediately tells us that these sites are the specific base pairs along the gene (Figure 10–1).

Many mutations are base-pair switches from, for example, AT to GC, CG, or TA (Figure 10–2). Thus, by studying the fine details of the genetic map very carefully, it is possible to obtain important information about the sequence of base pairs along

FIGURE 10–2 *Three classes of mutations result from introducing defects in the sequence of bases (A, T, G, C) that are attached to the backbone of the DNA molecule. In one class, a base pair is simply changed from one into another (i.e., G-C to A-T). In the second class, a base pair is inserted (or deleted). In the third class, a group of base pairs is deleted (or inserted).*

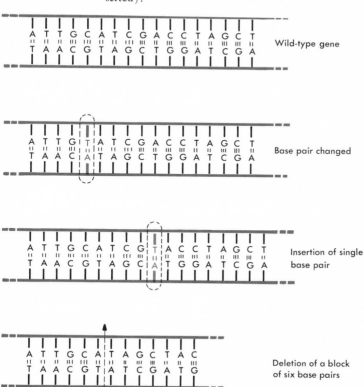

the DNA molecule, with one major reservation. There is no a priori reason to believe that all changes in the genetic code will necessarily cause functional changes in the corresponding proteins. The number of observed mutable sites, is, therefore, likely to be a serious underestimate of the number of nucleotide pairs.

Most single base switches are reversible, and often the rate of the "back" mutation to the normal nucleotide arrangement has an order of magnitude similar to that of the rate of change to the mutant arrangement. These mutations most likely reflect failures in the replication process. Either the correct hydrogen bonds do not form (Figure 10–3) or an adenine mistakenly pairs with guanine (or cytosine with thymine). There are other rare locations where the rates of forward (backward) mutation greatly exceed the reverse step. Most of these highly mutable nucleotide pairs—"hot spots"—probably do not arise by normal duplication, but as we shall see below, are connected with mispairing during crossing over.

Except for the hot spots, the general rate of spontaneous mutations agrees with our earlier guess about the accuracy of base pairing during replication. The average rate of detectable mutations per gene duplication is about 10^{-6}. This figure can be extended to the nucleotide level only if we guess what fraction of base pairs must remain unchanged for the maintenance of normal gene function. If we suppose that all the base pairs are essential, then in a gene containing 1000 nucleotides the error at the nucleotide level is approximately 10^{-9} mistakes per nucleotide replication. Only for the rII genes are there sufficient data to estimate the fraction of base pairs whose change leads to a detectable mutation. The 500 mutable sites known at present probably reflect at least one-fourth and possibly one-half of the total genetic map. Detectable mutations in the rII gene, however, occur at a higher rate than in many other loci. Here the total mutation frequency (even if we exclude the hot spots) is about 10^{-4} to 10^{-5}. This may mean that in most other genes many fewer nucleotide changes lead to detectable mutations than in the rII genes. If so, the general mistake level may be as high as 10^{-7} per nucleotide replication.

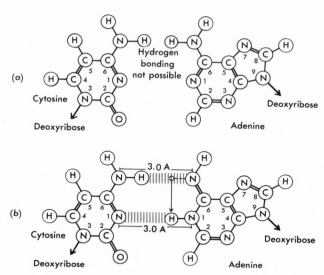

F I G U R E 10–3 *This demonstrates how the specificity of base pairing in DNA is determined by hydrogen bonding. The hydrogen atoms are indicated by solid circles, the bonds by ||||. (a) Shows why the pairing of cytosine with an adenine molecule, having the most stable distribution of its hydrogen atoms, cannot lead to hydrogen bonding. (b) Shows how the shift of a hydrogen atom in an adenine molecule, from the 6-amino group to the N_1 position, permits hydrogen bonding with cytosine. The normal position of the hydrogen atom is indicated by the small open circle. (The dimensions shown are only approximate.) (Redrawn from W. Hayes, The Genetics of Bacteria and Their Viruses, Blackwell, Oxford, 1964, p. 228, with permission.)*

Other spontaneous mutations involve the loss (deletions) or gain (insertions) of nucleotides. Sometimes hundreds to thousands of nucleotides are involved in deletions, and in rare cases, whole genes are lost. Reverse (back) mutation to the normal gene arrangement, clearly impossible for large deletions and insertions, occurs only at low rates for simple one-nucleotide mutations.

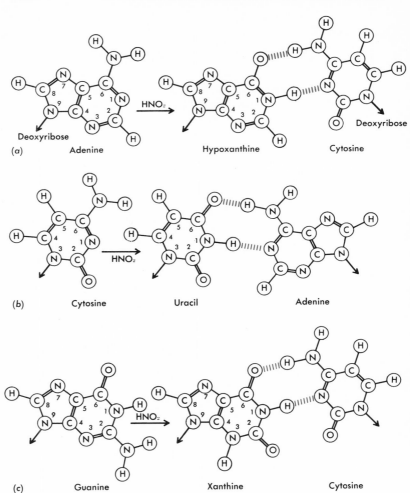

FIGURE 10–4 *The oxidative deamination of DNA bases by nitrous acid, and its effects on subsequent base pairing. (a) Adenine is deaminated to hypoxanthine, which bonds to cytosine instead of to thymine. (b) Cytosine is deaminated to uracil, which bonds to adenine instead of to guanine. (c) Guanine is deaminated to xanthine, which continues to bond to cytosine, though with only two hydrogen bonds. Thymine, and the uracil of RNA, do not carry an amino group and so remain unaltered. (Redrawn from W. Hayes, The Genetics of Bacteria and Their Viruses, Blackwell, Oxford, 1964, p. 280, with permission.)*

PRECISE STATEMENTS ABOUT
SOME CHEMICAL MUTAGENS

It is now possible to make intelligent statements about how some chemical mutagens produce changes in the genetic code. For example, nitrous acid (HNO_2) is a very powerful mutagen because it acts directly on the nucleic acids, replacing amino groups by keto groups. Thus, it directly alters the genetic code by converting one base into another (Figure 10–4). Other substances cause mutations as a result of their incorporation into the DNA molecule itself. These latter compounds are base analogues which, because of their structural similarity to the

FIGURE 10–5   *The base-pairing attributes of 5-bromouracil.   (a) In the normal keto state, with a hydrogen atom in the N_1 position, bromouracil bonds to adenine.   (b) In the rare enol state, a tautomeric shift of this hydrogen atom determines specific pairing with guanine.   (Redrawn from W. Hayes,* The Genetics of Bacteria and Their Viruses, *Blackwell, Oxford, 1964, p. 278, with permission.)*

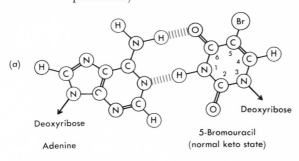

normal DNA bases, can be incorporated into DNA without destroying its capacity for replication. Their different structures, however, often cause less accurate base-pair formation than normal, leading to mistakes during the replication process. One of the most powerful base analogue mutagens is 5-bromouracil, an analogue of thymine. It is believed to cause mutations because its hydrogen atom at position 1 is not as firmly fixed as the corresponding hydrogen atom in thymine. Sometimes this hydrogen atom is bonded to the oxygen atom attached to carbon atom 6 (Figure 10–5). When this happens, the 5-bromouracil can pair with guanine.

GAPS BETWEEN GENES ARE RELATIVELY SHORT

Usually there is much less crossing over between mutations located at adjacent ends of two contiguous genes than between two mutations at extreme ends of even the shortest genes. This suggests that adjacent genes often are separated by relatively few nucleotide pairs. Confirmation of this point will not be possible until the exact nucleotide sequences of a number of contiguous gene sets are determined chemically. Until recently, this task seemed virtually impossible, but new techniques are now beginning to reveal long stretches of nucleotide sequences of certain viral chromosomes. As we shall see in Chapter 13, the first intergenic sequence data show a group of 30 nucleotide pairs separating the two genes.

AGREEMENT OF A GENETIC MAP WITH THE CORRESPONDING DISTANCE ALONG A DNA MOLECULE

Since crossing-over analysis began, geneticists have wondered how closely their genetic maps corresponded with actual physical length along the chromosome. The visualization in the 1930s of *Drosophila*'s highly extended salivary chromosomes permitted the exact mapping of the sites of mutations. Good correlations between the physical and genetic distances along some chromosomal stretches were shown. But these views of chromosomes in the light miscroscope tell us nothing about the arrangement of the constituent DNA molecules. Firm answers at the molecular level could come only when it became possible to locate the sites of specific mutations along a well-defined viral chromosome (DNA molecule).

The chromosome best studied so far is that of phage λ. Several methods have been used to assign physical locations to the various mutations. The first utilized our ability to break DNA helices into fragments of defined size by stirring them in a blender. A certain stirring speed will break λ DNA into halves, a higher speed will produce quarters, and so on. Fragments which have different densities can then be separated from each other by equilibrium centrifugation in a cesium chloride gradient. As fragments rich in GC have a higher density than those rich in AT, separation becomes routinely possible if the various fragments are constituted from different AT/GC ratios. This is the case in λ, where the left-hand side is much richer in GC than the right-hand side (Figure 15–9). Purified left and right halves can then be used in DNA transformation experiments to see which genes are in each fragment. The results show good correlation with the left and right halves of the genetic map.

Much more precise data come from the mapping of well-defined deletions of large numbers of nucleotides. This can be done using the technique of DNA-DNA hybridization. In this procedure, the two strands of the λ double helix are separated by heating the DNA to near 100°C. At that temperature virtually all the hydrogen bonds holding the molecule together break and the resulting free single strands unwind from each other (DNA denaturation). The "+" and "−" strands then can be separated by their density differences in a CsCl solution. Reformation of the double helices from separated single strands (renaturation) occurs if the single strands are mixed together, heated to near 100°C, and then gradually cooled. Under these conditions the original hydrogen bonds between the complementary chains reform and the resulting molecules are indistinguishable in the electron microscope from molecules which have never been heated.

If, however, renaturation occurs between a normal "+" strand and a "−" strand containing a deletion, the "+" strand section complementary to the deleted "–" section cannot form hydrogen bonds. It exists as a single-stranded loop extended out from the predominately double-stranded molecule (Figure 10–6). These loops are easily detectable in the electron microscope (Figure 10–7), allowing the location of a number of different deletions to be precisely spotted along the λ DNA molecule. Putting these data alongside the very extensively

FIGURE 10–6 *Mapping of deletions by electron-microscope vizualization of renatured DNA molecules.*

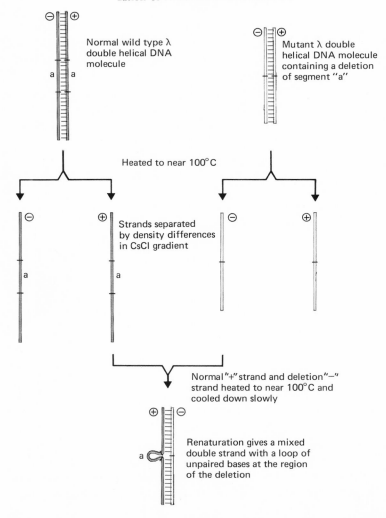

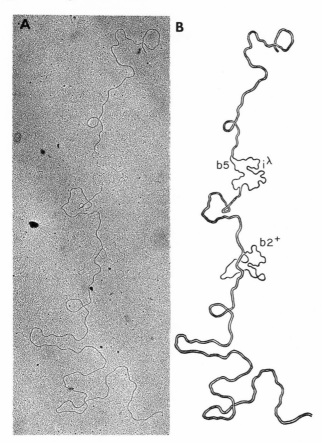

F I G U R E 10–7   An electron micrograph (left) of a heteroduplex formed between strand l of λ⁺ and strand r of λb2b5 together with an interpretive drawing (right). λb2b5 contains a deletion (b2) and a nonhomologous section (b5) unable to pair with its λ counterpart. [Reproduced with permission from Westmoreland, Szybalski and Ris, Science 163, 1343 (1969).]

studied λ genetic map gives the picture shown in Figure 10–8. It reveals a much closer correspondence between the genetic map and the actual physical structure of the DNA than had been anticipated. Thus, at medium resolution, the probability of crossing over is approximately equal throughout the DNA molecule. Exceptions to this point are obvious in Figure 10–8, and caution must be taken not to overinterpret genetic linkage data.

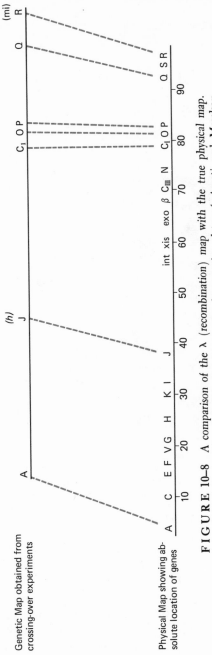

Genetic Map obtained from crossing-over experiments

Physical Map showing absolute location of genes

FIGURE 10–8 *A comparison of the* λ *(recombination) map with the true physical map. The recombination map was drawn using data of Amati and Meselson* [*Genetics* **51**, 369 (1965)], *while the physical map is redrawn from a recent map prepared by W. Szybalski (University of Wisconsin).*

THE AVERAGE GENE CONTAINS ABOUT 900 TO 1500 NUCLEOTIDE PAIRS

There are several ways to reach this conclusion. The most direct one divides the number of nucleotides in a chromosome by the number of genes located along it. For example, over 65 genes in the bacterial virus T4 chromosomes are already described. The chromosome has a molecular weight of 120 million, giving an average molecular weight of 2 million per gene. This is clearly an upper estimate, since a significant fraction of the T4 genes have probably not yet been discovered. In the more thoroughly studied bacterial virus λ, some 40 genes have been mapped. As the molecular weight of its DNA is 32 million, the upper limit of its average gene size is 0.8 million.

Similar size ranges are given by genetic mapping experiments. For example, the rIIA gene of T4 occupies about 1 per cent of the total genetic map (Figure 10–1). If it is of average size, there are about 100 genes in T4. The validity of this method also depends upon the assumption that crossing over occurs with approximately equal frequency in all regions along the chromosome. When this is not true, regions in which much crossing over takes place will genetically seem much farther apart than regions of equal physical size that have limited recombination.

Our first argument is eventually the more rigorous, suffering only the complication that not all the genes in T4 and λ are known. Hence, we should look closely at the rates at which new genes are still being discovered. It now looks as if the number for both T4 and λ will be at most doubled (the rate of discovery, especially for λ, is rapidly slowing down). Thus, the average gene size may be between a half and one million, depending upon the organism under study. Since the molecular weight of a pair of bases is slightly over 600, this means that an average gene is a linear arrangement of from around 900 to 1500 base pairs.

CROSSING OVER IS DUE TO BREAKAGE AND REJOINING OF INTACT DNA MOLECULES

Until recently, not even a superficial understanding of the molecular basis of crossing over existed. The classical picture of crossing over, developed in the 1930s from cytological observations, hypothesized that during meiosis the paired, coiled chromosomes were sometimes physically broken at the chromatid level as a result of tension created by their contraction. The broken ends could then relieve the tension by crossways reunion, creating two reciprocally recombinant chromatids as well as two parental chromatids (Figure 10–9). According to this model, recombination occurs after chromosome duplication is complete—that is, at the four-strand stage. This hypothesis

FIGURE 10–9 *Diagrammatic representation of two possible mechanisms of crossing over.*

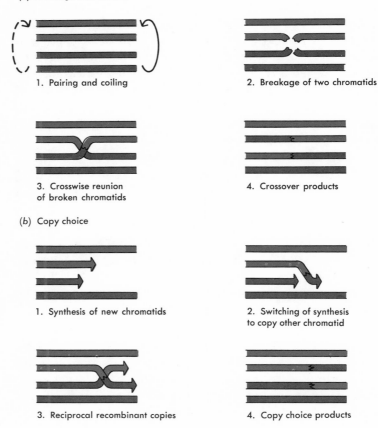

(a) Breakage and reunion

1. Pairing and coiling

2. Breakage of two chromatids

3. Crosswise reunion of broken chromatids

4. Crossover products

(b) Copy choice

1. Synthesis of new chromatids

2. Switching of synthesis to copy other chromatid

3. Reciprocal recombinant copies

4. Copy choice products

fell into disfavor about 1955 when geneticists found that crossing over occurred within the gene, by then realized to be part of a DNA molecule. A seemingly unpleasant consequence was that the effective breakage points must necessarily lie between the same nucleotides in the two homologous chromatids. Otherwise recombination would generate new DNA molecules differing in length from the parental molecules.

To avoid these dilemmas, enthusiasm developed for a hypothesis relating recombination to chromosome duplication. This alternative hypothesis proposed that during replication of the paired chromosomes, the new DNA strand being formed along the paternal chromosomes (for example) switches to the maternal one that it thereafter copies. If the complementary replica of the maternal strand also switches templates when it reaches the same point, two reciprocally recombinant strands would be formed. This hypothetical process is called *copy choice*. A fundamental distinction between the two hypotheses lies in their prediction of the physical origin of recombinant chromosomes. Following breakage and reunion, the recombinant chromosomes inherit physical material from the two parental chromosomes. In contrast, the recombinant chromosomes produced by copy choice are synthesized from new material.

These alternative hypotheses were recently tested by experiments using isotopically heavy (C^{13}, N^{15}) parental phage λ particles (Figures 10–10 and 10–11). Here again the heavy isotopes were used to allow a cesium chloride gradient to distinguish between parental and daughter DNA strands. Genetic crosses between heavy (or between heavy and light) phage particles were made in *E. coli* cells growing in a light (C^{12}, N^{14}) medium. Under these conditions, all of the newly synthesized viral DNA molecules are derived from light precursors; thus, if copy choice is the correct mechanism, all the recombinant particles should be light. On the contrary, if recombinants are derived by breakage and reunion, some of the recombinant phage particles will contain heavy atoms derived from the parental chromosomes. The progeny particles of these crosses were placed in dense CsCl solutions and rapidly centrifuged to

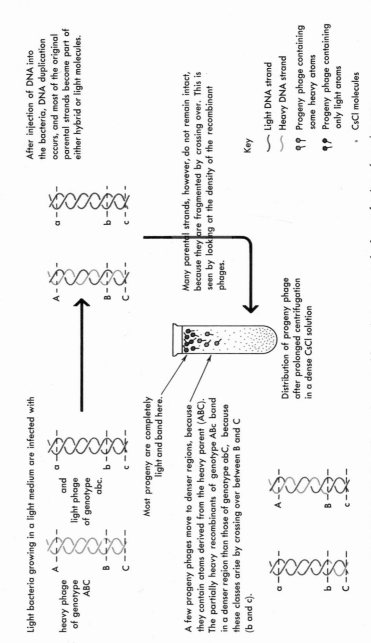

Light bacteria growing in a light medium are infected with

heavy phage of genotype ABC

and

light phage of genotype abc.

Most progeny are completely light and band here.

A few progeny phages move to denser regions, because they contain atoms derived from the heavy parent (ABC). The partially heavy recombinants of genotype ABc band in a denser region than those of genotype abC, because these classes arise by crossing over between B and C (b and c).

Distribution of progeny phage after prolonged centrifugation in a dense CsCl solution

Many parental strands, however, do not remain intact, because they are fragmented by crossing over. This is seen by looking at the density of the recombinant phages.

After injection of DNA into the bacteria, DNA duplication occurs, and most of the original parental strands become part of either hybrid or light molecules.

Key

～ Light DNA strand

～ Heavy DNA strand

Progeny phage containing some heavy atoms

Progeny phage containing only light atoms

• CsCl molecules

FIGURE 10–10   The employment of heavy isotopes to study the mechanism of crossing over.

After injection of the DNA molecules into the bacteria, most heavy strands become part of hybrid molecules. Rarely, however, an infecting molecule fails to duplicate and, when the new progeny particles are formed, these unreplicated molecules, in which the parental strands have never separated, become enclosed in new protein shells. This phenomenon enables us to ask whether the rare, completely heavy, DNA molecules are ever recombinants. Again use is made of a CsCl gradient to separate progeny particles of different density.

Key

⌒ Light DNA strand

⌒ Heavy DNA strand

· CsCl molecule

Progeny phage containing only light atoms

Progeny phage containing some heavy atoms

Light bacteria growing in a light medium are infected with

several particles, heavy phage, of genotype AB

and several particles, heavy phage, of genotype ab

A — a
B — b

Most progeny are light and band here.

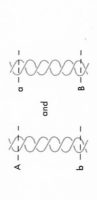

Distribution of progeny phage.

This is where the very rare progeny particles, containing completely heavy DNA, band. Some of these phage are recombinants of the classes

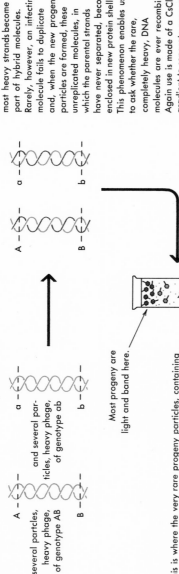

A — a
B — b

and

A — a
b — B

This shows that crossing over occurs between intact double helices and that extensive DNA synthesis is not involved in crossing over.

FIGURE 10–11 An experimental demonstration that crossing over and DNA duplication are independent phenomena.

separate particles of different density. Phage particles of vary-ing density were then collected and genetically tested to see which were recombinants. The experimental results (Figure 10–10) were clear-cut and, to the surprise of most molecular biologists, showed that some recombinant particles contained heavy atoms. Moreover, further experiments (Figure 10–11) revealed that recombination can occur between nonreplicating DNA molecules. Breakage and reunion of intact double helices must, therefore, be the primary mechanism of crossing over in bacteriophage. Crossing over in both bacteria and higher or-ganisms will most likely have a similar basis.

INVOLVEMENT OF SPECIFIC ENZYMES IN THE RECOMBINATION PROCESS

Two assumptions underlie most current experiments designed to disclose the exact way(s) in which the strands recombine. The first assumption is that two homologous double-helical DNA molecules will not attract each other at specific points. No obvious pairing force can be imagined. The second assump-tion is that recognition involves hydrogen bond formation be-tween complementary regions of single-stranded chains.

One way by which single-stranded regions might arise starts with the production by an endonuclease of single-stranded cuts. This creates free ends at which DNA polymerase can add new nucleotides, thus displacing the preexisting strands to form a number of single-stranded tails (Figure 10–12). Random col-lisions of tails with complementary sequences lead to the for-mation of double-helical junctions between different DNA molecules. If subsequent endonuclease cuts occur as shown in Figure 10–12, followed by gap filling, then a recombinant DNA molecule is produced together with two partial molecules. Exonuclease attack on the remaining fragments will then pro-duce the complementary single-stranded regions (Figure 10–12) necessary to bring about their union. The gaps in the individual strands can then be filled by an enzyme with the specificity of DNA polymerase. The final result is a second recombinant molecule whose genetic structure is essentially reciprocal to the first recombinant.

Solid evidence implicating nucleases in recombination comes

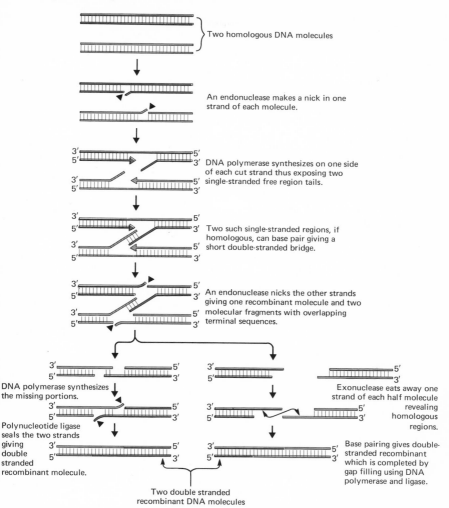

FIGURE 10–12   *The hypothesis that crossing over starts with pairing between complementary single-stranded tails growing out from double-helical DNA molecules.*

from the study of phages T4 and λ. When they multiply, much more crossing over occurs than is observed in corresponding lengths of *E. coli* DNA. Simultaneously, several viral specific nucleases appear. Each is coded by a specific gene on the viral chromosome (see Chapter 15). In T4 infection, both a viral

specific endonuclease and a new enzyme with specificity like
DNA polymerase have so far been discovered, while λ infection
is marked by the appearance of both new exonuclease and endonuclease activity. Most importantly, mutations which block
the synthesis of the λ exonuclease also block the increase in
recombination which normally accompanies λ infection.

STABILIZATION OF EXTENDED SINGLE-STRANDED TAILS BY A RECOMBINATION-PROMOTING PROTEIN

Apparently at variance with the above theory is the strong
tendency of all known DNA single strands to form hydrogen-
bonded hairpin loops like those of single-stranded RNA chains
(see Chapter 11). At 37°C outside of cells the majority of
bases in single-stranded DNA are part of hydrogen-bonded loops
(Figure 11–11) which normally break only when the temperature is raised to above 50°C. Thus many people found it very
hard to believe that freely extended single DNA chains were a
common intracellular feature. This dilemma vanished, however, with the very recent discovery of a protein which, by
binding tightly to single-stranded DNA, opens up the hairpin
loops. The resulting extended polynucleotide chains thereby
immediately become easily able to form double helices when
they collide with a similarly extended strand of complementary
sequences. Besides being involved with recombination, the protein also seems to play a necessary role in DNA replication—
possibly to keep the single-stranded regions at the growing
forks in the extended form necessary for template function.

HETERODUPLEXES

Perhaps the strongest support for the hypothesis that the fundamental recombination event involves pairing between single-
stranded tails is the existence of heteroduplex segments. These
are regions where the two strands are not exactly complementary. They arise when the pairing region encompasses the
site(s) of genetic differences between the two parental chromosomes. Evidence exists for heteroduplex regions in all viruses
whose genetics have been extensively analyzed. On the average,

one such region, several thousand nucleotides long, exists on each T4 DNA molecule. Heteroduplexes have also been well characterized in phage λ and again are much longer than at first expected. Thus, the intersecting tails should be large enough for direct electron-microscope visualization. Conceivably, this will occur very soon.

Heteroduplex lifetime is usually very short, for when the recombinant DNA molecules duplicate, the alternative alleles segregate out (Figure 10–13). This was first observed in phage systems, where mere inspection of recombinant plaques reveals mixtures of two genetically distinct types. When the DNA of a parental T4 phage particle contains a heteroduplex rII region, the resulting plaque has a mottled appearance with some sections characteristic of the rII phenotype, others of the wild-type r⁺ phenotype (Figure 10–14).

FIGURE 10–13   *Heteroduplex segregation with and without repair event.*

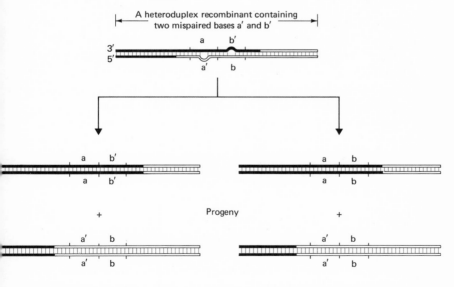

(a) Segregation following replication
with no repair event

(b) Segregation following replication with a
single repair event b′ → b

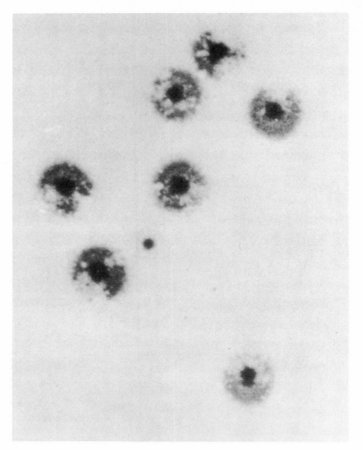

FIGURE 10–14   *Photographs of several mottled plaques arising from segregation of a heteroduplex DNA molecule containing both rII⁺ and rII markers on opposing strands. (Kindly supplied by A. D. Hershey.)*

RECOMBINATION IS NOT ALWAYS RECIPROCAL AT THE SITE OF CROSSING OVER

Early investigations of crossing over between different genes revealed the seemingly obligatory occurrence of reciprocal recombinants (Figure 10–15). Exceptions to this feature, however, were discovered when the recombinants studied arose between nearby sites in the same gene. Then, nonreciprocal behavior

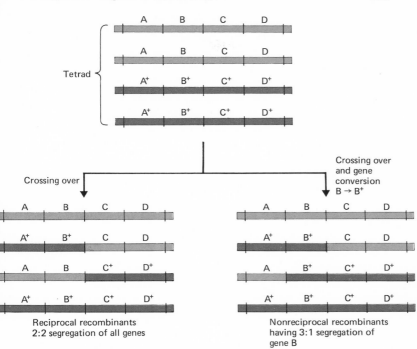

FIGURE 10–15 *Reciprocal and nonreciprocal recombination following crossing over.*

was often observed. This phenomenon, called "gene conversion," is best studied in those organisms, like yeast or *Neurospora*, where all the products of a single meiotic event can be seen. Here instead of always observing equal (2:2) segregation of the entering alleles, cases of 3:1 segregation are found.

The crossing-over hypothesis outlined above permits such exceptions. This is shown in Figure 10–13, where the final segregation pattern of genes localized around the crossing-over site may be affected by repair processes which recognize heteroduplex distortions in the double helix and randomly remove one of a mismatched base pair. Depending on the bases removed, either 2:2 or 3:1 ratios will be found. We do not yet know which fraction of gene conversion is actually due to repair synthesis. Other explanations involve complicated series of endonuclease and exonuclease cuts during recombination which may also produce disturbed segregation patterns. Seen from a broad perspective, however, the most striking thing about recombination, even at the molecular level, is the prevalence of reciprocal recombinants.

INSERTIONS (DELETIONS) ARISING FROM ERRORS IN CROSSING OVER

The extreme accuracy of most crossing-over events depends on the correct juxtaposition of the complementary single-stranded regions during reformation of the hydrogen bonds. This results from the uniqueness of most long nucleotide sequences. When a random chain of polynucleotides contains more than 12 nu-

FIGURE 10–16   *Origin of a many-nucleotide insertion through pairing of nearly homologous sequences within the same gene.*

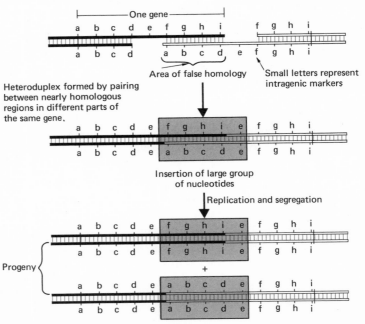

The two progeny molecules contain different insertions of a large group of nucleotides.

cleotides, it will virtually never have the same sequence as another fragment of similar length. Thus, as long as the single-stranded segments are relatively long, it is very, very unlikely that a fragment of one gene will mistakenly be linked up to the wrong part of its own gene or a different gene. In those rare cases, however, where two different regions have considerable homology, we should expect occasional misjoinings, leading to the insertion (deletion) of large blocks of nucleotides (Figure 10–16).

Deletions of single base pairs are the consequences of mispairing like that shown on the right in Figure 10–17. The resulting double helix has two mispaired bases which is uncor-

FIGURE 10–17   *The possible origin of deletions and insertions during crossing over by mispairing of regions containing stretches of identical bases.*

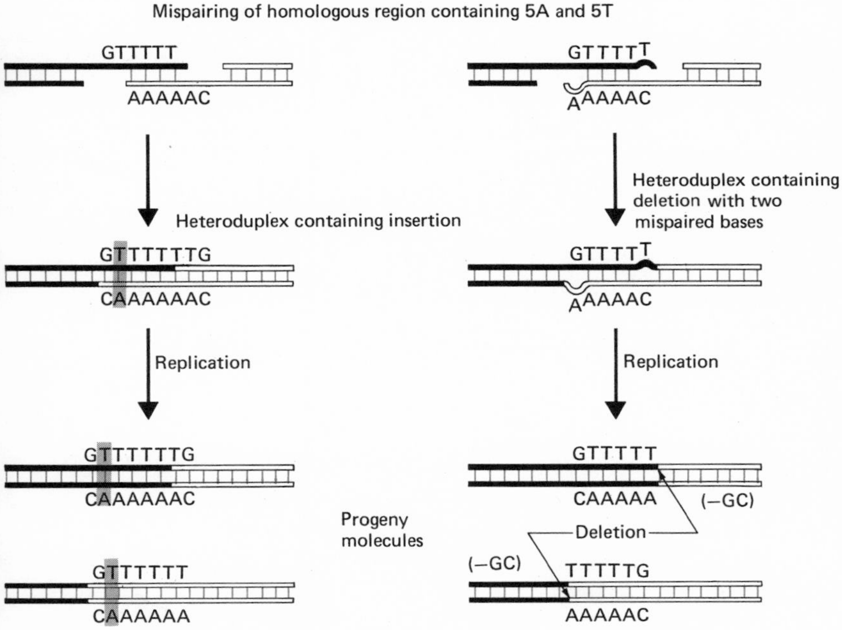

Mispairing of homologous region containing 5A and 5T

Heteroduplex containing insertion

Heteroduplex containing deletion with two mispaired bases

Replication

Replication

Progeny molecules

(–GC)

(–GC)

Deletion

(a) Segregation of recombinant gives two molecules containing an identical AT insertion.

(b) Segregation of recombinant gives two molecules each containing a different GC deletion.

rected by any repair process will give rise to two progeny helices, each containing a different nucleotide pair deletion. In contrast, if pairing occurs as on the left in Figure 10–17, the final result will be two progeny helices, each with the same single base-pair insertion.

With T4 it seems likely that most insertions (deletions) arise during crossing over. In contrast, during normal *E. coli* replication, there is much less crossing over, so the frequency of insertion (deletion) mutations is very much lower than with T4.

HOT SPOTS ARE OFTEN SITES OF MISMATCHING

The above model implies that the probability of an insertion (deletion) arising is dependent upon the base sequence around it. The longer the stretch of repeating bases, the higher the frequency of mutation. Evidence supporting this hypothesis came from studies on the T4-specific enzyme lysozyme, which is coded by the T4 DNA. Nucleotide sequence data obtained from insertion and deletion experiments like those described in the next section suggest that one highly mutable spot (hot spot) involves the deletion of an A from a stretch of 6 A residues. The reverse mutation, in which an additional A adds on to a 5A region, occurs at a 100-fold lower frequency. Thus, the freguency of the insertion (deletion) mutation most probably is a function of a very high power of the number of identical repeating bases (base doublets, etc.).

THE GENETIC CODE IS READ IN GROUPS OF THREE

An obvious consequence of the fact that there are 20 amino acids and only 4 bases is that each amino acid must be coded for by groups of nucleotides. There cannot be a one-to-one correspondence between the DNA bases and the amino acids. Genetic evidence tells us that groups of three nucleotides are fundamental units and that the code is read linearly starting from one end. These results arise from crosses between mutants with deletions (or insertions) of one or more nucleotides. Deletion or insertion mutations generally lead to completely nonfunctional genes. In contrast, simple nucleotide switches often lead to "leaky" genes, in which the mutant protein has partial enzymatic activity because of a single amino acid replacement. The virtually complete absence of enzymatic activity in the deletion (insertion) mutants tells us that their protein product is completely changed.

This striking qualitative difference arises from the fact that during protein synthesis the reading of the genetic code starts from one end of the protein template and occurs in consecutive blocks of three bases. As a result, if a deletion or insertion occurs, the reading frame is completely upset (Figure 10–18). For example, if normally the gene sequence ATTAGACAC . . . is read as (ATT), (AGA), (CAC), . . ., then the insertion of a new nucleotide ATTCAGACAC . . . leads to reading in the following groups: (ATT), (CAG), (ACA), (C . .). A similar consequence follows from a deletion. Crossing of two deletion (or two insertion) mutants yields double mutants in which the reading frame is still misplaced.

Partially active genes, however, can be produced by crossing over between an insertion and a nearby deletion. Crossing over between the deletion and insertion restores the correct reading frame except in the region between them (Figure 10–18). When the resulting protein product is normal except for several amino acid replacements, it may have some enzymatic activity. It is also sometimes possible to obtain functional genes by producing recombinants containing three closely spaced insertions (deletions). Recombinants containing four close insertions (deletions), however, produce only completely nonfunctional proteins. It is these latter two experiments that tell us that the reading group contains three nucleotides, since by combining three deletions (insertions), the reading frame is restored except for the deletion (insertion) region (Figure 10–19).

Thus an average gene containing 900 nucleotide pairs is subdivided into 300 reading units, each of which codes for a single amino acid. This corresponds very nicely with the average size of known proteins, somewhere around 30,000 (300 amino acids). Inasmuch as each estimate (average gene size and average protein size) is uncertain by 50 to 100 per cent, this

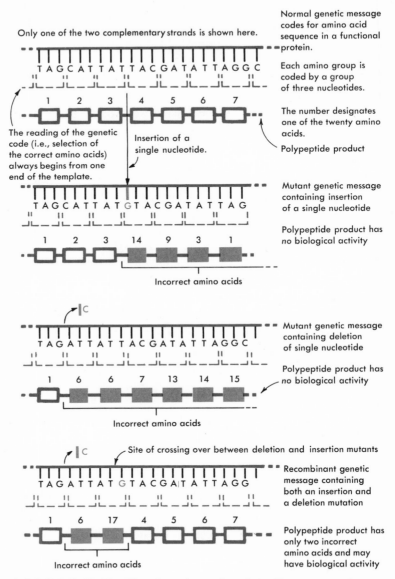

FIGURE 10–18   *The effect of mutations that add or remove a base is to shift the reading of the genetic message.*

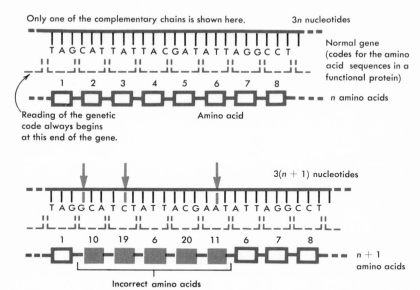

Only one of the complementary chains is shown here.   3n nucleotides

TAGCAT TATTACGATATTAGGCCT

Normal gene
(codes for the amino
acid sequences in a
functional protein)

1   2   3   4   5   6   7   8

Reading of the genetic   Amino acid   n amino acids
code always begins
at this end of the gene.

3(n + 1) nucleotides

TAGGCAT CTAT TACGAATATTAGGCCT

1   10   19   6   20   11   6   7   8   n + 1
                                               amino acids

Incorrect amino acids

Polypeptide chain contains four incorrect amino acids; its chain length is increased by one
amino acid. It may have some biological activity depending upon how the five wrong amino
acids influence its 3-D structure.

FIGURE 10–19 *The effect of the addition of three nucleotide pairs on the reading of the genetic code. When the three nucleotides are added close together, the genetic message is scrambled only over a short region. The same type of result is achieved by the deletion of three nearby nucleotides.*

level of agreement is almost better than the experimental evidence demands.

SUMMARY

The genetic information of a DNA molecule resides in the linear sequence of the four bases. Theoretically, a very, very large number of different sequences can exist, since the number of possible permutations is 4^n where n is the number of nucleotides along a DNA chain. All mutations involve changes in the sequence of base pairs. Many mutations are single base-pair replacements at a definite location, while others involve insertions or deletions of one to many nucleotide pairs. Replacements of a single base pair by another often result from mistakes in normal hydrogen bonding during replication, while insertion or deletion events frequently are connected with mistakes in crossing over.

Most nucleotides along a DNA molecule comprise genes coding for specific polypeptide chains. The distance between the end of one gene and the start of the adjacent one may be very short, sometimes only several nucleotides in length. Most DNA molecules contain a large number of genes, each of which usually contains between 600 and 1800 nucleotides. As groups of three successive nucleotides code for an individual amino acid, most polypeptides are composed of 200 to 600 amino acids.

Crossing over arises from breakage and rejoining of double-stranded DNA molecules. It is not directly connected with replication and must be mediated by specific cutting enzymes that expose long segments of single-stranded DNA. Formation of hydrogen bonds between these single-stranded regions of DNA may lead to the formation of recombinant molecules. Most molecular events involved in crossing over remain unknown.

REFERENCES

Benzer, S., "The Fine Structure of the Gene." A lucid 1962 *Scientific American* article, reprinted in *The Molecular Basis of Life*, p. 130, R. H. Haynes and P. C. Hanawalt (eds.), Freeman, San Francisco, 1968.

Stahl, F., *The Mechanics of Inheritance.* 2nd ed., Prentice-Hall, Englewood Cliffs, N.J., 1969. Mutation and recombination as seen by one of the more incisive phage workers. Particularly valuable are the questions accompanying each chapter.

Swanson, C. P., T. Merz, and W. J. Young, *Cytogenetics*, Prentice-Hall, Englewood Cliffs, N.J., 1967. A brief introduction to many of the cytological facts necessary for interpreting recombination experiments in higher organisms.

Whitehouse, H. K. L., *Toward an Understanding of the Mechanism of Heredity*, 2nd ed., Edward Arnold, London, 1969. The most complete treatment of the mechanism of crossing over to be found in any text.

Meselson, M., and J. J. Weigle, "Chromosome Breakage Accompanying Genetic Reconstruction in Bacteriophage," *Proc. Natl. Acad. Sci. U.S.*, **47**, 857–868 (1961). A classic paper which told the molecular biologists that chromosomes break during crossing over.

Strauss, B., "DNA Repair Mechanisms Related to Mutation and Recombination," in *Current Topics in Microbiology and Immunology*, Vol. 44, Springer, Berlin, 1968. A review that emphasizes both genetic and biochemical data.

Emerson, S., "Linkage and Recombination at the Chromosomal Level," in *Genetic Organization*, E. W. Caspari and A. W. Ravin (eds.), Academic, New York, 1969. The first thorough review which analyzes gene conversion in terms of DNA repair processes.

Crick, F. H. C., "The Genetic Code," *Sci. Am.*, October, 1962, pp. 66–74. A description of the original Crick-Brenner frameshift experiments with phage T4 revealing that the genetic code is read in groups of three nucleotides. Reprinted in *The Molecular Basis of Life*, p. 198, R. H. Haynes and P. C. Hanawalt, (eds.), Freeman, San Francisco, 1968.

Streisinger, G., Y. Okada, J. Emrich, J. Newton, A. Tsugita, E. Terzaghi, and M. Inoye, "Frameshift Mutations and the Genetic Code," *Cold Spring Harbor Symp. Quant. Biol.*, **31**, 77 (1966). A most elegant proof of the frameshift hypothesis involving amino acid sequence analysis.

Drake, John W., *The Molecular Basis of Mutation*, Holden-Day, San Francisco, 1970. A new and extensive summary about how mutations occur.

11

THE TRAN-
SCRIPTION OF
RNA UPON
DNA
TEMPLATES

WE ARE NOW READY TO APPROACH THE problem of how DNA controls the sequence of amino acids in proteins. Compared with DNA replication, we should anticipate this selection procedure to be a more chemically sophisticated task, since many of the amino acid side groups neither form specific hydrogen bonds nor have surfaces obviously complementary in shape to any nucleotide or nucleotide group. Yet somehow the correct amino acids are inserted into a given polypeptide chain with less than 1 error per 1000 amino acids. It is, then, not surprising that the solution of this problem (commonly known as the coding problem) has required much theoretical insight, produced many unanticipated results, and employed a greater variety of experimental approaches than those needed in understanding the mechanism of DNA replication.

THE CENTRAL DOGMA

We should first look at the evidence that DNA itself is not the direct template that orders amino sequences. Instead, the genetic information of DNA is transferred to another class of molecules, which then serve as the protein templates. These intermediate templates are molecules of ribonucleic acid (RNA), large polymeric molecules chemically very similar to DNA. Their relation to DNA and protein is usually summarized by the formula (often called the central dogma)

330

$$\underset{\text{(duplication)}}{\overset{\text{(transcription)}}{\text{DNA}\xrightarrow{\hspace{3cm}}\text{RNA}\xrightarrow[\hspace{3cm}]{\text{(translation)}}\text{protein}}}$$

where the arrows indicate the direction of transfer of the genetic information. The arrow encircling DNA signifies that it is the template for its self-replication; the arrow between DNA and RNA indicates that all cellular RNA molecules are made on DNA templates.[1] Correspondingly, all protein sequences are determined by RNA templates. Most importantly, both these latter arrows are unidirectional, that is, RNA sequences are never copied on protein templates; likewise, RNA never acts as a template for DNA.

PROTEIN SYNTHESIS IN ABSENCE OF DNA

Many experiments now exist which show that proteins can be constructed in the absence of DNA. The most obvious demonstration comes from nucleated cells where most protein synthesis occurs in the cytoplasm; almost all the DNA is found in the chromosomes within the nucleus. This observation unambiguously tells us that an intermediate template must carry genetic information to the cytoplasmic sites of synthesis. No such simple *in vivo* demonstration can exist for bacterial cells that lack a nucleus but the use of *in vitro* cell-free systems (see below) shows that DNA's lack of direct participation is a general phenomenon.

The intermediate is clearly RNA. In the first place, there is evidence from many types of nucleated cells that all cellular RNA synthesis is restricted to the DNA-containing nucleus (Figure 11–1).[2] No RNA strands are made in the cytoplasm, from which DNA is absent.[3] RNA is thus synthesized where it should be if it is made on DNA. After their synthesis, many of

---

[1] Although this statement holds for normal cellular RNA, it does not hold for cells infected with certain RNA viruses (See Chapter 13).

[2] This statement does not hold for certain virus-infected cells (see Chapter 15).

[3] This statement must now be qualified to take into account the recently discovered facts that both the mitochondria and chloroplasts contain small amounts of DNA which may serve as templates for the RNA molecules involved in the synthesis of specific mitochondria and chloroplast proteins.

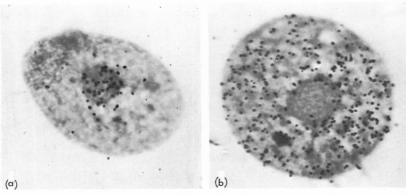

(a)   (b)

FIGURE 11-1 (a) Autoradiograph of a cell (*Tetrahymena*) exposed to radioactive cytidine for 15 min. Superimposed on a photograph of a thin section of the cell is a photograph of an exposed silver emulsion. Each dark spot represents the path of an electron emitted from an H³ (tritium) atom that has been incorporated into RNA. Almost all the newly made RNA is found within the nucleus. (b) An autoradiograph of a similar cell, exposed to radioactive uridine for 12 min and then allowed to grow for 88 min in the presence of nonradioactive cytidine. Practically all the label incorporated into RNA in the first 12 min has left the nucleus and moved into the cytoplasm. [Photographs courtesy of D. M. Prescott, University of Colorado Medical School; reproduced from *Progr. Nucleic Acid Res.*, **III**, 35 (1964), with permission.]

the RNA molecules move to the cytoplasm in which most protein synthesis is taking place.

In the second place, the amount of protein synthesized is directly related to the cellular content of RNA. Cells rich in RNA synthesize much protein, whereas little protein is made in RNA-poor cells. For example, the RNA-rich pancreas (Figure 11–2) synthesizes large quantities of proteolytic enzymes which are secreted into the digestive tract. Correspondingly, little RNA is found in muscle cells, in which little protein is made. The significance of this correlation is strengthened by isotopic experiments designed to locate accurately the synthetic sites within the cytoplasm. In these experiments cells are very

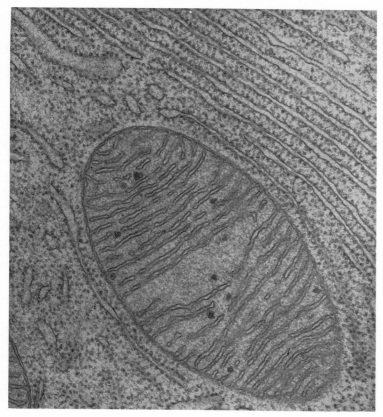

FIGURE 11-2   *Electron micrograph* ($\times$ 105,000) *of a portion of a cell in the pancreas of a bat, showing a mitochondrion and large numbers of ribosomes. Some ribosomes exist free; others (especially in the upper right) are attached to a membranous component, the endoplasmic reticulum. (Courtesy of K. R. Porter.)*

briefly exposed to amino acids labeled with radioactive isotopes. During these short intervals ("pulses"), some radioactive amino acids become incorporated into proteins. The cells are then quickly broken open to see in which cellular fraction the newly made protein (identified by its possession of radioactive amino acids) is found. In all cells the results are the same: Newly synthesized polypeptide chains are found associated with spher-

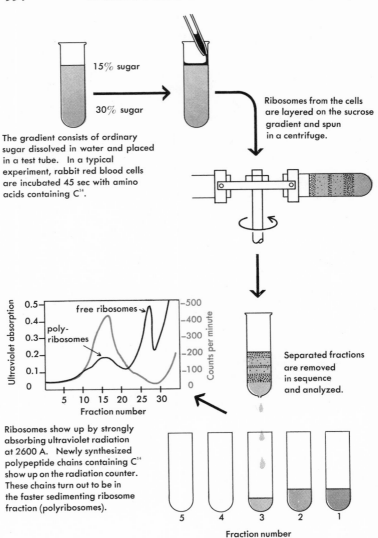

15% sugar

30% sugar

The gradient consists of ordinary sugar dissolved in water and placed in a test tube. In a typical experiment, rabbit red blood cells are incubated 45 sec with amino acids containing C^{14}.

Ribosomes from the cells are layered on the sucrose gradient and spun in a centrifuge.

Separated fractions are removed in sequence and analyzed.

Ribosomes show up by strongly absorbing ultraviolet radiation at 2600 A. Newly synthesized polypeptide chains containing C^{14} show up on the radiation counter. These chains turn out to be in the faster sedimenting ribosome fraction (polyribosomes).

free ribosomes

poly-ribosomes

Ultraviolet absorption

Counts per minute

Fraction number

FIGURE 11-3   *Sucrose gradient demonstration that protein synthesis occurs on ribosomes. [Redrawn from A. Rich, Sci. Am., 209, 46–47 (December 1963).]*

ical RNA-containing particles, the ribosomes (Figure 11–3). Likewise, a small amount of protein can be made *in vitro* in carefully prepared extracts of cells, and here also use of radio-

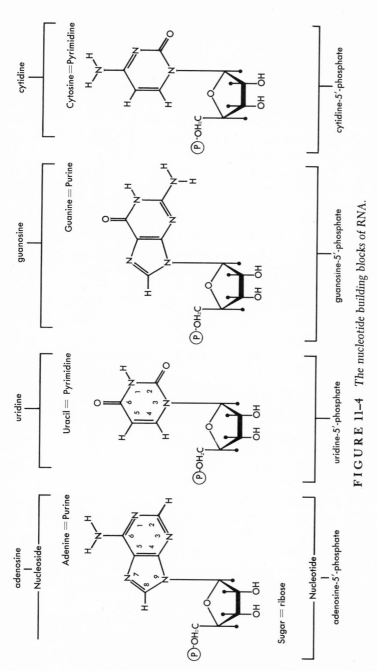

FIGURE 11-4 *The nucleotide building blocks of RNA.*

335

active isotopes shows attachment of much of this new protein to the RNA-rich ribosomes.

RNA IS CHEMICALLY VERY SIMILAR TO DNA

Mere inspection of RNA structure shows how it could be exactly synthesized on a DNA template. Chemically it is very similar to DNA. It is also a long, unbranched molecule containing four types of nucleotides (Figure 11–4) linked together by 3′–5′ phosphodiester bonds (Figure 11–5). Two differences in its chemical groups distinguish RNA from DNA. The first is a minor modification of the sugar component (Figure 11–6). The sugar of DNA is deoxyribose, whereas RNA contains ribose, identical to deoxyribose except for the presence of an additional OH (hydroxyl) group. The second difference is that RNA contains no thymine but instead contains the closely related pyrimidine uracil. Despite these differences, however, polyribonucleotides have the potential for forming complementary helices of the DNA type. Neither the additional hydroxyl group nor the absence of the methyl group found in thymine affects RNA's ability to form double-helical structures held together by hydrogen-bonded base pairs.

RNA IS USUALLY SINGLE-STRANDED

RNA molecules do not usually have complementary base ratios (Table 11–1). The amount of adenine does not often equal the amount of uracil, and the amounts of guanine and cytosine also usually differ from each other. This tells us that most RNA does not possess a regular hydrogen-bonded structure but, unlike double-helical DNA, exists as single polyribonucleotide strands. Because of the absence of regular hydrogen bonding, these single-stranded molecules do not have a simple regular structure like DNA. This structural uncertainty initially caused much pessimism, for there was general belief that we should have to see the template before we could attack the problem of how it selected amino acids during protein synthesis. Fortunately, as we show later, this hunch was wrong.

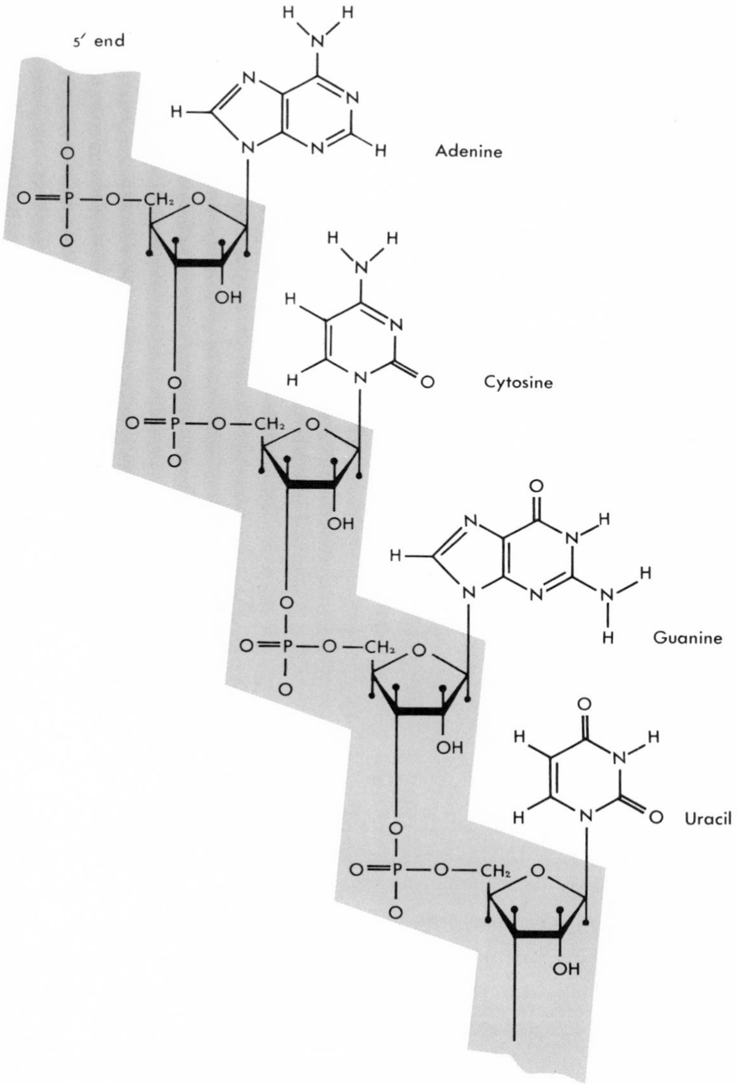

FIGURE 11–5   *The chemical formula of a polyribonucleotide.*

ENZYMATIC SYNTHESIS OF RNA UPON DNA TEMPLATES

The fact that RNA, like DNA, is a long, unbranched chain using four different nucleotides immediately suggests that the genetic information of DNA chains is transferred to a comple-

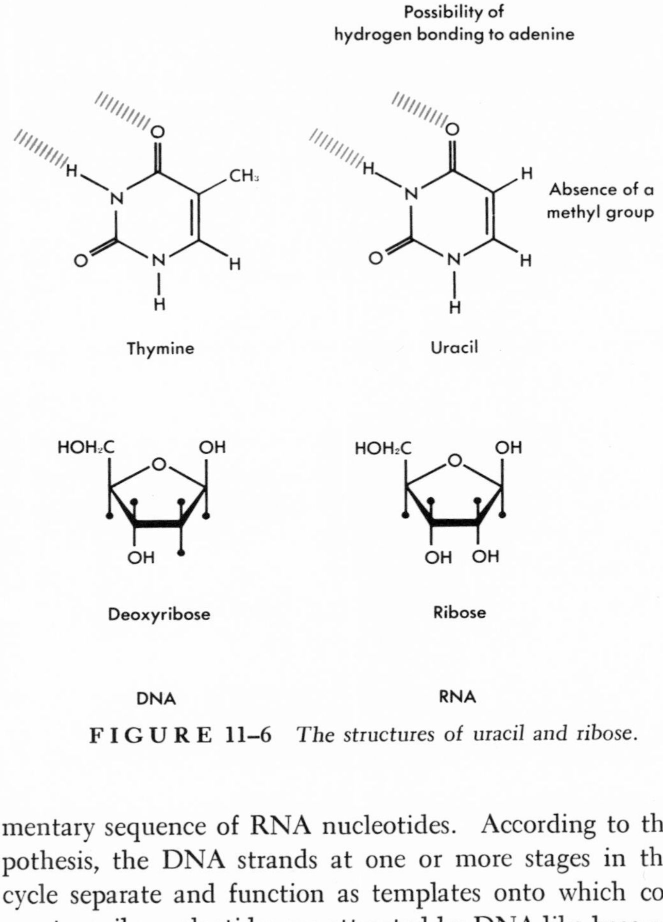

Possibility of
hydrogen bonding to adenine

Thymine

Uracil

Absence of a
methyl group

Deoxyribose

Ribose

DNA

RNA

FIGURE 11–6   *The structures of uracil and ribose.*

mentary sequence of RNA nucleotides. According to this hypothesis, the DNA strands at one or more stages in the cell
cycle separate and function as templates onto which complementary ribonucleotides are attracted by DNA-like base pairing
[adenine with thymine (uracil) and guanine with cytosine]. It
further tells us that some control mechanism must dictate
whether the separated DNA strands will function as templates
for a complementary DNA strand or a complementary RNA
strand.

Direct evidence for the hypothesis comes from the discovery
of the appropriate enzyme, RNA polymerase, which exists in
virtually all cells. This enzyme links together ribonucleotides
by catalyzing the formation of the internucleotide 3′–5′ phosphodiester bonds that hold the RNA backbone together (Fig-

T A B L E 11–1   *The base composition of RNA from various sources*

RNA Source	Proportion of the four main bases			
	Adenine	Uracil	Guanine	Cytosine
E. coli	24	22	32	22
Proteus vulgaris (a bacterium)	26	19	31	24
Euglena (an alga)	22	21	30	27
Turnip yellow mosaic virus	23	22	17	38
Poliomyelitis virus	30	25	25	20
Rat kidney	19	20	30	31

ure 11–7). It does so, however, only in the presence of DNA, a fact that suggests that DNA must line up the correct nucleotide precursors in order for RNA polymerase to work. Proof for this idea comes from seeing how the RNA base composition varies with the addition of DNA molecules of different AT/GC ratios. In every enzymatic synthesis, the RNA AU/GC ratio is roughly similar to the DNA AT/GC ratio (Table 11–2).

F I G U R E 11–7   *Enzymatic synthesis of RNA upon a DNA template.*

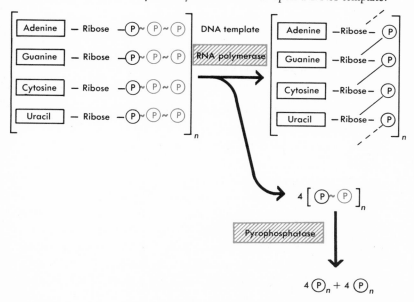

T A B L E   11-2   *Comparison of the base composition of enzymatically synthesized RNAs with the base composition of their double-helical DNA templates*

Source of DNA template	Composition of the RNA bases				$\dfrac{A+U}{G+C}$ observed	$\dfrac{A+T}{G+C}$ in DNA
	Ade-nine	Uracil	Gua-nine	Cyto-sine		
T2	0.31	0.34	0.18	0.17	1.86	1.84
Calf thymus	0.31	0.29	0.19	0.21	1.50	1.35
E. coli	0.24	0.24	0.26	0.26	0.92	0.97
Micrococcus lyso-deikticus (a bacterium)	0.17	0.16	0.33	0.34	0.49	0.39

Further experiments directly demonstrate that the template is a single DNA strand. One of the clearest experiments uses DNA from the virus $\phi \times 174$. This virus belongs to one of the very special viral classes that contain single-stranded DNA instead of the customary double-helical form. Only one of the two possible complementary DNA strands is present, and when it is used as the template for RNA polymerase, the enzymatic product has a complementary base sequence (Table 11-3).

T A B L E   11-3   *Base composition of enzymatically synthesized RNA using single-stranded $\phi \times 174$ DNA as template*

	$\phi \times 174$ DNA	Observed values of RNA product	Predicted RNA composition
Adenine	0.25	0.32	0.33
Uracil	0.33 (thymine)	0.25	0.25
Guanine	0.24	0.20	0.18
Cytosine	0.18	0.23	0.24
Total	1.00	1.00	1.00

Moreover, in this special case the RNA product remains attached to its DNA template, allowing the isolation of a hybrid DNA-RNA double helix. This result contrasts with experiments using double-helical DNA. Here the RNA product

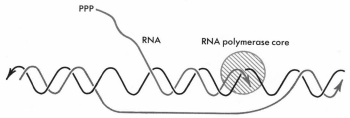

FIGURE 11–8   *Transcription of an RNA molecule upon a unique strand of its DNA template. The attachment of the enzyme RNA polymerase to a DNA molecule opens up a short section of the double helix, thereby allowing free bases on one of the DNA strands to base pair with the ribonucleoside—℗~℗~℗ precursors. As RNA polymerase moves along the DNA template, the growing RNA strand peels off, allowing hydrogen bonds to reform between two complementary DNA strands. Thus almost immediately after the synthesis of an RNA strand commences, its front end becomes available to bind to a ribosome (see Chapter 12).*

quickly detaches from its template and the two DNA strands again come together in specific register. Apparently the double helix made from two complementary DNA strands is energetically more stable than the hybrid DNA-RNA structure, so that the free single DNA strand quickly displaces the RNA product soon after RNA polymerase has moved over the corresponding template region (Figure 11–8).

We thus see that the fundamental mechanism for the synthesis of RNA is very similar to that of DNA. In both cases, the immediate precursors are nucleoside triphosphates that use the energy in one of their pyrophosphate bonds to drive the reaction toward synthesis. Also in both cases, a single enzyme works on all four possible nucleotides, whose correct selection is dictated by the obligatory need to base pair with a polynucleotide template. The transcription of RNA on DNA may, therefore, be as accurate as the self-replication of DNA. In any case, the very rare mistakes that do occur in RNA transcription are not passed on to many subsequent cell generations since cellular RNA is not a self-replicating molecule.

ALONG EACH GENE ONLY ONE DNA STRAND ACTS AS AN RNA TEMPLATE

If each of the two DNA strands of a given gene serves as an RNA template, each gene would produce two RNA products with complementary sequences which should code for two different proteins. Since our genetic evidence tells us that each gene controls only one protein, we must assume that either only one of the two possible RNA strands is made or, if both are synthesized, that only one is functional for some special reason. It appears that the former possibility is correct—*in vivo* only one of the two possible gene products is found. This can clearly be seen by examining the RNA synthesized *in vivo* under the direction of the virus SP8, which multiplies in the bacterium *Bacillus subtilis*. The two complementary DNA strands of the SP8, unlike those of most viruses, have quite different base compositions and can be relatively easily separated. It is thus possible to ask whether the RNA products have base sequences complementary to one or both the DNA strands.

To answer this question, use was made of our ability to form artificial DNA-RNA hybrid molecules by mixing RNA molecules with single-stranded DNA molecules formed by heating of double-helical DNA. Heating DNA molecules to temperatures just below 100°C breaks the hydrogen bonds holding the complementary strands together; they then quickly separate from each other (DNA denaturation). If the temperature is gradually lowered, the complementary strands again form the correct hydrogen bonds and the double-helical form is regained (renaturation of DNA). If, however, this gentle cooling is done in the presence of single-stranded RNA that has been synthesized on homologous DNA, then DNA-RNA hybrids form as well as renatured DNA double helices (Figure 11–9). These DNA-RNA hybrids are very specific and form only if some of the nucleotide sequences in the DNA are complementary to the RNA nucleotide sequences. This technique lets us ask whether the *in vivo* RNA products will form hybrids with only one or with both of the complementary SP8 DNA strands. A clear result emerges: Only one DNA strand is copied.

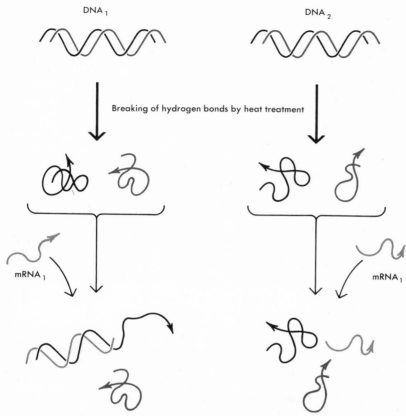

FIGURE 11-9 *The use of DNA-RNA hybrids to show the comple-
mentarity in nucleotide sequences between an RNA
molecule and one of the two strands of its DNA
template. The left side of the diagram shows the
formation of a hybrid molecule between an RNA
molecule and one of the two strands of the template.
The specificity of this method is shown on the right
side of the diagram. Here the same RNA molecule
is mixed with unrelated DNA. No hybrid molecules
are formed.*

The copying of only one DNA strand within a given gene
allows us to understand why the base ratios of RNA need not
be complementary even though RNA is made on a DNA template. In a given DNA strand, there is no reason why the A

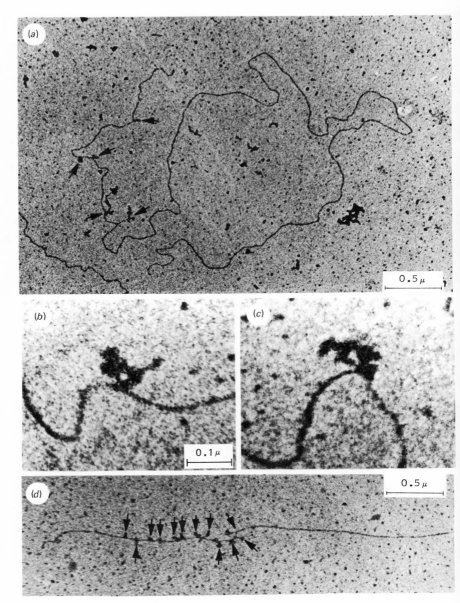

should equal T or G equal C. These ratios need be one-to-one only when the corresponding bases on the two complementary chains are added together. Thus, in general, we must assume that only in the exceptional DNA molecule will the single strands be found on close inspection to have the complementary ratios. Correspondingly, only rarely will single-stranded RNA molecules be found in which A equals U and G equals C.

Differential copying of the two strands of a DNA molecule can also be observed *in vitro*. This result depends on the use of DNA templates which have not been severely damaged. If, for example, T7 DNA has been denatured to produce single strands or if it has broken to produce single-stranded regions, then both strands are copied. When, however, intact molecules of T7 DNA (MW $= 2.6 \times 10^7$) are used as *in vitro* templates, the DNA strand which is copied is the same one copied during *in vivo* viral reproduction (Figure 11–10).

The transcription patterns along other chromosomes are often not as clear-cut as with T7 or SP8. Both strands of the T4 and λ chromosomes are transcribed, one strand serving as the template for some genes (usually contiguous groups) while the remaining genes are transcribed along the other strand (Figure 15–16). The same picture holds for the *E. coli* chromosome, which can be transcribed both clockwise and counterclockwise. Many more genes (e.g., lactose, tryptophan, and galactose groups) are read counterclockwise than clockwise. Whether this has any real significance remains to be ascertained. Since

FIGURE 11–10   *Electron micrographs of in vitro transcription of T7 DNA. In (a) several growing RNA chains can be seen attached to the DNA template. All of the RNA chains are transcribed off the same T7 strand, initiating their growth at a unique site near the end visible at the right side. Total synthesis time is 5 min at 37°C. In (b) and (c) views of two attached RNA chains are shown at higher magnification. In (d) synthesis was terminated after 2½ min at 37°C. −12 nascent chains all at one end can be seen. (Kindly supplied by Dr. R. Davis, California Institute of Technology.)*

the replicating bacterial chromosome is constantly rotating in a fixed direction, unwinding the nascent RNA chains might appear to be connected with the rotation of their templates. But this does not seem to be true. An example is known where the orientation of lactose genes within the E. coli chromosome is reversed so that they must be read clockwise instead of counterclockwise. As far as we can tell, their transcription rates are the same and so independent of gene orientation.

RNA CHAINS ARE NOT CIRCULAR

All RNA chains examined so far have a linear shape. No example of circular RNA, even from the RNA-containing viruses, has been found despite quite extensive searches.[4] The sizes of these linear molecules show much greater variation than those observed for DNA chains. Some are built up from as few as 75 nucleotides, while others may contain over 10,000. Independent of their length, they generally do not have a completely random shape. A majority of the bases are hydrogen bonded to each other using DNA-type base pairing (A with U, G with C). This is accomplished by hairpin folds (Figure 11–11) that bring bases of the same chain into a DNA-like double-helical arrangement. Such configurations are possible when the number of adenine residues along a given chain section is approximately equal to the number of uracil residues, or when the guanine number is approximately equal to the cytosine number.

SYNTHESIS OF RNA CHAINS OCCURS IN A FIXED DIRECTION

Each RNA chain, like DNA chains, has a direction defined by the orientation of the sugar-phosphate backbone. The chain end terminated by the 5′ carbon atom is called the 5′ end, while the end containing the 3′ carbon atom is called the 3′ end (Figure 11–5). Until recently, there was no evidence as to whether RNA chains grow in the 3′ to 5′ direction or vice versa. If they

[4] Since the writing of this section, Agol, Drygin, Romanova, and Bogdanov [FEBS Letters, 8:13 (1970)] have reported finding a circular replicating form of the RNA of the mouse encephalomyocarditis (EMC) virus.

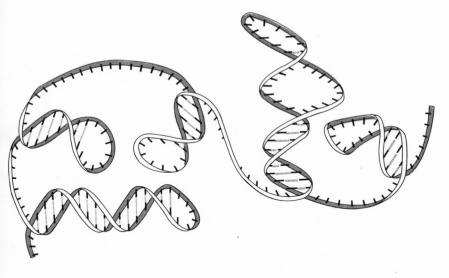

An actual example of an RNA loop from the
RNA of the virus R17

FIGURE 11–11 *Schematic folding of an RNA chain showing several double-helical regions held together by hydrogen bonds.*

grow 5′ to 3′, then we expect the beginning nucleotide to possess a (P)~(P)~(P) group (Figure 11–12). If the chains grow 3′ to 5′, then the nucleotide at the growing end will contain the (P)~(P)~(P) group. Firm evidence now shows that the direction of growth is 5′ to 3′. Newly inserted nucleotides are found at the 3′ ends, while the (P)~(P)~(P) groups are found attached to the nucleotides which commenced chain growth.

Work with the metabolic inhibitor 3′-deoxyadenosine confirms the 5′ to 3′ direction of growth. When added to cells, it is first phosphorylated to 3′-deoxyadenosine-(P)~(P)~(P) and then joined to the 3′ growing end. Because it contains no 3′-OH group, further nucleoside-(P)~(P)~(P) cannot attach, and RNA synthesis stops.

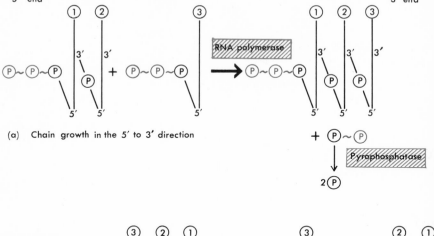

(a)   Chain growth in the 5' to 3' direction

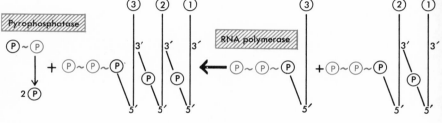

FIGURE 11-12   *Alternative directions for the synthesis of an RNA chain. Newly performed experiments suggest that chains always grow in the 5' to 3' direction.*

CONSTRUCTION OF RNA POLYMERASE FROM SUBUNITS

In contrast to DNA polymerase, which is built up from only a single polypeptide chain, RNA polymerase has a very complicated subunit structure. The active form, which sediments at about 15 S, contains 5 different polypeptide chains, β', β, σ, α, and ω, with respective molecular weights of 160,000, 150,000, 90,000, 40,000, and 10,000. No covalent bonds run between the various chains; aggregation results from the formation of secondary bonds. Each specific chain, with the exception of

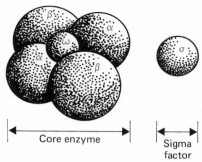

Core enzyme | Sigma factor

FIGURE 11–13   *Schematic picture of RNA polymerase showing subunit construction.*

a, which appears twice, is present once within the active molecule, giving the complete enzyme ($\beta'\beta a_2 \omega \sigma$) a molecular weight slightly over a half million (Figure 11–13).   The attachment of σ to the other chains is not very firm, so it is relatively easy to isolate a $\beta'\beta a_2 \omega$ aggregate.   This specific grouping is known as the *core enzyme*, for it catalyzes the formation of the internucleotide phosphodiester bonds equally well in the presence or absence of σ.

RECOGNITION OF START SIGNALS BY σ

Thus, σ by itself has no catalytic function; its role is the recognition of start signals along the DNA molecule.   *In vitro* experiments show that in the absence of σ, the core enzyme will sometimes initiate RNA synthesis, but this is the result of starting mistakes.   RNA chains made by the core enzyme alone are started randomly along both strands of a given gene. When σ is present, however, the correct strand is selected, indicating that somehow σ recognizes a specific nucleotide sequence coding for initiation of an RNA chain.   We do not yet know whether in a given cell all the σ molecules are identical or whether a number of different σ's exist, each of which can combine with the core enzyme and can recognize a different start signal.   In Chapter 15, we shall show conclusively that new viral specific σ's are present in cells infected by certain viruses.

After σ has recognized a proper start signal and chain elongation has started, σ dissociates from the core-enzyme–DNA complex and is free to attach to another core molecule. RNA synthesis in cells thus involves the cycle illustrated in Figure 11–14.

CHAINS START WITH EITHER pppA OR pppG

Apparently, all normal RNA chains start with either adenine or guanine. In *E. coli*, more chains start with a G, while when T4 DNA is the template, more chains start with A. These results tell us that the first DNA base to be copied must be a pyrimidine, either T or C. In fact, evidence from several viral chromosomes indicates the existence of a number of successive pyrimidine bases near the start signals. In λ DNA the number of poly C groups closely approximates the number of start points. Most of these pyrimidine residues, however, must not be transcribed, since the second RNA residue at the 5′ end of the RNA chain is frequently a pyrimidine.

Some apparent exceptions to obligatory A or G starts have a simple explanation. After synthesis, many RNA chains are cleaved by endonucleases to yield smaller fragments, many of which start with a pyrimidine. For example, although some tRNA chains start with U (see Chapter 13), they never contain terminal triphosphate groups, strongly suggesting their origin through *in vivo* cleavage of longer chains. As virtually all cells contain a variety of nucleases, unambiguous data about initiating nucleotide sequences is likely to come from *in vitro* experiments where, using highly purified enzymes, it is possible to exclude nuclease effects.

RELEASE FACTORS PRODUCE
CHAINS OF FINITE LENGTH

There also exist stop signals whose function is to terminate RNA synthesis at specific points along the DNA template.

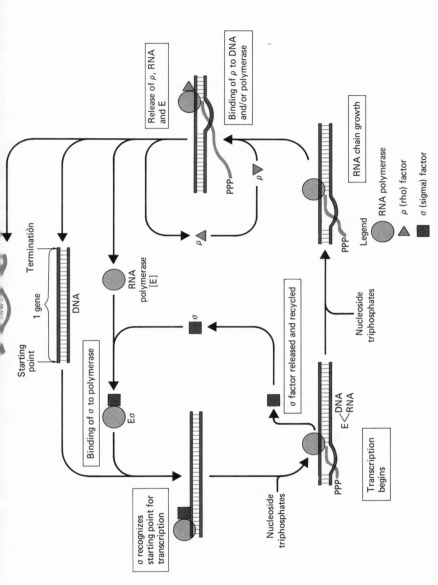

FIGURE 11-14 *RNA synthesis—outline diagram.*

The reading of these stop markers is not done by RNA polymerase, but by a specific protein—the ρ factor. How this protein, which has a molecular weight of about 60,000, functions has not yet been determined. Since it is stable and relatively easy to isolate, however, we should soon know whether it binds directly to the DNA stop signals or whether it first combines with RNA polymerase. In the absence of a ρ factor, chain elongation is not blocked at the stop signal, but proceeds through it, thereby resulting in transcription of the adjacent genetic region. There are now no data saying whether only one type of ρ factor exists. Nor do we know if all the stop signals are identical, or if some always result in chain termination and others permit occasional read-through to adjacent genes.

SUMMARY

DNA molecules are not the direct templates for protein synthesis. The genetic information of DNA is first transferred to RNA molecules. In turn, RNA molecules act as the primary templates that order amino acid sequences in proteins ($DNA \rightarrow RNA \rightarrow protein$). The covalent structure of RNA is chemically very similar to that of DNA, and its genetic information is also stored in the sequences of its four bases. In contrast to DNA, however, most RNA molecules are single-stranded and linear. The synthesis of RNA upon DNA templates shows many similarities to the DNA duplication process. Most importantly, the selection process involves formation of complementary base pairs. The enzyme RNA polymerase links together the monomeric precursors, which are the ribonucleoside triphosphates (ATP, GTP, CTP, and UTP). In a given gene, only one of the two DNA strands is copied.

RNA polymerase is constructed from five types of polypeptide chains. One of these chains, σ, easily dissociates from the other four, which collectively make up the core enzyme. The core catalyzes the formation of the phosphodiester linkages, while σ is responsible for recognition of start signals along DNA molecules. *After initiation occurs, σ dissociates from the DNA-RNA core complex, becoming free to attach to another core.*

Synthesis of all chains starts with either adenine or guanine, depending on the specific start signal in the DNA template. Elongation proceeds in the 5' to 3' direction, so the 5' terminal nucleotides always contain a Ⓟ~Ⓟ~Ⓟ *group. Synthesis ends upon reaching stop signals, which, like start signals, are specific nucleotide sequences. Termination also depends on the presence of a specific protein, the ρ factor. The molecular mode of ρ action has yet to be solved.*

REFERENCES

Prescott, D. M., "Cellular Sites of RNA Synthesis," in J. N. Davidson and W. E. Cohn (eds.), *Progr. Nucleic Acid Res.*, **III**, 35–37 (1964). A very clear discussion of the techniques of cell biology which have established the nucleus as the site of most RNA synthesis.

Spiegelman, S. S., "Hybrid Nucleic Acids," *Sci. Am.*, May, 1964, pp. 48–56. Here are clearly explained many of the experimental techniques that have been so elegantly used to demonstrate homology in nucleotide sequences between DNA and RNA.

Marmur, J., C. Greenspan, F. Palacek, F. M. Kahan, J. Levine, and M. Mandel, "Specificity of the Complementary RNA Formed by *B. subtilis* Infected with Bacteriophage SP8," *Cold Spring Harbor Symp. Quant. Biol.*, **28**, 191–199 (1963). A description of an experiment showing that, *in vivo*, only one of the two SP8 DNA strands is a template for RNA synthesis.

Taylor, K., Z. Hradecna, and W. Szybalski, "Asymmetric Distribution of the Transcribing Regions on the Complementary Strands of Coliphage λ DNA," *Proc. Nat. Acad. Sci. U.S.*, **57**, 1618 (1967). Use of the DNA-RNA hybridization technique to establish the transcription pattern of phage λ.

Geiduschek, E. P., and R. Haselkorn, "Messenger RNA," *Ann. Rev. Biochem.*, **38**, 647 (1969). A very clear summary of how RNA chains are synthesized with much emphasis on the mechanism of action of RNA polymerase.

Burgess, R., A. A. Travers, J. J. Dunn, and E. K. F. Bautz, "Factor Stimulating Transcription by RNA Polymerase," *Nature*, **222**, 537 (1969). The classic announcement of the separation of RNA polymerase into the core and σ components.

RNA Polymerase and Transcription, L. Silvestri (ed.), North Holland Publ. Co., Amsterdam (1970). A collection of papers arising out of a meeting held in Florence soon after the discovery of σ.

"Transcription of Genetic Material," *Cold Spring Harbor Symp. Quant. Biol.*, **35.** (1970). Here are found over 90 articles revealing the state of the transcription problem as of June, 1970. The most extensive collection of facts now available about the synthesis of RNA.

12

INVOLVEMENT OF RNA IN PROTEIN SYNTHESIS

WE NOW BEGIN TO LOOK AT HOW single-stranded RNA molecules function during protein synthesis. When the general validity of the central dogma (DNA → RNA → protein) was becoming obvious in the mid-1950s, there was general belief that all RNA was template RNA. Hope also existed that, when the RNA general structure was solved, mere inspection might tell us how RNA ordered amino acid sequences. Now, however, we realize that these views were very naive and that protein synthesis is a much more complicated affair than the synthesis of nucleic acid. Moreover, not all RNA molecules are templates. In addition to a template class, there exist two additional classes of RNA, each of which plays a vital role in protein synthesis.

AMINO ACIDS HAVE NO SPECIFIC AFFINITY FOR RNA

The fundamental reason behind this complexity has been mentioned before. There is no specific affinity between the side groups of many amino acids and the purine and pyrimidine bases found in RNA. For example, the hydrocarbon side groups of the amino acids alanine, valine, leucine, and isoleucine do not form hydrogen bonds and would be actively repelled by the amino and keto groups of the various nucleotide bases. Likewise, it is hard to imagine the existence of

355

specific RNA surfaces with unique affinities for the aromatic amino acids phenylalanine, tyrosine, and tryptophan. It is thus impossible for these amino acids in unmodified form to line up passively in specific accurate order against an RNA template prior to peptide bond formation.

AMINO ACIDS ATTACH TO RNA TEMPLATES BY MEANS OF ADAPTORS

Before the amino acids line up against the RNA template, they are chemically modified to possess a specific surface capable of combining with a specific number of the hydrogen-bonding groups along the template. This chemical change consists of the addition of a specific adaptor molecule to each amino acid through a single covalent bond. It is this adaptor component that combines with the template; at no time does the amino acid side group itself need to interact with the template. Adding a specific adaptor residue to an amino acid is much more economical than chemically modifying the side group itself. The latter process might require many enzymes for just a single amino acid. Conceivably, a similar number would be required to change the adapted side group back to its original configuration after it becomes part of a polypeptide chain. On the other hand, only a single enzyme is needed either to attach or to detach an amino acid from its specific adaptor.

SPECIFIC ENZYMES RECOGNIZE SPECIFIC AMINO ACIDS

There need not be any obvious relation between the shape of the amino acid side group and the adaptor surface. Instead the crucial selection of an amino acid is done by a specific enzyme. The enzyme that catalyzes the attachment of the amino acid to its adaptor must be able to bind specifically to both the amino acid side group and the adaptor. For this task, proteins are extremely suitable, because their active regions can be rich in either hydrophilic or hydrophobic groups. There is no difficulty in folding a suitably sequenced polypeptide chain to produce a cavity that is specific for the side group of one specific amino acid. For example, tyrosine can be distinguished from phenylalanine by an enzyme having a specific cavity containing an atom that can form a hydrogen bond to the OH group on tyrosine. Here the formation of one specific hydrogen bond yields about 4 to 5 kcal/mole of energy. This would be lost if phenylalanine were chosen instead. Thus, with the help of a physical chemical theory, we can predict that the probability that tyrosine is found in the "tyrosine cavity" is about 1000 times greater than the probability that phenylalanine is found in the tyrosine cavity.

There is more difficulty in immediately seeing how a similar accuracy can be achieved in distinguishing between amino acids differing only by one methyl residue, a group incapable of either salt linkages or hydrogen bonding. For example, glycine must be distinguished from alanine and valine from isoleucine. There is, of course, no difficulty in understanding why the larger alanine side group cannot fit into the cavity designed for the smaller amino acid valine. The problem arises when we ask why glycine will not sometimes fit into the alanine cavity or valine into the isoleucine hole. If this should happen, there would be loss of the van der Waals forces arising out of a snug fit around a methyl group. These forces are now thought to be about 2 to 3 kcal/mole, by themselves too small in value to account for the general accuracy by which amino acids are ordered during protein synthesis. Now we suspect that the maximum frequency at which a wrong amino acid is inserted into a growing polypeptide chain is about 1 in 1000. This means that the energy gained by selecting the correct amino acid must be at least 4 to 5 kcal, a value about twice that provided by only the van der Waals energy. This difference provided an apparent paradox until consideration was also given to the relative difficulty of inserting glycine and alanine molecules into an aqueous solution. The water molecules in the liquid phase are held together by a relatively regular arrangement of hydrogen bonds ($O—H \cdots O$). Virtually all the hydrogen and oxygen atoms in water are hydrogen bonded. This arrangement is disturbed by the presence of the nonhydrogen-bond-forming CH_3

groups, whose introduction necessarily causes the loss of the energy gained by forming hydrogen bonds. We should thus look at an aqueous solution as a collection of molecules which will try to expel unwanted hydrophobic groups. This tendency provides the added energy difference (2 kcal/mole) to allow the correct selection of alanine (isoleucine) since there is a very marked difference in the rate at which water solutions will expel alanine (isoleucine) in comparison to the more water-soluble glycine (valine).

THE ADAPTOR MOLECULES ARE THEMSELVES RNA MOLECULES

The molecules to which the amino acids attach are a group of relatively small RNA molecules called transfer RNA (tRNA).[1] It is really not surprising that the adaptors are also RNA molecules, since a prime requirement for a useful adaptor is the ability to attach specifically to the free keto and amino groups on the single-stranded template RNA molecules. This attachment is ideally accomplished by having the adaptor also be a single-stranded RNA molecule, since this opens the possibility of having very specific hydrogen bonds (perhaps of the base-pair variety) to hold the template and adaptor together temporarily. The tRNA adaptors for the twenty different amino acids all have different structures, each uniquely adapted for fitting a different nucleotide sequence on the template. Thus, a large number of different types of tRNA exist.

Each of the tRNAs contains approximately 80 nucleotides (MW ~ 25,000) linked together in a single covalently bonded chain (Figure 12–1). One end of the chain (3′ end) always terminates in a CCA sequence (cytidylic acid, cytidylic acid, adenylic acid). The terminal nucleotide of the other end (5′) is usually guanylic acid. Though there is only one chain, a majority of the bases are hydrogen bonded to each other. Hairpin folds bring bases on the same chain into a DNA-like double-helical arrangement. Hydrogen-bond formation can then

[1] Some authors prefer the name soluble RNA (sRNA) for the adaptor molecule.

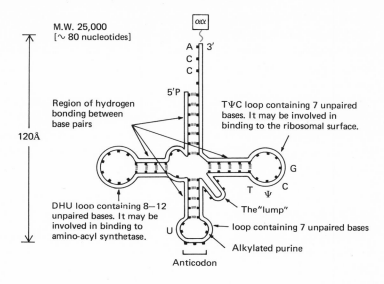

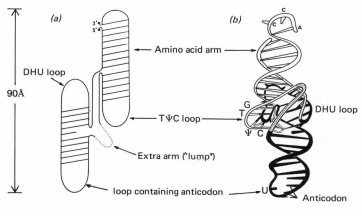

FIGURE 12-1 *Diagram of an amino-acyl tRNA molecule showing the cloverleaf convention of layout, and schematic diagram (a) and drawing (b) of proposed tertiary structure. [Redrawn from M. Levitt, Nature, 224, 759 (1969).]*

occur because the number of adenine residues approximates the number of uracil residues and the guanine number almost equals the cytosine number. The correspondence is not exact, however, and some nucleotides that do not internally base pair are available to fit to the template.

At first, it was thought that the three-dimensional shape of different tRNAs might be radically different. The finding that a mixture of all tRNAs can form very regular three-dimensional crystals, however, tells us that the basic three-dimensional arrangement is the same for all molecules.

YEAST ALANINE tRNA CONTAINS 77 NUCLEOTIDES

During December, 1964, the first nucleotide sequence of a specific tRNA molecule (from yeast) was worked out. This tRNA specifically attaches to alanine and, therefore, is called *alanine tRNA*. It contains 77 nucleotides arranged in a unique sequence (Figure 12–2). The most striking aspect of this sequence is the high content (9/77) of unusual bases (Figure 12–3). ("Unusual" means a base other than A, G, C, or U.) Many of these unusual bases differ from normal bases by the presence of one or more methyl ($—CH_3$) groups. Most, if not all, of the methyl groups are enzymatically added after the nucleotides are linked together by 3′–5′ phosphodiester linkages. Very probably, the other unusual bases also arise by the enzymatic modification of a preexisting polynucleotide.

The function of the unusual bases is not yet clear. They are not limited to alanine tRNA but occur in varying proportions in all tRNA molecules. Our only hint of their role is the fact that several unusual bases cannot form conventional base pairs. Some of the unusual bases may thus have the function of disrupting double-helical hairpin regions, thereby exposing free keto and amino groups which can then form secondary bonds. Depending upon the specific bases, the free groups may form secondary bonds to template RNA, to a ribosome, or to the enzyme needed to attach a specific amino acid to its specific tRNA molecule.

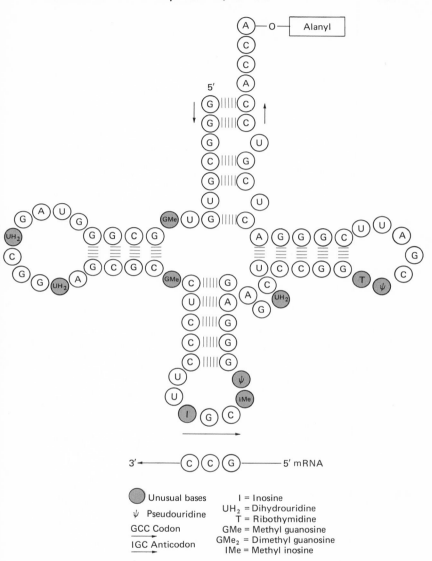

FIGURE 12–2   *The complete nucleotide sequence of alanine tRNA showing the unusual bases and codon/anticodon position.*

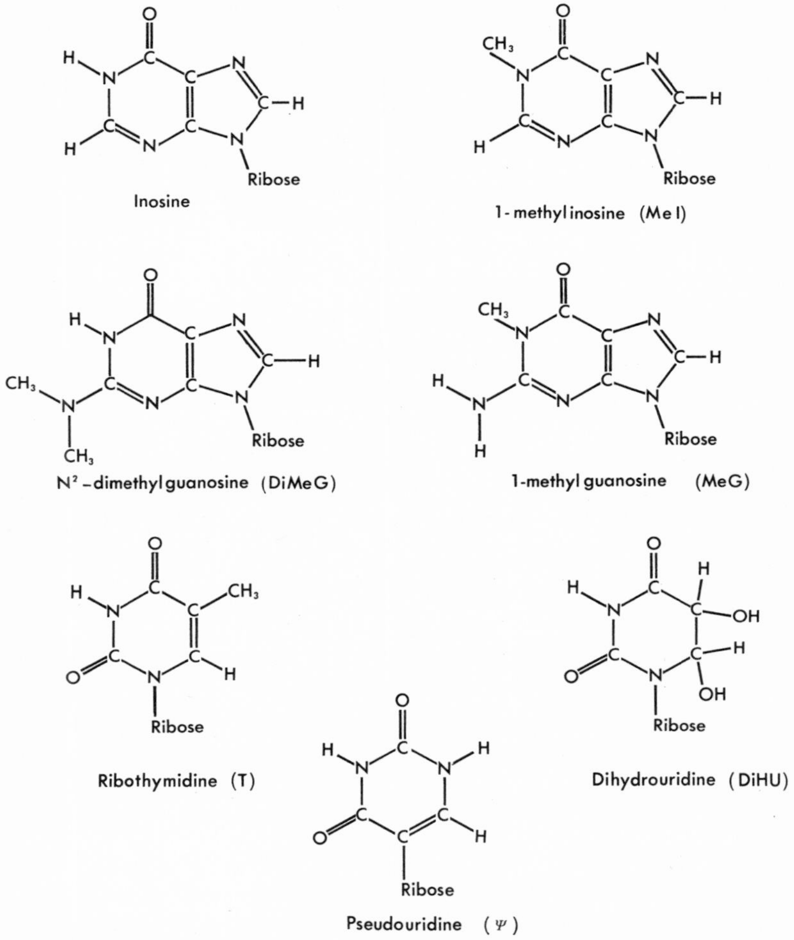

Inosine

1-methyl inosine   (Me I)

N²-dimethyl guanosine   (DiMeG)

1-methyl guanosine   (MeG)

Ribothymidine (T)

Dihydrouridine (DiHU)

Pseudouridine   (Ψ)

FIGURE 12–3   *The structures of the rare nucleotides found in yeast alanine tRNA.*

CLOVERLEAF FOLDING OF tRNA MOLECULES

The exact nucleotide sequence of alanine tRNA does not provide sufficient information to guess unambiguously the way various bases hydrogen bond to each other. Given only this structure, a number of possible hairpin configurations could be imagined. But after several other yeast tRNA sequences had been determined, it was realized that certain sequences were common to all types of tRNA molecules. There was only one way (the cloverleaf) to fold the chain which maximized the number of base pairs and led to a common shape (Figure 12–1). Each cloverleaf contains the following nonhydrogen-bonded sections:

1. The 3' end consists of ACC plus a variable fourth nucleotide. The amino acid always becomes attached to the 3' terminal A.

2. As one moves along the backbone away from the 3' end, one encounters the first loop of the cloverleaf. It is made up of seven unpaired bases and always contains the sequence 5'-T pseudo UCG-3'. Binding to the ribosomal surface may involve this region.

3. Next appears a loop of highly variable size, often called "the lump."

4. The third loop, which consists of seven unpaired bases, contains the anticodon—the three adjacent bases which bind (by base pairing) to the successive bases comprising the codon. The anticodon is bracketed on its 3' end by a purine and on its 5' end by U. The purine is often alkylated.

5. The fourth loop contains eight to twelve unpaired bases and is relatively rich in dihydro-U. It is thought to be involved in the binding to the specific activating enzyme (amino-acyl synthetase).

Over the past few years, tRNAs from a variety of organisms in addition to yeast have been worked out. All show the same general features favoring the formation of the cloverleaf. The fact that some yeast tRNA molecules can be activated (see below) by enzymes from quite unrelated organisms is thus not surprising.

CRYSTALLINE tRNA

Discovery of the cloverleaf pattern does not by itself tell us how the various loops are arranged in space. This information can only come from x-ray diffraction studies of tRNA crystals. Fortunately, the gloomy impression of former years that tRNA might be impossible to crystallize is gone. In fact, very good crystals of many tRNA species can now be routinely obtained (Figure 12–4). Thus, within the next several years, its general shape should be worked out. Tentative hints that the shape changes when an amino acid becomes attached will also make it necessary to study the structure of the tRNA–amino acid complex.

FIGURE 12–4 X-ray diffraction pattern of a mixed tRNA crystal. This crystal was formed by the co-crystallization of an unfractionated tRNA preparation from yeast. The ability of the unfractionated material to crystallize so regularly (the reflections extend out to about 10 A, and in other photographs, order to the 3-A level has been observed) indicates that the shapes of all tRNA species are very similar. [From Blake, Fresco, and Langridge, *Nature*, **225**, 32 (1970). Photograph kindly supplied by Dr. Robert Langridge, Princeton University.]

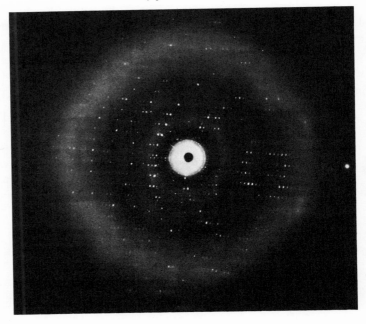

ADDITION OF THE ADAPTOR ALSO
ACTIVATES THE AMINO ACID

The link between the 3′ terminal adenosine and the amino acid is a covalent bond between the amino acid carboxyl group and the terminal ribose component of the RNA (Figure 12–5). The use of the amino acid carboxyl group to attach to the adaptor has several interesting implications. In the first place, before the carboxyl can form a peptide bond, the tRNA adaptor must be released. Thus, peptide-bond formation and adaptor removal occur in a coordinated fashion. In the second place, the bond linking the tRNA to its specific amino acid is a high-energy bond, making these complexes "activated" precursors. The energy in the amino acid–tRNA bond (an amino-acyl bond) can be used in the formation of the lower-energy peptide bond.

The energy required for forming the amino-acyl bond has come from a high-energy pyrophosphate linkage ($\circledP\sim\circledP$) in ATP. Prior to formation of the AA$\sim$tRNA compounds, the amino acids are activated by enzymes (amino-acyl synthetases) to form amino acid adenylates (AA$\sim$AMP) in which the amino acid carboxyl group is attached by high-energy bonding to an adenylic acid (AMP) group (Figure 12–5).

$$\text{AA + ATP} \quad \xrightleftharpoons[\text{synthetase}]{\text{amino acyl}} \quad \text{AA}\smile\text{AMP} + \circledP\smile\circledP \qquad (12\text{–}1)$$

The AA$\sim$AMP intermediate normally remains tightly bound to the activating enzyme until collision with a tRNA molecule specific for the amino acid. Then the same activating enzyme transfers the amino acid to the terminal adenylic acid residue of the tRNA.

$$\text{AA}\smile\text{AMP + tRNA} \quad \xrightleftharpoons[\text{synthetase}]{\text{amino acyl}} \quad \text{AA}\smile\text{tRNA + AMP} \qquad (12\text{–}2)$$

We therefore see that the activating enzymes are able to recognize (bind to) specifically both a given amino acid and its tRNA adaptor. For this purpose, the enzymes must have two different combining sites: one that recognizes the side group of an amino acid, and another that recognizes the tRNA

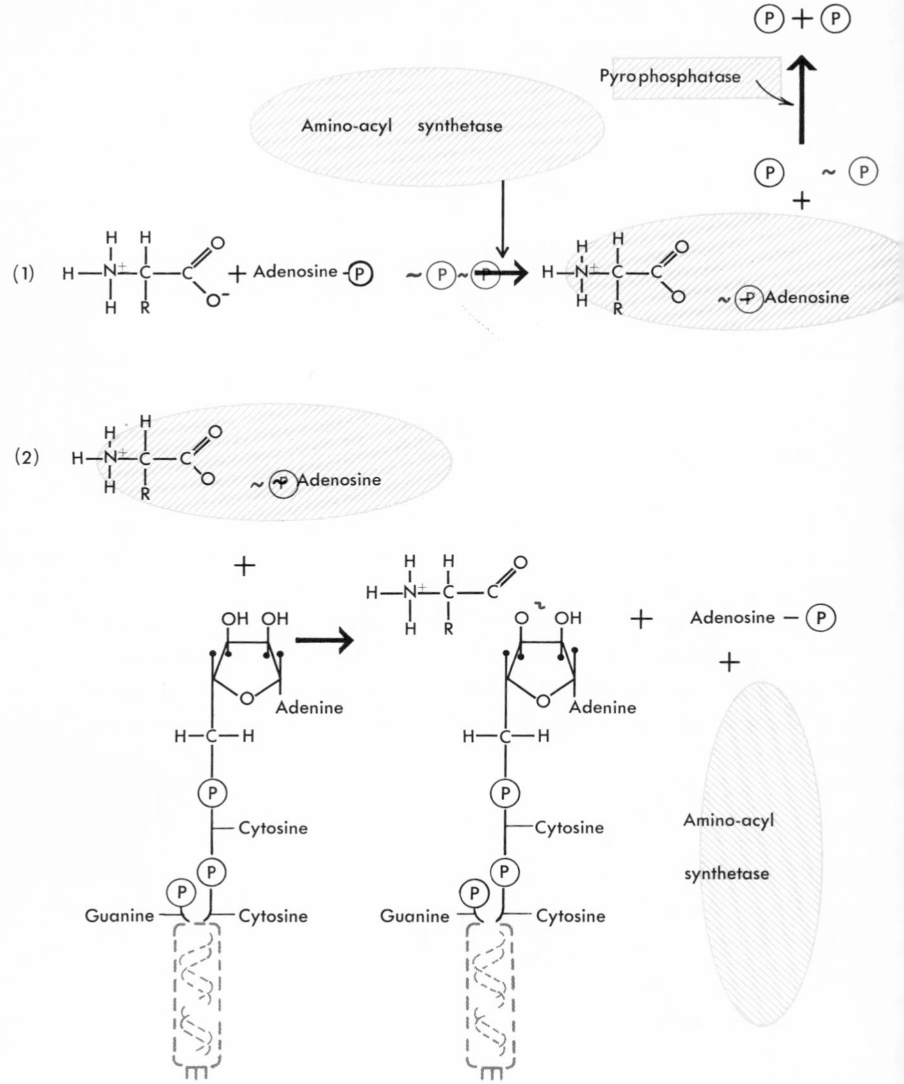

FIGURE 12–5   Activation of an amino acid by ATP and its transfer to the CCA end of its specific tRNA adaptor.

specific for that amino acid. Similarly, each tRNA molecule must have two specific recognition sites: one for its activating enzyme, the other for a specific group of template nucleotides. It follows that the amino acid side group itself never has to come into contact with a template molecule. It needs only to bind specifically to the correct activating enzyme.

Every cell needs at least twenty different kinds of activating enzymes and at least twenty kinds of tRNA molecules. There must be at least one of each for every amino acid. It was first thought that only twenty different tRNA molecules were used, but now it is clear that several cases exist in which at least two different types of tRNA molecules are specific for the same amino acid. This is connected with the fact that the genetic code often uses more than one nucleotide sequence (codon) for a given amino acid (degeneracy; see Chapter 13). Frequently, there is a unique tRNA molecule for each functional codon. There need not be, however, a separate activating enzyme for each of the several tRNAs corresponding to a given amino acid. Since the tRNA binds to the templates and to the activating enzymes at two distinct sites, tRNA molecules that differ in their template-binding nucleotides can possess identical nucleotide sequences in the region that combines with the enzyme. Thus, tRNA molecules that bind to different codons can bind to the same activating enzyme.

PEPTIDE-BOND FORMATION OCCURS ON RIBOSOMES

Once the amino acids have acquired their adaptors, they diffuse to the ribosomes, the spherical particles on which protein synthesis occurs. Protein synthesis never takes place free in solution, but only on the surfaces of the ribosomes, which might be regarded as miniature factories for making protein. Their chief function is to orient the incoming AA~tRNA precursors and the template RNA so that the genetic code can be read accurately. Ribosomes thus contain specific surfaces that bind the template RNA, the AA~tRNA precursors, and the growing polypeptide chain in suitable stereochemical posi-

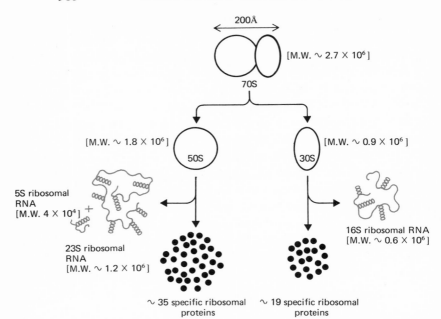

FIGURE 12–6   *The structure of the E. coli ribosome. It is usually called the 70-S ribosome since 70 S (Svedbergs) is a measure (the sedimentation constant) of how fast this ribosome sediments in the centrifuge. Likewise, the designations 30 S and 50 S are the sedimentation constants of the smaller and larger ribosomal subunits; 16 S and 23 S are the sedimentation constants of the smaller and larger ribosomal RNA molecules. All bacterial ribosomes have sizes similar to those of E. coli, possessing 30-S and 50-S subunits. In higher organisms (including yeast, etc.), ribosomes are somewhat larger (80 S), with 40-S and 60-S subunits. For convenience below, we shall use 30 S to designate all smaller particles and 50 S for larger particles.*

tions.   There are approximately 15,000 ribosomes in a rapidly growing *E. coli* cell.   Each ribosome has a molecular weight of slightly less than 3 million.   Together the ribosomes account for about one-fourth of the total cellular mass, and hence a very sizable fraction of the total cellular synthesis is devoted to the task of making proteins.   Only one polypeptide chain can be formed at a time on a single ribosome.   Under optimal conditions, the production of a chain of MW = 40,000 requires about ten seconds.   The finished polypeptide chain is then released and the free ribosome can be used immediately to make another protein.

All ribosomes are constructed from two subunits, the larger subunit approximately twice the size of the smaller one (Figure 12–6). Both subunits contain both RNA and protein. In *E. coli* ribosomes the RNA/protein ratio is about 2 : 1; in many other organisms, it is about 1 : 1. Most of the protein serves a structural role (as opposed to an enzymatic role). Both the large and small subunits contain a large number of different proteins whose chief function is to help bring the template RNA and the AA~tRNA precursors together correctly. So far, intensive work has been done only with the ribosomal proteins from *E. coli*. All nineteen proteins from the smaller subunit (30 S) have been characterized (Figure

FIGURE 12–7   *Reconstitution of the 30-S ribosome from a mixture of 19 specific ribosomal proteins and a 16-S rRNA molecule.*

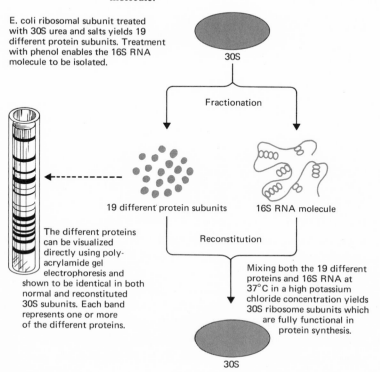

E. coli ribosomal subunit treated with 30S urea and salts yields 19 different protein subunits. Treatment with phenol enables the 16S RNA molecule to be isolated.

30S

Fractionation

19 different protein subunits

16S RNA molecule

The different proteins can be visualized directly using poly- acrylamide gel electrophoresis and shown to be identical in both normal and reconstituted 30S subunits. Each band represents one or more of the different proteins.

Reconstitution

Mixing both the 19 different proteins and 16S RNA at 37°C in a high potassium chloride concentration yields 30S ribosome subunits which are fully functional in protein synthesis.

30S

12–7) and show a variety of sizes. Most, if not all, are present in only one copy per ribosome. Characterization of the 35 proteins in the larger 50-S subunit is less complete. It appears, however, that like 30-S proteins, most are present only once in a given ribosome. Ribosomes are thus remarkably complicated structures whose complete chemical characterization may lie decades in the future.

RIBOSOME RECONSTITUTION

Recently, the complete reassembly of the smaller subunit from its RNA and protein constituents was accomplished. These reconstituted particles are active in protein synthesis, showing identical behavior to the normal 30-S subunits. While complete reconstitution has not yet been obtained for the larger subunits, there seems no real reason why this should not occur very soon. Finding the right conditions for reconstitution is a very important achievement, opening up the possibility of preparing particles lacking one or more specific proteins and seeing the effects of their absence on specific ribosomal functions (e.g., binding of tRNA, peptide-bond formation, etc.).

RIBOSOME-ASSOCIATED RNA DOES NOT USUALLY CARRY GENETIC INFORMATION

When ribosomes became implicated in protein synthesis (1953), it seemed natural at first to suppose that their tightly bound RNA component was the template that ordered the amino acids. In fact, it was initially supposed that all cellular RNA was located in the ribosomes and that the lighter, slowly sedimenting, soluble fraction (~20 per cent of total RNA) was a degradation product of the ribosomal RNA templates. The identification (1956) of the soluble RNA fraction as the adaptor molecules corrected this faulty guess, but it did not remove the belief that all the remaining 80 per cent of cellular RNA functioned as templates. In 1960, however, RNA isolated from purified ribosomes (rRNA or ribosomal RNA) was unambiguously shown not to have a template role.

TEMPLATE RNA (mRNA) REVERSIBLY ASSOCIATES WITH RIBOSOMES

The active templates are instead an RNA fraction comprising only one to several per cent of total RNA. This RNA reversibly binds to the surface of the smaller ribosome subunit and, in media of low Mg^{2+} ion concentration, can be removed without affecting ribosome integrity. Because it carries the genetic message from the gene to the ribosomal factories, it is called messenger RNA (mRNA). By moving across the ribosomal site of protein synthesis, it brings successive codons into position to select the appropriate AA~tRNA precursors. The existence of mRNA was first unambiguously established in experiments with T2-infected *E. coli* cells. After T2 DNA enters a host cell, it must turn out RNA templates for the many viral specific proteins needed for viral reproduction (see Chapter 15 for more details). Many biochemists were, therefore, surprised by the 1959 finding that no new rRNA chains and hence no new ribosomes were synthesized following T2 infection. This result could only mean that T2-specific proteins are not synthesized on rRNA templates, and further hinted that perhaps in normal cells rRNA chains were not the templates for protein synthesis. Searches begun when the T2 result became known quickly revealed the presence of mRNA, first in viral infected cells, and soon afterward in normal *E. coli* cells.

rRNA EXISTS IN TWO MAJOR SIZE CLASSES

Two major size classes of rRNA are found in all bacterial ribosomes. They are an integral component and, unlike mRNA, cannot be removed without the complete collapse of the ribosome structure. The smaller rRNA molecule, found in the smaller ribosome subunit, has a molecular weight of about one-half million, whereas the larger molecule, a component of the larger ribosome subunit, has a molecular weight of about one million. Each larger subunit contains in addition one very short rRNA molecule which sediments at 5 S. All are single-stranded and have unequal amounts of guanine and cytosine and of adenine and uracil. Nonetheless there is enough equivalence of base pairs, so that many rRNA bases on the same chain are hydrogen bonded into the hairpin-type turns found in tRNA. The joint presence of single-stranded and double-helical regions gives individual rRNA molecules irregular 3-D shapes. As a result, it has not yet been possible to obtain rRNA preparations in which the molecules are regularly arranged in space. Thus, x-ray diffraction pictures of rRNA are much more distorted than the corresponding DNA diagrams and cannot tell us precise details of rRNA structure. Similar dilemmas probably exist for elucidation of mRNA molecules by x-ray analysis.

THE FUNCTION OF rRNA IS NOT YET KNOWN

Even with the possibility of reconstitution experiments, the function of rRNA remains a major mystery. Not even a semi-satisfactory hypothesis now exists for why ribosomes contain rRNA as well as protein. Part of the reason may be that the unpaired bases in rRNA are in some way involved in the binding of tRNA and mRNA to ribosomes. In cells, much of RNA's negative phosphate charge is neutralized by Mg^{2+} ions. It is thus possible that the divalent Mg^{2+} ions sometimes form temporary bridges between mRNA and rRNA, or mRNA and tRNA, thereby helping to keep their components correctly aligned during polypeptide synthesis.

ALL THREE FORMS OF RNA ARE MADE ON DNA TEMPLATES

Since both tRNA and rRNA chains have very special roles in protein synthesis, the idea was proposed (several years ago) that perhaps these RNA forms were not make on DNA templates but were instead self-replicating, like the RNA in the single-stranded RNA viruses (see Chapter 15). This idea has been shown to be wrong by DNA-RNA hybridization experiments. In these experiments, rRNA (or tRNA) chains are mixed at a high temperature (near 100°C) with DNA isolated from the same organism. At this temperature, the double-helical regions of rRNA (tRNA) fall apart. Likewise, all hydrogen bonds in DNA break and complementary strands separate. When the temperature is then slowly dropped, stable double helices form again. In addition to reformation of many complementary DNA double helices, some single DNA strands specifically combine with rRNA (tRNA) chains to form hybrid DNA-RNA helices. These DNA-RNA complexes are very specific, for they do not form if DNA from an unrelated species is used. Hence, tRNA and rRNA are synthesized exactly as mRNA is, using DNA molecules as templates. Most interestingly, even though rRNA and tRNA together comprise over 98 per cent of all RNA, less than 1 per cent of the total DNA functions as their templates.

There is probably only one specific sequence of DNA nucleotides (a gene) coding for each of the 30 to 40 different tRNA molecules. In contrast, both the larger and smaller rRNA chains appear to be coded by several genes. Whether each of these separate genes for small or large rRNA has identical nucleotide sequences is not known. They certainly cannot possess radically different sequences since their rRNA products must have very similar 3-D shapes in order to fit in a ribosome.

The use of DNA to code for tRNA (and for rRNA, if future experiments reveal it never assumes a template role) tells us that all genes need not code for specific amino acid sequences. We must thus ask the question whether other RNA forms, as yet undiscovered, may play important metabolic roles. Certainly we now cannot automatically assume that for each gene there exists a corresponding protein.

mRNA MOLECULES EXIST IN A LARGE VARIETY OF SIZES

In contrast to tRNA molecules, which have molecular weights of about 2.5×10^4, and to rRNA molecules, which are either 5×10^5 or 10^6 in molecular weight, mRNA molecules vary greatly in chain length, and hence in molecular weight. Some of this heterogeneity reflects the large size spread in the length of polypeptide chain products. Not many polypeptide chains contain fewer than 100 amino acids, and so almost all mRNA molecules must contain at least 100×3 (because there are three nucleotides in a codon) nucleotides. In *E. coli* the average size of mRNA is 900 to 1500 nucleotides, corresponding to the fact that the average *E. coli* polypeptide chain contains from 300 to 500 amino acids.

Some molecules, however, code for more than one polypeptide chain. Their length is the sum of the lengths of the chains required to code for each protein for which they serve as templates. This summing provides another basis of variation in mRNA chain lengths. In most, if not in all, of these polygenic messengers, the polypeptide products have related functions. For example, there exists an mRNA molecule that codes for the ten specific enzymes needed to synthesize the amino acid histidine. It has approximately 12,000 nucleotides (MW ~4,000,-000) or an average of 1200 nucleotides coding for each enzyme.

RIBOSOMES COME APART INTO SUBUNITS DURING PROTEIN SYNTHESIS

The construction of all ribosomes from easily dissociable subunits suggested a cycle during which the large and small subunits come apart at some stage in protein synthesis. This hunch has recently been confirmed by experiments with *E. coli* and yeast which show that most ribosomes are constantly dissociating into subunits and reforming. Growth of cells in heavy isotopes followed by transfer to light medium was the technique used to settle this point. Soon after transfer to the light medium, hybrid (heavy 50-S–light 30-S, light 50-S–heavy 30-S) ribosomes began to appear, the rate of their appearance suggesting that the subunits exchange once during every cycle of polypeptide synthesis. Confirmatory evidence comes from *in vitro* studies of protein synthesis (see the next chapter) where the fate of "heavy" ribosomes can be followed in the presence of a great excess of light ribosomes. Within a minute or so (the time required to synthesize a complete polypeptide chain) almost all heavy ribosomes disappear, with the simultaneous appearance of hybrid ribosomes (Figure 12–8). The obligatory dependence

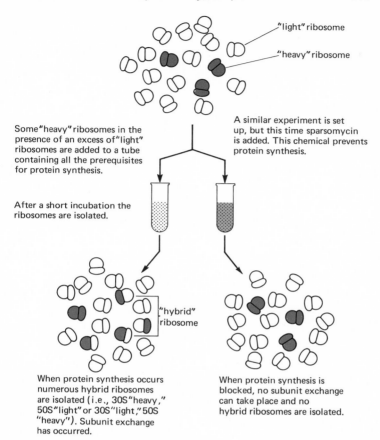

Some "heavy" ribosomes in the presence of an excess of "light" ribosomes are added to a tube containing all the prerequisites for protein synthesis.

A similar experiment is set up, but this time sparsomycin is added. This chemical prevents protein synthesis.

After a short incubation the ribosomes are isolated.

"hybrid" ribosome

When protein synthesis occurs numerous hybrid ribosomes are isolated (i.e., 30S "heavy," 50S "light" or 30S "light," 50S "heavy"). Subunit exchange has occurred.

When protein synthesis is blocked, no subunit exchange can take place and no hybrid ribosomes are isolated.

FIGURE 12–8 *The obligatory dependence of subunit exchange on protein synthesis.*

of subunit exchange on protein synthesis is confirmed by *in vitro* experiments with the antibiotic sparsomycin. This compound, which blocks polypeptide chain elongation, also prevents any subunit exchange.

It is not yet conclusively known whether the subunits separate simultaneously with the completion of a new polypeptide, or whether they come off an mRNA molecule in the form of a 70-S ribosome which subsequently dissociates into the subunit form.

POLYPEPTIDE CHAIN GROWTH STARTS
AT THE AMINO TERMINAL END

At one end of a complete polypeptide chain is an amino acid bearing a free carboxyl group, and at the other end is one bearing a free amino group. Chains always grow by the stepwise addition of single amino acids, starting with the amino terminal and ending with the carboxyl terminal (Figure 12–9). This point is clearly shown by brief exposure of hemoglobin-synthesizing reticulocytes to radioactively labeled amino acids, followed by immediate isolation of newly completed hemoglobin chains. Very little radioactivity is found in the amino acids of the amino terminal end; most is found in the amino acids of the carboxyl end (Figure 12–10). Moreover, a clear gradient of increasing radioactivity is observed as one moves from the amino to the carboxyl end.

FIGURE 12–9   *Stepwise growth of a polypeptide chain.   Initiation begins at the free NH_3^+ end with the carboxyl growing point terminated by a tRNA molecule.*

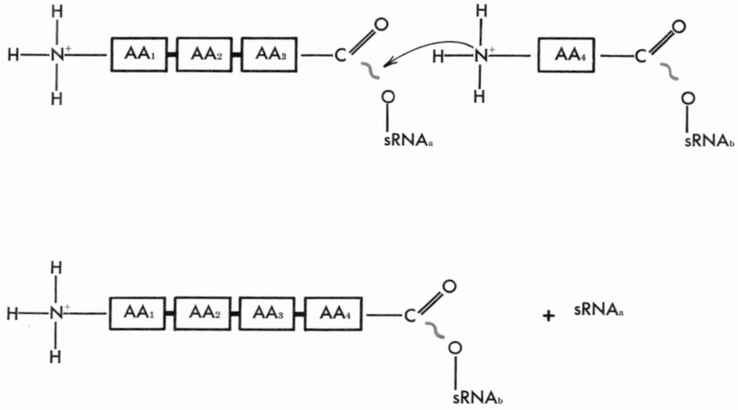

(Peptide bonds between amino acids
are indicated by a heavy line.)

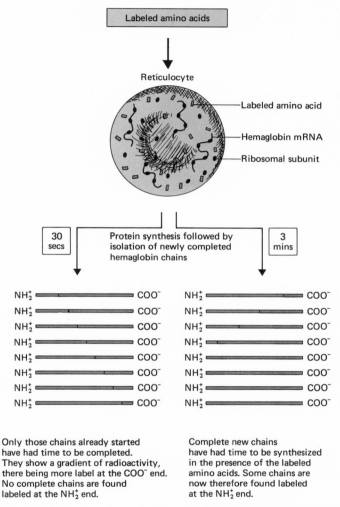

Labeled amino acids

Reticulocyte

Labeled amino acid

Hemaglobin mRNA

Ribosomal subunit

| 30 secs | Protein synthesis followed by isolation of newly completed hemaglobin chains | 3 mins |

NH_2^+ ══════════ COO^- NH_2^+ ══════════ COO^-
NH_2^+ ══════════ COO^- NH_2^+ ══════════ COO^-
NH_2^+ ══════════ COO^- NH_2^+ ══════════ COO^-
NH_2^+ ══════════ COO^- NH_2^+ ══════════ COO^-
NH_2^+ ══════════ COO^- NH_2^+ ══════════ COO^-
NH_2^+ ══════════ COO^- NH_2^+ ══════════ COO^-
NH_2^+ ══════════ COO^- NH_2^+ ══════════ COO^-
NH_2^+ ══════════ COO^- NH_2^+ ══════════ COO^-

Only those chains already started have had time to be completed. They show a gradient of radioactivity, there being more label at the COO^- end. No complete chains are found labeled at the NH_2^+ end.

Complete new chains have had time to be synthesized in the presence of the labeled amino acids. Some chains are now therefore found labeled at the NH_2^+ end.

FIGURE 12–10 *Experimental demonstration that hemoglobin chains grow in the $NH_2 \rightarrow COOH$ direction.*

STARTING OF ALL BACTERIAL POLYPEPTIDE CHAINS WITH N-FORMYL METHIONINE

Several years ago, the fact emerged that the starting amino acid in synthesis of all bacterial polypeptides is N-formyl methionine. This is a modified methionine which has a formyl group

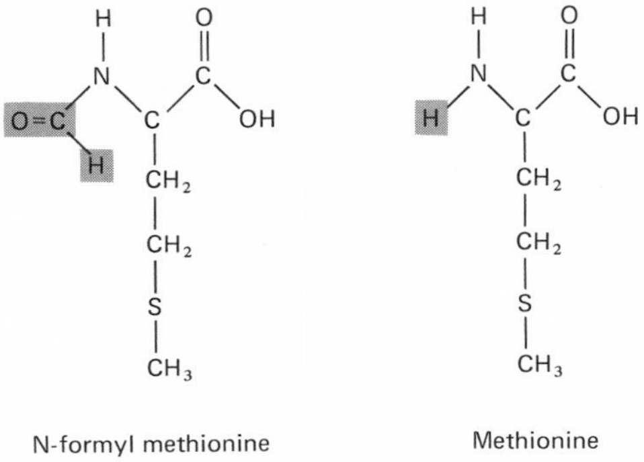

N-formyl methionine   Methionine

F I G U R E 12–11 *The structure of N-formyl methionine.*

attached to its terminal amino group (Figure 12–11). A blocked amino acid like N-formyl methionine can be used only to start protein synthesis. The absence of a free amino group would prevent this amino acid from being inserted during chain elongation. The formyl group is enzymatically added onto methionine after the methionine has become attached to its tRNA adaptor.

Not all methionine-tRNA molecules can be formylated. Instead, there exist two types of met-tRNA, only one of which permits the formylation reaction. Just completed sequence analysis of both of these met-tRNAs reveals that they have the same anticodon sequences (Figure 12–12), exposing the dilemma of how the same codon (AUG) can code for two different amino acids.

The discovery that synthesis of bacterial protein starts with a blocked amino acid was most unexpected because isolation of pure protein from growing bacteria revealed essentially no formylated end groups. This means an enzyme exists which removes the formyl group from the growing chain very soon after synthesis commences (Figure 12–13). In addition, another enzyme (an amino peptidase) exists which subsequently removes the terminal methionine from many proteins. It does not act on all proteins, so a large fraction of bacterial proteins commence with methionine.

Our picture of initiation in protein synthesis is less clear

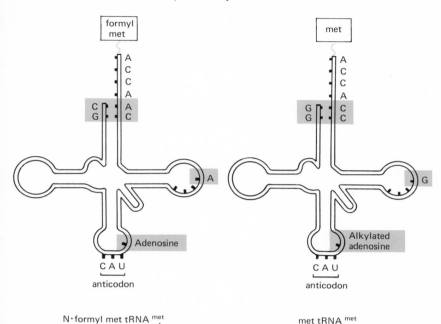

FIGURE 12-12   *The three main points of difference between N-formyl-met-tRNA and met-tRNA.*

in those organisms (eucaryotic as distinct from procaryotic) where cells contain discrete nuclei and have 80-S ribosomes. Though there are hints that synthesis also starts with methionine, it does not seem to be blocked with a formyl group. Continued investigation should soon clarify this situation.

**BINDING OF THE SMALLER
RIBOSOMAL SUBUNIT TO SPECIFIC
POINTS ALONG mRNA MOLECULES**

Initiation starts with the formation of a complex between the smaller 30-S ribosomal subunit, f-met-tRNA, and an mRNA molecule. Then 50-S subunits attach to form the functional 70-S ribosome. Each specific mRNA chain contains one to several spots where the free 30-S particles can stick. These points contain the nucleotide sequences which code for the first

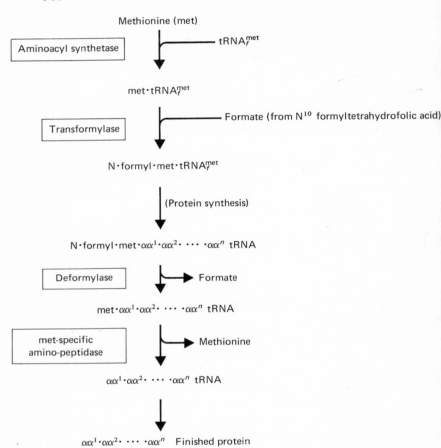

FIGURE 12–13   *Enzymatic steps involving formyl methionine initiation of protein synthesis.*

amino acids in the polypeptide chain. There is at most one sticky point per polypeptide chain coded by a given messenger. If there were more than one sticky point per polypeptide product, incomplete polypeptides would be produced. A few months ago, the first partial sequences for sticky regions were worked out. Their isolation was achieved by binding ribosomes to the RNA messenger of phage R17 (see Chapter 15) and then adding the enzyme ribonuclease which breaks down all sequences except those protected by binding of ribosomes to the

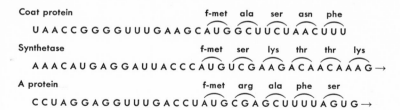

FIGURE 12–14   *The ribosome binding sites of the three genes along the phage R17 RNA molecule. At these sites ribosomes can attach and protein synthesis starts at the initiation triplet AUG.*

initiating sites. Nucleotide sequence methods were then used upon the protected fragments to give the results shown in Figure 12–14.

These sequences are still too fragmentary to tell us why the 30-S subunits attach only at specific points. The correct explanation may be connected with the fact that all natural messenger (as distinct from synthetic messenger; see Chapter 13) has considerable double-helical regions formed by hairpin turns similar to those in tRNA and rRNA. Now it is guessed that sticky areas contain one or more single-stranded regions, perhaps with specific sequences. If so, the sequence of nucleotides within each natural mRNA must cause it to assume a configuration in which long single-stranded regions are effectively absent over most of its length.

Once a ribosome attaches to a messenger and polypeptide synthesis commences, the ribosome comes into contact with regions of mRNA to which it could not bind prior to synthesis. In some way, the presence of an attached ribosome temporarily disrupts nearby hairpin double-helical regions, creating single-stranded regions which are able both to bind to the ribosome and to select the correct AA~tRNA precursors.

INITIATION FACTORS

A mixture of N-formyl-met-tRNA, mRNA, and the 30-S and 50-S subunits by itself is not sufficient for initiation. At least three separate proteins, not normally part of ribosomes, are

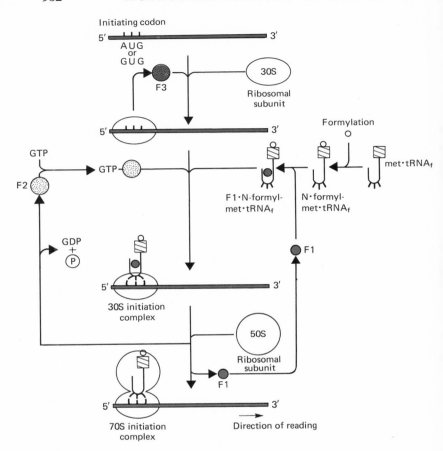

F1 [MW 8000] probably involved in binding 50S to 30S initiation complex.
F2 [MW 75,000] probably involved in binding N-blocked amino acyl tRNA.
F3 [MW 30,000] probably binds 30S ribosomal subunit to mRNA.

FIGURE 12–15   *Diagrammatic view of the initiation process in protein synthesis. [Only one of the two tRNA binding sites is shown on the ribosome. It is not known which site (A or P) the f-met-tRNA enters first.]*

necessary (Figure 12–15). One of these proteins (F3) is required for the binding of 30-S particles to mRNA. A second protein (F1) attaches to f-met-tRNA and helps it bind to the 30-S–mRNA initiation complex. It is released when the 50-S subunit joins the complex. How the third (F2) protein exactly operates remains unclear, though it is known to bind GTP and also to be needed in the formation of the 30-S initiation complex.

THE DIRECTION OF mRNA READING IS 5' TO 3'

After an mRNA molecule has stuck to a ribosome, it must always move in a fixed direction during protein synthesis. It does not have the alternative of moving both to the right or to the left, which reflects the fact that RNA molecules have a direction defined by the relative orientations of the 3' and 5' ends. The end which is read first, the 5' end, is also synthesized first. This opens up the possibility that a ribosome can attach to an incomplete mRNA molecule in the process of synthesis on its DNA template. If, on the contrary, polypeptide synthesis went 3' to 5', then a length of mRNA corresponding to a complete polypeptide chain would have to be synthesized before it could stick to a ribosome. The fact that protein synthesis goes 5' to 3' most likely means that long sections of mRNA unattached to ribosomes do not normally exist in rapidly growing cells.

EACH RIBOSOME HAS TWO tRNA BINDING SITES

Each 70-S ribosome contains two cavities into which tRNA molecules can be inserted (Figure 12–16). They are the "P" (peptidyl) and the "A" (amino-acyl) sites. Each hole is bounded partly by a 30-S region and a 50-S region and by a specific mRNA codon. Although the ribosomal bounded surface can accept any of the specific AA~tRNAs since it binds to an unspecific region of the tRNA molecule, the codon-bounded surface is specific for a unique tRNA molecule.

We do not yet know whether the initiating f-met-tRNA first enters the "P" site or whether it first goes into the "A" site and subsequently moves into the "P" site. It is clear, however, that it must be in the "P" site before the second AA~tRNA can bind specifically to the ribosome. For all AA~tRNAs except f-met-tRNA, it has been firmly established that entry to the ribosome occurs through the "A" site. After the second AA~

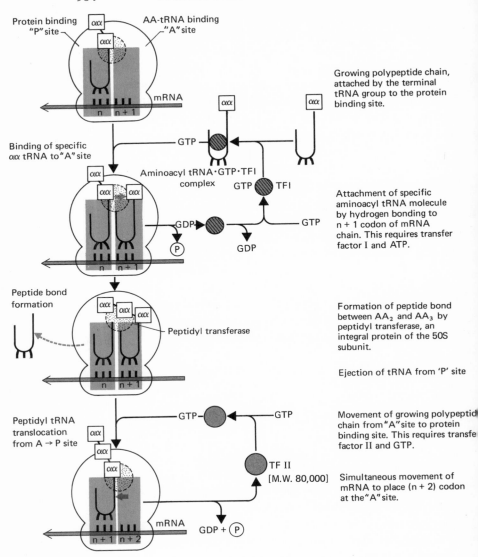

Protein binding "P" site

AA-tRNA binding "A" site

mRNA

Binding of specific αα tRNA to "A" site

Aminoacyl tRNA·GTP·TFI complex

Peptide bond formation

Peptidyl transferase

Peptidyl tRNA translocation from A → P site

mRNA

GTP

GTP·TFI

GDP

GTP

GDP

GTP

TF II [M.W. 80,000]

GDP + P

Growing polypeptide chain, attached by the terminal tRNA group to the protein binding site.

Attachment of specific aminoacyl tRNA molecule by hydrogen bonding to n + 1 codon of mRNA chain. This requires transfer factor I and ATP.

Formation of peptide bond between AA_2 and AA_3 by peptidyl transferase, an integral protein of the 50S subunit.

Ejection of tRNA from 'P' site

Movement of growing polypeptide chain from "A" site to protein binding site. This requires transfer factor II and GTP.

Simultaneous movement of mRNA to place (n + 2) codon at the "A" site.

FIGURE 12–16 *Diagrammatic view of peptide-bond formation showing the role of the transfer factors.*

tRNA is correctly placed in the "A" site, a peptide bond is formed enzymatically to yield a dipeptide (two amino acids linked by a peptide bond) terminated by a tRNA molecule, the adaptor of the second amino acid. This process of amino acid addition then repeats over and over, adding one amino acid at a time to form a complete chain (Figure 12–16). In these events, the following steps should be emphasized.

1. The growing carboxyl end is always terminated by a tRNA molecule. The binding of this terminal tRNA to either the "P" or "A" site is the main force holding a growing polypeptide chain to the ribosome.

2. Formation of the peptide bond moves the attachment point of the growing chain from the "P" to the "A" site.

3. Soon after, if not coincident with, the formation of the peptide bond, the released tRNA molecule is ejected from its "P" site.

4. The new terminal tRNA molecule then moves (translocates) from the "A" to the "P" site. At the same time, the mRNA template bound to the smaller ribosome subunit moves to place codon $n + 1$ in the position previously occupied by codon n.

5. The now vacant "A" site becomes free to accept a new AA~tRNA molecule whose specificity is determined by correct base pairing between its anticodon and the relevant mRNA codon.

EXISTENCE OF TRANSFER FACTORS

Because the amino acid carboxyl groups are activated by their attachment to their tRNA adaptors, the initial guess was that perhaps only one specific enzyme would be needed for making the peptide bond. Furthermore, there was no reason to suspect that more energy would be needed for the polymerization reaction. Both these hunches, however, were wrong. First, the energy-rich molecule GTP (analogous to ATP with adenine replaced by guanine) is required for the synthesis of all peptide bonds in protein. Second, two proteins (the transfer factors) have been isolated which are not normally part of ribosomes but which are also necessary. Moreover, neither of these two proteins itself precipitates the actual formation of peptide bonds.

BINDING OF AA ~ tRNA TO THE ''A'' SITE REQUIRES TRANSFER FACTOR I

The attachment of the AA~tRNA precursor to ribosomes was initially believed to be a nonenzymatic event occuring when the correct AA~tRNA randomly bumped the "A" site and its specific binding mRNA codon. Recent experiments, however, indicate that the binding reaction is far from simple. It starts when one of the transfer factors (TF I) reacts with GTP and AA~tRNA to form an AA~tRNA–GTP–TF I complex. This complex then transfers its AA~tRNA component to the "A" site with release of a free TF I–GDP complex and ℗. Each binding step thus requires the splitting of one of GTP's high-energy bonds. How this energy facilitates the binding remains unknown.

THE PEPTIDE-BOND-FORMING ENZYME IS AN INTEGRAL COMPONENT OF THE 50-S PARTICLE

Enzymatic catalysis of the peptide bond itself is caused by one of the proteins of the larger ribosomal subunit. It is called peptidyl transferase and is believed to be present in one copy per 50-S subunit. All attempts so far to dissociate this enzyme from 50-S particles have failed. When complete reconstitution of a 50-S particle is achieved, it should be possible to pinpoint a specific 50-S protein as the active catalyst.

PEPTIDYL-tRNA TRANSLOCATION REQUIRES TRANSFER FACTOR II

The movement of peptidyl-tRNA from the "A" to the "P" site is brought about by transfer factor II (TF II), often called the translocase. In this process, a TF II–GTP–ribosome complex first forms. Translocation, coupled with hydrolysis of GTP to GDP and ℗ then occurs, with subsequent release of free reusable TF II. The splitting of the high-energy bond is obligatory for the movement, with precise experiments showing that one GTP is split for every translocation act. Whether translocation is coupled in time with the stepwise movement of three mRNA nucleotides over the ribosomal surface remains to be worked out. At present, we have no hints about how the relative movement of mRNA chains over ribosomes occurs. Formulation of any precise model must undoubtably await further knowledge of ribosomal 3-D structure.

INHIBITION OF SPECIFIC STEPS IN PROTEIN SYNTHESIS BY ANTIBIOTICS

A number of antibiotics have proved very useful in delineating the steps by which proteins are built up. For example, puromycin, a very powerful inhibitor of the growth of all cells, acts by interrupting chain elongation. Its structure (Figure 12–17) resembles the 3′ end of a charged tRNA molecule and so it is able to enter the "A" ribosomal binding site very efficiently, competitively inhibiting the normal entering of AA~tRNA precursors. More importantly, peptidyl transferase will use it as a substitute, thereby transferring nascent chains to puromycin acceptors. Since the puromycin residues bind only weakly to the "A" site, the puromycin-terminated nascent chains fall off the ribosomes, thereby producing incomplete chains of varying lengths.

Another very useful antibiotic is fusidic acid, which specifically inhibits the translocation function of transfer factor II. The peptidyl transferase reaction itself is inhibited by the antibiotics sparsomycin and lincomycin, both of which specifically bind to the 50-S subunit. In contrast, streptomycin, which binds to the 30-S subunit, is a powerful inhibitor of chain initiation.

POLYPEPTIDE CHAINS FOLD UP SIMULTANEOUSLY WITH SYNTHESIS

Under optimal conditions, the time required for the synthesis of an *E. coli* polypeptide chain containing 300 to 400 amino acids

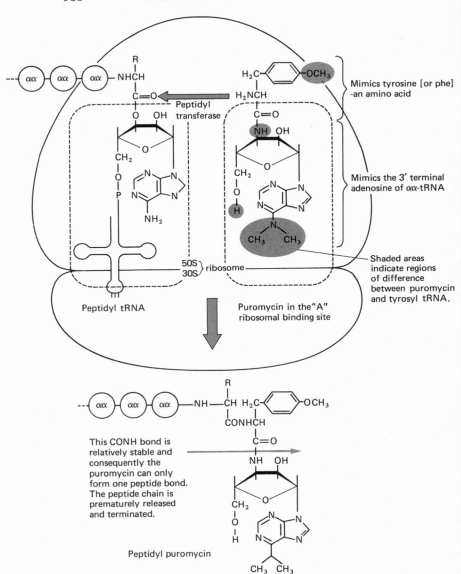

FIGURE 12–17 *Premature peptide chain termination by puromycin.*

is 10 to 20 seconds. During this time, the elongating chain does not remain a random coil, but quickly assumes much of its final 3-D shape through the formation of many of its secondary bonds. Thus, with many proteins, most of the final shape may be achieved before the last few amino acids are added on. As a result, trace amounts of many enzyme activities are found on ribosomes which have not yet released their polypeptide products.

CHAIN RELEASE DEPENDS UPON SPECIFIC RELEASE FACTORS WHICH NEED CHAIN-TERMINATING CODONS

Two conditions are necessary for chain termination. One is the presence of a codon that specifically signifies that polypeptide elongation should stop. The other is the presence of a release factor which reads the chain-terminating signal. Behind all this complexity is the fact that after a polypeptide chain has reached its full length, its carboxyl end is still bound to its tRNA adaptor. Termination must thus involve the splitting off of the terminal tRNA. When this happens, the nascent chain quickly dissociates since its binding to the ribosome occurred principally through its tRNA component.

Elucidation of the genetic code (see Chapter 13) revealed three codons specifically signifying stop. Their existence initially led to the expectation of chain-terminating tRNA molecules; that is, tRNAs which would specifically bind to the stop codon but which had no amino acid attached to their 3'-adenosine and which in some way promoted the release of the terminal tRNA group. New experiments, however, conclusively rule out the existence of such molecules. The stop codons are instead read by specific proteins (the release factors). Whether the release factors are enzymes and directly catalyze the splitting off of terminal tRNA residues remains to be elucidated.

BREAKS IN POLYPEPTIDE CHAINS AFTER CHAIN TERMINATION

Many examples are known where specific enzymes are modified after synthesis. We mentioned earlier the removal of formyl and methionine groups from many bacterial proteins. Very likely, cases will soon be found where more than one amino acid is removed from either the amino or carboxyl ends through the action of exopeptidases (enzymes which sequentially remove terminal amino acids). Equally important are the endopeptidases, which cut internal peptide bonds. Insulin, for many years thought to be constructed by aggregation of independently synthesized A and B chains, is synthesized first as a single chain (proinsulin) whose 3-D shape is attained after formation of several disulfide (S—S) bonds. Subsequently, two internal cuts remove 33 amino acids, leaving the formerly contiguous polypeptide fragments held together only by the S—S bonds. It is thus very clear that knowledge of the amino acid sequence of a purified enzyme may not necessarily reveal the true initiating and terminating amino acids.

AN mRNA MOLECULE WORKS ON SEVERAL RIBOSOMES SIMULTANEOUSLY

The section of an mRNA molecule that is in contact with a single ribosome is relatively short. This allows a given mRNA molecule to work on several ribosomes at once. Single mRNA molecules can move over the surfaces of several ribosomes simultaneously (the collection of ribosomes bound to a single mRNA chain is called a polyribosome), thus functioning as a template for several polypeptide chains at once. At a given time, the lengths of chains attached to successive ribosomes in the polyribosome vary in direct proportion to the fraction of the messenger tape to which each ribosome has already been exposed (Figure 12–18). This means that at any moment the polypeptide chains being produced along the length of the mRNA are shortest at the front of the strand, and gradually lengthen toward the end. There is great variation in polyribosome size, which depends upon the size of the mRNA chain. At maximum utilization of an mRNA chain, there is one ribosome for every 80 mRNA nucleotides. Thus the polyribosomes that make hemoglobin molecules usually contain 4 to 6 ribosomes (Figure 12–19), while approximately 12 to 20 ribosomes

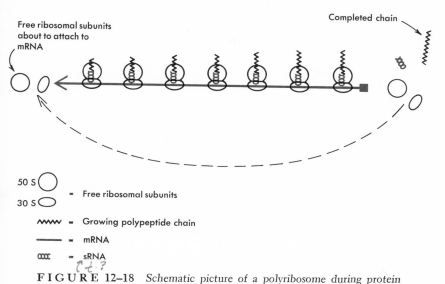

FIGURE 12–18 *Schematic picture of a polyribosome during protein synthesis. The mRNA molecule is moving from right to left.*

are attached to the mRNA molecules concerned with the synthesis of proteins in the 30,000 to 50,000 MW (300 to 500 amino acids) range.

The ability of a single mRNA to function on several ribosomes simultaneously explains why a cell needs so relatively little mRNA. Before polyribosomes were discovered, and when only one ribosome was thought to be attached to a given mRNA molecule, the fact that mRNA comprised only 1 to 2 per cent of the total cellular RNA seemed highly paradoxical. This followed from the fact that if the average mRNA chain were of MW about 5×10^5, then at a given instant at most only 10 per cent of the ribosomes in a cell could be making protein.

MUCH MORE MUST BE LEARNED ABOUT RIBOSOMES

It is very likely that the broad general outlines of protein synthesis are now established. Each of the key features shown in Figure 12–20 has been established by a variety of experiments.

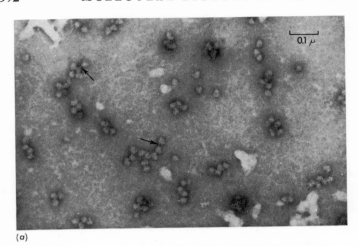

(a)

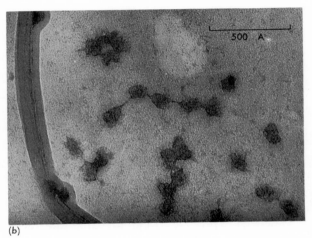

(b)

FIGURE 12–19   Electron-microscope photographs of polyribosomes from rabbit reticulocytes. (a) Shows that many of the observed polyribosomes contain 4–6 ribosomes. The smaller groups are most likely breakdown products produced during their isolation from cells. The arrows show material that seems to connect two ribosomes. (b) At higher magnification, the existence of a connecting thin mRNA strand is very clear. [Photographs by H. S. Slayter; reproduced from H. S. Slayter et al., J. Mol. Biol., 7, 652 (1963), with permission.]

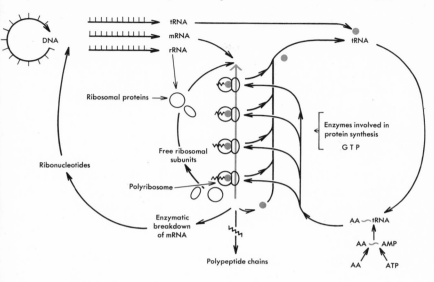

FIGURE 12–20   *Schematic view of the role of RNA in protein synthesis.*

Nonetheless, much new information must be obtained before we can honestly state that protein synthesis is understood at the molecular level. At the heart of our uncertainty is the role of the ribosome. Though a few physical parameters such as molecular weight and RNA content have been accurately established, almost nothing is known about the exact structures of rRNAs or ribosomal proteins, or how they combine with tRNA or mRNA.

Recent spectacular advances in technique for determining nucleotide and amino acid sequences may allow a successful assault within the next decade on the sequences of both the 16-S and 23-S rRNA chains, as well as on most of the ribosomal proteins. But even these data will probably provide little useful information about their spatial arrangements. Though high-resolution electron-microscope research may soon be able to tell us facts like the location of the "P" and "A" tRNA binding sites, it cannot show details at the atomic level. This will come only when it is possible to apply x-ray diffraction analysis. For many years this approach seemed almost hopeless, for no one has been able to grow ribosome crystals and doubts existed whether it would be possible.

Recently, however, numerous examples have been found where ribosome crystals form within living cells. The cells in which they occur are those where protein synthesis has temporarily stopped. For example, excellent crystals (Figure 12–21) are obtained in chick embryo cells when incubation at high temperature ceases and the cells are allowed to cool slowly. Under such conditions, nascent chains are completed, no new initiation occurs, and mRNA dissociates from the individual ribosomes. The resulting free ribosomes can then aggregate spontaneously. The existence of this *in vivo* crystallization makes it probable that, not too far in the future, crystals can be grown in the test tube. This, however, will just be the first step in a horrendous endeavor, since x-ray methods have not yet been used to solve structures of anywhere near this complexity. We must thus be prepared for a long wait and much hard work be-

FIGURE 12–21   *Crystals of ribosomes revealed in a thin-section electron micrograph of a chick embryo cell cooled for 6 hr at 5°C. [From Byers, J. Mol. Biol., 26, 155 (1967). Plate kindly supplied by B. Byers, The Biological Laboratories, Harvard University.]*

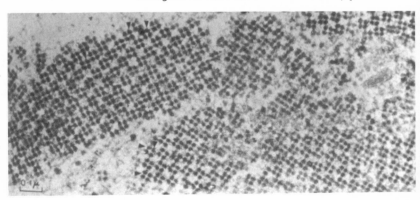

Rereal this
review

fore we understand why such a complicated structure is necessary for protein synthesis.

SUMMARY

Amino acids do not attach directly to RNA templates. They first combine with specific adaptor molecules to form AA~adaptor complexes. The adaptor component has a strong chemical affinity for RNA nucleotides. All the adaptors are transfer RNA molecules (tRNA) of MW~25,000. A given tRNA molecule is specific for a given amino acid.

All tRNA chains are folded into a cloverleaf pattern whose stems contain hydrogen-bonded base pairs and whose loops contain several unpaired bases. One of the loops contains the anticodon, the group of 3 bases which base pair to three successive template bases ("codon"). Amino acids attach through their carboxyl groups to the 3' terminal adenosine of tRNA molecules by high-energy covalent bonds. Adapted amino acids are thus "activated." There is a specific activating enzyme (amino-acyl synthetase) for each amino acid and so it is an enzyme, not tRNA, which recognizes the amino acid. The overall accuracy of protein synthesis can thus be no greater than the accuracy with which the activating enzymes can selectively recognize the various amino acids.

After activation, the AA~tRNA molecules diffuse to the ribosomes, which are spherical particles on which the peptide bonds form. Ribosomes have molecular weights of about 3×10^6 and consist of about half protein and half rRNA. They are always constructed from a large (MW $\sim 2 \times 10^6$) and a small (MW $\sim 10^6$) subunit. About 60 different proteins are found in a single ribosome in addition to major RNA chains (16-S and 23-S RNA). rRNA does not contain genetic information and its function remains an important mystery. The template itself is a third form of RNA, messenger RNA (mRNA). Messenger RNA attaches to ribosomes and moves across them to bring successive codons into position to select the correct AA~tRNA precursors.

Protein chains grow stepwise, beginning at the amino terminal end. This means the growing end is always terminated by a tRNA molecule. Attachment of the nascent chain to the ribosome occurs through binding of the chain's terminal tRNA group to a hole in the ribosomal surface. Each ribosome has two holes, the "P" (peptidyl) and the "A" (amino-acyl). Precursor AA~tRNA molecules normally first enter the "A" site, allowing the subsequent formation of a peptide bond to the growing chain held in the "P" site. This transfers the nascent chain to the "A" site. Action of the enzyme translocase then moves the nascent chain back into the "P" site where another cycle can begin. Both the attachment of AA~tRNA to the "A" site and the translocation process require the splitting of GTP to GDP and Ⓟ. Movement of successive codons over the ribosomal surface may occur simultaneously with the translocation step but nothing is known about how this happens. Initiation of synthesis requires separate enzymes from those involved in chain elongation. With bacterial ribosomes, initiation always involves N-formyl-methionine-tRNA. Chain termination results from the reading of specific stop signals by specific proteins (the release factors).

Completion of chain synthesis is followed by the dissociation of ribosomes into the large and small ribosomal subunits. Reunion of subunits occurs only after the initiating amino acid has first combined with an mRNA–small subunit complex. A given mRNA molecule generally works simultaneously on many ribosomes (a polyribosome). Thus, at a given moment, many codons of the same template are "at work."

REFERENCES

Crick, F. H. C., "On Protein Synthesis," *Symp. Soc. Exptl. Biol.*, **12**, 138–163 (1958). A presentation of the ideas that led the author to propose the adaptor hypothesis.

Watson, J. D., "The Involvement of RNA in the Synthesis of Proteins," *Science*, **140**, 17–26 (1963). A history of work between 1953 and 1962 that established how RNA participates in protein synthesis.

Holley, R. W., "The Nucleotide Sequence of a Nucleic Acid." A description of how the author worked out the structure of alanyl tRNA. A 1966 *Scientific American* article reprinted in *The Molecular Basis of Life*, R. H. Haynes and P. C. Hanawalt (eds.), Freeman, San Francisco, 1968.

Levitt, M., "Detailed Molecular Model for Transfer Ribonucleic Acid," *Nature*, **224**, 759 (1969). The most intelligent attempt so far to formulate a 3-D form for tRNA.

"Mechanism of Protein Synthesis," *Cold Spring Harbor Symp. Quant. Biol.*, **34**, (1969). The most up-to-date and comprehensive collection of facts about how polypeptide chains are put together.

Nomura, M., "Ribosomes," *Scientific American*, December 1969. A very nice introductory survey about how ribosomes can be taken apart and then put back together.

Spirin, A. S., and L. P. Gavrilova, *"The Ribosome,"* Springer, Berlin, 1969. A very complete and informative summary of the structure of ribosomes and how they function during protein synthesis.

Steitz, J. Argetsinger, "Polypeptide Chain Initiation: Nucleotide Sequences of the Three Ribosomal Binding Sites in Bacteriophage R17 RNA," *Nature*, **224**, 957 (1969). The first look at the nucleotide sequences at the beginning of genes.

Anfinsen, C. B. (ed.), *Aspects of Protein Biosynthesis*, Academic Press, New York, 1970. A collection of review articles.

13

THE GENETIC
CODE

EVEN WHEN THE GENERAL OUTLINE OF how RNA participates in protein synthesis had been established (1960), there was little optimism that we would soon know details of the genetic code itself. At that time we believed that identification of the codons for a given amino acid would require exact knowledge of both the nucleotide sequences of a gene and the corresponding amino acid order in its protein product. As mentioned earlier, the elucidation of amino acid sequences, though a laborious objective, was already a very practical one. But on the other hand, the then current methods for determining DNA sequences were very primitive, and even today no extensive DNA base sequence information exists. Fortunately, this apparently firm roadblock did not prove a real handicap. In 1961, just one year after the discovery of mRNA, the use of artificial messenger RNAs partially cracked the genetic code with the unambiguous demonstration of a codon for the amino acid phenylalanine. To explain how this discovery was made, we must first describe some details of how biochemists study protein synthesis in cell-free systems.

ADDITION OF mRNA STIMULATES *IN VITRO* PROTEIN SYNTHESIS

The need for three RNA forms (tRNA, rRNA, and mRNA) for protein synthesis was demonstrated largely by ex-

periments using cell-free extracts prepared from cells actively
engaged in protein synthesis.   In these experiments carefully disrupted cells were fractionated to see which cell components were
necessary for incorporation of amino acids into proteins.   All
these experiments utilized radioactively labeled (H^3, C^{14}, or S^{35})

FIGURE 13–1   *Experimental details of in vitro studies of protein
synthesis.*

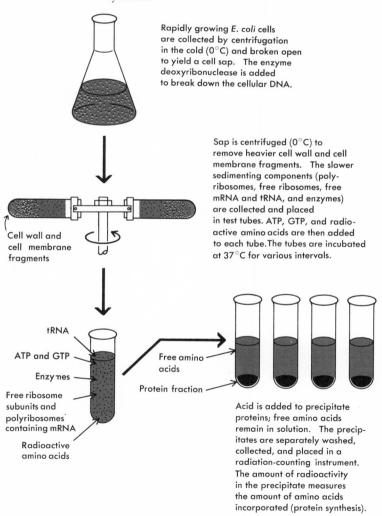

Rapidly growing *E. coli* cells
are collected by centrifugation
in the cold (0°C) and broken open
to yield a cell sap.   The enzyme
deoxyribonuclease is added
to break down the cellular DNA.

Sap is centrifuged (0°C) to
remove heavier cell wall and cell
membrane fragments.   The slower
sedimenting components (polyribosomes, free ribosomes, free
mRNA and tRNA, and enzymes)
are collected and placed
in test tubes. ATP, GTP, and radioactive amino acids are then added
to each tube. The tubes are incubated
at 37°C for various intervals.

Cell wall and
cell membrane
fragments

tRNA

ATP and GTP

Enzymes

Free ribosome
subunits and
polyribosomes
containing mRNA

Radioactive
amino acids

Free amino
acids

Protein fraction

Acid is added to precipitate
proteins; free amino acids
remain in solution.   The precipitates are separately washed,
collected, and placed in a
radiation-counting instrument.
The amount of radioactivity
in the precipitate measures
the amount of amino acids
incorporated (protein synthesis).

amino acids because *in vitro* protein synthesis is still very inefficient; that is there is no detectable net synthesis. Only by using labeled precursors can the incorporation of precursors into proteins be convincingly demonstrated (Figure 13–1).

A typical time course of the *in vitro* incorporation of radioactive amino acids into proteins is illustrated by the graph in Figure 13–2. It shows that synthesis in an *E. coli* extract proceeds linearly for several minutes and then gradually stops. During this interval there is a corresponding loss of mRNA, owing to the action of degradative enzymes present in the extract. This suggests that the major cause of the inefficiency of cell-free protein synthesis is loss of the template component. The correctness of this supposition is shown by adding new mRNA to extracts that have just stopped making protein. Such an addition causes an immediate resumption of synthesis. mRNA-depleted extracts are very valuable in testing mRNA activity. Because they contain very little functional mRNA, they can be used to detect small amounts of template activity in externally added mRNA.

FIGURE 13–2   *Effect of addition of mRNA on the in vitro incorporation of amino acids into protein by an E. coli cell extract (37°C).*

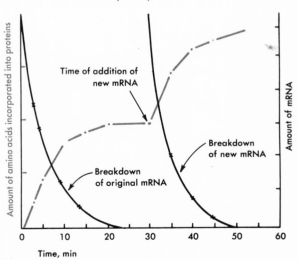

VIRAL RNA IS mRNA

In Chapter 15 we shall show that in many viruses the genetic component is single-stranded RNA. When these viruses infect a cell, their infecting RNA molecule must first act as a template for the synthesis of the specific proteins needed to initiate the life cycle of the virus. Among these necessary proteins is the RNA-replicating enzyme RNA synthetase. It is thus impossible for the infecting single-stranded molecule to act as a template for its complementary strand until it has *first* acted as a template for some protein synthesis. This means that the infecting viral RNA must itself be able to attach to its host's ribosomes and direct the synthesis of viral specific proteins (i.e., that it must act as mRNA). This point is neatly shown with cell-free systems. For example, the addition of TMV RNA to an mRNA-depleted *E. coli* extract immediately stimulates the incorporation of amino acids into proteins.

SPECIFIC PROTEINS CAN BE MADE IN CELL-FREE SYSTEMS

Even with addition of excess mRNA, there is still only a small amount of amino acid incorporation into polypeptide chains in our *in vitro* systems. This means that we do not yet know the conditions that permit normal *in vivo* synthesis. Doubts were initially raised about whether, in fact, the newly made proteins had structures at all similar to those of natural proteins. Fortunately, the use of specific viral RNA showed that these doubts were unfounded and that the genetic code can be accurately read in cell-free systems. In the first successful experiments, the RNA isolated from the bacterial virus F2 was added to pre-incubated *E. coli* extracts. It acted as a template and promoted the incorporation of amino acids into protein. Some complete polypeptide chains were made and released from the ribosomes. These newly made protein products were then compared with the F2 coat protein, which has a molecular weight of 14,000. Some of the *in vitro* products were found to have amino acid sequences identical to those of the *in vivo* synthesized coat protein, thus demonstrating that, under cell-free conditions, mRNA molecules can select the appropriate AA~tRNA precursors.

More recently the cell-free synthesis of a variety of other viral and bacterial proteins has been achieved. One of the most successful cases is that of T4 lysozyme, the enzyme which helps digest bacterial cell walls. Its synthesis in biologically active form shows the great fidelity of translation now possible in *in vitro* systems. Although hemoglobin has been successfully made in cell-free extracts of immature red blood cells (reticulocytes), attempts to make many other cell proteins have often failed. Conceivably, the chief factor limiting more complete success is our failure to understand the initiation mechanism operating in higher cells. But this may soon be understood and the cell-free synthesis of important mammalian proteins (e.g., immunoglobulins) will be routinely possible.

STIMULATION OF AMINO ACID INCORPORATION BY SYNTHETIC mRNA

While the foregoing experiments with viral RNA tell us that reading specificity is preserved in cell-free systems, by them-

T A B L E   13–1   *The 64 possible three-letter codons*

First position (5' end)	Second position				Third position (3' end)
	U	C	A	G	
U	UUU	UCU	UAU	UGU	U
	UUC	UCC	UAC	UGC	C
	UUA	UCA	UAA	UGA	A
	UUG	UCG	UAG	UGG	G
C	CUU	CCU	CAU	CGU	U
	CUC	CCC	CAC	CGC	C
	CUA	CCA	CAA	CGA	A
	CUG	CCG	CAG	CGG	G
A	AUU	ACU	AAU	AGU	U
	AUC	ACC	AAC	AGC	C
	AUA	ACA	AAA	AGA	A
	AUG	ACG	AAG	AGG	G
G	GUU	GCU	GAU	GGU	U
	GUC	GCC	GAC	GGC	C
	GUA	GCA	GAA	GGA	A
	GUG	GCG	GAG	GGG	G

selves they say nothing about the exact form of the genetic code. They cannot tell us which three-letter words (out of the possible 64) (Table 13–1) code for any particular amino acid. To obtain such data, use was made of synthetic polyribonucleotides, whose formation involves the enzyme, polynucleotide phosphorylase. This enzyme, found in all bacteria, catalyzes the reaction

RNA $+ \textcircled{P} \rightleftharpoons$ ribonucleoside $- \textcircled{P} \sim \textcircled{P}$ (13-1)

Under normal cell metabolite concentrations, the equilibrium conditions favor RNA degradation to nucleoside diphosphates, so that the main cellular function of polynucleotide phosphorylase may be to control mRNA lifetime (see Chapter 14). By use of high initial nucleoside diphosphate concentrations, however, this enzyme can be made to catalyze the formation of the internucleotide 3′–5′ phosphodiester bond (Figure 13–3) and thus make synthetic RNA molecules. Since it is not a biosynthetic enzyme, no template RNA is involved in the RNA synthesis; the base composition of the synthetic product depends entirely upon the initial concentration of the various ribonucleoside diphosphates in the reaction mixture. For example, when only adenosine diphosphate is used, the resulting RNA contains only adenylic acid, and thus is called polyadenylic acid or poly A. It is likewise possible to make poly U, poly C, and poly G. Addition of two or more different diphosphates produces mixed copolymers such as poly AU, poly AC, poly CU, and poly AGCU. In all these mixed polymers, the base sequences are approximately random, with the nearest-neighbor frequencies determined solely by the relative concentrations of the initial reactants. For example, poly AU molecules with two times as much A as U are formed in sequences like (UAAUAU AAAUAAUAAAAUAUU . . .).

Almost all these synthetic polymers will attach to ribosomes and function as templates. Some polymers are not efficient templates. This does not necessarily mean that they lack functional base sequences (codons). Instead, they may be inactive because most of their bases are hydrogen bonded, so that they cannot attach to the ribosomes.

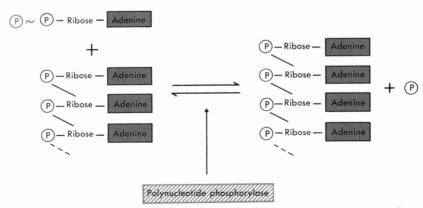

FIGURE 13-3 *Synthesis (degradation) of RNA molecules using the enzyme polynucleotide phosphorylase.*

POLY U CODES FOR POLYPHENYLALANINE

Poly U was the first synthetic polyribonucleotide discovered to have mRNA activity. None of its bases are normally hydrogen bonded in solution, and it binds well to free ribosomes. It selects phenylalanine tRNA molecules exclusively, thereby forming a polypeptide chain containing only phenylalanine (polyphenylalanine). Thus, we know that a codon for phenylalanine is composed of a group of three uridylic acid residues (UUU) (the group number 3 initially came from the genetic experiments described in Chapter 10). Similarly, we are able tentatively to assign (CCC) as a proline codon and (AAA) as a lysine codon on the basis of analogous experiments with poly C and poly A. Unfortunately, the guanine residues in poly G firmly hydrogen bond to each other and form multistranded triple helices that do not bind to ribosomes. Thus, this type of experiment cannot tell us whether (GGG) is a functional codon.

MIXED COPOLYMERS ALLOW
ADDITIONAL CODON ASSIGNMENTS

Poly AC molecules can contain eight different codons (CCC), (CCA), (CAC), (ACC), (CAA), (ACA), (AAC), and

(AAA), whose proportions depend on the copolymer A/C ratio. When CA copolymers attach to ribosomes, they cause the incorporation of asparagine, glutamine, histidine, and threonine, in addition to the proline expected from (CCC)

T A B L E 13–2 *Amino acid incorporation into proteins*[a]

Amino acid	Observed amino acid incorporation	Tentative codon assignments	Calculated triplet frequency				Sum of calculated triplet frequencies
			3A	2A1C	1A2C	3C	
Poly AC (5:1)							
Asparagine	24	2A 1C		20			20
Glutamine	24	2A 1C		20			20
Histidine	6	1A 2C			4.0		4
Lysine	100	3A	100				100
Proline	7	1A 2C, 3C			4.0	0.8	4.8
Threonine	26	2A 1C, 1A 2C		20	4.0		24
Poly AC (1:5)							
Asparagine	5	2A 1C		3.3			3.3
Glutamine	5	2A 1C		3.3			3.3
Histidine	23	1A 2C			16.7		16.7
Lysine	1	3A	0.7				0.7
Proline	100	1A 2C, 3C			16.7	83.3	100
Threonine	21	2A 1C, 1A, 2C		3.3	16.7		20

[a] The amino acid incorporation into proteins was observed after adding random copolymers of A and C to a cell-free extract similar to that described in Figure 13–1. The incorporation is given as a percentage of the maximal incorporation of a single amino acid. These values were then used to make tentative codon assignments, which were then used to calculate the frequencies with which three nucleotides would have positions in the same codon. In these calculations the sum of the frequencies of the triplets coding for the maximally incorporated amino acid was set at 100. Lysine, the maximally incorporated amino acid when A is in excess, is believed to be coded for by 3 A's. The relative frequencies of these codons is a function of the probability that a particular nucleotide will occur in a given position of a codon. For example, when the A/C ratio is 5:1, the ratio of AAA/AAC $= 5 \times 5 \times 5 : 5 \times 5 \times 1 = 125 : 25$. We thus assign to the 3A codon a frequency of 100 and to the 2A and 1C codon a frequency of $25 : 125 = 20$.

codons and the lysine expected from (AAA) codons. The proportions of these amino acids incorporated into polypeptide products depend on the A/C ratio. Thus, since an AC copolymer containing much more A than C promotes the incorporation of many more asparagine than histidine residues, we conclude that asparagine is coded by two A's and one C and histidine is coded by two C's and one A (Table 13–2). Similar experiments with other copolymers have allowed a number of additional assignments. These experiments, however, cannot reveal the order of the different nucleotides within a codon. There is no way of knowing from random copolymers whether the histidine codon containing two C's and one A is ordered (CCA), (CAC), or (ACC). Moreover, because of the difficulty of interpreting small amounts of incorporation, a few of the assignments made in this way were wrong. For example, the experiments with AU (1:5) suggested that lysine is coded by two A's and one U, as well as by (AAA). Later experiments, however (see below), showed that U is absent from all lysine codons.

ORDERING CODONS BY tRNA BINDING

A direct way of ordering the nucleotides within some of the codons was developed in 1964. It utilizes the fact that, in the absence of protein synthesis, specific tRNA molecules bind to ribosome–mRNA complexes. For example, when poly U is mixed with ribosomes, only phenylalanine tRNA will attach. Correspondingly, the attachment of poly C to ribosomes promotes the binding of proline tRNA. Most important, this specific binding does not demand the presence of long mRNA molecules. In fact, the binding of a *trinucleotide* to a ribosome is sufficient. The addition of the trinucleotide UUU results in phenylalanine-tRNA attachment, whereas lysine tRNA specifically binds to ribosomes if AAA is added. The discovery of the trinucleotide effect immediately opened the possibility of relatively easily determining the order of nucleotides within many codons. Before this discovery, it seemed obvious that the order could not be determined unless organic chemists could syn-

T A B L E 13–3 *Binding of specific tRNA molecules to tri-nucleotide–ribosome complexes*

Trinucleotide						tRNA bound
5'UUU3'	UUC					Phenylalanine
UUA	UUG	CUU	CUC	CUA	CUG	Leucine
AAU	AUC	AUA				Isoleucine
AUG						Methionine
GUU	GUC	GUA	GUG	UCU		Valine
UCU	UCC	UCA	UCG			Serine
CCU	CCC	CCA	CCG			Proline
AAA	AAG					Lysine
UGU	UGC					Cysteine
GAA	GAG					Glutamic acid

thesize long polynucleotides with regular repeating sequences. Now, however, the possession of trinucleotides of known sequence is sufficient to order many codons. For example, the trinucleotide $^{5'}GUU^{3'}$ promotes valine-tRNA attachment, $^{5'}UGU^{3'}$ stimulates cysteine-tRNA binding, and $^{5'}UUG^{3'}$ causes leucine-tRNA binding. After massive effort, all 64 possible trinucleotides were synthesized with the hope of definitively assigning the order of the majority of codons. In Table 13–3 some of the codons determined in this way are listed. It now seems likely that not all the correct combinations can be determined this way. Some of the trinucleotides bind much less efficiently than UUU or GUU, making it impossible to know whether they code for a specific amino acid.

CODON ASSIGNMENT FROM REGULAR COPOLYMERS

At the same time as the trinucleotide binding technique became available, methods were developed using a combination of organic chemical and enzymatic techniques to prepare synthetic polyribonucleotides with known repeating sequences. These regular copolymers direct the incorporation of specific amino acids into polypeptides. For example, the repeating sequence CUCUCUCU . . . is the messenger for a regular polypeptide in which leucine and serine alternate. Similarly UGUGUG

TABLE 13-4   *Assignment of codon orders using regular co-polymers building from two bases*

Copolymer	Amino acids incorporated	Codon assignments
CUC|UCU|CUC . . .	Leucine	$5'CUC3'$
	Serine	UCU
UGU|GUG|UGU . . .	Cysteine	UGU
	Valine	GUG
ACA|CAC|ACA . . .	Threonine	ACA
	Histidine	CAC
AGA|GAG|AGA . . .	Arginine	AGA
	Glutamine	GAG

. . . promotes the synthesis of a polypeptide containing two amino acids, cysteine and valine. And ACACAC . . . directs the synthesis of a polypeptide alternating threonine and histidine (Table 13-4). Use of the copolymer built up from repetition of the three-nucleotide sequence AAG (AAGAAGAAG) directs the synthesis of three types of polypeptides: polylysine, polyarginine, and polyglutamic acid. Appearance of all three chains tells us that ribosomes attach to this mesenger randomly, starting equally well at its AAG, AGA, and GAA codons. Poly $(AUC)_n$ behaves the same way, being a template for poly-isoleucine, polyserine, and polyhistidine. By now, a large number of such copolymers have been analyzed, giving the results shown in Table 13-5. Only a few polymers having repeating

TABLE 13-5   *Assignment of codon orders using regular co-polymers building from three bases*

Copolymer	Codon recognized	Polypeptide made	Codon assignment
$(AAG)_n$	AAG|AAG|AAG . . .	polylysine	$5'AAG3'$
	AGA|AGA|AGA . . .	polyarginine	AGA
	GAA|GAA|GAA . . .	polyglutamic acid	GAA
$(UUC)_n$	UUC|UUC|UUC . . .	polyphenylalanine	UUC
	UCU|UCU|UCU . . .	polyserine	UCU
	CUU|CUU|CUU . . .	polyleucine	CUU
$(UUG)_n$	UUG|UUG|UUG . . .	polyleucine	UUG
	UGU|UGU|UGU . . .	polycysteine	UGU
	GUU|GUU|GUU . . .	polyvaline	GUU

T A B L E   13–6   *Assignment of codon orders using regular co-polymers building from four bases*

Copolymer	Amino acids incorporated	Codon assignments
UAU|CUA|UCU|AUC|UAU . . .	Tyrosine	5'UAU3'
	Leucine	CUA
	Serine	UCU
	Isoleucine	AUC
UUA|CUU|ACU|UAC|UUA . . .	Leucine	UUA
	Leucine	CUU
	Threonine	ACU
	Tyrosine	UAC

tetranucleotide sequences have been looked at so far. The codon assignments obtained from two of them are revealed in Table 13–6. The sum of all these observations permits the definite assignments of specific amino acids to 61 out of the possible 64 codons (Table 13–7). The remaining three codons, as shown below, code for chain termination.

T A B L E   13–7   *The genetic code*

First position (5' end)	Second position				Third position (3' end)
	U	C	A	G	
U	Phe	Ser	Tyr	Cys	U
	Phe	Ser	Tyr	Cys	C
	Leu	Ser	Term[a]	Term	A
	Leu	Ser	Term	Trp	G
C	Leu	Pro	His	Arg	U
	Leu	Pro	His	Arg	C
	Leu	Pro	GluN	Arg	A
	Leu	Pro	GluN	Arg	G
A	Ileu	Thr	AspN	Ser	U
	Ileu	Thr	AspN	Ser	C
	Ileu	Thr	Lys	Arg	A
	Meth	Thr	Lys	Arg	G
G	Val	Ala	Asp	Gly	U
	Val	Ala	Asp	Gly	C
	Val	Ala	Glu	Gly	A
	Val	Ala	Glu	Gly	G

[a] Chain terminating (formerly called "nonsense").

THE CODE IS DEGENERATE

Many amino acids are selected by more than one codon (degeneracy). For example, both (UUU) and (UUC) code for phenylalanine, while serine is coded by (UCU), (UCC), (UCA), (UCG), (AGU), and (AGC). The present data suggest that when the first two nucleotides are identical, the third nucleotide can be either cytosine or uracil and the codon will still code for the same amino acid. Often adenine and guanine are similarly interchangeable. However, not all degeneracy seems to be based on equivalence of the first two nucleotides. Leucine, for example, seems to be coded by (UUA) and (UUG), as well as by (CUU), (CUC), (CUA), and (CUG) (Figure 13-4).

Codon degeneracy, especially the frequent third-place equivalence of cytosine and uracil and guanine and adenine, under-

FIGURE 13-4 *Two different tRNA molecules which accept leucine residues. Each recognizes a different code word.*

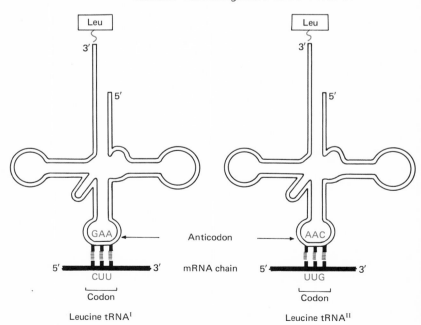

lies the fact that the AT/GC ratios can show very great variations (see Chapter 9) without correspondingly large changes in
the relative proportion of amino acids found in these organisms.
The original explanation was that these similarities in amino
acid composition were meaningless, reflecting the sequences of
only those genes coding for proteins present in large quantities.
But as the analysis of more individual proteins revealed no real
correlation between amino acid composition and evolutionary
position, this interpretation became untenable.

It was also at first guessed that a specific anticodon would
exist for every codon. If so, at least 61 different tRNAs, possibly with an additional three for the chain-terminating codons,
would be present. Evidence soon began to appear, however,
that highly purified tRNA species of known sequence (e.g.,
alanyl-tRNA) could recognize several different codons. Several
cases also arose where an anticodon base was not one of the four
regular ones, but a fifth base, inosine. Like all the other minor
tRNA bases, this arises through enzymatic modification of a
base present in an otherwise completed tRNA. The base from
which it is derived is adenine, whose 6-amino group is deaminated to give the 6-keto group of inosine.

THE WOBBLE IN THE ANTICODON

To explain these observations, the wobble concept was devised.
It states that the base at the 5′ end of the anticodon is not as
spatially confined as the other two, allowing it to form hydrogen
bonds with any of several bases located at the 3′ end of a
codon. Not all combinations are possible, with pairing re-

T A B L E 13–8 *Pairing combinations with the wobble concept*

Base in anticodon	Base in Codon
G	U or C
C	G
A	U
U	A or G
I	A, U, or C

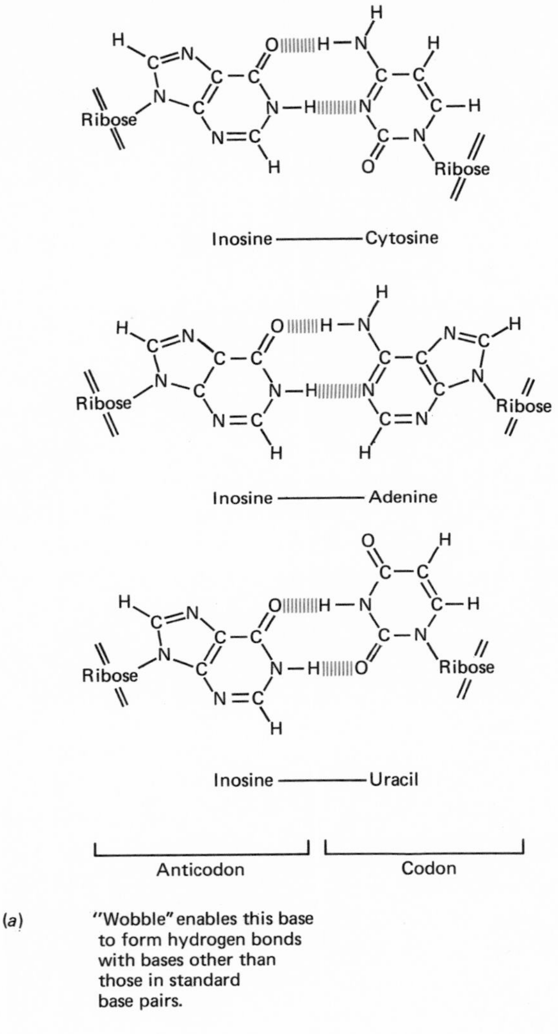

Inosine ——————— Cytosine

Inosine ——————— Adenine

Inosine ——————— Uracil

Anticodon   Codon

(a)   "Wobble" enables this base
             to form hydrogen bonds
             with bases other than
             those in standard
             base pairs.

FIGURE 13-5 *Examples of wobble pairing.*

stricted to those shown in Table 13-8. For example, U at the wobble position can pair to adenine and guanine, while I can pair with U, C, and A (Figure 13-5). These rules do not permit any single tRNA molecule to recognize four different

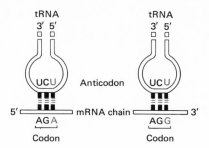

(b)   U in the third anticodon position can pair with A or G.

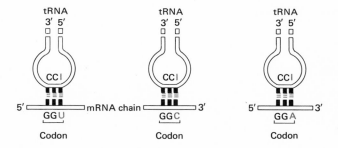

(c)   I in the third anticodon position can pair with U, C, or A.

FIGURE 13-5

codons, and three codons are recognized only when inosine occupies the third position.

Virtually all evidence now available supports the wobble concept. For example, it predicted correctly that at least three tRNAs existed for the six serine code words (UCU, UCC, UCA, UCG, AGU, and AGC). The other two amino acids (leucine and arginine) whose degenerate codons differ in the first or second position also have different tRNAs for each set.

While wobble permits a given base to recognize several bases, the binding efficiencies show considerable variation. In a given organism, one base is preferentially used to signify a given amino acid. When the code word used has a much lower binding efficiency, we might expect the rate at which the corresponding amino acid is inserted into proteins to be lower. If this conjecture proves correct, the rate of synthesis of a given protein will be controlled in part (see Chapter 14) by which codons construct its particular amino acid sequence.

Recently, a specific molecular model has been proposed for the anticodon loop. The various atoms have been arranged to maximize the formation of internal secondary bonds (between atoms in the same chain). Particularly important is placing the flat surface of the bases in as close contact as possible. In the resulting model, the third anticodon base has much more freedom of movement than the other two bases—hence, third-position wobble. This point cannot be considered proven, however, until several 3-D structures are worked out in detail.

MINOR tRNAs

Sometimes several chemically distinct tRNA forms have the same anticodon. Often the only difference between two forms is the presence or absence of the 3′ terminal adenylic acid. Within cells this difference is not permanent, for an "adding enzyme" exists which puts terminal adenylic acid residues on those molecules which lack them. Why some tRNA molecules lack their 3′ terminal residues is still a total mystery. Perhaps the original absence was caused by an accidental exonuclease attack, in which case the adding enzyme has a repair function. But conceivably the absence is somehow involved in controlling the general rate of protein synthesis, as the deficient molecules are unable to accept their specific amino acids.

Much more intriguing are cases where internal sequence differences occur and where one species is present in very large amounts compared to the other species. There are, for example, a major and a minor tyrosine tRNA, both having the anticodon ³′AUG⁵′. Origin of the minor component by enzymatic modification of the major component following gene transcription is ruled out by the nature of the sequence differences. They cannot arise by any known enzymatic transformations. The normal function played by these minor tRNA species remains unresolved, but as we see below, they are frequently involved in suppressor gene action.

AUG AND GUG AS INITIATION CODONS

The discovery of a tRNA specific for N-formyl methionine initially suggested that it would recognize a codon different from the AUG methionine codon. But even at first, the conjecture seemed strained since no unassigned codon existed which could specifically bind to f-met-tRNA. As shown in Figure 12–12, elucidation of the f-met-tRNA sequence revealed that its anticodon $^{3'}UAC^{5'}$ was identical to that of met-tRNA. Both f-met and met must, therefore, directly be coded by AUG. So, in some way, the signal for the starting amino acid must be more complex than the signal for all other amino acids. A further complication is the suggestion, obtained from *in vitro* studies with regular copolymers, that f-met-tRNA will bind to and initiate synthesis at GUG as well as AUG codons. Normally, GUG is a valine codon and its recognition by f-met-tRNA suggests a different sort of wobble at the f-met-anticodon. It would have ambiguity at the first as opposed to the third position. A possible reason for this lies in the f-met-tRNA sequence. The nucleotide adjacent to the 3' end of the anticodon is an unmodified adenine, not the bulky alkylated derivative found in almost all other tRNAs.

In vitro, GUG starts are much less efficient than AUG starts. More genes must be analyzed before the role of GUG becomes clear. If it is used, its lower affinity for f-met-tRNA might be a device which helps control the rate at which a given gene functions.

CODONS FOR CHAIN TERMINATION

The three codons UAA, UAG, and UGA do not correspond to any amino acid. Instead, they signify chain termination. As mentioned in Chapter 12, these codons are read not by special chain-terminating tRNAs but by specific proteins, the release factors. Two release factors have so far been identified, each of which recognizes two codons. One is specific for UAA and UAG and the other for UAA and UGA. Knowledge of how two different codons can be recognized by each release factor must await detailed knowledge of their 3-D structures. The use of proteins to read the stop signals emphasizes a fact ignored by many biochemists. The specific hydrogen bond-forming groups along a polynucleotide can also be recognized by those amino acids which have groups prone to hydrogen bonding.

ENDING OF A POLYPEPTIDE MESSAGE WITH TWO SUCCESSIVE STOP CODONS

Initially it was thought that all genes would end with a single stop codon. Thus, much speculation abounded about why three different ones existed and which one was the most frequently used. So the elucidation of the nucleotide sequences at the ends of actual genes was eagerly awaited. Now the first answer has just emerged from analysis of the gene which codes for the coat protein of the RNA phage R17. The nucleotide sequence determined (Figure 13-6) contains the codons for the last six amino acids of the coat protein, as well as the initial nucleotides in the adjacent gene coding for the phage-specific synthetase (see Chapter 15). Most surprisingly, the coat protein gene concludes UAAUAG. Two stop codons thus end this gene. Whether this will be a common occurrence will not be known until a number of genes have been similarly analyzed.

Certainly two stop codons are not always required. The frequent occurrence of nonsense mutations (see below) which generate new stop signals within preexisting genes shows that a single stop codon will terminate the growth of most polypeptide chains. Thus, it is possible that successive stop codons have come into existence as a safety feature to take care of the rare cases where the first stop codon fails. Whether the efficiency of codon reading by the release factors is as great as by tRNA is an important point to work out.

NONSENSE VERSUS MISSENSE MUTATIONS

An alteration in a codon specific for a given amino acid so that it specifies another amino acid is called a *missense mutation*.

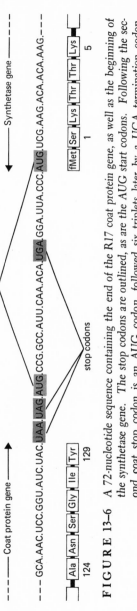

FIGURE 13-6 A 72-nucleotide sequence containing the end of the R17 coat protein gene, as well as the beginning of the synthetase gene. The stop codons are outlined, as are the AUG start codons. Following the second coat stop codon is an AUG codon, followed six triplets later by a UGA termination codon. Whether this segment codes for the hexapeptide fMet-Pro-Ala-Ile-Gln-Thr is not yet established.

417

On the other hand, the change to a chain-termination codon is known as a *nonsense mutation*. Given the existence of only three chain-terminating codons, most mutations involving single-base replacements are likely to result in missense rather than nonsense. As new proteins arising by missense mutations contain only single amino acid replacements, they frequently possess some of the biological activity of the original proteins. The abnormal hemoglobins (see Chapter 4) are the result of missense mutations.

Table 13–9 shows that the amino acid replacement data obtained from these changed hemoglobin molecules strongly support the idea that these mutations result from the substitution of single nucleotides. A companion replacement series (Table 13–10) obtained from mutant TMV protein molecules points to the same conclusion. Moreover, the fact that only certain specific changes are observed (e.g., glycine to aspartic acid) also supports the hypothesis that these altered proteins arise from

T A B L E   13–9   *Examples of possible codon changes underlying some amino acid replacements in the mutant hemoglobins*

Amino acid in normal hemoglobin		Amino acid in mutant hemoglobin	
Lysine (AAA)	⟶	Glutamic acid (GAA)	A → G
Glutamic acid (GAA)	⟶	Glutamine (CAA)	G → C
Glycine (GGU)	⟶	Aspartic acid (GAU)	G → A
Histidine (CAU)	⟶	Tyrosine (UAU)	C → U
Asparagine (AAU)	⟶	Lysine (AAA)	U → A
Glutamic acid (GAA)	⟶	Valine (GUA)	A → U
Glutamic acid (GAA)	⟶	Lysine (AAA)	G → A
Glutamic acid (GAA)	⟶	Glycine (GGA)	A → G

T A B L E 13–10 *Amino acid replacements induced by nitrous acid treatment of TMV*[a]

Proline (CCC)	⟶	Serine (UCC)	C → U
Proline (CCC)	⟶	Leucine (CUC)	C → U
Isoleucine (AUU)	⟶	Valine (GUU)	A → G
Isoleucine (AUA)	⟶	Methionine (AUG)	A → G
Leucine (CUU)	⟶	Phenylalanine (UUU)	C → U
Glutamic acid (GAA)	⟶	Glycine (GGA)	A → G
Threonine (ACA)	⟶	Isoleucine (AUA)	C → U
Threonine (ACG)	⟶	Methionine (AUG)	C → U
Serine (UCU)	⟶	Phenylalanine (UUU)	C → U
Serine (UCG)	⟶	Leucine (UUG)	C → U
Aspartic acid (GAC)	⟶	Glycine (GGC)	A → G

[a] All the observed changes can be fitted both with possible codon assignments and with the postulated mutagenic action of nitrous acid (C → U, A → G).

single nucleotide changes. If most observed mutations reflected changes in each of several adjacent nucleotides, a larger variety of amino acid switches would be observed.

NONSENSE MUTATIONS PRODUCE INCOMPLETE POLYPEPTIDE CHAINS

When a nonsense mutation occurs in the middle of a genetic message, incomplete polypeptides are released from ribosomes. Very often these incomplete chains have no biological activity (e.g., no enzymatic action), making most nonsense mutations in vital genes easily detectable. In contrast, the majority of missense mutations have some biological activity and are usually overlooked. Thus, after treatment with a mutagen, a sizeable fraction of the *detectable* mutations is of the nonsense variety.

The size of the incomplete polypeptide chain produced depends upon the relative site of the nonsense mutations. Mutations occurring near the beginning of a gene result in very short fragments, while if the site is near the end, the fragment is of almost normal length and may have some biological activity. This fact provides a way for precisely locating a mutation within a given gene. Isolation of a series of incomplete fragments and measurements of their length unambiguously tells us the sites of the corresponding mutations.

READING MISTAKES CAN OCCUR IN CELL-FREE PROTEIN SYNTHESIS

Under certain conditions reading mistakes can be very frequent in cell-free systems. Soon after the discovery that poly U is the template for polyphenylalanine, the apparent paradox arose that in the absence of phenylalanine, poly U templates directed the synthesis of polyleucine. This meant that the (UUU) codon was selecting leucine-specific tRNA molecules. At first, the possibility was considered that a fundamental ambiguity in the (UUU) codon might exist. Now, however, it is clear that the anomalous leucine incorporation was due to the use of excessive amounts of Mg^{2+} in the incorporation experiments. When the Mg^{2+} levels are lowered, poly U-directed leucine incorporation becomes much less frequent. The result is important, as it underlines the necessity of using normal physiological conditions in experiments with cell-free systems if we want to extrapolate the events occurring within a normal cell.

SUPPRESSOR GENES UPSET THE READING OF THE GENETIC CODE

Mistakes in reading the genetic code also occur in living cells. These mistakes underlie the phenomenon of suppressor genes. Their existence was for many years very puzzling and seemingly paradoxical. Numerous examples were known where the effects of harmful mutations were reversed by a second genetic change. Some of these subsequent mutations were very easy to understand, being simple *reverse* (or back) mutations which change an altered nucleotide sequence back to its original arrangement. Much more difficult to understand were other mutations occurring at different locations on the chromosome which suppress the change due to a mutation at site A by producing an additional genetic change at site B. Such *suppressor mutations* fall into two main categories: those due to nucleotide changes within the same gene as the original mutation but at a different site on this gene (intragenic suppression), and those occurring in another gene (intergenic suppression). Those genes which cause suppression of mutations in other genes are called *suppressor* genes.

Now we realize that these two types of suppression both work by causing the production of good (or partially good) copies of the protein made inactive by the original harmful mutation. For example, if the first mutation caused the making of inactive copies of one of the enzymes involved in making arginine, then the suppressor mutation allows the synthesis of arginine by restoring the synthesis of some good copies of this same enzyme. However, the mechanisms by which intergenic and intragenic suppressor mutations cause the resumption of the synthesis of good proteins are completely different.

Those mutations which can be reversed through additional changes in the same gene often involve insertions or deletions of single nucleotides. These shift the reading frame (see Chapter 10) so that all the codons following the insertions (or deletions) are completely changed, thereby generating new amino acid sequences. More rarely, the shifted reading frame generates premature nonsense codons, and as a result the mutant polypeptides are correspondingly shorter (Figure 13–7).

Intragenic suppression may occur when a second mutation deletes (or inserts) a new nucleotide near the original change and thus restores the original codon arrangement beyond the second change (Figure 13–7). Even though there are still scrambled codons between the two changes, there is a good

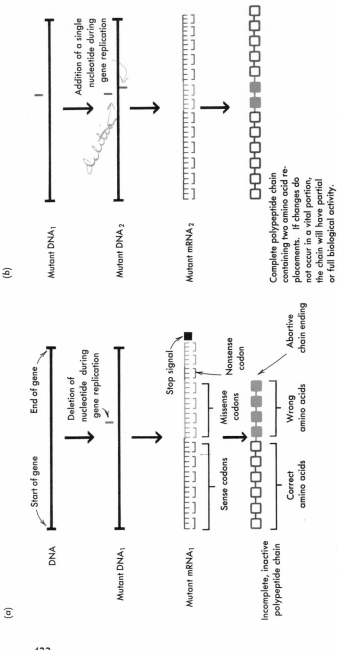

FIGURE 13-7 (a) The effect of a single nucleotide deletion (insertion) mutation upon the reading of the genetic message. (b) The mechanism by which a nucleotide addition (deletion) mutation can suppress the havoc caused by a previous deletion (insertion) mutation.

probability, because of degeneracy, that the scrambled codons all code for some amino acid. If so, full-length, often functional, proteins may be produced.

Intragenic suppressors can also result from a second missense mutation. In these cases, the original loss of enzymatic activity is due to an altered 3-D configuration resulting from the presence of a wrong amino acid. A second missense mutation in the same gene brings back biological activity if it somehow restores the original configuration around the functional part of the molecule. An example of this type of suppression in the tryptophan synthetase system was shown in Chapter 8 (Figure 8–13).

SPECIFIC CODONS ARE MISREAD BY SPECIFIC SUPPRESSOR GENES

Suppressor genes do not act by changing the nucleotide sequences of the mutant DNA. Instead they change the way in which the mRNA templates are read. There are a number of different suppressor genes in *E. coli*. Since each causes the misreading of specific codons, they can reverse the effects of only a small fraction of the single nucleotide changes within a given gene. For example, if we collect a large number of mutations blocking the synthesis of the enzyme β-galactosidase (see Chapter 14), only several per cent of these mutations will be suppressed by a given suppressor gene a. These few mutations would be due to changes in codons whose reading is specifically affected by gene a. Similarly, a completely different small fraction of β-galactosidase mutations can be suppressed by suppressor gene b.

It is generally observed that a given suppressor gene can suppress mutations in a number of different genes. This fact is easily understood by the misreading concept. For example, the ability to synthesize both arginine and tryptophan in certain double mutants unable to make either amino acid can be restored by a single change in a suppressor gene. We merely need to postulate that both these growth requirements are caused by the same specific changes to missense or nonsense.

NONSENSE SUPPRESSION INVOLVES MUTANT tRNAs

Suppressor genes exist for each of the three chain-terminating codons. They act by reading a stop signal as if it were a signal for a specific amino acid. There are, for example, three well-characterized genes which suppress the UAG codon. One suppressor gene inserts serine, another glutamine, and a third, tyrosine, at the nonsense position. All act by producing anti-codon changes in a tRNA species specific for a given amino acid. For example, the tyrosine suppressor arises by a mutation at the anticodon site which changes it from $^{3'}AUG^{5'}$ to $^{3'}AUC^{5'}$, thereby enabling it to recognize UAG codons (Figure 13–8).

tRNA-mediated suppression was first demonstrated with a nonsense mutation which blocked synthesis of the coat protein of the RNA phage R17. When mutant RNA containing this nonsense codon was used in an *in vitro* system, no coat protein was produced unless purified tRNA from the correct suppressor strain was added.

Discovery of tRNA-mediated suppression raised the question of how the normal tyrosine codon, for example, could continue to be read. The answer lies in the discovery that two genes normally code for tyrosine tRNA. One codes for the major component, the other codes for a component present in much smaller amounts and is the site of the suppressor mutation. Moreover, it was observed that the suppressor mutations most frequently occur in strains in which the minor tRNA gene is duplicated (present as two copies). Selections of those strains having the duplication occurs because loss of the minor component, while not lethal to a host cell, slows its growth. The true function of the minor component remains a tantalizing mystery. Conceivably it plays a regulatory role and thus only small numbers need be present.

Suppression of both the UAG and UGA codons is very efficient. In the presence of the suppressor tRNAs over half the chain-terminating signals are read as specific amino acid codons. In contrast, supression of the UAA codon is always very ineffi-

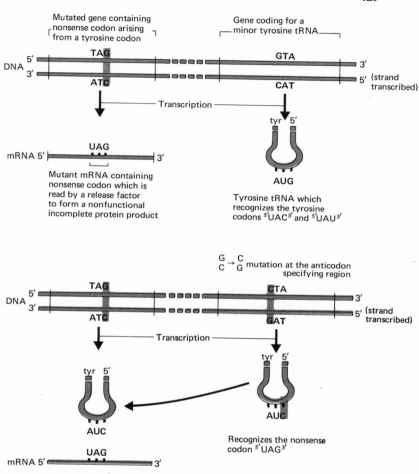

FIGURE 13-8 *Scheme to show the action of a minor tyrosine tRNA component as a nonsense suppressor.*

cient, usually averaging between 1 per cent and 5 per cent. At first it was believed that the efficient suppression of UAG and UGA meant that they seldom, if ever, served as a normal terminator signal. If they were frequently used, the presence of their specific suppression would prevent much normal chain termination, leading to the production of aberrantly long polypeptides and cessation of cell growth. Now, however, that a double stop signal has been seen, it is easier to understand why the UAG and UGA suppression have no effect on bacterial growth. We need merely postulate that the stop codons almost never occur singly. The case of the UAA suppressor is less clear since its acquisition always slows down the growth rate. Perhaps some gene terminates with UAA alone. Much more sequence data are necessary for clear answers to emerge.

tRNA-MEDIATED MISSENSE SUPPRESSION

Suppression of missense mutations can also be mediated by mutant tRNAs. This was recently demonstrated for a mutation in the tryptophan synthetase A gene which replaces glycine with arginine (see Chapter 8), thereby giving rise to an inactive enzyme. Suppressor mutations exist which cause the insertion of glycine at the newly made arginine site and thus restore enzyme function. The efficiency of suppression is low, so in the presence of the suppressor gene both active and inactive forms of the enzyme are made. The nature of this suppression was investigated using an *in vitro* protein synthesizing system in which the mRNA was the regular copoylmer polyAG. Normally polyAGAG . . . codes only for glutamic acid and arginine, but in the presence of tRNA extracted from the suppressor strain, traces of glycine were also incorporated into polypeptides. Furthermore, the level of glycine appearance corresponded well with the frequency of *in vivo* suppression. The suppressor tRNA cochromatographs with a glycine-tRNA fraction, suggesting that the mutation probably involves a change in a glycine-tRNA anticodon. If so, we must again be dealing with a situation where the mutant gene normally codes a minor as opposed to a major tRNA fraction. Arguing against a change in a major fraction is the fact that such a change would most likely be lethal.

RIBOSOMAL MUTATIONS ALSO AFFECT THE READING ACCURACY

The level of both nonsense and missense suppression is also determined by the exact ribosome structure. Specific mutations in several of the 30-S proteins affect the accuracy of reading. A number of different amino acid replacements each must distort the ribosome structure so that the disturbed template-ribosome complex is not always able to choose the correct tRNA molecule (Figure 13–9). One such mutation, ram (ribosomal ambiguity), will suppress weakly all three nonsense codons in the complete absence of any suppressing tRNAs.

STREPTOMYCIN CAUSES MISREADING

The belief that distorted ribosomes may misread the genetic code is strongly supported by experiments showing that the addition of the antibiotic streptomycin to either *in vitro* systems or living cells promotes mistakes in the translation of the genetic code. It does this by combining with the ribosomes, thereby disturbing the normal mRNA–tRNA–ribosome interactions. The extent of the misreadings depends upon whether the streptomycin is added to streptomycin-sensitive or streptomycin-resistant cells. Addition of the antibiotic to sensitive cells results in large-scale misreadings. The mutation to streptomycin resistance alters the ribosomes in such a way that misreadings occur much less commonly. They are, nonetheless, frequent enough to suppress a number of mutations by causing the synthesis of a small number of active enzyme molecules (Figure 13–10).

It now appears that streptomycin does not cause indiscriminate misreading. When poly U is used as a template with sensitive ribosomes, the most frequent error is the replacement of phenylalanine (UUU) by isoleucine (AUU). This hints that the presence of streptomycin normally disturbs the position of only one out of three nucleotides in the (UUU) codon (Figure 13–11).

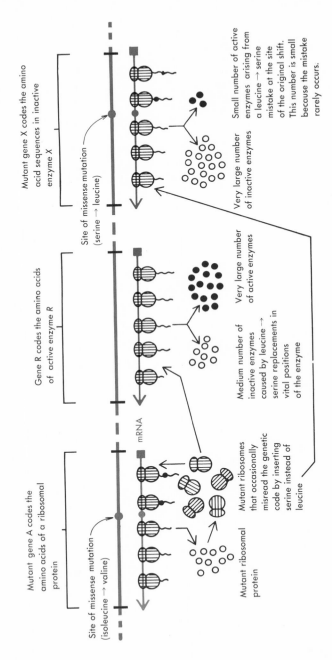

FIGURE 13–9 *Schematic drawing showing how a missense mutation in a gene coding for one of the ribosomal proteins acts as a suppressor mutation.*

Mutant gene A codes the amino acids of a ribosomal protein

Site of missense mutation (isoleucine → valine)

mRNA

Mutant ribosomal protein

Mutant ribosomes that occasionally misread the genetic code by inserting serine instead of leucine

Gene R codes the amino acids of active enzyme R

Very large number of active enzymes

Medium number of inactive enzymes caused by leucine → serine replacements in vital positions of the enzyme

Mutant gene X codes the amino acid sequences in inactive enzyme X

Site of missense mutation (serine → leucine)

Very large number of inactive enzymes

Small number of active enzymes arising from a leucine → serine mistake at the site of the original shift. This number is small because the mistake rarely occurs.

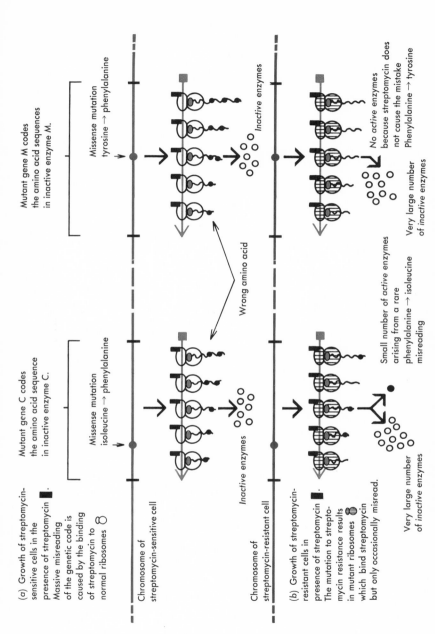

FIGURE 13-10 Schematic drawing illustrating the action of streptomycin upon streptomycin-sensitive and streptomycin-resistant E. coli cells.

429

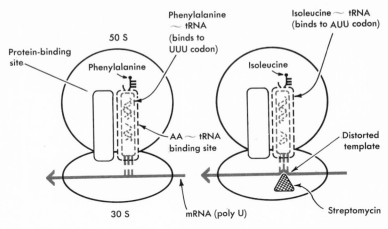

FIGURE 13-11 *Selection of an isoleucine~tRNA molecule by a ribosome–poly U–streptomycin complex. Here the streptomycin-induced misreading involves an isoleucine~tRNA molecule which normally attaches to the (AUU) codon.*

SUPPRESSOR GENES ALSO MISREAD GOOD GENES

We thus see that suppressor genes do not specifically misread mRNA templates made on mutant genes. In fact, they affect the synthesis of essentially all proteins. Most suppressor mistakes, therefore, occur in the copying of good mRNA templates, which hinders the synthesis of sound proteins. These changes are generally not very harmful to the growing cell, since many more good copies of each protein than bad ones are produced. There is, however, no advantage for a normal cell to harbor suppressor mutations which cause it to produce even a small fraction of bad proteins. Suppressors tend to be selected against in evolution, unless a harmful mutation is present for whose effect they must compensate.

It is now possible to make a general prediction about the normal function of suppressor genes. A gene becomes a suppressor gene by mutation. Before this mutation occurs, the gene is normal and active, coding for a specific tRNA, for one of the ribosomal proteins, or for one of the enzymes involved in protein synthesis. It has evolved so that its product has the optimal configuration for accurate reading of the genetic code. If a mutation changes such a gene so that its altered product increases the misreading level, this gene becomes a suppressor gene. Only when an increased mistake level is necessary for cellular existence do its mutant products have a selective advantage over their normal counterparts.

THE CODE IS LARGELY, IF NOT ENTIRELY, UNIVERSAL

Poly U stimulates polyphenylalanine incorporation in cell-free extracts from a variety of different organisms ranging from bacteria to higher mammals. Likewise, poly C promotes proline incorporation and poly A causes lysine incorporation in all extracts tested, regardless of their cellular source. Such indications of the universality of the code among contemporary organisms hint that the genetic code has remained constant over a long evolutionary period. But until all the codons in several organisms have been unambiguously worked out, this point will be neither rigorously proved nor disproved. Invariability in most of the code is expected. Consider what a mutation which changed the genetic code would result in. Such a mutation might, for example, alter the sequence of the serine-specific tRNA molecules of the class that corresponds to (UCU), thereby causing them to attach to (UUU) sequences instead. This would be a lethal mutation in haploid cells containing only one gene directing the production of each type of tRNA: No normal serine-specific tRNA of that class would be produced, and serine would not be inserted into many of its normal positions. Even if there were more than one gene for each tRNA type (e.g., in a diploid cell), this type of mutation would still be lethal, since it would cause the simultaneous replacement of many phenylalanine residues by serine in most cell proteins.

SUMMARY

The most direct way to study the genetic code is to examine protein synthesis in cell-free extracts. The most useful in vitro systems employ cell extracts that have been depleted of their original messenger component. Addition of new mRNA to these extracts results in the production of new proteins whose amino acid sequences are determined by the externally added mRNA. For example, the introduction of phage F2 RNA produces new proteins virtually identical to the F2 coat protein. Thus, viral genetic RNA also acts as mRNA.

The first (and probably most important) step in cracking the genetic code occurred when the synthetic polyribonucleotide poly U was found to code specifically for polyphenylalanine. A codon for phenylalanine is thus (UUU). Use of other synthetic polyribonucleotides, homogeneous (poly C, etc.) and mixed (poly AU, etc.) then produced a number of tentative codon assignments for various amino acids.

Unambiguous determination came from a study of specific trinucleotide–tRNA–ribosome interactions and the use of regular copolymers as messengers. All 64 codons have been firmly established. Sixty-one signify specific amino acids; the remaining three are stop signals. The code is highly degenerate, with several codons usually corresponding to a single amino acid. A given tRNA can sometimes specifically recognize several codons. This ambiguity arises from wobble in the base at the 5' end of the anticodon.

The codon for the starting amino acid, N-formyl methionine, is AUG, the same codon as for methionine. How one codon serves both purposes is unclear. The stop codons UAA, UAG, and UGA are read by specific proteins, not specialized tRNA molecules. Why three different stop codons need exist is unknown, though recent nucleotide sequence analysis reveals that at least one gene ends with two successive stop codons.

Certain mutations (intergenic suppressor mutations) appear to increase the frequency of mistakes in reading the genetic code. As a result of this increase of the mistake level, a mutant gene may occasionally produce a normal product. Suppressor genes exist for both missense (amino acid replacement) and nonsense (chain-terminating) codons. tRNAs with altered anticodons are the molecular basis of many suppressor gene actions.

The genetic code appears to be essentially the same in all

organisms. *This is not surprising: Variations in it from organism to organism would mean that the code had evolved by mutation, and it is almost impossible to imagine a mutation which would change the letters in a codon without being lethal.*

[handwritten marginalia: Some argument could be used for design.]

REFERENCES

Nirenberg, M. W., and J. H. Matthaei, "The Dependence of Cell-Free Protein Synthesis in *E. coli* upon Naturally Occurring or Synthetic Polyribonucleotides," *Proc. Natl. Acad. Sci. U.S.*, **47**, 1588 (1961). This is the classic paper which demonstrated that poly U codes for polyphenylalanine.

Crick, F. H. C., "The Recent Excitement in the Coding Problem," *Prog. Nucleic Acid Res.*, **I**, 164, (1963). A superb analysis of the state of the coding problem as of late 1962.

Leder, P., and M. W. Nirenberg, "RNA Code Words and Protein Synthesis II: Nucleotide Sequence of a Valine RNA Code Word," *Proc. Natl. Acad. Sci. U.S.*, **52**, 420 (1964). An elegant paper that establishes the order of nucleotides within a codon for valine.

Nishimura, S., D. S. Jones, and H. G. Khorana, "The *in Vitro* Synthesis of a Copolypeptide Containing Two Amino Acids in Alternating Sequence Dependent upon a DNA-like Polymer Containing Two Nucleotides in Alternating Sequence," *J. Mol. Biol.*, **13**, 302 (1965). Another classic paper on the genetic code. Here is found an unambiguous demonstration that each codon contains three nucleotides.

Gorini, L., "Antibiotics and the Genetic Code." A 1966 *Scientific American* article reprinted in *The Molecular Basis of Life* R. H. Haynes and P. C. Hanawalt (eds.), Freeman, San Francisco, 1968.

"The Genetic Code," *Cold Spring Harbor Symp. Quant. Biol.*, **31** (1966). A most impressive collection of papers, presented in June, 1966, just after the general features of the code became clear.

Crick, F. H. C., "Codon-Anticodon Pairing: The Wobble Hypothesis," *J. Mol. Biol.*, **19**, 548 (1966). An important argument which led to the understanding of how a single tRNA species binds to more than one codon.

Woese, C. R., *The Genetic Code*, Harper and Row, New York, 1967. A recent summary of current data, written from a historical point of view.

Garen, A., "Sense and Nonsense in the Genetic Code," *Science*,

160, 149 (1968). Reviews much of what is known about how suppressor genes act.

Ycas, M., *The Biological Code*, Wiley (Interscience), New York, 1969. The most complete monograph on the code written by one of the early workers in the field.

Nichols, J. L. "Nucleotide Sequence from the Polypeptide Chain Termination Region of the Coat Protein Cistron in Bacteriophage R17," *Nature*, **225**, 147 (1970). The first analysis of *in vivo* stop codons.

14

REGULATION OF PROTEIN SYNTHESIS AND FUNCTION

THE WORKING OUT OF THE GENERAL features of the participation of nucleic acid molecules in protein synthesis provides a solid base from which we can examine how the rate of synthesis of the various protein molecules is controlled. Within a given cell a great variation exists in the number of molecules of its different proteins; thus, devices to ensure the selective synthesis of those proteins needed in large numbers must exist. Until recently this problem was approached chiefly with ignorance, speculation, and hope. Now, however, we realize that the rate of the synthesis of a protein is itself partially under internal genetic control and partially determined by the external chemical environment. To show how these factors can interact, we shall focus attention on microbial systems, since they have been the basis of most of the important concepts up to now.

ALL PROTEINS ARE NOT PRODUCED IN THE SAME NUMBERS

Earlier we estimated from its length that the *E. coli* chromosome codes for between 2000 and 4000 different polypeptide chains. Exactly how many different proteins are simultaneously present in a given cell is not yet known. Based upon the probable number of enzymes needed to make the various necessary metabolites, general estimates argue for the presence of at least 600 to 800 different enzymes in a cell growing with glucose as its sole carbon source. Some of these enzymes, particularly those connected with the first steps in glucose degradation and with the reactions which make the common amino acids and nucleotides, are present in relatively large amounts. Also required in large amounts are the enzymes needed to produce the energy-rich bonds in ATP. In contrast, other enzymes, particularly those involved in making the much smaller amounts of the necessary coenzymes, are present in trace quantities. There must also be relatively large amounts of the various structural proteins used to construct the cell wall, the cell membrane, and the ribosomes.

VARIATIONS IN THE AMOUNTS OF DIFFERENT *E. COLI* PROTEINS

Precise values for the number of protein molecules normally present within a bacterial cell are known for only a few proteins. The best-studied case is the *E. coli* enzyme β-galactosidase ($MW = 5.4 \times 10^5$), which splits the sugar lactose into its glucose and galactose moieties (Figure 14-1). Each active molecule has a tetrameric structure, being composed of four identical polypeptide chains of molecular weight 135,000. This is a very important enzyme because lactose cannot be used as either a carbon or energy source unless it is first broken down to the simpler sugars galactose and glucose. *E. coli* cells growing with lactose as their exclusive carbon source generally contain about 3×10^3 molecules of β-galactosidase, which represents about 3 per cent of the total protein. This is the maximum quantity that can be synthesized if just one gene coding for the β-galactosidase amino acid sequence is present on each *E. coli* chromosome. If this gene is present in two copies, 6 per cent of the total protein produced by the cell can be β-galactosidase. There exist, in fact, superproducing mutant strains, probably containing many copies of this gene, that can synthesize almost 15 per cent of their protein as β-galactosidase. This supersynthesis, however, is achieved only at the expense of making too

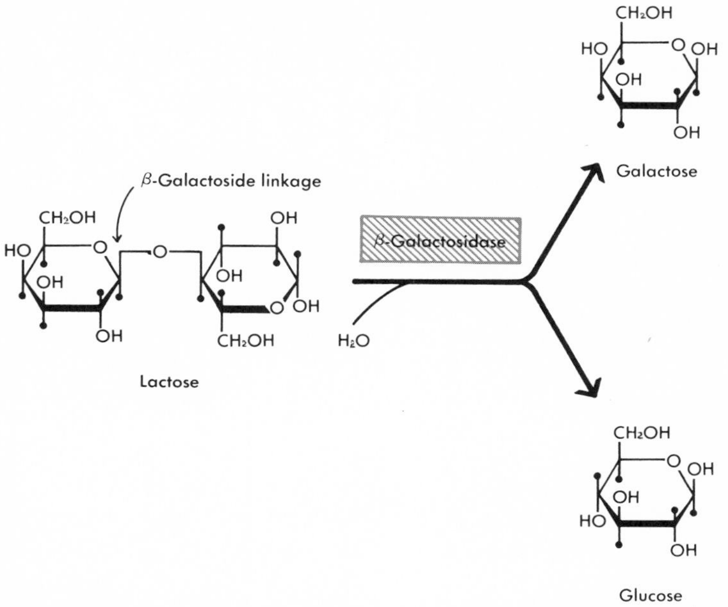

FIGURE 14–1 *The sugar lactose can be hydrolytically cleaved to galactose and glucose by the enzyme β-galactosidase. Mutants that fail to make this protein cannot utilize lactose as a carbon source.*

little of other necessary proteins. Cells making excessively large amounts of β-galactosidase grow poorly and tend to be replaced by mutants that have a balanced protein synthesis.

Good data also exist for the amounts of the structural proteins of the ribosomes. There are approximately 55 of these proteins (average MW ~ 20,000) that collectively comprise about 10 per cent of the total protein in rapidly growing cells. Thus the average ribosomal protein represents 0.2 per cent of the total *E. coli* protein. No similar quantitative data have yet been obtained for the enzymes required in the biosynthesis of the coenzymes. In some cases we expect that only very few molecules will be present. This point, however, will be hard to establish, since the isolation of even one of these enzymes in the amounts necessary for a molecular weight determination will require very large amounts of cells.

RELATION BETWEEN AMOUNT OF
AND NEED FOR SPECIFIC PROTEINS

Great variation can exist between the amount of a protein
present when it is needed and when the environmental conditions are such that it would serve no useful function. For example, there are approximately 3000 β-galactosidase molecules
in each normal E. coli cell growing in the presence of β-galac-
tosides, such as lactose, and less than one one-thousandth of
this number in cells growing upon other carbon sources. Substrates like lactose, whose introduction into a growth medium
specifically increases the amount of an enzyme, are known as
inducers; their corresponding enzymes are called inducible enzymes. An entirely different form of response is shown by
many enzymes involved in cellular biosynthesis. For example,
E. coli cells growing in a medium without any amino acids
contain all the enzymes necessary for the biosynthesis of the
20 necessary amino acids. When, on the other hand, the
growth medium contains these amino acids, their corresponding biosynthetic enzymes are almost entirely missing. Biosynthetic enzymes whose amount is reduced by the presence
of their end products (e.g., histidine is the end product of the
histidine biosynthetic enzymes) are called repressible enzymes.
Those end-product metabolites whose introduction into a
growth medium specifically decreases the amount of a specific
enzyme are known as corepressors. The inductive and repres-
sive responses are equally useful to bacteria: when enzymes are
needed to transform a specific food molecule or to synthesize a
necessary cell constituent, they are present; when they are unnecessary, they are effectively absent.

Adaptation is not, however, an all-or-nothing response, for
under conditions of intermediate need, there may be an intermediate enzyme level (Figure 14–2). Similar variation can
exist in the quantities of structural proteins. This is best shown
by the variation in the number of the ribosomes themselves.
When bacteria are growing at their maximum rate, ribosomes
amount to 25 to 30 per cent of the cell mass. If, however,
their growth rate is cut down by unfavorable nutritional condi-

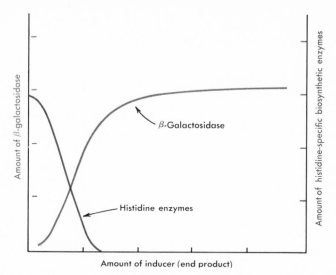

FIGURE 14–2 Variation in the amount of enzyme per cell as a function of the amount of inducer (end product) present in the growth medium.

tions, the bacteria need fewer ribosomes to maintain their slower rate of protein synthesis, and the ribosome content can drop to as little as 20 per cent of its maximum value.

VARIATION IN PROTEIN AMOUNT CAN REFLECT THE NUMBER OF SPECIFIC mRNA MOLECULES

In actively dividing bacteria, most individual protein molecules, once synthesized, are quite stable. Variation in the amount of proteins thus generally reflects rates of synthesis, not relative stability. This variation in the rate of synthesis is in turn partially related to differences in the number of available mRNA templates. The number of β-galactosidase templates in cells actively making β-galactosidase, for example, greatly exceeds the number found in cells not engaged in synthesizing this enzyme. Now our best estimate is that during maximal β-galactosidase synthesis, 35 to 50 β-galactosidase mRNA molecules are present in each cell. In contrast, when no lactose is present, the average cell contains fewer than one mRNA molecule specific for β-galactosidase synthesis.

REPRESSORS CONTROL THE RATE OF MUCH mRNA SYNTHESIS

A special group of molecules called *repressors* decides when mRNA molecules which code for the inducible and repressible enzymes are made. Each repressor blocks the synthesis of one or more proteins, and like all other proteins, repressors are coded by chromosomal DNA. The genes which code for them are called *regulatory genes*. A number of mutant regulatory genes, unable to code for functional repressors, have been isolated. Cells containing inactive regulatory genes produce their respective proteins independent of need (Figure 14–3). These mutants are called *constitutive mutants*, while those proteins produced in fixed amounts, independent of need, are called *constitutive proteins*.

Some mutations in regulatory genes can be suppressed by the occurrence of suppressor mutations in other genes. That is, the presence of a suppressor gene can restore the synthesis

FIGURE 14–3 *The control of repressors by normal and mutant genes.*

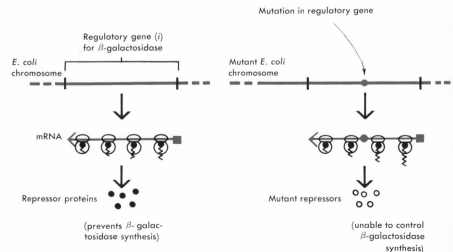

Mutation in regulatory gene

Regulatory gene (*i*)
for β-galactosidase

E. coli
chromosome

Mutant E. coli
chromosome

mRNA

Repressor proteins

Mutant repressors

(prevents β- galactosidase synthesis)

(unable to control β-galactosidase synthesis)

of functional repressors. This finding suggested that mistakes in the reading of the mRNA message change the structure of repressors, which in turn hinted that some, if not all, repressors are protein molecules.

REPRESSORS ARE PROTEINS

The protein nature of repressors has now been confirmed by the recent isolation of two different repressors—one which controls the synthesis of E. coli β-galactosidase, and one which controls the synthesis of phage λ specific proteins when the λ chromosome is inserted as a prophage in the E. coli chromosome (see Chapter 15). The β-galactosidase repressor is so far the best characterized. Its fundamental polypeptide chain of molecular weight 40,000 aggregates into tetramers of molecular weight 160,000. The active form appears to be the tetramer, of which only 10 to 20 copies are usually present for each E. coli chromosome. This very small number made their original detection and isolation a remarkable feat. Now, fortunately, there exist mutations (see below) which result in very much larger amounts (> 1 per cent of total cellular protein), making possible isolation of sufficient quantities for amino acid sequence determination. The complete sequence should be known within the coming year (1971).

REPRESSORS ACT BY BINDING TO DNA

Both the β-galactosidase and λ repressors bind at specific sites on their respective DNA molecules, stopping the transcription of the corresponding mRNA molecules. The specific nucleotide sequences which bind the repressors are called *operators*. In general, an operator must be at least 10 to 12 bases long in order to interact specifically with the appropriate hydrogen bond-forming groups on a repressor. A base number this large avoids the possibility that by random chance a similar sequence will exist somewhere else along the same chromosome. If a smaller number were used, too many false bindings would occur. Use of a large number of specific interactions has the added consequence that the binding can be very strong. Once an active β-galactosidase repressor has bound to DNA, it effectively remains attached until subsequent interaction with its inducer.

COREPRESSORS AND INDUCERS DETERMINE THE FUNCTIONAL STATE OF REPRESSORS

Repressors must not always be able to prevent specific mRNA synthesis. If they could, they would permanently inhibit the synthesis of their specific proteins. Instead, all repressor molecules can exist in both an active and an inactive form, depending on whether they are combined with their appropriate *inducers (corepressors)*. The attachment of an inducer inactivates the repressor. For example, when combined with a β-galactoside[1] (inducer), the β-galactosidase repressor cannot bind to its specific operator. Thus, the addition of β-galactosides to growing cells permits β-galactosidase synthesis by decreasing the concentration of active β-galactosidase repressors. In contrast, the binding of a corepressor changes an inactive repressor into an active form. For example, the addition of amino acids to cells activates repressors which control the synthesis of enzymes involved in amino acid biosynthesis. This quickly shuts off synthesis of their specific mRNA molecules (Figure 14–4).

No covalent bond is formed between repressors and their specific inducers or corepressors. Instead, a portion of each repressor molecule is complementary in shape to a specific portion of its inducer (corepressor). Weak secondary bonds (hydrogen bonds, salt linkages, or van der Waals forces) then form between a repressor and an inducer (corepressor). Since these bonds are weak, they are rapidly made and broken, allowing the repressor state (active or inactive) to adjust quickly to the physiological need. For example, the synthesis of β-galactosidase mRNA ceases almost immediately after the removal of lactose.

[1] Now there are suspicions that lactose itself is not the true inducer of β-galactosidase synthesis. Instead, some lactose molecules are first transformed into a related compound, which in turn attaches to the repressor.

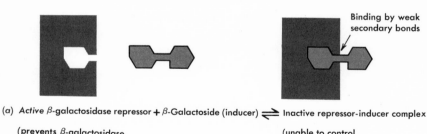

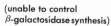

(a) *Active* β-galactosidase repressor + β-Galactoside (inducer) ⇌ Inactive repressor-inducer complex

(prevents β-galactosidase
synthesis)

(unable to control
β-galactosidase synthesis)

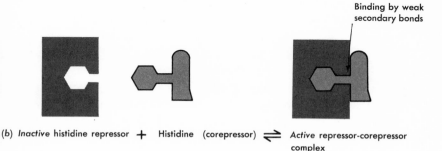

(b) *Inactive* histidine repressor + Histidine (corepressor) ⇌ *Active* repressor-corepressor complex

(unable to control synthesis
of enzymes
for histidine synthesis)

(controls rate of synthesis
of enzymes
for histidine synthesis)

FIGURE 14-4 *Schematic drawing illustrating the opposite effects of corepressors and inducers upon the activity of repressors. We see here that, depending upon whether the enzymes are inducible or repressible, the free repressors are either active or inactive.*

REPRESSORS CAN CONTROL MORE THAN ONE PROTEIN

In some cases, repressors may control the synthesis of only one protein. Often, however, a single repressor affects the synthesis of several enzymes. The β-galactosidase repressor of *E. coli*, for example, controls at least three enzymes: β-galactosidase itself; galactoside permease, which controls the rate of entry of β-galactosides into the bacteria; and galactoside acetylase, whose function is not yet known. When active β-galactoside per-

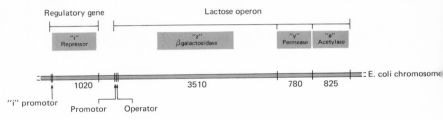

FIGURE 14–5   *The lactose operon and its associated regulatory gene drawn to scale based on known sizes of their gene products. The numbers give the number of base pairs found in the several genes. Now the exact distance between the regulatory gene and the lactose operon is still undetermined. They may be separated by only several nucleotides.*

mease is absent, *E. coli* cells are unable to concentrate β-galactosides within themselves. Since β-galactosidase and β-galactoside permease and galactoside acetylase (?) are ordinarily needed to metabolize β-galactosides, their *coordinated* synthesis is clearly desirable. Coordinated synthesis is brought about by having the respective enzymes coded by adjacent genes (Figure 14–5), thereby allowing a single mRNA molecule to carry all their genetic messages (Figure 14–6). An even larger number of genes (10) is coordinately repressed by the repressor of the amino acid histidine. Again, this is achieved by having a single mRNA molecule carry the messages of all these genes.

The collections of adjacent nucleotides that code for single mRNA molecules (under the control of a single promoter; see below) are called *operons*. Some operons thus contain one gene, others two, and still others, several genes. At first, it was thought that repressors were specific for single operons. Several years ago, a case was found that is most simply interpreted by assuming that a specific repressor can act on three different operons: the genes responsible for *E. coli* arginine biosynthesis have been found distributed among three unlinked operons. Nonetheless, there is evidence that one regulatory gene controls the level of enzymes belonging to all the operons. Likewise, the λ repressor can act at more than one site. It specifically binds

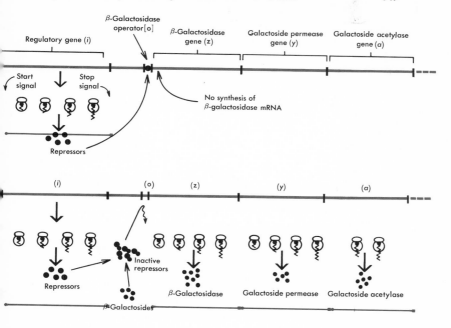

FIGURE 14-6 *How the interaction of repressor, inducer, and operator controls the synthesis of the E. coli proteins β-galactosidase, β-galactoside permease, and galactoside acetylase.*

to two operators, one to the left and one to the right of the corresponding regulatory gene.

ABSENCE OF AN OPERATOR LEADS TO CONSTITUTIVE SYNTHESIS

Operators (repressor binding sites) are all located very close to the regions where mRNA transcription starts. In fact, they are so closely linked that at first it was suspected that the operator region might overlap with the nucleotides coding for the first several amino acids in β-galactosidase. Now there is firm evidence against any overlap.

Presence of a bound repressor prevents only mRNA initiation, having no effect on chain growth where elongation has already commenced. Thus operators have essentially *negative* functions: If a functional operator is absent, the corresponding repressor cannot inhibit the synthesis of the specific mRNA, and as a result, there is constitutive synthesis of its corresponding protein product(s).

The existence of operators was first revealed by genetic analysis. The structure of the operator can mutate to an inactive form, preventing the working of repressors. When this happens, constitutive enzyme synthesis results. These mutants are, therefore, called O^c (constitutive) mutants. O^c mutations can

FIGURE 14-7 *The use of partially diploid cells to show that the presence of functional repressors is dominant over the presence of inactive repressors. No significant amounts of β-galactosidase molecules will be produced in these cells in the absence of externally added β-galactosides.*

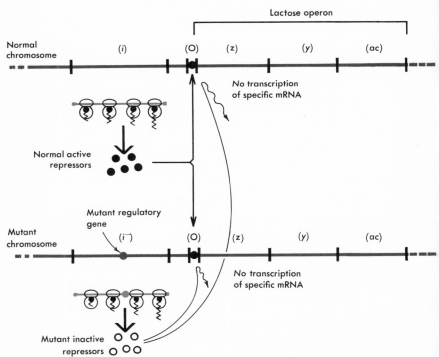

(a) Haploid cell containing mutant operator (O^c)

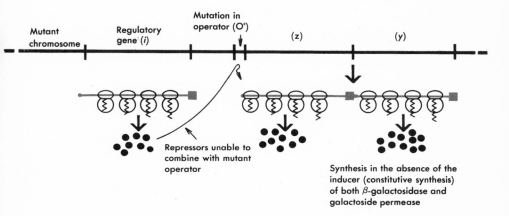

(b) Partially diploid cell containing a normal
operator (O) and a mutant (O^c) operator.
Here the O^c is dominant over the O form.

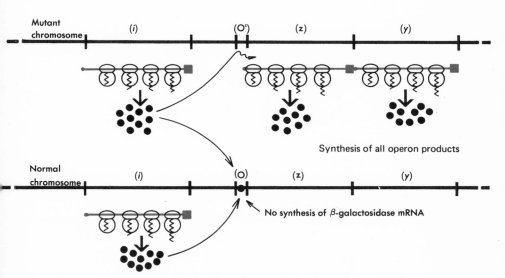

FIGURE 14-8   The control of specific mRNA synthesis by normal
and mutant operators.

easily be distinguished from mutations in the repressor genes by measuring enzyme synthesis in special partially diploid cells containing two copies of the relevant chromosomal regions. Cells containing one nonfunctional and one functional repressor gene are still respressible, since good repressor molecules can act on both operators (Figure 14–7). In contrast, cells containing only one bad operator will always be constitutive, no matter what the condition of the repressor gene (Figure 14–8).

FIGURE 14–9   (a) *Binding of RNA polymerase to the promoter for the lactose operon. (b) Electron micrograph of a β-galactosidase (lactose) repressor bound specifically to the promoter for the lactose operon. (Photograph kindly supplied by Jack Griffiths of Cornell University Physics Department.)*

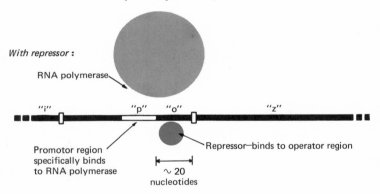

With repressor :

RNA polymerase

"i"   "p" "o"   "z"

Promotor region
specifically binds
to RNA polymerase

Repressor–binds to operator region

~ 20
nucleotides

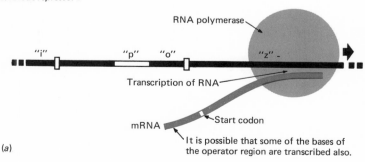

Without repressor :

RNA polymerase

"i"   "p" "o"   "z" -

Transcription of RNA

mRNA

Start codon

It is possible that some of the bases of
the operator region are transcribed also.

(a)

mRNA SYNTHESIS STARTS NEAR THE PROMOTER

The sites along DNA molecules where RNA polymerase molecules specifically bind are called *promoters* (Figure 14–9). The existence of promoters became known from the isolation of mutants which transcribed the β-galactosidase operon with highly reduced efficiency even in total absence of the corresponding repressor or in the presence of operator constitutive mutations (Figure 14–10). Not all promoter mutations need reduce specific binding by RNA polymerase. Cases are known

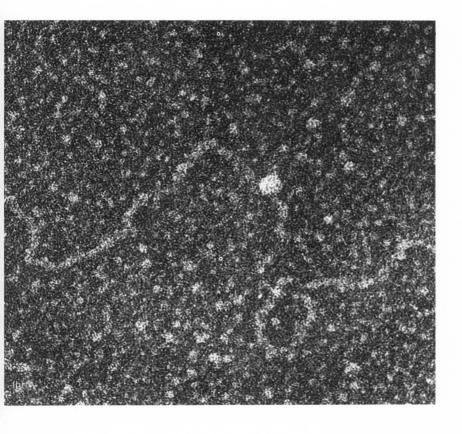

(b)

where the binding efficiency is instead increased by a promoter mutation. Strong supporting evidence for the promoter concept comes from *in vitro* experiments with RNA polymerase. Phage λ DNA containing specific promoter mutations fails to make certain RNA molecules made by DNA molecules with normal promoters.

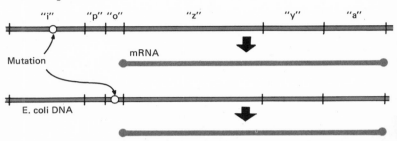

(a) In the absense of an active repressor or with a mutant operator, the wild-type promoter permits high-level synthesis of lac mRNA.

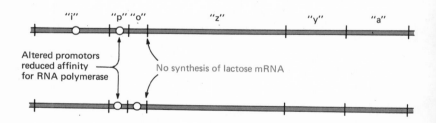

(b) A promotor mutation that blocks any synthesis of lac mRNA even in the absense of a functional repressor or a nonfunctional operator.

F I G U R E   14–10   *Genetic demonstration of the promoter for the lactose operon.*

A priori, there seems no reason why a promoter and its corresponding operator should not share some common nucleotides. One or all of the nucleotides recognized by the specific repressor might overlap some of those which make up a promoter. But with the β-galactosidase operon, there is no overlap detectable by genetic means. In this case, the operator lies between the β-galactosidase gene and the promoter. With other operons, however, we can see no reason why the promoter could not lie immediately next to its corresponding gene.

Before the emergence of these genetic results, the common belief was that only those nucleotide sequences corresponding to amino acids would be transcribed. Now the possibility exists that, in some cases, the operator itself will be transcribed. This, however, is not a firm conclusion, for as RNA polymerase is among the largest known proteins, the site at which it binds (the promoter) may be 10 to 20 nucleotides (30 to 60 A) from the base pair which codes for the initiating mRNA nucleotide (Figure 14–9). In any case, recent nucleotide sequence analysis reveals that many mRNA chains do not start with either of the initiation codons (AUG and GUG).

UNEQUAL PRODUCTION OF PROTEINS CODED BY A SINGLE mRNA MOLECULE

Variation in the number of molecules of different proteins arises also from the fact that the proteins coded by a single mRNA molecule need not be produced in similar numbers. This point is demonstrated by the study of the lactose operon proteins: Many more copies of β-galactosidase than of galactoside permease or galactoside acetylase are synthesized. The ratios in which they appear are $1 : \frac{1}{2} : \frac{1}{5}$ respectively. This may mean that ribosomes attach to the different starting points along a given mRNA molecule at different rates, depending upon the starting nucleotide sequences. Alternatively they may attach only at the β-galactosidase gene with translation of subsequent genes depending upon the frequency of ribosome detachment following the reading of a chain terminating signal. This hypothesis fits in nicely with the observation that the β-galactosidase gene is translated the most often and the acetylase the least often. Another factor conceivably affecting translation is the existence of codons whose corresponding tRNA species is present in very limiting amounts. Hypothetically, ribosomes might jam up at such codons waiting for the limiting tRNA to diffuse to them. We must emphasize, however, that so far no evidence exists for such tRNA species. In any case, it seems reasonable that mechanisms may exist that permit differential reading rates along single mRNA molecules. Although the coordinated appearance of related enzymes is obviously of great advantage to a cell, there is no reason why equal numbers should be produced. An equal number would be useful only if the specific catalytic activity rates (turnover numbers) of related proteins were equal. In general, however, there are great variations in individual turnover numbers.

BACTERIAL mRNA IS OFTEN METABOLICALLY UNSTABLE

When corepressor (inducer) molecules are added to or removed from growing bacteria, the rate of synthesis of the respective proteins is altered rapidly. This rapid adaptation to a changing environment is possible not only because growth requires continual synthesis of new mRNA molecules, but even more significantly, because many bacterial mRNA molecules are metabolically unstable. The average lifetime of many $E.$ $coli$ mRNA molecules at 37°C is about 2 minutes, after which they are enzymatically broken down. The resulting free nucleotides are then phosphorylated to the high-energy triphosphate level and reutilized in the synthesis of new mRNA molecules.

There is thus virtually complete replacement of the templates for many proteins every several minutes. For example, within several minutes after addition of suitable β-galactosides, $E.$ $coli$ cells synthesize β-galactosidase at the maximum rate possible for that particular inducer level. If on the contrary all mRNA molecules were metabolically stable, the maximum synthetic rate would not be reached until cell growth had effectively diluted out previously made mRNA molecules. Correspondingly, the existence of unstable lactose mRNA also means that, once β-galactosides are removed, synthesis of β-galactosidase quickly halts and does not resume until it is again necessary (Figure 14–11).

It now seems as if the average lifetime of different specific mRNA molecules may vary greatly. If true, this means that the mRNA lifetime is itself genetically determined. That is,

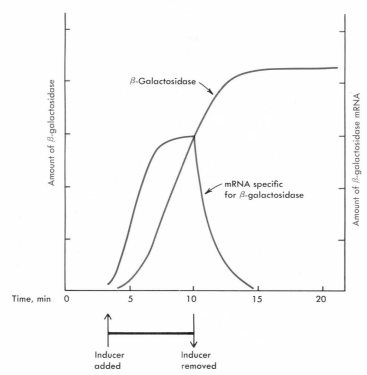

FIGURE 14–11 *Rapid rise (fall) of β-galactosidase mRNA upon the addition (removal) of β-galactosidase inducers. The E. coli cells in this experiment were grown at 37°C under conditions where the cells divided every 40 minutes.*

the nucleotide sequence (perhaps at one end) of an mRNA molecule determines the chance of enzymatic digestion. The enzymatic mechanism by which individual mRNA molecules are broken down has not yet been clarified, though it is clear that the direction of breakdown is 5′ to 3′ (Figure 14–12a and b). The end which is made first is digested first. Breakdown this way will not lead to the synthesis of incomplete chains. On the contrary, if breakdown were 3′ to 5′, then the ends of many messengers would be destroyed before ribosomes had translated their sequences. There are suggestions that mRNA molecules are stable as long as they are bound to ribosomes. Perhaps after the 5' ends of mRNA molecules finish moving across the ribosomes, there is a choice as to whether they attach to new ribosomes or to degradative enzymes which break them down.

PROTEINS NOT UNDER DIRECT ENVIRONMENTAL CONTROL

There are a variety of proteins within the cell whose amount does not seem to be influenced by the external environment. As an example, in E. coli the amounts of the enzymes controlling the degradation of glucose do not radically change when glucose is either removed from or added to the growth medium. Thus the glucose degradative enzymes seem to be *constitutive enzymes* whose rate of synthesis is controlled by neither inducers nor corepressors. We do not yet understand why this is so, since there should be a selective advantage to the cells that can change the amounts of these enzymes. We must, of course, consider that further experiments may demonstrate an inducer or corepressor. On the other hand, it now seems wiser to pose the more general question: Must all genes have repressor-operator control, or is it possible that the amounts of proteins can be controlled in other ways?

The answer is straightforward. The constitutive synthesis of any enzyme at either high or low levels is easy to imagine. High-level constitutive synthesis is what we observe when mutations cause the loss of a repressor or operator. The resulting invariant synthesis of the respective proteins occurs at the same rate as under optimal conditions of induction or repression. This tells us that repressors and operators per se are not required for the synthesis of mRNA molecules.

In general, the amount of constitutive synthesis is a reflection of four factors: (1) The rate at which a specific mRNA molecule can be made in the absence of repressors or operator(s) (this is now understood to be a function of its promoter sequence); (2) the rate at which ribosomes attach to the starting point of the mRNA template; (3) the rate at which a message itself is read; and (4) the lifetime of the particular template.

Unfortunately, because we still understand very little about

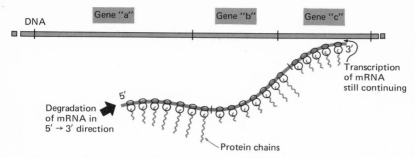

DNA

Gene "a"   Gene "b"   Gene "c"

3'

Transcription
of mRNA
still continuing

5'

Degradation
of mRNA in
5' → 3' direction

Protein chains

FIGURE 14–12   *Breakdown of an mRNA in the 5'-to-3' direction. Degradation of long mRNA molecules frequently begins at the 5' end even before the 3' end has been synthesized.*

the factors controlling any of these rates, it is difficult to assess the absolute or even relative importance of any of them. Nonetheless, the knowledge that so many factors influence the rate of constitutive synthesis suggests that the synthesis of the many proteins needed in small amounts might be regulated without the involvement of repressors or operators.

REPRESSOR SYNTHESIS IS USUALLY UNDER PROMOTER NOT OPERATOR CONTROL

At a given time, there are only about 1000 mRNA molecules in a single *E. coli* cell. A guess at the minimal number of operons influenced by corepressors (inducers) is 100 to 200. It is thus hard to imagine that more than 1 or 2 specific mRNA molecules exist for each repressor. A larger number of mRNA molecules coding for repressors (regulatory mRNA) would greatly restrict the amount of mRNA coding for necessary structural and enzymatic proteins. We conclude that the synthesis of regulatory mRNA is probably carefully controlled. This cannot be done, however, by an entirely new group of repressors, since an infinite number of different repressors would be required to repress each other's synthesis. Thus, either a repressor itself can repress its own synthesis, or repressors are constitutively synthesized. The latter explanation holds for the β-galactosidase system, where many promoter mutations

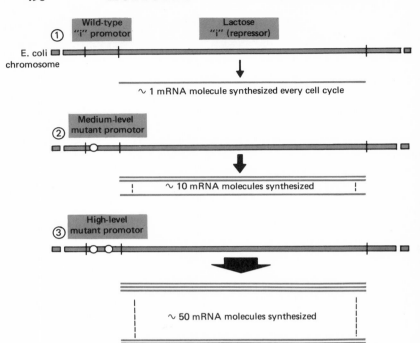

FIGURE 14-13 *Increase in the number of lactose repressor mRNA molecules through promoter mutations. The high-level promoter is thought to arise by several additive mutational changes.*

have already been mapped. Some of these increase the repressor number more than 50 times the number found in wild-type cells (Figure 14-13).

THE QUESTION OF POSITIVE CONTROL

The functioning of repressors in preventing mRNA synthesis is an example of *negative control,* for in the absence of the controlling factor, synthesis proceeds more rapidly than in its presence. But there are also metabolic pathways where current experiments indicate *positive* as opposed to *negative control.* The arabinose operon is the classic case now studied. Its mRNA codes for three proteins involved in the transformation

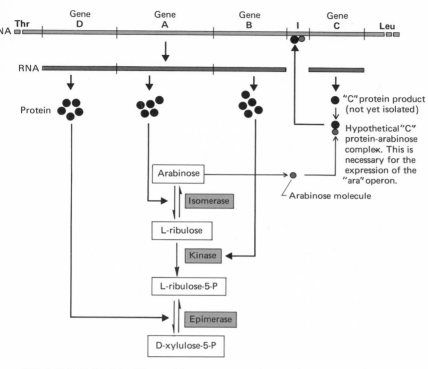

FIGURE 14-14   *The arabinose operon of E. coli: an example of positive control.*

of arabinose to more metabolizable breakdown products (Figure 14–14). In the absence of arabinose, all of these enzymes are present in small amounts, but upon addition of arabinose to growing cells, all three enzymes coordinately increase in amounts. This induction is controlled by a fourth gene, "C," which is immediately adjacent to the other three. The "C" product, however, seems not to be a repressor, since induction does not occur in its absence. Further genetic analysis reveals that "C" must play some positive role. As nonsense mutations occur within the "C" gene, it must produce a protein product, ruling out the possibility that "C" is not a gene but only the promoter where arabinose mRNA synthesis commences. Although much effort has been made to isolate the "C" product, all results are negative so far.

SPECIFIC σ FACTORS MAY BE USED TO TURN ON LARGE BLOCKS OF UNRELATED GENES

Earlier, when discussing how RNA polymerase acts, we emphasized that it is the dissociable σ factors, not the RNA polymerase core, which recognize start signals (promoters). No one knows how many different (possessing a specific nucleotide sequence) start signals exist in *E. coli*, and, if several exist, whether they are all read by σ's of identical structure. Conceivably during cell growth and division, a progression of different σ's appear for relatively short times and turn on specific sets of genes. They in turn would be replaced with σ's of different specificity which start the transcription of still other genes. The intriguing possibility also exists that rRNA and tRNA synthesis involve different σ factors than mRNA synthesis. This would provide a simple explanation for those cases where rRNA and tRNA synthesis almost stops while the rate of mRNA synthesis remains unaffected. Of course, these observations may eventually be explained by a repressor-operator control system. But as we shall see in the next chapters, displacement of one σ by another plays a vital role in controlling the correct sequential appearance of some viral specific enzymes. And there are hints that they may play a major role in the embryological development of higher organisms.

THE EXISTENCE OF GLUCOSE-SENSITIVE OPERONS

The functioning of a number of operons, each controlling the breakdown of a specific sugar, is virtually blocked when *E. coli* cells are growing in the presence of glucose. For example, when *E. coli* is grown in the presence of both glucose and lactose, only the glucose is utilized and none of the lactose operon proteins are synthesized. Similarly, when both glucose and galactose are present, the galactose operon is inactive. This phenomenon is not limited to operons with negative control systems. The arabinose and the maltose operons, both under positive control, likewise cannot operate in the presence of glucose.

The reason that glucose breakdown is preferred over that of the other sugars now can only be guessed. Most likely it is energetically preferable, reflecting the fact that bacteria more often find themselves in a glucose-rich environment than in one dominated by other sugars.

Glucose inhibition does not operate by influencing the rate of entry of the various sugars into the cell. Instead, the effect occurs at the level of RNA transcription. This is shown by the existence of promoter mutations, which render the lactose operon insensitive to glucose effects. With such mutants, the lactose operon can be maximally induced even in the presence of large amounts of glucose.

GLUCOSE CATABOLISM AFFECTS THE CYCLIC AMP LEVEL

The action of glucose on transcription is not mediated directly. Instead, one of its breakdown products (*catabolites*) controls the amount of *cyclic AMP* (Figure 14–15). This key metabolite is required for the transcription of all the operons which are inhibited by glucose catabolism (*catabolite-sentitive operons*). How cyclic AMP functions is just being elucidated. Now it appears that for RNA polymerase to recognize the catabolite-sensitive promoters, a specific protein factor as well as cyclic AMP must be present. Whether this protein will turn out to be a specific σ factor will soon be known.

The manner in which a glucose catabolite controls the cyclic AMP level within a cell is unknown. ATP is the direct metabolic precursor for cyclic AMP and the enzyme responsible for this transformation, adenylcyclase (Figure 14–15), may be directly inhibited by a specific catabolite. Alternatively, since there exists an enzyme which specifically converts cyclic AMP to AMP, inhibition might well be controlled by the rate of

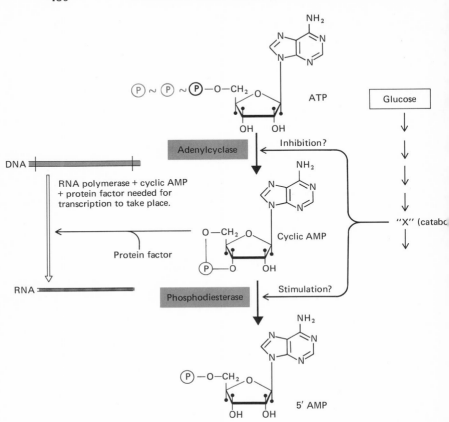

FIGURE 14–15 *Control of catabolite-sensitive transcription through cyclic AMP.*

cyclic AMP breakdown. Hopefully, the correct picture will soon emerge.

REGULATION OF PROTEIN FUNCTION BY FEEDBACK INHIBITION

The catalytic activity of many proteins is affected by their binding to specific small molecules. In this way, the activity of enzymes may be blocked when they are not needed. Consider, for example, what happens when an *E. coli* cell growing on minimal glucose medium is suddenly supplied with the amino acid isoleucine.   Immediately the synthesis (functioning?) of the mRNA molecules needed to code for the specific enzymes utilized in isoleucine biosynthesis ceases.   Without a further control mechanism, preexisting enzymes could cause continued isoleucine production, now unnecessary because of the extra-cellular supply.   Wasteful synthesis, however, almost never occurs, because high levels of isoleucine block the activity of the enzyme involved in the first step of its biosynthesis starting from threonine (Figure 14–16).   This inhibition is due to the binding of isoleucine to the enzyme threonine deaminase.   Thus bound, this enzyme is unable to convert threonine to α-keto-butyrate.   Because the association between the enzyme and

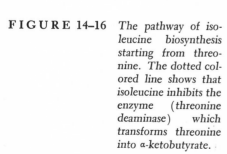

FIGURE 14–16   *The pathway of iso-leucine biosynthesis starting from threo-nine. The dotted col-ored line shows that isoleucine inhibits the enzyme (threonine deaminase) which transforms threonine into α-ketobutyrate.*

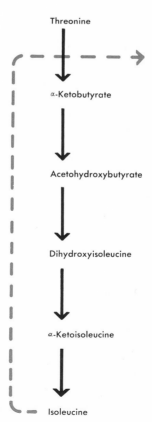

isoleucine is weak and reversible, relatively high isoleucine concentrations must exist before most of the enzyme molecules are inactivated. This very specific inhibition is called *feedback (end-product) inhibition,* because accumulation of a product prevents its further formation. Only the first step in a metabolic chain is blocked. With the first reaction blocked, there is no accumulation of unwanted intermediates, so that inhibition of the remaining enzymes would serve no end.

The final enzymatic step in the synthesis of an end-product feedback inhibitor is often separated by several intermediate metabolic steps from the substrate (or from the product) of the enzyme involved in the first step of its biosynthesis (Figure 14–

FIGURE 14–17 *Schematic diagram showing how feedback inhibition controls the biosynthesis of pyrimidines in E. coli.*

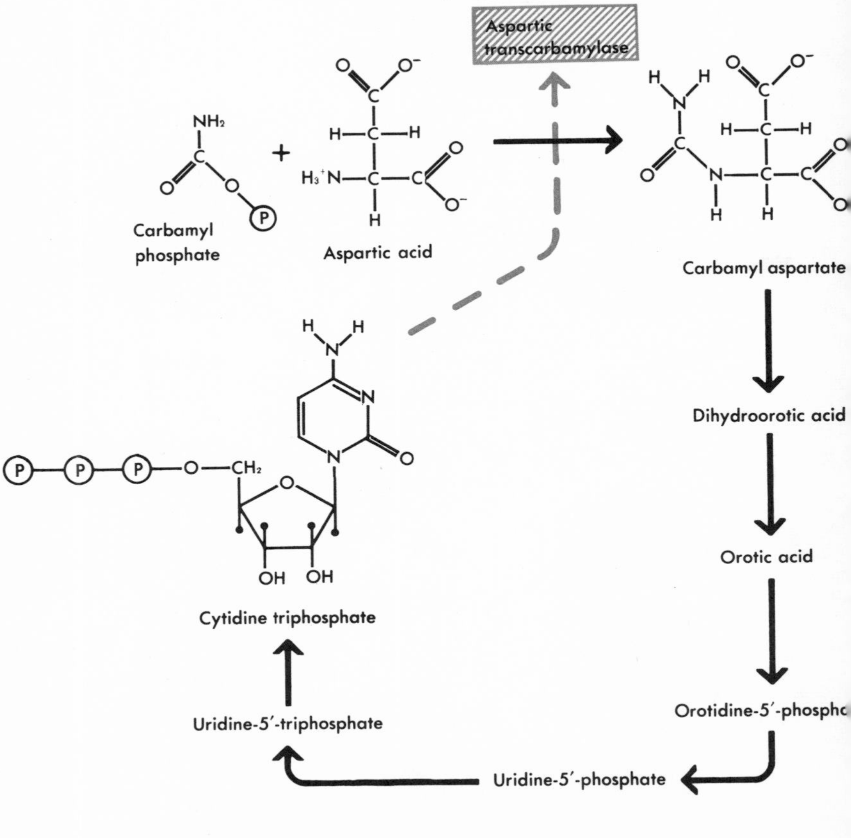

17). The structure of the inhibitor may thus only loosely resemble that of the substrate of the inhibited enzyme, so that
one would not expect an end-product inhibitor to combine with
the enzymatically active site (region that binds the substrate)
of the enzyme it inactivates. Instead, there is the suspicion
that it reversibly combines in some cases with a second site on
the enzyme and yet causes the enzyme activity to be blocked,
perhaps by causing a change in the precise enzyme shape (allosteric transformation) and thus preventing the enzyme from
combining with its substrate (Figure 14–18). Such proteins,
whose shapes are changed by the binding of specific small molecules at sites other than the active site, are called *allosteric proteins,* and, correspondingly, those small molecules that bring
about allosteric transformations are called *allosteric effectors.*

FIGURE 14–18   *Schematic view of how the binding of an end-product inhibitor inhibits an enzyme by causing an allosteric transformation.*

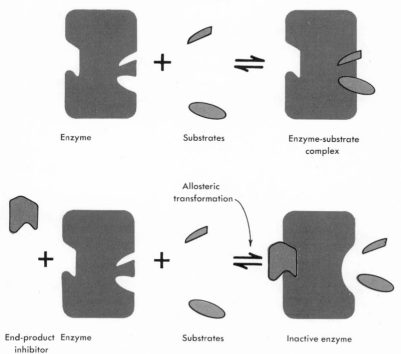

Enzyme   Substrates   Enzyme-substrate
complex

Allosteric
transformation

End-product Enzyme   Substrates   Inactive enzyme
inhibitor

There are now only scant data on the chemical forces binding specific feedback inhibitors to proteins. As in the postulated repressor–corepressor union, the binding is believed to depend upon weak secondary forces (hydrogen bonds, salt linkages, and van der Waals forces), and not to involve any covalent bonds. Hence, feedback inhibition can be quickly reversed once the end product is again reduced to a low level.

SUMMARY

Cells have control mechanisms to ensure that proteins are synthesized in the required amounts. Only very recently have we begun to understand their molecular basis. Most of our knowledge is limited to bacterial cells, in particular to E. coli. Bacteria contain many enzymes whose rate of synthesis depends on the availability of external food molecules. These external molecules (corepressors or inducers) control the rate of protein synthesis by contolling the synthesis of specific mRNA templates. Corepressors (inducers) act by binding to specific molecules, the repressors. Repressors exist in an active state when they have combined with a corepressor and in an inactive state when they have combined with an inducer. Active repressors act by combining with specific regions of the DNA (operators). This binding in turn prevents specific binding of RNA polymerase to its DNA binding sites (its promoters) and so specifically stops the initiation of mRNA synthesis. The length of DNA controlled by a specific repressor, the operon, often comprises several genes with related metabolic functions (e.g., the production of successive enzymes in the synthesis of an amino acid or nucleotide). A still-undiscovered mechanism brings about the differential synthesis of different proteins coded by the same mRNA molecules; some of the proteins are made much more frequently than others.

The control of operon function by repressor–operator systems is negative in character. Other operons are under positive control. They function only in the presence of a protein which specifically promotes their mRNA synthesis. How this happens at the molecular level remains very mysterious.

Cells that have metabolically unstable mRNA molecules can quickly shift their spectrum of protein synthesis in response to a radical change in their surrounding environment (e.g., food supply). This is true especially for bacteria, where the average lifetime for most mRNA molecules may be as short as 2 to 3 minutes.

The rate of synthesis of many protein molecules is not controlled by repressors and inducers (constitutive synthesis). Some proteins are synthesized at fixed high rates, others at very low rates. Frequently this control is accomplished through the specific nucleotide sequence comprising their promoters. Some promoter sequences have great affinity for RNA polymerase, and others have low affinity. As repressors are usually made in very small amounts, their promoters have low affinity.

Many bacterial operons involved in the breakdown of specific sugars, like lactose and arabinose, function much less efficiently when glucose is being catabolized. Somehow these catabolic processes lower the intracellular level of cyclic AMP, a key metabolite necessary for transcription of the catabolite-sensitive operons. Cyclic AMP acts at the initiation stage of transcription in conjunction with a specific protein. Whether this protein is a specific σ factor remains to be worked out.

Control over cell metabolism is also quickly effected by end-product inhibition of enzyme function. An end-product metabolite can reversibly combine with the first enzyme involved in its specific biosynthetic pathway. This combination transforms the enzyme into an inactive form. Now it is suspected that the end-product inhibitor does not combine with the enzymatically active site but binds instead to a second site on the enzyme, causing a change in the enzyme shape. Proteins whose shapes and activities are changed by combination with other molecules are called allosteric proteins.

REFERENCES

Jacob, F., and J. Monod, "Genetic Regulatory Mechanisms in the Synthesis of Proteins," *J. Mol Biol.*, **3**, 318 (1961). A beautiful review that ties together the concept of messenger-RNA with the problem of the control of protein synthesis.

Gilbert, W., and B. Müller-Hill, "Isolation of the Lac Repressor," *Proc. Natl. Acad. Sci., U.S.* **56**, 1891 (1966). How the first repressor was isolated.

Ptashne, M., "Specific Binding of the λ Phage Repressor to λ DNA," *Nature*, **214**, 232 (1967). The first proof that a repressor acts by attaching to DNA.

Martin, R. G., "Control of Gene Expression," *Ann. Rev. Genetics*, **3**, 181 (1969). A very up-to-date review giving evidence from a variety of bacterial operons.

The Lactose Operon, J. Beckwith and D. Zipser (eds.), Cold Spring Harbor Laboratory, 1970. A collection of papers giving a very clear analysis of the most important system so far developed to understand the control of protein synthesis in bacteria.

Morse, D. E., R. D. Mosteller, and C. Yanofsky, "Dynamics of Synthesis, Translation, and Degradation of *trp* Operon Messenger RNA in *E. coli*," *Cold Spring Harbor Symposium of Quant. Biol.*, **34**, 729 (1969). The most complete study so far of the kinetics of mRNA synthesis and breakdown.

Monod, J., J. P. Changeux, and F. Jacob, "Allosteric Proteins and Cellular Control Systems," *J. Mol. Biol.*, **6**, 306–329 (1963). A comprehensive review of the problem of allostery.

Gerhart, J. C., and A. B. Pardee, "The Effect of the Feedback Inhibitor, CTP, on Subunit Interactions in Aspartate Transcarbamylase," *Cold Spring Harbor Symp. Quant. Biol.*, **28**, 491 (1963). A summary of an enzyme system, the study of which was important in developing the concept of allostery.

15

THE

REPLICATION

OF VIRUSES

GENETICISTS USUALLY HAVE FOCUSED ON viruses because they have seemed so simple. In the beginning they were thought of as naked genes, but gradually it became obvious that the correct analogy was the naked chromosome. Many of the viruses first thought to be so uncomplicated now are seen to contain several hundred genes. And when we began to discover the ways bacteria can prevent unwanted synthesis, it seemed probable that the essence of a virus's existence was the lack of any such regulatory devices. Being so constituted, they would be able to multiply rapidly at the expense of their host cells' metabolism. Again the first hunches proved wrong. The replication of even the smallest of viruses is a very complicated affair, achieved only with the aid of highly evolved regulatory systems designed to see that the right molecules are synthesized at just the right time in the life cycle of a virus. But before we look into the details of this problem, some more general principles of viral structure and multiplication must be examined.

THE CORE AND COATING OF VIRUSES

Both the size and structural complexity of viruses show great variation. Some have molecular weights as small as several million, whereas others approach the size of very small bacteria.

467

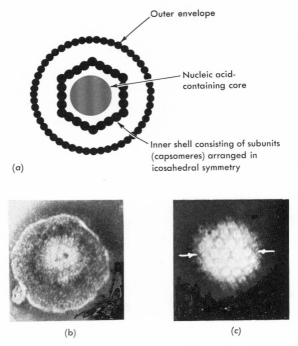

FIGURE 15–1   *The morphology of Herpes, a large DNA-containing virus which multiplies in animal cells. (a) A schematic view of its general structure showing the DNA-containing core embedded in a regular shell (capsid), and an outer envelope. (b) An electron micrograph showing the 1000-A diameter capsid surrounded by a 1500-A envelope. (c) A high-resolution electron micrograph of the capsid. It contains 162 subunits (capsomeres) arranged about fivefold, threefold, and twofold axes of symmetry. [(b) and (c) reproduced from Wildy et al., Virology,* **12,** *204 (1960), with permission.]*

However, all viruses differ fundamentally from cells, which have both DNA and RNA, in that viruses contain only one type of nucleic acid, which may be either DNA or RNA. The genetic nucleic acid component is always present in the center of the virus particle, surrounded by a protective coat (shell). Some of the shells are quite complex; they contain several layers and are built up from a number of different proteins, as well as from lipid and carbohydrate molecules (Figures 15–1, 15–2, 15–3).

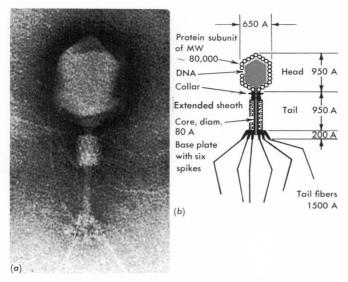

FIGURE 15-2   *The structure of the T-even (2, 4, and 6) phage
particle. (a) An electron micrograph of T2 [repro-
duced from R. W. Horne et al., J. Mol. Biol., 1,
281 (1959), with permission]. (b) A schematic
drawing showing detailed features revealed by electron
microscopy.*

In other cases, for example in tobacco mosaic virus (TMV)—a
virus that multiplies in tobacco plants—or in the small RNA
bacterial viruses F2, R17, and Qβ, the shell contains only one
type of protein and no lipid or carbohydrate.

All shells contain many copies of the protein component(s),
often arranged with either helical symmetry or cubical (or
quasi-cubical) symmetry. Thus the TMV shell has about 2150
identical protein molecules (MW ∼ 17,000) helically arranged
around a central RNA molecule containing approximately
6000 nucleotides (Figure 15-4). In F2 (or R17) there are 180
identical proteins (MW ∼ 14,000) cubically arranged about
an inner RNA molecule with 3300 nucleotides.

The use of a large number of identical protein molecules in
the construction of the protective shell is an obligatory feature
of the structures of all viruses. This follows from their limited
nucleic acid content, which in turn places an absolute

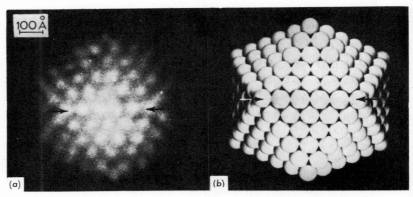

FIGURE 15–3   *Adenovirus structure. These DNA-containing viruses, which multiply in animal cells, have very regular structures. (a) A particle at high magnification. 252 capsomeres are used to construct the outer shell. (b) A model of an icosahedron in the same orientation. [Reproduced from R. W. Horne et al., J. Mol. Biol.; 1, 86 (1959), with permission.]*

restriction on the maximal number of amino acids in the proteins coded by the viral chromosome. For example, the ~6000 nucleotides in a TMV RNA chain can code for ~2000 amino acids, corresponding to a protein molecular weight of about 2.5×10^5. This is very much smaller than the molecular weight

FIGURE 15–4   *A high-resolution electron micrograph of one end of a TMV particle. The diameter is approximately 180 A, whereas the length of a complete particle is 3000 A. The particle is covered with a dark stain which penetrates the hollow central core. [Photograph reproduced from J. T. Finch, J. Mol. Biol., 8, 872 (1964), with permission.]*

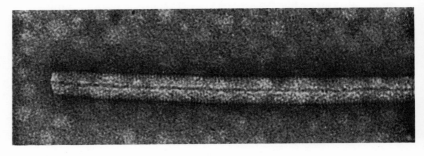

of TMV's protein shell (3.5×10^7). Thus, even if the entire TMV RNA chain coded for its coat protein (which it does not), approximately 150 identical protein molecules would be needed. This use of a large number of identical protein subunits is why the simpler viruses, which often contain only one type of protein molecule in their coat, have either helical or cubical (or quasi-cubical) symmetry. Only these two types of symmetry permit the identical protein subunits to be packed together in a regular (or quasi-regular) fashion and thus to have virtually identical (except for their contacts with the nucleic acid core) chemical environments.

NUCLEIC ACID: THE GENETIC COMPONENT OF ALL VIRUSES

Viruses afford some of the best demonstrations that genetic specificity is carried by nucleic acid molecules. Many viral nucleic acids are easily isolated from their protein shell and prepared in highly purified form. When they are added to host cells, new infective virus particles are produced; each is identical to those from which the nucleic acid was isolated (Figure 15–5). These very important experiments definitively show that the viral nucleic acid carries the genetic specificity to code both for its own replication and for the amino acid sequences in its specific coat proteins.

This is true not only for the DNA viruses, but also for viruses containing RNA. In fact, the first demonstration of infectious viral nucleic acid was made by using RNA isolated from TMV. Before this demonstration, doubts had persisted whether the RNA component of TMV was really genetic. This uncertainty existed because the large majority of TMV particles are not ordinarily infectious. Usually fewer than one in a million particles enters the tobacco leaf and serves as parent for progeny particles. It could thus be argued that perhaps this rare particle contained DNA. However, the isolation of infectious TMV RNA dispelled this uncertainty and clearly showed that sequences of nucleotide bases in RNA, like those in DNA, carry genetic messages.

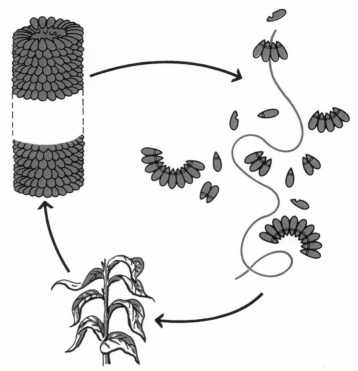

FIGURE 15–5 *Proof that RNA is the genetic component of TMV. The rod-shaped TMV particles can easily be separated into their protein and RNA components, which can then be separately tested for their ability to initiate virus infection. Only the RNA molecules have this ability. The virus particles produced by infecting with pure RNA are identical to those resulting from infection with intact virus.*

VIRAL NUCLEIC ACID MAY BE EITHER SINGLE- OR DOUBLE-STRANDED

The nucleic acid of most viruses has the form of its cellular counterparts. Thus all the best-known DNA viruses, such as smallpox (or its harmless relative *Vaccinia*), polyoma, and the T2, T4, and T6 group of bacterial viruses, have the double helical structure. Correspondingly the RNA of TMV, influenza virus, poliomyelitis virus, and the bacterial viruses F2 and R17 is single-stranded. There are, however, several groups of bacterial viruses in which the DNA is single-stranded and there is at least one group of RNA viruses (the Reoviruses) in which the RNA assumes a complementary double-helical form.

Fundamentally, it does not matter whether the genetic message is initially present as a single strand or as the double helix; for the single strand can quickly be used to form a complementary replica soon after it enters a suitable host cell. The really important fact is that the genetic information is present as a sequence of nucleotide bases.

VIRAL NUCLEIC ACID AND PROTEIN SYNTHESIS OCCUR INDEPENDENTLY

Exactly what happens after a viral nucleic acid molecule enters a susceptible host cell depends on the specific viral system. Particularly important is whether the virus contains DNA or RNA. If the genetic component is DNA, then during viral replication the DNA serves as a template both for its own replication and for the viral specific RNA necessary for the synthesis of its specific proteins. Similarly, if RNA is the genetic component, the RNA molecules have two template roles, the first to make more RNA molecules and the second to make the viral specific proteins. In both cases the end result of virus infection is the same: the production of many new copies of both the viral nucleic acids and the coat proteins. The new progeny molecules then spontaneously aggregate to form mature virus particles. Enzymes usually play no role in these final aggregation events, since with most viruses the formation of new covalent bonds is not needed either to build a stable protein coat or to affix it firmly to the nucleic acid core. Only weak secondary bonds (salt linkages, van der Waals forces, and hydrogen bonds) are involved. This last point is shown clearly with TMV. Here the rod-shaped particles can be gently broken down and their free RNA and coat protein components separated. When they are again mixed together, new infectious particles, identical to the original rods, quickly

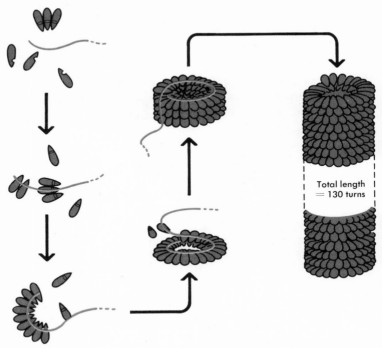

Total length
= 130 turns

FIGURE 15–6　Formation of a TMV particle from its protein subunits and its RNA molecule. (Redrawn from H.
Fraenkel-Conrat, Design and Function at the Threshold of Life: The Viruses, Figure 18, Academic, New
York, 1962.)

form (Figure 15–6). We thus see that the essential aspects of
virus multiplication are known once we understand the principles by which viral nucleic acid and protein components are
individually synthesized.

VIRAL NUCLEIC ACIDS CODE FOR
BOTH ENZYMES AND COAT PROTEINS

The viral nucleic acid genetic component must code the amino
acid sequences in the protein(s) that make(s) up the protective coat. These coat proteins are never found in normal uninfected cells and are completely specific to a given virus. In ad-

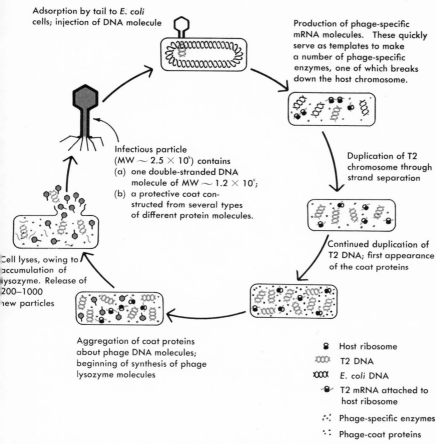

Adsorption by tail to *E. coli* cells; injection of DNA molecule

Production of phage-specific mRNA molecules. These quickly serve as templates to make a number of phage-specific enzymes, one of which breaks down the host chromosome.

Infectious particle (MW ∼ 2.5 × 10⁸) contains
(a) one double-stranded DNA molecule of MW ∼ 1.2 × 10⁸;
(b) a protective coat constructed from several types of different protein molecules.

Duplication of T2 chromosome through strand separation

Continued duplication of T2 DNA; first appearance of the coat proteins

Cell lyses, owing to accumulation of lysozyme. Release of 200–1000 new particles

Aggregation of coat proteins about phage DNA molecules; beginning of synthesis of phage lysozyme molecules

Host ribosome
T2 DNA
E. coli DNA
T2 mRNA attached to host ribosome
Phage-specific enzymes
Phage-coat proteins

FIGURE 15–7   *Chemical details in the life cycle of the double-stranded DNA virus T2 (T4).*

dition, the synthesis of one or many new enzymes usually occurs to permit successful viral multiplication.

Now there are many examples where DNA viruses carry information for the amino acid sequences of enzymes connected with the synthesis of their precursor nucleotides. One of the most striking cases involves T4 multiplication (Figure 15–7). No cytosine is present in its DNA, a fact that initially suggested that T4 DNA might be very different from normal DNA. Instead there is always present the closely related base

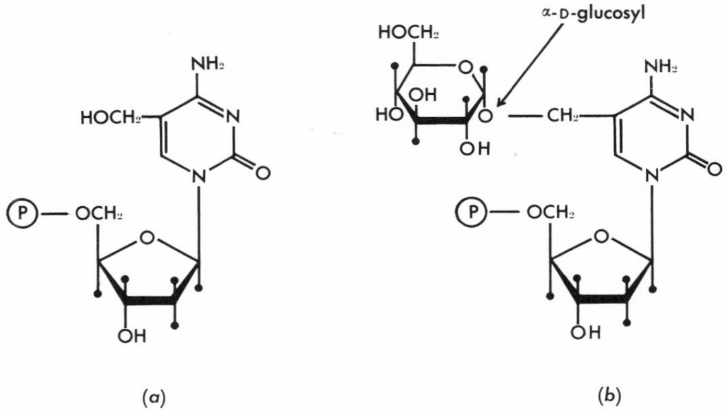

(a)   (b)

F I G U R E 15–8   *Phages of the T-even group do not contain cytosine in their DNA. Instead they contain the related base 5-OH-methylcytosine (a), which base pairs exactly like cytosine. One or more glucose residues are attached to some of their 5-CH₂OH groups. (b) Shows this base with one glucose molecule attached. The biological significance of these unusual bases has not yet been clearly established. One speculative hypothesis asserts that their function is to protect T-even DNA from a phage specific enzyme which only breaks down unmodified DNA. This hypothesis would explain how the E. coli DNA is selectively broken down during viral synthesis.*

5-OH-methylcytosine, which, like cytosine, forms base pairs with guanine. The 3-D structure of T4 DNA is thus basically the same as that of normal double-helical DNA (Figure 15–8).

No 5-OH-methylcytosine is found in uninfected E. *coli* cells, and so the several new enzymes required for its biosynthesis must be coded for by the T4 DNA. In addition, the rate of DNA synthesis in T4-infected cells is several times faster than in normal cells. This faster rate is achieved by having other T4 genes code for many of the enzymes involved in normal nucleotide metabolism, as well as for a DNA polymerase-like enzyme (Figure 15–9).

A new viral specific enzyme is also frequently needed to ensure the release of progeny virus particles from their host cell. This is a vital need for those bacterial viruses multiplying in bacteria with rigid cell walls. Since these walls do not spontaneously disintegrate, they could effectively inactivate progeny

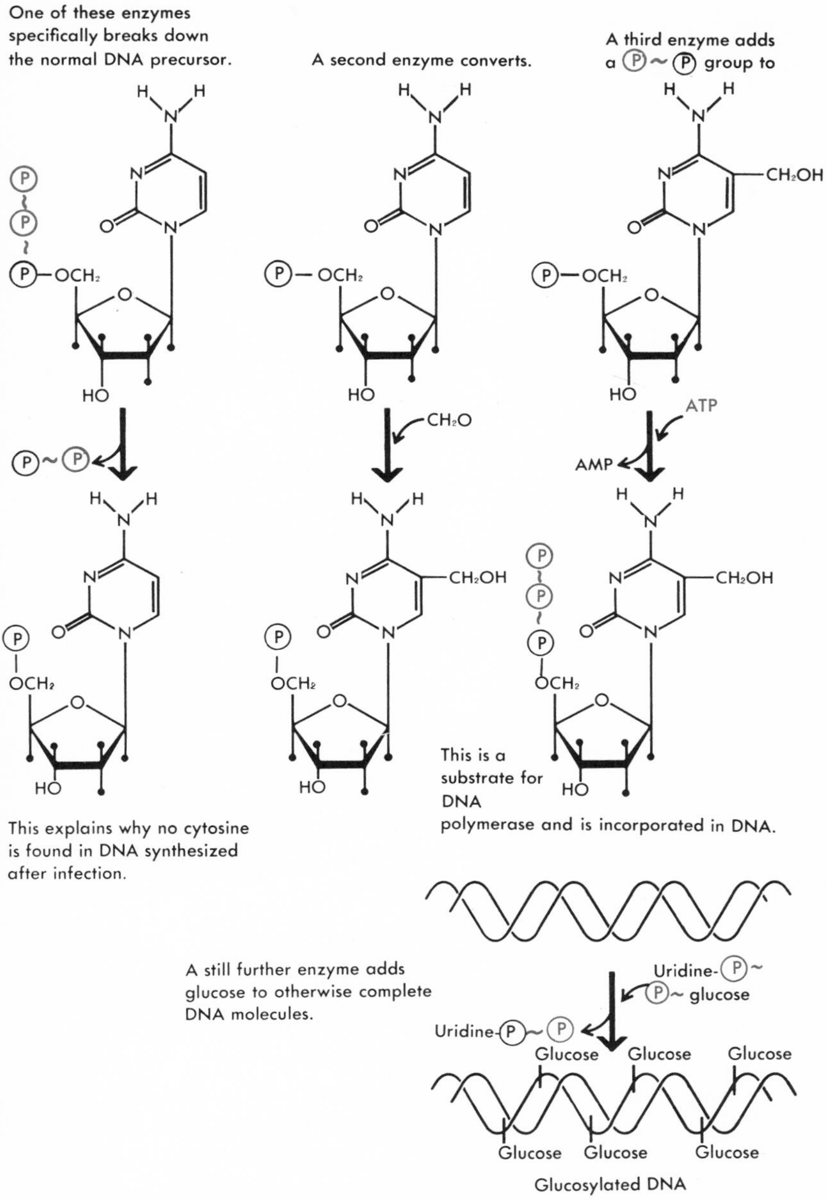

One of these enzymes specifically breaks down the normal DNA precursor.

A second enzyme converts.

A third enzyme adds a (P) ~ (P) group to

CH₂O

ATP

AMP

This explains why no cytosine is found in DNA synthesized after infection.

This is a substrate for DNA polymerase and is incorporated in DNA.

A still further enzyme adds glucose to otherwise complete DNA molecules.

Uridine-(P)~ (P)~ glucose

Uridine-(P)~(P)

Glucose   Glucose   Glucose

Glucose   Glucose   Glucose

Glucosylated DNA

FIGURE 15-9   The biochemical mechanism that brings about the synthesis of DNA lacking cytosine and containing instead 5-OH-methylcytosine and its glucose derivatives. Immediately after infection, a number of specific enzymes are synthesized. These are coded for by the viral DNA, and each has a specific role in ensuring the successful multiplication of the virus.

477

particles by preventing their release and transfer to new host cells. To take care of this problem, many phages have a gene that codes for the amino acid sequence of lysozyme, a cell-wall-destroying enzyme. This enzyme begins to be synthesized when the coat proteins appear, and causes the rupture of the cell wall at about the time virus maturation is complete.

MORPHOGENETIC PATHWAYS

The assembly of structurally complex viruses like λ and T4 is much more involved than the simple aggregation process needed for simple viruses like TMV. Some 40 different T4 gene products, each coded by a specific T4 gene, interact to produce the mature virus particle. Many of the genes code for the various structural proteins, while at least one other codes for an enzyme which most likely converts a precursor protein into the form found in mature T4 particles. In the assembly process the various components do not associate with each other randomly in time. Instead the assembly occurs in a definite sequence (a morphogenetic pattern) and devices not yet understood prevent the occurrence of a specific step until the preceding step has occurred. Three different branches, the first concerned with the head, the second with the tail, and the third with the tail fibers, come together as shown in Figure 15–10 to produce the final infectious particles.

VIRAL INFECTION OFTEN RADICALLY CHANGES HOST CELL METABOLISM

Sometimes the synthesis of viral specific nucleic acids and proteins goes hand in hand with normal cell synthesis. The chromosomes of the host cell often continue to function throughout a large fraction of the viral life cycle. In many cases, however, soon after infection, most of the cellular metabolism is directed toward the synthesis of new molecules connected exclusively with the appearance of new virus particles. In the most extreme cases, all DNA and RNA synthesis on the host chromosomes ceases, the preexisting RNA templates are

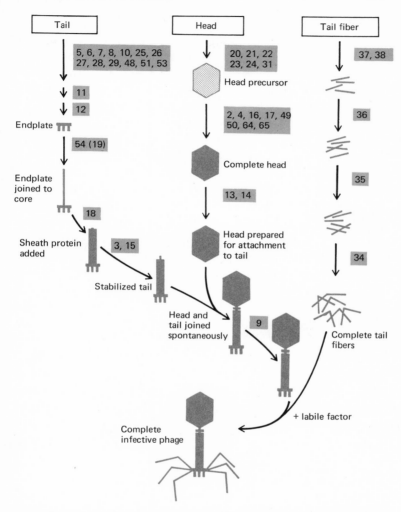

FIGURE 15–10 *The morphogenetic pathway leading to the formation of T4 particles. The numbers refer to the
various genes involved in each step. (Redrawn from
Wood and Edgar,* Scientific American, *July 1967.)*

degraded, and all subsequent protein synthesis occurs on new
RNA templates coded by the viral nucleic acid.

The extent to which a virus is able to control its host's synthetic facilities varies greatly, depending both on the nature of

the infecting virus and on the type of host cell. In general, the larger the viral nucleic acid content, the larger the number of viral genes directed toward stopping host cell functions unnecessary for the production of new viral particles. How these viral specific genes redirect cellular metabolism is only beginning to be understood. For example, during T4 multiplication, the host *E. coli* chromosome is enzymatically broken down, most likely by an enzyme coded for by T4 DNA. In contrast, the T4 chromosome is not attacked enzymatically, most likely because it contains the unusual base 5-OH-methylcytosine. This differential destruction of the host chromosome, however, is not the sole, if even major, cause of the metabolic dominance of the viral chromosome. Long before evidence of its breakdown can be detected, the host chromosome has ceased to serve as a template for *E. coli* mRNA. Recent experiments (see below) suggest that this is due to the inactivation of the host σ factors.

SYNTHESIS OF VIRAL SPECIFIC PROTEINS

Viral specific proteins are synthesized in the same basic way as normal cellular proteins. The viral specific messenger RNA molecules attach to host ribosomes, forming polyribosomes to which the AA ⁓ tRNA precursors are attached. F-met-tRNA also starts all phage proteins and the terminating signals are those of their host cells. Changes may occur, however, in the structure of the host's ribosomes. After T4 infection, the *E. coli* ribosomes are so modified that they work better with T4 messenger than with host messenger. The exact nature of the modifications induced by the virus remains to be worked out. In addition, several cases are now known where after viral infection new tRNA species arise by enzymatic modification of preexisting tRNA molecules. Totally new tRNA molecules also appear in some virus infected cells. And so viral, as well as host, genes can code for tRNA.

The significance of these new tRNA species is still very unclear. In some cases, they may be adaptations to the modifications in ribosome structure induced by the virus. In other cases, they may be connected with differences in base composition between the viral chromosome and the host chromosome. For example, T4 DNA has twice as many A-T base pairs as G-C base pairs, while *E. coli* DNA has roughly similar amounts of both types. As not all potential wobble pairs are equally strong, growth of an AT-rich virus using tRNAs adapted for a chromosome with equal amounts of the four bases might slow down the translation of many viral specific proteins. Hence the possible selective advantage of new tRNA species with altered anticodons.

THE DISTINCTION BETWEEN
EARLY AND LATE PROTEINS

After a viral chromosome enters a cell, all of its genes do not usually begin working at the same time. Instead there is a regular time schedule by which they function. Some viral proteins appear immediately after infection, while the synthesis of others may not begin until more than halfway through a viral growth cycle. Also, some genes start working early and continue to do so throughout viral growth, while others function for only several minutes and then shut off (Figure 15–11).

FIGURE 15–11   *Time of synthesis of various T4-specific proteins and DNA at 37°.*

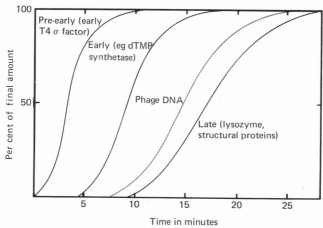

There are obvious advantages to such sequential appearance. Some of the early gene products are enzymes necessary to direct cellular synthesis from host to viral genes (they clearly must be turned on early), while others, such as the viral coat proteins or the lysozyme needed for cell lysis, must only appear late. For example, if lysozyme were an early enzyme, cell lysis would occur prematurely, aborting the construction of progeny virus particles. Hence, even the most cursory knowledge of a viral life cycle suggests that quite intricate control systems must exist to guarantee that the right proteins appear just when they are needed. As far as we know, these control systems usually operate at the transcription level. Thus, some specific mRNA molecules appear early, while others are found only late in the growth cycle. At first it was convenient to subdivide the various mRNAs into just two categories—early and late mRNAs—and likewise to classify a particular protein as either early or late. But often the situation is more complex, and the literature is filled with terms like pre-early, early-late, and so on.

CONTROLLING GENE TIMING THROUGH GENE ORDER

Under optimal growth conditions, the time needed to synthesize a mRNA molecule of molecular weight ~2 million is of the order of 3 to 4 minutes. Molecules of this size (6000 nucleotides) can code for 4 to 5 average-size proteins. But synthesis of these proteins will not begin at the same time—the proteins coded at the 5′ end can be completely translated before the transcription of the gene at the 3′ end has even started. Genes which need to function first thus tend to occur at the start of operons. Likewise, when the optimal time for the beginning of a gene's function is 3 to 4 minutes after viral infection, it sometimes makes sense to place it toward the 3′ end of a fairly large operon (Figure 15–12).

The delayed appearance of the "late" proteins, however, is not completely explained by the existence of very long operons. For example, in T4 most operons are relatively short and few have more than several thousand base pairs. Yet per-

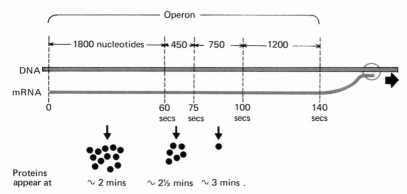

FIGURE 15-12   *Sequential functioning of contiguous genes along an operon. At 37° in vivo E. coli mRNA chains grow at about 30 nucleotides per second. Complete transcription of a DNA segment containing 4200 base pairs will take about 2 minutes and 20 seconds. Attachment of the first ribosomes begins seconds after transcription starts. Since ribosome movement during translation occurs at roughly the same rate as transcription, functional gene products begin to appear in less than a minute after transcription of the corresponding gene has been completed.*

haps one-third of its 200 or so genes do not begin to function until about 10 minutes after its chromosome has entered the host cell.

THE SEARCH FOR THE ABSENT T4 REPRESSORS

To explain why these late operons were not transcribed, the hypothesis was put forward that the promoters for the "late" operons were blocked by highly specific repressors, viral coded and synthesized immediately after penetration of the viral chromosomes into their host cell. By binding to the operator for late operons, they could specifically prevent appreciable amounts of late mRNA from being made until they were neutralized by an inducer, itself the product of a viral specific early enzyme. Proof for such a scheme would come with the finding of mutants which upset the normal time schedule by preventing repressor synthesis and so allowing all the late proteins to be made early. But, despite the isolation of a very large number of T4 nonsense mutations, not the slightest hint of a T4 repressor has been found.   Instead, increasing evidence indicates that positive control, not negative control, is the key to T4 development.

SIGMA FACTORS SPECIFIC FOR LATE mRNA

Just recently viral specific σ factors have been shown to be the heart of this positive control.   Several phages are already known where the changeover from early to late mRNA synthesis is caused by the replacement of one RNA polymerase σ factor by another.   In general, the promoters for the early genes are read by the σ('s?) present in the uninfected cells, while the promoters controlling the late ones are read by viral specific σ's. This means that one or more viral genes code for σ factors.

The moderately complicated T4 life cycle requires two different viral specific σ factors.   Immediately after the T4 chromosome enters a host cell, a group of genes, called "pre-early," begins to function using a host σ factor to read their respective promoters.   One of these pre-early genes codes a viral specific σ, which reads the so-called "early" genes.   These begin to function 3 to 4 minutes after infection.   At the same time, the host σ factors disappear so that transcription of all host mRNA as well as pre-early T4 mRNA ceases.   About 10 minutes after infection, a second T4 σ factor, coded for by one of the early genes, appears and begins to read the promoters for the "late" genes.   This late σ largely displaces the early σ so that most early synthesis stops soon after the late σ appears in appreciable amounts.

Parallel with these changes in the σ pattern, two successive modifications occur in the structure of the polymerase core component.   The first modification most likely prevents the host σ('s) from attaching to the core, while the second modification may promote the switchover from early to late synthesis.   An active search is underway for the T4 genes coding for both the early and late σ's as well as the core-modifying proteins.

Synthesis of late T7 mRNA, however, is achieved by the synthesis of a completely new polymerase coded for by gene 1.   In this phage, only 4 genes (including gene 1) are under the control of an E. coli σ, with the reading of the remaining 25 to 30 dependent on the presence of the T7-specific polymerase. About 5 minutes after infection, reading of the early genes stops, so we suspect that the functioning of host σ core factor is somehow blocked by the action of an *anti-σ* core factor coded by another T7 gene. How such anti-σ (core) factors act is now under intensive investigation.

THE λ REPRESSOR MAINTAINS THE PROPHAGE STATE

The situation with phage λ (Figure 15–13) is more complex. A repressor exists which specifically blocks λ mRNA synthesis. But its presence does not differentiate early from late RNA. Instead, the repressor blocks virtually all λ-specific mRNA synthesis. To understand its role, we must remember (see Figure

FIGURE 15–13   *The genetic map of λ showing the function of many of its genes.*

λ *map*

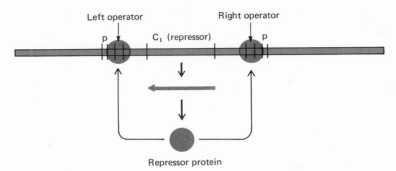

(a) In the lysogenic state, the λ repressor binds to both left and right operators preventing transcription from starting at either its left or right promotor.

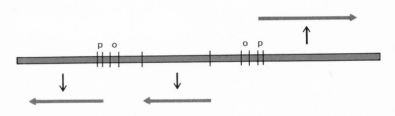

(b) When the λ repressor becomes inactivated transcription starts to move towards the left from the left promotor and towards the right from the right promotor.

FIGURE 15–14 *Action of the λ repressor in preventing synthesis of both early (left) and early (right) classes of λ mRNA.*

7–10) that λ is a lysogenic phage capable both of ordinary lytic multiplication in *E. coli* and of existence in the prophage stage as part of the *E. coli* chromosome. When λ is located on the host chromosome, the transcription of almost all of its genes is blocked. The λ repressor is responsible for this inhibition. Thus, the only gene functioning in the prophage state is that (C_1) coding for the repressor itself (Figure 15–14). Normally present in only a few copies, this repressor binds to two specific operators, each of which controls a specific early mRNA molecule.

Inactivation of the λ repressor frequently occurs under conditions where DNA synthesis is inhibited (e.g., after treatment with uv light). This allows mRNA transcription of the two early operons to begin (Figure 15–14). One of these operons is largely occupied by genes coding for proteins necessary for the recombination events which free the λ chromosome (see Chapter 7) from the E. coli chromosome. The other early operon contains, among others, the genes specifically needed for the replication of λ DNA.

One of the first early genes to be read somehow stops further synthesis of the C_1 (repressor) mRNA. The exact gene involved has not yet been found, though there are hints that it lies just to the right of C_1. Shutting off repressor mRNA synthesis clearly makes sense since no new repressors are needed or wanted throughout the remaining part of the life cycle.

POSITIVE CONTROL DIRECTED BY THE "N" GENE ANTITERMINATION FACTOR

Release of repression, however, does not by itself lead to the complete transcription of the early operons. For this to occur, the key λ gene "N" must work. In the absence of the "N" gene product, mRNA synthesis starts at the two respective promoter sites, but elongation proceeds for only relatively short distances, as nearby stop signals are read by an E. coli RNA ρ (termination) factor. The "N" protein somehow specifically antagonizes the action of the termination factor, thereby allowing much, much larger portions of both operons to be read (Figure 15–15). It is still unclear what terminates the synthesis of these much longer chains. Perhaps more than one stop signal (and corresponding termination factor) exists in E. coli, only one of which is neutralized by the "N" protein.

A SINGLE PROMOTER FOR ALL LATE λ GENES

Almost half of λ's genetic material (∼20 genes) codes for "late" proteins, most of them involved in the synthesis of λ's head and tail components. All these "late" genes belong to a

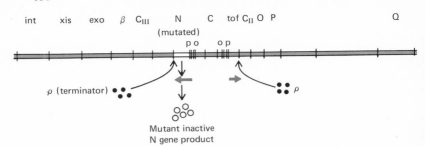

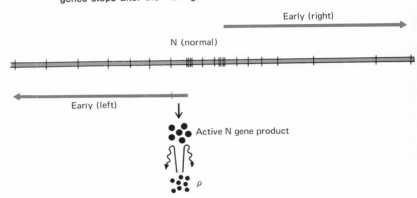

(a) In the absence of the "N" gene product, reading of early (left) genes stops after the "N" gene and reading of the early (right) genes stops after the "tof" gene.

(b) When "N" gene product is present, ρ action is inhibited and both the early operons are transcribed.

FIGURE 15-15 *Current scheme for the action of the λ "N" gene as an antitermination factor.*

single operon which begins before the "S" gene and ends after gene "J" (Figure 15–16). This operon only functions in the presence of a protein made by the "early" gene "Q." Conceivably, "Q" product is a σ-like factor necessary for reading of the "late" promoter. This point should soon be settled experimentally.

The "Q" gene is located some 4 minutes transcriptional time away from its promoter. Thus, its first protein product only begins to appear 5 minutes after the start of infection and it is not until 10 minutes after infection that enough "Q" prod-

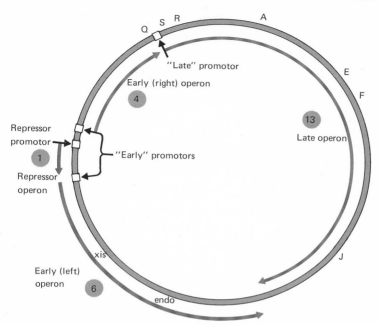

FIGURE 15–16 *The four operons of the phage* λ. *The numbers give the approximate times needed at 37° for complete transcription of the respective operons.*

ucts are present to allow appreciable transcription of late mRNA. Further control over the λ life cycle is achieved by the putting together of all the "late" genes in a single operon. For example, some 10,000 base pairs separate the genes for the main head protein from the ones coding for the tail fibers. This means that the final tail assembly can begin only 5 minutes after that of the heads.

With so much potential timing control possible through use of very long operons, the question should be posed why in fact a separate operon for the late proteins has come into existence. The answer lies in the fact that much larger amounts of "late" mRNA than of "early" are required. Most, if not all, of the early gene products are enzymes, while many of the late proteins are structural proteins needed in very large quantities. A device is thus required to turn on large-scale late mRNA synthesis some 8 to 10 minutes after the early operons start functioning. Evolution of a gene product permitting a new promoter to operate accomplishes this objective in a simple fashion.

A SINGLE OPERON FOR THE VERY SMALL DNA PHAGES

A much, much simpler transcription picture holds for the very small DNA phages like $\phi \times 174(S13)$ and Fl (fd, M13). Each has a circular chromosome containing about 5500 (6000) nucleotides, which *a priori* we would guess to code for six to eight proteins of average chain length between 200 and 300. In fact, eight genes have already been characterized within both $\phi \times 174$ and M13 and the pleasant possibility exists that almost all their genes have already been found.

Four of the $\phi \times 174$ genes are used to code for its structural proteins. Originally, because of its very small size, the protein coat was thought to be built up from the regular aggregation of only one protein. But now four distinct proteins—of molecular weights 60,000, 36,000, 19,000, and 5,000—have been identified. Their coding requires 3300 nucleotides or some 60 per cent of the total chromosome. One of the remaining four genes is known to be involved in the replication of the double-helical DNA intermediate (Figure 9–10), another functions in the production of the progeny single-stranded circles, and still another brings about cell lysis. Hopefully, within the next decade, the exact task of all its genes should be known.

Synthesis of viral specific mRNA begins as soon as the double-helical intermediates are made. All this mRNA is complementary to the viral "−" strand and apparently is transcribed as a single linear unit resulting from one complete reading of the genome. So far, the location of the promoter has not been determined. The relative location of the various genes is unlikely to be an important control factor—transcription of the entire genome takes only 2 minutes at 37°, while the corresponding virus life cycle occupies some 20 minutes. Further intensive research on these viruses is obviously in order since, given their small size, the working out of all the essential details of their replication is an achievable objective.

VIRAL RNA SELF-REPLICATION: REQUIREMENTS FOR A NEW VIRAL SPECIFIC ENZYME

Cellular RNA molecules never serve as templates for the formation of new RNA strands. The replication of most RNA viruses demands the participation of a completely new enzyme capable of forming new RNA strands upon parental RNA templates. This enzyme, called RNA synthetase (replicase), is usually formed just after the viral RNA enters the cell and attaches to

FIGURE 15–17   *An electron micrograph (by P. H. Hofschneider of Munich) of three double-helical replicative forms of the single-stranded RNA virus M12. Each molecule is approximately 1 μ in length. [Reproduced from P. H. Hofschneider, J. Mol. Biol., 10, 559 (1964), with permission.]*

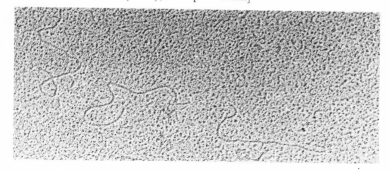

host ribosomes. Like both DNA polymerase and RNA polymerase, RNA synthetase catalyzes the formation of a complementary strand upon a single-stranded template. The fundamental mechanism for the copying of all nucleic acid base sequences is thus the same. Pairing of complementary bases is always used to achieve accurate replication of specific nucleotide sequences.

Soon after their formation, complementary RNA double helices (Figure 15–17) serve as templates for new strands, some of which become part of progeny particles, while others are used as templates for specific protein formation (Figure 15–18). Exactly how this happens depends on whether the mature virus

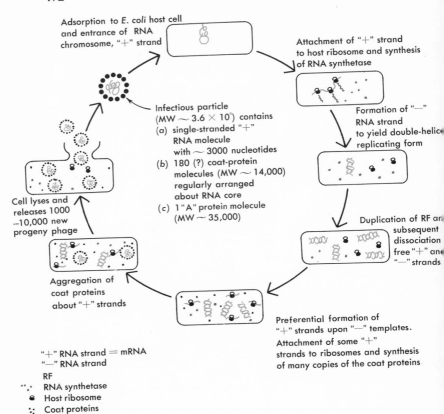

Adsorption to *E. coli* host cell and entrance of RNA chromosome, "+" strand

Attachment of "+" strand to host ribosome and synthesis of RNA synthetase

Formation of "—" RNA strand to yield double-helical replicating form

Infectious particle (MW ~ 3.6 × 10⁶) contains
(a) single-stranded "+" RNA molecule with ~ 3000 nucleotides
(b) 180 (?) coat-protein molecules (MW ~ 14,000) regularly arranged about RNA core
(c) 1 "A" protein molecule (MW ~ 35,000)

Duplication of RF and subsequent dissociation free "+" and "—" strands

Cell lyses and releases 1000 –10,000 new progeny phage

Aggregation of coat proteins about "+" strands

Preferential formation of "+" strands upon "—" templates. Attachment of some "+" strands to ribosomes and synthesis of many copies of the coat proteins

"+" RNA strand = mRNA
"—" RNA strand
RF
RNA synthetase
Host ribosome
Coat proteins

FIGURE 15–18   *The life cycle of a single-stranded RNA virus of the F2 (R17, M12, etc.) family.*

contains single-stranded or double-stranded RNA. In both cases, however, only one of the two complementary strands is used to make the protein template (i.e., mRNA) for a given gene. A close parallel thus exists between the formation of mRNA in both DNA and RNA viral systems.

During the reproduction of most single-stranded RNA viruses, the strand having the template function is the same strand found in the mature particles (i.e., "+"). This allows the infectious strand to code for the RNA synthetase molecules necessary to initiate viral RNA replication. Behaving quite differently, however, is the vesicular stomatitis virus, a single-stranded RNA virus. In this case, the template for its viral specific proteins is the "−" strand. This raised the question of the origin of the RNA synthetase molecules necessary to make the "−" strands upon the infecting "+" strands. Just recently their origin has been found to be the infecting virus particles themselves. Each vesicular stomatitis particle has packaged within it a synthetase molecule made in the previous cycle of viral infection.

RNA PHAGES ARE VERY, VERY SIMPLE

All the RNA phages (R17, F2, Qβ, etc.) so far characterized have a nucleic acid chain containing slightly over 3300 nucleotides. They are the simplest viruses known, being able to code for only about 1100 amino acids. The R17 and F2 protein coats are made of two types of polypeptide chains. One, the coat protein (CP), has a molecular weight of 14,700 and is present 180 times in each virus particle. Its sequence of 129 amino acids is now completely worked out. The other structural protein is the "A" (attachment) protein needed for adsorption of these phages to their host bacteria. One copy is found in each virus particle. It has a molecular weight of about 35,000 and is made from about 320 amino acids. Thus, approximately one-half of RNA phage genetic material is used to code for its structural proteins. A third viral specific protein is the RNA synthetase (replicase) involved in the self-replication of their RNA chains. Between 500 and 600 amino acids are found in the single synthetase polypeptide chain, leaving only 300 to 600 nucleotides whose coding role is not yet clear. Thus, if a fourth gene exists, it must be very small, coding only for a relatively short polypeptide chain.

The existence of three main gene products receives further direct support from genetic analysis. Use of mutagens produces nonsense mutations which fall into three complementation groups which have been assigned to the CP, "A," and synthetase (SYN) genes. Their gene order, however, cannot be obtained directly by genetic tricks, since no genetic recombination occurs during RNA phage replication. Recently, the order

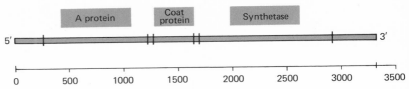

FIGURE 15–19   *The known genes of the phage R17 drawn to scale with their sizes and relative positions as established through recent nucleotide sequence analyses. The numbers refer to the actual nucleotide distance from the 5′ end of the RNA chain.*

INITIAL BINDING OF RIBOSOMES AT TWO INDEPENDENT SITES

($^{5'}$A-CP-SYN$^{3'}$) has been established through nucleotide sequence studies (Figure 15–19).

During R17 (Qβ) multiplication, ribosomes initially attach at two different sites— at the beginning of the "A" gene and at the beginning of the CP gene. They cannot initially attach to the synthetase gene since its binding site is not exposed because of secondary structure; it becomes accessible only when reading of the CP gene temporarily disrupts the inhibitory hydrogen-bonded hairpin loops. Functioning of the synthetase gene thus depends on prior ribosome attachment at the CP binding site (Figure 15–20). This restriction was first suggested by the existence of *polar nonsense mutations* in the CP gene which prevented functioning of the synthetase gene. In contrast, nonsense mutations in the synthetase gene never affected the CP gene. Further experiments showed that nonsense mutations in the "A" gene never had any effect on reading of either the CP or SYN genes. At first, this was interpreted to mean that the "A" protein lay at the distal (3′) end. Now, however, we realize that when more than one ribosome binding site exists, polarity experiments do not necessarily give clear conclusions about gene locations.

POLARITY GRADIENTS

Not all nonsense mutations are polar. In general, only those at the 5′ ends of a given gene are extreme polars, with a gradient

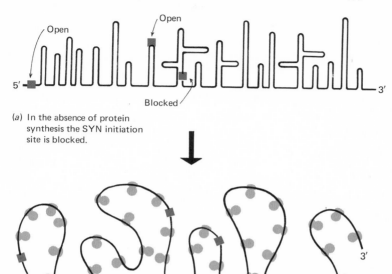

(a) In the absence of protein synthesis the SYN initiation site is blocked.

(b) The passage of ribosomes opens up the secondary structure thereby making the SYN gene available for translation.

FIGURE 15–20 *Schematic diagram showing how secondary structure affects the accessibility of ribosome binding sites.*

of polarity extending toward the 3' end. When a ribosome reads a chain-terminating codon, releasing an incomplete polypeptide chain, it generally detaches from its mRNA template. It or another ribosome will not have a high probability of working on a distal gene unless that gene's binding site is exposed. And the probability that it will be exposed depends on how much of its 5' neighboring gene has been read. Thus, nonsense mutations at the 3' end of a gene will in general not affect the reading of distal genes. By the time a ribosome reads such nonsense mutations, the hairpin loops encompassing the next ribosome binding site have been opened up.

UNEQUAL PRODUCTION OF THE THREE R17 PROTEINS

The RNA phage coat-protein molecules are made in much greater numbers than the other two viral specific proteins (approximately 10 CP : 1 A : 1 SYN). These differences arise in several ways. In the first place, ribosomes have a much, much lower affinity for the "A" binding site than for the CP binding site. Most likely, they also have lower affinities for the SYN site. But direct measurements are very difficult to interpret since the SYN site is normally blocked except when the CP

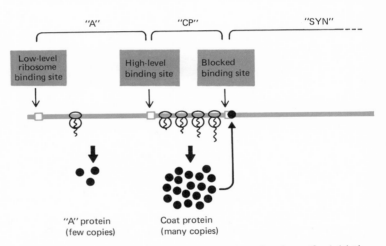

FIGURE 15–21   *Binding of a coat-protein molecule to the initiation site of the SYN gene.*

gene is being translated. As far as we can tell, not more than 10 per cent of the ribosomes which have moved across the CP gene move onto the SYN gene. Equally, if not more improtant as a control device, newly made CP subunits can specifically attach to the SYN binding sites and prevent further translation of the SYN gene (Figure 15–21) *in vivo*. This effect blocks further synthetase synthesis by 10 minutes following infection. Thus, CP subunits should be regarded as specific repressors working at the translational level.

Specifically stopping synthetase synthesis halfway through the life cycle makes obvious sense. For by this time enough enzyme has accumulated for viral RNA replication and the primary process needed in the last half of the life cycle is the production of the structural proteins of the virus.

TEST-TUBE SYNTHESIS OF BIOLOGICALLY ACTIVE Qβ RNA

Recently the test-tube synthesis of biologically active RNA phage chromosomes was achieved. Cells infected with the phage Qβ were the source of the enzyme RNA synthetase. Success depended on careful synthetase purification, freeing it from contaminating nucleases. This enzyme first uses the parental "+" strand to form a complementary "−" strand, thereby creating the double-helical intermediate (Figure 15–22). Now it appears that the double-helical intermediate, for

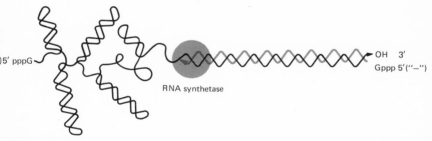

FIGURE 15–22 *Schematic view of the synthesis of a "−" strand upon a parental Qβ "+" strand.*

reasons not yet clear, is not stable and generally falls apart to free "+" and "−" strands. These, in turn, serve as templates to make more "+" and "−" strands. Both the "+" and "−" strands are made in the 5′ to 3′ direction, using ribonucleoside triphosphates as the precursors. Much larger numbers of the "+" strands are made than of the "−" strands. This hints that the RNA synthetase preferentially binds to the 3′ end of the Qβ "−" strand.

Test-tube "+" strands sediment at the same rate as *in vivo* chains and have equal infectivity when added to growing bacteria. Moreover, the frequency of mutants is similar to that found in nature. This means that the copying achieved *in vitro* is just as accurate as that occurring within cells.

ELUCIDATION OF THE COMPLETE NUCLEOTIDE SEQUENCES OF Qβ AND R17 MAY SOON OCCUR

For many years almost no one thought that the complete nucleotide sequence of a virus could be worked out. The nucleotide number seemed just too large to be tackled. But a variety of new methods for determining nucleotide sequences has radically changed everyone's attitude. Of great help is the fact that many of the nucleotide sequences so obtained can be checked by the amino acid sequences they predict. Conceivably, the complete sequence of both R17 and Qβ will be known two to three years from now. Already, the sequence of the first 150 Qβ nucleotides has been worked out as has the sequence of the first 80 R17 nucleotides; so there appears to be no real obstacle to total success which sustained work cannot overcome. One very important new experimental trick lets RNA synthetase act for variable times, thereby producing incomplete chains of increasing length. This allows easy ordering of many of the polynucleotide fragments produced by limited enzymatic digestion. Also very helpful in sequence analysis is the ability of the various ribonucleases to cut specifically the intact chain into smaller pieces of well-defined size. Frequently, the first cut creates a 40 per cent piece bearing the 5' terminal with a 60 per cent piece containing the original 3' end. In this way, it first became clear that the CP gene could not be the 5' terminal gene.

Already several important results have emerged (Figure 15–23) in addition to the gene order. First, we realize that translation need not start right at the 5' end, and that many terminal nucleotides have no coding function. The first possible Qβ AUG triplet is at position 60 but the following nucleotides do not code for the starting amino acids of the "A" protein. So its start most likely lies at a more distal AUG codon. Second, a chain-terminating codon is not found exactly

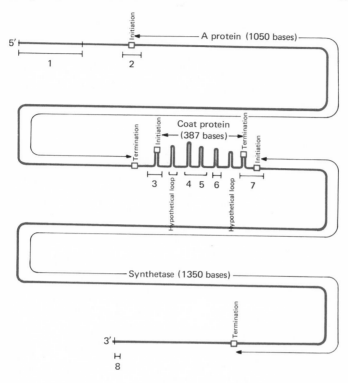

FIGURE 15-23 *The genetic map of R17 at the nucleotide level. (Continued on next page.)*

at the 3′ end, but must be separated from the end by a minimum of some 20 nucleotides. Now we guess that the nucleotides immediately adjacent to both 5′ and 3′ ends function specifically to recognize the viral specific RNA synthetase. Both ends must be coded for the synthetase binding step, since the same enzyme molecules replicate both the "+" and "−" strands. This means that the 3′ ends of both the "+" and "−" strands must look quite similar and hence the 5′ end of the "+" strand (on which the 3′ end of the "−" strand is made) has a sequence almost complementary to that found at its 3′ end.

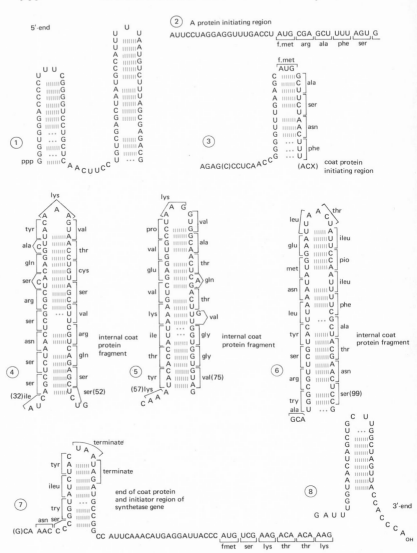

FIGURE 15–23 (Continued)

SATELLITE RNA CODES ONLY
FOR COAT-PROTEIN MOLECULES

Even smaller RNA-containing virus particles are found in tobacco cells infected with a tobacco necrosis virus. Their single-
stranded nucleic acid chains contain only about 1000 nucleotides, just enough to code for the protein component which
makes up their structural coat. These tiny particles (often
called "satellites") are never found alone but are made only
when susceptible cells are simultaneously infected with a different, larger (6000-nucleotide) RNA virus. This situation
suggests that the RNA of the very small virus is replicated
using viral specific enzymes (in particular, RNA synthetase)
coded for by the RNA of the larger particle. So, whether these
particles should be considered the smallest known viruses is a
somewhat arbitrary and perhaps not important question. Certainly relevant is the fact that their nucleic acid chains make
very favorable objects for future sequence studies.

THE SMALLEST KNOWN VIRUSES ARE ALMOST
AT THE LOWER LIMITS FOR A VIRUS

The need ordinarily to code for a viral specific RNA synthetase,
as well as their protein coats, effectively places a lower limit on
how small an RNA-containing virus can be. First, it would be
surprising if a synthetase molecule much smaller than 30,000
could carry out all the tasks involved in RNA self-replication.
Second, it is hard to imagine stable coat-protein subunits made
up of less than 50 to 75 amino acids. Thus the smallest complete RNA virus likely now to exist most probably contains at
least 1500 nucleotides (half the R17 number). The expectation of anything much smaller seems highly unrealistic.

Analogous reasoning for the lower size of a DNA virus is not
yet possible, since it is possible that a circular viral DNA molecule might be replicated using only host enzymes. If so, then
someday we might find a DNA virus whose only gene codes
for its coat protein. Conceivably, such a DNA chain might
contain as few as 300 to 500 base pairs.

Making intelligent guesses on the upper size for a virus is much more difficult. The largest viruses now known code for some 200 to 300 genes, but there seems to be no theoretical reason why a much larger number could not be coded for. Perhaps above a certain size, there is no substantial need for new genes to manipulate the host cell in favor of viral products.

Always very clear, however, is the absolute difference between a virus and a cell. As few as 10 years ago, however, much confusion existed. Then a key criterion for a virus was still its ability to pass through membrane filters which hold back bacteria. Under this definition, the very small disease-causing bodies known as *Rickettsiae* were generally treated as if they were viruses. But now they have been found to contain DNA and RNA, as well as a protein-synthesizing system, and so are realized to be very small bacteria. / The essence of viruses is thus the absence of protein-synthesizing systems. Hence their multiplication must always involve the breakdown of their surrounding protective coats, thereby letting their chromosomes come into contact with cellular enzymes. /

A LOWER SIZE LIMIT EXISTS FOR DIVIDING CELLS

Thus, a lower size limit exists for a cell even if it is growing in an external environment containing essentially all its required small molecules. It must be large enough to contain a functional semipermeable membrane, a protein-synthesizing apparatus, and sufficient genetic material to code for the various enzymes required to make its necessary proteins and nucleic acid components. In addition, its chromosomes must carry the information for the enzymes needed to make the small molecules that cannot be transported across the semipermeable cell membrane. For example, even though all the amino acids and purine and pyrimidine bases can be supplied to most cells as food, phosphorylated compounds such as ATP usually cannot be supplied. Their biosynthesis must normally take place in cells, and hence genes must exist for the enzymes needed to build them up from their smaller purine and pyrimidine building blocks. It is not yet possible to say exactly what the lower size limit for a cell is. The amount of DNA in *Rickettsiae* is still not accurately known, but a conservative guess is that one *Rickettsia* chromosome contains 15 to 20 per cent as much DNA as an *E. coli* chromosome. Its gene content is thus probably between 750 and 1000. There are reports of still smaller cells, but such statements must be viewed with disbelief because, if taken at face value, they imply that as few as 100 different proteins can maintain the living state.

SUMMARY

All known viruses contain a nucleic acid core (either DNA or RNA) surrounded by a protective shell that always contains protein and, in some of the more complicated particles, also lipids or carbohydrates (or both). The viral DNA may be either single-stranded or double-stranded. Likewise, both single- and double-stranded RNA viruses exist. The presence of nucleic acid is not surprising, since a genetic component must be present. What is surprising at first glance is that RNA is the genetic component of many viruses (e.g., tobacco mosaic virus and influenza). This means that viral RNA molecules serve as templates for their own formation.

After the viral nucleic acid enters a host cell, synthesis of both viral specific nucleic acid and the specific components found in the viral protective coat occurs. These components then specifically aggregate to form new infectious viruses identical with the infecting parental particle. The selective synthesis of virus components in a host cell is often aided by prior synthesis of viral specific enzymes involved in nucleic acid metabolism. For example, the duplication of single-stranded RNA needs the presence of RNA synthetase. This enzyme converts the infecting single-standed RNA molecule into a double-stranded molecule. It now appears likely that the basic rules involved in the duplication of RNA molecules are the same as the rules for DNA. In all cases, new polynucleotide strands are made by the formation of complementary copies using DNA-like base pairs.

The timing by which the specific proteins of DNA viruses appear at the right phase of their growth cycle is sometimes controlled by the order of their genes along their respective operons. Also of key importance is the use of viral specific σ factors to bring new operons into function at specific times. In general, repressor–operator systems are not important for the lytic phase of viral growth. In contrast, maintenance of the lysogenic state is directly controlled by specific repressors.

The simplest viruses now known are the RNA phages. Along their 3300-nucleotide-long chromosomes are three main genes—two coding for structural proteins, the other for RNA synthetase. The rates at which these genes function is controlled in part by the availability of their ribosome binding (initiation) sites. Also, an important control device is the specific binding of newly synthesized coat-protein molecules to the initiation site of the synthetase gene, thereby preventing functioning of the synthetase gene in the second half of the virus life cycle. New methods for nucleotide sequence analysis should soon allow the working out of the complete nucleotide sequence of several RNA phage chromosomes.

REFERENCES

Crick, F. H. C., and J. D. Watson, "Virus Structure: General Principles," *Ciba Found. Symp. Nature Viruses,* **1957,** 5–13. An early statement explaining the structural consequences of the limited nucleic acid content of viruses.

Fraenkel-Conrat, H., *Design and Function at the Threshold of Life: The Viruses,* Academic, New York, 1962. A paperback introduction to some simple ideas about TMV.

Klug, A., and D. L. D. Caspar, "The Structure of Small Viruses," *Advan. Virus Res.,* 7, 225 (1960). A beautiful exposition of the principles of virus construction, with special emphasis on TMV.

Stent, G. S., *Molecular Biology of Bacterial Viruses,* Freeman, San Francisco, 1963. Among other good features, it contains a very clear discussion of the role played by viral specific enzymes.

Luria, S. E., and J. E. Darnell, *General Virology,* 2nd ed. Wiley, New York, 1968. An intelligent treatment of all aspects of virus multiplication.

Fenner, F., *The Biology of Animal Viruses*, Academic, New York, 1968. A thorough two-volume treatment of animal viruses from a biological viewpoint.

Cohen, S. S., *Virus Induced Enzymes*, Columbia University Press, New York, 1968. A complete and individualistic summary of how viruses employ specific enzymes to direct cellular synthesis toward viral products.

Wood, W. B., and R. S. Edgar, "Building a Bacteria Virus." A beautifully illustrated *Scientific American* article reprinted in *Molecular Basis of Life*, R. H. Haynes and P. C. Hanawalt (eds.) Freeman, San Francisco, 1968.

Molecular Basis of Virology, H. Fraenkel-Conrat (ed.), Reinhold, New York, 1968. An excellent series of review articles on all forms of viruses stressing the molecular approach.

Roberts, J. W., "Termination Factor for RNA Synthesis," *Nature*, **224:** 1168 (1969). How the discovery of termination factor ρ simultaneously led to the idea of antitermination factors.

Travers, A. A., "Positive Control of Transcription by a Bacteriophage," *Nature*, **225:** 1009 (1970). Elegant experiments showing the involvement of a T4-specific σ factor in the synthesis of early T4 mRNA.

Schmidt, D. A., A. J. Mazaitis, T. Kasai, and E. K. F. Bautz, "Involvement of a Phage T4 σ Factor and an Antiterminator Protein in the Transcription of Early T4 Genes *in vivo*," *Nature*, **225:** 1012 (1970). The T4 life cycle imaginatively analyzed in terms of σ, ρ, and antitermination factors.

"Transcription of Genetic Material," *Cold Spring Harbor Symp. Quant. Biol.* **35** (1970). Virtually everything known by June, 1970, about the transcription of viral genes is found in this very comprehensive collection of papers.

16

EMBRYOLOGY AT THE MOLECULAR LEVEL

THE CAREFUL READER WILL HAVE NOticed that many statements in the preceding chapters were qualified; our understanding of how bacterial cells control the synthesis of specific proteins is less complete than our general knowledge about the mechanism of protein synthesis, and much less complete than our understanding of the structure of DNA. Although we can state unambiguously that the genetic information of cellular chromosomes resides in the nucleotide sequences of DNA molecules and are almost sure that all tRNA molecules are folded into a cloverleaf, we are not at all certain whether the majority of operons will follow the lactose example and be controlled by repressors or whether positive control systems will be the rule. These uncertainties, however, do not seriously annoy us. There is every reason to believe that within the next several years most of our speculations about bacterial control mechanisms will harden into facts.

We must not, however, be mesmerized by our past successes into asserting uncritically that our achievements at the molecular level with bacteria can automatically be extended to the cells of higher plants and animals; we must remember that bacteria and viruses were chosen because of their simplicity, that higher plants and animals are exceedingly complex objects, and that much wisdom must be exercised in deciding which of the genetic processes of higher organisms can be investigated profitably at the molecular level within the next ten to twenty years. In particular, we should ask if we have sufficient background at this time to attack embryology at the molecular level.

AMOUNT OF DNA PER CELL INCREASES ABOUT EIGHT HUNDREDFOLD FROM E. COLI TO MAMMALS

Before experts climb a high mountain, they carefully measure its height and try to anticipate how difficult the ascent will be. Likewise, it would be most useful to know how much more complex, genetically speaking, the mammalian cell is than the *E. coli* cell. One obvious approach is to determine how much DNA is present per mammalian cell; the answer (Table 16-1) is approximately 800 times that in *E. coli*. This number gives us an *upper limit* of the number of different genes, since there is no reason to believe that protein size (and hence, gene size) increases from the lower to the higher forms of life. Thus under the assumption that each gene is present in only one copy per haploid genome, a mammalian cell would be capable of synthesizing over two million different proteins. If so, the task of relating a given mutant character to a specific mutant protein will be much, much more formidable than the corresponding job with bacteria.

In some cases, however, the amount of DNA is certainly misleading; there are groups of amphibians that contain 25 times more DNA in their cells than is present in mammalian cells. Here there is no obvious reason to believe that greater biological complexity is involved; instead we suspect that many of these amphibian genes are present in very many identical copies. And if gene redundancy is a common feature of amphibian chromosomes, then many mammalian genes may also be present in highly duplicate form. In fact, as we shall show below, this is most certainly the case.

We must thus be very cautious about relating DNA content

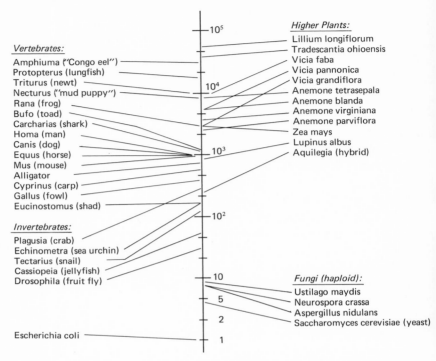

FIGURE 16–1 *Haploid amounts of DNA in various cells expressed as multiples of the amounts found in E. coli* $(4 \times 10^{12} \text{ mg} = 2.4 \times 10^9 \text{ MW})$. *Many of these values should be taken as approximate.* [*Redrawn from Holliday, Symp. Soc. Gen. Microbiol. 20:362 (1970).*]

directly to the number of different proteins that may be synthesized by a given cell. Nonetheless, mere morphological examination with the electron microscope tells us that a much larger variety of subcellular structures exists in the vertebrate cell than in *E. coli*. So we must expect a correspondingly larger number of structural proteins and enzymes to be necessary for their construction and function. It would be surprising if the vertebrate cell were not at least 20 to 50 times more complex genetically than *E. coli*.

CONCENTRATION ON ORGANISMS WITH EASILY OBSERVABLE CLEAVAGE DIVISIONS

The mechanisms by which fertilized eggs develop into multi-cellular organisms have been a continuous source of mystery to biologists for almost a hundred years. During this time, experimental studies have been concentrated on echinoderms (especially the sea urchin) and amphibians, in particular various frogs, salamanders, and toads. The reason for such polarization lay in the ease with which echinoderm and amphibian eggs could be procured, fertilized, and subsequently observed as they passed through their regular developmental stages. In contrast, birds and mammals—where all the embryological stages take place within the egg (female parent)—are much more tricky to work with. Only recently has real progress been made in opening up the early stages of mouse embryogenesis to experimental manipulation.

A very important feature of both urchin and frog embryology is that all the nutrients (mostly stored in the form of yolk) required for development through the blastula and gastrula stages (Figure 16–2) must be present in the unfertilized egg. Only when the developing embryo becomes able to feed itself, the frog, for example, at the tadpole stage, does real growth in mass occur. Consequently, echinoderm and amphibian eggs are very, very large in comparison with their respective adult cells, and the cell divisions that occur after fertilization progressively produce smaller and smaller cells. Hence the name "cleavage divisions." Early cleavage divisions occur in rapid succession, characterized by short interphase periods during which DNA synthesis occurs at a very accelerated rate: the amount of DNA in each of 1000 or more small daughter cell nuclei of a gastrula is the same as that in the nuclei of the newly fertilized egg.

THE HEART OF EMBRYOLOGY IS THE PROBLEM OF CELL DIFFERENTIATION

The cleavage divisions by themselves, of course, do not lead to embryological development. Its real essence instead is the

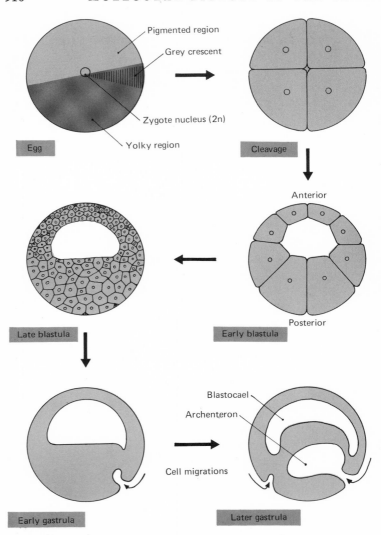

FIGURE 16-2 *Early stages in the development of an amphibian egg.*

process of cell differentiation. All higher plants and animals are constructed from a large variety of different cell types (e.g., nerve cells, muscle cells, thyroid cells, blood cells) which must arise in a regular way. In some organisms, specialization begins with the first few cell divisions after fertilization. In other organisms, a large number of divisions occur before any progeny cell is fixed in its fate. Irrespective of the exact time that differentiation occurs, however, it always results in the transformation of the parental cell into a large number of morphologically different progeny cell types.

Differentiation can be examined from three viewpoints. First, what are the external forces acting upon the original undifferentiated cell which might initiate a chain of events resulting in two progeny cells of different constitution? Sometimes the existence of asymmetrically acting external forces is easy to perceive. For example, gravity forces the yolk of a fertilized amphibian egg to the bottom. Thus, after the first few cell divisions, some of the progeny cells have more yolk than others.

The second way to analyze differentiation is to ask, What are the molecular differences between differentiated cells? Are they extreme, or do the morphological differences arise from the presence of only a few unique proteins in abnormally large numbers? Now all our evidence indicates the former conclusion: each type of differentiated cell contains many types of molecules peculiar to that cell type. Thus, a complete description of differentiation at the molecular level would necessarily be a most formidable task.

Third, we may ask whether the various changes which bring about differentiation are irreversible, and if so, how they are hereditarily perpetuated. The answering of these questions has always been a prime goal of most biologists. But until very recently, embryology has been largely studied as an isolated subject, apart from modern genetic or biochemical ideas. Now, however, it is clear that the morphological tools of the classical embryologist cannot give satisfying answers. Instead, as in genetics, the fundamental answer must lie at the molecular level. The parallel with modern genetics may, in fact, be very close, since embryologists now believe that many of the basic control mechanisms that fix a cell's potential chemical reactions act at the level of the gene. Thus, the recent methodological advances which have made aspects of biochemistry and genetics indistinguishable may soon encompass developmental biology.

But here we must point out a most disquieting fact: compared to higher organisms like *Drosophila* or the mouse, the genetics of sea urchins is virtually nonexistent, and that of frogs, salamanders, and toads is almost as bad.

DIFFERENTIATION IS OFTEN IRREVERSIBLE

At present, it is possible to isolate a large variety of differentiated cells and grow them (like bacteria) outside living organisms under well-defined nutrient conditions. This technique of "tissue culture" allows us to ask, for example, whether a nerve cell continues to look like a nerve cell when growing outside its normal cellular environment: the answer in this case is yes. Something has happened that has permanently destroyed this cell's capacity to synthesize proteins other than those found in nerve cells. Similar results come when many other cell types from higher animals are studied. But with higher plants, the opposite answer is more often found. A complete plant can often be regenerated, starting from either highly differentiated root or epidermal cells.

DIFFERENTIATION USUALLY IS NOT DUE TO CHROMOSOME GAIN OR LOSS

An obvious hypothesis to explain irreversible differentiation proposes that only a fraction of the genes of the fertilized egg are passed on to a nerve cell, and so on. This sort of scheme, however, appears to be completely wrong. As far as we can tell, all cells of most organisms, with the obvious exception of the haploid sex cells, contain roughly the same chromosomal complement. Virtually all cell divisions are preceded by a regular mitosis, so that daughter cells generally receive identical chromosome groups. We cannot say, however, that no permanent changes have occurred at the level of individual genes. The question remains whether it is possible to mutate specific genes selectively, thereby making them nonfunctional (or functional). Our problem is to devise methods that can test this possibility. Unfortunately, this task seems very difficult at present.

MULTICELLULAR ORGANISMS MUST HAVE DEVICES TO CONTROL WHEN GENES ACT

Irrespective of the molecular mechanism (i.e., whether a chemical change in the gene itself is involved), there is now very good evidence that, in multicellular organisms, as in bacteria, not all genes in a cell function at the same time. Something must dictate that a muscle cell, for example, selectively synthesize the various proteins used to construct muscle fibers, and so forth.

The understanding of embryology will thus, in one sense, be the understanding of how genes selectively function. Moreover, we must ask not only what causes two progeny cells to synthesize different proteins, but also what makes them *continue* to synthesize exclusively the same group of proteins. With the problem phrased in this way, it is clear that *no one* will ever be able to work out *all* the chemical details that accompany embryological development of any higher plant or animal. For even a modest approach to a comprehensive understanding, we would have to look at the behavior of hundreds of different proteins. Nonetheless, common sense tells us that, as in bacteria, there may exist some general principles governing the selective occurrence of specific proteins. For example, some differentiation might occur largely at the chromosome level by devices that control the amount of specific mRNA synthesis. In fact, there is now excellent evidence (see below) for differential rates of RNA synthesis along different regions of many chromosomes. Most important, regions which are active at one time often are inactive at another stage in development.

So now a growing number of embryologists are beginning to ask whether the fundamental control mechanisms act negatively, like the lactose repressor, or positively, like the specific viral sigma (σ) factors. The dilemma exists, however, that most of the characters which embryologists study are hopelessly complex from the chemical viewpoint (consider the eye); only a few can be related to the occurrence of well-defined chemical reactions. For example, although nerve cells are easy to identify on morphological grounds, almost nothing is known about their structure on the molecular level, and not one protein molecule in nervous tissue has been well characterized. Although our familiarity with several muscle proteins is more complete, our primitive knowledge of their detailed chemistry again is likely to make the analysis of precise gene–protein relationships a most tricky endeavor.

NECESSITY OF FINDING SIMPLE MODEL SYSTEMS FOR STUDYING DIFFERENTIATION

We must ask whether any of the embryologists' systems for studying differentiation are appropriate for a serious attack at the present time. To begin with, let us emphasize the fact that merely cataloging obvious protein and nucleic acid differences between the various differentiated cells is unlikely to yield any fundamental answer. We already know from classical morphology that there are differences. Instead, incisive answers are likely to come only from more meaningful questions. One of the most important goals is the identification of the external factors (embryonic inducers) which cause the directed transformations of many undifferentiated cells. For example, the differentiation of many nerve cells depends on an external factor received from nearby cells. A second important goal is to discover how the inducer changes the undifferentiated cell. In particular, we wish to understand the chain of events that relates inducers to the functioning of specific genes.

These problems are likely to be solved only when undifferentiated cells growing in tissue cultures can be specifically transformed by the addition of their embryonic inducers. Even though there exist many claims that *in vitro* differentiation has been obtained, careful examination of the experiments reveals that they are usually overinterpreted. For example, undifferentiated chicken cells can often be transformed into nerve cells by the addition of a distinct chemical compound. At first sight, this is a most spectacular result. Unfortunately, there is no single distinct compound that induces the differentiation of a nerve cell, but rather a large variety of seemingly unrelated molecules, all of which have the same result.   Under certain concentration conditions, even NaCl is an inducer. Most embryologists suspect that all currently known chemicals which induce *in vitro* act unspecifically and that the true specific embryonic inducers have not yet been observed.

BACTERIAL SPORULATION AS THE SIMPLEST OF ALL MODEL SYSTEMS

The colossal magnitude of the task of attempting to understand the molecular basis of a complex differentiation process (e.g., the origin of a nerve cell) has led many people to look for cell systems much, much simpler than those studied by the classical embryologist.   Some biochemists have gone so far as to focus their attention on the formation of bacterial spores. These are highly dehydrated cells which form inside certain bacteria (e.g., the genus *Bacillus*) as a response to a suboptimal environment.   As spores possess virtually no metabolic activity, they resemble seeds of higher plants.   Compared to vegetative bacteria, they are highly resistant to adverse treatments like extremes of heat or drying.   Thus, those bacteria which can produce spores have a much higher capacity to survive the extreme environmental conditions under which many forms of bacteria must live.

Some steps in the development of a spore are shown in Figures 16–3 and 16–4, which indicate that an early state involves an invagination of a portion of the bacterial membrane to enclose a chromosome and a small amount of cytoplasm. Afterward, a very thick and tough surface layer of protein is laid down on the outside.   It has a completely different composition from the surface of the corresponding vegetative forms. Parallel with these morphological transformations are important changes in enzyme composition.   The various cytochrome molecules responsible for aerobic metabolism completely disappear and a new electron transport system appears.   Ribosome content is also reduced, with an even greater decrease in the number of messenger RNA molecules. Small numbers of the enzymes necessary for protein synthesis remain—these are necessary for the resumption of new protein synthesis when the spore germinates under the stimulus of more favorable nutritional conditions.

Sporulation thus involves the stopping of the synthesis of virtually all the proteins necessary for vegetative existence; conversely, germination converts spores to a condition in which they

FIGURE 16–3   *Diagrammatic representation of the stages in sporulation. Key:—(1) Preseptation—cell with axial chromosome (2) Septation—plasma membrane infolds and cuts off an area containing intact chromosome (3) and (4) Stages of protoplast envelopment (5) Cortex formation—material laid down between two membranes (6) Coat formation and maturation— eventually the spore is released.*

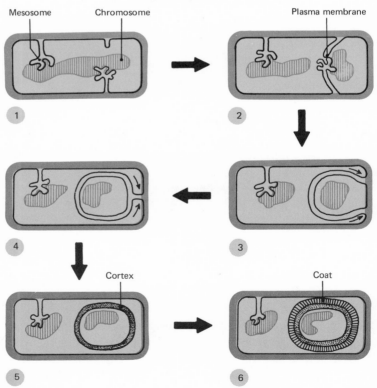

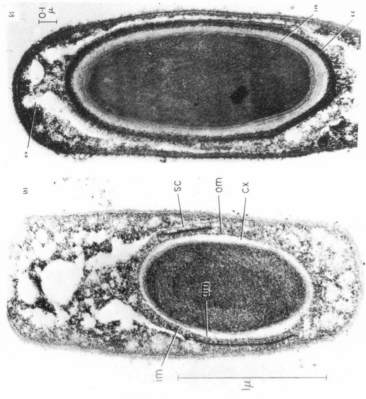

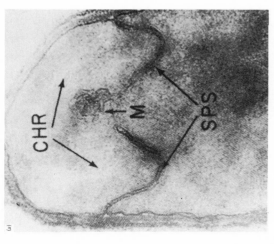

FIGURE 16–4 *Electron micrographs of thin sections of sporulating Bacillus cereus cells showing* (a) *septation,* (b) *cortex development, and* (c) *coat formation: chr, chromosome; m, mesosome; sps, transverse spore septum; cx, cortex; sc, spore coat; ex, exosporium; im and om, inner and outer membranes (courtesy of Dr. W. G. Morrell).*

can make the vegetative proteins. So the making of a spore must entail an inhibition of most, if not all, vegetative mRNA synthesis, replacing it with the synthesis of mRNA specific for spore specific proteins.

Until very recently the molecular basis of this changeover was a total mystery. Now very recent experiments tell us that sporulation is accompanied by the appearance of a new RNA polymerase σ factor which reads the genes necessary for sporulation. At the same time, there is a disappearance of one (or more?) vegetative σ's. Thus, the key control device which regulates the sequential development of phage proteins is also the crucial factor in sporulation. Of course, many, many questions remain unanswered (e.g., elucidation of the way the stimulation for sporulation (or germination) brings about a change in the σ pattern). But after years of real frustration, there is good reason for believing that the biochemistry behind the differentiation of a vegetative cell into a spore is now amenable to successful analysis.

THE DIFFERENCE BETWEEN EUCARYOTIC AND PROCARYOTIC CELLS

But a bacterium is not a higher cell, and so the question must be raised, Can any mircoorganism be a valid model system for studying differentiation of higher cells? In turn, this raises the question, Is there any essential difference between the cells of bacteria and higher plants and animals? The answer is clearly yes. Bacteria and their close relatives, the blue-green algae, have no nuclei. Collectively they are called *procaryotes*. In contrast, those organisms having nucleated cells are called *eucaryotes*. All procaryotes lack both nuclear membranes and membrane-bound organelles, such as mitochondria and chloroplasts. In addition, there are more subtle chemical differences; for example, some fatty acids are found only in eucaryote membranes—others, only in procaryote membranes.

Also very characteristic are the sizes of their respective ribosomes. Procaryotic ribosomes sediment at 70 S while eucaryotic ribosomes are always larger, sedimenting at about 80 S.

Correspondingly, the rRNA chain found in the larger ribosomal subunit is about 50 per cent longer in eucaryotes than in procaryotes. Why these various differences exist no one knows. The important point is that, at the structural level, a larger gap exists between the procaryotic and eucaryotic microorganisms (e.g., yeast, *Neurospora, Aspergillus*) than between the very extreme classes of eucaryotic cells.

THERE ARE NOW MANY REASONS TO INTENSIFY WORK ON ORGANISMS LIKE YEAST

The very concentrated effort which has gone into the study of all aspects of *E. coli* is one of the major reasons why molecular biology has advanced so rapidly over the past two decades. Clearly, similar attention will soon be placed on one or more types of eucaryotic cells. For many reasons it is natural that much emphasis must go toward the study of several types of human cells. But at the same time, it may be wise to concentrate equally on the molecular biology of one or two of the simplest eucaryotes. Several reasons dictate this approach. One is that these microorganisms most certainly contain much less DNA (Figure 16–1) than human cells. Only a five- to tenfold increase in genetic complexity is noticed in escalating to yeast or *Aspergillus* from *E. coli*. A second reason is economic: work with higher cells is at least an order of magnitude more expensive than with microorganisms. If a choice exists between solving the same problem with human tissue culture cells or with yeast or *Neurospora*, common sense tells us to stick with the simpler system. A third, and perhaps the most important reason, is the ease with which detailed genetic analysis can be applied to many microorganisms. Despite the great advantages now brought about by the cell-fusion technique (see below), detailed genetic analysis of human cells will be extraordinarily difficult to bring about.

Thus, even if our primary interest is the human cell, this may be the time for many more biologists to work with organisms like yeasts. They are very easy to grow as single cells, exist in either the haploid or diploid state, and are already very well studied genetically. Mutations are as easy to obtain as with *E. coli*, with the various genes of yeast cells being located on some 15 to 18 different chromosomes. The average length of DNA per yeast chromosome is much shorter than the single *E. coli* chromosome. Therefore, it should soon be possible to isolate yeast chromosomes, visualize them in the electron microscope, and hopefully learn what they look like at the molecular level.

Unfortunately, good techniques have not yet been developed for the isolation of intact yeast nuclei. Much of the difficulty lies in finding ways to easily break open the very tough yeast cell wall. But this obstacle will probably soon be overcome, allowing us to learn how eucaryotic ribosomes are assembled, in particular, whether mRNA passes to the cytoplasm as part of polyribosomes or whether mRNA chains attach to the smaller ribosomal subunits only after penetration through the nuclear membrane.

MITOCHONDRIA AS DEFECTIVE PROCARYOTIC SYMBIONTS

Eucaryotic microorganisms also offer excellent systems for studying mitochondria. Until several years ago, the mechanism of mitochondrial multiplication was very obscure. Then all mitochondria were found to contain circular DNA molecules, usually of MW $\sim 8 \times 10^6$, as well as ribosomes, tRNA, and the various enzymes needed to make proteins. Even more important for our ideas about mitochondrial biogenesis was the additional observation that the mitochondrial ribosomes sedimented at the 70-S value characteristic of procaryotic cells. This immediately suggested that some time early in evolution mitochondria evolved from parasitic bacteria capable of growth within much larger primitive eucaryotic cells. Why and how these bacteria evolved from parasites to become important cell organelles is not easily open to test. One obvious speculation is that they were so efficient in supplying ATP to their hosts that their obligatory presence was selected for.

A basically similar origin is now hypothesized for chloro-

plasts. Like mitochondria, they possess both DNA and procaryotic ribosomes, suggesting an origin from one of the several
bacterial groups capable of photosynthesis. Both types of organelles grow by increasing in length, followed by a fission
process similar to that of bacteria. But outside of cells, they
have never been made to grow and divide. This suggests that
some vital mitochondrial (chloroplast) proteins are coded by
nuclear DNA, with their synthesis occurring on cytoplasmic
80-S ribosomes, followed by movement to specific organelle
sites. Recent experiments confirm this conjecture.

Realization that cell organelles also possess functional genetic DNA has provided an explanation for many of the cases
of cytoplasmic (maternal) inheritance in plants, which for
several decades seemed to contradict the basic tenets of Mendelian genetics. Chloroplasts are present in large numbers in
virtually all cells, except for the male sex cells. Hence chloroplast genes are inherited only through the female parent.

REVERSIBLE STATES OF THE SLIME MOLD CELL

Clearly the most interesting microorganisms to the embryologist are those in which cell differentiation is an important aspect of the life cycle. Thus, much attention has recently been
given to a cellular slime mold, *Dictyostelium discoideum*, whose
life cycle is illustrated in Figure 16–5. The cycle begins with
spores germinating to yield ameboid cells called myxoamebae.
These irregular-shaped cells behave like small amebae, living
largely on bacteria and reproducing by fission. When their
food supply diminishes, they aggregate with each other to form
conical masses which eventually topple over on their sides.
These sluglike bodies then slowly move along the surface before coming to rest. Later, they form a fruiting structure made
of a basal disc, a stalk, and a mass of spores. All these components arise by the direct transformation (differentiation) of
ameboid cells into more specialized cells. The cell type to
which they change depends on the order in which they became
part of the initial aggregation. The first cells to come together
form the lower stalk, the next group changes into upper stalk

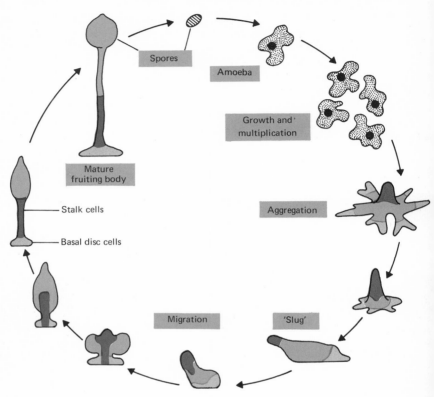

FIGURE 16–5 *The life cycle of the slime mold Dictyostelium discoideum.*

and spore cells, while the basal disc is formed from the last cells to come together. With time, all the disc and stalk cells die, leaving the spores capable of initiating a new life cycle when favorable nutritional conditions reappear.

Except for the final steps of spore formulation, all of the foregoing examples of differentiation are completely reversible. For example, when stalk cells are isolated from the fruiting body before cell disintegration begins, they may transform back to the ameboid phase and subsequently divide by fission. No one has any real clues about the molecular basis of the various differentiation processes. Most likely, serious work will soon start to see whether the RNA polymerase σ factors from the stalk, disc, and spore cells differ from those of their ameboid cell precursors.

GROWTH OF HIGHER ANIMAL CELLS IN TISSUE CULTURE

Until recently there was much mysticism about growing cells in tissue culture. Success apparently demanded very precise experimental conditions, and even worse, not everyone seemed to possess the necessary magic touch. Only special cell lines could be maintained and the suspicion existed that these cells

FIGURE 16–6   *Clones of the human tissue culture strain HeLa growing on the agar-covered surface of a petri dish (photo supplied by Dr. T. T. Puck, Univ. of Colorado Medical School).*

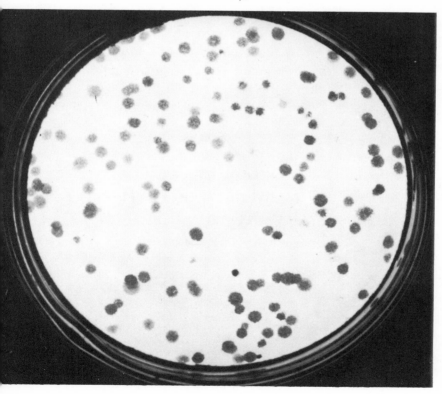

had lost many of the characteristic features of the various tissues from which they originally came. Over the last few years, however, the picture has radically changed. It is becoming easier and easier to grow a large variety of cells in well-characterized media in which the only undefined component is a serum protein fraction. Growth will generally occur both in liquid culture and on solid medium surfaces, and the single cell cloning techniques used with bacteria now also are a routine feature of modern tissue culture work (Figure 16–6).

But it is also clear that, in most cases, the cells growing in established lines have some real, if not important, differences from their *in vivo* cellular progenitors. One of the most common adaptations made to the tissue culture state is an increase in the chromosome number, often to a number almost twice that normally found. For example, cells from one of the best-known human cell lines, the HeLa strain, usually have some 70 to 80 chromosomes in comparison to the normal 46 count (Figure 16–7). Apparently, the possession of extra chromosomes (*aneuploidy*) somehow gives tissue culture cells a selective advantage over those with the normal diploid number. Most cells, when first placed in tissue culture, have the diploid number. During their initial period of slow growth, they occasionally give rise to mutant cells with extra chromosomes. These grow faster than their diploid companions and so eventually dominate the resulting cell line.

CLONING OF HIGHLY DIFFERENTIATED CELLS

Parallel with the tendency toward aneuploidy, some tissue culture cell lines seem much less differentiated than their *in vivo* precursors. They lack specialized functions present in their parental cells and often show many similarities to the undifferentiated embryonic cells present very early in development. They have also been compared with cancer cells, some types of which also seem to represent dedifferentiated states. This latter parallel becomes more plausible when we realize that continued cell growth in tissue culture may often have to be achieved by

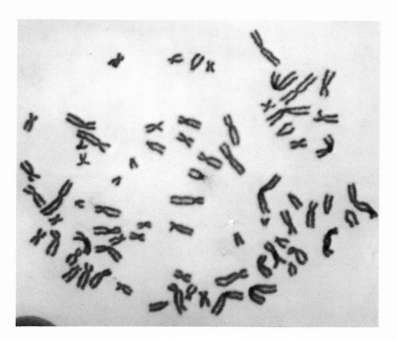

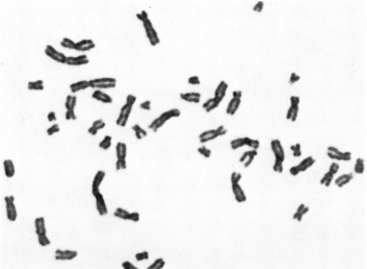

FIGURE 16–7 *The 73 chromosomes (top) of a HeLa cell contrasted with the normal 46 complement (bottom) of a cell from a normal human male (Courtesy of Dr. T. T. Puck, Univ. of Colorado, Denver).*

a loss of some of the devices which slow down, if not inhibit, the division of most of the cells in a multicellular organism. Isolation of some tissue culture strains may thus be dependent on selection of mutants less able to respond to signals telling them to stop multiplying.

But there are now also many cell lines which retain the ability to make specialized products; for example, cells which continue to synthesize collagen are very easy to obtain. Equally simple to maintain are cells which synthesize the key mucoproteins characteristic of cartilage tissue. And endocrine tumors (e.g., adrenal and pituitary) are the source of many cell lines which continue to synthesize their respective hormones. Moreover, there are reports of the synthesis of both the thyroid hormone and insulin in cell lines derived from normal tissues. There also have been great advances in the culture of the various cellular precursors of the white and red blood cells. Not only have many lymphoid cells been cloned, but there is now convincing evidence of specific antibody synthesis and, even more important, of the induction of an immunological response (see Chapter 17) in tissue culture.

DIVISION OF THE CELL CYCLE INTO M, G_1, S, AND G_2 PHASES

A most important tool for the analysis of the cell cycle is synchronization of growth so that virtually all cells are in the same phase of growth. Now most people divide cell cycles into the M (mitosis), G_1 (period prior to DNA synthesis), S (period of DNA synthesis), and G_2 (period between DNA synthesis and mitosis) phases (Figure 16–8). M is the shortest stage, usually lasting only an hour or so in a complete cycle of some 18 to 24 hours (the minimum time usually observed for the reproduction of mammalian cells in culture). The length of the other phases varies considerably from one cell type to another with G_1 and S often of about equal 8- to 10-hour durations. But in other strains, G_1 lasts only 1 to 2 hours.

One of the best methods for synchronization uses the fact

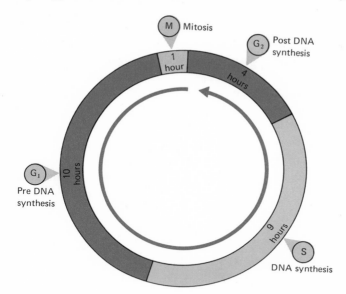

FIGURE 16–8 *Phases in the life cycle of a mouse hepatoma cell growing in tissue culture and dividing once every 24 hours.*

that M-phase cells attach much less firmly to glass surfaces than do interphase cells. This trick allows the isolation of large numbers of cells in the various phases of growth and the measurement of the rate at which different important compounds are made. In HeLa cells, RNA and protein synthesis occur throughout interphase (G_1, S, G_2), but both show abrupt decreases, if not actual stoppage, during the mitotic phase when the chromosomes contract and line up along the spindle fibers. While the cessation of RNA synthesis may be a consequence of shape changes in DNA concomitant with metaphase chromosome contraction, why protein synthesis declines is not at all clear. Perhaps the supply of mRNA rapidly decreases when RNA synthesis stops; but if this is the case, then the lifetime of mRNA in higher animals must be shorter than the 3 to 4-hour period commonly suggested. In any case, virtually no polyribosomes are seen by electron-microscopic examination of animal cells in metaphase.

TRANSCRIPTION AS A MEASURE
OF BIOLOGICAL TIME

That tissue culture cells tend to divide at constant intervals suggests that eucaryotes as well as procaryotes have accurate clock mechanisms at the cellular level. Earlier we saw that bacterial viruses can use the distance between genes for timing, a consequence of the relatively slow rate at which RNA polymerase molecules move along DNA templates (DNA replication occurs some 100 times faster!). At 37° C the rate of movement of *E. coli* RNA polymerase is only 30 to 40 nucleotides per second, and so a complete transcription of a λ molecule would require over 25 minutes. Because of the simultaneous transcription of several operons, this much time is not required for a single cycle of replication. Nevertheless, transcription of the very long "late" λ operon by itself counts out some 15 minutes.

Similar analysis applied to the *E. coli* chromosomes gives a total possible transcription time of 33 hours. Thus only 1 per cent of its total genome would have to be used to separate periodic events occurring once every 20-minute division cycle. And even the 3 to 4 hours required for a spore to germinate could easily be directly measured out on a DNA tape. There is, of course, no reason why such relatively long intervals need be coded along one contiguous DNA section. Several operons, each coding for a specific σ factor necessary for the reading of the subsequently transcribed operon, would also do the job (Figure 16–9).

Most likely all such biological clocks will also depend on the regular appearance of anti-σ factors, that is, gene products that specifically prevent certain σ factors from functioning. Such factors provide the most direct way of curtailing the synthesis of specific proteins to restricted periods in a life cycle. That they exist is already known from the life cycle of the phage T4 (see page 484) where at least one viral gene codes for a product that inhibits the functioning of an *E. coli* σ factor. The obviously much more complicated bacterial life cycles must involve

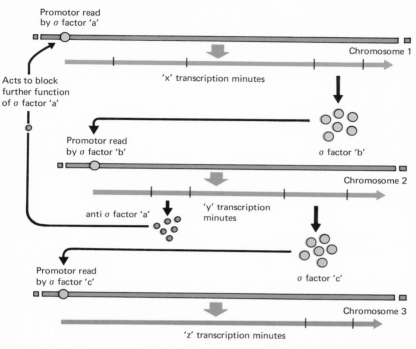

FIGURE 16-9   *A mechanism by which sequential synthesis of different σ factors might be used to count time.*

a number of different anti-σ's, each working at a different time to block specifically the functioning of certain genes.

Though the division cycles of higher cells are much longer, their DNA contents are correspondingly much greater; one polymerase molecule would require some 1000 days at 37° to completely transcribe the haploid complement of human genes. So, much of the timing required for a 24-hour human cell cycle is easily imagined to be at the transcription level, as may be the timing for many of the crucial steps in the embryological development of all higher organisms.

THE EUCARYOTIC CHROMOSOME

Fundamental knowledge about the structure of the chromosomes of higher plants and animals is very meager.   Still very confusing is the relation of individual DNA molecules to the chromosomes visible in microscopes. With viruses and bacteria, the answer is very clear: The chromosome is a pure DNA molecule, usually of circular form. But no one knows either how many DNA molecules are found within a single eucaryotic chromosome or how, at the molecular level, they relate to centromeres (themselves a total puzzle at the molecular level).

Most of this uncertainty comes from the highly irregular configuration of chromosomes as they are found in most cells. Generally they are visible in the light microscope only when they contract during mitosis and meiosis. But the resulting compacted masses are virtually impossible to decipher with the electron microscope. In contrast, when they are highly extended during interphase, their configurations often are so irregular that it has usually proved impossible to follow them for even short fractions of their total length. Moreover, while these electron-microscope studies frequently reveal long thin fibers, they often have diameters severalfold larger (50 A to 75 A) than that of single DNA fibers.

The favorite chromosomes, so far available, for structural analysis are found in vertebrate oocytes just before the first meiotic division. At this stage (which can last hundreds of days!) oocytes synthesize most of the mRNA which functions after fertilization during the early stages of development. To accomplish this synthesis, oocyte chromosomes are in a state of only partial contraction, with most of their DNA contracted into tight masses (chromomeres) but with a small fraction in a highly extended functional state. This functional DNA extends as very long lateral loops from the main chromosomal axis (Figures 16–10 and 16–11). Hence the name "lampbrush chromosomes."

Our best guess now is that at any point along a given chromosome there is only one DNA molecule. This conclusion certainly holds for the looped-out regions where single DNA molecules can directly be seen in the electron microscope. Still unproven is the theory that a single DNA molecule runs from

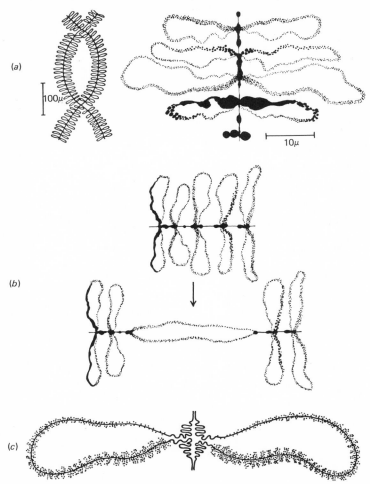

FIGURE 16–10   *Diagrammatic view of lampbrush chromosomes. (a) The two homologous meiotic chromosomes (left) are joined together by two chiasmata. A portion of the central chromosome axis (right) shows that two loops with identical morphology emerge at a given point, evidence that each chromosome has already split into two chromatids. (b) Accidental stretching of a chromosome reveals the continuity of the loop axis with the central axis (compare with Figure 16–11). (c) A single loop pair showing the single DNA molecules upon which RNA chains are being made. [From J. Gall, Brookhaven Symp. in Biol., 8:17 (1955)].*

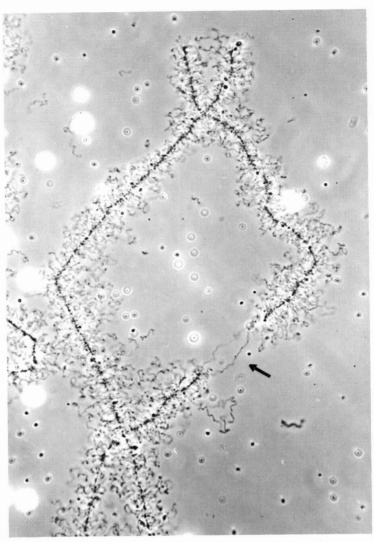

FIGURE 16-11 A partial view of a pair of highly extended lamp-brush chromosomes from an oocyte of the newt *Triturus viridescens*. Two chiasmata are seen in this photograph, taken in the diplotene phase of meiosis. The arrow points to a section where the double-stranded character of each premeiotic chromosome is revealed. (Courtesy of J. Gall, Yale University.)

one loop to another through the intervening axial chromo-mere(s). Hopefully this question will fall out from further electron-microscope work.

Clearly distinguishing procaryotic from eucaryotic chromosomes is the apparent total absence of histones (small basic proteins) from procaryotic chromosomes. In contrast, usually at least half the mass of eucaryotic chromosomes is histone. Initially, the suspicion existed that there were very many different histones, perhaps one type for every different gene. This led to proposals equating histones with the specific repressors of bacteria. Now it is clear, however, that only a few types of histones exist within a given organism. Moreover, the amino acid sequence of one specific mammalian histone is identical to that of a histone found in higher plants. Thus, no possibility exists that histones specifically combine with even large groups of related genes.

REPLICATION OF DNA STARTS AT A NUMBER OF DIFFERENT SITES ALONG A GIVEN CHROMOSOME

There are now several lines of evidence which indicate that DNA replication is initiated at a number of different sites along a given chromosome. In mammalian chromosomes there are hints that on the average there is one starting point every 100 μ along a given chromosome. Most interestingly, direct auto-radiographic evidence indicates that growth proceeds in both directions from a single initiation site (Figure 16–12). That is, the fundamental replication mechanism in eucaryotes strongly resembles that of E. coli and its viruses where synthesis also proceeds in both directions. Crucial to further understanding is whether more than one starting site exists along a single DNA molecule.

ACTIVE (EUCHROMATIN) VERSUS INACTIVE (HETEROCHROMATIN) CHROMOSOMAL REGIONS

Some of the best evidence for the selective functioning of different regions along chromosomes comes from the study of the

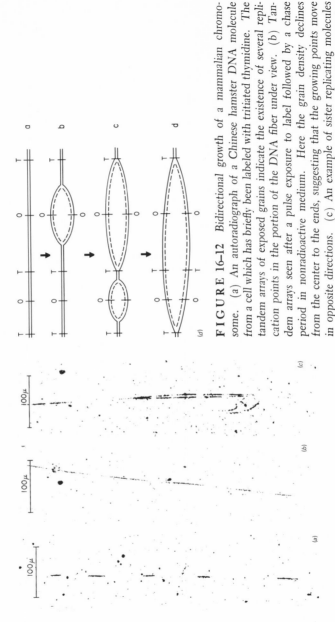

FIGURE 16-12 Bidirectional growth of a mammalian chromosome. (a) An autoradiograph of a Chinese hamster DNA molecule from a cell which has briefly been labeled with tritiated thymidine. The tandem arrays of exposed grains indicate the existence of several replication points in the portion of the DNA fiber under view. (b) Tandem arrays seen after a pulse exposure to label followed by a chase period in nonradioactive medium. Here the grain density declines from the center to the ends, suggesting that the growing points move in opposite directions. (c) An example of sister replicating molecules held together by a replicating fork. (d) A schematic model interpreting pictures (a) through (c). [The photographs in (a), (b), and (c) are courtesy of J. Huberman and originally appeared in Huberman and Riggs, J. Mol. Biol. **32**, 327 (1968).]

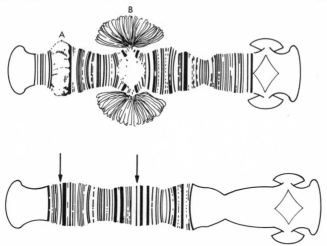

FIGURE 16–13 A diagrammatic view of part of a giant insect chromosome (from the salivary gland of Chironomus) at two different stages in development. The two puffs (A and B) observed in stage one are not visible at a later stage. The origin of the puffs A and B can be traced to single bands in the unexpanded phase. [Redrawn from W. Beermann, Chromosoma, 5 (2); Table 1 (1952), with permission.]

giant chromosomes of the flies *Drosophila* and *Chironomus*. These chromosomes are easy to observe even in interphase because each consists of a collection of about 1000 identical chromosomes neatly stuck sidewise to each other in lateral register (a *polytene chromosome*). Where the genes are closely stuck to each other to form well-defined bands, they are in a nonfunctional state, since autoradiographic experiments using radioactive precursors of RNA suggest that very little RNA is synthesized in these regular regions. Band sizes vary tremendously: some are so thin that they are hardly visible, whereas others occupy several per cent of the length of a given chromosome. In contrast, there are other regions along these chromosomes at which a much more disorganized arrangement of the individual chromosomes occurs (Figure 16–13). The more striking of these regions, which are called "puffs," are sites of intense RNA synthesis (Figure 16–14), and so are clearly very active genes. Most important, the locations of puffs do not remain constant during embryological development. Instead, some genes appear to function only at specific stages of development.

The term *euchromatin* is frequently employed to designate

FIGURE 16–14   *An autoradiograph (courtesy of W. Beermann) of a giant chromosome from an insect injected with radioactive uridine. Most of the RNA synthesis, as demonstrated by incorporation of radioactive uridine, occurs at the puffs. (a) Chromosome 4 from the salivary gland of Chironomus tentans with three large puffs. (b) Autoradiograph of the same chromosome with the same three puffs after a half-hour pulse of tritiated uridine.*

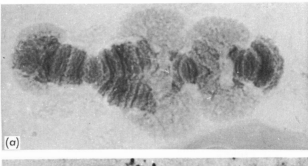

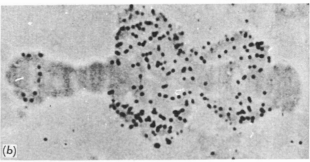

the functional diffuse regions, while the large masses of compacted DNA, some of which even remain visible during interphase, are called *heterochromatin*. There are many instances when a gene loses activity because of a chromosomal rearrangement which inserts it into a heterochromatic region. This suggests that control devices exist which can turn on or off the functioning of a very long section of a given chromo-some. This point, first demonstrated for *Drosophila*, holds equally well for mammalian systems. The most striking findings concern the sex chromosomes. Recently, the unexpected dis-covery was made that in female mammals the two homologous x chromosomes look quite different. One always appears highly condensed (hinting that it does not function), whereas the other is extended. This suggestion is confirmed by biochemical analysis, which shows that in the x chromosomes of a given cell only one gene from each pair is active. Surprisingly, the inert chromosome varies from one cell to another; so female tissue is in reality a mosaic containing mixtures of two different cell types. Though the molecular basis for this bizarre condition is still unknown (it appears to be restricted to the x chromo-some), it is quite important in showing that there are devices that can specifically block the functioning of an entire chromo-some.

While the other mammalian chromosomes do not show all-or-none effects, they also can have extended sections of hetero-chromatin whose extent again depends upon when in the life cycle they are examined. Most important, many regions com-pletely heterochromatic in later life appear as euchromatin early in development. Thus they most likely contain genes pro-grammed to function in one of the early embryological stages.

Initially, it seemed likely that the nonfunctional heterochro-matic regions might contain more histones, thereby being less accessible for RNA polymerase binding. But the limited meas-urements so far made reveal almost equal histone binding to both heterochromatin and euchromatin, thereby leaving wide open the real function of histone in higher cells.

EVEN THE SMALLEST BANDS (LOOPS) MUST CONTAIN MANY, MANY GENES

When they were first seen in the early 1930s, the bands along the salivary chromosomes were thought to be the individual genes, with the number of genes equal to the number of bands. But this type of analysis gives *Drosophila* only some 5000 genes, a number just slightly larger than that postulated for *E. coli*.

Clearly it must be an underestimate, since we now realize that the interband regions are likely to contain many, many genes.

Even more to the point, recent measurements of the amounts of DNA within even the smallest bands reveal that each of the single chromosome fibers which make up the polytene chromosome contains sufficient DNA to make up hundreds of normal-sized genes. This could mean that each band represents an operon comprising a large number of genes with related functions and whose genes products appear coordinately. Alternatively, bands could contain many identical copies of a single gene or gene cluster (operon) tandemly arranged. Favoring this latter explanation is the fact that the DNA contents of homologous bands in closely related species can show great variation in size, suggesting that the larger bands arise by duplication of originally smaller bands.

The same uncertainties exist about the DNA making up the loops of lampbrush chromosomes. Minimum estimates of the DNA lengths found in the loops give lengths (10 μ to 100 μ) much, much longer than that needed ($< 1 \mu$) to code for average-sized proteins. Now we have no way of knowing whether each loop represents a long operon or whether it is made up of many identical copies of the same gene. All that is now clear is that single RNA products are very, very long, representing the transcription of the entire loop (Figure 16–15). One end of a loop thus always looks much thicker than the other, with the thicker end containing the very long, almost completed RNA products.

In theory, it is possible to directly measure the extent of redundancy for those genes whose corresponding mRNA molecules can be isolated. Most likely, pure hemoglobin and pure immunoglobulin (antibody) mRNAs will soon become available. They are the predominant mRNA species within their respective cells. Then a direct titration can be made of the number of hemoglobin (immunoglobulin) genes capable of forming specific DNA–RNA hybrid molecules. Clearly, these hybridization experiments should be done with DNA from those cells actively synthesizing hemoglobin (immunoglobulin), as well as with DNA from cells which normally do not make

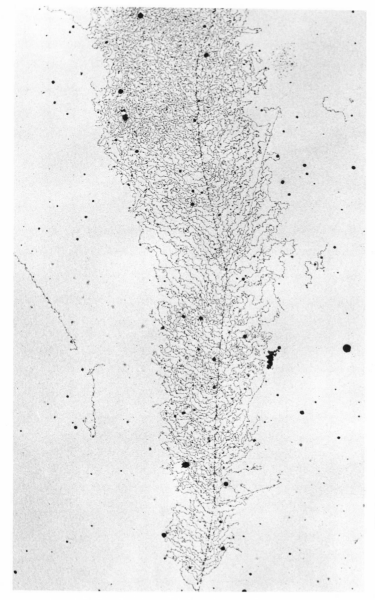

FIGURE 16-15 A section along a loop of a *Triturus* lampbrush chromosome showing a gradient of increasingly long RNA chains attached to their DNA template. The black dots at the sites where the RNA chains attach are RNA polymerase molecules. (Courtesy of O. L. Miller and Barbara Beatty, Oak Ridge National Laboratory.)

any hemoglobin (immunoglobulin). The results, using DNA from nonhemoglobin- (nonimmunoglobulin-) producing cells, will give the most straightforward answer. A positive answer of redundancy will strongly imply redundancy of chromosomally located genes. But, if many identical copies are found only in the corresponding differentiated cells, the explanation may be selective multiplication of a single chromosome gene to give rise to a large number of extrachromosomal DNA fragments.

HIGHLY REPETITIVE DNA SEQUENCES

A more general way of looking for repetitive DNA sequences measures the rate at which separated single strands hybridize with their complements to form double helices. This technique easily allows genes present in only a few copies per genome to be distinguished from those present in very great numbers. Most unexpectedly, it reveals that certain sequences are present 10,000 to 100,000 times in a single genome. What these repeated sequences code for is most unclear, for in certain cases the fundamental sequence, which repeats over and over, is less than 300 nucleotides in length. In some species these repeating sequences have base compositions unlike that of most DNA and so are easily separated by centrifugation in a CsCl gradient. When this happens, this DNA is referred to as *satellite* DNA. Often a satellite present in one species appears completely absent in a closely related species. Most likely, this difference is not meaningful, merely signifying that the base composition of the repetitive material does not greatly differ from the majority of cellular DNA.

Just recently, new experiments have shown that some repetitive sequences are preferentially located within heterochromatic regions, usually in close proximity to the centromeres. Whether this means that all such DNA sequences only infrequently, if ever, code for specific amino acid sequences is an unresolved question. More experiments must be done before this point becomes clear.

In addition to sequences present in very large number, there is also evidence in many organisms for some sequences (genes) present between 100 to 1000 times per genome. Conceivably all the copies of one type are situated next to each other on loops or puffs and function at the same time.

VARIATION IN DNA AMOUNTS BETWEEN CLOSELY RELATED SPECIES

After the coding significance of DNA became understood, the expectation existed that as we go from the simple to more complicated organisms, the amount of DNA per haploid genome would increase in proportion to the increase in true biochemical complexity. But this is not always the case. While higher plants and animals have much more DNA than the lower forms (Figure 16–1), no one anticipated the finding that certain fish and amphibia would have 25 times more DNA than any mammalian species. And as more and more plants were examined, closely related species were sometimes found to vary in their DNA contents by a factor of five to ten.

These variations usually do not arise by increases in chromosome number, but instead by increases in the amount of DNA per chromosome. How this happens is not known, though there are hints that much of the increase occurs by increasing the sizes of the tandemly arranged functional gene families, not by disproportionately increasing the amounts of the heterochromatic satellite sequences. Forms like salamanders of the genus *Necturus*, whose nucleic acid content is one of the largest among amphibia, have correspondingly some of the longest lampbrush loops.

THE NUCLEOLAR LOCATION OF rRNA SYNTHESIS

One gene which unambiguous evidence indicates to be present in tandem duplicate form is that coding for rRNA. In all eucaryotes examined, at least 100 to 1000 copies are present on

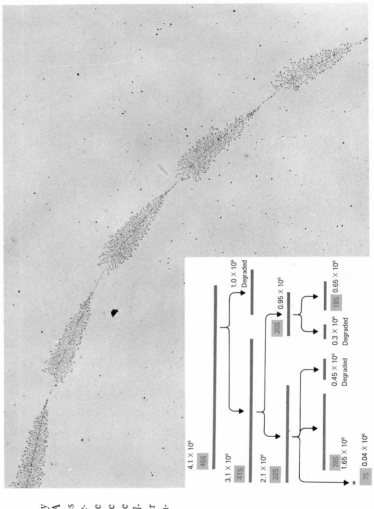

FIGURE 16–16 *A tandemly arranged series of nucleolar rRNA genes from Triturus viridescens showing growing 45-S rRNA precursor chains. The insert at the lower left shows the steps in the transformation of the 45-S molecule into mature mammalian rRNA molecules. (Courtesy of O. L. Miller and Barbara Beatty, Oak Ridge National Laboratory.)*

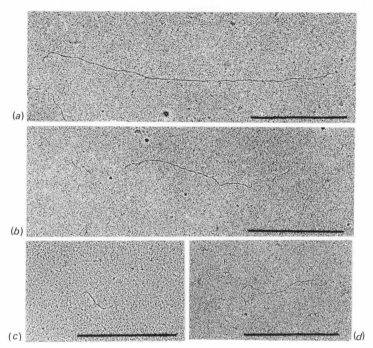

(a)

(b)

(c)   (d)

FIGURE 16–17   *Electron micrographs of HeLa cell rRNA precursors and the mature rRNA molecules which are derived from them: (a) = 45 S, (b) = 32 S, (c) = 18 S, and (d) = 28 S. The line marks off 1 μ. (Courtesy of N. Granboulan and K. Scherrer, Swiss Institute for Cancer Research, Lausanne, Switzerland.)*

one or more chromosomes. This DNA is usually looped off the main chromosomal fiber mass as highly extended threads which seem to coalesce with specific proteins to form the nucleoli. Some organisms have only one nucleolus per haploid complement, while others have several. In every case, however, the nucleoli are attached to highly specific chromosomal sites. Within each nucleolus the multiple rRNA genes are tandemly linked together (Figure 16–16), each gene having a molecular weight of some 8×10^8. They are transcribed separately, the rRNA product sedimenting at 45 S and having a molecular weight of about 4×10^6.

These 45-S molecules are precursors for the 28-S and 18-S rRNA chains found in all eucaryotic ribosomes (Figure 16–17). After being released from its DNA template, the 45-S molecule is broken down in several stages (Figure 16–16) to yield rRNA of the size usually present in ribosomes. Surprisingly, it is found that almost half of the initial 45-S precursor does not end up as rRNA. The discarded portions are thought to be degraded to the nucleotide level by intracellular nucleases.

Within the nucleoli, the 28-S chains combine with newly made ribosomal proteins to form the larger (60-S) ribosomal subunit. Synthesis of the ribosomal proteins does not take place in the nucleoli nor, for that matter, anywhere in the nucleus. They are made instead on cytoplasmic polyribosomes, afterward somehow migrating into the nucleoli. In contrast, the smaller (40-S) eucaryotic ribosomal subunits are apparently not assembled in the nucleoli. Whether they form in other parts of the nucleus or in the cytoplasm remains to be worked out. Similarly unclear is the form in which mRNA reaches the cytoplasm (as free mRNA, or attached to 40-S subunits, or as part of polyribosomes, or conceivably bound to still undiscovered proteins whose primary function is the mRNA transport from the nucleus to the cytoplasm).

THE VERY LARGE FORMS OF MUCH NEWLY MADE RNA IN HIGHER CELLS

Very large RNA molecules like those transcribed along the lampbrush loops also are made in many other, if not all, higher plant and animal cells. Conceivably they are the sole form in which mRNA is made. Though smaller ($< 10^6$ MW) molecules also appear in the nucleus, many if not all may arise from the breakdown of larger precursors. Even when cytoplasmic mRNA within a given cell is quite small (for example, the 9-S mRNAs for the 17,000-MW hemoglobin chains), it seems likely that they are first made as part of very, very long chains (Figure 16–18).

It is very tempting to consider the possibility that the cor-

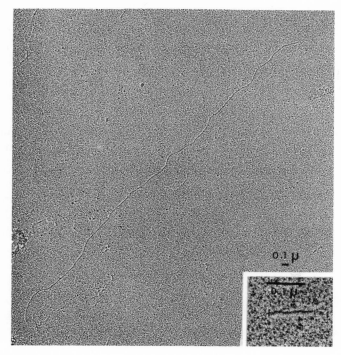

FIGURE 16–18   *A very long RNA molecule isolated from the nucleus of a duck erythroblast.   In the insert is a smaller (9-S) molecule isolated from a duck reticulocyte polyribosome and which is presumed to be a messenger for a hemoglobin chain.   (Courtesy of N. Granboulan and K. Scherrer.)*

responding DNA templates of these very, very long mRNA precursors are tandemly linked gene duplicates.   If so, the very long mRNA precursors may be the direct products of these duplicate genes with their final maturation process entailing nuclease-induced cuts between the individual messengers.

MOST RNA NEVER LEAVES THE NUCLEUS

Much mystery surrounds the fact that most of the RNA initially present in very large molecules never leaves the nucleus to become part of polyribosomes.   One possible explanation is that

the functioning of these molecules is under translational control (see below). Only in the presence of specific inducer-like
molecules might they be able to combine with ribosomes; otherwise they may be totally degraded by nucleases. Alternatively,
a large fraction of the nucleotide sequences on each very large
precursor may have no coding function. Instead they may
serve only as spacers. That spacer DNA can exist is clear from
electron micrographs like those of Figure 16–16. They show
that the duplicate genes coding for rRNA are usually separated
by 5000 or more base pairs (a distance two-thirds of the length
of the rRNA gene itself!). What the selective advantage is
for the spacer nucleotides between the successive rRNA genes
is not at all clear.

We suspect, however, that spacer DNA between other genes
sometimes might be used to count time. For example, inserting some 200,000 base pairs (65 μ) of spacer DNA between
two genes separates the time when they begin to function by at
least 100 minutes. But whether most of the RNA which fails
to reach the cytoplasm in fact has a timing function is a completely open question.

POLYRIBOSOME LIFETIMES IN RAPIDLY DIVIDING CELLS

Compared to what we know about bacterial messengers, our
knowledge of the lifetimes of functioning mRNA in higher
cells is very limited. It seems clear that many have a limited
lifetime, and estimates of 3 hours are frequently given for
mRNA in rapidly growing HeLa cells which are dividing about
once a day. If these figures are correct, then their relative lifetimes are not dissimilar to those of many bacterial mRNA
molecules which turn over some 10 times during a cell cycle.

STABLE mRNA MOLECULES EXIST IN NONDIVIDING DIFFERENTIATED CELLS

In contrast, it has begun to appear more and more likely that
much of the mRNA of the highly differentiated cells of higher
animals is metabolically stable. Immature reticulocytes (red

blood cells) provide a good example. These cells produce virtually no RNA while they are synthesizing their principal protein, hemoglobin. If their mRNA molecules were rapidly made and broken down, it would be possible to detect incorporation of RNA precursors into RNA; none is detected. This stability has an obvious advantage, particularly since the very constant environment of red blood cells, as contrasted with the highly fluctuating growth conditions of bacteria, makes great flexibility unnecessary. Red blood cells are designed to synthesize largely (> 90 per cent) hemoglobin. There is no reason to break down hemoglobin mRNA chains only to resynthesize them. Similarly, most of the mRNA found in the cytoplasm of the adult liver makes plasma protein to be released into the circulatory system. Correspondingly, much cytoplasmic mRNA in liver cells is relatively stable. There is, however, a slow turnover in which not only mRNA, but also the ribosomes themselves seem to be broken down. Recent measurements of the lifetime of ribosomes give a value of about 100 hours, much shorter than the average cellular lifetime of some 100 days. Why and how these processes occur is as yet totally unexplored. Particularly puzzling is the rRNA breakdown. While it can happen in bacteria, it does so only under unfavorable nutritional conditions. Yet in the liver, as far as known, rRNA breakdown occurs in perfectly "normal" cells.

SELECTIVE MULTIPLICATION OF THE rRNA GENES WITHIN OOCYTES

The number of rRNA genes within vertebrate oocytes is about a hundred to a thousandfold greater than within other vertebrate cells. But this extra DNA does not result from an increase in chromosome number, which remains 4N, characteristic of oocytes prior to the first meiotic division. Instead, almost all the increase is due to large numbers of extrachromosomal nucleoli. Each contains a single circular DNA molecule with lengths varying from 20 to 1000 μ. Corresponding large numbers of tandemly arranged rRNA genes are present, each capable of transcribing the 45-S rRNA precursors. Figure

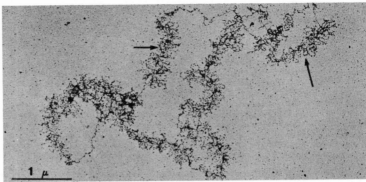

FIGURE 16–19 *Electron-microscope visualization of an extrachromosomal nucleolar core from an oocyte of the African toad Xenopus laevis. It contains 10 rRNA genes tandemly arranged along the circular DNA molecule. The arrows point to individual genes. (Courtesy of O. L. Miller and B. R. Beatty, Oak Ridge National Laboratory.)*

16–19 shows a most elegant electron-microscope picture of one of these extrachromosomal nucleoli to which are attached over 1000 growing rRNA precursor molecules.

How these circular DNA molecules are synthesized is unclear, though at least one must originate from a chromosomally situated rRNA gene. Release by crossing-over events similar to those which release λ prophages from the *E. coli* chromosomes obviously should be seriously considered. This could account for the wide variation in the lengths of nucleolar DNA found within a single nucleus, since crossing-over events should occur at many tandem sites along the relevant oocyte chromosome.

Why oocytes need so many rRNA genes now can only be guessed. Most likely it is an adaptation to the need for very rapid protein synthesis during early stages of development, when cell divisions occur much more rapidly than in later life. In the frog, for example, all the ribosomes present up to gastrulation are synthesized before fertilization in the oocytes. Without the presence of extra rRNA genes, this might be impossible to achieve.

DIFFERENTIATED SOMATIC CELLS WITH EXTRACHROMOSOMAL GENES

There is an increasing number of reports of selective gene multiplication and release in somatic cells. Most of the convincing cases so far involve the giant polytenic chromosomes of insects. Certain bands (genes?) not only increase in size at specific stages in development, but even more important, much of the newly synthesized DNA is released from its respective chromosome. At first almost everyone ignored these observations, but now, with the beautiful electron-microscope pictures of extrachromosomal nucleolar DNA, it seems unwise to deny the possibility that the large scale synthesis of many other gene products is achieved by producing more copies of their DNA templates.

DIFFERENTIATION IS USUALLY NOT IRREVERSIBLE AT THE NUCLEAR LEVEL

Even if selective gene multiplication proves of widespread importance in differentiation, nuclear transportation experiments provide conclusive evidence against the notion that extrachromosomal DNA necessarily irreversibly differentiates a cell toward the selective synthesis of a restricted set of gene products. In these experiments diploid nuclei from differentiated cells were transplanted into unfertilized eggs whose haploid nuclei had been previously removed. The resulting genetically complete diploid eggs were then artificially induced to divide and grow, often to form adult organisms whose chromosomal makeup derives entirely from clonal reproduction of donor nuclei (Figure 16–20). So far, the frog is the most complex organism for which nuclear transplantation has allowed "clonal" reproduction. Successes in this case owe much to the very large amphibian egg, which allows conventional microsurgical removal of the maternal nuclei. Eventually, however, we are likely to witness positive results with virtually "all vertebrates for which this goal seems worth achieving."

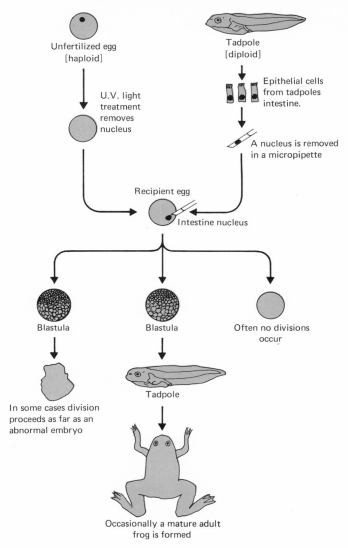

Unfertilized egg
[haploid]

Tadpole
[diploid]

U.V. light
treatment
removes
nucleus

Epithelial cells
from tadpoles
intestine.

A nucleus is removed
in a micropipette

Recipient egg

Intestine nucleus

Blastula

Blastula

Often no divisions
occur

In some cases division
proceeds as far as an
abnormal embryo

Tadpole

Occasionally a mature adult
frog is formed

FIGURE 16–20   *Steps in the origin of a "clonal" frog (redrawn from J. R. Gurdon,* Scientific American, *December, 1968.)*

IRREVERSIBLE CYTOPLASMIC DIFFERENTIATION CONCOMITANT WITH LOSS OF ABILITY TO DIVIDE

Many cells contain nuclei that, under normal conditions, will never divide again. Often they represent cases of extreme differentiation where a very large fraction of the total synthesis is devoted to making just a few different proteins. Mature red blood cells (erythrocytes) are perhaps the most striking example. These cells never divide, having as their only function the production of hemoglobin molecules able to combine reversibly with oxygen. Moreover, in some species, including all mammals, the nuclei of these cells eventually disintegrate, leaving the resulting mature erythrocytes unable to make any more hemoglobin. Erythrocytes generally live only several months and must be replaced by more recently synthesized cells. Behaving somewhat similarly are the adult plasma cells, which produce specific antibodies. They likewise never divide, but produce their products for several days and die. During this time their nuclei remain fully functional, producing the mRNA molecules coding for their antibody products. In contrast, many other specialized cells (e.g., nerve cells), though never dividing, may live many, many years. The functioning of such long-lived cells always depends on the presence of a nucleus able to make mRNA. Some protein synthesis, even at a very low level, seems to be necessary for the continued functioning of all cells.

REVIVAL OF DORMANT NUCLEI THROUGH FUSION WITH MORE ACTIVE CELLS

The dormancy of many nuclei is reversed when their respective cells are fused with other cell types. Until several years ago, fusion between cells growing in tissue culture was a rare event, not at all obtainable at the command of the biologist. Then the observation was made that the adsorption of certain viruses (in particular, a flu-like virus called *Sendai*) caused many cells to fuse. Somehow, the infecting virus particles modify cellular

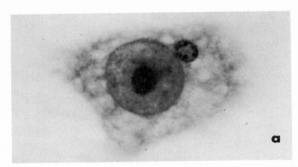

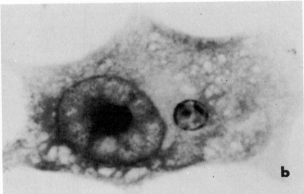

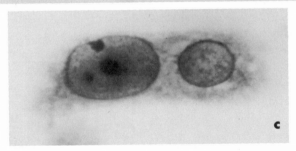

FIGURE 16–21   (a) A recently fused cell containing a very small hen erythrocyte nucleus and a HeLa nucleus. (b) A later stage showing enlargement of the erythrocyte nucleus. (c) A still later stage revealing still further enlargement. (Photographs by Dr. H. Harris and reproduced with the permission of the J. Cell. Science.)

surfaces in a way which promotes their fusion. Even more important, ultraviolet-killed viruses also promote fusion, allowing the metabolism of fused cells to be studied without the many disrupting complications which characterize viral infections. Now, as a result of the introduction of the "Sendai helpers," meaningful cell-fusion experiments are very easy to carry out, and important new insights into higher cell regulation already have been obtained.

For example, when a nucleated hen erythrocyte cell is fused with the human tissue culture strain HeLa, the erythrocyte nucleus resumes both DNA and RNA synthesis. Nuclear reactivation starts with an increase in nuclear volume allowing the tightly compacted hen chromosomes to expand and become capable of RNA synthesis (Figure 16–21). In some not yet understood way, the HeLa cytoplasm must supply components to the hen nucleus which permit it to function. Superficially at least, both DNA and RNA synthesis must be under some form of positive control. For, if the control mechanism were of the negative variety, the erythrocyte cytoplasm would prevent functioning of the HeLa nucleus. No such inhibition, however, is observed with this particular fusion pair or with any of the other cell pairs looked at so far. Further support for the hypothesis that DNA synthesis is under positive control comes from experiments in which a HeLa cell in the G_1 phase of the cell cycle is fused with one in S phase. Soon after fusion, DNA synthesis commences in the previously dormant G_1 nucleus.

POSITIVE CONTROL OF GENE FUNCTION

A key question thus becomes, What compounds directly cause specific genes of higher organisms to function? Here our ignorance is almost complete. While addition of certain substances may either initiate DNA synthesis or stimulate the synthesis of well-defined proteins, the way they do so is not known. The best-studied cases involve several hormones. The addition of estrogens, for example, to uterine tissue quickly stimulates RNA synthesis. But the target molecules which

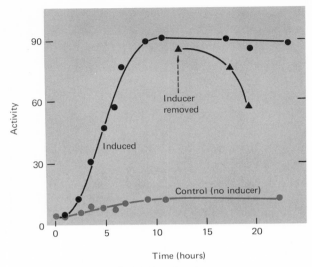

FIGURE 16–22 *Induction of tyrosine amino transferase in rat hepatoma cells by the synthetic adrenal hormone dexamethasone phosphate.*

interact with the estrogens are not known. Conceivably the estrogen acts directly at the chromosomal level, making some genes more accessible for RNA transcription; however, it might act only at the cell surface, setting into play metabolic events which eventually affect RNA synthesis.

An obvious goal is the finding of *in vitro* systems where hormones directly influence DNA or RNA synthesis. Unfortunately, no clear system has yet been worked out. There do exist, however, tissue culture cells which respond specifically to hormones. One of the best-studied cell lines derives from hepatomas (liver tumors). When hepatoma cells are grown in the presence of adrenal hormones, there is a five- to fifteen-fold increase in the activity of the enzyme tyrosine amino transferase over that present in the absence of these hormones (Figure 16–22). This stimulation is highly specific, since the level of total RNA and protein synthesis is unaffected by hormone addition.   Moreover, this increase in activity represents new protein synthesis, since no increase occurs if inhibitors of protein synthesis, like puromycin or cycloheximide, are added.   But it is totally unclear whether this induction requires synthesis of new mRNA molecules or whether the hormone somehow affects the translation of an already existing mRNA template.   Again we see the crucial need for development of workable *in vitro* systems before real answers are to be established.

PREFORMED mRNA ON THE WAY TO GASTRULATION

Whether translational control is an important factor in the lives of eucaryotic cells remains unclear.   The obvious thought, Why waste energy making an RNA molecule which you may never use?, may have greater validity for bacterial than for nucleated cells, in which a much longer time may be required for newly synthesized mRNA molecules to take up suitable positions for protein synthesis.   Quick metabolic responses by higher cells may thus require the preexistence of complete mRNA chains at suitable cytoplasmic sites.   In this way protein synthesis could begin immediately upon receipt of a molecular signal.

This is, in fact, the situation in unfertilized echinoderm eggs, which begin rapid protein synthesis immediately following fertilization.   Most of the mRNA chains used up to gastrulation have been synthesized before fertilization, and so subsequent blockage of RNA synthesis with actinomycin does not at all inhibit the early cleavage divisions.   So, we must conclude that the unfertilized egg is filled with mRNA waiting for a signal to start serving as templates.   This signal does not operate through control of the number of ribosomes since they are also present in large numbers.   Most ribosomes, however, are not combined with mRNA to form polyribosomes.   Instead, fertilization releases a signal which allows specific polyribosomes to form, thereby setting into motion the rapid series of cleavage divisions which lead, first, to blastulation and, finally, gastrulation. Throughout the early cleavage divisions, some new mRNA species are synthesized, largely for function at the gastrulation stage.

Existence of preformed mRNA within unfertilized eggs immediately makes us ask whether it is also of widespread occurrence in other cells. But before this question can be tackled, the state of the preformed mRNA within eggs must be elucidated. There are claims that it is combined with specific proteins, but none of the experiments are really convincing. Hopefully, solid experiments soon will be forthcoming.

FURTHER DECIPHERING OF THE EUCARYOTIC CHROMOSOME

It is thus very clear that the molecular biologist no longer regards embryology as a hopeless problem from which only basically untestable theories can emerge. If the right questions are asked, real answers will emerge at the molecular level, admittedly after much, much work. The key to this new feeling of optimism is the discovery of the σ factors and the emergence of well-defined theories for positive control of gene function. Now a most pressing task is to find the proper higher cells for rigorous testing of these new control concepts. At this moment these ideas still rest almost completely upon procaryotic systems. In this search much emphasis must be placed on the choosing of experimental organisms whose chromosomes can be studied in detail at both the genetic and molecular level. When these organisms emerge, embryology will at last be on a solid molecular course.

SUMMARY

All too little is known about the molecular basis of the control of protein synthesis in the cells of multicellular higher organisms. In particular, little information exists as to mecha-

nisms that bring about cell differentiation. Once a cell has become differentiated, all its descendants usually continue to produce a specific group of unique proteins. There are hints that this selective protein synthesis, like that of microbial cells, is sometimes based on the selective synthesis of unique types of RNA. Thus, differentiated cells must have mechanisms that control the rate at which specific DNA regions are read. A major difficulty that now hinders basic understanding is our current inability to easily study differentiation outside an intact organism. Though embryonic differentiation can be made to occur in tissue culture, it has not yet been possible to isolate the specific external factors that normally induce a cell to differentiate in a given direction.

In bacteria the differentiation process which leads to spore formation is triggered by suboptimal nutrition. This signal initiates a chain of events which causes the disappearance of one or more normal RNA polymerase σ factors and its (their?) replacement by a sporulation-specific σ factor which only reads those genes involved in spore production. Whether similar temporal displacements of one σ factor by another will be the basis of other differentiation processes (e.g., the slime mold life cycle, insect metamorphosis) soon should be testable.

A vast gulf still separates the depth of our knowledge of eucaryotic (nucleated) cells from our knowledge of the more simple procaryotic cells. Evolution of the eucaryotic cells ← oh? brought about a completely new method for chromosome separation (the spindle), the appearance of centromeres and a histone covering for many genes. Still almost a complete mystery is the structure of higher chromosomes and the way in which their DNA replication can start at many different sites along a single chromosome. There are hints of considerable gene redundancy but the only thoroughly proven example involves the genes coding for rRNA. Large numbers of rRNA genes are found tandemly attached to each other in the one-to-several chromosomally attached nucleoli of somatic cells. Many oocytes also contain large numbers of extrachromosomal nucleoli, each containing a circular DNA molecule made up of some 10 to 1000 tandemly attached rRNA genes. There are strong hints that in many insect somatic cells other genes can also selectively replicate themselves to form extrachromosomal copies. This very important point, however, is far from proven.

In many highly specialized cells, the nuclei normally do not divide. But this property does not reflect irreversible nuclear differentiation, as these nuclei sometimes spring back into action if they are introduced into less differentiated cytoplasm, either by microsurgery or by cell-fusion techniques. Nuclear behavior is thus largely a function of the molecular signals received from the surrounding cytoplasm. Though certain hormones are known to selectively influence either DNA or RNA synthesis, how or where they act is not known. While the belief exists that most control of protein synthesis in higher organisms is at the transcriptional level, in the unfertilized egg, many fully synthesized mRNA molecules somehow remain dormant until fertilization occurs. Whether "translational control" is an important feature of somatic cell existence remains to be learned.

REFERENCES

Sussman, M., *Growth and Development*, 2nd ed., Prentice-Hall, Englewood Cliffs, N.J., 1964. A brief paperback introduction to embryology that ties in the problems of the classical embryologist with the ideas of modern genetics.

Ebert, J., *Interacting Systems in Development*, 2nd ed., Holt, New York, 1970. An excellent, quite detailed paperback introduction to embryology with emphasis on the desirability of explanations on the molecular level.

Brachet, J., *Biochemical Cytology*, Academic, New York, 1957. An excellent, but now partially out-of-date, survey of the biochemical facts relevant to the problems of cytologists and embryologists.

The Bacterial Spore, G. W. Gould and A. Hurst (ed.), Academic, New York, 1969. A most thorough summary of the modern state of bacterial spore research.

Losick, R., and A. L. Sonenheim, "Changes in the Template Specificity of RNA Polymerase During Sporulation," *Nature*, **224**, 35 (1969). Sigma factors and the first real wedge toward understanding the differentiation of spores.

Organization and Control in Prokaryotic and Eukaryotic Cells:
Twentieth Symp. Soc. Gen. Microbiol., Cambridge University
Press, London, 1970. A very recent collection of papers em-
phasizing unique features of eucaryotes.

Roodyn, D., and D. Wilkie, *The Biogenesis of Mitochondria,*
Methuen, London, 1968. An introduction to mitochondria
which emphasizes genetic properties.

Cells and Tissues in Culture (3 vols.), E. N. Willmer (ed.), Academic, New York, 1965. A broad and very complete survey
of tissue culture ideas and methods.

Beermann, W., and O. Clever, "Chromosome Puffs," *Sci. Am.,*
April, 1964. A beautifully illustrated discussion of the functioning of the giant chromosomes of insects.

Gall, J. G., "Chromosomes and Cytodifferentiation," in M. Lock
(ed.), *Cytodifferentiation and Macromolecular Synthesis,* Academic, New York, 1963. A review providing an excellent
introduction to lampbrush chromosomes.

Brown, S. W., "Heterochromatin," *Science,* **151,** 477 (1966). A
review which introduces the general reader to the many complexities of this highly condensed form of chromosomal material.

Thomas, C. A., "The Theory of the Master Gene," in *Neuro-
sciences II: A Study Program,* Rockefeller University Press,
1970. An imaginative article which considers the implication
of gene redundancy in the life of higher organisms.

Britten, R. J., and D. A. Kohne, "Repeated Sequences of DNA,"
Sci. Am., April, 1970. Evidence for the presence of repetitive
sequences in a variety of organisms.

Brown, D. D., "The Genes for Ribosomal RNA and Their Transcription during Amphibian Development," *Current Topics
Develop. Biol.,* **2,** 47 (1967). A clear summary of experiments
which show nucleoli to be sites of ribosomal RNA synthesis.

"Nuclear Physiology and Differentiation," *Genetics,* **61,** Suppl.
(1969). A collection of papers asking how genes function
in higher organisms.

Miller, O. L., Jr., and B. R. Beatty, "Portrait of a Gene," *J. Cell.
Physiol.,* **74,** *Suppl.* **1,** 225 (1969). A summary of the authors'
extraordinarily beautiful electron micrographs showing amphibian genes in the process of synthesizing RNA chains.

Brown, D. D., and I. B. David, "Developmental Genetics," *Ann.
Rev. Genetics,* **3,** 127 (1969). A review which surveys all
aspects of embryology that look promising at the molecular
level.

Gurdon, J. B., "Transplanted Nuclei and Cell Differentiation,"
Sci. Am., December, 1968. A description of the most mean-

ingful nuclear transplantation experiments so far accomplished.

Harris, H., *Nucleus and Cytoplasm*, Clarendon Press, Oxford, 1968. An introduction to control problems in higher organisms which emphasizes the great value of cell-fusion experiments.

Ephrussi, B., and M. Weiss, "Hybrid Somatic Cells," *Sci. Am.*, April, 1969. The ways in which cell-cell fusion experiments can be utilized to say important things about the genetics of higher cells.

Harris, H., *Cell Fusion*, Harvard University Press, Cambridge, Mass., 1970. The most recent summary of the cell-fusion field.

Krooth, R. S., G. A. Darlington, and A. A. Velazques, "The Genetics of Cultured Mammalian Cells," *Ann. Rev. Genetics*, **2**, 141 (1968). An excellent advanced review about how hybrid cells are used in the study of mammalian genetics.

Tompkins, G. M., T. D. Gelehrter, D. Grannder, D. Martin, H. Samuels, and E. Thompson, "Control of Specific Gene Expression in Higher Organisms," *Science*, **166**, 1474 (1969). An essay article about enzyme induction in tissue culture cells that favors the possibility of translational control.

Gross, P., "The Control of Protein Synthesis in Embryonic Development and Differentiation," *Current Topics Develop. Biol.*, **2**, 1 (1967). A review which emphasizes RNA metabolism at early stages of development.

Davidson, E. H., *Gene Activity in Early Development*, Academic, New York, 1969. A complete summary of recent biochemical experiments which relate to embryology.

17

THE PROBLEM OF ANTIBODY SYNTHESIS

HOW ORGANISMS ARE ABLE TO GENERATE specific immunological responses has intrigued biologists all through this century. At first, their interest had purely practical considerations. The better we understand antigens and antibodies, the easier it might be to make our immunological responses more effective in defending ourselves against dangerous disease agents. In recent years, however, much attention has been focused upon immunology because of the realization that the induction of specific antibody synthesis involves specific irreversible cell differentiation. Particularly appealing was the fact that methods had become available for the isolation of large amounts of highly purified antibodies, thereby opening up the possibility of chemical work on their detailed structures. The belief now exists that, if antibody synthesis can be understood at the molecular level, a profound breakthrough might be achieved, not only with implications for medicine, but also for all aspects of the biology of multicellular organisms.

ANTIGENS ARE AGENTS WHICH STIMULATE ANTIBODY SYNTHESIS

Antibody synthesis is a defense response found in higher vertebrates that helps combat the harmful effects of pathogenic microorganisms. Antibodies accomplish this task by combining with the microorganisms to form complexes that are then destroyed by phagocytosis (digestion by certain scavenger white blood cells, such as macrophages) (Figure 17–1). For example, the introduction of a virus into the circulatory system of a higher vertebrate stimulates production of specific antibodies that combine specifically with the virus particles to prevent their further multiplication. An individual is *immune* to a virus as long as the corresponding antibodies are present in his circulatory system. Those objects which stimulate antibody synthesis (e.g., a virus particle) are called *antigens*. The study of antibodies and their interaction with antigens is called *immunology*.

An object is potentially antigenic when it possesses an arrangement of atoms at its surface that differs from the surface configuration of any normal host component. The immunological defense system is thus based on the ability of an organism to distinguish between its own molecules and foreign ones. Antibodies are produced against a virus not because the system realizes that the virus will produce a disease, but rather because it recognizes that the virus is a foreign object and hence must be eliminated from the circulatory system.

This immediately raises the question, What are the requirements for an object to have antigenic properties? One major requirement is that an antigen must either be a macromolecule or must be built up from macromolecules (e.g., a virus particle). Most proteins and some polysaccharides and nucleic acids are antigens. Small molecules by themselves can seldom induce specific circulating antibodies. The lack of response to small molecules is not based on lack of specificity. Many small molecules, nonantigenic by themselves, when coupled covalently to a larger molecule (e.g., to a protein), change the antigenic properties of the large molecule.

It seems unlikely that the entire surface of a large molecule is necessary for its antigenicity. Most probably, the immunological system responds to specific groups of atoms (antigenic determinants) located at a number of sites about a molecular surface (Figure 17–2). A given protein molecule is thus likely to induce the formation of several types of antibodies, whereas objects the size of bacteria possess a very large number of different antigenic determinants.

At present, we are still very uncertain exactly how many unique antigenic determinants exist. The number is certainly large, perhaps larger than 10,000. We make this guess on the basis of experiments that test whether antibodies induced by

FIGURE 17–1 *Diagrammatic view of the sequence of events between the injection of an antigen and the appearance of circulating antibodies.*

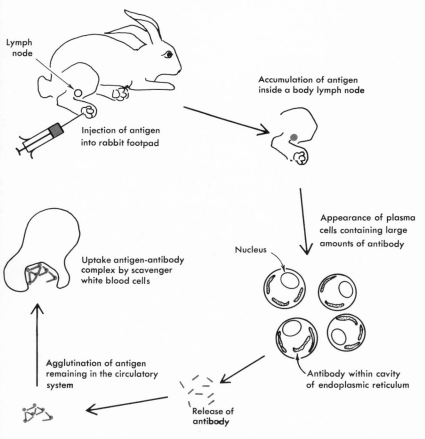

Lymph node

Injection of antigen into rabbit footpad

Accumulation of antigen inside a body lymph node

Appearance of plasma cells containing large amounts of antibody

Nucleus

Uptake antigen-antibody complex by scavenger white blood cells

Antibody within cavity of endoplasmic reticulum

Agglutination of antigen remaining in the circulatory system

Release of antibody

FIGURE 17–2   *Diagrammatic view of an antigen. The symbol R represents a single determinant of immunological specificity and is the actual group that combines with an antibody molecule.*

a given protein ever accidentally combine with a completely unrelated protein. Most strikingly, cross reactions almost never occur. If there were as few as 1000 different antibodies, there should now be numerous examples of cross reactions.

ANTIBODIES ARE ALWAYS PROTEINS

All antibodies are proteins. The selective synthesis of a specific antibody thus represents the selective synthesis of a specific protein molecule (frequently called an *immunoglobulin*). Within a given species, antibodies fall into several size groups, the major ones being the γG(MW $\sim$ 150,000), the γA(MW $\sim$ 180,000 to 500,000), and the γM(MW $\sim$ 950,000). Each is built up from regular aggregates of two size classes of polypeptide chains, usually called the light and heavy chains. The light chains found in all the major groups (γG, γA, and γM) have the same size, and it is the nature of the heavy chain which distinguishes the various groups from each other. The predominant antibody group within mammals is the γG, the principal antibody in blood serum. The amounts of γA and γM are usually about tenfold less. As yet, the different biological roles played by the three different classes is unclear, though the first stage of specific antibody response is usually mediated by γM molecules. By far the best-characterized group is γG, and in subsequent sections we shall restrict ourselves to it.

CONSTRUCTION OF THE γG ANTIBODY MOLECULE FROM TWO LIGHT AND TWO HEAVY CHAINS

Gamma globulin (γG) antibodies sediment in the ultracentrifuge at 7 S (Svedbergs) and have molecular weights of about 150,000. Four polypeptide chains are present in each molecule. They fall into two pairs: two heavy chains (MW ∼ 53,000) and two light chains (MW ∼ 22,500). In a given molecule the two heavy chains are identical, as are the two light chains. Each light chain is linked to a heavy chain by one covalent S—S bond, while two S—S bonds run between the two heavy chains to give the schematic picture shown in Figure 17–3. Most likely, several weak secondary bonds also hold the four chains together.

The chains are so arranged that each antibody molecule contains two identical, widely separated sites, each of which

FIGURE 17–3 *A model of the structure of a human γG antibody molecule. Interchain and intrachain disulfide bonds are indicated, and CHO marks the approximate position in the heavy chain of the carbohydrate moiety.*

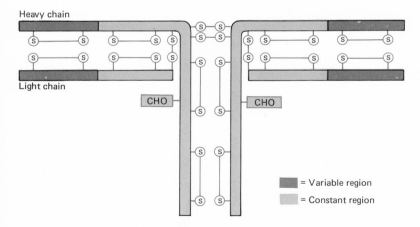

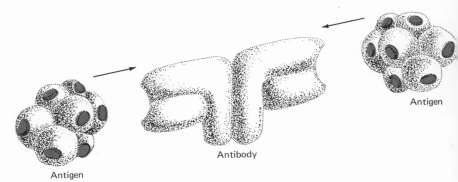

Antigen

Antibody

Antigen

FIGURE 17–4   *Existence of two identical antigen-combining sites on each 7-S antibody molecule. Both light- and heavy-chain atoms are used to form the combining sites.*

can combine with an antigen, using secondary bonds to hold their complementary surfaces together (Figure 17–4). In the electron microscope, the active sites can be seen at the ends of elongated molecules some 150 A in length. Not until the x-ray diffraction technique gives a three-dimensional structure,

FIGURE 17–5   *A diagrammatic view of how antigens and antibodies combine to form large aggregates.*

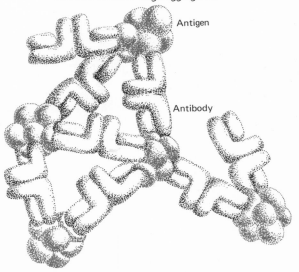

Antigen

Antibody

however, will we know the exact molecular details around the active sites.

The existence of two identical binding sites permits a single antibody molecule to link together two similar antigens; this feature is of great advantage in allowing antibodies to defeat an infection by a microorganism. This is because all micro-organisms contain a large number of identical antigenic deter-minants. Thus, in the presence of specific antibodies, a microorganism becomes linked to a large number of similar microorganisms through antibody bridges (Figure 17-5). These aggregates then tend to be taken up and destroyed by scavenger white blood cells.

ANTIBODY SPECIFICITY RESIDES IN AMINO ACID SEQUENCES

Until recently two competing hypotheses existed to explain what distinguishes one γG antibody molecule from another. One theory stemmed from the fact that the gross molecular structure of all γG antibodies is similar. This resemblance led some people to believe that the amino acid sequences of all antibody molecules are the same, and to postulate that the essential difference between different antibodies resides in the precise three-dimensional structure: the folding of the iden-tical chains. If this were true, the antigen would determine which antibody should be formed by combining with a newly synthesized antibody chain before it had folded to the final three-dimensional form. The interaction would allow part of the antibody molecule to fold around the antigen, automatically creating a complementary shape between the two molecules. Because, according to this scheme and most variants of it, the antigen directly determines the shape of the antibody, such models are called *instructive theories* of antibody formation (Figure 17-6).

Now, however, instructive theories are in disfavor. Instead, virtually everybody believes that there are not only three-dimen-sional differences, but also differences in primary structure (amino acid sequences) between different antibodies. One of

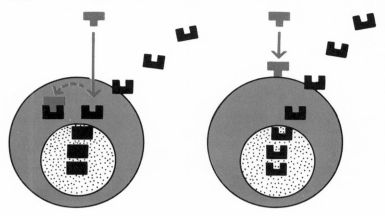

FIGURE 17–6   A schematic comparison of the instructive and selective theories of antibody formation.   Under the
instructive theory, an antigen enters a plasma cell
and forms a template on which a complementary
antibody is laid down.   Selective theories propose
that mere contact of a given antigen with a potential
antibody-producing cell signals the cell nucleus to
produce mRNA chains specific for a complementary
antibody.   (Redrawn from G. J. V. Nossal, Sci. Am.,
December 1964, p. 112, with permission.)

the most compelling types of evidence comes from experiments
in which the three-dimensional structure is temporarily destroyed (denatured) and allowed to reform in the absence of
antigen: the antibody molecules resume their specificity!
There is also a growing body of direct chemical evidence
based on analysis of amino acid sequences of purified antibodies. Here definite differences exist, revealing that antibodies
have two distinct regions: one common to all antibodies, which
accounts for the impression that all antibodies are chemically
very similar; and one whose amino acid sequence (and, hence,
three-dimensional form) differs from one antibody to another.

The existence of distinct amino acid sequences for each
specific antibody immediately raises the question whether
there is a distinct gene for each antibody. Since a given anti-

body-producing animal can produce a very large number of antibodies, it is possible that a very large number of genes might code for the amino acid sequences of antibodies. For many years this possibility has seemed repugnant to many immunologists, aware of the immense number of different antigenic determinants. Now, however, the dilemma can no longer be avoided. Since the amino acid sequences are different, there must exist corresponding differences in their mRNA templates, and thus in the relevant DNA regions.

We are also faced with the problem that, if different genes exist, there must be a control mechanism by which the presence of an antigen tells the gene controlling a corresponding antibody to function. In some way the presence of an antigen must cause the selective synthesis of unique amino acid sequences (*the selective theory of antibody formation*).

MYELOMA PROTEINS AS MODELS FOR SINGLE ANTIBODIES

At any given time the antibodies present in the serum of any individual are a collection of many, many different species directed against a large variety of different antigens. Even after continued immunization with a single strong antigen, no single antibody species is present in pure enough form to allow its isolation. Not only do traces remain of the many, many different antibodies previously induced in that individual's history, but even more important, a given single antigen seems always to promote the synthesis of several different antibodies, each with a different amino acid sequence, yet all able to specifically bind to the same antigen.

Single antibody species can, however, be obtained from the blood of certain individuals affected with the bone marrow disease, *multiple myeloma*. The disease, a form of cancer, involves the uncontrolled multiplication of antibody-producing cells. Most important, a given specific tumor produces only one antibody type characterized by a specific amino acid sequence. Moreover, the antibodies produced by different myeloma tumors each have different amino acid sequences, therefore permitting the comparative study of many different antibody sequences. Up till now no one has found any antigen with a strong affinity for any myeloma protein. But when sufficient numbers are looked at, we would expect this to occur. In every way examined, myeloma proteins have *identical* characteristics to well-defined antibodies.

The amounts of a given myeloma protein made in a myeloma patient are very large, easily permitting amino acid sequence studies. There are, moreover, similar tumors in a number of laboratory animals. Mice, in particular, offer an excellent system for work with myeloma proteins because of the possibility of extensive genetic analysis.

BENCE-JONES PROTEINS ARE SPECIFIC LIGHT CHAINS

Many myeloma patients excrete in their urine large amounts of specific proteins named after their discoverer, a nineteenth-century English physician. They were initially found because, unlike most proteins, they do not precipitate at boiling temperatures. Now we realize that a given Bence-Jones protein is identical to the light chain of its corresponding myeloma antibody. Its excretion into the urine is the result of overproduction of light antibody chains by the myeloma cells. Somehow the biological control device which normally ensures equal production of heavy and light antibody chains is lost and excessive light-chain synthesis results. The presence in very large amounts of Bence-Jones proteins, together with their abnormal solubility, makes their isolation extremely simple, and the first important insights about antibody amino acid sequences arose from their study.

LIGHT AND HEAVY CHAINS HAVE CONSTANT AND VARIABLE PORTIONS

Elucidation of the amino acid sequences of the first several light chains isolated revealed variable amino terminal sequences

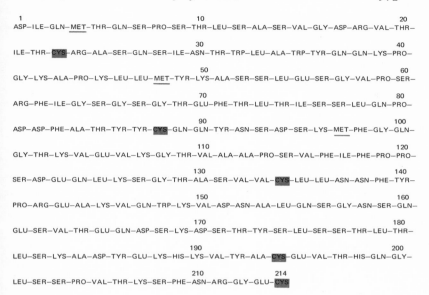

ASP—ILE—GLN—MET—THR—GLN—SER—PRO—SER—THR—LEU—SER—ALA—SER—VAL—GLY—ASP—ARG—VAL—THR—

ILE—THR—CYS—ARG—ALA—SER—GLN—SER—ILE—ASN—THR—TRP—LEU—ALA—TRP—TYR—GLN—GLN—LYS—PRO—

GLY—LYS—ALA—PRO—LYS—LEU—LEU—MET—TYR—LYS—ALA—SER—SER—LEU—GLU—SER—GLY—VAL—PRO—SER—

ARG—PHE—ILE—GLY—SER—GLY—SER—GLY—THR—GLU—PHE—THR—LEU—THR—ILE—SER—SER—LEU—GLN—PRO—

ASP—ASP—PHE—ALA—THR—TYR—TYR—CYS—GLN—GLN—TYR—ASN—SER—ASP—SER—LYS—MET—PHE—GLY—GLN—

GLY—THR—LYS—VAL—GLU—VAL—LYS—GLY—THR—VAL—ALA—ALA—PRO—SER—VAL—PHE—ILE—PHE—PRO—PRO—

SER—ASP—GLU—GLN—LEU—LYS—SER—GLY—THR—ALA—SER—VAL—VAL—CYS—LEU—LEU—ASN—ASN—PHE—TYR—

PRO—ARG—GLU—ALA—LYS—VAL—GLN—TRP—LYS—VAL—ASP—ASN—ALA—LEU—GLN—SER—GLY—ASN—SER—GLN—

GLU—SER—VAL—THR—GLU—GLN—ASP—SER—LYS—ASP—SER—THR—TYR—SER—LEU—SER—SER—THR—LEU—THR—

LEU—SER—LYS—ALA—ASP—TYR—GLU—LYS—HIS—LYS—VAL—TYR—ALA—CYS—GLU—VAL—THR—HIS—GLN—GLY—

LEU—SER—SER—PRO—VAL—THR—LYS—SER—PHE—ASN—ARG—GLY—GLU—CYS

F I G U R E 17–7 *The amino acid sequence of the light chain of the human immunoglobulin EU.*

(residues 1 to about 108), specific for each type of antibody, linked to constant carboxyl terminal regions (residues 109 to 214) common to all antibodies. More recently, when data began to appear on heavy chains, the same feature emerged: variability at the amino terminal end and constancy at the carboxyl end. The constant region of the heavy chain is proportionally much larger, being three times (~ 330 amino acids) longer than the heavy variable region (~ 110 amino acids). Thus, the lengths of the variable regions of both the light and heavy chains are approximately the same.

Figure 17–7 shows the light chain sequence and Figure 17–8, the heavy chain sequence of EU, the first antibody whose complete two-dimensional structure has been worked out. A total of 660 residues were ordered, a major achievement, for EU is the largest protein so far whose sequence has been totally elucidated.

1   10   20

PCA—VAL—GLN—LEU—VAL—GLN—SER—GLY—ALA—GLU—VAL—LYS—LYS—PRO—GLY—SER—SER—VAL—LYS—VAL—

                     30   40

SER—CYS—LYS—ALA—SER—GLY—GLY—THR—PHE—SER—ARG—SER—ALA—ILE—ILE—TRP—VAL—ARG—GLN—ALA—

                     50   60

PRO—GLY—GLN—GLY—LEU—GLU—TRP—MET—GLY—GLY—ILE—VAL—PRO—MET—PHE—GLY—PRO—PRO—ASN—TYR—

                     70   80

ALA—GLN—LYS—PHE—GLN—GLY—ARG—VAL—THR—ILE—THR—ALA—ASP—GLU—SER—THR—ASN—THR—ALA—TYR—

                     90   100

MET—GLU—LEU—SER—SER—LEU—ARG—SER—GLU—ASP—THR—ALA—PHE—TYR—PHE—CYS—ALA—GLY—GLY—TYR—

                     110   120

GLY—ILE—TYR—SER—PRO—GLU—GLU—TYR—ASN—GLY—GLY—LEU—VAL—THR—VAL—SER—SER—ALA—SER—THR—

                     130   140

LYS—GLY—PRO—SER—VAL—PHE—PRO—LEU—ALA—PRO—SER—SER—LYS—SER—THR—SER—GLY—GLY—THR—ALA—

                     150   160

ALA—LEU—GLY—CYS—LEU—VAL—LYS—ASP—TYR—PHE—PRO—GLU—PRO—VAL—THR—VAL—SER—TRP—ASN—SER—

                     170   180

GLY—ALA—LEU—THR—SER—GLY—VAL—HIS—THR—PHE—PRO—ALA—VAL—LEU—GLN—SER—SER—GLY—LEU—TYR—

                     190   200

SER—LEU—SER—SER—VAL—VAL—THR—VAL—PRO—SER—SER—SER—LEU—GLY—THR—GLN—THR—TYR—ILE—CYS—

                     210   220

ASN—VAL—ASN—HIS—LYS—PRO—SER—ASN—THR—LYS—VAL—ASP—LYS—ARG—VAL—GLU—PRO—LYS—SER—CYS—

                     230   240

ASP—LYS—THR—HIS—THR—CYS—PRO—PRO—CYS—PRO—ALA—PRO—GLU—LEU—LEU—GLY—GLY—PRO—SER—VAL—

                     250   260

PHE—LEU—PHE—PRO—PRO—LYS—PRO—LYS—ASP—THR—LEU—MET—ILE—SER—ARG—THR—PRO—GLU—VAL—THR—

                     270   280

CYS—VAL—VAL—VAL—ASP—VAL—SER—HIS—GLU—ASP—PRO—GLN—VAL—LYS—PHE—ASN—TRP—TYR—VAL—ASP—

                     290   300

GLY—VAL—GLN—VAL—HIS—ASN—ALA—LYS—THR—LYS—PRO—ARG—GLU—GLN—GLN—TYR—ASX—SER—THR—TYR—

                     310   320

ARG—VAL—VAL—SER—VAL—LEU—THR—VAL—LEU—HIS—GLN—ASN—TRP—LEU—ASP—GLY—LYS—GLU—TYR—LYS—

                     330   340

CYS—LYS—VAL—SER—ASN—LYS—ALA—LEU—PRO—ALA—PRO—ILE—GLU—LYS—THR—ILE—SER—LYS—ALA—LYS—

                     350   360

GLY—GLN—PRO—ARG—GLU—PRO—GLN—VAL—TYR—THR—LEU—PRO—PRO—SER—ARG—GLU—GLU—MET—THR—LYS—

                     370   380

ASN—GLN—VAL—SER—LEU—THR—CYS—LEU—VAL—LYS—GLY—PHE—TYR—PRO—SER—ASP—ILE—ALA—VAL—GLU—

                     390   400

TRP—GLU—SER—ASN—ASP—GLY—GLU—PRO—GLU—ASN—TYR—LYS—THR—THR—PRO—PRO—VAL—LEU—ASP—SER—

                     410   420

ASP—GLY—SER—PHE—PHE—LEU—TYR—SER—LYS—LEU—THR—VAL—ASP—LYS—SER—ARG—TRP—GLN—GLU—GLY—

                     430   440

ASN—VAL—PHE—SER—CYS—SER—VAL—MET—HIS—GLU—ALA—LEU—HIS—ASN—HIS—TYR—THR—GLN—LYS—SER—

FIGURE 17–8   *The amino acid sequence of the heavy chain of the human immunoglobulin EU.*

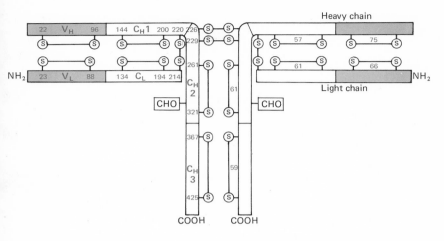

F I G U R E 17–9 *Internal homologies in the* γG *antibody molecule. The variable regions* V$_L$ *and* V$_H$ *are homologous to each other, as are the constant regions* C$_L$, C$_H$1, C$_H$2, *and* C$_H$3.

HEAVY-CHAIN ORIGIN THROUGH REPETITIVE DUPLICATION OF A PRIMITIVE ANTIBODY GENE

Analysis of the foregoing sequences strongly suggests that the heavy chain evolved by successive duplication of a primitive antibody gene. To show this, its sequence is divided into four parts, as shown in Figure 17–9. The first, the variable portion, shows similarity to the variable part of the light chain. In turn, the three regions of the constant portion show strong homologies both among themselves and to the constant region of the light chain. These relationships can easily be seen in Figure 17–10, which compares the sequences of C$_L$, C$_H$1, C$_H$2, and C$_H$3. Along a 100-residue length, identity between any two regions occurs at some 30 positions. Moreover, each region contains one intraregion S—S bond with the two sulphur atoms separated by some 50 to 60 amino acids. By contrast, there are no S—S bonds joining together residues on different regions of the same chain. This suggests that each homologous region exists as a fairly separate mass, not closely bound to any

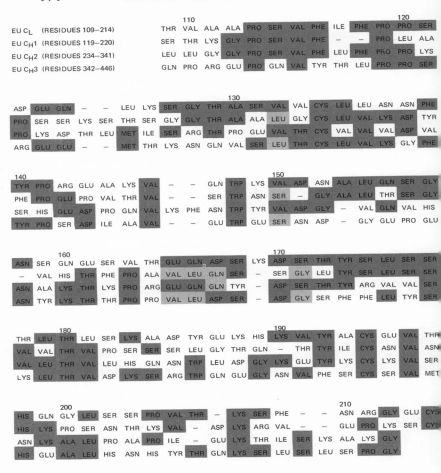

EU C_L (RESIDUES 109–214)
EU C_H1 (RESIDUES 119–220)
EU C_H2 (RESIDUES 234–341)
EU C_H3 (RESIDUES 342–446)

FIGURE 17–10   Sequence homology in the constant regions of the EU antibody molecule. Deletions indicated by dashes have been introduced to maximize the homology. Identical residues are darkly shaded; both dark and light shadings are used to indicate identities which occur in pairs in the same positions. (Redrawn from G. M. Edelman, et al., Proc. Nat. Acad. Sci., **63**:78 1969).

of the others. This conjecture, of course, must await future x-ray studies for its eventual proof or disproof.

It is tempting to speculate whether the fact that all variable regions also contain a single intraregion S—S bond implies that the constant and variable portions had a common ancestor. If so, the first step in immunoglobulin evolution may have been the duplication of a primitive gene to form a compound gene with two identical nucleotide sequences. One sequence, not significantly altered further, would remain as the constant region, while the other could evolve into the variable section.

LIGHT AND HEAVY CHAINS BOTH INFLUENCE THE SPECIFICITY OF ANTIBODIES

The region of the antibody that combines with an antigenic determinant includes the variable parts of both light and heavy chains (Figure 17-5). At first it was suspected that most of the specificity was due to variations in the amino acid sequence of the heavy chain, but now it has been realized that in most cases the amino acid sequence of the light chain is also involved. The discovery that both the light and heavy chains have specific variable regions could mitigate the dilemma posed earlier about the great number of genes needed to code for different antibodies. Since each antibody must be coded for by two genes (one for the light chain, the other for the heavy chain), the number of possible antibodies may be the number of different light chains multiplied by the number of different heavy chains. Thus, a million different antibodies may be formed by only two thousand genes, coding for a thousand different light chains and a thousand different heavy chains.

PLASMA CELL SITE OF ANTIBODY SYNTHESIS

It is obvious that before we can seriously test the selective theories of antibody formation, we must know which types of cells produce antibodies. For a long time it has been known that the spleen and the lymph nodes are sites of antibody synthesis. At first it was thought that a scavenger white blood cell, the macrophage, produces antibodies. Now, however, it is clear that another type of white blood cell, the plasma cell, is the main, if not sole, site of antibody production. When an antigen is injected into an animal, there appears within several days an increased number of immature plasma cells, called *plasmablasts*. These new cells arise from the division of a still-undiscovered precursor cell (perhaps a small lymphocyte) as a result of the injection of the antigen. Each plasmablast exists but a short time before dividing to form new progeny cells. The progeny cells are not, however, morphologically identical to their parents. Each successive division cycle results in cells having a more pronounced cytoplasm filled with an increasing number of ribosomes. By the fifth day after the antigen is injected, the cycle of successive cell divisions has produced adult plasma cells, which are by then rapidly turning out antibody molecules (Figure 17–11).

Thus the injection of an antigen into the bloodstream has two separate effects. One is the transformation of the inert ribosome-poor plasma cell precursors into the ribosome-rich plasma cells capable of rapid protein synthesis (Figure 17–12). This development is common to all antibody synthesis. The second effect of the antigen is probably far more specific; it is most likely the production of the specific messenger-RNA molecules, which code for the unique amino acid sequences of the specific antibody molecules.

A GIVEN PLASMA CELL USUALLY PRODUCES ONE TYPE OF ANTIBODY MOLECULE

When a number of different antigens are injected simultaneously into an animal, the question naturally arises whether a given plasma cell produces antibodies against all the foreign antigens or, instead, produces only one type of antibody. According to instructive theories, we might expect that many different types of antigen would enter a single plasma cell, and so each cell should produce a variety of antibodies. The ex-

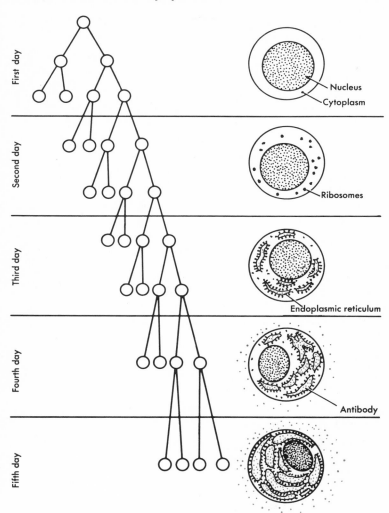

FIGURE 17-11 *Successive stages in the development of mature plasma cells. At least 8 cell generations and 5 days of growth are required before the appearance of cells producing a great deal of antibody. The most noticeable feature of the mature cells is the extensive endoplasmic reticulum whose internal cavity is filled with antibody molecules. (Redrawn from G. J. V. Nossal, Sci. Am., Dec. 1964, p. 109, with permission.)*

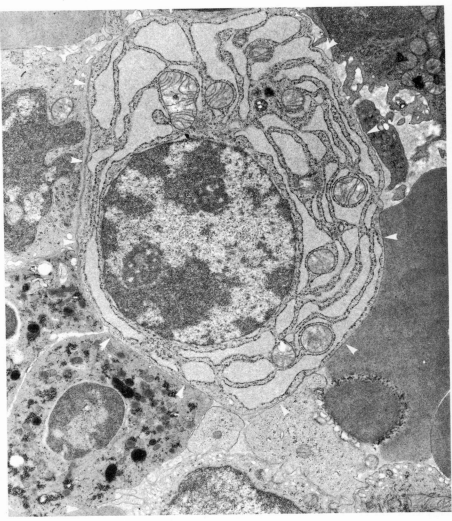

FIGURE 17–12   Electron micrograph of a plasma cell from the spleen of a guinea pig (courtesy of K. R. Porter, Biological Laboratories, Harvard). The cell margins are indicated by white arrows. The cavity of endoplasmic reticulum is greatly distended by the presence of large amounts of antibody molecules. Ribosomes are visible as black dots attached to the endoplasmic reticulum. The objects around the edges are other types of white blood cells.

perimental answer, however, seems to be the opposite. When the antibodies produced in a single cell are examined (this can be done by isolating single plasma cells after they have begun to produce antibody), most cells are found to produce only one specific antibody. Thus, almost every antibody-producing plasma cell represents a most highly specialized factory, devoting much of its protein synthesis to the production of only one product.

SECOND INJECTION OF ANTIGEN INCREASES THE NUMBER OF ANTIBODY-PRODUCING CELLS

Several days after a single injection of an antigen, the number of plasma cells which are producing the corresponding antibody is relatively small. For still unclear reasons, only a small number of the plasmablast precursors become transformed into antibody-producing plasma cells. When, however, the first injection is followed some weeks later by a second injection, a much larger number of antibody-producing plasma cells is found. Correspondingly, very many more antibody molecules are made and released. This is the reason that immunization is usually carried out by repeated injections of the same antigen.

The foregoing results hint that a first antigen injection may transform some of the *unspecific precursor cells* into *transformed precursor cells* which, when subjected to a second contact with the same antigen, multiply to produce plasma cells with the corresponding antibody. Some inactive plasmablasts may thus possess immunological memory. In some very precise way, they seem to know that they have previously had contact with a specific antigen.

ANTIBODY-PRODUCING CELLS NEED NOT CONTAIN ANTIGENS

We might guess that both immunological memory and the production of specific antibodies are based upon contact with specific antigen molecules. Now, however, there is sound evidence that very little, if any, specific antigen is present inside an antibody-producing plasma cell. Such evidence arises from experiments in which a highly radioactive antigen is injected into an animal. Some days later, thin sections of antibody-producing regions are examined by autoradiographic techniques to find out where the antigens have gone. Much of the labeled antigen is found inside the scavenger macrophage cells, which have no direct connection with antibody synthesis. In contrast, most plasma cells seem to contain not even a single antigen molecule, and only a few antigens can be seen in the plasmablasts. This observation, if confirmed, independently rules out any instructional theory. Each antibody-producing cell is simultaneously making thousands of antibodies. Given the instructional model, we would expect that thousands of antigens would be found in each cell, perhaps bound to the ribosomal sites of protein synthesis. Thus, this observation strongly supports the idea that the antigen either directly or indirectly *selects* the synthesis of a specific mRNA molecule.

It remains unclear, however, whether the antigen need be present to ensure the massive synthesis of mRNA templates. The fact that the precursor plasmablasts contain only a few antigen molecules hints that antigen need not be present, but the question must still be considered open. If no antigen is present, then we must consider the possibility that the genetic apparatus itself has been transformed.

THEORY OF CLONAL SELECTION

The fact that the presence of an antigen leads to a great increase in the number of cells which produce the corresponding specific antibody has suggested to some immunologists that the sole function of the antigen is to stimulate specific cell division. This *clonal selection theory* (a clone is a group of identical cells, all descended from a common ancestor) presumes that the antigen need provide no information other than the fact that it is present. This theory assumes that there *preexists*, prior to the appearance of the antigen, a large variety of differ-

ent plasma cell precursors, each class endowed with the capacity to form only one (or sometimes, two) specific type of
antibody. The antigen then acts to select the appropriate class
by causing its selective division. Some of the newly divided
precursors give rise after several cell generations to mature
plasma cells. Others may continue to divide without producing antibody. These would be the cells responsible for immunological memory.

These speculations bring us again to the problem raised
earlier of whether there exists a separate gene for each of the
different light and heavy antibody chains. Certainly the total
population of plasma cells within a single animal must contain
a large number of different antibody genes. This fact, however,
does not help us with the crucial point of whether every plasma
cell possesses each gene. In fact, it is possible to distinguish
two broad categories of hypotheses about genes coding for antibodies. One category emphasizes the above-mentioned possibility that each haploid chromosome set contains a large number
of antibody genes. If this is the case, then a given plasma cell
must be restricted (at random?) to the production of only one
type of antibody. How this might happen is not at all obvious.

The alternative set assumes that, in the fertilized egg, each
haploid chromosome set contains only one, or at most a few,
genes for the light and heavy chains. Under this set of schemes,
during the many cell divisions following fertilization, these antibody genes are randomly modified to produce a large number
of different antibody genes, each present in only a very small
fraction of the total population of plasma cell precursors.
These cells are then triggered to divide and produce their specific antibody whenever they come into contact with the appropriate antigen.

There are a variety of ways by which a small number of
antibody genes could give rise to a very large number of different antibody genes. One way presupposes that the genes for
the light and heavy chains are much more mutable than other
genes. This is hard to imagine, not only because other genes
must not be mutated, but also because the high mutability
must be restricted to approximately one-half of the "light" gene

and one-fourth of the "heavy" gene. Otherwise, we should not find that all light (heavy) chains have identical amino acid sequences in the COO⁻ terminal regions. Another way to generate a large number of different genes is for each cell to possess several different genes for the light (and heavy) chains. Each of the genes would have identical nucleotide sequences at one end (the COO⁻ end) and quite different sequences at the other (the NH_3^+ end). Crossing over (mitotic recombination) between these related genes would then produce new nucleotide sequences, each coding for a new set of amino acid sequences. Now there is no clear way to decide between recombination hypotheses and those based upon mutation. However, when the amino acid sequences for a number of distinct antibodies become available, it may be apparent that regularities in amino acid sequences exist that favor recombination models over those based on random mutations.

IMMUNOLOGICAL TOLERANCE

Up to now, we have avoided mentioning a very important characteristic of the immunological response. How does an antibody-forming system know that a molecular surface is present on a *foreign* molecule? How is it able to avoid making antibodies against its own proteins and nucleic acids? This lack of responsiveness has nothing to do with the inherent lack of antigenicity of these molecules. For example, almost any human protein, if injected into a rabbit, will induce the formation of specific antibodies. Likewise, rabbit proteins are antigenic in humans. These facts lead to the conclusion that an immunological system learns how to recognize native molecules. Such a learning process occurs very early in life, before the development of an active immune response to foreign proteins. If a foreign antigen is injected into a newly born animal before it possesses an antibody-forming system, then, in adult life, the animal is unable to form antibodies against the early-injected foreign antigen. The foreign antigen is recognized as though it were a host protein. This lack of immunological responsiveness to all those antigens present when the antibody-forming system was being developed is called *immunological tolerance.*

It would indeed be surprising if the seemingly opposite behaviors of specific tolerance and specific antibody response were in fact completely unrelated. One hypothetical way to relate the two responses rests on the fact that a cell making large amounts of antibody is usually unable to multiply and thus lives for only several days. Perhaps if the theory of clonal selection is correct, then very early in life there exist only a few cells genetically competent to form antibodies against a specific antigen. Immunological tolerance might result if at this early time the presence of an antigen, instead of somehow causing a significant antibody response, resulted in immediate cell death.

INDUCTION OF ANTIBODIES IN VITRO

It is obvious to even the most enthusiastic immunologist that neither the formation of a specific antibody nor the development of immunological tolerance as a result of the injection of a specific antigen is understood at either the cellular or the molecular level. This fact leads to the immediate question: Why not study the induction of antibodies with isolated cells outside the intact animal? Such a procedure would automatically enable us not only to identify unambiguously the precursors to the plasmablast intermediates, but even more important, to tell whether they were already differentiated as to which antibody they would produce. At first, virtually all *in vitro* experiments were so completely negative that the occasional positive report of tissue culture antibody induction was greeted with almost universal skepticism. Over the last two years, however, there have been fairly convincing claims of having achieved not only a secondary response, but also genuine primary responses by cells never before exposed to that specific antigen. However, whether the system can be exploited to give some fundamental answers remains to be seen.

There are also many attempts now being made to synthesize antibodies in cell-free systems. The limited success so far achieved has always involved use of cell-free systems made from cells already making antibodies. So many, if not all, of the "antibody systems" now observed involve only the completion of partially synthesized chains. Unfortunately, cell-free protein synthesis using mammalian systems has, up till now, proved much less efficient than that achieved in many bacterial systems. But when more people decide to concentrate on mammalian systems, this picture should improve.

So at the present moment, the only direction in which the immunologist can move at the molecular level with some prospects of obvious success is the study of the antibody itself. Our knowledge of detailed antibody structure is still incomplete, and much more work is required to understand antibody structure at the level at which we now look at myoglobin or hemoglobin. Here, however, even though the detailed protein structure information may in itself be quite interesting, there is no reason to believe that it will necessarily yield information relating to the primary problem of how the antigen induces the synthesis of a specific antibody. We thus see that the molecular biologists who have decided to concentrate on antibody synthesis as a means of understanding cell differentiation have chosen a problem that, upon close examination, seems even more complicated than embryological differentiation seen from afar. Even so, there is no reason to believe that the really fundamental embryological problems, when properly posed, will prove any easier to solve.

SUMMARY

There is a great need to find a "simple" system in which cells become irreversibly differentiated to produce a well-defined protein in response to the addition of a specific, well-understood external molecule. One system, initially thought to be "simple," is the synthesis of specific antibodies as a result of the injection of specific foreign objects. Those objects that induce the synthesis of specific antibodies are called antigens. Many macromolecules, including most proteins and some carbohydrates and nucleic acids, are antigens. Antibodies inactivate antigens by combining with them to form complexes that are engulfed by scavenger white blood cells.

It was originally thought that an antigen induced the formation of a specific antibody by combining with a nascent antibody before it acquired its final three-dimensional shape. According to this hypothesis, the antibody would fold around the antigenic surface, thereby forming a region complementary in shape to the antigen's specific surface (instructive theories). Now, however, it is known that each specific antibody possesses a unique sequence of amino acids which folds in a unique three-dimensional shape. The function of the antigen is thus to select the synthesis of the specific mRNA templates that code for the desired amino acid sequence (selective theories).

The commonest form of antibody, the γG group, are proteins with molecular weights of about 150,000. They are constructed from two identical light chains ($MW \sim 22,500$) and two identical heavy chains ($MW \sim 53,000$) which are linked together regularly by disulfide bonds. Both the light and heavy chains have variable sequences at the amino terminal end and constant regions at their carboxyl ends. Their dimeric structure gives each antibody two active sites at which they can specifically combine with antigens using secondary bonds. Most, if not all, active sites are bounded by variable portions of both the light and heavy chains.

The antibodies present in normal blood serum are a collection of many, many types of proteins with different amino acid sequences. Single antibody species, however, are produced by myeloma tumors, now the source of virtually all antibodies used in amino acid sequence studies. Some myelomas produce many more light chains than heavy. The excessive light chains, excreted into urine, are called the Bence-Jones proteins.

The site of antibody synthesis is the plasma cell. It is a highly differentiated cell that arises (from small lymphocytes?) by means of intermediate plasmablast cells. Little, if any, antigen is present in antibody-producing cells. Most plasma cells can make only one type of antibody. This fact suggests that each plasma cell is hereditarily restricted to the production of only one (two) type(s) of antibody. The number of plasma cells producing a given antibody increases with repeated antigen injections. This hints that the presence of an antigen stimulates the division of cells capable of giving rise to the plasma cells which produce the corresponding antibody (theory of clonal selection). This theory assumes the preexistence, prior to the injection of an antigen, of a very large variety of cells differentiated with respect to the antibody their progeny can produce.

Since antibodies are formed only against foreign proteins, an animal's immunological system must be able to recognize its own proteins. This learning process occurs early in life, before circulating antibodies exist. If a foreign protein is injected into a newborn animal, the animal in later life is unable to form antibodies against the foreign protein (immunological tolerance).

REFERENCES

Landsteiner, K., *The Specificity of Serological Reactions*, rev. ed., Dover, New York, 1964. A paperback reprint of a scientific classic, last revised in 1943. Still a beautiful introduction to immunology.

Lederberg, J., "Genes and Antibodies," *Science*, **129**, 1649 (1959). The problems of antibody synthesis as seen in 1959 by an inquisitive geneticist.

Nossal, G. J. V., "How Cells Make Antibodies," *Sci. Am.*, December, 1964, p. 106. A clear summary of the immunological dilemmas as of late 1964.

Davis, B. D., R. Dulbecco, H. N. Eisen, H. S. Ginsberg, and W. B. Wood, *Microbiology*, Harper and Row, New York, 1967. The section on immunology by Herman Eisen (over 250 pages) in every way surpasses all other textbook treatments.

"Antibodies," *Cold Spring Harbor Symp. Quant. Biol.*, **32** (1967). The most complete survey of ideas and experiments about all aspects of immunology. The concluding summary by Nils Jerne is a minor masterpiece.

Gamma Globulins, Structure and Control of Biosynthesis, J. Killander (ed.), Nobel Symp. 3, Wiley (Interscience), New York, 1967. Articles arising from a 1967 Stockholm meeting.

Smithies, O., "Antibody Variability," *Science*, **157**, 267 (1967).

The argument for the somatic recombination origin of multiple antibody gene sequences by its most astute proponent.

Edelman, G. M., B. A. Cunningham, W. E. Gall, P. D. Gottlieb, U. Rutishauser, and M. J. Waxdel, "The Covalent Structure of an Entire γG Immunoglobulin Molecule," *Proc. Natl. Acad. Sci. U.S.*, **63**, 78 (1969). The announcement of the first complete covalent antibody structure.

Edelman, G. M., and W. E. Gall, "The Antibody Problem," *Ann. Rev. Biochem.*, **38**, (1969). A very complete review emphasizing amino acid sequence results.

Burnet, F. M. *Cellular Immunology*, Cambridge University Press, London and New York, 1969. An extensive and perceptive discussion of all aspects of immunology which focuses on the clonal selection theory.

18

A GENETICIST'S VIEW OF CANCER

IN THE PREVIOUS TWO CHAPTERS, IT became glaringly obvious that the problem of understanding the genetic basis of cell differentiation at the molecular level may be exceedingly difficult to solve. Only today are we beginning to gain some confidence that we are close to understanding the essential molecular features upon which the life of even the simplest bacterial cell depends. The jump to an attempt to understand the much more complex mammalian cell with its thousand-fold greater amount of DNA has only begun. Though we can now grow some of these cells in tissue culture, we are always painfully aware that the normal environment of a cell from a multicellular organism is the intact organism, and that when we remove a cell from its normal cellular companions, we may so alter it that it is unable to function in the way that interests us.

Thus it might be thought that, if it is still very difficult to attack the molecular basis of normal differentiation, it should be even harder to understand failures in cell heredity which produce abnormal cells unable to integrate into organized multicellular complexes. That is, if we are still a colossally long way from understanding a healthy animal cell at the molecular level, have we any chance of gaining an insight into the diseased cell? Are we likely to understand soon the majority of diseases at a molecular level?

588

Fortunately, we already know that at least a few diseases can be so understood. The abnormal hemoglobin molecules (see Chapter 8) which cause various blood diseases (anemias) are a case in point. Here we are able to understand their molecular bases (but not yet cure them!) because we had prior, very detailed knowledge about the structure of normal hemoglobin. *Our chance to understand a disease depends greatly upon whether it is based upon abnormalities in molecules with which we are already familiar.*

From this viewpoint, we can look at the problem of cancer. The term *cancer* encompasses a large variety of different diseases, all characterized by the property that cells grow when they should not. We are thus dealing with the problem of *the control of cell division,* and so we must ask what tells a normal cell in a multicellular organism to stop dividing. This is a problem which does not exist at the bacterial level, for bacteria separate from each other soon after cell division has occurred. Our studies of bacterial cells, therefore, provide no direct hints. The problem must thus be attacked directly at the level of the higher eucaryotic cell. Here, unfortunately, despite much intelligently conceived effort, we are still essentially in the dark as to the molecular factors which ensure that cells cease to grow and divide at the correct time. Hence, many intelligent biochemists hold the view that now is not the time to work seriously on the biochemistry of cancerous cells. They argue that, even though cancer cells are the cause of enormous human suffering, nonetheless it does not make sense to put a disproportionate share of our scientific effort into trying to meet an unripe intellectual challenge. They compare the current situation with the desire to understand the nature of solar energy at the time of Newton.

I suspect, however, that this pessimism may not be justified and that an understanding of at least some aspects of uncontrolled cell growth may soon be achieved at the molecular level. Such optimism arises from some recent, spectacular results on the induction of tumors by viruses. Before we state the arguments, however, it may be well to try to define the problem more exactly.

CANCERS CAN ARISE IN ALMOST ALL DIFFERENTIATED CELLS

There are many distinct types of uncontrolled cell growth (cancer). Each appears to arise by an inheritable change in a specific cell. Almost all types of differentiated cells can be transformed into cancer (malignant) cells. Thus, liver cells, skin cells, nerve cells, kidney cells, blood cells, bone cells, and so on, can all become cancer cells. In general, cancer cells exhibit many morphological and functional characteristics common to their normal precursors. For example, cancer cells arising in the thyroid gland often produce the hormone thyroxin, which is specifically synthesized by normal thyroid cells.

Contiguous masses of cancer cells are called tumors. There is great variation in the rate at which tumors grow. Some grow relatively slowly, whereas others grow rapidly and, if not removed by surgery or radiation treatment, inevitably kill their host. Great differences also exist in the affinity of the various types of cancer cells for other cells. Some cancer cells tend to remain at the location where they arise. The tumors they produce are often not harmful, because they can usually be easily removed. Others quickly spread through an organism and invade a variety of normal tissues. Invasive cancers, after they have spread, usually cannot be completely removed by surgery or other treatment and so almost always lead to death unless detected soon after their origin.

CANCER CELLS GROW WHEN THEY SHOULD NOT

We cannot distinguish a cancer cell from a normal cell by the fact that the tumor cell is constantly dividing while the normal one divides only rarely. In fact, tumors most often arise in cells normally undergoing frequent division. In mature animals, many normal cells are in the process of constant growth and cell division. This is particularly true of the cells exposed to the external environment. For example, the epithelial cells of the skin and those lining the various cavities of the digestive system are constantly forming new cells to replace the large number of cells that die each day. Likewise, the various types of blood cells have relatively short lives and must be replaced by the division of preexisting precursor cells. On the other hand, organs such as the liver and the brain have cells which seldom divide in a mature adult. In addition to those two types, there are other cells, normally quiescent, which after the appearance of a specific hormone suddenly begin to divide and continue to do so as long as the hormone is present.

The difference between a cancer cell and a normal cell is thus often not an all-or-none matter, but is a question of the frequency of division. Either the cancer cell may divide more rapidly than a normal cell or, if the normal cell requires the stimulus of a specific hormone, then the cancer cell may not need this stimulus, or may require less hormone before commencing division. Thus, the only useful distinction is that the cancer cell is less subject to the normal control devices which tell a cell not to divide.

CONTACT INHIBITION

There is now growing evidence that, when two normal animal cells touch one another, a signal is often generated which stops both cells from further cell movement and in some cases from further cell division. This phenomenon of *contact inhibition* is revealed by noticing how isolated mouse cells grow on a solid glass surface. Normal cells have a great affinity for solid surfaces and stick to the glass rather than float freely in the nutrient medium. As long as there are relatively few cells about, division proceeds regularly about once every 24 hours. The division rate often slows down when the cells have formed a confluent monolayer. It is as if these cells are able to divide as long as they are not in close contact with several other cells. In contrast, when a variety of cancer cells (but not all) are observed, growth does not cease when a monolayer has formed. Instead, the cancer cells pile on top of each other, forming masses of cells several layers thick (Figure 18–1). The basis of these phenomena is still very unclear. It may be related to a greater stickiness of the normal cells. When they touch each

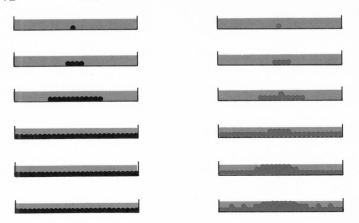

Normal cells   Cancer cells

FIGURE 18–1 *Schematic comparison of the multiplication of a normal cell and of a cancer cell upon a solid surface. The normal cells divide until they form a solid monolayer. Cancer cells, however, often have less affinity for the solid surface and form irregular masses, several layers deep.*

other, they often remain fixed, whereas many types of cancer cells have much less affinity for other cells and so do not form regular monolayers.

In vivo some control system may exist which allows normal cells to divide only so long as they have some freedom of movement. This would mean that the moment this freedom of movement were lost (e.g., through the formation of a continuous monolayer) cell growth would stop. In an obvious way, contact inhibition makes sense. Inside a multicellular organism, it would be disadvantageous for a cell to grow and divide if it had no room to move about.

MALIGNANCY AS A LOSS OF CELLULAR AFFINITIES

The "sticky" quality of cells, observed in contact inhibition, displays considerable specificity. A given type of cell (e.g., a liver cell) prefers to stick to others of its own kind (e.g., other liver cells) and shows very little, if any, affinity for other types (e.g., kidney cells). This type of specificity has been elegantly demonstrated in experiments in which small amounts of the proteolytic enzyme trypsin are used to break apart organs such as the liver and the kidney into single cell components. If these isolated cells are then incubated in the absence of trypsin, they reaggregate to form tissue fragments similar to those in the intact organ, that is, small fragments of liver tissue and small fragments of kidney tissue. When kidney and liver cells are mixed together, small fragments of liver and kidney are again observed. No mixtures of kidney and liver cells are detected. Thus, a kidney cells prefers to stick to a kidney cell, and a liver cell to a liver cell. If this experiment is repeated with cancer cells, however, the normal cellular affinities no longer hold. For example, the mixing of cells from a malignant skin cancer with normal kidney cells results in aggregates containing both kidney cells and skin cancer cells. A loss of normal cellular affinities is most likely the reason why many malignant cancer cells invade a variety of normal organs.

The results from both the normal and the cancer cells point to the same important conclusion. The outside surfaces of cells play a very important role in ensuring the correct positioning of cells in a multicellular organism. Moreover, if the current speculation about contact inhibition is correct, the formation of the correct cellular contact is of great importance in determining whether a cell will divide.

SEARCH FOR CHEMICAL DIFFERENCES BETWEEN NORMAL AND CANCER CELLS

Almost as soon as scientists began to describe molecules within normal cells, they also looked to see whether these same molecules were found in cancer cells. Now, when a new chemical reaction (or enzyme) is described in a normal cell, a search is very often made to see if the same reaction occurs in the cancer cell. Often these searches seem to be successful, with the tumor cells containing much more (or less) of a particular component than their normal equivalent. Further analysis, however, has so far invariably resulted in disappointment. One of the difficulties inherent in this type of analysis is that, if we observe a change, the question arises: Should we regard the change as the primary metabolic disturbance or as a secondary response to the changed metabolism caused by the primary changes? Moreover, in many such experiments, it is impossible to select a good control with which to compare the tumor cell, since we cannot be sure in what type of normal cell the cancerous transformation has occurred. Also, our only comparison must often be with isolated cells growing in tissue cultures. These are not necessarily good standards for comparison, however, since normal cells may have undergone a number of genetic changes during their adaptation to growth in the unnatural environment of tissue culture.

WARBURG AND THE MEANING OF INCREASED GLYCOLYSIS

Nonetheless, one biochemical difference of real significance may already be known. This is the fact that many types of tumor cells excrete much larger quantities of lactic acid than do their normal counterparts. They do this both when growing as solid tumors in animals or when multiplying as single cells in tissue culture. Interest in this phenomenon goes back almost fifty years to the 1920s, when the German biochemist Warburg first seriously investigated it. Since then the meaning of lactic acid overproduction (often called the _Warburg effect_) has been studied again and again, but its real significance remains tantalizingly elusive. The metabolic source of the excessive lactic acid, however, is known. It arises from glucose via the glycolytic pathway. But this increase in fermentation (nonoxygen-involving metabolism) does not result from an insufficiency of any enzymes involved in the various oxidative pathways (e.g., oxidative phosphorylation proceeds normally). Nonetheless, more glucose is consumed by these tumor cells than they need to grow and multiply.

This suggests the loss of a normal control device which regulates the rate at which glucose is taken into a cell. Unfortunately, despite years and years of many biochemists' careers, no one really knows how glucose consumption is regulated. Conceivably tumor cells lack one or more specific surface proteins which control both glucose uptake and the "sticky" quality that gives the cells the correct cellular affinity. But even if this hypothesis is correct, proof may not come for years since at the molecular level the real morphology of external cell membranes lies in almost total darkness.

TUMOR-SPECIFIC ANTIGENS

In the absence of any real chemical foothold for looking closely at cell surfaces, much attention has gone to see whether immunological methods might reveal specific antigenic differences between normal and tumor cells. While many, many positive reports of new tumor-specific antigens are in the literature, until recently they have not been taken seriously. Arguing against their relevance, if not existence, was the belief that the presence of new tumor antigens should induce the selective synthesis of antibodies which would destroy any newly arising cancer cells. And since, at first sight, tumors grow uncontrolled within their hosts, they must not have significant antigenic differences from the normal cells they have descended from.

Today, instead, there is the growing feeling that *in vivo* tumor growth occurs despite the acquisition of new antigenic markers. This argument further proposes that most animal tumors which start to grow are quickly destroyed and it is only the exceptional cancer cell against which host animals cannot react. Why the host antibody response fails in these rare cases is not clear, though it is known that the capacity to respond to well-defined antigens often shows great individual variability within the same species. Most likely, this variability has a strong genetic component. Certainly it is now clear that use of immunosuppressive drugs results in a great increase in the number of "spontaneous" tumors most of which we now believe would, under normal conditions, have undergone regression as a result of attack by their hosts' antibodies. Thus the evolution of vertebrates with their relatively long lives was dependent upon development of an immunological response against cancer. Conceivably the use of antibodies to combat microbial infections arose as an incidental side benefit of a system primarily selected to defend animals against cancer.

SELECTIVE PRECIPITATION OF CANCER CELLS BY A PLANT GLYCOPROTEIN

Another indication that tumor cell surfaces differ from normal ones comes from experiments which follow up the chance observation that a glycoprotein isolated from wheat seeds selectively agglutinates many types of tumor cells. In contrast, their normal cell progenitors do not combine with the glycoprotein. The cancer-specific surface site can be shown to contain N-acetyl-glucose amine. Its combination with the agglutinin is reversible, no enzymatic action is involved, and growth of the agglutinated cells is unaffected. These facts lead to the question whether the selective reaction of the tumor cells is due to the presence of a new component not found in normal cells or whether it involves components present in normal cells but somehow "masked" by the simultaneous presence of another compound. Now the "masking" hypothesis is preferred since brief treatment of normal cells with several different proteolytic enzymes (e.g., trypsin and chymotrypsin) converted them into forms agglutinatable by the specific glycoprotein. This strongly suggests that many cancer cells lack a normal protein component of the exterior cell membrane.

CANCER INDUCTION BY RADIATION AND CHEMICALS

It is obvious that a prime requirement for satisfactory chemical analysis of cancer cells is the availability of external agents whose application can change, *in vitro* (i.e., in tissue culture), a normal cell into a cancer cell. We already know of many examples of an externally added agent greatly increasing the incidence of tumors inside living animals. These cancer-causing agents are called *carcinogens*. Among the most potent carcinogens are various forms of radiation. Exposure of the thyroid gland to x rays, for example, greatly increases the occurrence of thyroid cancer. None of the various radiations, however, can be used to cause all the cells in an exposed population to become cancerous. Only a small fraction is affected. Thus, radiation does not yet seem to be a useful agent for studying the biochemistry of the primary events accompanying the changeover from the normal to the cancerous state. Similarly, most chemicals which cause tumors in animals transform only a small percentage of the exposed cell population.

A further difficulty in analyzing the biochemical events occurring during either radiation or chemical carcinogenesis is that both types of agents are quite toxic and undoubtedly cause many changes other than the cancerous change. What biochemists need is an agent whose primary effect is connected with the change to unrestrained growth. Fortunately, as we shall soon see, carcinogenesis induced by viral infection fills the requirement. Before we discuss how viruses act, however, we must first inquire how the cancer cell maintains its cancerous property.

CANCER AS A HEREDITARY CHANGE

When a cancer cell divides, the two progeny cells are usually morphologically identical to the parental cell. The factor(s) that gives cancer cells their essential quality of unrestrained growth is thus regularly passed on from parent to progeny cells. These changes persist not only in tumors growing in intact animals, but also in tumor cells growing in tissue culture. Hundreds of generations of growth can occur in tissue culture without appreciable reversion to a normal state. The permanence of such changes is shown not only by perpetuation of a typical morphology, but also by the ability of progeny cells to cause new tumors when injected into a tumor-free animal of genetic composition similar to the one from which the original tissue culture was obtained.

The heritability of the changes allowing unrestrained growth makes us consider the possibility that an alteration has occurred at the chromosomal level. Direct tests of this idea should soon be possible using the Sendai virus technique to fuse cancer and normal cells. Following formation of tetraploid (4n) fused nuclei, subsequent irregular mitotic divisions produce cells with lower chromosome numbers and, hopefully, the cancer property can be correlated with the presence of one or more specific chromosomes. Currently, much effort is being directed toward this goal, so perhaps within the next year or so we shall have a clear proof of this hypothesis.

Alternatively, we can imagine that the cancerous change is an example of irreversible differentiation. That is, the mechanism which makes the cancerous transformation permanent may be similar to the devices which, for example, ensure that a nerve cell always multiplies as a nerve cell. We cannot, however, really follow up this hypothesis, for, as we emphasized in the previous chapter, no one yet knows how cells are irreversibly differentiated.

SOMATIC MUTATIONS AS POSSIBLE CAUSES OF CANCER

If the essential changes that make cells cancerous are at the chromosomal level, it is possible to imagine two quite different mechanisms for their occurrence. The first mechanism postulates that somatic mutations (mutations occurring in cells not destined to become sex cells) constitute the essential change. Under this scheme, a somatic mutation could cause a cancer if its occurrence upset a normal control device regulating cell division. Proponents of this hypothesis believe that, in general, several somatic mutations are necessary to cause a cancer. This idea is based on the fact that the incidence of cancer greatly increases with age. This phenomenon would be explainable if a particular cell had to accumulate several mutations, each occurring randomly in time, before becoming a full-fledged cancer cell. At present there exists no direct evidence either for or against this theory, which we might best describe as cancer due to loss of an essential gene(s) function. Even without evidence, however, it is clear that somatic mutations must occur;

it would be surprising if at least some did not disrupt the normal control of cell division.

VIRUSES AS A CAUSE OF CANCER

Alternatively, there is the hypothesis that many cancers are caused by viruses. In a sense, this is not really a hypothesis since there is already convincing evidence that a number of specific cancers in animals, ranging from fish to mammals, are virus-induced. The relevant question is thus not whether viruses can cause cancer, but whether a sizable fraction of cancers are virus-induced. Until recently, there was no intellectual framework in which to consider how viruses might cause cancer. Now largely as a result of work with bacterial viruses, we realize that when a virus enters a cell, a new piece of genetic material is brought into the cell. Normally we think of viruses as objects whose multiplication inevitably kills cells. Addition of a tumor virus to a cell, however, often does not kill the host cell. It is thus possible, as we shall soon show, to believe that the essential aspect of viral carcinogenesis is *the introduction of new genetic material*, in contrast to somatic mutations which, we suspect, often cause a loss of functional genetic material.

At present it seems most likely that not all tumor viruses act in the same way. For example, a variety of cancers are caused by RNA-containing viruses. The best-known of these RNA viruses is the Rous sarcoma virus, which causes solid tumors in chickens (a sarcoma is a tumor of connective tissue). Certain other RNA viruses most likely cause leukemia in both birds and mammals, probably including man. Acting quite differently are several groups of DNA viruses. One group is responsible for wartlike growths on the skin in many different mammals, ranging from rodents to man. Other closely related DNA viruses, of which the best-known are a mouse virus called polyoma and a monkey virus called SV40, can cause a variety of tumors when injected into newborn animals. Below we shall focus attention first on polyoma (SV40) and then on the Rous virus to show that it is now possible to propose concrete hypotheses, at the molecular level, about how they cause cancerous transformations.

THE VERY SIMPLE STRUCTURE
OF A POLYOMA (SV40) PARTICLE

Polyoma is a spherical virus that normally multiplies in mice. It is among the smallest DNA-containing viruses, with a mo-

FIGURE 18–2   *An electron micrograph (courtesy of L. V. Crawford, Institute of Virology, Glasgow) of polyoma virus particles. The viral diameter is about 500 A. Careful observation reveals that 72 subunits are used to construct the external protein coat. Two of the particles (lower left) are held together by an antipolyoma antibody molecule.*

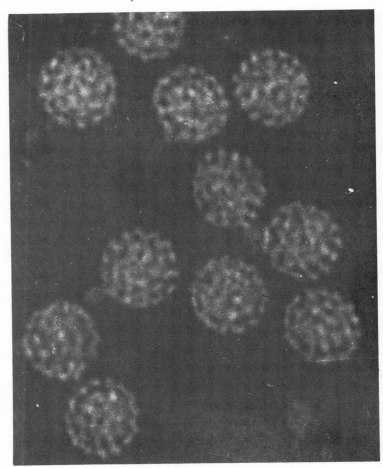

lecular weight of about 25 million. On the outside is a protein shell, which electron-microscope examination shows to be built up from 72 morphologically identical protein subunits (Figure 18–2). Each of these subunits in turn is built up from either five or six smaller protein molecules to give a grand total of 420 protein molecules in the shell. Whether these units of MW ~ 40,000 are built up from more than one polypeptide chain is not yet established. Within each shell is a single, circular, double-helical DNA molecule of molecular weight about 3 million with a length of 1.6μ (Figure 18–3). Also internally located is a small protein, basic in charge and most likely tightly bound to the DNA chromosome. Much less is known about it than of the shell proteins. A good guess for its molecular weight is 15,000.

Virtually identical in appearance and basic construction to polyoma is SV40, a virus that multiplies in monkeys. Like polyoma, it also can induce cancer and so is now very exten-

FIGURE 18–3   *An electron micrograph (coutresy of W. Stoeckenius, Rockefeller Institute) of several molecules of purified polyoma DNA. All clearly have a circular contour. The DNA contour length is 1.6 μ, corresponding to 3×10^6 daltons.*

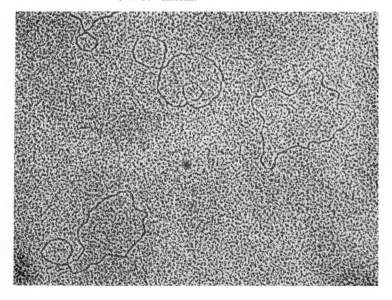

sively studied. In all the most important aspects (except for their host ranges), polyoma and SV40 behave in a biologically identical manner and so results gained with one virus usually hold for the other.

As only some 5000 nucleotides are present in the polyoma (SV40) chromosome, the maximum number of amino acids that it can code for ranges near 1600. Given the plausible assumption that both the shell and internal proteins are coded for by the viral chromosome, approximately 40 per cent of the total genome is used to specify structural protein. This leaves about 3000 nucleotides to code for the various enzymes specifically needed for polyoma reproduction. Even if they are of smaller-than-normal size, the number of polyoma-specific enzymes is unlikely to be more than five or six. Its gene number thus closely resembles that of the very small single-stranded DNA phages, each of whose chromosomes contain some seven to eight genes. Polyoma (SV40) thus has as simple a genetic structure as any known DNA virus (Figure 18–4).

FIGURE 18–4   *The genetic structure of polyoma (SV40). Still to be determined are the relative location and sizes of the various genes. The existence of 8 distinct genes is postulated. If the protein products are smaller than with other known genes, the gene number will be correspondingly larger.*

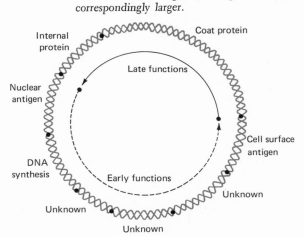

LYTIC VERSUS TRANSFORMING RESPONSE

When a polyoma virus enters a susceptive mouse cell, it generally disappears without trace. Less commonly (10^{-2}), it multiplies like conventional virus, producing a large number of new virus particles. The site of production within its host cell is the nucleus, which eventually becomes totally filled with a million or so progeny particles. During this process, which occupies some 24 to 48 hours at 37° C, the normal nuclear functions are disrupted and the infected cell necessarily dies (a lytic infection). Still less commonly (10^{-5}), the virus enters the cell but forms no progeny. Instead, the infected cell becomes transformed into a morphologically distinguishable cancer cell.

Both lytic and transforming responses can be observed outside living animals, in tissue culture. In these experiments, tissue culture cells (often derived from embryonic mice) are allowed to grow on a glass surface bathed in nutrient solution.

FIGURE 18–5 *Plaques of polyoma virus. Polyoma particles were added to embryonic mouse cells growing on a glass surface. The plaques, which became visible after 25 days of incubation, represent contiguous masses of dead cells which stain differently than growing cells. [From Crawford and Diamond, Virology, 22, 235 (1964), with permission.]*

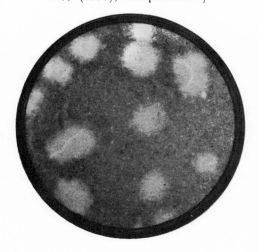

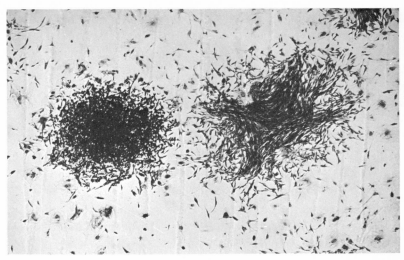

FIGURE 18–6   *Clones formed by transformed (left) and normal (right) mouse embryo cells. The transformed cells pile on top of each other, thereby forming a thicker (darker) mass than do normal cells (courtesy of M. Stoker, Institute of Virology, Glasgow, Scotland).*

A number of polyoma particles are then added. Some of these particles multiply in the cells to produce progeny particles which then absorb to nearby cells, producing a circular region of dead cells similar to the plaques formed by bacterial viruses (Figure 18–5). If, on the other hand, the virus transforms one of the tissue culture cells, the transformed cell then begins to multiply in the disorganized and easily identifiable fashion of a cancer cell (Figure 18–6). Particularly noticeable in the case of the transformed cells is their apparent lack of contact inhibition, which results in the formation of groups of cells piled irregularly on top of each other.

PERMISSIVE VERSUS NONPERMISSIVE CELLS

Cells in which a specific virus multiplies are called *permissive* cells, while cells in which viral growth does not occur are known as *nonpermissive* cells. A permissive cell line usually is derived from an animal in which a given virus normally reproduces.

In contrast, nonpermissive cell lines usually originate from animals incapable of multiplying a given virus. Thus, depending upon the specific virus, a cell can be either permissive or nonpermissive. For example, the very well-known mouse strain 3T3 is permissive for polyoma, a mouse virus, but nonpermissive for SV40, a monkey virus. In contrast, when SV40 infects a 3T3 cell, it never multiplies but occasionally induces cell transformation. And when polyoma infects the nonpermissive hamster cell line BHK (baby hamster kidney), it can transform but not multiply, and so BHK cells are frequently used in polyoma transformation experiments.

EARLY AND LATE POLYOMA MESSENGERS

The life cycle of polyoma, like that of phages, can be subdivided into early and late stages. The early stage is marked by the synthesis of several viral specific proteins, one of which is strongly antigenic (the "T" antigen), accumulating in the nucleus in large amounts. Exact metabolic roles for all the early polyoma proteins remain to be worked out. During the late stages of infection, synthesis of the progeny polyoma DNA and of the polyoma structural proteins occurs.

Correspondingly, the viral specific mRNA can be differentiated by DNA-RNA hybridization experiments into early and late components. Synthesis of the early mRNA occurs even if protein synthesis is blocked at the time of infection, suggesting that it is transcribed by a host-specific RNA polymerase molecule. No late mRNA molecule is synthesized if protein synthesis is blocked, suggesting that some viral specific enzyme must be made for reading of the late genes.

At first sight, a most appealing possibility is that one of the early polyoma genes codes for a σ factor specific for the late genes. But arguing against this suggestion is the size range of the various σ's found in bacteria. All have molecular weights of about 80,000 with single polypeptide chains made up of some 750 amino acids. If the mammalian polymerase cores require similar-sized σ's, a polyoma-specific σ would need for its coding almost all the polyoma genome not devoted to its structural proteins. So the probability remains that the transcription of the late, as well as the early, polyoma mRNA requires host-specific σ's. How the polyoma early-to-late transition is brought about thus remains a total mystery.

POLYOMA GENETICS IS STILL IN ITS INFANCY

The genetic organization of polyoma compared to that of the better-known phages is very incompletely understood. A number of temperature-sensitive mutants have been isolated after treatment with the mutagen nitrous acid and complementation experiments hint that mutations have been induced in four different genes. None of the protein products corresponding to these genes have been identified. Two appear to function early, being necessary for viral DNA synthesis, while the other two most likely code for the viral structural proteins. Much more genetic investigation is obviously necessary.

INDUCTION OF HOST ENZYMES INVOLVED IN DNA SYNTHESIS

Polyoma can reproduce either in cells actively synthesizing DNA (S_1 stage) or in contact-inhibited cells whose DNA synthesis has stopped. Growth in the inhibited cells occurs despite the fact that before infection these cells lack many of the enzymes (e.g., CDP reductase, dTMP synthetase, and DNA polymerase) used to make the various DNA nucleotide precursors or to link them together. Thus polyoma infection must specifically induce the synthesis of these enzymes. One of the early polyoma genes codes for an enzyme which unlocks the cellular control device which normally shuts off the synthesis of the "DNA enzymes" when their presence is no longer wanted. As to how this happens, we still are completely in the dark.

Induction of the "DNA enzymes", which occurs some 8 to 12 hours after infection, starts off not only polyoma DNA synthesis but also large-scale synthesis of host DNA (Figure 18–7). The specific signals which cause a circular polyoma chromosome to begin its replication also act upon the many host

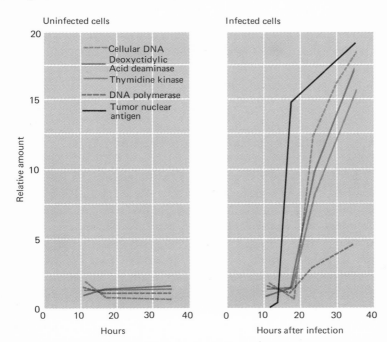

FIGURE 18–7 *Induction of enzymes involved with DNA synthesis following infection of permissive monkey cells by SV40 virus. Before these cellular-coded enzymes appear, synthesis of the viral specific protein, the "T" nuclear antigen, has begun. (Redrawn from Dulbecco, Scientific American, April, 1967.)*

chromosomes. This observation, surprising at first, makes sense when the genetic origin of the "DNA enzymes" is considered. They must be coded by host chromosomes since the polyoma chromosome is not nearly large enough to have this task. Coding for all these enzymes would require a size much more like that of λ DNA (10 times larger than polyoma).

ABORTIVE INFECTIONS PRECEDE TRANSFORMATION

Many of the polyoma particles infecting nonpermissive BHK cells go through the early stage of reproduction. Early polyoma mRNA is made, as is the polyoma nuclear antigen. Neither viral DNA nor the structural proteins, however, are synthesized. Likewise, no traces of late polyoma mRNA are detected. For some yet unknown reason, the nonpermissive cells do not permit late mRNA to be transcribed.

ONE PARTICLE CAN TRANSFORM A CELL

When polyoma particles are added to nonpermissive cells, the number of cells transformed is directly proportional to the amount of input virus. If a certain number of particles transforms one in a thousand cells, then ten times that number transforms one in a hundred cells. This relationship tells us that one particle by itself is completely sufficient to do the job. Furthermore, provided enough particles are added, virtually all the exposed cells can be transformed, indicating that all the cells growing in the culture were capable of being transformed. The probability of a single polyoma particle causing transformation, however, is very, very low. Some tens of thousands of infecting particles ordinarily must be present to give the average cell a 50 per cent probability of conversion to the cancer state.

ABSENCE OF INFECTIOUS POLYOMA PARTICLES FROM TRANSFORMED CELLS

No infectious polyoma particles are present in transformed cells. It is, of course, not surprising that the nuclei of transformed cells are not filled with viral particles. This would probably result in cell death. The fact is, however, that no particles *at all* can be detected. Here there is an obvious analogy to lysogenic bacterial viruses (see Chapter 7). Lysogenic phages also have two possible fates. They may multiply lytically or they may become part of the host chromosome by crossing over.

TRANSFORMATION INVOLVES INTEGRATION OF POLYOMA (SV40) DNA INTO HOST CHROMOSOMES

Some recent experiments, in fact, clearly show the existence of polyoma-specific (SV40-specific) DNA inserted into host chromosomal DNA. DNA-RNA hybridization studies reveal the presence of polyoma (SV40) DNA sequences in the DNA isolated from transformed cells. In contrast, when DNA from normal cells was tested, no polyoma DNA sequences were detected. This inserted DNA clearly originates from the nucleus, not from a cytoplasmic (mitochondria?) organelle. Moreover, within the nucleus, it must be covalently bound to chromosomal DNA since careful extraction techniques indicate that the DNA sequences that hybridize with polyoma mRNA are part of exceedingly long DNA molecules ($MW > 10^9$).

Within a single nucleus are some 5 to 60 copies of polyoma (SV40) DNA. Whether they are located next to each other, representing tandem duplications of an original copy, or whether they are present on many different chromosomes remains to be worked out. The fact, though, that transformation generally is caused by a single viral particle argues for the tandem copy hypothesis. Soon it should be possible to

FIGURE 18–8 *A schematic drawing showing how the circular polyoma chromosome might integrate into a host chromosome.*

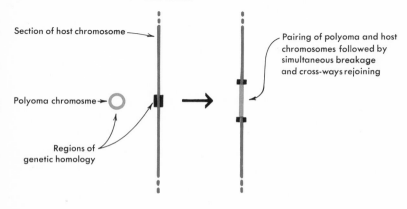

Section of host chromosome

Pairing of polyoma and host chromosomes followed by simultaneous breakage and cross-ways rejoining

Polyoma chromosme

Regions of genetic homology

separate the various host chromosomes into several size categories and see whether the polyoma genomes always attach to chromosomes of the same size.

The enzymes involved in the insertion process are not known, though it seems simplest to imagine a crossing-over process like that sketched in Figure 18–8. Both the very low transformation efficiency and the small polyoma genome size argue against use of an enzyme(s) coded by the virus.

LIBERATION OF INFECTIOUS PARTICLES FOLLOWING FUSION OF A TRANSFORMED NONPERMISSIVE CELL WITH A NONTRANSFORMED PERMISSIVE CELL

For many years, efforts were made to induce polyoma (SV40) tumor cells to yield infectious virus particles. But despite application of the several agents that induce the λ prophage to detach from the *E. coli* chromosome, all such attempts were unsuccessful. Just recently, however, the cell-fusion technique was found to work. When an SV40-transformed 3T3 cell is fused with a nontransformed cell, permissive for SV40, within 24 hours the fused cells almost always yield SV40 progeny. Something present in the permissive cell allows SV40 genes to detach from a host chromosome and carry out a complete multiplication cycle. As yet, this finding has not been duplicated with polyoma-transformed cells, but most likely the reason for this is trivial, not fundamental. With polyoma, as well as SV40, we believe that all the viral genome, not just an incomplete portion, is present within the transformed cells.

VIRAL SPECIFIC mRNA IN TRANSFORMED CELLS

Only a fraction of the polyoma (SV40) genome functions in transformed cells. The genes that function belong largely, if not entirely, to the early class; that is, the same genes which function immediately after polyoma particles infect the nonpermissive cells. Late genes either function not at all or at such

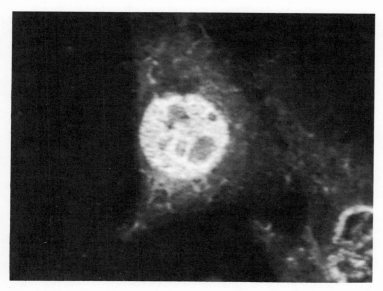

FIGURE 18–9 *Demonstration by the fluorescent antibody technique of the presence of the SV40 specific nuclear antigen within nonpermissive hampster cells transformed by SV40. (Courtesy of V. Defendi, Wistar Institute, Philadelphia.)*

low rates as to be so far undetectable. One of the early genes that functions in transformed cells is that which produces the tumor-specific nuclear antigen (Figure 18–9). There are also hints that another early gene functions which codes for a surface antigen (the transplantation antigen) which localizes at the cell surface and can be detected by failure of polyoma tumor cells to divide when they are transplanted into inbred mice not previously exposed to polyoma.

The presence of tumor-specific cellular antigens explains why polyoma, SV40, and many other tumor viruses usually induce tumors only in newborn animals. At the time of birth, most mammals have a very poor ability to make circulating antibodies. The tumor cells arising at birth are not destroyed by newly produced polyoma tumor-specific antibodies. In fact,

the presence of tumor cells often confers immunological tolerance, as the host's immunological system recognizes the tumor
cells as normal cells.

DO PERMISSIVE CELLS PROVIDE σ FACTORS NEEDED TO READ LATE GENES?

The fact that fusion with a permissive cell induces the transformed nuclei of nonpermissive cells to yield SV40 indicates
that, unlike the λ prophage, SV40 genomes are under positive,
not negative, control. In the case of λ, the prophage genome is
kept inactive by the presence of its repressor, which specifically
prevents transcription of early, as well as late, λ mRNA. But
if the failure to transcribe the late SV40 genomes were due to
a repressor, fusion with a permissive cell should not lead
necessarily to induction. The repressor should continue to
bind to the promoter for the late SV40 genes. Instead, the
permissive cell may contain a molecule necessary for late transcription, conceivably an RNA polymerase σ factor, normally
lacking in nonpermissive cells. This hypothesis should soon
be testable. Until now, very little work has gone toward char-
acterizing the RNA polymerases of mammalian cells, but this
situation is rapidly being rectified.

VIRUS-INFECTED CELLS LIKE TO SYNTHESIZE NUCLEIC ACID

Here we shall try to face up to the heart of the matter. Why
should a variety of DNA-containing viruses, many morphologically similar to polyoma, but others of very different structure (e.g., certain adenoviruses), all possess the ability to induce
tumors in newborn animals? Our answer will start with the
assumption that formation of tumors which *kill* the host is
essentially a laboratory accident. Outside a laboratory, animals
almost never become infected with polyoma before the time
that they can mount an effective immunological assault on the
incipient tumors. We further suspect that the antigenic specificity of virus-induced tumors is a necessary feature for ensuring

the survival in nature of the host of the virus and, hence, of the virus itself. If the tumors provoked did not contain specific antigens, then nearly all viral infections might result in host death due to cancer.

We shall further tentatively adopt the hypothesis that all transformed cells contain a viral chromosome (provirus) integrated by crossing over into one of the host chromosomes. If we assume a provirus is present, we can then ask whether knowledge of any of the properties of a virus-infected cell could lead to a crucial insight into the metabolism of a cancer cell.

At present, our knowledge of the metabolism of cells infected with the viruses that multiply in higher organisms is scant, so that we must base our argument on our knowledge of bacterial viruses. These systems have yielded the very important generalization that viruses tend to maximize their reproductive potential by altering the host cell so that they can synthesize viral nucleic acid at an extremely rapid rate. In Chapter 15, we discussed several examples in which the nucleic acid of the infecting virus codes for enzymes involved in nucleic acid metabolism. Sometimes, the enzymes involved are unique to the virus-infected cell, but in other cases, the viral specific enzymes have the same functions as preexisting host enzymes. For example, phage T2 codes for an enzyme similar to *E. coli* DNA polymerase, which allows the infected cell to synthesize DNA much faster than the uninfected cell.

It is likely that many other viruses, in addition to phages, also take active measures to ensure a rapid rate of viral nucleic acid synthesis. The tendency may even be more pronounced for viruses infecting organisms which have a high proportion of nondividing cells, because many nondividing cells (e.g., liver cells) are quite deficient in the enzymes involved in making the deoxynucleoside triphosphate precursors. When an animal virus enters such a cell, either it must code for all the missing nucleic acid-synthesizing enzymes or it must release the control mechanisms that prohibit a nondividing cell from making these enzymes. Many times, of course, viruses will enter metabolically satisfactory cells. On the other hand, they are likely to enter nondividing cells sufficiently often to confer a marked evolutionary advantage upon those particles which can multiply in either phase of a cell's life.

As we mentioned earlier, both polyoma and SV40 have the property of inducing host DNA synthesis concurrent with their own multiplication. This property is due to an early gene product and so is also likely to be expressed in the transformed cells containing integrated viral chromosomes. This may explain why DNA synthesis in a tumor induced by DNA viruses is not subject to the control devices operating in normal cells. Thus, a most immediate task is to identify the gene product responsible for induction of host DNA synthesis. Since there are so few early genes, there is a good chance that the polyoma nuclear antigen is, in fact, the protein which unlocks DNA synthesis. So, much effort now is being given to isolation of the nuclear antigen in pure form.

However, we would still be left with the problem of understanding what advantage there is for the tumor virus to insert itself into a host chromosome as a provirus. It seems hard to believe that insertion is a matter of chance, since it requires that homologies in nucleotide sequence exist between regions of the viral and host chromosomes. Our current failure to answer this enigma should, however, be seen in relation to a similar lack of understanding in bacterial lysogeny. Here also, we are as yet unable to pinpoint any selective advantage for the prophage state.

VIRAL-INDUCED CHANGES AT THE CELL SURFACE

Unlocking of DNA synthesis, however, is unlikely by itself to give the SV40 (polyoma) transformed cell all the essential properties of a cancer cell. Equally, if not more important, are specific chemical changes at the cell surface which result in loss of contact inhibition. The changes, first detected by immunological means, are now easily followed by the selective agglutination of transformed cells by the wheat germ glycoprotein. Now there are hints that the viral-induced specific changes at the cell surface are directly related to the replication of viral DNA. Evidence comes from a polyoma mutant that at high temperature specifically loses its ability to carry out viral DNA synthesis. Most importantly, there occurs parallel loss of the ability of the transformed cells at high temperature to be precipitated by the specific glycoprotein. Now, no one has any believable hypothesis to explain why a change of the cell surface should effect DNA synthesis (or vice versa). Nor is there any obvious reason why viral reproduction would be aided by specific membrane changes.

ROUS SARCOMA IS CAUSED BY A MYXOLIKE VIRUS

Specific alterations of the cell membrane of cells infected with the various RNA tumor viruses are much easier to relate to the way such viruses replicate. The best-known RNA tumor virus is the Rous sarcoma virus (RSV). Though it was discovered over fifty years ago, the state of our knowledge about how viruses multiply did not allow decisive experimentation with RSV until the past fifteen years. RSV is a medium-size virus, morphologically similar to a large group of animal viruses collectively called *myxoviruses*. These are viruses considerably more complex than the polyoma-SV40 variety. In the center of each myxovirus is a *single-stranded* RNA *chain* combined with a large number of protein subunits (the internal proteins), somewhat in the manner of tobacco mosaic virus. The RNA-protein complex is not rigid, as in TMV, but is flexible and is itself contained within a special outer membrane composed of both protein and lipid (Figure 18–10). The presence of the lipid gives the myxovirus the feature of being rapidly destroyed by lipid solvents. Among the best-known myxoviruses are the groups that cause influenza and the mumps.

There appears to be considerable range in the size of myxoviruses. The external diameter of some is as small as 700 A (e.g., influenza), whereas for others (e.g., mumps) it is about 1200 A. Likewise, there is a large spread in the amount of nucleic acid present per particle; it ranges between 2×10^6 and

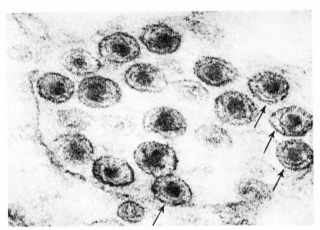

FIGURE 18–10   *An electron micrograph (by W. Bernhard, Institute of Cancer, Villejuif, France) of an ultrathin cross section of a chick cell infected with both RSV and a helper virus. The virus particles appear as circular bodies about 750 A in diameter. [Reproduced from* Bull. Cancer, **43**, 497 (1956), *with permission.]*

10^7 MW. Nucleotide base analyses show noncomplementary base ratios indicating single-chain structures.

MYXOVIRUSES MATURE ON CELL SURFACES

After their entrance into cells, the RNA chains of many myxoviruses move to the cell nucleus. There, progeny RNA chains, as well as specific internal proteins, accumulate. RNA-internal protein complexes then migrate to the cell surface where they are surrounded by the lipid and protein components that comprise the outer viral membrane. The newly formed virus particles appear to pinch off from the cell surface, quite possibly acquiring some normal cell components in the process (Figure 18–11). A distinctive feature of a myxovirus infection is that considerable viral multiplication and release can occur without causing cell death. Though the reproduction of many myxoviruses (e.g., influenza) does eventually lead to cell death, as we shall soon point out in the case of RSV, cell death is very

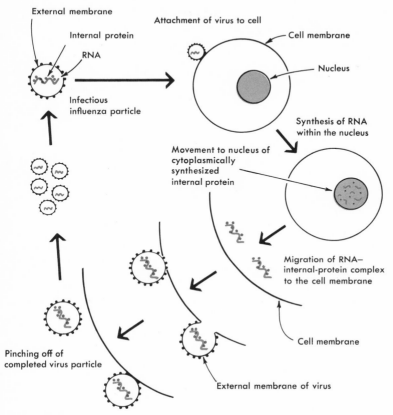

External membrane

Attachment of virus to cell

Internal protein

Cell membrane

RNA

Nucleus

Infectious
influenza particle

Synthesis of RNA
within the nucleus

Movement to nucleus of
cytoplasmically
synthesized
internal protein

Migration of RNA–
internal-protein complex
to the cell membrane

Cell membrane

Pinching off of
completed virus particle

External membrane of virus

FIGURE 18–11 *Diagrammatic view of the life cycle of a typical myxovirus (influenza virus).*

definitely not an obligatory consequence of the large-scale production of a myxolike virus by a cell.

GENOMES OF RNA TUMOR VIRUSES ARE RELATIVELY LARGE CODING FOR SOME 30–50 DIFFERENT PROTEINS

Recent measurements of RSV suggest that each particle contains about 10^7 MW units of RNA per particle. The genetic message of RSV (30,000 nucleotides) is thus about six times larger than that of polyoma (4800 base pairs). Approximately

10,000 amino acids are coded by the RSV genome. This number is sufficient for some 30–50 different proteins, many more than are found in its coat. This fact suggests that a large number of still-unidentified proteins are synthesized during RSV multiplication.

Similar genetic complexity is shared by a number of other tumor viruses which use RNA as their genetic material. Several mouse cancer viruses that induce leukemia (e.g., the Rauscher virus, the Maloney virus, and the Gross virus), as well as several chicken leukemia viruses, are morphologically identical to the Rous virus, each having RNA chains of MW's about 10^7.

INFECTION BY A SINGLE RSV PARTICLE LEADS TO A CANCER CELL

Infection of a susceptible chicken cell by a *single* RSV particle almost immediately converts the normal cell into a cancer cell. Within 48 hours after attachment of the virus, an RSV-

FIGURE 18–12   Photograph of a group (focus) of chicken cells (magnification × 30) transformed by RSV infection (supplied by H. Rubin, Department of Molecular Biology, University of California, Berkeley). The spherical transformed cells are easily distinguished from the background of normal cells.

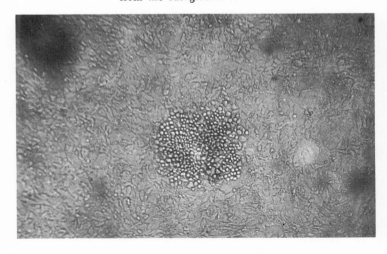

infected cell loses its normal shape, becomes more spherical, and acquires the invasive properties of a malignant cell. This rapid response is easily demonstrated by using tissue culture cells derived from chicken embryos. When RSV particles are added to a number of normal cells growing attached to a glass surface, the transformed cells are easily scored. They are not subject to contact inhibition and so do not stop growing after the glass surface is covered with cells. Instead, they continue to proliferate and pile up on top of each other to form discrete masses easily distinguishable from normal cells (Figure 18–12).

RSV-TRANSFORMED CELLS OFTEN PRODUCE OTHER ROUS-LIKE VIRUSES

Initially everyone thought that cells infected with RSV contained this virus and no other. But now it is realized that many transformed chicken cells are simultaneously infected with another very similar virus [e.g., the morphologically identical RAV (Rous Associated Virus)], and that such cells are producing both viruses at the same time. Most importantly, the presence of RAV profoundly affects the structure of the progeny RSV particles. When a chicken cell is infected with RSV only, progeny particles are budded off the cell surface but their outer membranes are somehow defective and unable to adsorb to most other chicken cells. In contrast, when RAV is simultaneously multiplying in the same cell, some of the progeny RSV genomes become surrounded with outer membranes containing RAV specific components and so become able to multiply easily in chicken cells. RAV multiplication thus helps the production of infectious RSV particles and so RAV is frequently called a *helper virus*.

HELPER VIRUSES BY THEMSELVES ALSO CAN CAUSE CANCER

RAV itself is a cancer (leukosis) virus, that is, when injected into a chicken it can cause a form of leukemia. Its infection, like that of other leukemia viruses, however, does not ordinarily transform its host cell into a malignant cell. Infected cells usually maintain a normal morphology except for the continuous production on their outer cell membranes of large numbers of new virus particles. Why cell transformation by leukemia viruses is a rare event remains a total mystery. The answer may be that only a very special class of defective particles can transform. If so, they may be very hard to detect because of the simultaneous presence of many, many normal leukosis genomes. So far, despite some searching, no evidence of helper virus involvement has been found for any known leukemia viruses. This finding contrasts with results obtained with several sarcoma (solid tumor) inducing viruses. In both chickens and mice, sarcoma viruses tend to be associated with helper viruses. Clearly work on this problem is still in its infancy.

Defectiveness *per se* thus may be a peculiarity of the sarcoma-inducing viruses, with no general applicability to most other RNA tumor viruses. Instead, the basic carcinogenic property of the RNA tumor viruses may arise from the way they mature at the cell surface. One or more of the proteins used to construct the outer membrane of RNA tumors may somehow upset the normal cell membrane, thereby preventing both contact inhibition and regulation of DNA replication.

DNA AS THE PROVIRUS FORM OF RNA TUMOR VIRUSES

RSV transformed cells almost never revert to the normal state. Thus either the number of RSV genomes must be very large, or those present must have a fixed arrangement in the cell so that they are regularly segregated at mitosis to both progeny cells. At first, it seemed easiest to believe that RSV RNA replicates like an RNA phage, using double-helical RNA molecules as intermediates. If this were the mechanism, then the nuclei of all transformed cells should contain large numbers of double-helical intermediates. Many excess copies would be needed to ensure that random segregation during mitosis did not occasionally produce a cell lacking an RSV genome. But extensive searches for such double-helical molecules gave completely negative results.

Instead, very recent data now strongly suggest that the RSV genome, like the SV40 genome, becomes part of one of the host chromosomes (a provirus stage) when it transforms a cell. It can then replicate as if it were a set of host genes. The evidence is of several sorts. Firstly, inhibitors of DNA synthesis prevent RSV from transforming cells. This fact hints that the RSV genome, after entry into the host nucleus, is used as a template to form a complementary DNA strand. Secondly, DNA isolated from RSV-infected cells contains a small region in which one of the chains is complementary in sequence to RSV RNA. In contrast, no homology is seen with uninfected cells. Thirdly and even more important, an enzyme has just been isolated (1970) from mature RSV particles which carries out the RNA→DNA copying process. Using an RSV RNA molecule as a template, this enzyme can link together deoxynucleoside triphosphates to form a single-stranded DNA chain. Whether a newly-made DNA chain serves as a template to make the complementary DNA strand before it recombines into a host chromosome remains to be worked out. Most excitingly, similar enzymes can be isolated from several other RNA tumor viruses, including the Rauscher mouse virus and a chicken leukosis virus.

The integrated RSV genome produces progeny RSV RNA molecules by the same mechanism used to transcribe host genes. Thus, the antibiotic actinomycin D, which specifically binds to DNA thereby inhibiting DNA-dependent RNA synthesis, also prevents transformed cells from producing progeny RSV particles. In contrast, actinomycin has no effect on the reproduction of many RNA viruses (e.g., poliomyelitis) whose replication involves a double-helical RNA intermediate.

The concept of a DNA provirus for an RNA virus is clearly a radical proposal. It overturns the belief that flow of genetic information always goes in the direction DNA to RNA, and never RNA to DNA. On the other hand, it offers an even greater variety of ways for cells to exchange genetic information. Considering the enormous complexity of biological systems, it would not be surprising if this device were uniquely advantageous in some situations.

THE BURKITT LYMPHOMA AND ITS
RELATIONSHIP TO MONONUCLEOSIS

Despite the many advances made in understanding viral cancer induction in several animal species, a clear-cut connection between a human cancer and a specific virus does not yet exist. All the evidence so far gathered is circumstantial. One of the most promising leads involves a lymphoma first observed in Uganda by the English surgeon Burkitt. Its incidence appeared limited to certain ecological zones, suggesting transmission by an insect vector. Electron microscope examination of tissue culture-grown Burkitt cells occasionally reveals Herpes II particles. Most intriguingly, antiserum against these DNA-containing viruses crossreacts with cells from patients suffering from infectious mononucleosis. In this disease there is widespread multiplication of lymphatic cells forming tumorlike masses, which subsequently regress, most likely due to an immunological response. Thus, it is very tempting to hypothesize that multiplication of the Burkitt cells is stimulated by a Herpes II-like virus, but that for some unknown reason, regression is much less likely than after mononucleosis infection.

HERPES II VIRUSES AND CERVICAL CANCER

There also exists circumstantial evidence linking another Herpes II-type virus with human cervical cancer. Patients with this disease have a very high probability of having antibodies against such viruses, while control sera much less frequently contain such antibodies. As in the Burkitt case, most tumor cells give no indication of viral infection. This suggests that the causative Herpes II virus acts as a carcinogen when in a provirus stage. Interestingly, the Herpes I-type viruses, which are responsible for cold sores, are commonly believed to exist in a latent (e.g., provirus) condition between the infectious periods, which are characterized by large numbers of progeny particles. But so far, no one has solid evidence to back up these conjectures. The impressions remain, however, that many other DNA viruses resemble SV40 in their ability to reside for long interludes on host chromosomes.

SEARCHING FOR HUMAN RNA TUMOR VIRUSES

Very many efforts now are being made to demonstrate that some human tumors are caused by RNA viruses morphologically similar to RSV. Attention in particular has been focused on those specific tumors where animal systems clearly implicate viruses. By now thousands of independently arising tumors have been looked at with the electron microscope to see if RSV-like particles are present. Occasionally some cells of a given tumor reveal virus-like particles, but they are also seen (though more rarely) in apparently normal cells. Thus attention has gone toward isolating such particles to see if they cannot only multiply like viruses but more importantly cause cell transformation. Just recently positive results have been obtained from several tumors which yield particles capable of multiplying in normal human cells grown in tissue culture. No evidence, however, yet exists that these viruses can transform normal cells into cancer cells and the possibility exists that they arrived on the scene after the tumor originated.

THEORY OF THE RNA ONCOGENE

Many virologists now are more struck by the failure to isolate mature viruses from most human tumors thought to be caused by RNA viruses (e.g., the various forms of leukemia) than by the occasional presence of virus-like particles in a small fraction of the tumors examined. Yet these same scientists strongly believe in the involvement of RNA viruses, proposing that most of these cancers are caused by defective RNA viruses which have become virtually a permanent part (oncogenes) of a human chromosome. Under this hypothesis, it is the functioning of the oncogenes which results in the production of the specific proteins (enzymes) that give their host cells their cancerous condition. Only when such tumor cells are simultaneously infected with helper viruses can their oncogenes occasionally be packaged into mature virus particles, thereby revealing the viral causation of the cancerous state.

A variant of this theory proposes that many oncogenes exist in a quiescent form and generally are only induced to work (e.g., be transcribed) by the action of external carcinogens like ionizing radiation, cigarette smoke, or conceivably the presence of another virus. In support of this idea is the fact that certain mouse leukemias induced by x rays often contain viruses that induce leukemia even in the absence of any radiation treatment. This suggests that the primary action of the x rays is to induce the functioning of a leukemia viral genome already present on a host chromosome. Now it is hard to avoid the idea that the genomes of many such viruses are normally present in most cells, often being passed through the germ cells from parent to offspring without being detected.

DNA TUMOR VIRUSES MOST LIKELY ACT DIRECTLY

An extreme form of the oncogene hypothesis proposes that all DNA viruses act by inducing RNA oncogenes to begin functioning, after which the genome of the DNA virus no longer need be present. This hypothesis, however, is incompatible with some new experiments in which cells transformed by a temperature-sensitive polyoma mutant lose their cancerous morphology at high temperatures, becoming unable to be agglutinated by the specific glycoprotein. This shows that a protein product (which in the temperature-sensitive mutant is inactive at high temperatures) must at all time be present for the transformed cell to remain cancerous. Thus, when these normal-appearing cells are returned to a lower temperature to multiply, they soon regain the cancerous morphology. If the polyoma genome merely induced an RNA oncogene to work, we need not expect that the continued presence of the DNA viral genome would be required for maintenance of the cancerous state.

STUDY OF CANCER AT THE MOLECULAR LEVEL

Until the recent work with polyoma and RSV, the search for chemical differences between normal and cancer cells resembled the search for a needle in a haystack. There may be more than a hundred thousand different genes in a mammalian cell, of which we now can assign functions to perhaps 1000. Thus, in the past biochemists studying cancer were most likely looking for changes in molecules that had not yet been discovered. This situation could only prevail as long as research was dominated by the concept of somatic mutation.

The increasing use of viruses as carcinogenic agents has greatly changed the picture. Now we can ask how an essential aspect of virus multiplication can be misdirected toward the production of a cancer. Attention can be concentrated on the fact that some of the most potent tumor viruses contain only several genes. A primary goal is thus to assign functions to each of these genes during viral multiplication. In particular, we hope to find the polyoma (SV40)-specific protein (enzyme?) that simultaneously releases the normal control of DNA replication and alters the outer cell membrane. In the case of RSV, we hope to learn the details of how the mature virus particles form at the cell surface and, hopefully, how viral proteins made by its genome upset contact inhibition. Naturally, we should not underestimate the difficulties ahead. These viruses multiply in cells that we are only beginning to study at the molecular level. Nonetheless, most important is the fact that at last the biochemistry of cancer can be approached in a straighforward, rational manner.

SUMMARY

A cancer cell is a cell that has lost the ability to control its growth and division. When it becomes a cancer cell, it divides both when and where it should not. Many cancer cells have lost a surface component which restricts the types of cell to which they may attach (loss of "selective stickiness"). Possibly connected with the disappearance of selective stickiness is a parallel loss of "contact inhibition" [inhibition of cell movement (and division?)].

At this time, tissue culture techniques are used in much cancer research. A single cancer cell can be isolated and the properties of all its progeny observed as they multiply in vitro. The technique allows a clear demonstration that the transformation of a normal cell to the cancerous state is a permanent change; all the cancerous properties are passed on to the descendants of a cancer cell. There are three main hypotheses about the origin of human cancers. One states that they are due to the accumulation of somatic mutations. An alternative hypothesis ascribes the occurrence of many cancers to viruses. Supporting this hypothesis has been the discovery of a variety of vertebrate viruses which transform normal cells into cancer cells. The third hypothesis is that the cancerous transformation is an example of irreversible differentiation.

Study of the biochemistry of the cancer cell often suffers from the fact that the original normal cell is not present for comparison. Systems are needed whereby addition of an external agent (carcinogen) will rapidly transform well-defined normal cells into cancer cells. Among the most useful carcinogenic agents known at present are several viruses. One is polyoma, a DNA virus which multiplies in mice; another is SV40, a DNA virus very similar to polyoma, that multiplies in monkeys; still another is the Rous sarcoma virus, an RNA virus which causes solid tumors in chickens.

Polyoma and SV40 have molecular weights of about 25 million and contain single circular DNA molecules of molecular weight about 3 million. This is a DNA amount sufficient to code for about 6 to 8 average-size genes. Both life cycles are divided into early and late phases. In the early phase, several viral specific proteins are produced which prepare the way for the synthesis, in the second stage, of progeny DNA molecules and of the structural proteins present in the infectious virus particles. Correspondingly, there are both early and late mRNA molecules.

A polyoma (SV40) particle, when it infects a susceptible (permissive) cell, multiplies lytically. In contrast, infection of

a nonpermissive cell leads to an abortive infection in which only
early polyoma mRNA and proteins molecules are made. A very
small fraction of abortive infections lead to transformation of
the host cell to a cancer cell. Transformation is marked by the
insertion of intact viral genomes (provirus) into host chromosomes. In the provirus state, several polyoma (SV40) genes
function, one of which controls the specific nuclear tumor antigen. Fusion of an SV40 transformed cell with a nontransformed permissive cell induces the transformed nucleus to produce progeny SV40 particles. This suggests that permissive
cells have molecules necessary for the reading of "late" genes.

Rous sarcoma virus (RSV) is a myxolike virus which rapidly
transforms normal chicken cells into cancer cells. Growth of
this virus does not kill its host cell when the virus particles are
released from the cell surface, the site of their final assembly.
Rous particles grown in chickens often produce particles unable
to grow in chickens. Whether this particular form of defectiveness relates to their cancer-inducing properties is unknown. It
is tempting to relate the conversion to the cancer state with the
appearance of coat-protein molecules which disturb the cell
membrane, thereby blocking contact inhibition.

REFERENCES

Huxley, J., *Biological Aspects of Cancer*, Harcourt, New York,
1958. A brief introduction to the cancer problem as seen by
a distinguished zoologist.

Burnet, F. M., "Cancer: Biological Approach. I. Processes of Control," *Brit. Med. J.*, **1**, 779 (1957). A superb appraisal of the
complexity of the cancer field with emphasis on the consequences of somatic mutation.

Harris, M., *Cell Culture and Somatic Variation*, Holt, New York,
1964. A very complete summary of how modern tissue culture
research is at the heart of both embryological and cancer research.

Gross, L., *Oncogenic Viruses*, Pergamon, New York, 1961. A
well-documented survey of the various viruses which cause
tumors.

Dulbecco, R., "The Induction of Cancer by Viruses", *Scientific
American*, April 1967. A very clear presentation of current

ideas about how the polyoma and SV40 viruses may cause cancers.

Black, P. H., "The Oncogenic DNA Viruses: A Review of in vitro Transformation Studies," *Ann. Rev. Microbiol.*, **391** (1968). The most complete recent review on many aspects of DNA tumor viruses.

Dulbecco, R., "Cell Transformation by Viruses," *Science*, **166**: 962 (1969). A very recent review that emphasizes the molecular biological approach to DNA tumor viruses.

Green, M., "Oncogenic Viruses," *Ann. Rev. Biochem.*, **39** (1970). A particularly strong review with much emphasis on the problems of transcription.

Burger, M. M. and Allan R. Goldberg, "Identification of a Tumor-Specific Determinant on Neoplastic Cell Surfaces," *Proc. Nat. Acad. Sci.*, **57**:359 (1967). How specific glycoproteins selectively react with cancer cell surfaces.

Mizutami, S. and H. M. Temin, "An Enzyme in Virions of Rous Sarcoma Virus that appears to Make DNA from an RNA Template, *Nature*, **226**:1211 (1970).

Baltimore, D., "An RNA-Dependent DNA polymerase in Virions of RNA Tumor Viruses, *Nature*, **226**:1209 (1970). This and the preceding paper give the first reports of the viral enzyme which makes DNA off RNA templates.

Huebner, R. J. and G. J. Todaro, "Oncogenes of RNA Tumor Viruses as Determinants of Cancer," *Proc. Nat. Acad. Sci.*, **64**: 1087 (1969). A brief summary of evidence suggesting the latent presence of RNA tumor virus genomes within many normal cells.

GLOSSARY

A + T/G + C Ratio. An expression of the relative amount of adenine-thymine pairs to guanine-cytosine pairs in a molecule of DNA.

Acidic Amino Acids. Amino acids having a net negative charge at neutral pH.

Actinomycin D. Antibiotic that blocks elongation of RNA chains.

Activating Enzmye. (See *Amino Acyl Synthetase.*)

Active Site. Region of protein directly involved in interaction with other molecules.

Adaptor Molecules. Small RNA molecules (sRNA) that bind amino acids to their proper positions on an mRNA template during protein synthesis. Each is specific for both an amino acid and a template codon.

Adenylcyclase. Enzyme that catalyzes production of cyclic AMP from ATP.

Allele. One of two or more alternate forms of a gene.

Allosteric Proteins. Proteins whose biological properties are changed by the binding of specific small molecules (allosteric effectors) at sites other than the active site.

Amino Acids. The building blocks of proteins. There are twenty common amino acids, each present as the L-stereoisomer. All amino acids have the same basic structure, but they differ in their side groups (R):

629

$$H-N^+-C-C{\overset{\displaystyle O}{\underset{\displaystyle O^-}{\diagdown}}}$$

Amino Acid Sequence.   The linear order of the amino acids in a peptide or protein.

Amino Acid Side Group(s).   (See *Amino Acids.*)

Amino Acyl Adenylate (AA ∼ AMP).   In protein synthesis, an activated compound that is an intermediate in the formation of a covalent bond between an amino acid and its sRNA adaptor.

Amino Acyl Synthetase.   Any one of at least twenty different enzymes that catalyze (1) the reaction of a specific amino acid with ATP to form amino acyl-AMP (activated amino acids) and pyrophosphate and (2) the transfer of the activated amino acid to sRNA forming amino acyl-sRNA and free AMP.

Amino Group. $-NH_2$, a chemical group, characteristically basic because of the addition of a proton to form $-NH_3^+$.

Amino Terminal.   The end of a polypeptide chain that has a free α-amino group.

Angstrom (A).   A unit of length convenient for describing atomic dimensions; equal to 10^{-8} cm.

Antigen.   Any object that, upon injection into a vertebrate, is capable of stimulating the production of neutralizing antibodies.

Antigenic Determinant.   Chemical structure (small compared to macromolecule) recognized by the active site of an antibody. Determines specificity of antibody-antigen interaction.

Anti-σ Factor.   Protein that prevents recognition of initiation sites by σ factor of RNA polymerase. An anti-σ factor is synthesized during phage T4 infection.

Antitermination Factor.   Protein that prevents normal termination of RNA synthesis, perhaps by interfering with action of ρ factor. Bacteriophage λ "N" gene product may be an antitermination factor.

Aromatic Amino Acids.   Amino acids whose side chains include a derivative of a phenyl group. The aromatic amino acids found in protein are phenylalanine, tyrosine, and tryptophan.

Autoradiographs.   When a photographic emulsion is placed in contact with radioactive material (e.g., thin sections of a cell), the radiation exposes the film, revealing details of the location and geometry of the radioactive components.

Autoradiography.   Detection of radioactive label in cytological preparations and macromolecules by exposure of photographic film.

Backbone. The atoms in a polymer that are common to all its molecules (e.g., the sugars and phosphates in RNA).

Bacterial Viruses. Viruses that multiply in bacteria.

Bacteriophages (Phages). (See *Bacterial Viruses.*)

Base Analogs. Purines and pyrimidines that differ slightly in structure from the normal nitrogenous bases. Some analogs (e.g., 5-bromouracil) may be incorporated into nucleic acids in place of the normal constituent.

Base-Pairing Rules. The requirement that adenine must always form a base pair with thymine (or uracil) and guanine with cytosine, in a nucleic acid double helix.

Basic Amino Acids. Amino acids having a net positive charge at neutral pH.

Bence-Jones Protein. Light chains of a single antibody species produced by myeloma cells. Commonly detected in urine of human multiple myeloma patients.

β-Galactosidase. An enzyme catalyzing the hydrolysis of lactose into glucose and galactose; in *E. coli*, the classic example of an inducible enzyme.

Biological Clocks. Mechanisms that allow expression of certain biological structures (genes) at periodic intervals. May involve σ and anti-σ factors.

Breakage and Reunion. The classical model of crossing over by physical breakage and crossways reunion of completed chromatids during meiosis. This model has recently been shown to be applicable in at least one case on the molecular level—crossing over between phage-DNA molecules proceeds by breakage and reunion.

^{14}C. A radioactive carbon isotope emitting a weak β particle (electron). Its half-life is 5700 years.

Calorie. A measure of energy, defined as the amount of energy necessary to raise 1 cc of water 1°C.

Cancer. The name given to a group of diseases that are characterized by uncontrolled cellular growth.

Carboxyl Group.
$$-\overset{\overset{O}{\|}}{C}-OH$$

A chemical group, characteristically acidic, as a result of the dissociation of the hydroxyl H to form

$$-COOH \rightleftharpoons -\overset{\overset{O}{\|}}{C}-O^- + H^+$$

Carboxyl Terminal. The end of a polypeptide chain that has a free α-carboxyl group.

Carcinogen. An agent that induces cancer.

Catabolite Repression. Decreased synthesis of certain enzymes in bacteria grown on glucose or other very good catabolite source. Caused by low levels of cyclic AMP in such cells.

Catabolites. Compounds that are breakdown products of food molecules.

Catalyst. A substance that can increase the rate of a chemical reaction without being consumed (e.g., enzymes catalyze biological reactions).

Cell. The fundamental unit of life; the smallest body capable of independent reproduction. Cells are always surrounded by a membrane.

Cell Cycle. The timed sequence of events occurring in a cell in the period between mitotic divisions.

Cell Differentiation. The process whereby descendants of a common parental cell achieve and maintain specialization of structure and function.

Cell-Free Extract. A fluid containing most of the soluble molecules of a cell, made by breaking open cells and getting rid of remaining whole cells.

Cell Fusion. Formation of a single hybrid cell with nuclei and cytoplasm from different cells. Often induced by treatment of mixed cell culture with killed Sendai virus.

Cellular Affinity. Tendency of cells to adhere specifically to cells of same type, but not of different types. This property is lost in cancer cells.

Central Dogma. The basic relationship between DNA, RNA, and protein: DNA serves as a template for both its own duplication and the synthesis of RNA; and RNA, in turn, is the template in protein synthesis.

Chromatids. The two daughter strands of a duplicated chromosome that are still joined by a single centromere.

Chromomere. A concentrated chromatin "bead" on eucaryotic chromosome. May be region of gene redundancy. Results from local coiling of a continuous thread.

Cleavage Divisions. Mitotic divisions of fertilized egg until stage when regions of egg shift relative to one another.

Clone. A group of cells all descended from a single common ancestor.

Coat Protein(s). The external structural protein(s) of a virus.

Codon. A sequence of three adjacent nucleotides that code for an amino acid (or chain termination ?).

Colony. A group of contiguous cells, usually derived from a single ancestor, growing on a solid surface.

Complementary Base Sequences. Polynucleotide sequences that are related by the base-pairing rules.

Complementary Structures. Two structures, each of which defines the other; for instance, the two strands of a DNA helix:

Complementation Test. The introduction of two mutant chromosomes (or sections of chromosomes) into the same cell for the purpose of seeing whether their respective mutations occurred in the same gene.

Conditional Lethal Mutations. A class of mutants whose viability is dependent on growth conditions (e.g., temperature-sensitive lethals).

Constitutive Enzymes. Enzymes that are synthesized in fixed amounts, irrespective of the growth conditions.

Contact Inhibition. The cessation of cell movement (division?) that is often observed when freely growing cells from a multicellular organism come into physical contact with each other.

Coordinated Enzyme Synthesis. Enzymes whose rates of production are observed to vary together. (For example, in *E. coli* cells growing in the absence of β-galactosides, the addition of lactose to the medium causes the coordinated induction of β-galactosidase and β-galactoside permease.)

Copolymer. A polymeric molecule containing more than one kind of monomer unit.

Corepressors. Metabolites, which by their combination with repressors specifically inhibit the formation of the enzyme(s) involved in their metabolism.

Coupled Reaction. A thermodynamically unfavorable reaction, which by association with a thermodynamically favorable reaction is driven in the direction of product formation.

Crossing Over. The process of exchange of genetic material between homologous chromosomes.

Cyclic AMP. Adenosine monophosphate with phosphate group bonded internally (phosphodiester bond between 3′ and 5′ carbon atoms) to form cyclic molecule. Active in regulation of gene expression in bacterial and eucaryotic cells.

Dalton. A unit of weight equal to the weight of a single hydrogen atom.

Defective Virus. A virus that by itself is unable to reproduce itself when infecting its host, but that can grow in the presence of another virus.

Degenerate Codons. Two or more codons that code for the same amino acid.

Deletions. Loss of a section of the genetic material from a chromosome. The size of the deleted material can vary from a single nucleotide to sections containing a number of genes.

Denaturation. The loss of the native configuration of a macromolecule resulting, for instance, from heat treatment, extreme pH changes, chemical treatment, or other denaturing agents. It is usually accompanied by loss of biological activity.

Deoxynucleoside. The condensation product of a purine or pyrimidine with the five-carbon sugar, 2-deoxyribose.

Deoxyribonucleotide. A compound which consists of a purine or pyrimidine base bonded to the sugar, 2-deoxyribose, which in turn is bound to a phosphate group:

Dimer. Structure resulting from association of two identical subunits.

Diploid State. The chromosome state in which each type of chromosome except for the sex chromosomes is always represented twice (2N).

Disulfide Bond. Covalent bond between two sulfur atoms in different amino acids of a protein. Important in determining secondary and tertiary structure.

DNA (Deoxyribonucleic Acid) A polymer of deoxyrinonucleotides. The genetic material of all cells.

DNA Polymerase. An enzyme that catalyzes the formation of polydeoxyribonucleotide strands from deoxyribonucleoside triphosphates, using DNA as a template.

DNA-RNA Hybrid. A double helix that consists of one chain of DNA hydrogen bonded to a chain of RNA by means of complementary base pairs.

Early vs Late Genes. Genes transcribed early and late after infection of bacteria by bacteriophage. May require different σ factors for recognition of promoters.

Early vs Late Proteins. During viral infection, viral-specific proteins are synthesized at characteristic times after infection in groups that can be classed as "early" and "late." Often under positive control of bacterial and viral sigma factors.

Electron Microscopy. A technique for visualizing material that uses beams of electrons instead of light rays and that permits greater magnification than is possible with an optical microscope. Resolutions of ~ 10 A are attainable with biological materials.

Electronegative Atom. An atom with a tendency to gain electrons.

End Product. A chemical compound that is the final product of a sequence of metabolic reactions.

Endonuclease. An enzyme that makes internal cuts in DNA backbone chains.

Enzymes. Protein molecules capable of catalyzing chemical reactions.

Episome. A genetic element that can exist either free or as part of the normal cellular chromosome. Examples of episomes are the sex(F^+) factor and lysogenic phage DNA.

Erythroblast. Nucleated cell in bone marrow that differentiates into red blood cell.

Established Cell Line. Cultured cells of single origin capable of stable growth for many generations.

Estrogen. Hormone produced by ovary.

Equilibrium Density Centrifugation. Separation of cell organelles or macromolecules of different densities by centrifugation in a density gradient. The gradient is a solution (for example of sucrose, or cesium chloride) that increases in concentration from top to bottom of the centrifuge tube.

Eucaryote. Organism with cells that have nuclear membranes membrane-bound organelles, 80 S ribosomes, and characteristic biochemistry.

Euchromatin. Diffuse form of chromatin active in RNA synthesis.

Exonuclease. An enzyme that digests DNA from the ends of strands.

Feedback (End-Product) Inhibition. Inhibition of the enzymatic activity of the first enzyme in a metabolic pathway by the end product of that pathway.

Fertility Factor (F^+). An episome that determines the sex of a bacterium. The presence of this factor in the cell makes it a male. (Female cells are called F^-.)

Fertilization. Fusion of gametes of opposite sexes to produce diploid zygote.

Fluorescent Antibody Technique.   Detection of specific antigen in cells by staining with a specific antibody conjugated with a fluorescent dye.

Gene Redundancy.   Presence in cell of many copies of a single gene. Multiple copies may be inherited or result from selective gene duplication during development.

Genetic Information.   The information contained in a sequence of nucleotide bases in a DNA (or RNA) molecule.

Genetic Map.   The arrangement of mutable sites on a chromosome as deduced from genetic recombination experiments.

Genotype.   The genetic constitution of an organism (to be distinguished from its physical appearance or phenotype).

Glycoprotein.   Protein in which a carbohydrate is covalently bonded to the peptide portion of the molecule.

Group (Functional).   Covalently bonded groups of atoms that behave as a unit in chemical reactions.

Group-Transfer Reactions.   Reactions (excluding oxidations or reductions) in which molecules exchange functional groups.

Growth Curve.   The change in the number of cells in a growing culture as a function of time.

Growth Factor.   A specific substance that must be present in the growth medium to permit a cell to multiply.

^{3}H *(Tritium).*   A radioactive isotope of hydrogen, a weak β emitter, with a half-life of 12.5 years.

Haploid State.   The chromosome state in which each chromosome is present only once.

Heavy Isotopes.   Forms of atoms containing greater than the common number of neutrons and thus more dense than the commonly observed isotope (e.g., ^{15}N, ^{13}C).

HeLa Cells.   An established line of human cervical carcinoma (cancer) cells. Has been used for many years in study of biochemistry and growth of cultured human cells.

Helix.   A spiral structure with a repeating pattern described by two simultaneous operations—rotation and translation. It is the natural conformation of many regular biological polymers.

Helper Virus.   A virus that, by its infection of a cell, is able to supply one or more functions that a defective virus lacks, thus enabling the latter to multiply.

Hemoglobin.   Protein carrier of oxygen found in red blood cells. Composed of two pairs of identical polypeptide chains and iron-containing heme group.

Hepatoma.   A specific form of liver cancer.

Hereditary Disease. A pathological condition whose cause is a gene mutation and that can therefore be transferred from one generation to the next.

Heterochromatin. Condensed form of chromatin relatively inactive in RNA synthesis.

Heteroduplex. Double-stranded DNA molecule in which the two strands do not have completely complementary base sequences. Can arise from mutation, recombination, or by annealing DNA single strands *in vitro*.

Hfr (High Frequency of Recombination). Strains of *E. coli* that show unusually high frequencies of recombination. In these cells the F factor is integrated into the bacterial chromosome, where it is thought to play some part in the transfer of the chromosome from Hfr to F⁻ cells. (See also *Fertility Factor*.)

High-Energy Bond. A bond that yields a large (at least 5 kcal/mole) decrease in free energy upon hydrolysis.

Histones. Proteins rich in basic amino acids (e.g. lysine) found in chromosomes of all eucaryotic cells except sperm where the DNA is specifically complexed with another group of basic proteins, the protamines.

Homologous Chromosomes. Chromosomes that pair during meiosis, have the same morphology, and contain genes governing the same characteristics.

Hormones. Chemical substance (often small polypeptide) synthesized in one organ of body that stimulates functional activity in cells of other tissues and organs. Many act by stimulating adenylcyclase in cell membrane to produce cyclic AMP.

Host Cell. A cell whose metabolism is used for growth and reproduction of a virus.

"Hot Spots." Sites in genes at which mutations occur with unusually high frequency.

Hydrocarbon Side Groups. Amino acid side chains consisting of carbon and hydrogen only.

Hydrogen Bond. A weak attractive force between one electronegative atom and a hydrogen atom that is covalently linked to a second electronegative atom.

Hydrolysis. The breaking of a molecule into two or more smaller molecules by the addition of a water molecule:

$$H_2O + A{-}B \rightarrow H{-}A + HO{-}B$$

Hydrophilic. Pertaining to molecules or groups that readily associate with H_2O.

Hydrophobic. Literally, water hater. Used to describe molecules or certain functional groups in molecules that are, at best, only poorly soluble in water.

Hydrophobic Bonding. The association of nonpolar groups with each other in aqueous solution, arising because of the tendency of water molecules to exclude nonpolar molecules.

Immunoglobulin. Protein molecule, produced by plasma cell, that recognizes and binds a specific antigen. Also called antibody.

Immunological Tolerance. Absence of immune response to antigens, resulting from recognition of "self" or induced by very large antigen dose.

Immunosuppressive Drug. Drug that blocks normal response of antibody-producing cells to antigen.

Inducers. Molecules that cause the production of larger amounts of the enzymes involved in their uptake and metabolism, compared to the amounts found in cells growing in the absence of an inducer.

Inducible Enzymes. Enzymes whose rate of production can be increased by the presence of inducers in the cell.

Infectious Viral Nucleic Acid. Purified viral nucleic acid that can infect a host cell and cause the production of progeny viral particles.

Initiation Factors. Three proteins (F_1, F_2, F_3) required for the initiation of protein synthesis.

Intergenic Suppression. Restoration of a lost function by a second mutation that is located in a different gene than the primary mutation.

Intermediary Metabolism. The chemical reactions in a cell that transform food molecules into molecules needed for the structure and growth of the cell.

Intragenic Suppression. Restoration of a lost function by a second mutation that is located within the same gene as the primary mutation.

In Vitro (Latin: in glass). Pertaining to experiments done in a cell-free system. Currently, the term is sometimes modified to include the growth of cells from multicellular organisms under tissue-culture conditions.

In Vitro Protein Synthesis. The incorporation of amino acids into polypeptide chains in a cell-free system.

In Vivo (Latin: in life). Pertaining to experiments done in a system such that the organism remains intact, either at the level of the cell (for bacteria) or at the level of the whole organism (for animals).

Label (Radioactive). A radioactive atom, introduced into a molecule to facilitate observation of its metabolic transformations.

Lampbrush Chromosome. Giant diplotene chromosome found in oocyte nucleus with loops projecting in pairs from most chromomeres. Loops are sites of active gene expression.

Leaky Protein. A protein coded by a mutant gene that shows some residual activity.

Leukemia. Form of cancer characterized by extensive proliferation of nonfunctional immature white blood cells (leukocytes).

Leukosis. Uncontrolled proliferation of mature forms of white blood cells.

Linked Genes. Genes that are located on the same chromosome and that therefore tend to be transmitted together.

Lymphoma. Cancer of lymphatic tissue.

Lysis. The bursting of a cell by the destruction of its cell membrane.

Lysogenic Bacterium. A bacterium that contains a prophage.

Lysogenic Viruses. Viruses that can become prophages.

Lytic Infection. Viral infection leading to lysis of cell and "burst" of progeny virus.

Lytic Viruses. Viruses whose multiplication leads to lysis of the host cell.

Macromolecules. Molecules with molecular weights ranging from a few thousand to hundreds of millions.

Map Units. A number proportional to the frequency of recombination between two genes. One map unit corresponds to a recombination frequency of 1 per cent.

Mesosome. An invagination of the bacterial cell membrane. Associated with DNA replication.

Messenger RNA (mRNA). RNA that serves as a template for protein synthesis.

Metabolic Pathway. A set of consecutive interacellular enzymatic reactions that converts one molecule to another.

Micron (μ). A unit of length convenient for describing cellular dimensions; it is equal to 10^{-3} cm or 10^5 A.

Missense Mutation. A mutation that changes a codon coding for one amino acid to a codon corresponding to another amino acid.

Mitotic Recombination. Crossing over between homologous chromosomes during mitosis, which leads to the segregation of heterozygous alleles.

Molecular Weight. The sum of the atomic weights of the constituent atoms in a molecule.

Monolayer. A layer of cells that is uniformly one cell thick.

Monomer. The basic subunit from which, by repetition of a single reaction, polymers are made. For example, amino acids (monomers) condense to yield polypeptides or proteins (polymers).

Mutable Sites. Sites along the chromosome at which mutations can occur. Genetic experiments tell us that each mutable site can exist in several alternative forms.

Mutagens. Physical or chemical agents, such as radiation, heat, or alkylating or deaminating agents, which raise the frequency of mutation greatly above the spontaneous background level.

Mutation. An inheritable change in a chromosome.

Myeloma. Cancer of antibody-producing cells characterized by proliferation of a single clone of plasma cells producing a pure immunoglobulin.

Negative Control. Prevention of biological activity by presence of a
specific molecule, prominent example is inhibition of mRNA initiation by binding of specific repressor to specific sites along a DNA
molecule.

Nitrogenous Base. An aromatic N-containing molecule having
basic properties (tendency to acquire an H atom). Important
nitrogenous bases in cells are the purines and pyrimidines.

Nonsense Mutation. A mutation that converts a codon that specifies some amino acid into one that does not specify any amino acid
(a nonsense codon). Nonsense codons may have the function of
terminating the polypeptide chain.

Nucleic Acid. A nucleotide polymer. (See also DNA and RNA.)

Nucleolus. Round, granular structure found in nucleus of eucaryotic cells, usually associated with specific chromosomal site. Involved in rRNA synthesis and ribosome formation.

Oocyte. Unfertilized egg cell.

Operator. A chromosomal region capable of interacting directly (or
indirectly?) with a specific repressor, thereby controlling the functioning of an adjacent operon.

Operon. A genetic unit consisting of adjacent genes that function
coordinately under the joint control of an operator and a repressor.

Organelle. Membrane-bound structure found in eucaryotic cell containing enzymes for specialized function. Some organelles, including mitochondria and chloroplasts, have DNA and can replicate
autonomously.

^{32}P. A radioactive isotope of phosphorus that emits strong β particles and has a half-life of 14.3 days.

Pairing. The sideways attachment of two homologous chromosomes
prior to crossing over.

Peptide Bond. A covalent bond between two amino acids in which
the α-amino group of one amino acid is bonded to the α-carboxyl
group of the other with the elimination of H_2O:

Permissive vs Nonpermissive Cells.   Permissive cells support lytic infection by a specific virus. Nonpermissive cells do not.

Phage.   (See *Bacterial Viruses.*)

Phage Cross.   Multiple infection of a single bacterium by bacteriophages that differ at one or more genetic sites. This leads to the production of recombinant progeny phage, which carry genes derived from both parental phage types.

Phenotype.   The observable properties of an organism; produced by the genotype in cooperation with the environment.

Phosphodiester.   Any molecule that contains the linkage

$$R - O - \overset{\displaystyle O}{\underset{\displaystyle O^-}{\overset{\|}{\underset{|}{P}}}} - O - R',$$

where R and R' are carbon-containing groups (e.g., nucleosides), O is oxygen, and P is phosphorus.

Plaques.   Round clear areas in a confluent cell sheet that result from the killing or lysis of contiguous cells by several cycles of virus growth.

Polar Mutation.   Mutation in one gene that reduces expression of genes further from promoter in the same operon. Nonsense mutations frequently are polar.

Polarity Gradient.   Quantitative effect of polar mutation in one gene on expression of later genes of operon. Function of the distance between the nonsense codon and the next polypeptide chain-initiation signal.

Polymer.   A regular, covalently bonded arrangement of basic subunit (monomers) that is produced by repetitive application of one or a few chemical reactions.

Polynucleotide.   A linear sequence of nucleotides in which the 3' position of the sugar of one nucleotide is linked through a phosphate group to the 5' position on the sugar of the adjacent nucleotide.

Polynucleotide Ligase.   Enzyme that covalently links DNA backbone chains.

Polypeptide.   A polymer of amino acids linked together by peptide bonds.

Polyribosome.   Complex of a messenger-RNA molecule and ribosomes (number depending on size of mRNA), actively engaged in polypeptide synthesis.

Polytene Chromosome.   Giant chromosome composed of many fibrils (up to 2000) arising from successive rounds of chromatid duplication. Pairing of many identical chromomeres gives rise to characteristic banding pattern.

Positive Control.   Control by regulatory protein—the presence of which, in correct conformation, is required for gene expression.

Primary Protein Structure.   The number of polypeptide chains in a protein, the sequence of amino acids within them, and the location of inter- and interachain disulfide bridges.

Procaryote.   Simple unicellular organism, such as bacterium or blue-green alga, with no nuclear membrane, no membrane-bound organelles, and characteristic ribosomes and biochemistry.

Promoter.   Region on DNA at which RNA polymerase binds and initiates transcription.

Prophage.   The provirus (see below) stage of a lysogenic phage.

Provirus.   The state of a virus in which it is integrated into a host cell chromosome and is thus transmitted from one cell generation to another.

Puromycin.   Antibiotic that inhibits polypeptide synthesis by competing with amino-acyl tRNAs for ribosomal binding site "A."

Radioactive Isotope.   An isotope with an unstable nucleus that stabilizes itself by emitting ionizing radiation.

Reading Mistake.   The incorrect placement of an amino acid residue in a polypetide chain during protein synthesis.

Recombination.   The appearance in the offspring of traits that were not found together in either of the parents.

Regulatory Genes.   Genes whose primary function is to control the rate of synthesis of the products of other genes.

Release factors.   Specific proteins involved in the reading of genetic stop signals for protein synthesis.

Renaturation.   The return of a protein or nucleic acid from a denatured state to its "native" configuration.

Repair Synthesis.   Enzymatic excision and replacement of regions of damaged DNA. Repair of thymine dimers by uv irradiation is best understood example.

Replicating Fork.   Y-shaped region of chromosome that is a growing point in DNA replication.

Replicating forms (RF).   The structure of a nucleic acid at the time of its replication—the term most frequently used to refer to double helical intermediates in the replication of single structured DNA and RNA viruses.

Repressible Enzymes.   Enzymes whose rates of production are decreased when the intracellular concentration of certain metabolites increases.

Repressor.   The product of a regulatory gene, now thought to be a protein and to be capable of combining both with an inducer (or corepressor) and with an operator (or its mRNA product).

Reticulocyte. Immature red blood cell active in hemoglobin synthesis.

Reverse (Back) Mutation. A heritable change in a mutant gene that restores the original nucleotide sequence.

ρ Factor. Protein involved in correct termination of synthesis of RNA molecules.

Ribonucleotide. A compound that consists of a purine or pyrimidine base bonded to ribose, which in turn is esterified with a phosphate group.

Ribosomal Proteins. A group of proteins that bind to rRNA by noncovalent bonds to give the ribosome its three-dimensional structure.

Ribosomal RNA (rRNA). The nucleic acid component of ribosomes, making up two-thirds of the mass of the ribosome in *E. coli*, and about one-half the mass of mammalian ribosomes. Ribosomal RNA accounts for approximately 80 per cent of the RNA content of the bacterial cell.

Ribosomes. Small cellular particles ($\sim$ 200 A in diameter) made up of rRNA and protein. Ribosomes are the site of protein synthesis.

RNA (Ribonucleic Acid). A polymer of ribonucleotides.

RNA Polymerase. An enzyme that catalyzes the formation of RNA from ribonucleoside triphosphates, using DNA as a template.

^{35}S. A radioactive isotope of sulfur, a β emitter with a half-life of 87 days; very useful in studying protein systems, since it can be incorporated into proteins via the sulfur-containing amino acids.

Serum Protein. Protein found in serum (cell-free) component of blood. Includes immunoglobulins, albumin, clotting factors, and enzymes.

σ Factor. Subunit of RNA polymerase that recognizes specific sites on DNA for initiation of RNA synthesis.

Soluble RNA (sRNA). (See *Transfer RNA.*)

Somatic Mutation. A mutation occurring in any cell that is not destined to become a germ cell.

Spontaneous Mutations. Mutations for which there is no "observable" cause.

Sporulation. The formation from vegetative cells of bacteria and other organisms of dry, metabolically inactive cells with thick surface coats (spores), which can resist extreme environmental conditions.

Stereoisomers. Molecules that have the same structural formula but different spatial arrangement of dissimilar groups bonded to a common atom. Many of the physical and chemical properties of stereoisomers are the same, but there are differences in their crystal structures, in the direction in which they rotate polarized light, and, very importantly for biological systems, in their ability to be used in an enzyme-catalyzed reaction.

Steric (Stereochemical). Pertaining to the arrangement in space of the atoms in molecules.

Suppressor Gene. A gene that can reverse the phenotypic effect of a variety of mutations in other genes.

Suppressor Mutation. A mutation that totally or partially restores a function lost by a primary mutation and is located at a genetic site different from the primary mutation.

Svedberg. The unit of sedimentation (S). S is proportional to the rate of sedimentation of a molecule in a given centrifugal field and is thus related to the molecular weight and shape of the molecule.

Synthetic Polyribonucleotides. RNA made *in vitro* without a nucleic acid template either by enzymatic or chemical synthesis.

"T" Antigen. Antigen found in nuclei of cells infected or transformed by certain tumor viruses (e.g., polyoma and SV40). May be an early viral-specific protein.

Tautomeric Shifts. Reversible changes in the localization of a proton in a molecule that alter the chemical properties of the molecule.

Temperature Sensitive Mutation. Mutation-yielding protein that is functional at low (high) temperature, but that is inactivated by temperature elevation (lowering).

Template. The macromolecular mold for the synthesis of another macromolecule.

Template RNA. (See *Messenger RNA.*)

Tertiary Structure (of a Protein). The three-dimensional folding of the polypeptide chains(s) that characterizes a protein in its native state.

Tetramer. Structure resulting from association of four subunits.

Three-Factor Crosses. Mating experiments involving three distinguishable genetic markers (e.g., $a^+b^+c^+ \times abc$).

Tissue Culture. The growth and maintenance of cells from higher organisms *in vitro*, outside the tissue of which they are normally a part.

Transcription. A process involving base pairing, whereby the genetic information contained in DNA is used to order a complementary sequence of bases in an RNA chain.

Transduction. The transfer of bacterial genes from one bacterium to another by a bacteriophage particle.

Transfer Factors. Two proteins required for peptide bond formation on ribosomes. Transfer factor I participates in binding of charged tRNAs to ribosomes. Transfer factor II moves peptidyl tRNAs from the "A" to the "P" ribosome site.

Transfer RNA (tRNA). Any of at least twenty structurally similar species of RNA, all of which have a MW $\sim$ 25,000. Each species of sRNA molecule is able to combine covalently with a specific amino acid and to hydrogen bond with at least one mRNA nucleotide triplet. Also called *adaptor RNA* or *transfer RNA* (tRNA).

Transferases. Enzymes that catalyze the exchange of functional groups.

Transformation. The genetic modification induced by the incorporation into a cell of DNA purified from cells or viruses.

Translation. The process whereby the genetic information present in an mRNA molecule directs the order of the specific amino acids during protein synthesis.

Translational Control. Regulation of gene expression by controlling rate at which specific mRNA molecule is translated.

Tumor Virus. A virus that induces the formation of a tumor.

Turnover Number (of an Enzyme). The number of molecules of a substrate transformed per minute by a single enzyme molecule, when the enzyme is working at its maximum rate.

Two-Factor Cross. A genetic recombination experiment involving two markers (e.g., $a^+b^+ \times ab$).

Ultracentrifuge. A high-speed centrifuge that can attain speeds up to 60,000 rpm and centrifugal fields up to 500,000 times gravity and thus is capable of rapidly sedimenting macromolecules.

uv Radiation. Electromagnetic radiation with wavelength shorter than that of visible light (3900-2000 A). Causes DNA base-pair mutations and chromosome breaks.

van der Waals Force. A weak attractive force, acting over only very short distances, resulting from attraction of induced dipoles.

Viral-Specific Enzyme. An enzyme produced in the host cell after viral infection from viral genetic information.

Viruses. Infectious disease-causing agents, smaller than bacteria, which always require intact host cells for replication and which contain either DNA or RNA as their genetic component.

Weak Interactions (also called Secondary Bonds). The forces between atoms that are less strong than the forces involved in a covalent bond (includes ionic bonds, hydrogen bonds, and van der Waals forces.)

Wild-Type Gene. The form of gene (allele) commonly found in nature.

Wobble.   Ability of third base in tRNA anticodon (5′ end) to hydrogen bond with any of two or three bases at 3′ end of codon. Thus, a single tRNA species can recognize several different codons.

X-Ray Crystallography.   The use of diffraction patterns produced by x-ray scattering from crystals to determine the 3-D structure of molecules.

Zygote.   The result of the union of the male and female sex cells. The zygote therefore has a diploid number of chromosomes.

INDEX

647

Mutations *(cont.)*
 missense, 416, 418-419, 426-428
 nonsense, 416, 418-420
  polypeptide fragments produced
   by, 419-420
  from shift in reading frame, 421
 polar, in phage R17, 494
 "reverse," in *E. coli* tryptrophan
  synthetase, 251, 252
 somatic, and cancer, 598
 suppressor, effect on repressor
  synthesis, 440
 and misreading of genetic code,
  420-426, 427, 430-431
 tryptophan synthetase, 244-252
Myeloma proteins, and antibodies,
 569
Myoglobin, 3-D structure, 172
Myxovirus, 615
 life cycle, 617
 RSV as, 615

Negative control, definition, 456-457
Nicotinamide adenine dinucleotide
 (NAD), as hydrogen-
 transfer coenzyme, 44
Nonpolar molecules, 111
Nucleases, viral, and genetic recom-
 bination, 316-318
Nucleolus, 3, 6
 and rRNA biosynthesis, 542
Nucleus, 2-4
 site of RNA synthesis, 332

Oncogene theory and carcinogens,
 624
Operator, 441
 binding of repressor to,
  441-442, 444
 constitutive enzymes and, 446, 448
 and control of mRNA bio-
  synthesis, 445-448
 controlling β-galactosidase
  synthesis, 445
 minimum size of, 442
Operon, catabolite-sensitive, 459,
 460
 and coordinate protein synthesis,
  443-444
 definition, 444

function, control of, 443-451
 lactose, catabolite repression of,
  459
 controlling β-galactosidase
  synthesis, 444, 445
 diagrammatic view, 444
 promoter of, 448, 449
Opposing rolling circle model, of
 DNA replication, 289-291
Oxidation-reduction reactions,
 coupled, in respiratory chain,
  54, 56
 role of coenzymes in, 42, 43
Oxidative phosphorylation, 56

Paper chromatography, 62
Peptide bond, hydrolytic breakdown,
 92
 partial double-bond character,
  104, 105
 planar shape, 104
 as structural feature of proteins,
  87, 90
Peptide bond formation, free-energy
 change during, 149, 150
 on ribosomes, 367-370, 385, 386,
  391
Phages *(see* Bacteriophages)
Phenotype, 14, 15, 17
Phosphate esters in energy storage,
 48
Phosphodiester bonds, in DNA, 269
 in RNA, 336
Photosynthesis, generation of ATP
 during, 58
 over-all chemical reaction, 39
Phytol, chlorophyll constituent, 165
Plaques, formation, mutations,
 affecting, 220-224
 phage multiplication and, 203,
  204
 from polyoma-infected cells, 603,
  604
 and segregation of heteroduplex
  DNA, 320
Plasma cell, antibody production in,
 575-579
 developmental stages, 576-577,
  579
 electron micrograph of, 578

I read this entire fat book and I never want to see
an RNA again. SFB. April 1. 973